Introduction to Human Ecology

Fifth Revised Printing

Edited by
George F. Clark

Kendall Hunt
publishing company

Cover image © PhotoDisc, Inc.

Kendall Hunt
publishing company

www.kendallhunt.com
Send all inquiries to:
4050 Westmark Drive
Dubuque, IA 52004-1840

Copyright © 2000 by George F. Clark

Revised Printing 2011

ISBN 978-0-7575-8582-1

Printed in the United States of America
10 9

Contents

Introduction   v
Preface II   **vii**
Preface III   **viii**
Preface IV   ix
Preface V   x
Preface VI   **xi**

Section One

1. *What Is Human Ecology?*   Bonnie McCay   05
2. *If Scientists Want to Educate the Public, They Should Start by Listening*   Chris Mooney   14
3. *Body Ritual among the Nacirema*   Horace Miner   17
4. *The Mysterious Fall of the Nacirema*   Neil B. Thompson   21
5. *Will the Flood Wash Away the Crees' Birthright?*   Clifford Krauss   26
6. *Athapaskans Along the Yukon*   Brad Reynolds   28
7. *The Meaning of Adaptation*   Ann McElroy and Patricia K. Townsend   36
8. *On New Guinea Tapeworms and Jewish Grandmothers*   Robert S. Desowitz   58
9. *The Historical Roots of Our Ecologic Crisis*   Lynn White, Jr.   62
10. *Our Treatment of the Environment in Ideal and Actuality*   Yi-Fu Tuan   71
11. *Preaching the Gospel of Green*   Paul Nussbaum   77
12. *New Demand Drives Canada's Baby Seal Hunt*   Clifford Krauss   80
13. *Wrong to Monkey with Human Rights*   Russell Paul La Valle   83
14. *Speaking for Critters Who Can't Speak*   B. G. Kelley   85
15. *Why Perch a Bird on Your Shoulder?*   Albert DiBartolomeo   87
16. *The Benefits of the Commons*   F. Berkes, et al   89
17. *Conservation and Conceptions of the Environment: A Manus Province Case Study*   James Carrier   94
18. *Interactions between People and Forests in East Kalimantan*   A. P. Vayda, et al   98

Section Two

19. *Countering a Major Blow to Garden State Economy*   Suzette Parmley   113
20. *Food That Travels Well*   James E. McWilliams   116
21. *Take a Short Route from Farm to Plate*   Froma Harrop   118
22. *Can Sustainable Agriculture Be Profitable?*   Patrick Madden   120
23. *Energy Conservation in Amish Agriculture*   Warren A. Johnson, et al   131
24. *Catalog of Woes*   Richard N. Mack   143

25. *Agricultural Change in Vietnam's Floating Rice Region*   R. C. Cummings   **147**

26. *Food Revolution That Starts with Rice*   William J. Broad   **161**

27. *The Great Sisal Scheme*   Daniel R. Gross   **164**

28. *Plants, Genes and People: Improving the Relevance of Plant Breeding in Africa*   Angelique Haugerud and Michael P. Collinson   **170**

29. *Three Ways Industrial Food Makes You Sick*   Turning Point Project   **188**

30. *Opposition to Biotech Crops Is Groundless*   John K. Carlisle   **191**

31. *Nutritional Ecology*   Bonnie McCay   **193**

32. *Why People Go Hungry*   Kenneth J. Arrow   **202**

33. *Facing Food Scarcity*   Lester R. Brown   **207**

34. *What Are the Real Population and Resource Problems?*   Julian J. Simon   **219**

35. *Growth in Population and Energy Consumption: More Than a Matter of Interest*   Courtland L. Smith   **227**

36. *Eating Fossil Fuels*   Dale Allen Pfeiffer   **233**

37. *What's Your Consumption Factor?*   Jared Diamond   **241**

Section Three

38. *Deal Is Reached to Save California Redwood Forest*   Frank Clifford   **249**

39. *A Revisionist View of Tropical Deforestation and Development*   Michael R. Dove, MA, PhD   **251**

40. *Social Forestry for Whom?*   Vandana Shiva, et al   **265**

41. *Organizing for Sustainable Development: Conservation Organizations and the Struggle to Protect Tropical Rain Forests in Esmeraldas, Ecuador*   Thomas K. Rudel   **271**

42. *The Price of Everything*   Thomas Michael Power and Paul Rauber   **281**

43. *Putting a Value on Environmental Quality*   John A. Dixon   **289**

44. *Solution, or Mess? A Milk Jug for a Green Earth*   Stephanie Rosenbloom   **296**

45. *Are People Acting Irrationally?*   Abraham H. Wandersman and William K. Hallman   **298**

46. *Black Lung: The Social Production of Disease*   Barbara Ellen Smith   **308**

47. *Multi-Party Responses to Environmental Problems: A Case of Contaminated Dairy Cattle*   George E. B. Morren, Jr.   **323**

48. *National Priorities List Sites in New Jersey*   United States Environmental Protection Agency   **336**

49. *Social Responses to Commodity Shortages: The 1973-1974 Gasoline Crisis*   Thomas K. Rudel   **337**

50. *Fueling National Insecurity (Advertisement)*   Washington Legal Foundation   **352**

51. *America's Green Recession (Advertisement)*   Washington Legal Foundation   **353**

52. *America's Apathy on the Environment*   Geneva Overholser   **354**

53. *Green Fatigue*   Susan Nielsen   **356**

54. *The Age of Eco-Angst*   Daniel Goleman   **358**

55. *The Elusive Process of Citizen Activism*   Celene Krauss   **360**

End Note   **368**

Introduction to Human Ecology

Welcome to *Introduction to Human Ecology*. Although I will be going over some of what follows in the first lecture, I also wanted to put it in writing at the beginning of our reader. For many years, this course was taught in individual sections of fifty to sixty students. Different faculty members taught the course, each of us in his/her own way. Over the decade of the 1990s, several changes occurred in the Department of Human Ecology generally and in this course specifically.

In terms of the course, one change was that I was given the responsibility of teaching "*Intro*" every semester. A second change was that we put together a reader for the course. Our faculty selected most of the articles in this book as being a representative cross-section appropriate for an introductory course. Over the years I have made some additions—including in this edition—and an occasional deletion or substitution. A third change was making this a lecture-recitation course so that we could accommodate more students. Course evaluations since this change seem to indicate that most students prefer this arrangement.

In terms of the Department of Human Ecology, larger changes were made as well. Where we once offered two majors—International Environmental Studies and Human Ecology—we now offer one, Environmental Policy, Institutions and Behavior. The name of our major was changed for two reasons. First, we wanted the consolidated major to subsume our two previous ones. Second, many of our majors felt that "human ecology" was largely unknown in the outside world (especially among prospective employers) and we needed a new name that more tangibly expressed what we did. The "EPIB" major has four options—U.S., International, Health, and Individual. The International Option is similar to our old IES major. The Individual Option allows students to put together their own unique curriculum, either so that they can graduate with teaching certification, so that they can best derive from their education a body of knowledge they wish to have, or for some other, similar reason. We also have a six-course minor, with "*Intro*" being one of its requirements. Many of the topics we touch on here are examined in greater depth in our upper level courses.

Early in the course we shall be discussing what human ecology is. Without getting into that here, much of its beauty lies in its diversity. You should find evidence of that here in the readings and in the books and films we also use. There is not only diversity in terms of the disciplines represented by the authors and the topics they write about, but also in their views concerning environmentally-related issues. Some students find this disconcerting at first and require a period of adjustment.

As a student, I always resented classes in which I felt I had to agree with the instructor in order to do well. As a teacher, I have attempted to avoid interjecting my views or judging students' opinions by mine. Our goal here is to teach you ***how*** to think in a human ecological perspective, not ***what*** to think. We are much more interested in how you arrive at your views than the views themselves. Maybe this course will change some of your opinions and how you see the world around you, maybe it won't. At the least, we hope it will make your opinions more informed ones. We also hope that you will continue to think about and perhaps act on some of the topics and issues we cover far beyond this course or your formal academic training. Education truly should be a life-long process that is by no means confined to the classroom.

While this reader and the course encompass numerous topics, it is and can only be a sampling of subjects of interest to human ecologists. Similarly, we will not be covering any topic in great depth—we can't, really, in an introductory course. Nonetheless, you should be able to gain familiarity with fundamental human ecological concepts, get a feel for the variety of relevant interests, and some sense of the spectrum of thought concerning environmental issues. You should also come away with an appreciation for the gamut of human-environment interactions across time and space. We can learn from the past and from other cultures in the present—both what we might try to do and what we should avoid.

The first section of the reader largely deals with the basics—what "human ecology" is, who human ecologists are, their role in the greater scheme of things. We'll also be looking at other cultures; by doing so perhaps we can learn more about our own culture and ourselves as individuals. This is true in terms of our relationship with the environment, but in a larger sense as well. As this is predominantly a social science enterprise, "human ecology" is an apt term.

The second section focuses on the constellation of food, agriculture, population and nutrition. We'll be looking at the interrelationships among these and their connection to other areas, too. Among other things, you should come to realize their interconnectedness and the fact that it is difficult to discuss one in isolation from the others. We'll examine the various perspectives on the role of population, one area where informed opinion ranges from population as "the" fundamental problem of the day to the view that it is no problem at all.

The third section generally returns closest to home and concentrates on resource and impact issues, strategies for promoting change, and policy. Here, too, there is widespread disagreement about not only what should be done, but also how to accomplish it. Unfortunately, we'll only be able to touch on a few of the significant issues. Much of what we'll discuss in this section can be applied to non-environmental issues and non-governmental settings (such as Rutgers).

I should note that the reader is discussed above in terms of "sections," even though while recognizing that this is an artificial division. The course is subdivided largely as a matter of convenience and emphasis. Many articles and other course materials have relevance to more than one "section." It has, however, proven easier to approach what we do here in this manner.

At times here I have used "I" and at other times "we." The former means that I was speaking only for myself, the latter means that I was speaking for both my teaching assistants and I. In the more than ten years that I have been teaching "*Intro*" I have had the good fortune to have TAs who have shared my philosophy and commitment to the course and to our students. To the extent that the course is successful and continues to evolve, past and present TAs deserve much of the credit.

Again, welcome to "*Introduction to Human Ecology*." We hope to expose you to some new concepts and ideas, to broaden your horizons a bit, and maybe to help you get a bit of insight about yourself and the world around you. If we can accomplish that, it will have been a successful semester.

George F. Clark

Preface II

As I write this in May, 2002, 1 would like to add to the original preface for the first edition of this reader two years ago. In our two year "test run" with Kendall-Hunt, student reaction has been generally favorable and the reader has proven to be a "win-win" situation. As opposed to the old course packet, students receive a higher quality book at a similar or even lower price and royalties from this reader are returned to the Department of Human Ecology for the benefit of our students; hence, this second edition.

Once again, in consultation with my colleagues and with my Teaching Assistants—and in response to comments by *"Intro"* students of the last two years, there are some new articles and a few deletions. I am also adding introductions to each section to highlight where each article "fits" into the course. Although I hand out review sheets before each exam, perhaps these will help a bit beforehand—you will better know what to look for as you read the articles for the first time.

I hope that you enjoy the articles in the reader and get something of value from them apart from the practicality of answering test questions. I also hope that you enjoy the course. The longer I teach, the more convinced I am of the need for Human Ecology and of its value. We often hear that the world is becoming a smaller place due to technological advances; e.g., you can be in touch with almost anyone anywhere in the world at any time. That notion is increasingly true in environmental terms as well—we truly are living in a global environment in which we affect and are affected by everyone else. What we do today as individuals and as a society will determine not only the conditions of future generations, but also their choices in terms of dealing with those conditions.

Having just read through this semester's course evaluations, I am well aware that many students find this course both "eye-opening" and "depressing." Academics in general and social scientists in particular *do* tend to be fascinated with and intrigued by "problems." In part, I think this is because problems are somewhat inherently more interesting than things that work well just as the news media focus on "bad news" rather than "good news" most of the time. In part, I think we gravitate toward problems because it is they that need to be recognized and addressed they're not likely to go away by themselves.

Environmental problems are often frustrating because they require long term attention even to make small gains. It is understandable why many lose patience and give up on them, though when someone does so, they are simply leaving important decisions to other parties who are not likely to decide them in other than their own interest. Each of us must choose our path for ourselves, including both our individual relationship with the environment and to what extent we become involved in larger causes—from voting, to signing a petition, to attending meetings, to donating to interest groups, to boycotting, to protesting, to tree-sitting. By the time the semester is over, I hope this course will contribute to your ability to make choices appropriate for you. *Not* making a conscious choice *is* a choice itself. As one of my former teaching assistants put it "now that you know, you can't *not* know."

George F. Clark
May, 2002

Preface III

This is the third version of the *Introduction to Human Ecology* reader done with the Kendall-Hunt Publishing Company. As my students have been happy with the first two editions, I am pleased to continue this mutually beneficial relationship.

I have added a few new and timely newspaper articles this time. They pose little additional burden on the student and complement other course materials nicely, I think. The introductions to the book's sections have also been re-done to reflect how the additions fit. I continue to make other changes in course materials in terms of books and films in response to students' comments and suggestions. Although the changes from year to year seem small and incremental, my first "*Intro*" students from the early 90s would see the course as being quite different from the one they had with me then.

I continue to enjoy teaching the course immensely. New generations of students, new issues, and new knowledge help to keep it fresh. Beyond that, I have always liked teaching introductory courses because that is where, in many respects, one can have the most impact as a teacher—where one can see the proverbial light bulb go on above people's heads. That happened to me when I took *Introduction to Sociology* many years ago; now, it is one of the major joys of teaching. I hope that light bulb clicks on for you in this course—and in others.

George F. Clark
June, 2004

Preface IV

We live in a time of rapid change, worldwide and locally. Even here at the University we are in the process of transformation and Cook College is morphing into the School of Environmental and Biological Sciences. Not surprisingly, this edition of the book also represents change. I would like to thank the students who took this course over the 2004–5 and 2005–6 academic years for their comments and suggestions. Most especially, I would like to thank Nick Martyniak, Satsuki Takahashi, Sheri Seminski, Emilie Stander, and Kristen Drusjack, who all worked with the course and who have offered their thoughts and materials to this edition.

Overall, the length is about the same as previous versions, but we've added some new articles, dropped a few, and moved others. Hopefully, this improves the flow of the materials and makes it easier on the current generation of *Intro* students. For as long as the course is offered, this book will be a work in progress — as will the course itself. I would also like to thank Kendall-Hunt for our continued partnership in bringing you this book.

I hope that you enjoy the course as much as I have enjoyed doing it over the years. I think of each semester as a new adventure — each class is unique, each generation of students is different, and often the unexpected happens. Let us begin...

George F. Clark
May, 2006

Preface V

This is the fifth incarnation of the *"Intro"* reader done with Kendall-Hunt. It continues to evolve, as does the course–and hopefully, your instructor. We are now the School of Environmental and Biological Sciences, and soon "Cook College" will be unknown to students and remembered only by us graybeards–just as the "College of Agriculture and Environmental Sciences" and before that the "College of Agriculture" and simply the "Ag School" are memories to only a few. Again, I have dropped some old articles and added some new ones, for like our name, environmental issues and interests, change, too.

I am more convinced than ever that Human Ecology in general and this course in particular are ever-more important. My generation has not made as good decisions as I would have hoped and expected when I was sitting where you are today. I know it's unfair to think that your generation should do better. Our challenges seem greater than ever before. On the other hand, we continually learn more and become increasingly capable of more wonderful–and more frightening–things. You will need to think in much more sophisticated and creative ways if you are to do any better than we have. We not only need to teach you many substantive things, but also to teach you to learn from our mistakes. I like to think that this course can play a small role in that process.

Perhaps because I'm more and more aware of the fact that I'm well into the second half of my teaching career, I find that I enjoy it more each year. I hope that's evident in the classroom and outside of it as well. It's been both a privilege and a pleasure to have the opportunity to touch so many young adult lives. In the years ahead, I hope your memory will be jogged by something that makes you recall this course and I hope we give you something of lasting value.

George F. Clark
September, 2008

Preface VI

This is the sixth incarnation of the *"Intro"* reader done with Kendall-Hunt. It continues to evolve, as does the course—and hopefully, your instructor. We are now the School of Environmental and Biological Sciences, and "Cook College" is unknown to students and will be remembered only by us graybeards—just as the "College of Agriculture and Environmental Sciences" and before that the "College of Agriculture" and simply the "Ag School" are memories to only a few. Again, I have dropped some old articles and added some new ones, for like our name, environmental issues and interests, change, too.

I am increasingly convinced that Human Ecology in general and this course in particular are ever-more important. My generation has not made as good decisions as I would have hoped and expected when I was sitting where you are today. I know it's unfair to think that your generation should do better. Our challenges seem greater than ever before. On the other hand, we continually learn more and become increasingly capable of more wonderful—and more frightening—things. You will need to think in much more sophisticated, holistic, and creative ways if you are to do any better than we have. We not only need to teach you many substantive things, but also to teach you to learn from our mistakes. I like to think that this course can play a small role in that process.

Perhaps because I'm more and more aware of the fact that I'm well into the second half of my teaching career, I find that I enjoy it more each year. I hope that's evident in the classroom and outside of it as well. It's been both a privilege and a pleasure to have the opportunity to touch so many young adult lives, just as so many of my instructors touched mine. In the years ahead, I hope your memory will be jogged by something that makes you recall this course and I hope we give you something of lasting value.

George F. Clark
August, 2010

Section One

1. *What is Human Ecology?*   **Bonnie McCay**   5

2. *If Scientists Want to Educate the Public, They Should Start by Listening*   **Chris Mooney**   14

3. *Body Ritual Among the Nacirema*   **Horace Miner**   17

4. *The Mysterious Fall of the Nacirema*   **Neil B. Thompson**   21

5. *Will the Flood Wash Away the Crees' Birthright?*   **Clifford Krauss**   26

6. *Athapaskans Along the Yukon*   **Brad Reynolds**   28

7. *The Meaning of Adaptation*   **Ann McElroy and Patrick K. Townsend**   36

8. *On New Guinea Tapeworms and Jewish Grandmothers*   **Robert S. Desowitz**   58

9. *The Historical Roots of Our Ecologic Crisis*   **Lynn White, Jr.**   62

10. *Our Treatment of the Environment in Ideal and Actuality*   **Yi-Fu Tuan**   71

11. *Preaching the Gospel of Green*   **Paul Nussbaum**   77

12. *New Demand Drives Canada's Baby Seal Hunt*   **Clifford Krauss**   80

13. *Wrong to Monkey with Human Rights*   **Russell Paul La Valle**   83

14. *Speaking for Critters Who Can't Speak*   **B.G. Kelley**   85

15. *Why Perch a Bird on Your Shoulder?*   **Albert DiBartolomeo**   87

16. *The Benefits of the Commons*   **F. Berkes, et al**   89

17. *Conservation and Conceptions of the Environment: A Manus Province Case Study*   **James Carrier**   94

18. *Interactions between People and Forests in East Kalimantan*   **A.P. Vayda, et al**   98

Introduction to Section One

In this first section we begin, logically enough, with McCay's article defining and describing "human ecology". It discusses ecology in its myriad forms, the relationship between natural and social science approaches to the study of ecology, and the key social sciences associated with human ecology. It also reveals what McCay describes as its "inter-/multi-/anti- disciplinary" nature, and an important part of what makes it unique. Mooney discusses the inadequate relationship between the public and scientists. Although he focuses on natural scientists, the same holds true for social scientists.

The Miner and Thompson articles illustrate how social sciences look at societies and cultures differently from how we do so in the usual sense. They will familiarize you with an important concept—"ethnocentrism". We in social science try to avoid ethnocentrism—judging other cultures by the standards of our own. To the extent you can appreciate and apply this concept, you will, in effect, be stepping outside yourself as a member of this society and culture—a valuable ability in everyday life as well as in social science.

As you will learn, words such as "culture" mean something different to social scientists than they do to others. That's because—unlike natural scientists—we can't easily coin our own terms (e.g., terms such as "quarks"), so we have to use ordinary words and give them our own unique and more specific definitions. For us, "culture" is non-biological inheritance, material and non-material—language, symbols, norms, values, and technology/things. Even "technology" has a different meaning for us—it's simply how we do things (and how we *choose* to do things), rather than meaning "high tech" or implying "progress" in the material sense. For us, it's at least partially *socially* determined and not merely the product of scientific and technical research and development. "Cultural lag"—what happens when nonmaterial culture has trouble keeping up with material culture—is a major concern of human ecology.

The Krauss article is an update on our first film of the semester—"*Cree Hunters*". Reynolds describes a similar group—the Athapaskans of Alaska—and allows comparison between the two groups in terms of their relationship with modern society and the consequences of their decisions. You may note that almost thirty years elapse between the film and the Krauss article—not unusual for the resolution of an environmental dispute.

McElroy and Townsend define the term "adaptation" and delineate its key types. We—and all societies—are continually adapting and have a variety of strategies at our disposal to do so. Desowitz offers two groups in similar circumstances—Jewish grandmothers and the Ekan of New Guinea, both suffering health problems from the introduction of new organisms into their environments. From a range of possibilities, each group makes its choice in response.

White and Tuan provide competing explanations for what both agree is our problematic relationship with our environment. These are not the only explanations, but they are illustrative of viewpoints on this issue. You may feel free to choose between them, disagree with both, or blend them through your own analysis. Nussbaum gives an example to ponder and to apply the White-Tuan debate.

La Valle, Kelley, and DiBartolomeo write about different aspects of our relationship with animals. In our second and third films, "*Sharkcallers of Kontu*" and "*Survival in the High North*" cover this topic, among others, as well. The Krauss article represents an update of the Canadian sealing issue and the renewed battle over it.

Berkes, et al, present an alternative view to "the tragedy of the commons", suggesting that government regulation and private property are not the only alternatives in avoiding this "tragedy". This is an important point to keep in mind, for issues are often presented for public consideration—in political campaigns, for example—in "either/or" terms. This is known as a "false dichotomy", meaning that we almost always have more than two options from which to choose. Human ecology is a vehicle for seeing less obvious solutions, ones that may be better than options "A" and "B".

Among the many dimensions of disputes about animals is the relationship (often, clash) between modern and traditional cultures and how the former affects the latter—intentionally and unintentionally. Carrier's article offers an illustration of this. Vayda, et al describe how the social scientific view of traditional cultures has evolved, and by implication how that view has changed in modern societies generally. The piece by Shiva, et al shows how this changing view has been applied in a practical sense—and what happened as a result.

By the end of this first section of the course, you should have some idea of what this creature called "human ecology" is about, some new vocabulary, and perhaps a new perspective on the world around you and your role in it.

What Is Human Ecology?

Bonnie McCay

I. What Is Human Ecology?

A. General Definition

Human ecology is the study of man-environment interactions and interrelationships.

The field of inquiry known as "human ecology" has diverse roots and branches. Biologists, for example, who use the term "human ecology" in their texts very often do so to introduce their discussion of world population problems, meaning two things: (1) application of principles of population biology to the human species; and (2) concern for the effects of human population growth on non-human species and the physical environment, i.e., species extinction, soil erosion, acid rain. This is part of "human ecology," but not the whole thing.

To many people both "human ecology" and "ecology" refer solely to policy and action in the solution of environmental problems such as pollution, wildlife preservation, and resource and energy conservation. While these policy and action concerns are definitely part of both "ecology" and "human ecology," they are not the whole story either. Just as "ecology" properly refers to a certain field of study in biology, so "human ecology" refers to a field of study bringing together a wide variety of traditional disciplines.

B. The Multi-disciplinary, Anti-disciplinary Nature of Human Ecology

Because most biologists, excluding human biologists (those who study only the biology of human beings), do not study people, by and large the enterprise known as "human ecology" has become the affair of social scientists. Thus, in many different social science disciplines, including psychology, anthropology, sociology, geography, economics, political science, and history we find groups of scholars and students concerned with the ecological and environmental aspects of people, their institutions, and their lives. Human ecology, or something with a closely related name (like "ecological anthropology/sociology/etc.") has emerged as a specialty within most of these disciplines. It is also, I must add, still considered a specialty within biology.

"Human ecology" is rarely considered an academic discipline in and of itself. Some people even consider it an "anti-discipline." They would like to get rid of the traditional disciplinary boundaries that often make it so hard for people to communicate and work together and that work against the development of a unified science (eg. Bruhn 1974). At its best, human ecology is inter- and multi-disciplinary. There is, however, a Society of Human Ecology and a journal called *Human Ecology*, and in a few places, including here at Rutgers University, there are Departments or Colleges of Human Ecology offering undergraduate majors. Students are trained with the understanding that they will go from college into jobs whose descriptions may include neither the term "human" nor that of "ecology or into graduate and professional school programs in one or another more traditional discipline where they will continue their training in the study of human/environment relationships.

This course is an introduction to human ecology. I am an "ecological anthropologist" by training. I got my graduate doctorate degree at Columbia University, New York, and did "fieldwork," required for anthropologists, for 2 1/2 years in Newfoundland, Canada, studying the interrelationships between fish resource dynamics and problems and the lives of people who live in small coastal communities. All faculty at a university like Rutgers are expected to carry on active research and writing, in addition to teaching, and therefore, whenever I can I do research. I have continued to do my research with fishing communities, and for obvious reasons now most of it is done with the commercial fishermen of New Jersey. I also visit Newfoundland every year or so, to keep up, and am involved in a research project in Puerto Rico.

Like most human ecologists and anthropologists, my training and interests are quite broad. Therefore, I also teach in the areas of medical ecology and medical anthropology. In addition, I have organized conferences and am editing a large book on the topic of the management of common property resources, a topic that we will address in this course. Some of my graduate and undergraduate students are also interested in research in agricultural systems, both here and abroad (especially Indonesia). So they have trained me in that area and I was co-editor of a journal called "Culture and Agriculture." Meanwhile, I am also writing a book on "nature, culture, and the law in New Jersey's fisheries," one that has made me into more of an historian and legal scholar than I ever thought I would be, and I have published a book on the issue of "the commons," about which more later.

My Department of Human Ecology, at Cook College, is made up of similar types, from sociology, geography, and anthropology. In addition, some of us are members of the Graduate Faculty in Ecology, which has a specialty in Human Ecology. We are very fortunate to have these opportunities at Rutgers University. That a Department of Human Ecology and a curriculum in Human Ecology exist is due to the ideas of the faculty and administration of what was once the College of Agricultural and Environmental Sciences and is now Cook College. In the late 1970s, partly in response to the "environmentalism" of that time and this, they decided that this "land-grant" college should have as its theme and one of its major emphases "man and the environment." And here we are.

C. The Science of Ecology

The word "ecology" was coined by Ernst Haeckel, a German zoologist, in 1870 (1866, Smith 1986:3),[1] to refer to the aspect of biology that was concerned with the relationships of animals (and plants) to their outside worlds. Ecology becomes "human ecology" when people become a central focus of this science (cf. Bruhn 1974:105).

1. Popularity and Scientific Uses of the Term Ecology

A specialized academic term until the environmental movement of the late 1960s and early 1970s, when it became a "household word" and as such was used, misused and abused. It was and is equated with "the environment" by most people, as in a phase such as "acid rain is very dangerous to the ecology of the Adirondack mountain lakes." But it properly, as an "-ology" word (theology, biology, anthropology), is the *study of* something, in this case, of *"oikos"* the Greek word for "family household." So it is the study of the household . . . but has been used instead to mean the broader, natural science studying *the relationship between organisms and their environment*, (just as "economics" refers to the "management of the household").

The word "ecology" was first used by Ernst Haeckel in 1870, in describing the science of studying the *context* of Darwinian evolution:

> *by ecology we mean the body of knowledge concerning the economy of nature—the investigation of the total relations of the animal both to its inorganic and to its organic environment, including above all, its friendly and inimical relation with those animals and plants with which it comes directly or indirectly into contact—in a word, ecology is the study of all the complex interrelations referred to by Darwin as the conditions of the struggle for existence.*

Ecology came to emphasize balance, equilibrium, and orderly change within natural communities, leading to theories about population regulation and the concept of the ecosystem.

Fuller senses of the terms: *Environment:* biological and also physical conditions of life for an organism (and in human ecology, the social conditions); *Relationship:* interrelationships with individuals of same species, different species, and physical world (Smith 1986:3).

a. Plant Ecology

Ecology derived (Smith 1986:3–15) from many sources, especially the study of plant geography and natural history. Plant geographers in the 18th and 19th centuries observed that although the species of plants differed in different parts of the world, the vegetation had broad similarities and differences that demanded explanation; interest in the role of *climate* on vegetation (eventually leading to Koeppen's climate types).

A scientist studying the vegetation of Hungary and Transylvania (Kemer) introduced the concept of vegetational change over time, or *succession.*

One of the plant ecologists, A. E. Tansley of Great Britain, introduced the term and concept of *ecosystem*. He emphasized the importance of physical as well as biological factors on plant and animal life (including energy) and stimulated the study of nature in terms of measurable inputs and outputs and rates of transformation, such as the conversion of chemical energy into forms useful for life.

Early important work in the U.S. was done on sand dune plant succession, and notions of *holism* or *organism* came to be applied to ecosystems such as prairies, sand dunes, lakes, and the like.

Ecosystems were viewed as economic organizations, as in the use of terms "*producers*" and "*consumers*," (introduced by A. Thienemann, 1931, who also introduced ideas of organic *nutrient cycling* and *trophic feeding levels* in his study of freshwater ecosystems). Focus on *photosynthesis* and *primary productivity* came, not surprisingly, from the study of Illinois cornfields (by Edgar Transeau, 1926), who also talked of "*energy budgets*," another economic term.

b. Population Ecology and Evolution

The development of ecology was also strongly influenced by Charles Darwin, who was in turn influenced by Thomas Malthus, an economist and preacher. Darwin was a naturalist who voyaged to the Galapagos and other parts of the world on the *Beagle* in the early 19th century, to collect biological specimens, take detailed notes, and formulate his view of causes for variation and similarity in life on earth. He was influenced by the works of the geologist Charles Lyell, who proposed that the earth changed *gradually* over time (versus those who gave credit to the God of Genesis about 4000 years before). Darwin noted that life too changed slowly through time.

He came up with his theory of *evolution and the origin of species*, which would be a powerful foundation for the study of *population dynamics*, The concepts of *adaptation* and *natural selection* are critical to his theory. In a later lecture we will further discuss his ideas, and those of other ecologists, as they were influenced by, and in turn influenced, the "human" side of the coin, public policy concerning population, wealth, and poverty. [History of Ideas lecture]

In the following remarks I will try to give you some idea of what the social scientists who talk about "human ecology" mean by the term. We will see that there are several different perspectives on the field, each of which contributes in different ways to the more general goal of understanding human interactions with their environments.

Psychological Human Ecology

Psychology emphasizes first and foremost the *individual as the unit of analysis* and those aspects of genetics, environment and personality that affect the individual's behavior and emotions.

Psychological human ecology includes the scientific study of "the interplay between human behavior and its environmental settings" (Craik 1973 in Young 1983:216). This enterprise is, of course, shared by many other types of academics, including researchers in environmental design and planning from architecture, urban design, landscape architecture, and regional planning perspectives; engineers; and many other kinds of social scientists (Ibid).

This field is so broad and diverse that I will arbitrarily restrict my introductory discussion to a few examples of what researchers do in it. One is the study of *human use of space*, or spatial behavior. Humans, like other animals, tend to be territorial, with varying degrees of mobility and boundaries of "home ranges" and the like. Some studies have shown that more "dominant" persons tend to be more mobile, that whether you own a bicycle (or a car if you are older) affects the size of your home range, and so forth. We also have notions of *personal space*, that may correlate with our sex, ethnic background, age, social status, and personality variables, and we react differently to violations of our personal space. Furniture arrangement, the number of persons in a room, and other environmental features may also affect our behavior and moods.

Psychologists (and geographers) are also interested in *human perceptions of environments and how people evaluate different environments* (i.e., what turns you on more, the beach at Sandy Hook on a summer weekend or a beach on the coast of Maine in the middle of the winter? Central Park on a Sunday afternoon or the solitude of the remote Adirondacks? Why?). In addition, they, as well as political scientists and others concerned with environmental policy and decision-making, are beginning to look at differences between professional environmentals, other decision-makers, and sectors of the "lay" public in terms of attitudes, beliefs, and perceptions of the environment (cf. Craik *op cit:* 219).

Psychological human ecologists tend to emphasize:

❏ the individual as the unit of analysis;
❏ the "environment" as the "built" or human-made physical environment, rather than rocks, trees, butterflies, etc. (unless they are studying perception of the environment, in which case almost anything goes);
❏ experimental, laboratory studies (although one "ecological" school in psychology, headed by Barker, emphasizes the importance of observing "natural streams of behavior" in unmanipulated settings, such as school, home, the neighborhood sandlot, etc.).
❏ the ways in which personality, sex, status, the internal workings of the mind, etc. affect how people evaluate and react to environmental problems (i.e., living in hazardous places or being exposed to horrendous noise while trying to study; geographers also study this question).
❏ the cognitive dimensions of risk perception.

Ecology and Economics

There are close connections between ecology and economics, not the least of which is semantic: "eco" is derived from the Greek word "Oikos," meaning "habitat," "house," or "household." Thus, "ecology" could mean the study of the habitat, house, or household, while "economics" could mean the management of the habitat, house or household (cf. Young 1974, 1983). In practice, ecology is concerned mostly with how plants and animals make their living, economics with how people make their living. The scientist Marston Bates (1964) has pointed to a central focus of both disciplines: how scarce resources are allocated among different users, or "looking at ecology in terms of the economy of nature" (cited in Young 1974:29). Going back much farther, we find that the great evolutionary biologist Charles Darwin took some of his basic ideas from the pastor/economist Thomas Malthus, both concerned over "the struggle for existence" in the context of scarce resources.

Many of the theoretical approaches used in economics are also used in ecology. Thus, for example, models of consumer choice behavior are used, with some modifications, in the study of animal foraging behavior (cf. Rapport and Turner 1977). Economic concepts and models are also used by human ecologists in the other disciplines (Young 1974:31). Most economists concerned with environmental problems apply economic cost-benefit analysis to the evaluation of environmental impacts or "externalities" of human activities, of polluting industries, of dams, of housing developments, etc. In addition, resource and environmental economics is concerned with how market mechanisms sometimes fail to protect longer-term environmental and societal interests while favoring short-term economic interests, particularly when the resources being used by people trying to make profits are either not owned at all or are owned "in common" with other individuals. This is the economists' version of what the biologist Garrett Hardin (1968) called "the tragedy of the commons." This opposition between short-term interests, and, we must add, the simple criterion of efficiency or profit-maximization and long-term interests and, again we must add, the complex structure and dynamics of human ecological systems, has posed real challenges to economists concerned to somehow synthesize their discipline with that of ecology (Bernstein 1981).

Economists, like other systems analysts, have worked with energy analyses of human ecological systems (Ibid). In energy analyses, "costs" are expressed in terms of energy inputs rather than monetary inputs. Thus, a human activity that may seem efficient in monetary terms may turn out to be less efficient, or to have hidden costs, in energy terms.

Economists concerned with environmental issues tend to emphasize:

❏ Cost-benefit relationships
❏ Abstract models of human behavior that assume humans wish to maximize profit
❏ Market as the regulator; breakdown of market regulation as cause of many problems

Sociological Human Ecology

A feature of the "ecological" approach within the discipline of sociology that distinguishes it from the rest of sociology is its focus on the characteristics of large aggregates of humans, as opposed to individuals, small groups, or even the communities we normally think of. The major unit of analysis is the **population**. A population is a subset of a species, usually defined in terms of the organisms of a species that inhabit one territory. (Similarly, the major unit of analysis in ecology is sometimes seen as the population, as opposed to the individual or the cell or the gene.)

Accordingly, sociologists are known for their work in "demography," or the description and analysis of human fertility, mortality, and migration as they affect population structure and change. The ecological aspect of demography includes interrelationships between environmental factors and population factors, e.g., how changes in resources (soil quality, the amount of energy available, etc.) affect fertility, mortality, and migration; or, how changes in population size affect natural resources (depletion, intensification of use, pollution, etc.). Sociologists are best known for their work in demography, but anthropologists and geographers are more likely to be interested in the ecological aspects of demography.

The ecological perspective in sociology, anthropology, and geography is a naturalistic way of understanding human life. By this I mean that the fundamental assumption is that

". . . the complexities of human life arise from the exigencies of obtaining a livelihood from available resources" (Hawley 1984:2). (See Netting: "ecological" versus "ideological" perspectives.) We cannot be the clever, ideological, social, complicated creatures that we sometimes are without interacting with the natural components of our universe and ecosystems, without eating, drinking, defecating, driving automobiles made out of iron ores, other minerals, and fueled by petroleum and emitting lead and other pollutants into the environment. This is an old intellectual tradition, going back very far, at least as far as the thinking of the 18th and 19th century philosophers such as Montesquieu, Malthus, Darwin, Spencer, Marx. In sociology, its 20th century proponents, those who actually used the term "human ecology" in this context, are known as "The Chicago School," including men named Park, Duncan, Burgess, and Hawley. The "naturalistic" perspective is opposed to the "social structural" one, in which human social facts should be discussed only in relation to other social facts, not to environmental ones; and an "ideological" perspective that focuses on the customs, beliefs, and values of human groups (cf. Netting 1977:4–6).

Here is a statement, taken from the writing of Amos Hawley (Ibid), of some of the basic ideas of sociological human ecology:

❏ human social systems are "territorially based," that is, they occur in specific times and places, rather than in ahistorical vacuums;
❏ human social systems are ways in which populations try to "adapt to their environments" (Note: they can be understood in other ways, too, i.e., as sources of socialization and stresses for individuals; as interactive systems; as repositories of ideas)
❏ therefore, a proper focus of study is the "interaction between a population and its environment" and how this is affected by the social system or how it might help explain some features of the social system;
❏ human ecology involves a "holistic" and "macro-level" mode of analysis. That is, to understand the adaptation of a human

population to its environment, we must look at the entire system, not just focus on some of its parts.

So far, sociological human ecology is very similar to ecological anthropology and geography: looking at the interactions between humans and their environments, taking a holistic perspective, focusing on populations as a major if not the major unit of analysis, and assuming above all that if we wish to understand our human lives, the ways we arrange them and deal with other people in "social systems," we must take into account the "naturalistic" basis of life.

Sociologists tend to emphasize the following:

❏ urban and suburban populations in the industrialized world;
❏ the organization of the social systems of those populations and how well different organizational forms respond to urban and suburban problems (i.e., "urban renewal" organizations in relation to urban blight and "gentrification").
❏ relationships of interdependence, competition, and division of labor in human social systems (reflecting analogous concepts in biological ecology).[1]

Geographical Human Ecology

Geographers are very similar to sociologists and anthropologists in emphasizing the larger picture, "holistic" systems of population-environment interactions. Traditionally the field of geography focused on questions concerning the spatial distribution of landform features and human and other populations. (So did ecological sociology, but in urban settings). To some extent this involved looking at the effects of human settlements and activities (such as burning and cutting down forests) on the natural environment, and how climatic regions affect the kinds of human settlements and activities possible. In addition, geography is known for its use of "central place theory," a variation on the sociologists' notions of "dominance" and functional interdependency used to account for the actual placement of human settlements of different sizes and types (i.e., metropolitan centers, bedroom communities, satellite small cities and towns, rural villages, etc.) in relationship to each other. Today geographers are also interested in the passing of time and in more complex processes occurring in ecological systems.

Geographers and anthropologists have worked the hardest to actually incorporate the biological concept of "ecosystem" into their studies. Because this is difficult, they too have tended, when doing this kind of ecological study, to deal with relatively small-scale human populations, such as farmers, pastoralists, etc. in the poorer regions of the world. Thus, some of the best "ecosystems" work done by human ecologists has been done by geographers and anthropologists working among "primitive" tribal societies in places such as East Africa and New Guinea. However, the simplifying ecosystems approach that involves the study of energy flows and distribution has enabled geographers (and others) to study urban communities and entire nations from this perspective.

Geography's concern with the spatial dimension helps us understand major problems such as natural hazards and the imbalance between population growth and economic development in the less affluent nations in the world, as well as that between population and consumption in the wealthier, industrialized nations (see Zelinsky 1970, cited in Micklin 1984:80). Thus, for example, the spatial distribution of a population (and the historical and economic processes that determined it) may have a major effect on the degree to which a natural hazard such as an earthquake becomes a human disaster—why are all of those poor people living in shanties in the shaky hills?

II. Human Ecology of Health and Disease

Geography also includes the study of human patterns of disease and death (morbidity and mortality) from a spatial as well as epidemiological perspective. All of the fields of study that I am discussing have subsectors that are concerned with health and disease, and "human ecology" is very much part of that social science tradition. Geographers, anthropologists, sociologists, and historians contribute to the medical sciences of epidemiology and medical ecology. They add holistic, environmental, social, and cultural perspectives that are often missing from strictly medical research.

Ecological Political Science

Some political scientists use ecological perspectives in their work. Harold and Margaret Sprout (1971) conceptualized foreign policy and international relationships in terms of ecological systems theory and the adaptational problem of obtaining and allocating resources (materials, energy, wealth). As our world becomes more interrelated and environmental and social problems become as much global as national or local, nations are increasingly involved both in competing for scarce resources and in trying to cooperate to solve common problems. Thus, from this perspective the unit of analysis is the world system of nations (see Micklin 1984:80).

Study of the politics of environmental and health issues may also be thought of as "political ecology" (Ibid). How do such issues rise and fall in political agendas? How do different formal or informal political decision-making structures and processes affect policy outcomes? What is the nature of "grass-roots" politics in relation to environmental and health issues, of citizen mobilization in response to perceived and real hazards to life and health and well-being? Once a public policy is established, how is it implemented? What effects do lobbyists and other political pressure groups have on policy formation and implementation? From this perspective, the unit of analysis varies according to the nature of the polity being studied (i.e., international agency, national government, local government, pressure group) and the specific issue or event involved.

In this course we will look at politics of many different environmental problems, with a special focus on the politics of contemporary toxic waste and industrial chemical hazards.

Political Scientists tend to emphasize:

❏ Formal government (i.e., state arid national legislatures; government agencies like Department of State or Environmental Protection Agency)
❏ People in interaction with formal government through the voting process or in other ways, like civil disobedience and organized lobbying.

Ecological Anthropology

Anthropologists have long included careful descriptions of the environment and how people interact with it in making their livings ("subsistence activities") in their case studies or "ethnographies" of diverse cultural groups. Ecological anthropologists tend to take the "naturalistic" perspective discussed in our section on sociology, holding that careful studies of man-environment relationships can tell us a lot about the nature of *Homo sapiens sapiens* that studies of more "ideological" aspects of human communities cannot do.

Here are some of the emphases found in ecological anthropology (Note: these are just emphases; as in other sections above there are many exceptions):

❏ rural, non-industrial societies;
❏ the population or the small society as a major unit of analysis;
❏ "holistic" and "contextual" approaches
❏ adaptability as one of the key relationships between humans and their environments

Note also that anthropology is distinctive among the social sciences for emphasizing:

❏ human biology (including physiology and anatomy; evolution and genetics; and nutrition and health)
❏ human culture and meaning

As noted above, ecological anthropology is very similar in many ways to sociological and geographical human ecology. They all emphasize the larger picture, "holistic" systems of population-environment interactions. In addition, both anthropology and geography have tried to incorporate the biological concept of "ecosystem" into their studies. "The task of the human ecologist is to describe systems and to explain the interconnections among people and environments which sustain the system and keep it equilibrated" (Porter 1978:19). This is a difficult task to do on a large scale, and thus human ecologists—geographers and anthropologists in particular—tend to do their work in ". . . the underdeveloped world, the tropical, colonial world, and areas that appear to be too hot, too cold, too dry, or too high for most people" (Ibid).

Anthropology is the most diverse of the social sciences that have been discussed, and in many ways is not a *social* science at all, but a science of "man" (in the generic sense) that includes human biology, evolution, language, culture, social structure, and more. Archaeologists, who study the remains of former societies, both prehistoric and historic, are also very much involved in ecological studies as are physical anthropologists who study fossil and other remains to discern the outlines of primate and human evolution. Some physical anthropologists also study living human populations, and are interested in how environmental factors, including nutrition, climate, and altitude, affect human growth, development, and health. The anthropological study of language and culture includes "ethnoecology," or the study of how different human groups categorize and order the world around them and then how this is related to their behavior.

Economic and ecological anthropologists also look at the specifics of people's relationships with their local environments, how they make a living and share the costs and benefits of their work, how their involvements in markets or other economic system affect their use of natural resources, how people cope with environmental problems and opportunities. The "systems" approach that is so often found in ecological studies fits naturally into anthropology, because anthropologists are most generally concerned with how the many different facets of human and nonhuman life and physical environments interact.

Note

1. Smith notes that the word did not come into general use until the appearance of Warming's *Plantesamfund: Grundtrak af den okologiske Plantegeografi,* 1895, the origin of its modern meaning. Smith emphasizes plant geography in his treatment of the history of ecology.

References

Bates, M. (1964) *Man In Nature.* Englewood Cliffs, N.J.: Prentice-Hall.

Bernstein, B. B. (1981) Ecology and economics: complex systems in changing environments. *Annual Review of Ecology and Systematics* 12:309–30.

Craik, K. H. (1973) Environmental psychology. *Annual Review of Psychology* 24:403–422, reprinted in G. L. Young (ed.) 1983 *Origins of Human Ecology.* Stroudsburg, PA. Hutchinson Ross Pub. Co.

Enger, E. D., J. R. Kormelink, B. F. Smith, R. J. Smith. (1983) *Environmental Science: The Study of Interrelationships.* Dubuque: Wm. C. Brown.

Hardin, G. (1968) The tragedy of the commons. *Science* 162:1243–48.

Hawley, A. H. (1984) Sociological human ecology: past, present, and future, pp. 1–15 in M. Micklin & H. M. Choldin (eds.) *Sociological Human Ecology: Contemporary Issues and Applications.* Boulder: Westview Press.

Micklin, M. (1984) The ecological perspective in the social sciences: a comparative overview, pp. 51–90 in M. Micklin & H. M. Choldin (eds.) *Sociological Human Ecology: Contemporary Issues and Applications.* Boulder: Westview Press.

Netting, R. McC. (1977) *Cultural Ecology.* Menlo Park, CA: Cummings.

Orlove, B. S. (1980) Ecological anthropology. *Annual Review of Anthropology* 9:235–73.

Porter, P. W. (1978) Geography as human ecology: a decade of progress in a quarter century. *American Behavioral Scientist* 22(1):15–39.

Rapport, D. J. and J. E. Turner. (1977) Economic models in ecology. *Science* 195:367–73.

Smith, Robert Leo. (1986) *Elements of Ecology.* 2nd ed. New York: Harper & Row.

Sprout, M. and H. Sprout. (1971) *Toward a Politics of the Planet Earth.* New York: D. Van Nostrand.

Steward, J. (1955) *Theory of Culture Change.* Urbana: University of Illinois Press.

Young, G. L. (1974) Human ecology as an interdisciplinary concept: a critical inquiry. *Advances in Ecological Research* 8:1–105.

2

If Scientists Want to Educate the Public, They Should Start by Listening

Chris Mooney

Whenever controversies arise that pit scientists against segments of the U.S. public—the evolution debate, say, or the fight over vaccination—a predictable dance seems to unfold. One the one hand, the nonscientists appear almost entirely impervious to scientific data that undermine their opinions and prone to arguing back with technical claims that are of dubious merit. In response, the scientists shake their heads and lament that if only the public weren't so ignorant, these kinds of misunderstandings wouldn't occur.

But what if the fault actually lies with both sides?

We've been aware for a long time that Americans don't know much about science. Surveys that measure the public's views on evolution, climate change, the big bang and even the idea that the Earth revolves around the sun yield a huge gap between what science tells us and what the public believes.

But that's not the whole story. The American Academy of Arts and Sciences convened a series of workshops on this topic over the past year and a half, and many of the scientists and other experts who participated concluded that, as much as the public misunderstands science, scientists misunderstand the public.

In particular, they often fail to realize that a more scientifically informed public is not necessarily a public that will more frequently side with scientists.

Take climate change. The battle over global warming has raged for more than a decade, with experts still stunned by the willingness of their political opponents to distort scientific conclusions. They conclude, not illogically, that they're dealing with a problem of misinformation or downright ignorance—one that can be fixed only by setting the record straight.

Yet a closer look complicates that picture. For one thing, it's political outlook—not education—that seems to motivate one's belief on this subject. According to polling performed by the Pew Research Center, Republicans who are college graduates are considerably less likely to accept the scientific consensus on climate change than those who have less education. These better-educated Republicans probably aren't ignorant; a more likely explanation is that they are politically driven consumers of climate science information. Among Democrats and independents, the relationship between education and beliefs about global warming is precisely the opposite—more education leads to greater acceptance of the consensus climate science.

In other words, it appears that politics comes first on such a contested subject, and better information is no cure-all—people are likely to simply strain it through an ideological sieve. In fact, more education probably makes a global warming skeptic more persuasive, and more adept at collecting information and generating arguments sympathetic to his or her point of view.

A similar story unfolds with public opposition to vaccination. Once again, on a technical level, skeptics get the science wrong. The body of epidemiological evidence overwhelmingly shows that vaccines don't cause autism. Furthermore, the principal agent accused of having this effect (a mercury-based preservative called thimerosal) has long since been removed from most childhood vaccines. Yet autism rates have not declined.

With public health at stake, it's no wonder medical experts get frustrated when they hear autism activists such as actress Jenny McCarthy attack vaccines. But once again, the skeptics aren't simply ignorant people. If anything, they seem to be more voracious consumers of the relevant medical information than the nation as a whole. According to a 2009 study in the New England Journal of Medicine, children who go unvaccinated by parental choice (rather than because of inadequate access to vaccines) tend to be white, from well-to-do families and with married, college-educated mothers. Parents in such families are more likely to go onto the Internet (what McCarthy calls the "university of Google") to research the health risks of inoculation than are other groups of parents.

Or consider the long-running controversy over plans to dispose of the nation's nuclear waste at Nevada's Yucca Mountain. Although many technical experts have long argued that the repository would be safe, this has hardly convinced frightened and angry Nevadans. In 1991, the American Nuclear Energy Council even launched an ad campaign to educate the public about the Yucca Mountain plan but it backfired. Nearly a third of viewers became more resistant to the repository, and among those who were already opposed, their resolve strengthened. (Just 15 percent had a more favorable opinion of the repository after seeing the ad, and half of viewers did not change their minds.)

These three controversies have a single moral, and it's that experts who want Americans to take science into account when they form opinions on contentious issues need to do far more than just "lay out the facts" or "set the record straight." What science says is important, but in controversial areas, it's only the beginning. It's critical that experts and policy makers better understand what motivates public concern in the first place; and in this, they mustn't be deceived by the fact that people often appear, on the surface, to be arguing about scientific facts. Frequently, their underlying rationale is very different.

Thus, for instance, resistance to climate science in the United States seems to be linked to a libertarian economic outlook: People who resist what experts tell them about global warming often appear, at heart, to be most worried about the consequences of increased government regulation of carbon emissions. Similarly, based upon my observation, vaccine skepticism seems closely connected to distrust of the pharmaceutical industry and of the federal government's medical research establishment. As for Yucca Mountain, much of the outrage appears to originate in the perceived unfairness of having Nevada proposed as the sole dump site for the waste of an entire nation.

For this reason, initiatives that engage the public about science policy in a two-way conversation—before controversies explode—show great promise. In Canada, for instance, the national Nuclear Waste Management Organization spent three years listening to the public's views about how to handle nuclear waste disposal and promised that no dump or repository would be sprung on a community without its consent. Throughout the process, even critics of waste storage efforts remained engaged and supportive of attempts to come up with the best possible solution. In the United States, meanwhile, the federally funded National Nanotechnology Initiative has sponsored a great deal of social science research to explore possible public concerns that may arise as this new field of technology advances.

Experts aren't wrong in thinking that Americans don't know much about science, but given how little they themselves often know about the public, they should be careful not to throw stones. Rather than simply crusading against ignorance, the defenders of science should also work closely with social scientists and specialists in public opinion to determine how to defuse controversies by addressing their fundamental causes.

They might, in the process, find a few pleasant surprises. For one thing, the public doesn't seem to disdain scientists, as scientists often suppose. A 2009 study by the Pew Research Center for the People & the Press found that Americans tend to have positive views of the scientific community; it's scientists who are wary of the media and the public.

3

Body Ritual among the Nacirema

Horace Miner

Most cultures exhibit a particular configuration or style. A single value or pattern of perceiving the world often leaves its stamp on several institutions in the society. Examples are "machismo" in Spanish-influenced cultures, "face" in Japanese culture, and "pollution by females" in some highland New Guinea cultures. Here Horace Miner demonstrates that "attitudes about the body" have a pervasive influence on many institutions in Nacireman society.

The anthropologist has become so familiar with the diversity of ways in which different people behave in similar situations that he is not apt to be surprised by even the most exotic customs. In fact, if all of the logically possible combinations of behavior have not been found somewhere in the world, he is apt to suspect that they must be present in some yet undescribed tribe. The point has, in fact, been expressed with respect to clan organization by Murdock. In this light, the magical beliefs and practices of the Nacirema present such unusual aspects that it seems desirable to describe them as an example of the extremes to which human behavior can go.

Professor Linton first brought the ritual of the Nacirema to the attention of anthropologists twenty years ago, but the culture of this people is still very poorly understood. They are a North American group living in the territory between the Canadian Cree, the Yaqui and Tarahumare of Mexico, and the Carib and Arawak of the Antilles. Little is known of their origin, although tradition states that they came from the east. . . .

Nacirema culture is characterized by a highly developed market economy which has evolved in a rich natural habitat. While much of the people's time is devoted to economic pursuits, a large part of the fruits of these labors and a considerable portion of the day are spent in ritual activity. The focus of this activity is the human body, the appearance and health of which loom as a dominant concern in the ethos of the people. While such a concern is certainly not unusual, its ceremonial aspects and associated philosophy are unique.

The fundamental belief underlying the whole system appears to be that the human body is ugly and that its natural tendency is to debility and disease. Incarcerated in such a body, man's only hope is to avert these characteristics through the use of ritual and ceremony. Every household has one or more

* From *American Anthropologist 58(3)*.

17

shrines devoted to this purpose. The more powerful individuals in the society have several shrines in their houses and, in fact, the opulence of a house is often referred to in terms of the number of such ritual centers it possesses. Most houses are of wattle and daub construction, but the shrine rooms of the more wealthy are walled with stone. Poorer families imitate the rich by applying pottery plaques to their shrine walls.

While each family has at least one such shrine, the rituals associated with it are not family ceremonies but are private and secret. The rites are normally only discussed with children, and then only during the period when they are being initiated into these mysteries. I was able, however, to establish sufficient rapport with the natives to examine these shrines and to have the rituals described to me.

The focal point of the shrine is a box or chest which is built into the wall. In this chest are kept the many charms and magical potions without which no native believes he could live. These preparations are secured from a variety of specialized practitioners. The most powerful of these are the medicine men, whose assistance must be rewarded with substantial gifts. However, the medicine men do not provide the curative potions for their clients, but decide what the ingredients should be and then write them down in an ancient and secret language. This writing is understood only by the medicine men and by the herbalists who, for another gift, provide the required charm.

The charm is not disposed of after it has served its purpose, but is placed in the charm-box of the household shrine. As these magical materials are specific for certain ills, and the real or imagined maladies of the people are many, the charm-box is usually full to overflowing. The magical packets are so numerous that people forget what their purposes were and fear to use them again. While the natives are very vague on this point, we can only assume that the idea in retaining all the old magical materials is that their presence in the charm-box, before which the body rituals are conducted, will in some way protect the worshipper.

Beneath the charm-box is a small font. Each day every member of the family, in succession, enters the shrine room, bows his head before the charm-box, mingles different sorts of holy water in the font, and proceeds with a brief rite of ablution. The holy waters are secured from the Water Temple of the community, where the priests conduct elaborate ceremonies to make the liquid ritually pure.

In the hierarchy of magical practitioners, and below the medicine men in prestige, are specialists whose designation is best translated as "holy-mouth-men." The Nacirema have an almost pathological horror of and fascination with the mouth, the condition of which is believed to have a supernatural influence on all social relationships. Were it not for the rituals of the mouth, they believe that their teeth would fall out, their gums bleed, their jaws shrink, their friends desert them, and their lovers reject them. They also believe that a strong relationship exists between oral and moral characteristics. For example, there is a ritual ablution of the mouth for children which is supposed to improve their moral fiber.

The daily body ritual performed by everyone includes a mouth-rite. Despite the fact that these people are so punctilious about care of the mouth, this rite involves a practice which strikes the uninitiated stranger as revolting. It was reported to me that the ritual consists of inserting a small bundle of hog hairs into the mouth, along with certain magical powders, and then moving the bundle in a highly formalized series of gestures.

In addition to the private mouth-rite, the people seek out a holy-mouth-man once or twice a year. These practitioners have an impressive set of paraphernalia, consisting of a variety of augers, awls, probes, and prods. The use of these items in the exorcism of the evils of the mouth involves almost unbelievable ritual torture of the client. The holy-mouth-man opens the client's mouth and, using the above mentioned tools, enlarges any holes which decay may have created in the teeth. Magical materials are put into these holes. If there are no naturally occurring holes in the teeth, large sections of one or more teeth are gouged out so that the supernatural substance can be applied. In the client's view, the purpose of these ministrations is to arrest decay and to draw friends. The extremely sacred and traditional character of the rite is evident in the fact that the natives return to the holy-mouth-men year after year, despite the fact that their teeth continue to decay.

It is to be hoped that, when a thorough study of the Nacirema is made, there will be careful inquiry into the personality structure of these people. One has but to watch the gleam in the eye of a holy-mouth-man, as he jabs an awl into an exposed nerve, to suspect that a certain amount of sadism is involved. If this can be established, a very interesting pattern emerges, for most of the population shows definite masochistic tendencies. It was to these that Professor Linton referred in discussing a distinctive part of the daily body ritual which is performed only by men. This part of the rite includes scraping and lacerating the surface of the face with a sharp instrument. Special women's rites are performed only four times during each lunar month, but what they lack in frequency is made up in barbarity. As part of this ceremony, women bake their heads in small ovens for about an hour. The theoretically interesting point is that what seems to be a preponderantly masochistic people have developed sadistic specialists.

The medicine men have an imposing temple, or *latipso*, in every community of any size. The more elaborate ceremonies required to treat very sick patients can only be performed at this temple. These ceremonies involve not only the thaumaturge but a permanent group of vestal maidens who move sedately about the temple chambers in distinctive costume and headdress.

The *latipso* ceremonies are so harsh that it is phenomenal that a fair proportion of the really sick natives who enter the temple ever recover. Small children whose indoctrination is still incomplete have been known to resist attempts to take them to the temple because "that is where you go to die." Despite this fact, sick adults are not only willing but eager to undergo the protracted ritual purification, if they can afford to do so. No matter how ill the

supplicant or how grave the emergency, the guardians of many temples will not admit a client if he cannot give a rich gift to the custodian. Even after one has gained and survived the ceremonies, the guardians will not permit the neophyte to leave until he makes still another gift.

The supplicant entering the temple is first stripped of all his or her clothes. In everyday life the Nacirema avoids exposure of his body and its natural functions. Bathing and excretory acts are performed only in the secrecy of the household shrine, where they are ritualized as part of the body-rites. Psychological shock results from the fact that body secrecy is suddenly lost upon entry into the *latipso*. A man, whose own wife has never seen him in an excretory act, suddenly finds himself naked and assisted by a vestal maiden while he performs his natural functions into a sacred vessel. This sort of ceremonial treatment is necessitated by the fact that the excreta are used by a diviner to ascertain the course and nature of the client's sickness. Female clients, on the other hand, find their naked bodies are subjected to the scrutiny, manipulation and prodding of the medicine men.

Few supplicants in the temple are well enough to do anything but lie on their hard beds. The daily ceremonies, like the rites of the holy-mouth-men, involve discomfort and torture. With ritual precision, the vestals awaken their miserable charges each dawn and roll them about on their beds of pain while performing ablutions, in the formal movements of which the maidens are highly trained. At other times they insert magic wands in the supplicant's mouth or force him to eat substances which are supposed to be healing. From time to time the medicine men come to their clients and jab magically treated needles into their flesh. The fact that these temple ceremonies may not cure, and may even kill the neophyte, in no way decreases the people's faith in the medicine men.

There remains one other kind of practitioner, known as a "listener." This witchdoctor has the power to exorcise the devils that lodge in the heads of people who have been bewitched. The Nacirema believe that parents bewitch their own children. Mothers are particularly suspected of putting a curse on children while teaching them the secret body rituals. The counter-magic of the witchdoctor is unusual in its lack of ritual. The patient simply tells the "listener" all his troubles and fears, beginning with the earliest difficulties he can remember. The memory displayed by the Nacirema in these exorcism sessions is truly remarkable. It is not uncommon for the patient to bemoan the rejection he felt upon being weaned as a babe, and a few individuals even see their troubles going back to the traumatic effects of their own birth.

In conclusion, mention must be made of certain practices which have their base in native esthetics but which depend upon the pervasive aversion to the natural body and its functions. There are ritual fasts to make fat people thin and ceremonial feasts to make thin people fat. Still other rites are used to make women's breasts larger if they are small, and smaller if they are large. General dissatisfaction with breast shape is symbolized in the fact that the ideal form is virtually outside the range of human variation. A few women afflicted with almost inhuman hyper-mammary development are so idolized that they make a handsome living by simply going from village to village and permitting the natives to stare at them for a fee.

Reference has already been made to the fact that excretory functions are ritualized, routinized, and relegated to secrecy. Natural reproductive functions are similarly distorted. Intercourse is taboo as a topic and scheduled as an act. Efforts are made to avoid pregnancy by the use of magical materials or by limiting intercourse to certain phases of the moon. Conception is actually very infrequent. When pregnant, women dress so as to hide their condition. Parturition takes place in secret, without friends or relatives to assist, and the majority of women do not nurse their infants.

Our review of the ritual life of the Nacirema has certainly shown them to be a magic-ridden people. It is hard to understand how they have managed to exist so long under the burdens which they have imposed upon themselves. But even such exotic customs as these take on real meaning when they are viewed with the insight provided by Malinowski when he wrote:

Looking from far and above, from our high places of safety in the developed civilization, it is easy to see all the crudity and irrelevance of magic. But without its power and guidance early man could not have mastered his practical difficulties as he has done, nor could man have advanced to the higher stages of civilization.

4

The Mysterious Fall of the Nacirema

Neil B. Thompson

Many archeologists consider themselves to be cultural anthropologists because their ultimate aim is to make interpretations about cultural systems. They use artifacts to infer the nature of both the social organization and cultural orientation of a people. The following article draws such inferences from the few artifacts left by the Nacirema. Neil Thompson attempts to explain why these people suddenly vanished from the face of the earth. His study suggests that a cultural drive to change the land, water, and air may have caused their demise.

The revival of concern in the recently extinct culture of the Nacirema is, to say the least, most interesting, and perhaps reflects an increasing state of concern for our own society. (Aspects of the Nacirema culture were first described by Horace Miner in "Body Ritual Among the Nacirema." *American Anthropologist* (1956) 58:503–507.) The use of a multidisciplined approach in deciphering this puzzling culture is gratifying, for it is only by bringing all our methodological techniques to bear on the fragments of evidence in our possession that we will be able to rationally study and understand the history of this apparently vigorous but short-lived culture.

Through exploratory digs by our archeological expeditions, we are able to say with some confidence that the Nacirema were the dominant group in the complex of North American cultures. Although the Nacirema left a large number of documents, our linguists have been unable to decipher any more than a few scattered fragments of the Nacirema language. Eventually, with the complete translation of these documents, we will undoubtedly learn a great deal about the reasons for the sudden disappearance of what, from the physical evidence, must have been an explosive and expansive culture. For the present, however, we must rely upon the physical evidence we have uncovered and analyzed in order to draw any conclusions concerning its extinction.

When we examine the area occupied by these people in a single overview, it is immediately apparent that the Nacirema considered it of primary importance to completely remake the environment of the lands they occupied. On studying the fringes of their territory, particularly their penetration of the Cree cultural area to the north, one is struck by the energy

* "The Mysterious Fall of the Nacirema" by Neil B. Thompson with permission from *Natural History,* Dec. 1972. Copyright the American Museum of Natural History 1972.

that they expended on this task. Trees, if in large enough numbers and size to influence the appearance of the landscape, were removed. In treeless regions, hills were leveled and large holes were dug and partially filled with water. In a few areas the Nacirema imported structural steel with which they erected tall, sculpturesque towers. Some of these towers were arranged in series, making long lines that extended beyond the horizon, and were linked by several cables running through the air. Others, particularly in the northern fringe area, were erected in no discernible geometric pattern and were connected by hollow pipes laid on the surface of the earth.

When one views areas normally considered to be within their cultural suzerainty, one sees evidence of similar activity. Most trees were removed. In some areas, however, trees were replanted or areas were allowed to reforest themselves without assistance. Apparently, the fetish against trees went by fits and starts, for the Nacirema would sometimes move into a reforested area and again remove the trees.

Most of the land, however, was kept clear of trees and was sowed each year with a limited variety of plants. Esthetic considerations must have led to the cultivation of plants poisonous to human life because, while the products of the cropland were sometimes used as food, few were consumed without first being subjected to long periods of complicated processing. Purifying chemicals, which radically changed the appearance and the specific weights of the seeds or fibers, were added. These purification rituals were seldom performed in the living quarters, but rather in a series of large temple-like buildings devoted to this purpose. A vast hierarchy of priests dressed in white (a symbol of purity) devoted their lives to this liturgy. Members of another group, the powerful ssenisub community (whose position will be explained later), constantly examined the efforts of the first group and, if they approved, would affix to the finished product one of several stamps, such as "ADSU" or "Doog Gnipeekesouh." Still a third group, the repeekkoobs, accepted and recorded on permanent memorial rolls

the gifts of the general population to their priestly order.

On a more limited territorial basis, the Nacirema spent great time and energy constructing narrow ribbons, called steerts, across the landscape. Some steerts were arranged and connected in patterns, and in regions with a great concentration of people, the patterns, when viewed from the air, increased in size and became more elaborate. Other ribbons did not follow any particular pattern but aimlessly pushed from one population center to another. In general, their primary function seems to have been to geometricize the landscape into units that could be manipulated by a few men. The steerts also served as environmental dividers; persons of a lower caste lived within the boundaries of defined areas while those of the upper caste were free to live where they chose. Exploratory digs have shown that the quality of life in the different areas varied from very luxurious to poverty stricken. The various areas were generically referred to as ottehgs.

The task of completely altering the appearance of the environment to fit the Nacirema's ideology was given such high priority that the ssenisub community completely controlled the amassing of resources, manpower, and intelligence for this purpose. This group, whose rank bordered on that of a nonregimented priestly caste, lived in areas that were often guarded by electronic systems. There is no evidence to suggest that any restraints—moral, sociological, or engineering—were placed on their self-determined enterprises.

For a period of about 300 solar cycles (a determination made on the basis of carbon-dating studies), the Nacirema devoted a major part of their effort to the special environmental problem of changing the appearance of air and water. Until the last 50 solar cycles of the culture's existence, they seemed to have had only indifferent success. But during the short period before the fall of the culture, they mastered their art magnificently. They changed the color of the waters from the cool end of the spectrum (blues and greens) toward the warm end (reds and browns).

The air was subjected to a similar alteration: it was changed from an azure shade to a uniform gray-yellow. This alteration of water and air was effected by building enormous plants in strategic locations. These are usually found by our archeologists in or near large population centers, although, as success rewarded the Nacirema's efforts, they seem to have built smaller plants in outlying areas where environmental changes had not yet been effected. These plants constantly produced a variety of reagents, each appropriate to its locale, which were then pumped into the rivers and lakes or released into the atmosphere in the form of hot gases. The problem of disposing of the many by-products of this process was solved by distributing them among the general population. which retained them as venerated or decorative objects in their living quarters for a short time, then discarded them in the huge middens that were established near every population center.

In regions where colder temperatures apparently prevented the reagents from changing the color of the water sufficiently, the Nacirema, near the end of their cultural explosion, built special plants that economically raised the water temperature to an acceptable level for the desired chemical reaction.

The idea of a man-made environment was so pervasive that in some areas, notably in the provinces called Ainrofilac and Anaisiuol, the Nacirema even tried to alter the appearance of the ocean currents. In these regions they erected steel sculptures in the sea itself and through them released a black and slick substance, which stained the waters and the beaches. This experiment, however, was relatively unsuccessful since the stains were not permanent and the Nacirema apparently never mastered a technique for constantly supplying the reagent.

Early research has disclosed the importance of ritualistic observance among the Nacirema. In support of these observations, we should note the presence of the quasi-religious Elibomotua Cult, which sought to create an intense sense of individual involvement in the community effort to completely control the environment. This pervasive cult was devoted to the creation of an artistic symbol for a man-made environmental system.

The high esteem of the cult is demonstrated by the fact that near every population center, when not disturbed by the accumulation of debris, archeologists have found large and orderly collections of the Elibomotua Cult symbol. The vast number of these collections has given us the opportunity to reconstruct with considerable confidence the principal ideas of the cult. The newest symbols seem to have nearly approached the ultimate of the Nacirema's cultural ideal. Their colors, material, and size suggest an enclosed mobile device that corresponds to no color or shape found in nature, although some authorities suggest that, at some early time in the development, the egg may have been the model. The device was provided with its own climate control system as well as a system that screened out many of the shorter rays of the light spectrum.

The object was designed to eliminate most sounds from the outside and to fill the interior with a hypnotic humming sound when the machine was in operation. This noise could be altered in pitch and intensity by the manipulation, through simple mechanical controls, of an ingenious mechanism located outside the operator's compartment. This mechanism also produced a gaseous substance that, in a small area, could change the appearance of the air in a manner similar to the permanent plant installations.

In the early stages of the symbol's development, this was probably only a ritualistic performance since the production plant was small and was fueled by a small tank. This function, however, may have been the primary reason for the cult's symbol: to provide each family with its own device for altering the environment by giving it a private microuniverse with a system of producing the much desired air-changing reagent.

The complete machined piece was somewhat fragile. Our tests of the suspension system indicate that it was virtually immobile on unimproved terrain: by all of our physical evidence, its movement was restricted to the surfaced steerts that the Nacirema had built to geometricize the landscape.

We are relatively certain that a specially endowed and highly skilled group of educators was employed to keep the importance of these enclosed mobile devices constantly in the public eye. Working in an as yet unlocated area that they referred to as Euneva Nosidam, these specialists printed periodical matter and transmitted electronic-impulse images to boxlike apparatus in all homes.

While some of the information was aimed at describing the appearance and performance characteristics of the various kinds of machines, the greatest portion of the material was seemingly aimed at something other than these factors. A distinguished group of linguists, social psychologists, and theologians, who presented the principal symposium at our most recent anthropological conference, offered the hypothesis that the elibomotua symbols, also known as racs, replaced the processes of natural selection in the courtship and mating rituals of the Nacirema. Through unconscious suggestion, which derived from Euneva Nosidam's "mcnahulesque" materials, the female was uncontrollably driven to select her mate by the kind of elibomotua he occupied. The males of the culture were persuaded to believe that any handicap to masculine dominance could be overcome by selecting the proper cult symbol. In this way, the future of the race, as represented by Nacirema culture, was determined by unnatural man-made techniques.

The symposium was careful to point out that we have not yet uncovered any hard evidence to show whether or not this cultural trait actually had any effect on the race or its population growth. We have found, however, one strange sculpture from the Pop Loohcs depicting a male and female mating in an elibomotua's rear compartment, indicating a direct relationship. The hypothesis has the virtue of corresponding to the standard anthropological interpretations of the Nacirema culture—that it was ritual ridden and devoted to the goal of man's control of the environment.

Further evidence of the Nacirema's devotion to the Elibomotua Cult has been discovered in surviving scraps of gnivom serutcip. Some of these suggest that one of the most important quasi-religious ceremonies was performed by large groups who gathered at open-air shrines built in imitation of a planetary ellipse and called a keartecar. There, with intensely emotional reactions, these crowds watched a ritual in which powerful gnicar racs performed their idealized concept of the correct behavior of the planets in the universe. Apparently, their deep-seated need for a controlled environment was thus emotionally achieved.

The racs did not hold a steady position in the planetarium, but changed their relationship to the other racs rather frequently. Occasionally a special ritual, designed to emphasize man's power over his universe, was enacted. On these unannounced occasions one or more of the planet symbols was destroyed by crashing two of them together or by throwing one against a wall. The emotional pitch of the worshipers rose to its highest level at this moment. Then on command of the high priest of the ceremony, all the gnicar racs were slowed to a funereal speed and carefully held in their relative positions. After an appropriate memorial period honoring man's symbolic control of the universe, the machines were given the signal to resume their erratic speeds and permitted to make unnatural position changes.

We can only speculate on the significance of this ritual, but it seems reasonable to conclude that it served as an educational device, constantly imprinting in the individual the society's most important values.

Many of the findings of archeological explorations suggest that these symbols of universal power took up a large portion of the time and energy of the Nacirema society. Evidence indicates that a sizable portion of the work force and enormous amounts of space must have been devoted to the manufacture, distribution, and ceremonial care of the devices. Some of the biggest production units of the economy were assigned this function;

extensive design laboratories were given over to the manipulation of styles and appearances, and assembly lines turned out the pieces in serial fashion. They were given a variety of names, although all of those made in the same time period looked remarkably alike.

Every family assumed the responsibility for one of the machined pieces and venerated it for a period of two to four solar cycles. Some families who lived in areas where a high quality of life was maintained took from two to four pieces into their care. During the time a family held a piece, they ritually cleansed it, housed it from the elements, and took it to special shrines where priests gave it a variety of injections.

The Nacirema spent much of their time inside their elibomotuas moving about on the steerts. Pictures show that almost everyone engaged, once in the morning and once in the evening, in what must have been an important mass ritual, which we have been unable to decipher with any surety. During these periods of the day, people of both sexes and all ages, except the very young and the very old, left their quarters to move about on the steerts in their racs. Films of these periods of the day show scenes analogous to the dance one can occasionally see in a swarm of honeybees. In large population centers this "dance of the racs" lasted for two or three hours. Some students have suggested that since the swarm dances took place at about the time the earth completed one-half an axial rotation, it may have been a liturgical denial of the natural processes of the universe.

In as much as we are reasonably certain that after the rite most of the adults and all of the children left the racs and were confined inside man-made structures variously called loohcs, eciffos, tnalps, or emohs and, when released, went immediately to their racs and engaged in the next swarming, the suggestion may be apropos. The ardent involvement of the whole population from ages six through sixty five indicates that it was one of the strongest mores of the culture, perhaps approaching an instinctual behavior pattern.

It should also be mentioned that, when inside their racs, people were not restricted to their ottehgs, but were free to go anywhere they chose so long as they remained on the steerts. Apparently, when they were confined inside a rac, the Nacirema attained a state of equality, which eliminated the danger of any caste contamination.

These, then, to the best of our present state of knowledge, were the principal familial uses of the Elibomotua Cult symbols. After a family had cared for a piece long enough to burnish it with a certain patina, it was routinely replaced by another, and the used rac was assigned to a gallery keeper, who placed it on permanent display in an outdoor gallery, sometimes surrounded by trees or a fence, but usually not concealed in any way. During their free time, many persons, especially those from the ottehgs of the lesser sorts, came to study the various symbols on display and sometimes carried away small parts to be used for an unknown purpose.

There seems to be little doubt that the Cult of the Elibomotua was so fervently embraced by the general population, and that the daily rituals of the rac's care and use were so faithfully performed, that the minute quantities of reagent thus distributed may have had a decisive effect on the chemical characteristics of the air. The elibomotua, therefore, may have contributed in a major way toward the prized objective of a totally man-made environment.

In summary, our evaluation of both the Nacirema's man-made environmental alterations and the artifacts found in their territories lead us to advance the hypothesis that they may have been responsible for their own extinction. The Nacirema culture may have been so successful in achieving its objectives that the inherited physiological mechanisms of its people were unable to cope with its manufactured environment.

5

Will the Flood Wash Away the Crees' Birthright?

Clifford Krauss

Mistissini, Quebec, Feb. 22—Jimmy Neeposh has been trapping beavers and martens and hunting moose and caribou along the Rupert River since he was 4 years old, his life moving with the migrations of the game on which Cree Indians have lived for centuries.

Now at age 45, Mr. Neeposh faces a transformation, one that may end once and for all the remaining nomadic customs of the 13,000 Crees in the snowy northern woods of Quebec Province.

The Rupert is to be flooded by a series of dams and dikes as part of a huge hydroelectric development project. Many of the traditional Cree trap lines will be sunken forever, and the fishing for walleyed pike and speckled trout will never be quite the same.

"I have a very uneasy feeling about this," Mr. Neeposh sighed "but the reality of the world is changing and we have to change with it."

Resigned to the project, the Crees signed an agreement with the Quebec provincial government this month that will open their vast territory—a third of the province—to expanded logging, mining and hydroelectric installations.

The Crees also agreed to drop $3.6 billion in environmental lawsuits, receiving in return promises of $3.5 billion in financing over 50 years, and thousands of jobs for their chronically underemployed youth.

This is the first agreement in Canada's history that recognizes the full autonomy of any Indian people as a "native nation," giving Quebec's Crees substantial powers to help manage mining, forestry and energy development.

Top Cree chiefs negotiated in secret with the Quebec premier, Bernard Landry, to bury a long, bitter conflict over land rights. When agreement was announced last October, it shocked Quebec's nine Cree communities. Eventually, in a leap of faith that Cree jobs could be created without eating into the essence of Cree culture, nearly 70 percent of 6,500 Cree voters supported the agreement in a referendum.

"Agreeing to hydroelectric development was very difficult for me," acknowledged the Cree grand chief, Ted Moses. "But if you are going to gain something in negotiations you have to give something."

Quebec's Crees have shown a strong pragmatic streak since the French and English arrived in the 17th and 18th centuries.

Faced with superior military might, the Crees put aside their warrior ways, struck up a lucrative fur trading relationship with the Hudson Bay Company and adapted to Anglican Protestantism.

In 1975, the Crees signed an agreement with Quebec that allowed for the flooding of hundreds of square miles of hunting lands in exchange for $232.5 million in compensation over 21 years, guaranteed incomes for Cree hunters and subsidized housing.

The drowning of vast herds of caribou, flooding of ancestral grave sites, and broken promises of forestry and wildlife protection made them bitter, although leaders acknowledge that government cash brought many benefits. Now far larger sums are on the way.

In a generation, the Crees have evolved from a nomadic people who lived in tepees, had arranged marriages and used dog teams into an increasingly suburban society with power tools, snowmobiles, cellular telephones and computers.

Few of the 470,000 people scattered across 2,250 Indian reserves in Canada have achieved the standard of living of Quebec's Crees in the last 25 years.

Like most of the other Cree communities, Mistissini now looks like a working-class suburb with neat and comfortable wooden houses, an indoor hockey rink, a lighted baseball diamond, three well-equipped school buildings, two day-care centers and a modern hardware store. A large, attractive grocery store is stocked with T-bone steaks, deluxe imported coffees, fashion candles and magazines ranging from Today's Bride to Business Week.

Yet the Crees have preserved important parts of their culture, and one-third of their work force still live off hunting, fishing and trapping.

The 1975 agreement gave the Crees control over the local school board, which has mandated school instruction through the third grade strictly in the Cree language. Teaching in English is introduced only after that.

Modern medical care has helped to double Mistissini's population, to 3,100, in the last 25 years. Sixty-five percent of the local population is under age 30—an explosion that has helped to produce high unemployment and alcoholism among the young, whom Cree leaders now hope to help.

The Mistissini chief, John Longchap, said the new government compensation would be used to develop a lumber mill and create hundreds of jobs in retail businesses. Low-interest mortgages should also augment existing subsidies for public housing.

"It's never easy to compromise on something we have always depended on like the Rupert River," Chief Longchap said. "But we are reasonable people who make rational decisions even if they are not perfect."

Most Crees seem to agree, if reluctantly. Sam Edwards is a 72-year-old trapper who speaks only Cree. Interviewed in his shack, which is heated by a cast-iron stove, he noted: "Our traditional way was hard. There were no houses and tents were cold."

He still fishes as his father taught him, draping a net under the lake ice between two poles dug through the ice cover. But he now travels to his fishing spots by snowmobile, allowing him to cast more nets over a larger territory.

"Modern life is easier," he said, warming his water-swollen hands on a cup of coffee. "When the hunting doesn't go well these days, we can always go to the grocery store or to restaurants."

6

Athapaskans Along the Yukon

Brad Reynolds

It's easy, they said. Nothing to it. Wearing snowshoes is just like walking, they said. But with my face two inches above the snow, my feet twisted over my head, and my body wedged between two willows in minus 20° weather on an island in the frozen Yukon River, it did not seem all that easy.

Ellen Peters, kneeling in front of me on snowshoes, looked up from her rabbit snare. "Are you OK?"

Ellen has been snaring rabbits most of her 70 years. Small, less than a hundred pounds, she agreed to take me, a man twice her size and half her age, along to help on this trip.

Athapaskan Indians like Ellen have trapped, fished, and hunted along the middle Yukon River in north-central Alaska for at least 2,500 years. It is called the Koyukon region, and the Athapaskans who live there refer to themselves as *Dena*, "the people."

In Ellen's village of Nulato, on the banks of the Yukon, we hooked a wooden sled behind the new Bravo snowmobile her son Mark had bought with money earned from fighting forest fires. I balanced on the runners of the sled while she drove the Bravo out of town, onto the frozen Yukon, and three miles upriver to her snares. Ellen has two stickers pasted onto her snowmobile's windshield: "Mothers Against Drunk Driving" and "Don't Drink and Drive."

She came to a stop at a small island, and we put on our snowshoes. I struggled. Ellen slipped hers on, dropped a hatchet into an Army pack, slung it over her back, and lit a cigarette while she patiently stood waiting for me. She wore quilted snow pants, a home-made parka, mittens, mooseskin mukluks. Sunglasses protected her eyes from the harsh snow glare.

We plunged into thick willow growth, following a snare line Ellen knows by heart. She pointed out willows that rabbits had gnawed and showed me broken branches where moose had brushed by with their huge racks of antlers. When she meets a moose on her trail, she stands quietly until the animal senses her presence, then she stamps her feet and whistles to scare it off. She also pointed out the tracks of fox, ptarmigan, and wolf.

As I pant and flounder in her wake, she moves steadily ahead, smoking cigarettes and whistling "Amazing Grace" as she peers through the willows at her snares. She ties a noose of wire onto a willow in a rabbit trail, setting out about 30 snares along a two-mile stretch. Today Ellen will find only two rabbits caught in her wire snares.

There used to be lots more rabbits, she tells me. Her people used the fur to make socks, coats, and mitten liners, roasting the meat or cutting it up for stews and soups.

Now she snares them just for the meat and for the pure enjoyment of being on the river.

"As long as my legs are good," Ellen says, "I'll keep doing this. I really like it."

Indians of the Athapaskan language family stretch from Alaska's interior across northern Canada to Hudson Bay. They have been traced as far South as northern Mexico. The Navajo and the Apache speak languages identified as Athapaskan. Whether their ancestors migrated from an original Athapaskan homeland across the Bering Strait or developed their culture in place in the Alaska-Yukon-British Columbia region is still a matter of debate. In either case the Athapaskans have occupied Alaska for a very long time, even longer than the Eskimos.

The Koyukon region, largest Athapaskan area in Alaska, is home to some 2,400 people. It stretches 375 miles along the Yukon River, from Beaver to Kaltag, and includes remote villages scattered up the Koyukuk River, which empties into the Yukon about 25 miles below Galena.

The population of these villages varies from under a hundred in Hughes to about a thousand in Galena, including the Air Force Personnel stationed there. Two F-15 fighter jets scramble out of Galena as part of our front-line defense system guarding the border between the United States and the Soviet Union.

No roads connect these villages, so transportation is by air or on the river. In summer riverboats and barges ply the Yukon, which flows brown with suspended sediment. Over a mile wide in places, the Yukon in winter becomes a winding white highway traversed by snowmobiles and dogsleds. The river ice can grow more than four feet thick.

In the 19th century the Russians discovered that the Koyukon region was prime country for beaver furs, and they established trading posts along the river, including one in the village of Nulato. The Russian influence lives on in Athapaskan families with names like Demoski and Demientieff. It is not unheard of to see Indian children with bright red hair running through a village.

I first crossed this country by plane, en route from Fairbanks to Yupik Eskimo villages on the Bering seacoast. The view below was mesmerizing. Snow-topped hills and mountains covered with spruce, birch, and aspen rolled down to the wide, white, frozen Yukon River dotted with islands thick with willow and spruce. Moose, chest high in snow, fed on the willows at river's edge.

On one of those trips to visit the Eskimos—the largest group of native Alaskans—I was informed, to my surprise, that the state is also home to nearly 23,000 Indians. Eager to explore the secrets of their survival in this beautiful but harsh land, curious to learn how they are adjusting to 20th-century changes, I returned with my partner, photographer Don Doll, to meet the Dena.

Dena, over the centuries, have learned to survive by living in harmony with nature. They learned to live off what the land and river provide. In the Koyukon region you do not try to dominate nature, but work with it. Everything along the river has its own time and season: Salmon are taken in the summer, moose in the fall; caribou herds pass through during winter. The surrounding forests provide fuel for stoves and lumber for building cabins and fish wheels.

Now the Athapaskans must learn new lessons of survival, but in an environment much stranger and harsher than any they are used to. In less than a generation's time they have moved away from their subsistence life-style along the river into the high risks and corporate stress of the late 20th century.

The Alaska Native Claims Settlement Act of 1971 allocated 962.5 million dollars and 44 million acres of land for distribution among 13 corporations representing the native peoples of Alaska. Each native village was also incorporated, and a hundred shares of stock were issued to each qualifying native person.

The settlement terms were, at the time, foreign concepts to most Alaska natives. As a villager in Nulato remarked, "One day we were Indians standing on the bank, watching the river go by. The next day we were corporation members."

In the old days no one would have dreamed of laying claim to the land. It belonged not just to Dena but to the moose, caribou, bears, and the birds as well. The river was shared by the fish in it and the people on it. But today strips of orange tape, marking plots and subplots, flutter along the banks of the Yukon. Signs nailed to trees warn of private property and against cutting wood. Villagers find themselves buried in a blizzard of corporate papers. Even the hunting and fishing they have depended on for thousands of years are increasingly subject to licenses, permits, and regulations.

Bankruptcy, unemployment, and alcoholism are making survival problematic for many Athapaskans. Faced with frightening changes in their life-style and an uncertain future, many find they are drowning, figuratively and literally.

Suicide among Athapaskans has reached epidemic proportions. The rate for young native men is more than five times the rate for non-native men. Alcohol floods their villages. Father Bill Cardy, a priest serving several villages on the middle Yukon, testified about the effects of alcohol on village life to Alaska's Alcoholic Beverage Control Board. He recounted that testimony to me. "Eighty percent of our people who use alcohol use it destructively. In two years I have buried 16 young men and women. Alcohol was reportedly involved in all 16 deaths. In 22 months I have witnessed only four natural deaths."

Beer and whiskey can be ordered from Fairbanks liquor stores that cater to the villages. Getting alcohol out to the Yukon is not cheap, but it finds a ready market once it arrives there. I saw one man in Galena pay $24 for a case of beer and another $24 to fly it to a village downriver.

At the Native Hospital in Anchorage I talked with Vicki Hild, who coordinates the fetal alcohol syndrome (FAS) program for the Alaska Native Health Board. Among Alaska natives the number of babies born with FAS is more than double the national average. "Right now we have one of the highest rates among the populations studied," she noted.

In one region she followed closely for a year, one out of every four babies was born with fetal alcohol syndrome.

Don Doll and I drove to that region. There in Gulkana, an Athapaskan village near the Copper River, we met Frank and Pauline George and their three children, Margaret, 15, Kelsey, 6, and Amy, 3.

Kelsey was born with FAS, three weeks premature, weighing only five pounds, his lungs and eyes permanently damaged. He had to remain in the hospital a month before being taken home—Kelsey and his sister Amy, three years younger, are about the same size. Both are energetic. But Kelsey suffers bouts of bronchitis and catches colds easily.

"It's a miracle he lived," Pauline said. "The rest didn't make it. They were too small." Four other babies born to the Georges all had FAS. "Their blood was too much alcohol," she explained. "I never knew anything about this FAS, or that drinking could be that bad."

Both Frank and Pauline are recovering alcoholics. Pauline, born of alcoholic parents, began drinking with them as a teenager. "It was my mom, my dad, and me," she said. At 19 she married Frank, who was 34. They moved into the little house at the bottom of the hollow and continued drinking together. "I used to go into the village every morning and get a bottle," Frank recalled.

Both went for treatment after Kelsey was born. They are still pulling their lives back together. "The kids are happy for us having stopped drinking," Frank said. Pauline nodded and looked at her son. "Every once in a while it makes me cry to see him suffer," she said. "He's got a lot of hyper in him. That's because of the alcohol. There is nothing the doctors can do."

On Mother's Day I climbed the hill above Nulato to the cemetery overlooking the river. Ellen Peters and her granddaughter Carla were at the graves to offer food to the spirits of Ellen's four children buried there.

The old woman and the young girl cleared a patch of ground near the white crosses and gathered a pile of dry twigs and sticks. A strong, cold wind coming off the still frozen river made it difficult to start the fire. It took several tries before they had a blaze, burning most of the cardboard box in which they had carried the food.

As the flames grew, Ellen put food onto four paper plates. She served roast moose, dressing, gravy, and salad, speaking to her dead young as she set plates of food into the fire: "Here my children, I hope you like this food." She explained to the dead Stephen that at present she had no money for cigarettes, so he would have to settle for the chewing tobacco she sprinkled over the fire.

With her fingers Ellen dug four holes in the mud around the edge of the fire. Pulling a whiskey bottle from a sack, she poured some into each hole. "Stephen must be thirsty," she told her granddaughter, "look how that goes down so quick." And she poured a little more into that hole.

Photographs of her children line the walls of the small frame house she shares with two of her grandchildren. Of the 15 children Ellen bore, only six are living. Five died in infancy. "Alcohol," Ellen said, waving her hand toward photographs of the others, "these all died from alcohol.

"People used to die when they were old, and we would go to say good-bye and they would tell us stories about their lives. Those were good, happy deaths." she recalled. "But now they die so quick. We don't have time to say good-bye. It's all that dope and alcohol. It's no good."

The river is quiet and smooth and strong at nine o'clock on a summer evening. The sun remains high over the Yukon as Pat Madros and I head upriver to start his fish wheel. Pat points out five red foxes playing on the shore. Trees starting to change color splash bright red and orange on the hills above us. "I love this river," Pat tells me over the drone of the motor. "I could ride it for weeks."

Arriving at his fish wheel, Pat ties his boat to a log. When he pulls out a plank wedged beneath one of the wire baskets, the wheel slowly begins to turn.

He explained that a fish wheel runs on the same principle as a paddle wheel. Floating logs are lashed together into a rectangular frame. Two wooden uprights support an axle that revolves with two wire-mesh baskets and two wooden paddles. Each dips into the river, being pushed by the current: first a basket, then a paddle, then the other basket. Salmon swimming upriver are scooped up by the baskets and dropped into a wooden box at the side of the wheel.

The fish wheel, turning by itself, requires no tending. We found something hypnotic in watching the big wheel turn, splashing into the cold, muddy Yukon. When the fish are lifted out of the water, they flop and thrash in the basket; the sound can be heard halfway across the wide river.

When Pat untied his boat, he did not start the engine, content to drift downriver toward home, enjoying the Yukon in the evening light. "In the fall when we're hunting moose," he said, "sometimes it's so dark when we come back, all you can see are the mountaintops."

The next morning, although it was cloudy and cold, we returned to the wheel with his wife, Mary. They tossed salmon into two plastic bins they had brought along. They had caught about three dozen, most about 20 inches long, a few closer to three feet.

Back home Mary flattened a cardboard box onto the table next to their smokehouse and began cleaning fish. She cut the head, tail, and fins with three deft slices, dumping them into a bucket to be boiled for dog food.

Pat watched for a while and offered to help. He picked up the curved fish knife and chopped at the tail, clearly not familiar with work usually reserved for women. Though his wife tried showing him how to do it, he soon cut his finger. Mary sent him inside, saying, "Men are not good for cutting fish."

In 1973 limited-entry commercial fishing permits were introduced to regulate Alaska's fishing industry. Along the middle Yukon permits are granted for 74 gill nets and 159 fish wheels. With many more applications than permits, these have become a valuable commodity. The going price for a gill-net permit is about $9,800; for a fish-wheel permit, nearly

$13,000. As the price escalates, fewer Athapaskan fishermen can afford permits, so outsiders buy them.

While most Athapaskan families in the Koyukon region still spend their summers drying fish for the winter, those with commercial permits spend their energy harvesting eggs from the fat bellies of female salmon ready to spawn. Processors from Japan have moved in to buy the roe. Salmon roe is as popular in Japan as sirloin steak in the U.S.

Jerry Felton is manager for Towa America, Inc., which operates out of Galena. "One hundred tons of roe go through this district each year," he told me, "and we get the majority of it." Each morning of the season he sends a boat up and down the river to buy roe from the commercial fishermen. Back in Galena it is cleaned, soaked in brine, sorted by size and quality, and crated to be flown first to Anchorage, then to Japan.

Competition for the roe has increased. Plants offer four to five dollars a pound. An average fish carries just under one pound.

Pat Madros has built his own roe plant near his father's traditional fish camp, 25 miles below Kaltag. A plywood cabin among the trees just above the Yukon serves as home for Pat and his family during the fishing season. Collaborating with the buyer for a Japanese company out of Anchorage, Pat pays cash for eggs delivered to his camp.

Felton admitted that harvesting the roe is sometimes looked upon with suspicion by Alaska natives, who are used to getting the most out of what they harvest. The temptation is to grab the roe and dump the fish, wasting good food.

In the village of Kaltag the commercial fishermen formed a cooperative. They sought a better price for gas and oil by buying in bulk and a better position to bargain with the roe companies. Not that that helped in 1987 when they signed a contract with a company offering to buy both roe and fish. The buyer cemented the deal with an initial $10,000, and the Indians began delivering their roe and fish to him. But at the end of the season the dealer told them he was broke, and the 15 members of the Kaltag

Fishermen's Association found themselves out $75,000 and with no stockpile of fish for the winter ahead.

The corporation for Alaska natives in the Koyukon region is Doyon, Limited, with acreage larger than Connecticut, Rhode Island, and Massachusetts combined; when title is conveyed, the corporation will be the largest private landholder in North America. "Doyon" is a Russian loanword meaning "chief."

Besides the corporate responsibilities to its shareholders, Doyon has the added responsibility of promoting their social, cultural, and personal interests in all its business ventures. For instance, any land deals must consider the subsistence needs of the villages included in the project.

Doyon has made major investments in oil exploration on Alaska's North Slope. Doyon Drilling Inc. Joint Venture owns four big oil-drilling rigs and leases them to companies like ARCO Alaska, which prefer the leasing arrangement to the expense of owning the rigs. Doyon Drilling's crews operate the rigs, and nearly half its employees are shareholders in the parent corporation.

In early spring Don Doll and I visited Doyon's Rig 14, drilling in the Kuparuk oil field. Daily flights shuttle ARCO and Doyon employees between Anchorage and the North Slope. A 90-minute jet flight took us to Prudhoe Bay, where we boarded a Twin Otter for a 20-minute hop to Kuparuk.

A Doyon truck took us the final 15 miles over gravel roads to the rig itself. Oil flows from the wells to a central processing facility that then pipes it to Prudhoe Bay. From there it is funneled into the trans-Alaska pipeline, which runs 800 miles to Valdez, in south-central Alaska.

Rig 14 rose up out of the flat, snow-covered tundra like a golden skyscraper. It stands 182 feet high, 100 feet long, 52 feet wide. Amazingly, this 2.4-million-pound structure moves from site to site on eight gigantic tires, each 12 feet tall and 3 feet wide.

Jim Spaulding, "tool pusher," or boss of the rig, took us to the "dog house," the rig's command central. The drill penetrates down 90 to

120 feet an hour, piercing as much as 10,000 feet of earth in a week. Its precise depth and location show up on the geograph, which records the drill's depth at one-foot intervals. "It costs ARCO $100,000 a day to drill a well," Jun yelled over the drill's pounding, "so they want to know they're getting their money's worth."

The crew numbers 50, counting those on the rig and the support staff in the three-story modular living quarters, also on wheels. Everyone works a 12-hour shift, which means two employees for every job: cooks, maids, janitors, roughnecks, and roustabouts. When not working, they can relax in the recreation center, playing pool, watching cable TV or a movie, or just unwinding in the sauna. Meals are served four times a day.

Athapaskans applying for work with Doyon Drilling far exceed the number hired. I met Lenny Lewis, a "roustabout pusher," or foreman, and a Doyon shareholder. Lewis commutes between the oil rig and his home in Quilcene, Washington, every two weeks. "Up here I work hard, and down there I play hard," he told me. "At home I like to kick back in my hot tub and drink beer.

"Oil rigs are rough on a marriage. My wife, she's glad to see me come home, but after two weeks she's glad to see me go."

Before signing on with Doyon, Lewis worked on oil rigs in Texas, where he earned $30,000 a year. With Doyon he has doubled his salary. "For guys coming out of villages, $60,000 is a lot of money," he said. No wonder young Athapaskans along the Yukon talk admiringly of their brothers and cousins working "on the slope" and dream of the day they can join them.

One cold, gray day I went to the state-run Alaska Vocational-Technical Center in Seward. Here I met the students—15 young Alaskans from villages in the interior, Doyon shareholders being trained for the oil rigs.

Robin Renfroe, from the Tanana Chiefs Conference, showed me around the campus. While the Doyon corporation can offer Athapaskans paying jobs, Tanana Chiefs (or TCC, as they call it) ensures that they gain the skills needed for those jobs.

Robin was TCC's director of training. She told me they had 120 applications for the 15 openings in the 11-week course and interviewed 45 young men and women. Once you are enrolled, TCC provides tuition, room and board, transportation, steel-toed boots, and a monthly stipend. Most of the $1,600 cost comes from federal grants.

While helping people learn specialized skills, TCC also promotes traditional native resources and crafts through its Alaskan Resources, Commodities, Trading and Investment Corporation (ARCTIC). One ARCTIC project was a candy company that provided jobs for village Athapaskans who gathered and shipped wild berries to their urban counterparts in Fairbanks and Anchorage to turn into delicious chocolate-covered candies.

ARCTIC's marketing and sales specialist, Kathy Mayo, showed me other company products, including potpourri, herbal teas, and spruce cones, all collected by villagers, packaged in birchbark baskets and miniature dogsleds made by them, and distributed for sale to department stores and souvenir shops.

In Galena I attended an agricultural fair sponsored by TCC. As people brought their entries to the community hall, Amy VanHatten, who organizes this fair and others in Athapaskan villages, showed me through a vegetable exhibit. Radishes were as big as fists, turnips the size of pumpkins. Amy said TCC sells seeds and tools to the villagers at cost. The Alaska soil is rich, and though the season is short—from early June until late August—the sun shines almost constantly.

"We have only one livestock entry," Amy said, leading me to a wire cage. Inside sat the biggest, blackest rabbit I have ever seen. A hand-lettered sign explained that Shadow was the pet rabbit of the kindergarten and first-grade students at the Galena school. Laughing, Amy said it probably deserved a purple heart in addition to the blue ribbon on its cage.

Most Athapaskan villages have primary and secondary schools, usually housed in the same building. Teachers, many from outside the state, arrive in the fall for the nine months of school. Students take the usual academic subjects, plus electives like home economics, woodworking, and computer studies. During the long winter months basketball games in the school gymnasium are a popular pastime for the entire village. Competition is fierce. Teams travel up and down the river by snowmobile for weekend tournaments.

Maurice McGinty, from Nulato, has served as teacher, counselor, and principal in schools along the Yukon. He earned his master's degree in education administration from the University of Alaska in Fairbanks. McGinty said that while the schools are good at what they do, they are not designed for teaching the skills needed in village life. "A lot of boys would like to go out and trap if they had the skills, but there's no one instructing them.

"We're teaching them academics for moving on out," he explained. "In some cases we have kids who bloom and shine—and they go into the outside world. But if they bomb out, we've got nothing to offer them back here in the community. And that's a real letdown. Once you lose motivation, you lose self-esteem. And once you've lost that, there's nothing. That's when they go for the bottle."

I attended the Spring Festival in Fairbanks, sponsored by the Yukon-Koyukuk School District. About 200 students—most of them Athapaskans from villages scattered throughout the interior—compete in spelling, reading, mathematics, speech, and performing arts.

Each of the 11 schools in the district holds its own competitions, then sends its champions to Fairbanks. Although the school district provides food and housing, each school has to pay for transportation. Kaltag sent 24 participants; its plane bill came to $7,300.

I heard the Kaltag children's choir on stage in Fairbanks' Alaskaland Civic Center. They were performing a song that urged Indian youth to achieve great things in their lives. Then they sang "La Bamba" in Spanish, accompanied by maracas and drums.

On the last night of the festival the organizers mounted an awards banquet and a fashion show. A dozen girls and four boys had volunteered to model clothes they selected from the racks at J C Penney. Staring hard into the dressing-room mirrors, they combed their hair and fiddled nervously with their unaccustomed apparel. The music started, and, as they had carefully rehearsed, they sauntered one by one onto the stage. In front of a wall-size mural of spruce and birch trees they turned and posed for their appreciative audience before scampering back to the safety of the dressing rooms. Flashes from the cameras of fellow students, teachers, and parents gave the feel of an opening in Paris.

Bruce Kleven calls such experiences learning "urban survival skills." He helps run a program to teach them to Athapaskan youths. High school students from the villages spend two weeks living and working at the school district's headquarters in Nenana, about an hour's car ride west of Fairbanks.

They work with a journeyman printer and professional reporter, studying graphic arts and journalism while producing an issue of the school district's newsletter, *Han Zaadl-itl'ee,* "we live on the river." The students provide stories, poems, and reports about their own villages.

They also take field trips into Fairbanks to sharpen such urban survival skills as using a bus schedule, obtaining a driver's license, making hotel reservations, filling out job applications, opening a bank account, ordering food in a restaurant and then calculating the tip.

"The idea is not to make seasoned city dwellers out of these students," Kleven explained. "The thrust is to expose students to situations and conditions they will face whenever they leave the village. Remember, our students live in one of the most remote areas in the U. S. They are ill-equipped to function in Fairbanks."

Don and I spend our final days with the Koyukon Athapaskans at the Stickdance—a traditional week-long memorial for their dead. It is said to have originated near the Yukon tributary of Bear Creek. There, according to legend, a man received a vision of the Stickdance in a dream after the rest of his family died, leaving him to mourn alone. Today the ceremony is observed in only two villages on the Yukon: Kaltag and Nulato.

It can take months and even years for a family honoring deceased members to prepare for a Stickdance—saving up gifts to distribute, choosing the people who will represent the dead they honor, making the clothes that will symbolize that identity.

Each evening of the week of the Stickdance we join the people who come to the community hall carrying traditional foods— moose, salmon, beaver, rabbit, ptarmigan— for the shared meal they call a potlatch. Afterward the women stand in a solemn circle, eyes downcast, swaying in place as they chant songs composed for the dead.

The hall becomes fuller each night as friends and relatives from other villages on the river arrive. Night by night the intensity of the mournful songs builds.

On Friday night, amid loud singing as the women dance in a circle around the hall, men carry a tall, thin spruce tree—stripped of branches and bark and wrapped in ribbons— to the center of the room. Wolf, fox, and wolverine furs are draped on it as the people surge around, chanting and dancing in a tight circle.

Their hypnotic chanting and dancing continues nonstop through the night. Laughter erupts and tears stream as the people remember and grieve for their dead during the long hours. Arguments and fights break out as some try to drown their grief and anger in alcohol.

By morning the exhaustion is tangible, some fall asleep despite the noise and constant movement around the stick. As part of the tradition, men force their way through the dancers to tear the skins and ribbons from the stick. Once it is stripped, they carry it out into the village, still chanting as they snake between the houses down to the Yukon. There they break the stick into pieces and hurl them onto the river ice.

Immediately the chanting stops. Eerie quiet descends over the village as people return to their homes to sleep.

On the final night—Saturday—those representing the dead are ritually dressed in their new clothes. With eyes downcast, they leave the village hall in a somber line to shake the spirits from their clothing at the river's edge.

I sit with Ellen Peters on the floor of the hall as we watch them leave. She tells me that she plans to honor her own dead children at Nulato's next Stickdance, which will be held in two years.

"I'll start getting ready this spring before I put my garden in," she continues. "Because it will take me a long time. I'm not young. And I'm tired." But it is more the weariness of grief, I think, than loss of vigor.

The departed return from the river, file in silently, and sit in a row in the hall.

Suddenly the mood changes. The excitement of the traditional distribution of gifts sparks a night of celebration.

The next morning those who have assumed the identity of the dead move through the village, shaking hands with the villagers, sharing food and drink, and saying farewell.

Although the villagers faithfully tried to adhere to the age-old rituals during the Stickdance, much of the meaning and symbolism behind the ceremonies appeared to have been lost. Originally there were 14 songs to honor the dead spirits. One has been forgotten, and today the other 13 are only vaguely remembered by a handful of elders. During the Stickdance these remaining songs were played on a cassette tape.

The Athapaskans we met along the mighty Yukon represent a culture that has struggled to survive for thousands of years. Their plaintive songs for the dead sound ever more poignant as parts of their heritage erode before their eyes. Amid calls for increased control over their own lives and welfare, Athapaskans recognize that, although as a people they are survivors, not all among them will weather the current cultural transitions. The unrecognized symbols and half-remembered chants of the Stickdance mourn not only those lost in the past but also those who will be lost to the future.

7

The Meaning of Adaptation

Ann McElroy and Patricia K. Townsend

Preview

A central concept of medical ecology is adaptation, the processes of adjustment and change that enable a population to maintain itself in a given environment. Because environments and ecological relationships change over time, adaptation is a continual process. Environmental pressures—such as climatic extremes, seasonal fluctuations, and natural or man-made disasters—evoke adaptive responses. Some responses are quickly made and quickly reversed if the environmental pressures are alleviated. Other responses take generations to become established in a population and are relatively irreversible.

The slowest and least reversible adaptive mechanisms are genetic changes. Natural selection, occurring through differences in mortality rates and reproductive success of individuals exposed to a specific disease such as malaria, brings about genetic adaptation to the disease. The chapter's first profile, concerning adaptation to malaria, discusses one of the best examples of how ecological change—in this case, development of agriculture in West Africa—is related historically to genetic change in a population.

A second type of adaptive mechanism is the constellation of physiological responses and developmental changes made within an individual life span. Some of these responses are very rapid, as when a person begins to sweat in a hot room. Others are incremental results of developmental processes, for example, the development of large chests and lungs by people who grow up at high altitudes. Because individuals must have the genetic potential for physiological adaptation, it is difficult to discriminate between physiological and genetic forms of adaptation.

A third type of adaptive response highly developed in human beings is the use of cultural information shared by a social group and transmitted through learning to each generation. Medical systems are one of cultural adaptation to health problems. Cultural customs, beliefs, and taboos also have an indirect effect on health, some positive and some negative. In a fourth type of adaptation, individuals adjust their behavior and attitudes to cope with the challenges of illness, disability, and aging.

The capacity of the group and the individual to adapt to environmental circumstances is very broad, but certain limits exist and compromises are often necessary between what is desired and what is possible. Adaptation is never perfect and often involves inherent risks along with potential benefits. Technological changes may increase the environment's carrying capacity, but these changes may also increase the risk of disease or hazard. Evolutionary changes giving resistance to disease in certain environments may create genetic difficulties for future generations, requiring new kinds of adaptive responses, as shown in the health profile on sickle cell anemia in the United States.

Now, here, you see, it takes all the running you can do, to keep in the same place.

The Red Queen, in Lewis Carroll,
Through the Looking-Glass

The Red Queen's explanation to Alice reflects a basic premise of medical ecology: Ecosystems are dynamic and living things are continually responding to change. According to the Red Queen Hypothesis (Ehrlich 1986:86), "in order to persist, a population must continue to evolve—otherwise the population's ever-changing environment, especially its evolving predators and competitors, will force the population to extinction."

Populations lacking variability in their adaptive potential can tolerate only limited change, and organisms that cannot respond flexibly and adapt to change often do not survive. In this chapter we consider the mechanisms that ensure that humans maintain flexibility and variability in response to environmental challenges.

While effective responses to environmental pressures often involve changes by the population or the individual, human biologists are discovering that *non-change* is also an effective physiological and genetic response. Population systems come into equilibrium and maintain plateaus for periods of time, and factors conducive to such stability are also adaptive. Maintaining equilibrium at an optimal point is a dynamic process that contributes to survival just as much as does change (Steegmann 1987: personal communication).

Adaptation can be defined as a set of processes of change and adjustment that increase a population's chances of continuing to exist through successive generations in a given environment. Adaptation occurs within two time frames: short-term adjustments and long-range evolution. The physiological and behavioral adjustments that a person makes in his or her lifetime in response to specific environmental problems are one component of adaptation. When the population itself undergoes genetic or cultural changes that enhance the group's success within its ecological niche or in new niches, it is adapting through evolutionary processes.

Adaptation occurs in response to a variety of environmental problems and challenges. Some habitats sustain life rather precariously, with poor soil, little rainfall, and extremes of heat and cold, and yet humans manage to live in these places. The diverse processes by which people manage to survive, even to thrive, in such environments indicate the human capacity for adaptation. . . .

The differences in the body size and shape of the two men, largely inherited but also influenced by diet and variable growth patterns, are related to the different climates of their home environments. The arctic hunter's short limbs and compact, bulky body may help conserve heat, while the relatively long limbs and linear physique of the East African may help him dissipate body heat (Howells 1960; Steegmann 1975).

Even more important than body type in coping with temperature extremes is the capacity to adjust physiologically to variations in temperature. As the dry heat of the grasslands increases during the day, the African maintains a fairly constant body temperature through sweating. The Inuk is also capable of throwing off excess body heat through sweating during exertion and when the microclimate of his fur parka or crowded snowhouse becomes too warm.

Both arctic and grasslands dwellers are able to respond to a decrease in air temperature through the constriction of peripheral blood vessels. This prevents loss of heat from the warm body core area. However, the, blood vessels of the Inuk's hands and feet quickly dilate again, allowing rewarming and giving protection against cold injury. The heat-adapted African's fingers and toes usually do not rewarm quickly, and he is more susceptible to

Table 7.1 Human Adaptation Mechanisms, Encompassing Both Biological an Sociocultural Mechanisms on the Population and Individual Level (examples of adaptive processes in *Ratios*)

	Population Processes	**Individual Processes**
Biological mechanisms	biological evolution *(change in gene frequencies)*	Physiological responses and developmental changes *(acclimatization)*
Sociocultural mechanisms	cultural change *(advances in health care)* behavioral adjustments *(coping with disease)*	

injury if exposed to severe cold (Steegmann 1975:144–146).

The houses that these people build also provide protection against the environment. The snowhouse insulates against wind and heat loss, while the mud-and-thatch house insulates against heat. Both dwellings make good use of principles of insulation and air convection. The snowhouse uses thick blocks of dense, dry snow, air pockets between hanging skins and outer walls, raised sleeping platforms, and right-angle tunnel entrances. The thick mud walls of the grasslands house have good insulating properties also. They absorb solar radiation during the day and radiate it during the cooler night, leveling the daily temperature variation.

Body type, sweating and vasodilation, and housing all give protection against the environment. They result from very different processes, yet each contributes to adaptation. Body type is highly influenced by heredity, which sets fairly narrow limits on variability. Sweating and cooling are flexible responses that occur automatically within a fairly wide range of external variation. The human ability to learn from others how to use tools and raw materials to build appropriate houses as buffers against the environment is very flexible and is limited only by available materials, technology, and human energy.

Not all habitats are as harsh as the Arctic or the hot, dry grasslands, but each habitat requires certain modifications and variations in human physiology and behavior. Every ecosystem has periodic fluctuations in tem-

perature and precipitation. Long-term or permanent changes occur, including those resulting from natural or man-made disasters. With these changes, new opportunities may arise for competition or cooperation between populations, and humans modify their technology in ways that change their ecological niche or increase their effectiveness in their present niche. Any of these changes—whether they are natural fluctuations, unexpected catastrophes, or human-induced changes—act as challenges for adaptation. They evoke a variety of human responses, some automatic and influenced by heredity, others the product of learning and innovation.

Table 7.1 illustrates various dimensions of human adaptation: population versus individual processes and biological versus sociocultural mechanisms. A third dimension of adaptation is long-term (genetic and cultural change) versus short-term time frames (physiological or developmental and individual adaptation). A fourth dimension is the degree of reversibility, ranging from the relatively irreversible nature of genetic change, to cultural change that is not easily reversed once a pattern becomes entrenched, to the relatively reversible categories of physiological and psychological adjustment. However, physiological adaptations made in the course of growth and development over one's lifetime are usually not reversible. For example, stunted adult size from chronic malnutrition during childhood is not reversible. However, many other behavioral and physiological or morphological attributes are partially reversible.

Adaptation in Biological Evolution

Evidence of evolutionary change can be found in the fossil record and in historical sources, as well as in the fact that populations in various geographic regions vary in height, skin color, blood types, resistance to certain diseases, and other physical characteristics. Populations differ over time and across space in part because of the adaptive process of biological evolution, defined as change over time in the genetically inheritable characteristics of a population. A population is a group of people, usually but not always of common ancestry, who live in the same general region and type of environment and who form mating relationships. They may or may not share a single cultural system, but they do share similar genetic characteristics. It is the population that evolves, not the individual, through changes in gene frequencies.

Genetic Codes

Genetic characteristics are derived from biochemical codes or instructions for life processes of the body—self-maintenance, repair, growth, use of energy. These instructions are contained within the set of twenty-three pairs of chromosomes found in the nucleus of each primary cell of the human body. Chromosomes contain molecules of DNA (deoxyribonucleic acid), double structures of alternating sugar and phosphate groups joined by chemical base pairs. The structure of DNA is shown in Figure 7.1. Bases always bond in pairs, and the sequence of base pairs provides the chemical instructions for synthesis of amino acids. The instructional codes are called genes. A **gene** is a length of DNA that codes for a complete chain of amino acids determining protein structure (Damon 1977:68). Each gene corresponds to a certain *locus*, or position, on the chromosome. Since chromosomes function in pairs, the genes are also paired, one inherited from the individual's father and one from the mother. The two genes may be almost identical or they may be slightly different, expressing two variants, or *alleles*, of the gene.

Using a hypothetical example, if you inherit allele M from your father and allele N from your mother, your *genotype* would be MN. If M is dominant and N is recessive, on laboratory tests you would show up as type M, and your *phenotype* would be M. A genotype expresses the actual genetic makeup, while the phenotype is the expressed or visible trait. Having two alleles at a locus is called a *heterozygous* condition; thus the MN individual is a *heterozygote.* The person who inherits M from both parents is *homozygous* for that trait and is designated MM. Because M is dominant over N, MN and MM are phenotypically similar even though they are genotypically different.

Many genes exist without variants; about two-thirds of all loci in the gene pool of a population (and about 90 percent in an average individual) are nonvariant loci. About one-third of all chromosomal loci are variable, and it is this variation that is the raw material for evolution (Birdsell 1972:55, 396; Nei 1975). While some elements of the genetic pool are standardized, others are variable, or *polymorphic*, in a population. Traits that vary polymorphically in populations are especially suitable for the study of factors that influence changes in allele frequencies in a gene pool.

Genetic changes occur partly because of *mutations*, abrupt changes in base pair sequences in the DNA molecules or breaks in chromosomes leading to rearrangements of gene positions and code sequences. Mutations create changes in biochemical activity that can have a significant metabolic effect on the individual. *Point mutations*, involving the substitution of a single base in a code sequence, may seem particularly insignificant, but these tiny alterations are the most important source of genetic variation. Most mutations are harmful, particularly in the homozygous condition. However, sometimes it is actually an advantage to be heterozygous for a trait, with one normal allele and one variant form. The first profile in this chapter will show how this can be so in the case of adaptation to malaria.

Mutation maintains variation within a species, but by itself, mutation is not inherently adaptive. It is simply a random process, only rarely producing a change that happens

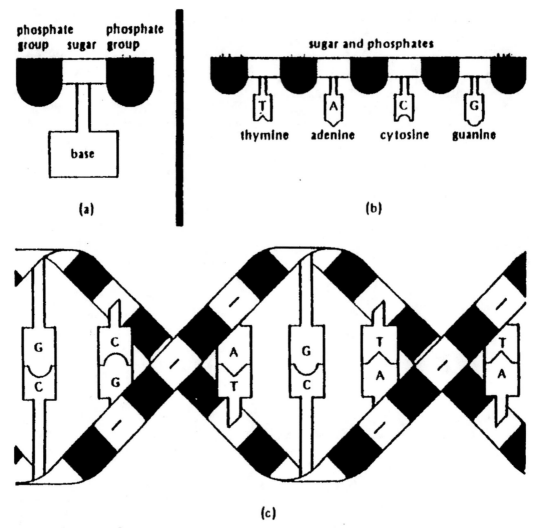

Figure 7.1 Each unit of DNA contains three parts shown in *(a)*: a base, bonded to a sugar, bonded to a phosphate, making the chain shown in *(b)*. DNA has four types of bases, which always bond in pairs, thymine (T) with adenine (A) and cytosine (C) with guanine (G), shown in *(c)*. It is the bonding of the bases that holds the DNA double helix *(c)* together.

to be of any adaptive value. Like mutation, the other genetic processes (for example, meiosis, crossing over, and genetic drift) that introduce variability are random, that is, undirected and not inherently adaptive.

A major directional force in evolution is **natural selection,** which occurs through differences in survival to reproductive age and differences in fertility. Natural selection works in this manner: Some individuals respond more effectively to environmental pressures than do others. They are more likely to survive and reproduce, and so are those who have inherited their genes. When differences

in survival and reproduction are due to a genetic variation, then that variation will increase in frequency in that population over time. This is termed "differential reproduction and differential mortality associated with genotype" (Simpson 1969:81).

In the term natural selection, "natural" refers to natural forces that cause death, especially death during childhood or before one has completed the reproductive years. These selective forces include famine, harsh climate, predators, and especially disease. It is the cumulative impact of these natural forces on birth and death that "selects" adaptive traits

(that is, allows them to be retained in the population and transmitted to future generations.)

It is important to understand that individuals, whose genetic traits are fixed before they are born, do not change genetically in response to natural selection pressures. What changes as a result of natural selection is the genetic makeup of the population and of future generations.

Some genetic factors do not affect survival or reproduction and also are not part of natural selection. It is only the phenotypic characteristics that give some advantage or degree of **Darwinian fitness** that are subject to selective action. Darwinian fitness, so called because Charles Darwin first developed the concept that variation in fitness was the key factor in evolution, is simply the ability to contribute one's genes to the next generation. Fitness need not have anything to do with strength, intelligence, or aggressiveness.

How does one measure Darwinian fitness? Take an example of two hypothetical phenotypes, A_1 and A_2, which differ in a single genetic characteristic. Equal numbers of A_1 and A_2 are born, but only 999 A_1s reach reproductive maturity, while 1,000 A_2s do. The difference in fitness is one in a thousand, or .001. This difference seems small, but in large populations it is enough to bring about changes in the gene pool over time (Birdsell 1972:397).

Selective Compromise

Selection operates at the same time on many genetic traits that affect survival and reproduction. When selective forces counteract each other, they set limits on genetic change. For example, selection for an optimal birth weight is continually operating. A seven-pound baby has a far better chance of surviving after birth than a three-pound one. If there were no balancing forces operating, birth weights might continue to increase. But in fact the optimal limits are rather narrow, for most women are more likely to have difficulty delivering a ten-pound baby. Such a high birth weight poses a hazard both to the infant and to the mother. The opposed selective forces stabilize a range of about five to eight pounds as optimal birth weight in most populations.

Selective forces operating on many traits affected the evolution of upright walking (bipedalism), female pelvis size, brain and skull size of infants, and birth weights in the transition to bipedalism through selection for a series of changes in the structure and mechanics of the pelvis . . . , selection for larger brains was also occurring. Cranial capacity doubled in the transition from australopithecines, hominids living 2 to 4 million years ago, to early humans (called *Homo erectus* or pithecanthropines), and it almost tripled through the evolutionary transition to true humans *(Homo sapiens)*.

Simultaneous selection for change in pelvis structure and change in brain size operated within certain constraints. The female pelvis had to be wide enough to permit the delivery of large-brained infants, but not so wide as to inhibit the woman's ability to walk and run. The major selective factors were mortality rates of women and infants at childbirth, as affected by pelvis size, head size, and birth weight, and survival rates for individuals with increased brain size and increased mobility. Perhaps one of the most important *selective* compromises coming out of this situation was selection for brain and skull growth after birth rather than before. The human infant's brain has reached only one-third of its potential adult size at birth. In contrast, the rhesus monkey is born with a brain almost three-fourths of adult size. There was selection not only for increased brain size and delayed brain growth but also for elaboration of the cerebral cortex, which facilitates learning, memory, imitation, and cognitive processing of environmental input.

Not all selective compromises are as advantageous as the example just discussed, however. Genetic adaptation often involves less-than-ideal evolutionary outcomes. The size and shape of the pelvis is not ideal; if it were, childbirth would be an easier and faster process, and backaches would not be such a common complaint.

Selection and Disease

Disease has played an important selective role in human evolution. Infectious diseases can be especially potent selective factors, depending on mortality rates or the effect of the disease on reproduction. Diseases with low mortality rates, and those affecting mostly older people (such as cancer, adult onset diabetes, and arteriosclerosis), are less subject to selection because the people affected by them usually have reproduced before the disease develops.

The cumulative effect of infectious and nutritional disease on fertility is significant. The sick or undernourished woman may not ovulate. Venereal disease may have damaged her fallopian tubes or obstructed the seminal tract in her husband. If she conceives but scarring in the fallopian tubes prevents passage of the fertilized ovum to the uterus, she may have an ectopic pregnancy, a life-threatening condition if surgery is not done.

Miscarriage can be caused by infectious diseases such as rubella (German measles), toxoplasmosis (a disease transmitted by cats), and African trypanosomiasis (sleeping sickness) (McFalls and McFalls 1984:55). Anemia in pregnant women can be caused by parasitic infections such as malaria and hookworm and leads to stillbirth, premature birth, low birth weight, and increased risk of death within the first month of life. Chagas' disease (also called American trypanosomiasis), transmitted by the "kissing bug" or "assassin bug," is a major cause of death in Brazil and other Latin American countries. This disease can infect the fetus through the placenta and cause fetal and infant death (McFalls and McFalls 1984:235).

Resistance to disease can develop in two ways: (1) through physiological mechanisms such as natural or acquired immunity responses of the body or passive immunity received from antibodies transmitted through the placenta or the mother's milk, and (2) through genetically inherited traits that promote resistance (Desowitz 1987). Genetic resistance, unlike the immune system, is specific to a given disease or category of diseases, and it plays an important role in childhood in the transition between passive immunity and active immunity. Genetic resistance is controlled by a specific gene or set of genes and does not promote overall adaptability in the way the immune system normally does.

Genetic factors may be responsible for increased resistance of populations over time to tuberculosis, plague, and other high-mortality diseases, but we have no conclusive evidence. Resistance to tuberculosis, for example, depends a great deal on diet, overall health, and degree of emotional stress. Although genetic factors may contribute to resistance, environmental factors appear to play an equally influential part.

Physical anthropologists have discovered puzzling statistical associations between the ABO blood group system and disease risk. (By "association," they mean that a certain disease affects people of a given blood type more often than one would expect due to chance. It does not mean, however, that that blood type causes the disease.) People with type A blood have a somewhat higher risk of developing stomach cancer, pernicious anemia, rheumatic diseases, myocardial infarctions (a type of heart attack), cirrhosis of the liver, high serum cholesterol, and certain other diseases. People with type O blood do develop the diseases we have listed, but at lower rates, and conversely, they are at higher risk of developing gastric and duodenal ulcers, skin cancer, manic-depressive illness, and a few other conditions (Vogel and Motulsky 1979:164–167; Stine 1977:429).

The reasons for associations between blood type and disease risk are not clear, but there is some evidence that blood type may be related to immune response. For example, type O individuals have a better immune response once they contract syphilis; that is, they are more easily treated and have less severe symptoms. The high O frequency among native peoples of Central and South America may be due to natural selection by the treponema infections (syphilis, yaws, and pinta) (Vogel and Motulsky 1979:409–412).

In the P blood group system, high frequencies of the P_2 blood type are found in the fishing and hunting populations of the Arctic, the Pacific Islands, and the Far East. It has been theorized that the P_2 allele is an adaptation that helps give humans resistance to disease due to the parasites that infest the animals they eat (Blangero 1982).

Natural selection increases disease resistance directly through genetic change in human populations, but it also does so indirectly through evolutionary change in the virus or parasite responsible for the disease. The microorganism undergoes adaptive change in response to the mortality rates of the host population, and there may be selection favoring organisms whose metabolic requirements inflict less harm on the host population.

When a disease organism has two hosts in its life cycle, it may be harmless for one but damaging to the other. This is the case with the malaria parasite, which has adapted to coexisting with the mosquito vector without harming it. As McNeill explains, in order for the parasite to reach a new human host, "the mosquito carrying it must be vigorous enough to fly normally. A seriously sick mosquito simply could not play its part in perpetuating the malarial cycle by carrying the parasite to a new human host successfully. But a weak and feverish human being does not interfere with the cycle in the slightest" (1976:11).

Of the many parasitical diseases that affect humans, malaria is one of the most ancient, and populations living in endemically malarial environments have evolved certain genetic characteristics that contribute significantly to malaria resistance. These characteristics include many hemoglobin variants. Some are relatively rare or localized, such as hemoglobin E in Southeast Asia and hemoglobin C in West Africa. Hemoglobin S, which is more widespread, is discussed in the following health profile.

Profile: Malaria and Agriculture

Ancient Chinese mythology describes three demons who bring malaria. One demon carries a hammer to cause a pounding headache, the second carries a pail of icy water to chill its victims, and the third carries a stove to produce fever. Thus the demons afflict humans with the three major symptoms of a disease that plagued the ancient civilizations of China, India, and Mesopotamia, afflicted Renaissance England and the nineteenth-century United States, and continues to kill millions of children every year (Russell et al. 1963; Motulsky 1971:235).

World-wide, about 2 million of the estimated 200 million who suffer from malaria die each year. In tropical Africa, malaria accounts for 15 percent of all clinically treated cases, and each year 1 million people, mostly children, are reported to have died of malaria. The disease also contributes to death from kidney failure, anemia, and pneumonia. The anemia caused by malaria is a serious hazard in pregnancy, and infection of the placenta by malaria parasites causes low birth weight in infants and in some cases miscarriage and stillbirth (McFalls and McFalls 1984:105–108).

Malaria is caused by a protozoan parasite of the genus *Plasmodium*, which lives in red blood cells. The protozoa cannot survive outside their hosts and completely depend on the enzymes and metabolism of red cells, consuming the glucose and enzymes needed by the cell for its own functioning. When the protozoa destroy the cells, usually at two- or three-day intervals, the release of waste products and pigment brings on severe intermittent bouts of chills and fever.

The name for the disease comes from the Italian words *mala* ("bad") and *aria* ("air"). For centuries, people believed that marsh air caused the illness, and a Roman author advised his readers against building a house near a marsh, which "always throws up noxious and poisonous steams during the heats, and breeds animals armed with mischievous stings . . . (Russell et al. 1963:2).

The "mischievous stings" come from mosquitoes, the vectors that transmit malaria from one person to another. A female mosquito of the genus *Anopheles* bites a person who is already infected and who carries male and female *Plasmodium* gametocytes (sexual forms in the life cycle) in the blood stream. The mosquito ingests the gametocytes and becomes infected, although with no negative effect on her health. Gametes develop in the mosquito, undergo fertilization, and release sporozoites (asexual forms in the life cycle of *Plasmodium*), which travel to the mosquito's salivary glands. When the mosquito feeds, she injects sporozoites into a new victim, thus completing the cycle of disease transmission. Each parasite depends on both an insect vector and a mammal host to live out its full life cycle, although it can reproduce asexually for an indefinite time in the host.

Four species of *Plasmodium* affect humans. The most severe of the four species is *P. falciparum,* which causes acute symptoms in victims, especially among small children. When untreated, the death rate among nonimmunes is about 25 percent. Since well-adapted parasites do not kill their hosts, falciparum protozoa may have begun to affect humans fairly recently. In contrast, the less severe forms *P. vicax, P. malariae,* and *P. ovale* have probably had a long evolutionary association with humans.

Two major groups of vector mosquitoes for falciparum malaria in sub-Saharan Africa are *Anopheles gambiae* and *Anopheles funestus.* The two species have very different ecological niches. Funestus mosquitoes breed along shaded river edges and in heavily vegetated swamps in undisturbed tropical forest. Gambiae mosquitoes breed best in open, sunny pools and in ditches with slow-running water. When African forest dwellers lived as small groups of hunters without permanent village sites and with no need to cut down trees, there were relatively few breeding or habitation areas for gambiae mosquitoes. Nor were humans in frequent contact with funestus mosquitoes, which fed on other mammals. Although the two vectors were present in the ecosystem, the incidence of malaria for humans was not high.

The introduction of agriculture into sub-Saharan Africa about 2,000 years ago set off a migration by Bantu tribes, which greatly changed the ecology of the tropical forests. Iron tools and iron-working techniques made it possible to clear the vegetation effectively (Livingstone 1958:549). Clearing of forests and cultivation of root and tree crops greatly increased the breeding opportunities of gambiae mosquitoes. Domestication of plants and storage of surplus meant that far more people could be supported in one place than had been possible with hunting-gathering subsistence. This shift in settlement pattern also benefited mosquitoes. Agricultural villages provided not only sunlit, stagnant pools for breeding, but also a feast of human blood. . . .

The malaria parasites also benefited from these changes, and the disease increased in prevalence. This may have been the period in which *P. falciparum* began to adapt to human red blood cells. Previous mammalian hosts decreased in number as human activities altered the ecosystem. With rapid population growth, theorizes Frank Livingstone, the human being became "the most widespread large animal" in West Africa and thus "the most available blood meal for mosquitoes and the most available host for parasites" (1958:556).

The changes in the mosquito and parasite niches created serious disease problems for the human population. With death rates as high as 25 percent and the debilitation of those chronically infected, the health costs of the new subsistence strategy were high. The death rate from malaria is highest among small children, and it also causes miscarriage and premature birth. Responsible for both high mortality and reduced birth rates, falciparum malaria operated as a major agent of natural selection (Russell 1963:391).

Infants in malarial areas are born with passive immunity to malaria acquired prenatally from their mothers. This immunity last about six months. Then they are highly susceptible until age 3, when they begin to develop active immunity to the parasite. Older children are frequently infected without experiencing severe symptoms (Motulsky 1971: 236). Any genetic factor that gives resistance to children from the age of 6 months to 3 years is favored by natural selection. In fact, up to 40 percent of the people of West Africa do have an inherited characteristic that provides a certain amount of resistance to malaria: the sickle cell trait for abnormal hemoglobin in the red blood cells.

Hemoglobin is a molecule of two alpha and two beta protein chains, which binds, carries, and releases oxygen and carbon dioxide in the tissues. Because the hemoglobin molecule is large, there is considerable potential for point mutations to occur. At some time in the past, a point mutation occurred in one of the DNA base pair codes for the hemoglobin protein chains. The copying error affected the synthesis of the amino acid at the sixth position on the beta chains. A simple reversal in the order of the base pairs changed the instructions for the sequence of amino acids. Instead of glutamic acid at the sixth position, as is found in normal hemoglobin, valine was produced.

The substitution of valine affected the hemoglobin's level of oxygen affinity. Glutamic acid has a negative charge, allowing easy change from high to low oxygen affinity, depending on the external environment of the red blood cell. But valine has no electrical charge and is structured

differently, so that in certain conditions the hemoglobin molecules containing valine at the sixth position tend to clump together. When there is a deficiency of oxygen, the molecules combine and form rigid bundles of needle-like crystals that distort the cell membrane into an irregular, sickled, or curved shape (Stini 1975b:37; Brodie 1975:453; Milner 1973). . . . This hemoglobin is designated hemoglobin S (Hb^s) because of the sickle shape of these red blood cells.

The abnormal hemoglobin differs from normal hemoglobin only by a single amino acid on the beta protein chain, but this small change is very important, for hemoglobin S greatly inhibits the metabolism and reproduction of the malaria parasite in the red blood cell. The normal red blood cell lasts about 120 days, while a cell with a combination of both genetic characteristics, Hb^A and Hb^s, may last only two to three weeks, which is not enough time for the parasite to reproduce. The parasite is also not well adapted metabolically to the type of red blood cell that contains both hemoglobins (Stini 1975:39).

Because they have the sickling trait, which is disadvantageous for *Plasmodium,* heterozygotes are unlikely to suffer greatly from malaria. Having the sickling trait does not give them immunity to the disease, but it does reduce the severity of infection. Individuals heterozygous for the sickle cell condition have both normal and abnormal hemoglobin in every red blood cell. Person homozygous for sickling also resist malaria, but their red cells contain only abnormal hemoglobin. This causes excessive sickling and severe anemia. Without medical care, sickle cell anemia is usually fatal for children, who rarely survive long enough to reproduce. In West African populations, the disease affects about 4 percent of the children.

The shift to agriculture in Africa had far-reaching ecological repercussions.

The new human ecological niche changed the adaptive opportunities of many animals and plants, including those of anophelines and *Plasmodium*, both of which moved into new niches created by human activities. We can see a series of concomitant adaptations by various species operating in this situation of ecological change. As humans adapted culturally through new and more efficient methods of subsistence, *A. gambiae* adapted behaviorally to the presence of humans in sedentary villages. Both the malaria parasite and the human population then underwent certain genetic adaptations. The parasites evolved into forms biochemically suited to the metabolism of the human red blood cell, while natural selection increased the frequency of mutant hemoglobin types resistant to the parasite, thus affecting the population's genetic makeup.

Two principles are illustrated in this chain of adaptations among interacting organisms. First, adaptation must always be assessed in the context of a specific environment. The sickling trait proved adaptive in a malarial environment. In regions where malaria has been eradicated, the sickling trait no longer gives any special advantage. This is why the frequency of the trait has declined sharply among blacks in the United States to an average of 8.5 percent and the disease to a fraction of 1 percent (Johnson 1984:20). Second, adaptation is rarely without costs. Sickle cell anemia was one of the costs of genetic adaptation, a negative effect that would continue to pose medical problems for people of African ancestry long after they had migrated to other continents.

Evidence of the differential fitness provided by the sickling trait is quite conclusive. Calculating the difference between the statistically expected and the actually observed frequencies of the normal hemoglobin in homozygous form (Hb_AHb_A) and the sickling trait in heterozygous form (Hb_AHb_S), the Darwinian fitness of Hb_AHb_A is 0.943 and that of Hb_AHb_S is 1.238. The heterozygous condition gives a slight selective advantage over the normal homozygous condition (Stini 1975b:42).

Edelstein (1986:53) has calculated that for the Igbo people of Nigeria, "only 9 AA individuals on the average for every 10 AS individuals survived to reproduce' over many generations in tropical environments. In drier climates less supportive of the Anopheles mosquito, malaria is less severe and the fitness of AA individuals is higher.

If having the sickling trait is advantageous, why hasn't this variant completely replaced the normal gene? The answer is that there is one chance in four that heterozygous parents will reproduce children who are homozygous for the trait (Hb_SHb_S). The affected child has double dose instructions for abnormal hemoglobin in each red blood cell and suffers from sickle cell anemia. Homozygotes have high mortality before adolescence, and about 16 percent of the sickle cell genes in the population are lost each generation, depending on the frequency of S in the population.

The heterozygote has a selective advantage over *both* types of homozygote. Hb_AHb_A has higher mortality and lower fertility because of malaria, while Hb_SHb_S is normally a fatal condition. Heterozygotes usually do not exceed 30 to 40 percent in a population, however, because selection against allele A by malaria is counterbalanced by even stronger selection against allele S by anemia and complications of sickle cell disease.

When two selective forces oppose one another in this manner, the frequencies of the two genes stabilize. This situation is called **balanced polymorphism** because the disadvantage for those in the population who have anemia is balanced by the advantage to others who can resist malaria. The system is in equilibrium, with more than one allele persisting over time.

Hemoglobin S is one of several mutations that act as genetic buffers against malaria. The distribution of these traits is shown in Figure 7.2. Hemoglobin C, resulting from a

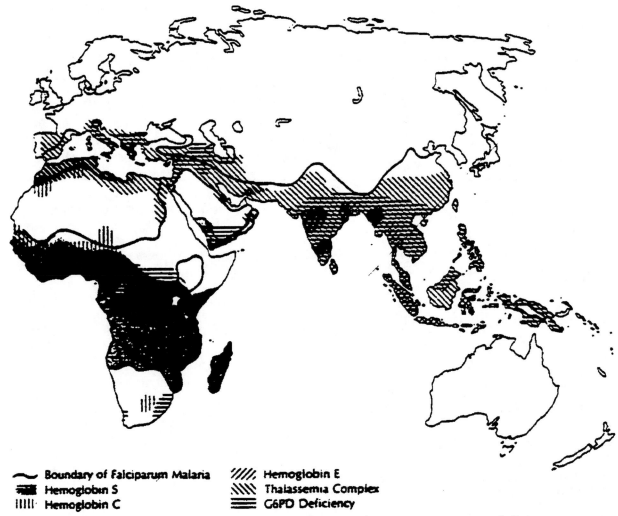

Figure 7.2 Four separate hemoglobin abnormalities and an enzyme (G6PD) deficiency represent favorable mutations that have acted as "genetic buffers" in malarial regions. (From *Human Evolution 2nd Ed.* By Joseph B. Birdsell. Copyright 1975, 1981 by Harper & Row, Publishers, Inc. Reprinted by permission of Addison Wesley Educational Publishers, Inc.)

substitution of lysine for glutamic acid at the sixth position of the beta chain, provides resistance to malaria without causing severe anemia in homozygotes. Two other types of defects produce some anemia in heterozygotes but also increase their resistance to malaria: the thalassemia complex, found in North and Central Africa, Mediterranean countries, India, the Middle East, and Southeast Asia, and G6PD deficiency, found in Central and South Africa, Italy, Greece, the Middle East, and India.

Deficiency of G6PD (the enzyme glucose-6-phosphate dehydrogenase) produces anemia only under special circumstances, as when persons with this deficiency eat raw fava beans, commonly grown in southern Europe and the Near East, or inhale fava pollen. This anemia is called *favism.* Anemia also develops if a person with the deficiency is given primaquine, an antimalarial drug, or if the person is suffering from certain infections. The adaptive value of this deficiency may be that malaria parasites do not grow well in red cells lacking the enzyme. Ironically, researchers believe that this deficiency provides resistance to malaria only when fava beans are regularly consumed (Huheey and Martin 1975). Fava contains strong oxidizing agents that inhibit growth of malaria parasites (Edelstein 1986:63).

Note that the mutations responsible for hemoglobin changes occurred before malaria became a severe problem. Edelstein (1986:55) estimates that the evolution of sickling began about 2,400 years (about 119 generations) ago. It is important to understand that selection operates on traits that already exist in the gene pool. Until these mutations proved advantageous because of some environmental change, they were without value and even deleterious for some individuals. But when human technological and demographic change led to an increase in malaria, individuals who had inherited the variant allele with the normal allele had an adaptive advantage. Not only did more of them survive childhood malaria, but they also suffered less from the disease as adults. Because of generally better health, their reproduction rates were slightly higher. With better health, heterozygotes could also be more productive in agriculture, compensating for losses in human productivity due to increased disease following the shift to agriculture (Wiesenfeld 1967).

Some of the staple crops in Africa and the West Indies contain the chemical compounds cyanate and thiocyanate, which may inhibit the sickling of red blood cells. Eating cassava (manioc), yams, sorghum, millet, sugar cane, and dark lima beans is believed to reduce the severity of symptoms of sickle cell anemia and to decrease the chances that heterozygotes will sickle under conditions of stress (Haas and Harrison 1977:78–79; Frisancho 1981:195). This may explain why the percentage of people in Africa and the West Indies who suffer from sickle cell anemia crises is lower than in the United States. Although it has been assumed that the low frequency in Africa is due to anemics dying in infancy, Frisancho argues that it is consumption of cyanate- and thiocyanate-containing foods that diminishes the clinical symptoms in Africa.

In Jamaica, people with sickle cell anemia often have mild symptoms, but when they migrate to the United States or Great Britain and change their diets, they experience severe sickling crises (Frisancho 1981:195).

Physiological and Developmental Adaptation

Step out of your air-conditioned room and jog along the pavement on a hot day, and your body makes certain adjustments to the heat. You begin to sweat: Evaporative cooling is taking place. Your face reddens as an expanded flow of blood through the capillary bed allows more heat to be lost. The body is working to maintain **homeostasis,** the inner balance that maintains an organism's internal environment despite external change.

We all have the capability to maintain homeostasis and to respond to climatic extremes of heat and cold, high or low humidity, ultraviolet radiation, excess or deficient nutrients, toxic substances, or disease-producing organisms. Some people are clearly more flexible than others in responding to different stressors. Some do better in heat and others in cold, for complex reasons of diet, physique, metabolism, and adjustments since infancy. But all people can tolerate a wide range of environmental conditions; our adaptability is part of our genetic programming.

In contrast to adaptive changes in gene frequency (discussed in the previous section), which require more than a generation to develop, physiological and developmental adaptations occur within a lifetime. Some changes are instantaneous, as when the pupil of your eye narrows in response to light. Other changes take longer, such as skin tanning after exposure to ultraviolet rays. Most types of physiological adaptation are reversible, but certain ones that develop over a long time may be irreversible, such as the barrel-chested physique that develops in people who grow up at high altitudes in the Andes and the Himalayas. Many scientists question whether all these physiological changes should even be called "adaptation." They try to reserve that term for evolutionary, genetic change. Others insist that adaptation has occurred only when there is conclusive evidence that a genetic change has led to differential mortality or differential fertility. However, we define adaptation broadly. It is not only the *effect* of genetic change but also the short- and long-term *processes* that lead to change: growth under different environmental conditions, metabolic responses to climatic and nutritional change, hormonal stress responses, and development of antibodies in response to antigens, to name a few of the physical processes that constitute adaptation.

Physiological changes, called *functional adaptation* by some human biologists, occur more rapidly than do genetic changes, and they are often more reversible. They form a graded response system in which short-term and long-term adjustments of different kinds are made by individuals, who vary in their genetically endowed ability to make those adjustments successfully. Three levels of physiological adaptation can be distinguished. *Acclimation* is rapid, short-term adjustment to a single stressor, usually experimentally induced. *Acclimatization* is a more pervasive but still reversible response to change over a more extended period. This acquired acclimatization can be contrasted with *developmental acclimatization*, which is the result of a lifetime of exposure to a given set of environmental stressors. It is often the case that *developmental acclimatizations* are irreversible. The differences among these concepts are seen in the ways people adapt to high altitudes.

High-Altitude Adaptation

Reduced oxygen pressure at high altitudes is one of the most severe forms of environmental stress that people tolerate. Lowlanders who visit the mountains at 10,000 feet (3,000 meters) above sea level may suffer mountain sickness due to *hypoxia*, insufficient oxygen reaching the tissues, especially if they exert themselves physically. The symptoms are nausea, shortness of breath, and headaches.

In adjusting to low oxygen pressure, faster breathing and a more rapid heartbeat are immediate responses. Later there is a gradual increase in the number of red blood cells circulating, which makes more hemoglobin available for carrying oxygen to the tissues. The capacity to adapt to high altitudes varies individually. Some people never do become successfully acclimatized, while others adjust but are not capable of full work effort. Most athletes participating in the 1968 Olympics in Mexico City, at 7,500 feet (2,300 meters), adapted well enough to compete, but only after a period of acclimatization at high-altitude training camps.

Lifetime residents of high altitudes make a set of characteristic anatomical and physiological adjustments that give them the capacity for sustained work in thin mountain air (Stini 1975b:53–64; Mazess 1975; Baker 1978; Baker and Little 1976). They tend to be short-legged, to grow slowly, and to have a large thoracic volume. A rounded rib cage and long sternum increase the chest volumes which accommodates larger lungs. They also have more red marrow, a tissue that produces red blood cells, in the ribs and sternum.

High-altitude populations also differ from sea level populations in their greater blood volume, red cell volume and concentration, total and relative hemoglobin, and greater acidity of the blood. Pumping this more viscous blood enlarges the heart muscle, especially the right ventricle, which pumps blood to the lungs. These blood features appear to be more characteristic of Andean high-altitude dwellers than of natives of the high Himalayas.

The hypoxia of high-altitude regions is believed to depress human reproductive potential through increased miscarriage and stillbirth rates and through higher neonatal mortality (Moran 1982:154–156). The alleged effect of hypoxia on reproduction has been disputed by some researchers. In the Andes of South America, fertility is high, perhaps for cultural reasons. There is little difference between high- and low-altitude groups in Peru, Chile, and Bolivia in the numbers of children whom women give birth to in their lifetimes (called completed fertility). Muslims living in a high-altitude Himalayan region of India have higher completed fertility rates than Buddhists in the region, suggesting that cultural influences on sexual behavior and family size preferences probably have greater impact on fertility than does hypoxia (Goldstein, Tsarong, and Beall 1983:35–43).

Placentas are generally larger in high-altitude regions than at sea level, which probably reduces hypoxic stress on the fetus (Moran 1979). Infants tend to have low birth weights, but survival rates for those under 2,500 grams (about 5.5 pounds) are better than for babies of equal weights in sea level populations. It is possible that natural selection favors low birth weights in hypoxic environments (Stini 1975b:63).

Climatic Adaptation

People who live at high altitudes must adapt to cold as well as to hypoxia, but adaptation to cold has been more thoroughly studied in arctic and subarctic regions. In experiments on cold response, Inuit and Indians perform better than do Europeans. The skin of natives' fingers, hands, and feet remains warmer for a longer period, and the tissues and joints are better protected (Steegmann 1975:145). Adults do better on these tests than children do, though, indicating that physiological adaptation to cold develops over one's lifetime.

Most tests of cold response are conducted in laboratory situations simulating natural conditions, for example, immersing the person's fingers in ice water and measuring his responses, but field studies of cold adaptation by Marshall Hurlich (1976) among Cree Indians and by A. T. Steegmann, Jr. (1977, 1983a) among Ojibwa Indians in northern Ontario (also see Hurlich and Steegmann 1979) combined these standard techniques with additional measures conducted outside the laboratory while the native men were riding snowmobiles, cutting firewood, hunting, and trapping. These human biologists found that adaptation to cold stress involves more than just physiological responses. Coping with the cold is affected by the kind of food consumed, by methods of handling equipment during travel, by knowledge of weather patterns, and by intelligence and judgment. In other words, response to an environmental stressor is never purely physiological in human beings; cultural

patterns and individual behavioral variation also influence the chances of survival. Physiological responses prove critical, however, in the unexpected emergency. The body's ability to conserve heat, to resist frostbite, and to keep active with very little food serves as a kind of emergency reserve, allowing the habitual response repertoire to stretch well beyond the usual limits.

After completing several seasons of field work in northern Ontario, Steegmann concluded that extreme cold was one of the more manageable of the environmental pressures faced by the Cree-Ojibwa people. The temperature of fingers or toes while hunting or fishing did not seem to give a significant advantage for survival. "One could live for years among the peoples of the northern forests and never see a case of serious frostbite, nor a death by hypothermia. In stark contrast, our field notes carry numerous accounts of death by drowning, fire, homicide, and disease" (Steegmann 1983b:4).

Learning survival skills in the northern forest "ranges in difficulty somewhere between learning to drive a car and learning a language," according to Louis Marano, an anthropologist who lived for five years in northern Ontario as an in-law of the native community. However, the skills are learned easily by children as they observe their elders in heat-conserving strategies. Among these strategies are choosing appropriate footwear (often rabbit-skin socks inside moosehide moccasins) and preventing the hands from freezing in the wind while ice-fishing by dipping them in ice water. Another strategy was to stop for frequent tea breaks on hunting trips to prevent dehydration and to dry the sweat from interior clothing (Marano 1983:279).

The responses of populations to extreme heat have been less well documented than responses to cold and high altitude, but desert environments include a number of climatic stressors: high solar and ground radiation, extreme variation in temperature, high aridity, dry winds, and small amounts of poor-quality water. The most critical health problem is dehydration (Briggs 1975).

The body responds to heat through sweating, a reduced flow of urine, and regulation of the rate of salt elimination in balance with salt consumption. During exposure to heat, the blood is diverted to the skin and muscles of the limbs, and cardiac output increases. As the individual becomes acclimatized to the desert, the symptoms of increased heart rate and rise in body temperature gradually decrease, although the person may develop chronic low blood pressure.

As in the Arctic, clothing provides an important cultural buffer against environmental stress in hot, dry climates. A nude person attains maximum sweat rate when the air temperature is 109°F (43°C), while a properly clothed person reaches a maximum sweat rate at 125°F (52°C). Appropriate clothing gives insulation, shielding the body from heat while allowing sweat to evaporate. Loose-fitting, loosely woven clothing that covers the body completely allows for a layer of air between the cloth and the skin and allows passage of evaporation. Saharan peoples traditionally have worn hooded robes and body-length veils, loose trousers, and full-sleeved shirts. Turbans are usually loose and made of lightweight, absorbent material (Briggs 1975:112, 115–116, 122).

The very young, especially newborn infants, are under special stress in the Sahara. Newborns have difficulty in adjusting to heat because their ratio of surface area to volume is far less than that of adults, and their rate of vasodilation, sweating, and blood flow is inadequate. The highest infant and child mortality rate is in summer. Mortality in general increases in summer, but heat stress in adults is usually just an additive factor imposed on diseases such as dysentery and on the risk of dehydration.

People of savannah environments, that is, grassland plains, also experience heat stress and intense solar and particularly ultraviolet radiation. People working in the heat have higher metabolism and thus higher energy intake requirements than those in temperate zones (Little 1980). However, periodic droughts and limited food resources reduce caloric intake.

Some savannah peoples, such as the Turkana pastoralists of East Africa studied by Michael Little and colleagues, tend to be tall and linear in physique. It is not certain whether this physique is due to climatic selection or to limited food energy. In theory, being thin and linear would help to dissipate heat. Studies of native desert groups have shown that they sweat less than acclimated whites, thus dissipating heat not so much through sweat evaporation as through radiation and convection (Frisancho 1981:36). Little and Johnson (1986) attempted to assess whether the Turkana were thin because of undernutrition by testing their hand grip strength and degree of muscle fatigue. While Turkana women were as strong as samples of U.S. women, Turkana men were weaker than U.S. men, suggesting that the women were better nourished than the men, even though they consumed an average of 800 calories less per day (Galvin 1985). Further, the women expended more energy in their daily work of gathering food and firewood, carrying drinking water, lifting and carrying children, milking and watering livestock; men's work, mostly supervising and managing grazing livestock, involved light to moderate energy output (Little 1980). Thus adaptation to heat stress does not seem to be the only factor involved in Turkana morphology.

Adaptation and Well-Being among Samoans

Despite the difficulties of studying environmental physiology in the field, laboratory studies of thermal response and acclimation are increasingly being viewed as too narrowly defined. As human biologists turn toward field studies of people's survival strategies, resource management, and general well-being, the theoretical paradigm of adaptation becomes broader and more interdisciplinary. But this shift has not led to abandonment of quantitative analyses or of controlled study designs. An example of a carefully designed study of a population's general well-being is Baker, Hanna, and Baker's *The Changing Samoans* (1986).

Samoans are a Polynesian people currently numbering about 270,000, many of whom have migrated from their native South Pacific Islands to New Zealand, Hawaii, and the U.S. mainland. Anthropologists are particularly interested in studying migrating populations because controlled comparisons of their adaptation to several environments can be carried out (see Little and Baker 1987).

Comparison of health patterns of migrant and nonmigrant, rural and urban Samoans allowed researchers working between 1975 and 1984 to compare data and to build a picture of the influence of migration and culture change on the population. Among the data collected were anthropometric measures, blood pressure readings, fertility patterns, blood lipid levels, measures of stress hormones (catecholamines) in urine samples, work capacity, blood genetic data, and cardiovascular risk date. Other researchers studied more qualitative indices of coping and adaptation, such as responses to economic problems, social support systems, response to illness, and management of anger.

Among the many findings of the study is the fact that fertility has not declined among Samoans, regardless of migration, education, or employment patterns of the women. The total average completed fertility per woman remains at five or more children, even in nonagricultural groups (Baker and Hanna 1986:424). Secondly, growth rates and adult heights have not significantly changed, although weight has increased and many of the migrants are obese. Average life expectancy has risen because infectious disease rates are lower. The types and quality of food eaten have changed little. Aerobic work capacity of the men remains low; neither migrant nor nonmigrant Samoan men are especially physically fit. Blood pressure is higher among migrants and urban groups, as is hormonal evidence of stress (Baker and Hanna 1986:424–429).

Given this mix of adaptive and seemingly maladaptive responses to change, what can we conclude about Samoan well-being? Are Samoans relatively adapted, as a population, to modern pressures and opportunities? Are nonmigrants better adapted than migrants? Using the biological criteria of high fertility, population growth, increased longevity, and nutritional adequacy, we would assess both groups as relatively well adapted. Using clinical criteria such as high blood pressure, physiological evidence of stress, obesity, and low aerobic ability, we would, on the other hand, assess the well-being of the population, and especially of migrants, to be less than optimal. Wisely, Baker and his colleagues do not attempt to judge adaptation in this study but simply present their findings for the reader to interpret.

This case shows how complicated it is to measure adaptation. Like health, adaptation is difficult to define, and paradoxically it is easier to know when a person is unhealthy or when a population has failed to adapt.

Cultural Adaptation

When environmental change occurs, humans can respond rapidly and flexibly by change in their behavior: They can come in out of the rain. Behavioral adaptation ranks along with genetic and physiological adaptation as a major type of response to environmental alterations. Some behavioral adaptations are specific to the individual regardless of cultural background. These *individual adaptations* are studied, for the most part, by psychologists. Other behavioral adaptations are shared by members of a society and are traditional; these *cultural adaptations* are the special focus of anthropologists (Carneiro 1968a).

A culture is often casually defined as a way of life, but inherent in this phrase is an ambiguity. On the one hand, it implies a lifestyle with shared rules and rituals full of symbolic meaning for some subgroup of humanity. On the other hand, the emphasis can be shifted to a culture as a way *of life*, in the sense of a strategy for survival, a population's means of staying alive under the pressures of natural selection. Depending on the balance between these two perspectives—the symbolic and the ecological—different anthropologists' priorities in cultural analysis may be very different.

Each culture, whether simple or complex, is composed of *technology, social organization*, and *ideology*. These components of culture evolve in interaction with each other and with the environment. The cattle-herding peoples adapted to the grasslands of East Africa, for example, share patterns of subsistence technology, settlement patterns, and religious beliefs that differ systematically from those of the West African tropical forest farmers mentioned in the malaria profile earlier in this chapter.

Many of the strategies used by humans to cope with environmental problems are based on information and skills that have been learned. In growing up, children learn how to get food, to avoid danger, to secure protection against the weather, to use raw materials for tools. They have not inherited this information genetically, and if one is abandoned by the group, he or she would find it almost impossible to learn all this through trial-and-error learning. Each generation has to learn basic survival techniques from the previous generation through a process of *cultural transmission.*

The culture of a group is an information system transmitted from one generation to another through nongenetic mechanisms. The information units are very diverse. Some are material objects, others are ideas and beliefs, and yet other units are ways of doing things—instructions or "recipes" in a broad sense. Tools, clothing, houses, weapons, music, laws, medicine, farming, raising children, regulating conflict—these and many more human behaviors and products of behavior form a complex informational system.

Although culture is nongenetic, three genetically based characteristics underlie the human capacity for culture. First, humans have evolved extensive and complex neural connections in the cerebral cortex of the brain, with considerable overlap between specific association areas for vision, hearing, touch, and motor coordination, This overlap allows learning to occur through transfer and correlation of information between association areas. A part of this learning is the acquisition of language in early childhood, made possible by neural connections between a portion of the auditory association area and an area controlling the motor actions of speech. Without some form of language, human groups could not maintain the complex informational systems through which they adapt, nor could they easily transmit this information to children.

Second, the human hand and fingers facilitate the manipulation of objects and making of tools. Our prehensile hands can easily grip, lift, and throw objects, and our opposable thumbs allow us to pick up and work with very small tools. Evolution of this type of hand accompanies evolution of fine visual-motor coordination in the brain; the selective factor may have been differential survival of individuals and groups that used tools.

Third, humans are born as altogether dependent beings, unable to walk, to hold onto the mother, or actively to search for food. The child remains dependent on the group for many years, and this allows a long time for learning. It also allows for intense attachments to form between infants and their caretakers. This *bonding* behavior occurs in other animals, especially primates, and in birds as well. Humans normally form social bonds throughout their lives—with their peers, mates, and children—and they work together, creating and coordinating group strategies for meeting problems.

These three characteristics—a brain capable of complex learning and speech, the ability to use and make tools and other objects, and social bonding—have allowed humans to generate an impressive diversity of cultural systems and to survive in a wide range of ecological niches. Each of these characteristics provides only a generalized framework for adaptation; that is, they do not specify what people must learn, how they must use tools, or how to organize themselves socially. The content of cultural adaptation varies from population to population and from generation to generation. A complex cultural pool of ideas, techniques, strategies, and rules developed over many generations encompasses far more knowledge and ideas than any one individual could learn or needs to learn. Living in cultural systems, people have at their disposal diverse sets of knowledge, skills, and innovative ideas.

Variability and Change in Cultural Systems

Just as the genetic pool of a population contains varied genotypes, some of which may prove over time to be more adaptive than others to environmental changes, so the informational pool of a cultural system contains considerable variation. Each person learns and replicates what he or she is taught imperfectly. Young people reinterpret rules they have learned from elders in terms of their own experiences and problems. Changes occur also through selective retention of new ideas and techniques that promote the effectiveness of the group or of the individual in dealing with problems, including situations that threaten the integration of the group and the self. These new ideas may be innovated within the group, but frequently they are borrowed from neighboring groups, travelers and traders, allies and enemies. Adaptation in this sense extends beyond ecological systems. It also involves adjustments and changes that increase the group's competence and security, maintain the community's physical and emotional health, and protect the individual and defend the ego.

We come to understand individual adaptation through psychological concepts, giving attention to how the mind works, how the person learns from his or her cultural system to cope emotionally with pressures exerted by that cultural system. The individual uses culture but is always a bit separate from it. A cultural system emerges from the interaction of two or more people. Thus the study of cultural adaptation focuses on the community or population rather than on the individual.

As a population process, cultural adaptation is analogous to genetic adaptation. Cultures evolve—that is, they undergo directed adaptive changes in response to environmental pressures and challenges—just as biological populations evolve, although the mechanisms that bring about the two types of evolution differ. Further, biological evolution in humans has paralleled cultural evolution; there has been natural selection for traits underlying the human ability to learn, to communicate, and to

work together—the fundamental requirements for a cultural system. In turn, cultural patterns have affected biological evolution, at times protecting humans against the selective forces of disease and climatic extremes, at other times intensifying natural selection through ecological changes that increase disease.

Cultural Adaptation and Health

Functionalism, a major orientation in anthropology that looks for the "function" (the role or purpose served in maintaining the whole system) of any custom, institution, or belief, has been part of adaptation theory. Functionalist hypotheses suggesting that apparently "irrational" ethnomedical customs have underlying, unconscious adaptive significance are very attractive to people of Western societies. We are eager to believe that the true significance of religious taboos on eating pork is to prevent trichinosis, or that circumcision of males, practiced for ritual reasons, later prevents cervical cancer in their wives.

Looking for ecological or adaptive functions in every ethnomedical custom reflects a major cultural bias of Westerners, namely, the view that health is a high priority and that disease can ultimately be prevented or controlled. However, if evil eye, or witchcraft, or soul loss is a major component of a culture's explanatory model of illness, it is less likely that a person from that culture will believe that one can control disease through pragmatic, preventive measures.

In developing his classic medical anthropology text, *Adaptation in Cultural Evolution* (1970), Alexander Alland recalls (1987:427) that he "felt that many adaptations, at least in the area of disease prevention, occurred alongside of, or in spite of, native theories" of disease. Alland's self-critique of this position is that "when disease functions in native theory as a metaphor for social problems, behavior concerning disease becomes a complex set of compromises involving social as well as ecological adaptation. It is therefore necessary to include social factors, as well as belief systems, in any attempt to unravel complex patterns of cultural adaptation" (1987:427).

Whether one prefers to do symbolic analysis or functional analysis of health practices and beliefs of a society, it is possible to see a number of unintended, adaptive benefits of various practices. When the effect of a custom is positive, anthropologists consider the pattern to be adaptive even though people may not be aware of the adaptive value of what they are doing. Positive biological feedback may have contributed toward selective retention of these practices.

For example, many societies have postpartum sex taboos, which prohibit a couple from having sexual intercourse for some months after a woman gives birth. People who practice this custom do not justify it in medical or contraceptive terms. Rather, they consider it a way of protecting the child, the mother, and the father from the mysterious forces associated with sexual and reproductive processes. But one adaptive function of the custom is birth spacing.

Dietary taboos often have adaptive components. Southeastern American Indians had taboos against the use of salt by menstruating and pregnant women, by adolescents during puberty rituals, and by warriors. Restriction of salt intake could be of benefit in reducing hypertension and water retention in pregnant women and thus in reducing complications of pregnancy and childbirth (Neumann 1977).

Some customs are deliberate attempts to reduce disease but are based on a "faulty" understanding of disease transmission differing from the Western model. In Peter Brown's study (1986) of genetic and cultural adaptations to *malaria* in Sardinia, the local explanatory model was based on the notion of "bad air" or malaria. Adaptations included restrictions on the movement of women, who were usually not allowed to leave the settlement, especially if they were pregnant. The settlements themselves were generally free of malaria-carrying mosquitoes; more mosquitoes were found in the agricultural areas surrounding the settlements, where mostly men worked. Consequently, women had lower malaria rates than men. Brown (1986:324) reasons that "threat of malaria-induced spontaneous abortions possibly acted in a mechanism of 'natural selection' of cultural restrictions on the geographical mobility of females." In this case, it did not matter that the people believed that "bad air" caused malaria, for the restrictions protecting pregnant women were effective preventive measures against the disease.

References

Alland, Alexander, Jr. 1987. Looking Backward: An Autocritique. Medical Anthropology Quarterly—New Series 1:424–431.

Baker, Paul T. 1978. The Biology of High-Altitude Peoples. Cambridge, England: Cambridge University Press.

Baker, Paul T., and Joel M. Hanna. 1986. Perspectives on Health and Behavior of Samoans. *In* The Changing Samoans. Paul T. Baker, Joel M. Hanna, and Thelma S. Baker, eds. Pp. 419–434. New York: Oxford University Press.

Baker, P. T., and Michael A. Little, eds. 1976. Man in the Andes: A Multidisciplinary Study of High Altitude Quechua. Stroudsburg, Pennsylvania: Dowden, Hutchinson & Ross.

Baker, Paul T., Joel M. Hanna, and Thelma S. Baker, eds. 1986. The Changing Samoans: Behavior and Health in Transition. New York: Oxford University Press.

Birdsell, Jose B. 1972. Human Evolution. Chicago: Rand McNally.

Blangero, John. 1982. The P Blood Group System: Genetic Adaptation to Helminthic Zoonoses. Medical Anthropology 6:57–69.

Brodie, Jessie Laird. 1975. Medical and Social Problems of Sickle Cell Anemia: The Patient and the Bearer of the Trait. Journal of the American Medical Women's Association 30:453–455.

Brown, Peter J. 1986. Cultural and Genetic Adaptations to Malaria: Problems of Comparison. Human Ecology 14:311–332.

Carneiro. 1968a. Full citation not provided in original article, [Ed. Note]

Damon, Albert. 1977. Human Biology and Ecology. New York: W. W. Norton.

Desowitz, Robert S. 1987. The Thorn in the Starfish: How the Human Immune System Works. New York: W. W. Norton.

Edelstein, Stuart J. 1986. The Sickled Cell: From Myths to Molecules. Cambridge, Massachusetts: Harvard University Press.

Ehrlich, Paul R. 1986. The Machinery of Nature. New York: Simon and Schuster.

Frisancho, A. Roberto. 1981. Human Adaptation: A Functional Interpretation. Ann Arbor, Michigan: University of Michigan Press.

Galvin, K. 1985. Food Procurement, Diet, Activities and Nutrition of Ngisonyoka Turkana Pastoralists in an Ecological and Social Context. Ph.D. dissertation, Department of Anthropology, State University of New York, Binghamton.

Goldstein, Melvyn C., Paljor Tsarong, and Cynthia M. Beall. 1983. High Altitude Hypoxia, Culture, and Human Fecundity/Fertility: A Comparative Study. American Anthropologist 85:28–49.

Haas, Jere D., and Gail G. Harrison. 1977. Nutritional Anthropology and Biological Adaptation. Annual Review of Anthropology 6:69–101.

Howells, William W. 1960. The Distribution of Man. Scientific American 203(3):112–127.

Huheey, J. E., and D. L. Martin. 1975. Malaria, Favism, Glucose-6-phosphate Dehydrogenase Deficiency. Experientia 31:1145–1147.

Hurlich, M. G., and A. T. Steegmann, Jr. 1979. Contrasting Laboratory Response to Cold in Two Subarctic Algonkian Villages: An Admixture Effect? Human Biology 51(3):255–278.

Hurlich, Marshall. 1976. Environmental Adaptation: Biological and Behavioral Response to Cold in the Canadian Subarctic. Ph.D. dissertation, Department of Anthropology, State University of New York at Buffalo.

Johnson, Carl J. 1984. Cancer Incidence in an Area of Radioactive Fallout Downwind from the Nevada Test Site. JAMA 251:230–236.

Little, Michael A. 1980. Designs for Human-Biological Research Among Savannah Pastoralists. In Human Ecology in Savannah Environments. D. R. Harris, ed. Pp. 479–503. London: Academic Press.

Little, Michael A., and Paul T. Baker. 1987. Migration and Adaptation. In Biological Aspects of Human Migration. C.G.N. Mascie-Taylor and C. W. Lasker, eds. Pp. 167–215. Cambridge, England: Cambridge University Press.

Little, Michael A., and Brooke R. Johnson, Jr. 1986. Grip Strength, Muscle Fatigue, and Body Composition in Nomadic Turkana Pas-

toralists. American Journal of Physical Anthropology 69:335–344.

Livingstone, Frank B. 1958. Anthropological Implications of Sickle Cell Gene Distribution in West Africa. American Anthropologist 60:533–562.

McFalls, Joseph A., Jr., and Marguerite Harvey McFalls. 1984. Disease and Fertility. New York: Academic Press.

McNeill, William H. 1976. Plagues and People. Garden City, New York: Anchor Press/Doubleday.

Marano, Louis. 1983. Boreal Forest Hazards and Adaptations: The Present. In Boreal Forest Adaptations. A. Theodore Steegmann, Jr., ed. Pp. 269–288. New York: Plenum Press.

Mazess, Richard B. 1975. Human Adaptation to High Altitude. In Physiological Anthropology. Albert Damon, ed. Pp. 167–209. New York: Oxford University Press.

Milner, Paul F. 1973. Functional Abnormalities of Sickle Cells: Uptake and Delivery of Oxygen. In Sickle Cell Disease. Harold Abramson, John F. Bertles, and Doris L. Wethers, eds. Pp. 155–163. St. Louis: C. V. Mosby.

Moran, Emilio. 1979. Full citation not provided in original article, [Ed. Note]

___. 1982. Human Adaptability: An Introduction to Ecological Anthropology. Boulder, Colorado: Westview Press.

Moran, Emilio, ed. 1984. The Ecosystem Concept in Anthropology. AAAS Selected Symposium 92. Boulder, Colorado: Westview Press.

Motulsky, Arno G. 1971. Metabolic Polymorphisms and the Role of Infectious Diseases in Human Evolution. In Human Populations, Genetic Variation, and Evolution. Laura Newell Morris, ed. Pp. 222–252. San Francisco: Chandler.

Nei, Masatoshi. 1975. Molecular Population Genetics and Evolution. New York: American Elsevier Publishing Co., Inc.

Neumann, Thomas W. 1977. A Biocultural Approach to Salt Taboos: The Case of the Southeastern United States. Current Anthropology 18:289–308.

Russell, Paul F., et al. 1963. Practical Malariology. London: Oxford University Press.

Simpson, George G. 1969. Organisms and Molecules in Evolution. In Evolutionary Anthropology. Hermann K. Bleibtreu, ed. Pp. 78–88. Boston: Allyn and Bacon.

Steegmann, A. T., Jr. 1975. Human Adaptation to Cold. In Physiological Anthropology. Albert Damon, ed. Pp. 130–166. New York: Oxford University Press.

___. 1977. Finger Temperatures During Work in Natural Cold: The Northern Ojibwa. Human Biology 49:349–362.

Steegmann, A. Theodore, Jr., ed. 1983a. Boreal Forest Adaptations. The Northern Algonkians. New York: Plenum Press.

___. 1983b. The Northern Algonkian Project and Changing Perceptions of Human Adaptation. *In* Boreal Forest Adaptations. A. Theodore Steegmann, Jr., ed. Pp. 1–8. New York: Plenum Press.

___. 1987. Personal communication.

Stine, Gerald James. 1977. Biosocial Genetics: Human Heredity and Social Issues. New York: Macmillan.

Stini, William A. 1975a. Adaptive Strategies of Human Populations Under Nutritional Stress. *In* Biosocial Interrelations in Population Adaptation. E. S. Watts, F. E. Johnston, and G. W. Lasker, eds. Pp. 19–41. The Hague: Mouton.

___. 1975b Ecology and Human Adaptation. Dubuque, Iowa: Wm. C. Brown.

Vogel, Friedrich, and Amo G. Motulsky. 1979. Human Genetics: Problems and Approaches. New York: Springer-Verlag.

Wiesenfeld, Stephen L. 1967. Sickle-Cell Trait in Human Biological and Cultural Evolution. Science 157:1134–1140.

8

On New Guinea Tapeworms and Jewish Grandmothers

Robert S. Desowitz

Some parasites take fantastic—and tragic—cross-cultural voyages

Even I confess to a certain coolness of heart toward tapeworms. But when the World Health Organization (WHO) calls, all parasites are equals regardless of race or region. And so I found myself in the central highlands of Irian Jaya, Indonesian New Guinea, the WHO consultant sent to advise on the control of a pig-transmitted tapeworm that was sending the Ekan of Enarotali into epileptic convulsions. Once again I was about to learn that in problems of public health, expert but alien reason is usually not reasonable to the peoples of another culture.

To the peoples of New Guinea the pig is more than pork. Throughout the large island, man and pig have a relationship that is intimate beyond domesticity. The pig is a quasi-family member, a source of food, and ultimately a gift to propitiate the spirit world. The great, gory festivals during which great numbers of pigs are consumed are held to gain prestige, to pay of obligations, or to celebrate a successful battle.

At other times the pig is in constant demand for ritual slaughter. One or more must be killed at the birth of a child or in any unfortunate circumstance or other perceived emergency requiring sacrifice to gods and ancestor spirits. Ritual slaughter represents something more than paying the premium for the insurance of spiritual good will; it reflects the absolute belief that life and sanity require harmony with the spirit world. Pig sacrifice is a major means of attaining that harmony. Thus, the introduction of the pig tapeworm. *Taenia solium,* into New Guinea was both a medical and cultural disaster.

Pig and man share not only more habits than we like to admit but also two helminth parasites, the nematode *Trichinella spiralis,* the cause of trichinosis, and the tapeworm *Taenia solium.* Trichinosis, once a common infection in the United States, can be an unpleasant, even fatal, disease but the tapeworm is the villain of this piece.

Tapeworms belong to the class Cestoidea, gutless flatworms that absorb nutriment directly through the integument. In a sense a tapeworm is a communal chain of individuals that keep in touch by means of common lateral nerve cords. Each mature segment in the chain comes complete with male and female sexual organs and an excretory pore to dispose of metabolic wastes.

The "head" of the tapeworm, a segment referred to as a scolex, has specialized structures, or suckers, augmented in some species with hooks, to anchor the worm to the host's intestinal wall. The scolex is also the germinal center from which all other segments of the tape arise. Near the scolex the segments are sexually immature, in the middle of the chain they are sexually functional; and at the terminal portion, gravid—mere sacs of eggs. The gravid segments separate and either disrupt and release their eggs inside the bowel or are passed whole with the feces.

To develop completely, tapeworms require one or more intermediate hosts. When a pig swallows the egg of a *Taenia* tapeworm, the egg hatches within the pig's intestine but the worm does not develop to the adult "tape." Instead, the microscopic embryo penetrates the intestinal wall and enters a small vein. Circulating blood carries the embryo to various parts of the pig where it will develop into a cysticercus, a bladderlike form with an invaginated structure that will eventually become the scolex. The tapeworm develops no further until a human ingests pork containing the cysticercus. Now safe in its final home, the scolex pops out, attaches to the human intestinal wall, and the worm begins to grow to its full complement of segments.

Most adult tapeworms have a strict host-specific relationship; only man can serve as definitive host (the host for the sexually mature stage) of *Taenia solium* and its close relative *Taenia saginata*. *Taenia solium* is known as the pig tapeworm and *Taenia saginata* as the beef tapeworm because the cysticerci are found in those animals.

Transmission of the disease occurs when infected humans defecate where cows or pigs feed. The animals ingest the eggs, which de-

velop into cysticerci; and the cycle is completed when humans eat undercooked pork or a tasty steak tartare. One highly important difference between the pig tapeworm and the beef tapeworm is that humans can also act as intermediate hosts for the pig tapeworm. If a person swallows an egg of the beef tapeworm, the worm embryo would die in that unsuitable host. But when a human ingests an egg of the pig tapeworm, the bladder stage of the parasite can develop into a disease known as cysticercosis.

While the harboring of a twenty-foot tapeworm may not be a pleasure (except perhaps that you could refer to yourself in the imperial style as "We"), most infections cause little discomfort. Those harboring a tapeworm are often unaware of the beast within, unless they notice segments in their stools.

It is not worms, but the cysticercus that can be devastatingly pathogenic. After hatching from the egg and entering the blood system, the embryo frequently flows to the brain where it grows into the bladder form. In time, an inflammatory reaction can lead to such neurological disorders as epileptic-like convulsions and bizarre personality changes mimicking psychosis. These pathogenic manifestations often do not appear until two to five years after a person has contracted the infection. The condition is like a time bomb inexorably ticking away in the brain.

In 1971, two physicians at the small Enarotali general hospital reported a bewildering "epidemic" of severe burn cases among the Ekari. Some of the twenty-five to thirty cases each month were so bad that limbs had to be amputated. All patients gave similar accounts. While sleeping, they had been overcome by an epileptic seizure and had fallen unconscious into the household fire.

Enarotali is piercingly cold at night. The village sits on the shore of one of the Paniai (Wissel) lakes at an altitude of 5,000 feet, surrounded by the wild barricade of the east-central mountain range. Hardly overdressed for this climate, the local Ekari men wear only a long gourd penis sheath and the women a brief string girdle. To ward off the night chill, they build a fire in the center of rude thatch huts and sleep on bunks around the fire.

The hospital staff had treated burn accidents before 1971 but never on this scale. The frequency of epileptiform attacks was also new, giving rise to the suspicion that some new infectious agent had been introduced.

The pathogen came to light during a survey for intestinal parasites by a team of scientists from the Department of Parasitology of the University of Indonesia School of Medicine in Jakarta. Along with the usual intestinal zoo, they were astonished to find that 8 percent of the fecal samples were positive for the eggs of the tapeworm *Taenia*. Although many parasitological surveys had been carried out in New Guinea for many years, this finding was the first instance of taeniasis. Moreover, the technique of microscopic examination of fecal specimens has a low diagnostic sensitivity for this parasite. Undoubtedly, many more cases existed. For example, in one African study 6 percent of the stools showed taeniasis, while autopsy examinations indicated that more than 60 percent of the population had the tapeworm.

Subsequent clinical examinations of the Ekari revealed cysts under the skin, a sign of heavy, disseminated cysticercosis, and the discovery of the deadly, pearly globules of the cysticerci studded in the brain of a patient who had died of the disease confirmed the cause of the neurological syndrome. Serological tests recently performed by my Indonesian colleagues and me indicate that, at present, at least 25 percent of the Ekari adults and children have cysticercosis.

But where did the parasite come from? How was it introduced into such a remote, isolated area? Reconstruction of historical events indicates that the tapeworm came unseen, riding the anticolonial wave; the vehicles of transport were men and pigs.

In 1969 the United Nations directed the peoples of West New Guinea to choose whether to join the Republic of Indonesia. The Ekari were uncertain, to say the least, about the change in regime, and during the plebiscite, or shortly thereafter, the Indonesians sent troops to Enarotali to help the vote along. Some of the soldiers came from Bali. Indonesia's President Suharto softened the military action by sending a gift of pigs. The pigs came from Bali, since pig rearing in mostly Muslim/Indonesia is largely concentrated on the Hindu island.

Whatever the political and social advantages of the gift, the medical results were an unforeseen tragedy. The pig tapeworm has been endemic in Bali for at least 60 years. A favorite Balinese dish is an undercooked pork preparation in which the cysticerci are cleverly disguised by the legendary spices of the Indies. However, the Balinese are fastidiously clean in their personal habits and so while the tapeworm infection is prevalent, cysticercosis is almost nonexistent. In contrast, the Ekari have Stone Age toilet habits and when the tapeworm came from Bali, they became infected via meat and human feces.

Transcultural tapeworm traffic hasn't been confined to Bali-New Guinea and I should like to digress for a moment to recount a somewhat similar occurrence much closer to home. Now that it is epidemiological history, the story is rather amusing. It might be entitled "A Tapeworm Tale of Two Cities," with a cast of characters that includes the fish tapeworm, Scandinavian fishermen, and Jewish grandmothers of New York City.

The fish tapeworm is big, up to forty-five feet in length, and its name, *Diphyllobothrium latum*, fits its size. The historical endemic focus of *D. latum* is Scandinavia, where the infected fishermen defecate in the lakes. The first intermediate host, a copepod, eats the eggs. A freshwater fish, the second intermediate host, eats the copepod. A wormlike larva develops in the muscles of the fish, and humans become infected by eating a Nordic version of sashimi.

When Scandinavian fishermen came to the United States during the nineteenth-century wave of immigration, many settled in the lake region of Minnesota and Wisconsin where they began to ply their trade (and habits). Shortly thereafter the fish in these lakes became infected.

Commerce in live fish took place regularly between the Midwest and New York City at least until the late 1930s. I recall that during my boyhood in New York almost every market had a large holding tank full of live pike, pickerel, and carp. The chief customers were Jewish housewives who magically transformed the fish into an ethnically ambrosial concoction called gefilte fish.

Basically, gefilte fish is an amalgam of minced fish, pressed into balls, and boiled until done. "Until done" is the tricky part. The grandmothers of that time, to whom the thermometer was considered high technology, would sample the fish until it was cooked just right. The early samples were still quite raw and if infected, contained a viable larval worm. In this way, several of the nice old ladies of Gotham unwittingly acquired a forty-foot Scandinavian immigrant in their digestive tracts. The introduction of fish inspection, sanitary practices, and thermometers, along with the gradual demise of the traditional Jewish grandmother's instinctive culinary arts have made *D. latum* infections rare in the United States.

But to return from New York to highland New Guinea. By 1973 the main epidemiological factors governing the transmission of tapeworm disease were known, but the problem of control remained. In technically advanced countries, refrigerating the pork for the proper length of time kills the cysticerci. Although this is impossible in primitive Enarotali, an effective method would be to cook the carcass thoroughly. Unfortunately, the traditional Ekari barbecue doesn't allow for this. The Ekari throw the dead pig on the fire just long enough to warm it up. One reason for this hasty cooking is that, except for the big feasts, when an Ekari knobbles a pig, he wants it to be all his. Neighbors are not customarily invited for dinner. The Ekari kills his pig secretly—or as secretly as a pig can be butchered—in the dead of night, following the kill with a quick turn on the fire. A fast-food meal takes place in stealth and gloom. (This and other traits have not endeared the Ekari to anthropologists who have described them as greedy, avaricious, and "primitive capitalists.")

The affliction of cysticercosis would seem a compelling enough reason for a change in cooking practice. With incontestable logic, the health educator from Jakarta, a dedicated woman trained at one of America's more prestigious schools of public health, tried to teach the new methods with all the zeal of a Cordon Bleu instructor. So there we were, the educator educating, the doctor expounding on the virtues of sanitation, and the Ekari nodding in pleasant agreement. After all, under the circumstances, who in his right mind could reject this appeal to common sense? Then one night it all fell apart and the cultural gap yawned into an abysmal chasm.

I was sitting by the fire drinking wine with the village elders. Through the translator, the chief expressed his bitterness that the disease introduced by foreigners had corrupted the tribe's pigs and religion. Then came the real shocker for me when he said: "We are not blind. We can see the seeds that give us the illness in the pig flesh. But no one lives forever and if we must die, then we must die. Life is no longer of pleasure. We are only half men. The Indonesians will not let us make the warfare that gave us manhood. I no longer care if I eat the corrupt pig flesh.

"Even if this were not so, we still could not do as you say. You tell us not to eat the infected pig, to be careful, to cook it long. How can we do this? If a child is born at night we must sacrifice a pig immediately, there is no time to look and see if it has the seeds. The pig must be killed and eaten at once.

"When the missionaries brought us the coughing sickness many years ago [a pertussis epidemic in 1956], we rose in anger. This time we have no heart to do so."

After he concluded, the wine was passed around again. I couldn't remember ever feeling so lonely and helpless.

After I left Enarotali I flew to Jayapura, the provincial capital, to discuss the situation with the governor. He was highly sympathetic and concerned, particularly since we had clear evidence that the infection had now spread to many parts of Irian Jaya. After going over the possible remedies and the difficulty in implementing them, he remarked, as I was about to leave the governor's mansion, "You know they are not like you and me. They are very primitive and it is extremely difficult to change their customs even for their better health." I was about to agree when I noticed that we were both smoking cigarettes.

9

The Historical Roots of Our Ecologic Crisis

Lynn White, Jr.

Man's attitude toward nature is the subject of this modern classic. White gives profound insight into the dominant Western tradition of arrogance toward nature. The roots of our environmental troubles are largely religous, he explains. The attitudes and actions of modern technological man contradict the reality that man is part of nature, not rightful master over nature: "Despite Copernicus, all the cosmos rotates around our little globe. Despite Darwin, we are not, in our hearts, part of the natural process. We are superior to nature, contemptuous of it, willing to use it for our slightest whim."

White concludes that "What we do about ecology depends on our ideas of the man-nature relationship. More science and more technology are not going to get us out of the present ecologic crisis until we find a new religion, or rethink our old one." The author includes Marxism and Islam as part of the Judeo-Christian tradition, and hence sharing the blame.

It should be noted that some other authors take issue with White's implied absolution of Oriental attitudes and actions. Yi-Fu Tuan (1968, 1970), for example, argues that the inconsistency and paradox between man's treatment of environment and his own well-being is a characteristic of all human existence, not just of Western cultures. He points out that the highminded ideals of Eastern cultures are frequently not practiced. He believes that at the level of actual impress of man on environment, both constructive and destructive, the pagan world and Oriental societies had as much impact as did European Christians, until the beginning of the modern period. Rhoads Murphey (1967) has shown that in contemporary China ideals are now being adjusted to this reality. With Western technology, China (like Japan and other Asian countries before her) is replacing the traditional notions of harmony with nature with the attitude that man is properly lord over the environment.)

(Editor's comments)

*   Reprinted with permission from *Science, vol. 155*, pp. 1203–1207 by Lynn White, Jr. Copyright © 1967 American Association for the Advancement of Science.

A conversation with Aldous Huxley not infrequently put one at the receiving end of an unforgettable monologue. About a year before his lamented death he was discoursing on a favorite topic: Man's unnatural treatment of nature and its sad results. To illustrate his point he told how, during the previous summer, he had returned to a little valley in England where he had spent many happy months as a child. Once it had been composed of delightful grassy glades; now it was becoming overgrown with unsightly brush because the rabbits that formerly kept such growth under control had largely succumbed to a disease, myxomatosis, that was deliberately introduced by the local farmers to reduce the rabbits' destruction of crops. Being something of a Philistine, I could be silent no longer, even in the interests of great rhetoric. I interrupted to point out that the rabbit itself had been brought as a domestic animal to England in 1176, presumably to improve the protein diet of the peasantry.

All forms of life modify their contexts. The most spectacular and benign instance is doubtless the coral polyp. By serving its own ends, it has created a vast undersea world favorable to thousands of other kinds of animals and plants. Ever since man became a numerous species he has affected his environment notably. The hypothesis that his fire-drive method of hunting created the world's great grasslands and helped to exterminate the monster mammals of the Pleistocene from much of the globe is plausible, if not proved. For 6 millennia at least, the banks of the lower Nile have been a human artifact rather than the swampy African jungle which nature, apart from man, would have made it. The Aswan Dam, flooding 5000 square miles, is only the latest stage in a long process. In many regions terracing or irrigation, overgrazing, the cutting of forests by Romans to build ships to fight Carthaginians or by Crusaders to solve the logistics problems of their expeditions, have profoundly changed some ecologies. Observation that the French landscape falls into two basic types, the open fields of the north and the *bocage* of the south and west, inspired Marc Bloch to undertake his classic study of medieval agricultural methods. Quite unintentionally, changes in human ways often affect nonhuman nature. It has been noted, for example, that the advent of the automobile eliminated huge flocks of sparrows that once fed on the horse manure littering every street.

The history of ecologic change is still so rudimentary that we know little about what really happened, or what the results were. The extinction of the European aurochs as late as 1627 would seem to have been a simple case of overenthusiastic hunting. On more intricate matters it often is impossible to find solid information. For a thousand years or more the Frisians and Hollanders have been pushing back the North Sea, and the process is culminating in our own time in the reclamation of the Zuider Zee. What, if any, species of animals, birds, fish, shore life, or plants have died out in the process? In their epic combat with Neptune have the Netherlanders overlooked ecological values in such a way that the quality of human life in the Netherlands has suffered? I cannot discover that the questions have ever been asked, much less answered.

People, then, have often been a dynamic element in their own environment, but in the present state of historical scholarship we usually do not know exactly when, where, or with what effects man-induced changes came. As we enter the last third of the 20th century, however, concern for the problem of ecologic backlash is mounting feverishly. Natural science, conceived as the effort to understand the nature of things, had flourished in several eras and among several peoples. Similarly there had been an age-old accumulation of technological skills, sometimes growing rapidly, sometimes slowly. But it was not until about four generations ago that Western Europe and North America arranged a marriage between science and technology, a union of the theoretical and the empirical approaches to our natural environment. The emergence in widespread practice of the Baconian creed that scientific knowledge means technological power over nature can scarcely be dated before about 1850, save in the chemical industries, where it is anticipated in the 18th century. Its acceptance as a normal pattern of action may mark the greatest event in human history since the invention of agriculture, and perhaps in non-human terrestrial history as well.

Almost at once the new situation forced the crystallization of the novel concept of ecology; indeed, the word *ecology* first appeared in the English language in 1873. Today, less than a century later, the impact of our race upon the environment has so increased in force that it has changed in essence. When the first cannons were fired, in the early 14th century, they affected ecology by sending workers scrambling to the forests and mountains for more potash, sulphur, iron ore, and charcoal, with some resulting erosion and deforestation. Hydrogen bombs are of a different order: a war fought with them might alter the genetics of all life on this planet. By 1285 London had a smog problem arising from the burning of soft coal, but our present combustion of fossil fuels threatens to change the chemistry of the globe's atmosphere as a whole, with consequences which we are only beginning to guess. With the population explosion, the carcinoma of planless urbanism, the now geological deposits of sewage and garbage, surely no creature other than man has ever managed to foul its nest in such short order.

There are many calls to action, but specific proposals, however worthy as individual items, seem too partial, palliative, negative: ban the bomb, tear down the billboards, give the Hindus contraceptives and tell them to eat their sacred cows. The simplest solution to any suspect change is, of course, to stop it, or better yet, to revert to a romanticized past: make those ugly gasoline stations look like Anne Hathaway's cottage or (in the Far West) like ghost-town saloons. The "wilderness area" mentality invariably advocates deep-freezing an ecology, whether San Gimignano or the High Sierra, as it was before the first Kleenex was dropped. But neither atavism nor prettification will cope with the ecologic crisis of our time.

What shall we do? No one yet knows. Unless we think about fundamentals, our specific measures may produce new backlashes more serious than those they are designed to remedy.

As a beginning we should try to clarify our thinking by looking, in some historical depth, at the presuppositions that underlie modern technology and science. Science was traditionally aristocratic, speculative, intellectual in intent; technology was lower-class, empirical, action-oriented. The quite sudden fusion of these two, towards the middle of the 19th century, is surely related to the slightly prior and contemporary democratic revolutions which, by reducing social barriers, tended to assert a functional unity of brain and hand. Our ecologic crisis is the product of an emerging, entirely novel, democratic culture. The issue is whether a democratized world can survive its own implications. Presumably we cannot unless we rethink our axioms.

The Western Traditions of Technology and Science

One thing is so certain that it seems stupid to verbalize it: both modern technology and modern science are distinctively *Occidental*. Our technology has absorbed elements from all over the world, notably from China; yet everywhere today, whether in Japan or in Nigeria, successful technology is Western. Our science is the heir to all the sciences of the past, especially perhaps to the work of the great Islamic scientists of the Middle Ages, who so often outdid the ancient Greeks in skill and perspicacity: al-Razi in medicine, for example; or ibn-al-Haytham in optics; or Omar Khayyam in mathematics. Indeed, not a few works of such geniuses seem to have vanished in the original Arabic and to survive only in medieval Latin translations that helped to lay the foundations for later Western developments. Today, around the globe, all significant science is Western in style and method, whatever the pigmentation or language of the scientists.

A second pair of facts is less well recognized because they result from quite recent historical scholarship. The leadership of the West, both in technology and in science, is far older than the so-called Scientific Revolution of the 17th century or the so-called Industrial Revolution of the 18th century. These terms are in fact outmoded and obscure the true nature of what they try to describe—significant stages in two long and separate developments. By A.D. 1000 at the latest—and perhaps, feebly, as much as 200 years earlier—the West began to apply water power to industrial processes other than milling grain. This was followed in the late 12th century by the harnessing of wind power. From simple beginnings, but with remarkable consistency of style, the West rapidly expanded its skills in the development of power machinery, labor-saving devices, and automation. Those who doubt should contemplate that most monumental achievement in the history of automation: the weight-driven mechanical clock, which appeared in two forms in the early 14th century. Not in craftsmanship but in basic technological capacity, the Latin West of the later Middle Ages far outstripped its elaborate, sophisticated, and esthetically magnificent sister cultures, Byzantium and Islam. In 1444 a great Greek ecclesiastic, Bessarion, who had gone to Italy, wrote a letter to a prince in Greece. He is amazed by the superiority of Western ships, arms, textiles, glass. But above all he is astonished by the spectacle of water-wheels sawing timbers and pumping the bellows of blast furnaces. Clearly, he had seen nothing of the sort in the Near East.

By the end of the 15th century the technological superiority of Europe was such that its small, mutually hostile nations could spill out over all the rest of the world, conquering, looting, and colonizing. The symbol of this technological superiority is the fact that Portugal, one of the weakest states of the Occident, was able to become, and to remain for a century, mistress of the East Indies. And we must remember that the technology of Vasco da Gama and Albuquerque was built by pure empiricism, drawing remarkably little support or inspiration from science.

In the present-day vernacular understanding, modern science is supposed to have begun in 1543, when both Copernicus and Vesalius published their great works. It is no derogation of their accomplishments, however, to point out that such structures as the *Fabrica* and the *De revolutionibus* do not appear overnight. The distinctive Western tradition of science, in fact, began in the late 11th century with a massive movement of translation of Arabic and Greek scientific works into Latin. A few notable books—Theophrastus, for example—escaped the West's avid new appetite for science, but within less than 200 years effectively the entire corpus of Greek and Muslim science was available in Latin, and was being eagerly read and criticized in the new European universities. Out of criticism arose new observation, speculation, and increasing distrust of ancient authorities. By the late 13th century Europe had seized global scientific leadership from the faltering hands of Islam. It would be as absurd to deny the profound originality of Newton, Galileo, or Copernicus as to deny that of the 14th century scholastic scientists like Buridan or Oresme on whose work they built. Before the 11th century, science scarcely existed in the Latin West, even in Roman times. From the 11th century onward, the scientific sector of Occidental culture has increased in a steady crescendo.

Since both our technological and our scientific movements got their start, acquired their character, and achieved world dominance in the Middle Ages, it would seem that we cannot understand their nature or their present impact upon ecology without examining fundamental medieval assumptions and developments.

Medieval View of Man and Nature

Until recently, agriculture has been the chief occupation even in "advanced" societies; hence, any change in methods of tillage has much importance. Early plows, drawn by two oxen, did not normally turn the sod but merely scratched it. Thus, cross-plowing was needed and fields tended to be squarish. In the fairly light soils and semiarid climates of the Near East and Mediterranean, this worked well. But such a plow was inappropriate to the wet climate and often sticky soils of northern Europe. By the latter part of the 7th century after Christ, however, following obscure beginnings, certain northern peasants were using an entirely new kind of plow, equipped with a vertical knife to cut the line of the furrow, a horizontal share to slice under the sod, and a moldboard to turn it over. The friction of this plow with the soil was so great that it normally required not two but eight oxen. It attacked the land with such violence that cross-plowing was not needed, and fields tended to be shaped in long strips.

In the days of the scratch-plow, fields were distributed generally in units capable of supporting a single family. Subsistence farming was the presupposition. But no peasant owned eight oxen: to use the new and more efficient plow, peasants pooled their oxen to form large plow-teams, originally receiving (it would appear) plowed strips in proportion to their contribution. Thus, distribution of land was based no longer on the needs of a family but, rather, on the capacity of a power machine to till the earth. Man's relation to the soil was profoundly changed. Formerly man had been part of nature; now he was the exploiter of nature. Nowhere else in the world did farmers develop any analogous agricultural implement. Is it coincidence that modern technology, with its ruthlessness toward nature, has so largely been produced by descendants of these peasants of northern Europe?

This same exploitive attitude appears slightly before A.D. 830 in Western illustrated calendars. In older calendars the months were shown as passive personifications. The new Frankish calendars, which set the style for the Middle Ages, are very different: they show men coercing the world around them—plowing, harvesting, chopping trees, butchering pigs. Man and nature are two things, and man is master.

These novelties seem to be in harmony with larger intellectual patterns. What people do about their ecology depends on what they think about themselves in relation to things around them. Human ecology is deeply conditioned by beliefs about our nature and destiny—that is, by religion. To Western eyes this is very evident in, say, India or Ceylon. It is equally true of ourselves and of our medieval ancestors.

The victory of Christianity over paganism was the greatest psychic revolution in the history of our culture. It has become fashionable today to say that, for better or worse, we live in the "post-Christian age." Certainly the forms of our thinking and language have largely ceased to be Christian, but to my eye the substance often remains amazingly akin to that of the past. Our daily habits of action, for example, are dominated by an implicit faith in perpetual progress which was unknown either to Greco-Roman antiquity or to the Orient. It is rooted in, and is indefensible apart from, Judeo-Christian theology. The fact that Communists share it merely helps to show what can be demonstrated on many other grounds: that Marxism, like Islam, is a Judeo-Christian heresy. We continue today to live, as we have lived for about 1700 years, very largely in a context of Christian axioms.

What did Christianity tell people about their relations with the environment?

While many of the world's mythologies provide stories of creation, Greco-Roman mythology was singularly incoherent in this respect. Like Aristotle, the intellectuals of the ancient West denied that the visible world had a beginning. Indeed, the idea of a beginning was impossible in the framework of their cyclical notion of time. In sharp contrast, Christianity inherited from Judaism not only a concept of time as nonrepetitive and linear but also a striking story of creation. By gradual stages a loving and all-powerful God had created light and darkness, the heavenly bodies, the earth and all its plants, animals, birds, and fishes. Finally, God had created Adam and, as an afterthought, Eve to keep man from being lonely. Man named all the animals, thus establishing his dominance over them. God planned all of this explicitly for man's benefit and rule: no item in the physical creation had any purpose save to serve man's purposes. And, although man's body is made of clay, he is not simply part of nature: he is made in God's image.

Especially in its Western form, Christianity is the most anthropocentric religion the world has seen. As early as the 2nd century both Tertullian and Saint Irenaeus of Lyons were insisting that when God shaped Adam he was foreshadowing the image of the incarnate Christ, the Second Adam. Man shares, in great measure, God's transcendence of nature. Christianity, in absolute contrast to ancient paganism and Asia's religions (except, perhaps, Zoroastrianism), not only established a dualism of man and nature but also insisted that it is God's will that man exploit nature for his proper ends.

At the level of the common people this worked out in an interesting way. In Antiquity every tree, every spring, every stream, every hill had its own *genius loci,* its guardian spirit. These spirits were accessible to men, but were very unlike men; centaurs, fauns, and mermaids show their ambivalence. Before one cut a tree, mined a mountain, or dammed a brook, it was important to placate the spirit in charge of that particular situation, and to keep it placated. By destroying pagan animism, Christianity made it possible to exploit nature in a mood of indifference to the feelings of natural objects.

It is often said that for animism the Church substituted the cult of saints. True; but the cult of saints is functionally quite different from animism. The saint is not *in* natural objects; he may have special shrines, but his citizenship is in heaven. Moreover, a saint is entirely a man; he can be approached in human terms. In addition to saints, Christianity of course also had angels and demons inherited from Judaism and perhaps, at one remove, from Zoroastrianism. But these were all as mobile as the saints themselves. The spirits *in* natural objects, which formerly had protected nature from man, evaporated. Man's effective monopoly on spirit in this world was confirmed, and the old inhibitions to the exploitation of nature crumbled.

When one speaks in such sweeping terms, a note of caution is in order. Christianity is a complex faith, and its consequences differ in differing contexts. What I have said may well apply to the medieval West, where in fact technology made spectacular advances. But the Greek East, a highly civilized realm of equal Christian devotion, seems to have produced no marked technological innovation after the late 7th century, when Greek fire was invented. The key to the contrast may perhaps be found in a difference in the tonality of piety and thought which students of comparative theology find between the Greek and the Latin Churches. The Greeks believed that sin was intellectual blindness, and that salvation was found in illumination, orthodoxy—that is, clear thinking. The Latins, on the other hand, felt that sin was moral evil, and that salvation was to be found in right conduct. Eastern theology has been intellectualist. Western theology has been voluntarist. The Greek saint contemplates; the Western saint acts. The implications of Christianity for the conquest of nature would emerge more easily in the Western atmosphere.

The Christian dogma of creation, which is found in the first clause of all the Creeds, has another meaning for our comprehension of today's ecologic crisis. By revelation, God had given man the Bible, the Book of Scripture. But since God had made nature, nature also must reveal the divine mentality. The religious study of nature for the better understanding of God was known as natural theology. In the early Church, and always in the Greek East, nature was conceived primarily as a symbolic system through which God speaks to men: the ant is a sermon to sluggards; rising flames are the symbol of the soul's aspiration. The view of nature was essentially artistic rather than scientific. While Byzantium preserved and copied great numbers of ancient Greek scientific texts, science as we conceive it could scarcely flourish in such an ambience.

However, in the Latin West by the early 13th century natural theology was following a very different bent. It was ceasing to be the decoding of the physical symbols of God's communication with man and was becoming the effort to understand God's mind by discovering how his creation operates. The rainbow was no longer simply a symbol of hope first sent to Noah after the Deluge: Robert Grosseteste, Friar Roger Bacon, and Theodoric of Freiberg produced startlingly sophisticated work on the optics of the rainbow, but they did it as a venture in religious understanding. From the 13th century onward, up to and including Leibnitz and Newton, every major scientist, in effect, explained his motivations in religious terms. Indeed, if Galileo had not been so expert an amateur theologian he would have got into far less trouble: the professionals resented his intrusion. And Newton seems to have regarded himself more as a theologian than as a scientist. It was not until the late 18th century that the hypothesis of God became unnecessary to many scientists.

It is often hard for the historian to judge, when men explain why they are doing what they want to do, whether they are offering real reasons or merely culturally acceptable reasons. The consistency with which scientists during the long formative centuries of Western science said that the task and the reward of the scientist was "to think God's thoughts after him" leads one to believe that this was their real motivation. If so, then modern Western science was cast in a matrix of Christian theology. The dynamism of religious devotion shaped by the Judeo-Christian dogma of creation, gave it impetus.

An Alternative Christian View

We would seem to be headed toward conclusions unpalatable to many Christians. Since both *science* and *technology* are blessed words in our contemporary vocabulary, some may be happy at the notions, first, that, viewed historically, modern science is an extrapolation of natural theology and, second, that modern technology is at least partly to be explained as an Occidental, voluntarist realization of the Christian dogma of man's transcendence of, and rightful mastery over, nature. But, as we now recognize, somewhat over a century ago science and technology—hitherto quite separate activities—joined to give mankind powers which, to judge by many of the ecologic effects, are out of control. If so, Christianity bears a huge burden of guilt.

I personally doubt that disastrous ecologic backlash can be avoided simply by applying to our problems more science and more technology. Our science and technology have grown out of Christian attitudes toward man's relation to nature which are almost universally held not only by Christians and neo-Christians but also by those who fondly regard themselves as post-Christians. Despite Copernicus, all the cosmos rotates around our little globe. Despite Darwin, we are *not,* in our hearts, part of the natural process. We are superior to nature, contemptuous of it, willing to use it for our slightest whim. The newly elected Governor of California, like myself a churchman but less troubled than I, spoke for the Christian tradition when he said (as is alleged), "when you've seen one redwood tree, you've seen them all." To a Christian a tree can be no more than a physical fact. The whole concept of the sacred grove is alien to Christianity and to the ethos of the West. For nearly 2 millennia Christian missionaries have been chopping down sacred groves, which are idolatrous because they assume spirit in nature.

What we do about ecology depends on our ideas of the man-nature relationship. More science and more technology are not going to get us out of the present ecologic crisis until we find a new religion, or rethink our old one. The beatniks, who are the basic revolutionaries of our time, show a sound instinct in their affinity for Zen Buddhism, which conceives of the man-nature relationship as very nearly the mirror image of the Christian view. Zen, however, is as deeply conditioned by Asian history as Christianity is by the experience of the West, and I am dubious of its viability among us.

Possibly we should ponder the greatest radical in Christian history since Christ: Saint Francis of Assisi. The prime miracle of Saint Francis is the fact that he did not end at the stake, as many of his left-wing followers did. He was so clearly heretical that a General of the Franciscan Order, Saint Bonaventura, a great and perceptive Christian, tried to suppress the early accounts of Franciscanism. The key to an understanding of Francis is his belief in the virtue of humility—not merely for the individual but for man as a species. Francis tried to depose man from his monarchy over creation and set up a democracy of all God's creatures. With him the ant is no longer simply a homily for the lazy, flames a sign of the thrust of the soul toward union with God; now they are Brother Ant and Sister Fire, praising the Creator in their own ways as Brother Man does in his.

Later commentators have said that Francis preached to the birds as a rebuke to men who would not listen. The records do not read so: he urged the little birds to praise God, and in spiritual ecstasy they flapped their wings and chirped rejoicing. Legends of saints, especially the Irish saints, had long told of their dealings with animals but always, I believe, to show their human dominance over creatures. With Francis it is different. The land around Gubbio in the Apennines was ravaged by a fierce wolf. Saint Francis, says the legend, talked to the wolf and persuaded him of the error of his ways. The wolf repented, died in the odor of sanctity, and was buried in consecrated ground.

What Sir Steven Ruciman calls "the Franciscan doctrine of the animal soul" was quickly stamped out. Quite possibly it was in part inspired, consciously or unconsciously, by the belief in reincarnation held by the Cathar heretics who at that time teemed in Italy and southern France, and who presumably had got it originally from India. It is significant that at just the same moment, about 1200, traces of metempsychosis are found also in western Judaism, in the Provençal *Cabbala.* But Francis held neither to transmigration of souls nor to pantheism. His view of nature and of man rested on a unique sort of pan-psychism of all things animate and inanimate, designed for the glorification of their transcendent Creator, who, in the ultimate gesture of cosmic humility, assumed flesh, lay helpless in a manger, and hung dying on a scaffold.

I am not suggesting that many contemporary Americans who are concerned about our ecologic crisis will be either able or willing to counsel with wolves or exhort birds. However, the present increasing disruption of the global environment is the product of a dynamic technology and science which were originating in the Western medieval world against which Saint Francis was rebelling in so original a way. Their growth cannot be understood historically apart from distinctive attitudes toward nature which are deeply grounded in Christian dogma. The fact that most people do not think of these attitudes as Christian is irrelevant. No new set of basic values has been accepted in our society to displace those of Christianity. Hence we shall continue to have a worsening ecologic crisis until we reject the Christian axiom that nature has no reason for existence save to serve man.

The greatest spiritual revolutionary in Western history, Saint Francis, proposed what he thought was an alternative Christian view of nature and man's relation to it: he tried to substitute the idea of the equality of all creatures, including man, for the idea of man's limitless rule of creation. He failed. Both our present science and our present technology are so tinctured with orthodox Christian arrogance toward nature that no solution for our ecologic crisis can be expected from them alone. Since the roots of our trouble are so largely religious, the remedy must also be essentially religious, whether we call it that or not. We must rethink and refeel our nature and destiny. The profoundly religious, but heretical, sense of the primitive Franciscans for the spiritual autonomy of all parts of nature may point a direction. I propose Francis as a patron saint for ecologists.

Additional References

Bouillenne, R. 1962. Man, the destroying biotype. *Science* 135:706–712.

Glacken, C. J. 1956. Changing ideas of the habitable world. Pp. 70–92 in *Man's role in changing the face of the earth,* ed. by William L. Thomas, Jr. Chicago and London: The University of Chicago Press.

Glacken, C. J. 1967. *Traces on the Rhodian shore.* Berkeley, California: University of California Press. Monumental history of man-nature relationships in Western thought.

Glacken, C. J. 1970. man against nature: An outmoded concept. Pp. 127–142 in *The environmental crisis*, ed. by H. W. Helfrich, Jr. New Haven and London: Yale University Press.

Matley, I. A. 1966. The Marxist approach to the geographical environment. *Annals Assoc. Am. Geograph.* 56:97–111.

Murphey, R. 1967. Man and nature in China. *Modern Asian Studies* 1(4):313–333.

Murray, E. G. D. 1954. The place of nature in man's world. *Am. Scientist* 42:130–135, 142.

Northrop, F. S. C. 1956. Man's relation to the earth in its bearing on his aesthetic, ethical, and legal values. Pp. 1052–1067 in *Man's role in changing the face of the earth,* ed. by William L. Thomas, Jr. Chicago and London: The University of Chicago Press.

Shepard, P. 1967. *Man in the landscape: A historic view of the esthetics of nature.* New York: Knopf. 290 pp.

Tuan, Y. 1966. Man and nature. *Landscape* 15(3):30–36. An extensive overview of literature on the subject of man in relation to nature.

Tuan, Y. 1968. Discrepancies between environmental attitude and behaviour: examples from Europe and China. *Canadian Geographer* XII(3).

Tuan, Y. 1970. Our treatment of the environment in ideal and actuality. *Am. Scientist.* 58(3):244, 247–249.

10

Our Treatment of the Environment in Ideal and Actuality

Yi-Fu Tuan

A geographer observes man's effect on nature in China and in the pagan and Christian West.

Ethnocentrism is characteristic of peoples all over the world. It is difficult for any viable culture to avoid seeing itself as the center of light shading into darkness. In Europe, to be sure, in the late seventeenth and early eighteenth centuries, this glorification of self was temporarily reversed. *La-bas on était bien.* In the spirit of that age Europe was viewed as a portion of the earth afflicted with the blight of tyranny and superstition; beyond lay unspoiled Nature, unspoiled and rational peoples still appareled in celestial light.[1] This romantic spirit has continued to affect the thinking of the West to the present day. Sensitive Westerners are wont to contrast their own aggressive, exploitative attitude to nature with the harmonious relationships of other times and other places. This view should be commended for generosity, but it lacks realism and fails to recognize inconsistency and paradox as characteristic of human existence.

In recent years two ideas that have bearing on our relationships to our environment are receiving greater recognition. One is that the balances of nature can be upset by people with the most primitive tools, the other that a wide gap may exist between a culture's ideals and their expression in the real world.

A current debate of interest in connection with the first point is the role of man in the extinction of Pleistocene mammals. Although the issue is far from resolution, I think we must admit that Paul Martin has made a good case for what he calls "prehistoric overkill."[2] We are readily persuaded that the disappearance of the bison was brought about by masterful and predatory white men, but find the thought that primitive hunters could cause the wholesale destruction of fauna somewhat unpalatable.

The second point is a commonplace of experience in daily life; that a high-minded philosopher should actually live his philosophy is a matter for surprise, and we take it for

---

* From *American Scientist, vol. 58* by Yi-Fu Tuan. Copyright © 1970 by Sigma Xi; The Scientific Research Society. Reprinted by permission.

granted that few of a politician's professed ideals are convertible into substance. But in the study of the ideas and ideals of cultures, especially non-Western cultures, there remains a tendency to assume that they have force and correspond to reality. It seems to go against the grain for a scientist to seek for polarities, dichotomies, and paradoxes; he would rather see unity and harmony. Contrarieties exist, however, in cultures as in individuals. A nonliterate, stable people such as the Zuñis of New Mexico do indeed make much of their aspiration to achieve harmonious order in the affairs of nature and of men, but their community is nonetheless wracked from time to time by bitter factionalism.[3]

If small and stable societies do not often work as harmonious wholes, it is not surprising that large and complex civilizations like those of Europe and China should contain numerous dysfunctions. One of these is ecological imbalance. This is a theme I wish to take up—but indirectly; my primary concern is with the gaps that exist between an expressed attitude toward environment and actual practice. Such gaps may be taken as one of the signs of maladjustment in society.

To the question, what is the basic difference between European and Chinese attitudes to nature, many people might answer that whereas the European sees nature as subordinate to man the Chinese sees himself as part of nature. Although there is some truth in this generalization, it cannot be pressed too far. A culture's publicized ethos about its environment seldom covers more than a fraction of the total range of its attitudes and practices pertaining to that environment. In the play of forces that govern the world, esthetic and religious ideals rarely have a major role.

Christianity has often been blamed for Western man's presumption of power over nature. Professor Lynn White,[4] for example, speaks of the Christian religion as the most anthropocentric the world has seen: it not only established a dualism between man and nature but insisted that it is God's will that man should exploit nature for proper ends. Christianity, White says, has destroyed antiq-

uity's feeling for the sacredness of places and of natural things, and has made it possible for man to exploit his environment indifferent to the spirits that once guarded the trees, hills, and brooks. The Christian religion he further credits with Western man's prideful faith in perpetual progress, an idea that was unknown to Greco-Roman antiquity and to the Orient.

Opinions such as these reenforce the view that Christianity constituted a great divide. But the official triumph of Christ over the pagan deities brought no revolutionary change to the organization either of society or of nature. At the level of the actual impress of man on environment, both constructive and destructive, the pagan world had as much to show as Christianized Europe did, until the beginning of the modern period. Contrary to the commonly accepted opinion of twentieth-century scholars, classical antiquity knew progressivism. As Ludwig Edelstein has recently noted, the pre-Socratic philosopher Xenophanes believed in progress; and his faith could well have been buoyed up by the engineering achievements of this time.[5] Lines in Sophocles' *Antigone* refer to the power of man to tear the soil with his plow. Plato in *Critias* described the negative side of that power—deforestation and soil erosion.[6] By the early Hellenistic period, technical ingenuity was performing feats that justified Aristotle's boast: "Vanquished by nature, we become masters by technique."[7]

But the Romans did far more than the Greeks to impose their will on the natural environment. "Public roads," as Gibbons wrote in admiration, "ran in a direct line from one city to another, with very little respect for the obstacles either of nature or of private property. Mountains were perforated, and bold arches thrown over the broadest and most rapid streams."[8] An even more overriding example of the triumph of the human will over the lineaments of nature is the Roman grid method of dividing up the land into *centuria quadrata,* each containing a hundred *heredia.* As John Bradford puts it,[9] centuriation well displayed the arbitrary but methodical qualities in Roman government. With absolute self-assurance and great technical competence the Romans imposed the same formal pattern of land division on the well-watered alluvium of the Po Valley as on the near-desert of Tunisia. Even today the forceful imprint of centuriation can be traced across thousands of square miles on both sides of the central Mediterranean, and it can still stir the imagination by its scale and boldness.

Against this back-ground of the vast transformations of nature in the pagan world, the inroads made in the early centuries of the Christian era appear relatively modest. Christianity teaches that man has dominion over nature—but for a long time this new dignity was more a tenet of faith than a fact of experience: for man's undisputed power over nature to become a realized fact Europe had to await the growth of human numbers, the achievement of greater administrative centralization, and the development and application of new technological skills. Farmsteads and arable fields multiplied at the expense of forests and marshes through the Middle Ages, but these lacked the permanence, the geometric order, and the prideful assertion of the human will that one can more readily read into the Roman road systems, aqueducts, and centuriated landholdings.

When we turn to China, we again find discrepancies between esthetic ideals and performance, as well as unforeseen conflicts and dysfunctions that are inevitable in a complex civilization. Western intellectuals who look at Chinese culture tend to be overgenerous, following the example of the eighteenth-century *philosophes* rather than the chauvinism of nineteenth-century European scholars.

Seduced by China's Taoist and Buddhist traditions, they like to compare the Oriental's quiescent and adaptive approach toward nature with the aggressive masculinity of Western man.

An adaptive attitude toward nature does indeed have ancient roots in China. Evidence of it occurs in diverse sources. Well known to the West is the concept of *feng-shui* or geomancy, aptly defined as "the art of adapting the residences of the living and the dead so as to co-operate and harmonize with the local

currents of the cosmic breath."[10] A general effect of the belief in feng-shui has been to encourage a preference for natural curves—for finding paths and structures that seem to fit into the landscape rather than to dominate it—and at the same time to promote a distaste for straight lines and layouts.

Ancient Chinese literature contains scattered evidence that the need to regulate the use of resources was recognized. Even as early as the Eastern Chou period (8th–3rd century B.C.) the deforestation resulting from the expansion of agriculture and the building of cities seems to have led to an appreciation of the value of trees. In the *Chou Li*—a work which was probably compiled in the third century B.C. but may well include earlier material—two classes of conservation officials are mentioned: the inspectors of mountains and of forests. They were charged with protecting certain species, and with seeing to it that the common people cut trees at the proper season, except when emergencies required making coffins or strengthening dykes.[11] Another ancient literary reference to conservation practice is Mencius' advice to Kiny Huai of Liang that he would not lack for wood if he allowed the people to cut trees only at the proper time.[12]

Throughout Chinese history perspicacious officials have on various occasions warned against the dire consequences of deforestation. They deplored the indiscriminate cutting of trees in the mountains not only because of its harmful effect on stream flow and on the quality of soil in the lowland but also because they believed that forested mountain ridges slowed down the horse-riding barbarians. As one scholar of the Ming dynasty put it, "I saw the fact that what the country relies on as strategically important is the mountain, and what the mountain relies on as a screen to prevent advance are the trees."[13] The scholar-officials also recognized the esthetic value of forested mountains. The Wu-tai mountains in northern Shan-hsi, for example, were famous, but shorn of their trees can they retain their fame?

These references suggest that an old tradition of forest care existed in China. On the other hand it is clear that the concern arose in response to damages that had already occurred, even in antiquity. Animistic belief and Taoist nature philosophy lie at the back of an adaptive attitude to environment; alone these might have produced a sequestered utopia. But China, with her gardens and temple compounds, was also a vast bureaucracy, a civilization, and an empire. Opposed to the attitude of passivity was the "male" principle of dominance. One of the greatest culture heroes of China was the semilegendary Yu, whose fame lay not in his precepts but in his acts—his feats of engineering.

An idea that lent support to the dominance side in Chinese culture was one which discerned a model of the cosmos in the earthly environment. It held that the regular motions of the stars could be expressed architecturally and ritually in space and time on earth. The walled city was given a rectilinear pattern, an orientation, and a grandeur that reflected the order and dimension of heaven.[14] The earth's surface itself lacks paradigms of geometric order. Mountains and water are irregularly disposed. Experience of them has led to such unaggressive precepts as the need to observe and placate the spirits of the earth, the need for man to contemplate terrestrial harmony and adapt himself to it. By contrast observation of the stars has encouraged the aggressive side of Chinese culture, nurturing its predilections for order, hierarchy, and control.

Visitors to China in the nineteenth and early part of the twentieth centuries have often commented on the treelessness of the North, and the acute problems of soil erosion on the loess-covered plateaus. These areas were once well wooded. Deforestation on a vast scale took place as population increased and more and more land was taken over by farmers. But this alone does not account for the extent of the clearing. Other factors militated against prudence. One was the ancient custom, first recorded in the fourth century B.C., of burning trees in order to deprive dangerous animals of their hiding places.[15] Even in contemporary China farmers are known to start fires for no evident purpose.

Asked why, they may say it is to clear land for cultivation—although the extent of burn-ing far exceeds the needs for this purpose—or it is to leave fewer places in which bandits may hide, or to encourage the growth of small-sized sprouts in the burnt-over area and avoid the labor of splitting wood.[16] The real reason for the burning is difficult to pin down.

Forests in North China were also depleted to make charcoal for industrial fuel. From the tenth century on, the expanding metallic industries swallowed up many hundred of thousands of tons of charcoal each year, as did the manufacture of salt, alum, bricks, tiles, and liquor. By the Sung dynasty (960–1279 A.D.) the demand for wood and charcoal as both household and industrial fuels had exceeded the timber resources of the country; the result was the increasing substitution of coal for wood and charcoal.[17]

An enormous amount of timber was needed for construction in the old Chinese cities, probably more than was required in European cities of comparable size. One reason for this is the dependence of traditional Chinese architecture on wood as the basic structural material. Great cities like Ch'ang-an, Lo-yang, and Hang-chou made severe demands on the resources of the surrounding country. The rapid expansion of Hang-chou in the thirteenth century to a metropolis of some one and a half million people led to the denuding of the neighboring hills. Despite the demand of the swelling urban population for food, some farmers found it more profitable to give up rice cultivation and grow trees.[18] Rebuilding the wooden houses after fires put a further strain on timber resources; but of greater consequence was the deliberate devastation of whole cities in times of upheaval, when rebels or nomadic invaders toppled a dynasty. The succeeding phase of reconstruction was normally achieved in haste by armies of men who made ruthless inroads on the forest.

In a complex society benign institutions can introduce effects that were no part of their original purpose. The indirect results of any major action or event are largely unpredictable, and we tend to see the irony only in retrospect. For example, Buddhism in China is at least partly responsible for the preservation of trees around temple compounds, islands of green in an otherwise denuded landscape. On the other hand Buddhism introduced into China the idea of cremation of the dead; and from the tenth to the fourteenth centuries cremation was common enough in the southeastern coastal provinces to create a timber shortage there.[19] Large parts of Mongolia have been overgrazed by sheep and goats. The most abused land appeared as sterile rings around the lamaseries, whose princely domains pastured large herds though the monks were not supposed to consume meat. In Japan, the seventeenth-century official and conservationist Kumazawa Banzan was inclined to put most of the blame for the deforestation of his country on Buddhism; the Buddhists, he contended were responsible for seven-tenths of the nation's timber consumption. One reason for this grossly disproportionate consumption was that instead of living like "grass hermitages" they built themselves huge halls and temples.[20]

Another example of fine irony concerns that most civilized of the arts, writing. Soot was needed to make black ink, and soot came from burnt pine. As E. H. Schafer has put it, "Even before T'ang times, the ancient pines of the mountains of Shan-tung had been reduced to carbon, and now the busy brushes of the vast T'ang bureaucracy were rapidly bringing baldness to the T'a-hang Mountains between Shansi and Hopei."[21]

Although ancient pines may already have disappeared from Shan-tung by the T'ang dynasty, from the testimony of the Japanese monk Ennin we know that large parts of the peninsula were still well wooded in the ninth century.[22] The landscapes described by Ennin provide sharp contrast to the dry, bare scenes that characterize so much of Shan-tung in modern times. Shan-tung has many holy places; the province includes the sacred mountain T'ai-shan and the ancient state of Lu, which was the birthplace of Confucius. The numerous shrines and temples have managed to preserve only tiny spots of green amid the brown. Around Chiao-chou Bay in eastern Shan-tung a conspicuous strip of forest lies behind the port of Ch'ing-tao. It is ironic that this patch of green should owe its existence not to native piety but to the conservation-minded Germans.

The unplanned and often careless use of land in China belongs, one hopes, to the past. The Communist government has made an immense effort to control erosion and to reforest. Besides such large projects as shelterbelts along the semiarid edges of the North, forest brigades of the individual communes have planted billions of trees around villages, in cities, along roads and river banks, and on the hillsides. A visitor from New Zealand reported in 1960 that as seen from the air the new growths spread "a mist of green" over the once bare hills of South China.[23] For those who admire the old culture, it must again seem ironic that the "mist of green" is no reflection of the traditional virtues of Taoism and Buddhism; on the contrary, it rests on their explicit denial.[24]

Problems of despoliation of the environment must be attacked along several fronts. Engineers offer technical solutions. Social scientists need to examine those societal dysfunctions that leave strains and scars on our habitats. One symptom of maladjustment lies in the conflicts between an ideal of nature or environment and our practice. Such conflicts are embarrassing to observe for they expose our intellectual failure to make the connection, and perhaps also our hyposcisy; moreover, they cannot always be resolved. Contradictions of a certain kind may be inherent in the human condition, and not even stable and simple cultures are exempt. Ideals and necessities are frequently opposed as, for example, on the most fundamental level, keeping one's cake and eating it are incompatible. Some consume beauty for gain; but all of us must consume it to live.

Notes

1. Willey, B. 1962. *The eighteenth-century background* (Penguin Books), pp. 19–21.
2. Martin, P. S. 1963. *The last 10,000 years* (Tucson: Univ. of Arizona Press), pp. 64–65, 70; P. S. Martin and H. E. Wright, Jr., eds.,

Pleistocene extinctions, Proc. of the 7th Congress of the Internat. Assoc. for Quaternary Research, vol. 6. New Haven: Yale Univ. Press, 1967.

3. Vogt, E., and E. M. Albert, eds. 1966. *People of Rimrock: A study of value in fire cultures* (Cambridge: Harvard Univ. Press), pp. 201–2.

4. White, L. 1967. The historical roots of our ecologic crisis, *Science* 155:1205.

5. Edelstein, L. 1967. *The idea of progress in classical antiquity* (Baltimore, Md.: The Johns Hopkins Press), pp. 3, 11–13.

6. Sophocles, *Antigone,* trans. by Gilbert Murray, quoted in Arnold Toynbee, *Greek historical thought* (New York: New American Library, 1952), p. 128; Plato, *Critics,* ibid, pp. 146–47). On the theme of man-nature relationships in Western thought, see Clarence Glacken's monumental *Traces on the Rhodian shore,* Berkeley, Cal.: Univ. of California Press, 1967.

7. Aristotle, *Mechanics* 847, a 20.

8. Gibbons, E. *The decline and fall of the Roman Empire,* chap. 2.

9. Bradford, J. 1957. *Ancient landscapes* (London), p. 145.

10. Chatley, H. 1917. "Feng Shui," in *Encyclopaedia Sinica,* ed. by S. Couling (Shanghai), p. 175.

11. *Chou Li,* trans. by E. Biot as *Le Techeou-li* (Paris: 1851) 1: 371–74.

12. Mencius, Bk. 1, pt. 1, 3:3.

13. Chen Teng. 1596. Gazetteer. Quoted by W. C. Lowdermilk and D. R. Wickes, *History of soil use in the Wu T'ai Shan area,* Monograph, Royal Asiatic Soc., North China Branch, 1938, p. 8.

14. Wright, A. F. 1965. Symbolism and function: reflections on Changan and other great cities, *J. Asian Studies* 24: 670.

15. Mencius, Bk. 3, pt. 1, 4:7.

16. Steward, A. N., and Y. Cheo. 1935. Geographical and ecological notes on botanical exploration in Kwangsi province, China, *Nanking Journal* 5:174.

17. Hartwell, R. 1962. A revolution in Chinese iron and coal industries during the Northern Sung, 960–1126 A.D., *J. Asian Studies* 21:159.

18. Gernet, J. 1962. *Daily life in China on the eve of the Mongol invasion 1250–1276* (London: Allen & Unwin), p. 114.

19. Moule, A. C. 1957. *Quinsai* (Cambridge Univ. Press), p. 51.

20. McMullen, J. 1967. "Confucianism and forestry in seventeenth-century Japan." Unpublished paper, Toronto. I am grateful to Professor McMullen for allowing me to read this.

21. Schafer, E. H. 1962. The conservation of nature under the T'ang dynasty, *J. Econ. and Soc. Hist. of the Orient* 5:299–300.

22. Reischauer, E. O. 1955. *Enmin's travels in T'ang China* (New York: Ronald Press), pp. 153–56.

23. Buchanan, K., 1960. The changing face of rural China, *Pacific Viewpoint* 1:19.

24. Murphey, R. 1967. Man and nature in China. *Modern Asian Studies* 1, no. 4:313–33.

11

Preaching the Gospel of Green

By Paul Nussbaum

Increasingly, Evangelicals are Embracing Environmentalism

One of Calvin DeWitt's favorite Bible verses is Revelation 11:18:

"... *The time has come for judging the dead ... and for destroying those who destroy the Earth.*"

DeWitt, a professor of environmental studies at the University of Wisconsin, is a leader in a growing evangelical Christian movement to protect the environment in the name of God.

"This comes right out of the Christian calling of how we should live our lives on Earth," DeWitt said. "Christians are coming on board more and more because there really is an interest in seeking the kingdom of God beyond just individual needs."

On such issues as global climate change, endangered species, and mercury hazards to the unborn, many evangelical Christians are parting ways with conservatives. They are embracing environmental protection as "stewardship" of God's creation.

One such expression was to take place Saturday, when President Bush was to give the commencement address at Calvin College, a small school in the Reformed tradition in Grand Rapids, Mich. A third of the faculty of the college signed an open letter to Bush, citing "conflicts between our understanding of what Christians are called to do and many of the policies of your administration."

Among the concerns, the faculty wrote: "As Christians we are called to be caretakers of God's good creation. We believe your environmental policies have harmed creation and have not promoted long-term stewardship of our natural environment."

The environmental awakening among evangelicals has prompted some to seek common ground with other faiths. A group of evangelical Protestant scientists is working with Jewish scholars and scientists to form a "Noah Alliance" to protect endangered species — and the Endangered Species Act.

"Ours is the time for a concert of religious voices to proclaim our privilege and responsibility for not allowing the great lineages of God's living creatures to be broken," says a draft statement being circulated this month among Christian and Jewish scientists.

Broadly defined, evangelicals are Christians who have had a personal or "born-again" religious conversion, believe the Bible is the word of God, and believe in spreading their faith. Millions of Americans fit the definition, although estimates vary on exactly how many: Forty-two percent of Americans described themselves as evangelical Christians in a 2003 Gallup poll, while only 19 percent said they met all three criteria in a 1995 Gallup poll. The National Association of Evangelicals says about 25 percent of adult Americans are evangelicals.

Evangelicals — especially white, Protestant evangelicals — have been considered reliable supporters of a conservative agenda that focuses on "values" issues such as abortion and gay marriage. In last year's presidential election, Bush received 78 percent of the vote of white evangelicals, according to the National Election Pool exit poll.

Historically, many evangelical Christians have been suspicious of environmentalism as a liberal, godless movement more interested in scenery than souls.

But in recent months, a number of evangelical leaders have advocated for strong measures to protect the environment, based on biblical teachings of stewardship, helping the poor, and loving one's neighbors.

A group of 30 prominent evangelicals — including the Rev. Ted Haggard, chairman of the NAE; David Neff, editor of Christianity Today magazine; the Rev. Jo Anne Lyon, executive director of the aid organization World Hope International; and the Rev. Dwight McKissic, senior pastor of Cornerstone Baptist Church in Arlington, Texas — met last summer to pledge to "motivate the evangelical community to fully engage environmental issues in a biblically faithful and humble manner, collaborating with those who share these concerns, that we might take our appropriate place in the healing of God's creation, and thus the advance of God's reign."

"We are persuaded that we must not evade our responsibility to care for God's creation," the evangelical leaders wrote after a three-day retreat at Sandy Cove, Md. "We recognize that there is much more we need to learn, and much more praying we need to do, but that we know enough to know that there is no turning back from engaging the threats to God's creation."

The group said it would seek by this summer to find a consensus among evangelical leaders on how best to tackle global warming.

Richard Cizik, vice president for governmental affairs of the NAE, said recent polling showed 48 percent of evangelicals rated the environment as an important priority, nearly as high a proportion — 52 percent — as those who cited abortion as a priority.

"That's an amazing statistic, considering that we've been talking about abortion for 30 years and we haven't even begun to make a case to a lot of our folks about environmental issues," Cizik said.

John Green, director of the Ray C. Bliss Institute of Applied Politics and coauthor of *The Bully Pulpit: The Politics of Protestant Clergy and Religion and the Culture Wars: Dispatches From the Front*, sees a steady growth in environmental consciousness among evangelicals.

"Historically, evangelical Protestants have been slow to pick up the cause of environmentalism. The more traditional they were, the less interested they were. And some fundamentalists were, in fact, quite hostile to environmentalism.

In recent times, though, evangelicals have developed an interest in the environment.

"Part of that may be that as more evangelicals have attained middle-class status, they have grown more interested in middle-class issues, and one of those is the environment."

In polling by the Bliss Institute last year, 52 percent of evangelicals agreed with the statement, "Strict rules to protect the environment are necessary even if they cost jobs or result in higher prices."

The Rev. Jim Ball, a Baptist minister who is executive director of the Evangelical Environmental Network and organizer of the "What Would Jesus Drive?" campaign, says evangelical Christians are more receptive to environmental messages "when we talk about things in terms of family and kids."

So one powerful environmental topic among evangelicals has become the threat of mercury, emitted by coal-burning power plants, to the unborn.

And environmental messages resonate more loudly when they are addressed in Christian language, he said.

"I quote the Golden Rule. I remind people that reducing pollution is loving your neighbor. I quote [the Gospel of] Matthew: '[W]hatever you do to the least of these, you do to me.' I remind people that if something we're doing impacts the poor, we're doing that to Jesus."

Some evangelicals remain leery of associating with environmental activists, concerned about what they regard as liberal solutions to environmental problems: big government and oppressive regulations.

The conservative Focus on the Family organization reacted warily to the NAE's attention to global warming, saying in a statement, "Focus and the broader evangelical movement have viewed such issues as the protection of marriage, the sanctity of human life, and the related issue of judicial reform as paramount. Our friends at the National Association of Evangelicals, with whom we agree on these and so many other issues, have now staked out a position in the very controversial area of global warming. This is despite the fact that significant disagreement exists within the scientific community regarding the validity of this theory. . . . Any issue that seems to put plants and animals above humans is one that we cannot support."

Evangelicals should not be taken for granted by any political party or movement, said Paul Gorman, executive director of the National Religious Partnership for the Environment, in Amherst, Mass.

"Religion isn't red or blue and it isn't green, either," Gorman said. "Engagement of the religious community can be a powerful force for the common good."

12

New Demand Drives Canada's Baby Seal Hunt

Clifford Krauss

CAP-AUX-MEULES, Quebec, March 30—Commercial hunting of baby seals is back and even bigger than when it stirred a global outcry two decades ago.

Horrified by the clubbing of infant harp seals, animal rights advocates swayed public opinion against the hunt. Environmentalists joined the campaign, fearing that the species was being depleted. World sales collapsed. Even Canada reacted with revulsion and began stiffening regulations on the kill.

Now, Canada has lifted the quota to a rate unheard of in a half century, buoyed by new markets in Russia and Poland, and changing environmental calculations. A recovering market has turned into a quiet boom.

Here on ice patches of the Gulf of St. Lawrence, the hunt looks nearly as brutal as ever. For as far as the eye can see, dozens of burly men bearing clubs roam the ice in snowmobiles and spiked boots in search of silvery young harp seals. With one or two blows to the head, they crush the skulls, sometimes leaving the young animals in convulsions. The men drag the bodies to waiting fishing vessels or skin them on the spot, leaving a crisscross of bloody trails on the slowly melting ice.

On the trawler Manon Yvon, one hunter, Jocelyn Theriault, 35, said, "My father hunted for 45 years, so I was born with the seal." His colleagues utter a sarcastic "welcome aboard" as they throw the skins on their 65-foot boat. "We do it for the money," Mr. Theriault said, "but it's also a tradition in our blood."

Animal rights advocates aroused the world in the 1970's and 1980's with grim films of Canadian seal hunters clubbing white-coated seal pups not yet weaned from their mother's milk and then skinning some alive. That campaign—complete with photographs of Brigitte Bardot snuggling an infant seal—succeeded in shutting down American and European markets and forcing a virtual collapse of the hunt.

But over the last six years, Canada's seal hunt, by far the world's largest and commercially most valuable, has undergone a gradual revival that has virtually escaped world attention. That trend is making an extraordinary jump this year, when the federal government will allow the killing of up to 350,000 baby harp seals, or more than one in three of all those born, largely for their valuable fur.

That is an increase of more than 100,000 from recent years, and the largest number hunted in at least a half century.

Rising prices for the skins and contentions that the growing seal population is contributing to a shrinking codfish population have eased the revival of an industry once roundly seen as barbaric. Meanwhile, tougher hunting rules, including stiffer regulations to avert skinning the seals alive, have muted the effort to stop the hunt and eased the consciences of Canadians.

"This slaughter that everyone thinks has disappeared is back with a vengeance," said Rebecca Aldworth, an antihunt advocate with the International Fund for Animal Welfare.

A majority of the seals killed are under a month old, she said, and, "at that age, the seals haven't eaten their first solid foods and have not learned to swim so they have no escape from the hunters."

The seal hunt never completely shut down. After the United States banned the importation of all seal products in 1972 and the European Union banned the importation of the white pelts of the youngest pups in 1983, killings fell to as low as 15,000 harp seals in 1985, mostly for meat and local handicrafts.

Embarrassed by all the publicity accusing Canada of inhumane treatment of animals, the government banned killing whitecoats—the youngest pups up to 12 days old. Now only the seals who have shed their white coats and become "beaters," at about three weeks old, are killed in these waters for their black-spotted silvery fur. The killing of those young seals has so far raised fewer hackles, although critics say hunting methods have not been substantially changed.

The surprising rebound of the hunt off the Îles de la Madeleine and the northern coast of Newfoundland, where the harp seals migrate south from the Arctic every spring to give birth and then mate again, results in large part from a robust revival in the price of sealskin.

Seal products remain banned in the United States, and they find only limited acceptance in most of Western Europe. But new markets have emerged in Russia, Ukraine and Poland, with a fashion trend for sealskin hats and accessories. Fur experts expect the Chinese market to grow, perhaps raising prices higher.

"Markets are good, acceptance is growing and prices are well up," said Tina Fagen, executive director of the Canadian Sealers Association. She said the price for a top-grade harp sealskin had more than doubled since 2001, to about $42, approaching the prices of the early 1970's.

But the revival is also made possible by a Canadian seal population that was replenished during the long hunting slump. The Canadian harp seal population has tripled in size since 1970, according to the Department of Fisheries and Oceans, to more than five million today.

Fishermen contend that the abundance of seals is hindering a revival of shrinking cod stocks since each adult seal eats an estimated ton of sea life annually. The fishermen get support from politicians who want to help revive economically depressed regions of Canada, and some scientists say their position is reasonable.

Animal rights advocates are revving up a campaign against the hunt, reviving calls for a tourism boycott of Canada and flying journalists over the ice fields to photograph hunters killing the seals. The New York Times did not take part in any of those flights.

A new generation of celebrities has taken up the cause, including Paris Hilton, Christina Applegate and Nick Carter of the Backstreet Boys pop group. At the last Sundance Film Festival, some people wore a new T-shirt that said, "Club sandwiches, not seals."

But so far the outrage has not echoed the way it once did, in part because Canada outlawed the killing of the youngest pups to follow Western European import guidelines and stiffened rules and enforcement to ensure that seals are killed quickly and not skinned alive. The government requires novice seal hunters to obtain an assistant's license and train under the supervision of veterans for two years before qualifying for a professional license.

The government this year added a requirement that hunters thoroughly examine the skull of the seal or touch the eyes of animal to test for reflexes to guarantee a seal is brain dead before skinning.

"The industry needed to be cleaned up and it was, though perceptions persist," said Roger Simon, the Department of Fisheries and Oceans area director for the Îles de la Madeleine.

Some prominent environmental groups that opposed the hunt in years past because of concerns over the sustainability of the Canadian harp seal population have dropped their active opposition. Greenpeace, once one of the most active groups against the hunt, now says it is satisfied that Canada is not allowing infant whitecoat seals to be killed.

But Mads Christensen, a Greenpeace seals expert, said he was concerned about this year's large hunt. "We don't have enough science, and that calls for caution," he added.

Canadian officials say they will regularly review the seal population and adjust the hunt accordingly. "If you are going to have an annual harvest you have to maintain a sustainable number," said Geoff Regan, the minister of fisheries and oceans, in an interview. "We are going to come up with these numbers on the basis of what the herd can sustain."

Seal hunting is worth about $30 million annually to the Newfoundland economy, which has been hurt by the collapse of the cod fishery. About 5,000 hunters and 350 workers who process skins rely on the industry. Hundreds more hunting jobs are created in Quebec and Nova Scotia.

"I love it that the market is back," said Jason Spence, the 32-year-old captain of Ryan's Pride, a fishing boat that set sail from Newfoundland a few weeks ago for the seal hunt in the Gulf of St. Lawrence.

Arguing that hunting seals is no worse than "people taking the heads off chickens, butchering cows and butchering pigs," he added, "People are just trying to make a living."

13

Wrong to Monkey with Human Rights

Russell Paul La Valle

In Spain, a funny thing is happening on the way to the circus—all of the monkeys are disappearing.

At least, that is what a group of legislators on an environmental committee is hoping will happen now that parliament is considering a resolution to grant certain human rights to "our nonhuman brothers"—great apes, gorillas, bonobos, chimpanzees and orangutans. The measure has broad support and, barring the unexpected, is likely to become law within a year. After enactment, harmful experimentation on apes, as well as their use for circuses, television commercials and films, will be prohibited. It will be legal for the 350 apes in Spanish zoos to stay there, but their conditions will have to be drastically improved.

With one stroke, Spain will also become the first country to acknowledge unequivocally the legal rights of nonhumans.

The resolution urges parliament to adopt the recommendations of the Great Ape Project, a consortium of philosophers, ethicists, primatologists and psychologists formed in 1993 to ensure the protection of apes from "abuse, torture and death."

"This is a historic moment in the struggle for animal rights," Pedro Pozas, the Spanish director of the Great Ape Project, told the Times of London. "It will doubtless be remembered as a key moment in the defense of our evolutionary comrades."

The real force behind the initiative is Peter Singer, a professor of bioethics at Princeton University and co-founder of the Great Ape Project. Singer is widely viewed as the father of the international animal rights movement. His rationale is simple: "There is no sound moral reason why possession of basic rights should be limited to members of a particular species."

Singer is no stranger to controversy. His appointment at Princeton in 1999 caused widespread protests because of his publicly stated contention that parents should have the right to euthanize children—within 28 days of birth—who have severe handicaps. "Killing a defective infant is not morally equivalent to killing a person," he has written. "Sometimes it is not wrong at all."

Apparently, though, killing an animal is.

Should animals have rights? The quick and only logical answer is no. A "right" is a moral principle that governs one's freedom of action in society. This concept is uniquely and exclusively human—man is the only being capable of grasping such an abstraction, understanding his actions within a principled framework and adjusting his behavior so as not to violate the rights of others. The source of rights is man himself, his nature and his capacity for rational thought. To give rights to creatures that are irrational, amoral and incapable of living in a rights-based environment makes a mockery of the very concept of rights and, ultimately, threatens man.

Unlike most mammals or other types of creatures, humans are not born with instinctual, inherited knowledge of how to survive. Rather, man's survival is achieved through reason, which allows him to integrate the facts of his surroundings and apply this knowledge to use and shape the natural world for his preservation and advancement. This includes the use of animals, whether for food, shelter or other necessities.

As the Nobel laureate Joseph Murray has observed, "Animal experimentation has been essential to the development of all cardiac surgery, transplantation surgery, joint replacement and all vaccinations." Indeed, animal research and clinical study are paramount in the discovery of the causes, cures and treatments of countless diseases, including AIDS and cancer.

Cruelty to animals is, of course, repugnant and morally indefensible. Yet we should not lose sight of who we are or of our place in the world. Yes, humans have a responsibility as stewards of our domain but not at our own expense or with the mentality that a cat is a rat is a chimp is a person.

I'm all for the humane treatment of animals. I support better conditions in zoos. But let's let apes be apes and no try to teach them how to recite the Bill of Rights.

14

Speaking for Critters Who Can't Speak

B. G. Kelley

A Washington march protests animal cruelty in hunt and lab.

Several years ago, I saw a video of an experiment using baboons in head-trauma research. In the film, the animals were drooling and their arms and legs were flapping uncontrollably after having had their heads smashed by a projectile device accelerated to the force of a freight train.

This horrific treatment of animals would affect anyone whose sense of morality wasn't as rough as sandpaper. It galvanized me to speak out in defense of sentient creatures who couldn't speak out for themselves.

So, tomorrow, I'll be among those gathering in Washington, D.C., for the national March for the Animals—the largest gathering of animal protectionists ever to confront a wide range of animal issues, from vivisection and genetic engineering to factory farming and bloodsports.

I'll be there to protect against cruelty to animals in general and experimental tinkering with animals in research labs in particular.

Each year in the United States, the maw of the research machine is fed millions of animals, from rats to man's best friend, the dog, to primates—all to come up with causes and cures for everything from heart disease to drug addiction to AIDS to cancer.

Yet, each year more people get sick, more people die. Something isn't working here.

For example, millions of animals suffer and die in the on-going war on cancer, yet statistics show that a human is more likely to contract cancer today than at any other time.

I remember the words of Dr. Irwin Bross, the former director at the Roswell Memorial Institute for Cancer Research in Buffalo, N.Y.: "From a scientific standpoint, what are called animal model systems in cancer research have been a failure." I remember the six members of my family who died from cancer.

I admit, when growing up, to having bought into—accepting without question—all the reasons, explanations and rationales for using animals in experimental research: "Cures to disease would be discovered"; "Animals can't feel pain anyway"; "Results can easily be extrapolated to humans"; "We have dominion over the animals, it's right here in Genesis."

But for 20 years now I've been skeptical. Biological, physiological and behavioral

---

responses are, to me, not common across species. I see distinction and difference rather than likeness and uniformity. A rat is not a pig. A pig is not a dog. A dog is not a boy.

Furthermore, I can't understand the intransigence of scientists who refuse to explore the possibility of alternatives to animal-based research, alternatives that now are increasingly proving reliable: cell, tissue and organ cultures derived from humans; mathematical, mechanical and computer models of living organisms; computer-assisted drug design; epidemiological and clinical studies; post-mortem investigations.

All these alternatives would spare millions of animals pain and death.

I have an idea why researchers refuse to look at alternatives. The financial interests of the monolithic research industry are tied in a symbiotic sort of way to the use of animals.

And tradition is a factor. The 17th-century French mathematician and scientist Rene Descartes likened animals to machines—merely unfeeling, unthinking "things" whose lives are tantamount in value to throwaway bottles.

But I know that there are some scientists today who believe animals share with humans higher mental abilities, that they do think; they do feel pain, joy, grief, anger; they do possess intelligence.

Those who have companion animals, like me, know this.

Finally, I imagine that ringing in the ears of the animal protectionist on the march to the Capitol tomorrow will be the words that 19th century English philosopher Jeremy Bentham used to challenge the rationale of Descartes: "The question is not, 'Can they reason?' nor, 'Can they talk?' but, 'Can they suffer?'"

And I know the answer.

15

Why Perch a Bird on Your Shoulder?

Albert DiBartolomeo

Recently, I returned home from a New Jersey shore town where I several times saw a white cockatoo riding the shoulder of a young man. How cute! And the bird didn't seem to mind at all.

I suppose if the bird did mind, it would have bitten the guy's ear with its pointed beak. But the two of them, man and bird, seemed to be chums, although of course I had no way of knowing the bird's true opinion. It was real, that bird, not a Disney animation with a celebrity's voice to tell me how it felt.

That was not the first time I saw an exotic bird perched on a person's shoulder; however it was my first cockatoo. I've seen large, multicolored parrots taking in the sights of Philadelphia while clinging to a collarbone. I've also seen snakes draped around necks. I've seen a white rat closer to the face of a young man than I would ever want a rat to be, domesticated or not. I once saw a pig on a leash on Lombard Street. I must admit, I stared at that, wondering: Why?

I mean, I understand why dog owners walk their dogs, and I suppose a pig would have to be walked for the same reason. But why would anyone even want a pig as a pet, and why does somebody feel the need for the company of exotic birds and reptiles on their traipse through the city?

No matter how much affection those owners may have for their unconventional pets, it seems to me that the animals have been brought out into the air less for their well-being than to serve as a kind of live ornamentation, something to catch the eye of passersby—like, perhaps, Dennis Rodman's spectral hair. I don't know how exotic birds feel about an environment of concrete instead of flora, and if snakes are happy to be necklaces in surroundings completely foreign to them it would be a revelation to me.

About the pig's opinion of city life, I can't begin to guess. Upon returning to Philadelphia from the New Jersey shore, with thoughts of the cockatoo lingering in my head, I soon learned that the circus was in town. I never went to a circus and, though perhaps as an ignorant child, I wanted to, I would not go to one now. I would suspect too strongly that the clowns are really a comic diversion from any dark suspicion in the audience that the circus animals should not be made to do all those ridiculous tricks, that the animals would not be doing them if they had not been "disciplined" into doing them.

An elephant does not naturally stand on its head, after all, or sway to some cheap concertina music. And I'm not so sure that if I

* From *The Philadelphia Inquirer,* June 22, 1996, by Albert DiBartolomeo. Copyright © 1996 by the Philadelphia Inquirer. Reprinted by permission of Ellen Levine Literary Agency.

were a tiger I would want to jump through a flaming hoop.

I'm no radical animal rights person. I eat a little meat now and then, and I would not throw red dye on somebody's mink coat, but I'm really depressed at how animals, particularly those not given to easy domestication, are often treated, whether in the circus or elsewhere. For instance, why "game" animals are allowed to be set "free" on ranches and then pursued and killed by sports hunters is something I simply cannot fathom. I have a hard enough time grasping the allure of killing animals in their natural habitat.

All I can think of is that killing an animal in this manner must reassert the need in some of us to feel our superiority—our dominion—over the "lesser" animals. In this light, I un-derstand the appeal of that part of the circus where animals are put through their paces.

It's for our amusement, yes, and we can't fail but to recognize the skill, even courage, of a person manipulating an animal that could quite easily crush or maul the "tamers." But is it amusement or are we at bottom gratified to see that the human being is so powerful that he or she can make elephants "dance" and lions leap through fire rings?

If I sound like somebody quite happy to deprive thousands of little children the joys of watching elephants, lions, bears, and horses performing absurd feats—well, I'm sorry. But we have no right to strip these animals of their dignity, nor to disrespect them by treat-ing them as objects, playthings, or eye-catchers, whether cockatoos or pachyderms.

16

The Benefits of the Commons

F. Berkes, D. Feeny, B. J. McCay, and J. M. Acheson

Conventional wisdom holds that resources held in common will invariably be overexploited—the "tragedy of the commons." A number of examples show that this is not necessarily so.

It has become a truism that resources held in common are vulnerable to overexploitation. Twenty-one years ago, Hardin popularized this dilemma—calling it the "tragedy of the commons"—by the use of a metaphorical village common in which each herdsman "is locked into a system that compels him to increase his herd without limit."[1] Hardin argued that such problems have no technical solutions, and emphasized the need for government controls to limit "freedom in the commons [which] brings ruin to all."[1] Hardin and others[2] have subsequently pointed to privatization of common resources as another solution consistent with the analysis of many resource economists.[3]

It is usual to assume that resource degradation is inevitable unless common property is converted into private property or government regulations are instituted. The prevalence of this view is reflected by an article in *The Economist* of 10 December 1988 about fisheries, typically viewed as a common-property resource: ". . . it is possible to manage fisheries successfully," the author asserts, "provided three facts are kept in mind." Two of these are relevant here: "left to their own devices, fishermen will overexploit stocks" and "to avoid disaster, managers must have effective hegemony over them."

Nevertheless, research carried out in the 21 years since Hardin's article often leads to conclusions that challenge this conventional wisdom. Such results are of interest to resource managers, applied natural and social scientists, policy-makers and development planners. Many case studies, including our own, show that success can be achieved in ways other than privatization or government control.[4-7] Communities dependent on common-property resources have adopted various institutional arrangements to manage those resources, with varying degrees of success in achieving sustainable use. We use ecological sustainability[8] as a rough index of management success without necessarily implying resource use that is ecologically or economically optimal.

As a first step in the analysis, it is necessary to define the kind of resources under

---

consideration. Common-property (or common-pool[9]) resources share two key characteristics. First, these are resources for which exclusion (or control of access) of potential users is problematic. The physical nature of the resource is such that controlling the access of potential users is costly and, in some cases, virtually impossible. Migratory or fugitive resources such as fish and wildlife pose obvious difficulties. Similarly, ground water, range and forest lands, and global commons[8] such as the high seas, the atmosphere and the geosynchronous orbit, pose problems of exclusion.

The second key characteristic of common-property resources is subtractability; each user is capable of subtracting from the welfare of others. This characteristic creates a potential divergence between individual and collective economic rationality in joint use.[3] As one user continues to pump water from an aquifer, others experience increased pumping costs; as the number of fishing boats increases, the catch per unit of effort for each declines. On the basis of these two characteristics, we define common-property resources as a class of resources for which exclusion is difficult and joint use involves subtractability.

As a second step in the analysis, a taxonomy of property-rights regimes is needed.[9-11] Common-property resources are held in one of four basic property-rights regimes. (1) Open access is the absence of well-defined property rights. Access is free and open to all, as with ocean fisheries of the past century. This is the regime implied in Hardin's model. (2) Private property refers to the situation in which an individual or corporation has the right to exclude others from using the resource and to regulate its use. (3) Under communal property, the resource is held by an identifiable community of users who can exclude others and regulate use. Some shellfish beds, range lands, forests, irrigation and ground water have been managed as communal property. (4) State property or state governance means that rights to the resource are vested exclusively in government, which controls access and level of exploitation. Examples include crown lands and resources such as fish and wildlife held in public trust. These

four categories are ideal, analytical types. In practice, resources are often held in overlapping combinations of these four regimes, and there is variation within each.

We now briefly summarize selected case studies. These studies show the workings of communal-property systems not recognized in Hardin's model, as well as the limitations to the use of state governance in some situations.

Our first case concerns wildlife hunting territories in James Bay, Quebec, in northeastern Canada.[12] Hunters in this subarctic area have traditionally used resources communally, as do many Amerindian groups, and have a rich heritage of customary laws to regulate hunting. Beaver is an important species both for food and, since the start of the fur trade in James Bay in 1670, for commerce.

The beaver is vulnerable to depletion because colonies are easily spotted. A community-based hunting territory system, with senior hunters and their families acting as stewards of specific territories, at present ensures sustainable use. The beaver resource in James Bay, however, has not always been used sustainably. In the 1920s, a large influx of non-native trappers followed the new railroad into the area to take advantage of high fur prices. Amerindian communities lost control over their territories and all trappers, including natives, contributed to a "tragedy of the commons." Conservation laws were eventually enacted after 1930, when beaver populations were at an all-time low, and outsiders were banned from trapping in James Bay. Amerindian community and family territories were legally recognized and customary laws became enforceable, resulting in productive harvests after about 1950.[12] The experience of the 1920s and 1930s is not unique. Periods of cut-throat rivalry among fur companies had led to non-sustainable use of resources twice before: in the mid-1700s and in 1825–29. Gradually, however, local control was restored and stocks recovered.[12]

Our second and third cases deal with lobster and fish management on the east coast of the United States[13,14] and show that communal territories exist even in societies that subscribe to the ideal of freedom in the commons. In the U.S. tradition, marine resources belong to all citizens but are controlled by state governments as a public trust. Privatization of some marine resources such as shellfish beds is feasible but not always socially desirable or politically acceptable.[15] Government management is similarly difficult: limiting the number of licenses is considered an infringement of citizens' rights. Even so some groups of users are able to restrict access and manage common-property resources.

The lobster resource is vulnerable to overharvesting. but lobster stocks in Maine have remained sustainable. Although some managers have for decades been predicting a resource collapse, the Maine lobster catch has been remarkably stable since 1947.[13] The state government establishes lobstering regulations but does not limit the number of licenses. In practice, however, there is exclusion through a system of traditional fishing rights; to go lobster fishing at all, one has to be accepted by the community. Once accepted, a lobsterman is only allowed to fish in the territory held by that community. Interlopers are usually discouraged by surreptitious violence.

One cannot say if the resource could have been used sustainably in the absence of such locally enforced exclusion and regulation. But we have compared the productivity of exclusively used territories with areas in which claims of adjacent communities overlap. We found that fishermen in the exclusive territories catch significantly more and larger lobsters with less overall effort.[13]

The third case, a trawl fishery in the New York Bight region, provides an alternative community-based solution to the commons dilemma.[14] The fishermen who belong to a cooperative specialize in the harvest of whiting. They have ready access to the best whiting grounds in the region, and often dominate the regional whiting market in the winter months.

The cooperative maintains relatively high prices for members through supply management; it limits entry into the local fishery and establishes catch quotas among members. Limited entry is achieved through a closed membership policy and the control of docking space, effectively excluding non-members from access to whiting grounds and markets.

Quotas are based on the estimates of what the cooperative can sell to the regional market, and are achieved in ways that reward individual initiative but also discourage "free-riding." By contrast with government-imposed regulations, which are considered by fishermen to be inflexible and which in any case are ineffective because they do not address the fundamental problem of access, self-regulation through the cooperative is considered to be both flexible and effective in maintaining sustainable use.[14]

Forests in Thailand comprise our fourth case.[16] Traditionally the exploitation of high-value timber was regulated by local governments; the use of low-value timber was essentially unregulated. The rapid commercial exploitation of teak in Thailand in the late nineteenth century led to the nationalization of all forests. State ownership fails to provide consistent enforcement, but it also serves to deny users the authority to manage local forests. Illegal logging, followed by further land clearing for cultivation, is widespread. Although much of this land is suitable for cultivation, there are few safeguards for conserving environmentally sensitive areas; this results in overall damage to land.

The lack of enforcement of state-forest property rights leading to accelerated degradation is not unique to Thailand. The nationalization of forests in Nepal (1957) and Niger (1935) produced a similar outcome.[17] In Nepal, the situation is being ameliorated by the re-creation of communal management at the local level.[18] Without effective control by government, nationalization has often converted traditional communal property into *de jure* state property but *de facto* open-access.

Having reviewed a few cases, we return to the tragedy of the commons model to explore its problems in relation to the findings. Hardin asks the reader to assume a pasture "open to all."[1] Each herdsman acts in an individually rational fashion by adding animals to the common pasture. For him, the private benefits of adding one more animal exceed the private cost. Because each herdsman does the same, the overall result is overgrazing and disastrous losses for all.

Hardin's model provides insight about the divergence between individual and collective rationality. But it fails to take into account the self-regulating capabilities of users. It assumes that the herdsmen are unable to limit access or institute rules to regulate use. Therefore, overexploitation is inevitable—unless privatization or government controls are imposed. These conclusions have been used as part of the justification for nationalization,[18] privatization of land resources,[19] and the widespread practice of top-down development planning that ignores local institutions.[4,6] The social and ecological costs of these practices have often been tragic in their own right.

Recognition that users have the potential and, under some conditions, the motives and means to act collectively opens up other policy alternatives and provides questions about why some communal management systems fail and others succeed. The success or failure of common-property resource management has to do with the exclusion and regulation of joint use. Forest destruction in Thailand, for example, occurs because villagers do not own the forest and cannot exclude others. Local people therefore have little incentive to conserve and every incentive to cut down trees before someone else does.[16]

By contrast, in other examples—hunters in James Bay, lobstermen in Maine, trawlermen in the New York Bight area, communal forest users in Nepal, and irrigation water users in South India[20]—groups are able to exclude other potential users and regulate their own joint use. They are therefore able to reap the benefits of their own restraint. Our examples are not isolated, but are consistent with a large body of literature on grazing lands,[21] forests,[22] water[23] and coastal marine resources,[24] covering a wide range of regions and cultures throughout the world.

What accounts for the many exceptions to the predictions of the conventional theory? How can Hardin's model be improved to obtain a more comprehensive theory of common-property resource management? First, the Hardin model confuses common-property resources with open access—the absence of property rights. By equating common-property

resources with open access, and then assuming that open access leads to overexploitation, the model falls into the trap of equating the commons with overexploitation.

Second, the model assumes that the individual interest is unconstrained by existing institutional arrangements. In many communities, common-property resource users are compelled by social pressure to conform to carefully prescribed and enforced rules of conduct.

Third, the model assumes that resource users cannot cooperate toward their common interests. This is not necessarily so; under certain circumstances, voluntary collective action is feasible,[25] and sustainable outcomes are not unusual.[4-7,20-24]

More fundamentally, the model overlooks the role of institutions that provide for exclusion and regulation of use. Cultural and historical factors underlying such institutional arrangements are a key to the success of communal management of coastal marine resources in Japan and several Pacific-island nations,[24] in addition to the cases we describe above.

Finally, the set of solutions offered by the model is too limited. Privatization or the imposition of government control are not the only viable policy options. In fact, the conventional reliance on these approaches is overly sanguine. By definition, common-property resources are ones for which exclusion is difficult and so privatization is often not feasible. Although dividing a commons and assigning individual property rights can increase efficiency under some circumstances, it might not in others. Similarly, state control has worked in some cases, but the example of Thailand forests illustrates its potential for failure.

In general, we propose that successful approaches to the commons dilemma are found in complementary and compatible relationships between the resource, the technology for its exploitation, the property-rights regime and the larger set of institutional arrangements. We also propose that combinations of property-rights regimes may in many cases work better than any single regime. The success of local-level management, for example, often depends on its legitimization by central government; James Bay[12] and recent experience in Nepal[18] are examples. Such nested relationships are also found in fisheries in Japan and Oceania.[24] In some cases, cooperative management arrangements (co-management) are needed, involving the sharing of power between governments and local communities.[26]

In sum, sustainable common-property resource management is not intrinsically associated with any particular property-rights regime. Successes and failures are found in private, state and communal-property systems. Recent research highlights the potential viability and continued relevance of communal-property regimes, nested systems and co-management. Studies after that of Hardin have shown the dangers of trying to explain resource use in complex socio-ecological systems with simple deterministic models.

Notes

1. Hardin, G. *Science 162,* 1243–1248 (1968).
2. Hardin, G. & Baden, J. (eds) *Managing the Commons* (Freeman, San Francisco, 1977).
3. Gordon, J. S. *J. Polit. Econ. 62,* 124–142 (1954).
4. *Proc. NRC Conf. Common Property Resource Management* (National Academy, Washington, DC, 1986).
5. McCay, B. J. & Acheson, J. M. (eds) *The Question of the Commons: The Culture and Ecology of Communal Resources* (University of Arizona Press, Tucson, 1987).
6. Ostrom, V., Feeny, D. & Picht, H. (eds) *Rethinking Institutional Analysis and Development* (Institute for Contemporary Studies, San Francisco, 1988).
7. Berkes, F. (ed.) *Common Property Resources: Ecology and Community-Based Sustainable Development* (Belhaven, London, 1989).
8. World Commission on Environment and Development, *Our Common Future* (Oxford University Press, 1987).
9. Ostrom, E. in *Proc. NRC Conf. Common Property Resource Management* 599–615 (National Academy, Washington, DC, 1986).
10. Bromley D. W. in *Proc. NRC Conf. Common Property Resource Management* 593–598 (National Academy, Washington, DC, 1986).
11. Bromley, D. W. *Economic Interests and Institutions* (Blackwell, Oxford, 1989).
12. Berkes, F. in *Common Property Resources: Ecology and Community-Based Sustainable Development* 70–78 (Belhaven, London, 1989).
13. Acheson, J. M. *The Lobster Gangs of Maine* (University Press of New England, 1988).
14. McCay, B. J. *Anthrop. Q. 53,* 29–38 (1980).
15. McCay, B. J. in *The Question of the Commons: The Culture and Ecology of Communal Resources* 195–216 (University of Arizona Press, 1987).
16. Feeny, D. in *World Deforestation in the Twentieth Century* (Duke University Press, 1988).
17. Thomson, J. T., Feeny, D. H. & Oakerson, R. J. in *Proc. NRC Conf. Common Property Resource Management* 391–424 (National Academy, Washington, DC, 1986).
18. Arnold, J. E. M. & Campbell, J. G. in *Proc. NRC Conf. Common Property Resource Management* 425–454 (National Academy, Washington, DC, 1986).
19. Peters, P. in *The Question of the Commons: The Culture and Ecology of Communal Resources* 171–194 (University of Arizona Press, 1987).
20. Wade, R. *Village Republics: Economic Conditions for Collective Action* (Cambridge University Press, 1987).
21. Netting, R. M. *Balancing on an Alp: Ecological Change and Continuity in a Swiss Mountain Community* (Cambridge University Press, 1981).
22. Fortmann, L. & Bruce, J. W. (eds) *Whose Trees? Proprietary Dimensions of Forestry* (Westview, Boulder, 1988).
23. Maass, A. & Anderson, R. L. *. . . and the Desert Shall Rejoice* (MIT, Cambridge, 1978).
24. Ruddle, K. & Akimichi, T. (eds) *Maritime Institutions in the Western Pacific* (National Museum of Ethnology, Osaka, 1984).
25. Ostrom, E. in *Rethinking Institutional Analysis and Development* 101–139 (Institute for Contemporary Studies, San Francisco, 1988).
26. Pinkerton, E. (ed) *Co-operative Management of Local Fisheries* (University of British Columbia Press, 1989).

17

Conservation and Conceptions of the Environment: A Manus Province Case Study

James Carrier

Introduction

Any efforts to conserve species not threatened by commercial exploitation almost certainly rely on the cooperation of villagers in rural areas. But this cooperation is not automatic. People hunt, gather, farm and fish the way they do for reasons. Usually it is necessary to provide good reasons for people to change, reasons that make sense to them.

Finding such reasons may not be simple. I illustrate this by way of a case study of an effort to encourage conservation in a Manus Province society, and the difficulties encountered (Carrier and Carrier 1980). The society is Ponam, a small island of about 300 fishing and trading people about 5 kilometres off the north-central coast of Manus.[1]

Conservationist Environmental Model

First I shall sketch the basics of the conservationist model, bringing out aspects of significance, not for commercial management but for the question of the extinction of species. The core of the model is this: the biological environment is made up of a variety of unique species, functionally integrated into a whole.

First is the idea that every species is unique, and that it does a special thing, and occupies a special niche. Failure of a species to occupy such a position will force it into competition with other species, with the result that all but one of them will die out or be forced into another niche. Further, these species depend on each other. Each forms a part of the environment of other species. Elimination of one will affect the others.

* James Carrier, "Conservation and Conceptions of the Environment: A Manus Province Case Study," from L. Morauta, J. Pernetta, and W. Heaney (eds.) *Traditional Conservation in Papua New Guinea: Implications for Today. NRI Monograph 16*, the National Research Institute, Waigani. Copyright © 1982. Reprinted by permission.

Thus, a change in any one part of the environment has effects which ripple outward, extending in principle to all parts. An underlying web of interdependence connects the seemingly separate parts of the environment. Which is to say, in the conservationist model the environment is a functionally integrated whole.

If you accept this model, then you would see the introduction or extinction of species as a disruption, almost inevitably undesirable. And generally this is the case. We are presented with stories of how things get worse when *Salvinia* weed, the mink, or a new species of seaweed is brought into an ecosystem. The introduction of a new species is usually applauded only when it restored a balance previously upset.

Likewise, the extinction of a species is generally taken to be undesirable, according to the assumption that each species makes a unique contribution to the environment. Loss of the species upsets the environment, and the unfortunate results will be permanent, as the species is gone forever. This is true whether or not we are aware of the contribution—the model assumes usefulness.

The last element of the conservationist model I want to mention here is the impact of human action on the environment. Human beings are seen to be the agency of disruption of the functional integration and balance of the environment.

We have, then, four basic elements of the conservationist model of the environment. First, each species is unique. Second, all species are part of a functionally integrated whole—the ecosystem. Third, any change in this is undesirable until proven otherwise. Fourth, human action is the most significant source of disruption.

From this view, efforts at conservation make good sense. There are two parts to this. First, conservation efforts are *possible*, because we think that we, as humans, can correct our own disruptive actions. Second, the sacrifices we make will produce a real benefit, maintaining environmental stability.

The Ponam example illustrates all this. The conservationist argument goes thus: the elimination of dugong, and to a lesser extent sea turtles, will reduce pressure on the lagoon sea-grasses. This will lead to a disruption of the fish population, with presumably undesirable consequences for Ponam fishing.[2] Notice the elements of this argument: there is a functional integration of fish, sea-grasses, dugong and turtles, and ultimately the people of Ponam; the presumed consequences of disruption are undesirable; and the significant agent is human action. Given this model, the conservationist has good reason to want a change in the human activity: a restriction on the hunting of turtle and the killing of dugong. Efforts were made to present this argument in truncated form to Ponam Islanders.

My own observation was that islanders were unpersuaded by the plea for conservation because, I think, their basic view of the environment is very different from the conservationist view. Good reason to a government conservation expert was no reason at all to a Ponam. To see why, I need to turn to what I have uncovered of the Ponam environmental model.

Ponam Environmental Model

The first point is that Ponams are not very interested in the ways that species of fish are unique. They are more interested in their suitability as food, and where and how to catch them. Their dominant orientation is their requirement for survival, and not the various minor unique aspects of marine life.

Moreover, Ponams see different species pursuing their existence more or less independently. Of course, Ponams are perfectly aware that certain species do interact in certain ways. They know that dugong and sea turtles eat grasses. But they do not have any notion of an integrated environment. They do not see that a few turtles and dugong have any important effect on the survival of sea grasses, much less indirectly on the survival of fish.

Further, Ponams do not see human activity as having an especially important impact on species. They hold that individual species were created by God, and they do not presume to speculate upon His reasoning. Further, species will exist for so long as God desires. In the face of the divine, the importance of a few hundred fishing people is petty indeed.

Ponams are aware that areas can be overfished; they see it happening in the lagoons of some north coast Manus islands. They have two related accounts of why less fish are caught. First, the fish become wary; they learn how to hide, and so become that much harder to find and catch. Second, the fish move away to areas where they are not harassed. Although overfishing can be a serious inconvenience, it is no more than that. The fish as species are in no way threatened. The fish are continuing their fishy existence in safer waters, and will continue to do so until God changes His mind.

Thus we can contrast the Ponam model of the environment with the four points of the conservationist model. First, uniqueness of species is not important. Second, species are not interrelated in a functionally integrated whole. Third, any change in species is the result of God's will, and its desirability is not an issue. Fourth, human action is not a source of disruption.

Given all of this, now do Ponams interpret conservationist pleas? They are being asked among other things, to give up sea turtle, and it is important to their lives. As they see it, if turtles are going to die out, it is because God wills it. Stopping hunting would not change God's mind, and would mean only that they would be giving up turtle sooner than necessary. They would incur a cost with no benefit. We can see, then, that good reason for the conservationist is no reason at all for the Ponam.

Alternatively, when Ponams have been presented with what were good reasons to them, they have responded. Sea turtle eggs are a good illustration. A few years ago officials asked them to stop eating the eggs as a conservation measure. Ponams agreed to this. The eggs were not important to them, and they

were ready to sacrifice them for the likelihood of larger numbers of the more desirable sea turtles. So when the likely benefits outweigh the costs, Ponams are happy to comply. However, when the cost is high and the benefits are uncertain at best, from their point of view, they will continue as they have before.

Bases of the Ponam Environment Model

The reasons why Ponams see their environs as they do are quite complex. While I feel that elements of social structure and practice bear on this matter, I shall limit myself here to some fairly straightforward environmental considerations.

The first of these has to do with supply and demand. The reef around Ponam is large, and islanders fish outside it as well. In any event, Ponams do not have an unlimited need for fish. In the pre-colonial period they produced shell money, and after colonization they made use of the wages earned by employed islanders. So, for at least the past hundred years, they have not had to rely on the fish they catch for the necessities of life (Carrier and Carrier, in press).

Furthermore, they do not sell large numbers of fish for money. There is not much demand at the local weekly market, and transport to the Lorengau market is expensive, slow and uncertain. People seldom go, and rarely earn more than the costs of transport and their stay in town. Moreover, while Ponam does have a fish freezer, it has been used only twice since November 1978 at great inconvenience to the islanders who were obliged to fish all night for a week to fill it.

All this indicates that Ponams make relatively little demand on the resources of reef and sea. It follows that they are unlikely to see human activity as having significant impact on fish stocks.

A second factor which may be quite important is that fish move. Thus any bad effects from fishing practices in one particular area of the reef would be hidden, as fish from adjacent areas would move into the relatively depopulated parts of the lagoon. Likewise, a number of important fish spend only a part of their time inside the reef. This reduces islanders' impact on them, and with it the chance that Ponams would notice whatever impact they make.

Conclusion

Because Ponams see their environment so differently from those using the conservationist model, they do not see the sense of arguments that draw their force from that view of the environment. Quite often, good sense to the conservationist is no sense at all to the Ponam. This state of affairs likely will continue so long as islanders live in an environment fairly impervious to their actions, and so long as conservationists produce arguments that rely on unspoken assumptions about the way the environment works.

This Ponam case study illustrates a point that has more general applicability. The success of conservation programmes relies in part on the compliance of people living in the rural areas of Papua New Guinea. To gain their consent, and so their compliance, one has to present good reasons why the conservation programme is useful and effective. But as this Manus Province case study shows, "good reasons" can vary from society to society. The more important it is that people comply, the more important it is to take those people's conceptions of the environment into account.

Notes

1. A brief social and economic description of Ponam can be found in Carrier (in press) and in Carrier and Carrier (in press). A description of the social and technical aspects of Ponam fishing is in Carrier 1980. All are available from the author.
2. Empirical evidence in support of this model is partial at best (cf. Heinsohn *et al.* 1977). I do not present this model, nor was it presented to me, as definitive. My thanks to R. Johannes for bringing this matter to my attention.

References

Carrier, J., 1980. "Seafood production on Ponam Island." Typescript.

___. in press. "Labour migration and labour export on Ponam Island," *Oceania*, 51(4).

Carrier, J. and Carrier, A., 1980. "Dugongs and Ponam Island," *Wildlife in Papua New Guinea,* 80/13, Papua New Guinea Department of Lands and Environment, Wildlife Division.

___. in press. "Colonization and adaptation: Ponam Island, 1900–1980," in R. Gordon and D. Townsend, eds., *Problems of Peripheral People in Papua New Guinea.* Port Moresby: Institute of Papua New Guinea Studies, and Boston: Cultural Survival.

Heinsohn, G. E., Wake, J., March, H., and Spain, A. V., 1977. "The dugong (*Dugong Dugon* [Müller]) in the seagrass system," *Aquaculture,* 12:235–248.

18

Interactions between People and Forests in East Kalimantan

A. P. Vayda, Carol J. Pierce Colfer and Mohamad Brotokusumo

There follow a brief discussion of the setting of an Indonesian/United States Man and Biosphere project in East Kalimantan, an elaboration of the rationale for the research currently underway in this region and some illustrative examples drawn from the findings to date. The authors describe the project at an early stage because the approach they advocate has important implications for both development policy and research, and the approach is eminently workable and productive.

I

East Kalimantan is a large, economically booming Indonesian province on the island of Borneo (see map, Fig. 18.1). It covers a total land area of 21,144,000 hectares (ha) or about 11 per cent of the total land area of Indonesia. Natural forest accounts for 17,292,000 ha of East Kalimantan's land. Tropical rain forests are among the last remaining reserves of economically valuable land in the world,[1] and East Kalimantan has, predictably, become a prime target for development.

The potential timber volume of East Kalimantan's production forest is about 530 million cubic metres of commercially exportable timber and about 270 million cubic metres of non-exportable timber.[2] Stimulated by such factors as the greatly increased Japanese demand for tropical hardwoods and the passage of Indonesian laws conducive to foreign investment in the forestry sector,[3, 4] logging in East Kalimantan developed quickly after 1967. Of the almost 13 million ha of production forest allocated for mechanical logging, about 2 million have already been logged, and there are now some 100 timber concessionaires operating in East Kalimantan.

This rapid development in logging has led to extensive ecological and social disruptions, including some associated with movements of people attracted by the economic boom. Sixty-two per cent of the increase from a population of 725,000 in East Kalimantan in 1971 to 960,000 in 1976 resulted

* From *Impact of Science on Society, vol. 30, no. 3* by A. P. Vayda, et al. © UNESCO 1980. Reprinted by permission of UNESCO.

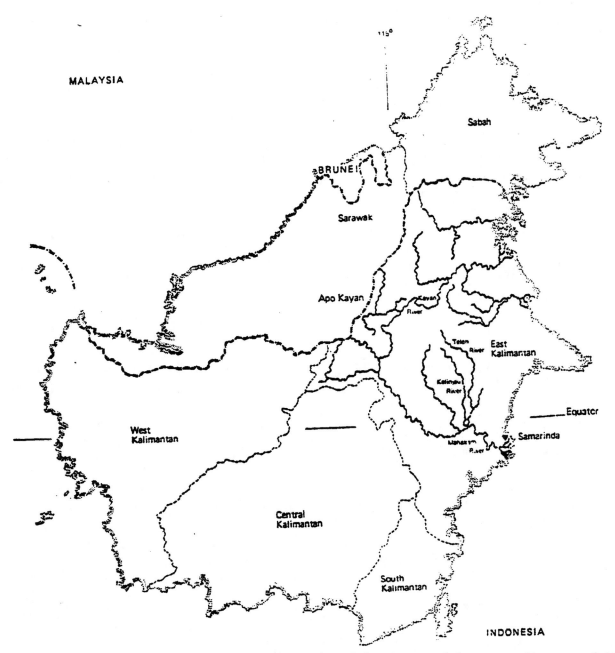

Figure 18.1 Map of Borneo, indicating major political divisions and the East Kalimantan field locations.

from immigration from other provinces; many more migrants, especially farmers from the island of Sulawesi (Celebes), have come since the new road between East Kalimantan's two largest cities, Samarinda and Balikpapan, was opened to the public in 1976.[5] Because of the rapidity with which social and ecological changes are occurring in East Kalimantan, it has become urgent to make forest management in the province more effective and to combine it with development that benefits the people who live in or by the forest and use it.

Policy-makers attempting to achieve these objectives have been handicapped by the lack of information on existing uses of forests by people in East Kalimantan. Such information is needed especially to enhance the social and ecological soundness of policies with respect to the following:

Containing, eliminating, or improving shifting cultivation, depending on the various forms it takes and consequences it has.

Resettlement of forest-using people in East Kalimantan.

The use of existing local-level knowledge and existing practice in agriculture, forest-product collection, and trade as foundations for integrated agroforesty (or forest-farming) development.

The nature and extent of participation by people in their development and in the management of resources on which they depend.

Recognizing this need for information, Indonesian and American social and biological scientists jointly began a project of research in September 1979 entitled "Interactions between People and Forests in East Kalimantan." Broadly, this research, which is part of Indonesia's Man and Biosphere Programme,[6] is intended to show: (a) the range of people's forest-related knowledge; (b) their repertoire of forest-related activities; (c) the variety of situations in which decisions to engage in these activities or to change them are made; and (d) the environmental and socioeconomic effects that these activities have.

Foci of the Research

Three main locations were chosen for the research because of the opportunities they afford for studying significant variations in shifting cultivation and other forest-related activities, and in the conditions under which they are practised. One location, the Apo Kayan, is a lofty interior plateau isolated from commercial centres and timber concessions in the lowlands by extensive and impassable river rapids. It is the home of nearly ten thousand Dayak people living in long-house communities, possessing a wealth of forest-related knowledge, and practising an apparently stable, long-fallow, forest-maintaining form of shifting cultivation.

A second location is the Telen River lowland area where settlements of Dayak migrants from the interior plateau were established prior to the timber boom and where the subsequent granting of timber concessions has led to further changes in the physical and socio-economic conditions to which the Dayak migrants are adapting. The third location is the vicinity of East Kalimantan's booming capital city of Samarinda. Lands along the new roads constructed by the government and by timber companies have become readily accessible for the first time here, and the agriculture practised in logged-over forests in the vicinity of Samarinda by newly arrived inter-island migrants as well as by long-established residents of East Kalimantan includes the dry-field farming which, because of long cropping periods and/or short fallows, is apparently the most damaging to the tropical forest environment. In addition to the investigations specific to each of these locations, research is also proceeding in all of them (and along the trade routes connecting them) on the collection and trading of rattan, incense wood, and other so-called minor forest products.

Explication of the rationale of this project calls for a discussion of the relationship between our research and certain issues in development theory and anthropology. It is appropriate to review here three general models or views that have been dominant at various times concerning the economic behaviour of such rural and tribal people as are among the important subjects of research in the project.

The first two of these models were formulated and gained adherents largely in the absence of substantial information about the diversity, variability and situational specificity of the economic behaviour in question, i.e., in the absence of the kind of information being collected in this research project. All three models or views may be said to vary with respect to two important issues. These are the rationality or irrationality of people's behaviour, and their capacity for or resistance to change. Important policy and research implications of the models are discussed below.

II

A common but possibly now waning view portrays rural and tribal people as unquestioning traditionalists, lacking in initiative and decision-making capabilities, kept from modern technology either by superstition and ignorance or by cultural barriers, docile prisoners of age-old customs and magical or mystical ideas that make them use their land irrationally and inefficiently.[7] In recent years much evidence has accumulated to cast doubt on this view,[8] but many policy-makers, developers, and researchers still subscribe to it.[9]

A frequent concomitant of this view is an acceptance of a unilineal view of human history and development. From this perspective, hinterland people gaining their subsistence by hunting and gathering are, for example, at an earlier, less advanced stage of evolutionary development. The policy implication of the view is that wholesale change of the beliefs and behaviour is required, to draw people from their backwardness and (further up the evolutionary ladder) towards that highest stage represented by modern metropolitan society.

Though few anthropologists explicitly subscribe to this view, the traditional anthropological conceptualization of culture as an integrated whole—a persisting system in a specific community or some comparable unit—as well as the evolutionary theories that have waxed and waned in the field over the years, have served to reinforce this first model of human beliefs and behaviour. The focus of much of applied anthropology on the identification of cultural barriers to change, proceeding from the assumption that "the major problems in technological development are embedded in the society and culture of the community itself,"[10] has meshed nicely with prevalent notions about rural traditionalism and resistance to change.

We find this view to be of little value for realizing our project's goal of obtaining policy-relevant information on interactions between people and forests in East Kalimantan. Traditionlism is hardly what is demonstrated by some of the activities and processes in which we are most interested in this project—

for example, the spontaneous migration of thousands of Bugis farmers from the island of Sulawesi in order to convert East Kalimantan forest land into plantations of pepper, a crop the people had not grown in their homeland; the movement of Dayak from the interior plateau to lowland areas where they have eagerly taken to using chain-saws and *peraku* (canoes) with outboard motors in their activities as shifting cultivators; and the greatly increased allocation of time and effort to the collection of incense wood by Dayak from Apo Kayan when the price traders were paying for that commodity rose.

Evolutionary Integration of Cultures

These examples are also indicative of difficulties with (a) assigning the way of life of a people to a particular evolutionary level, and (b) construing this way of life as necessarily a functionally interconnected whole that maintains its integrity by resisting change. According to commonly accepted evolutionary schemes, shifting cultivation belongs to a "primitive" level[11] whereas use of chain-saws and outboard motors and participation in a cash economy would be considered indicators of a more "advanced" level. Yet the same people engage in various combinations of these so-called primitive and advanced activities. In the Samarinda area, there even are shifting cultivators—recent migrants from the island of Buton (Butung)—who commute to their fields in shared taxis from their urban residences. Such examples, illustrative of the behaviour we are trying to understand in the project, must be interpreted by means of concepts and approaches other than those used to show the integration of cultures at particular evolutionary levels.

In a somewhat different view that has gained currency in economic and development circles in recent years, present-day rural land use is seen as efficient and rational but stagnant because trial-and-error development over many generations has made it impossible for the small farmers to effect further significant improvements in the allocation of traditionally available means and resources. In the words of one economist subscribing to this view, traditional farmers are "caught in a technical and economic equilibrium trap."[12] The development policy associated with this view concentrates on making new means in the form of modern agro-chemical inputs available to the traditional farmers. In this view, then, the people have no irrational resistance to change, but the means for change must be provided from the outside.

The implications in anthropological research, in this view, are minimal or nonexistent. The economist Schultz says, for instance, that "since differences in profitability are a strong explanatory variable, it is not necessary to appeal to differences in personality, education, and social environment."[13] The main research task, in this view, would then be economic investigations of "differences in profitability" rather than anthropological studies encompassing the social contexts or situations in which economic behaviour operates. Whereas the first model discussed above exaggerates the differences between modernized and traditional people, this second model attributes undue universality to the ends that people seek and the means that are suitable for attaining them.

Pertinence of Economic Motivation

So far, most of the people we have been studying have been found to be responsive to economic opportunity. Being responsive does not mean, however, that they are ready to consider all possible alternative uses of their labour, land, or capital, and then to choose from them those likely to be most profitable. If there is an opportunity to gain profit in a particular way, the people frequently respond to that without necessarily considering whether or not there might be other ways even more profitable.

Thus, some, like most of the Bugis migrants, see the new roads through the forests in the Samarida vicinity as presenting opportunities for pepper farming. The path towards profit seen by others, including poorer members of the Banjar and Kutai ethnic groups, lies in combining shifting cultivation

with the removal of wood from the forests in the form of beams, planks, and shingles for sale. Yet others, including urban as well as rural residents in East Kalimantan, concentrate on having logged-over forest cleared so that they can establish their claims to land either simply to be sold for profit in the future or else to be worked by wage labourers or share-croppers.

The motivations of the farmers vary as much as their means. Some are the poor, subsistence-orientated, land-hungry farmers who have been characterized in other parts of the world as "shifting cultivators by necessity";[14] others, including many of the migrants from Sulawesi, seek to gain enough wealth to be able to advance themselves socially by such means as making the pilgrimage to Mecca; and others have turned to farming as a supplementary occupation because their incomes from urban wage-earning are inadequate for maintaining middle-class creature-comforts. Miracle's comment on the view put forward by Schultz is apt: "We can ill afford to use an economic shorthand which implies that the critical characteristics of all small-scale farmers are the same."[15]

III

The third and most current view—and the out most congruent with our research perspective—focuses on continuing responsiveness to changing circumstances. Associated with this view is attention to the following kinds of phenomena, among others.

First, the continuing exercise of decision-making capabilities by rural people.[16] Some observers have concluded that a lack of obvious long-term planning by people in some rural areas implies an absence of decision-making capabilities. But the people we are observing in this project repeatedly demonstrate their willingness to use their minds actively rather than slavishly following a plan. Indeed, one can argue that in the absence of a firm, comprehensive plan, more, not less, decision-making is required.

For example, in Long Segar, a Dayak settlement on the Telen River, where a variety of options exist for productive activity, each individual makes daily decisions about how to allocate his or her time, taking into consideration such factors as current household and agricultural labour needs, exchange obligations within the village, cash requirements, and personal preference, as well as a number of more external factors such as the market price of various products, the weather, the current labour needs of the nearby plantation and timber company, and so on. Compare this with the decision-making demands awaiting a factory worker in an industrialized nation as a new day dawns.

The absence of rigid planning among the Kenyah people among whom our research is being conducted seems to be accompanied by a recognition of the advantages to be gained by decision-making in the course of action.[17] Thus an Apo Kayan man, when asked by a project investigator what he would do for the day, laughed and said, "I don't know now . . . I have many plans." When another man was asked how long his trading trip to Malaysia would take, the answer was maybe a month, maybe two or three, depending on what happened along the way.[18]

Secondly, the rationality of the rejection of some externally advocated innovations.[19] The Banjar farmers who left the government-subsidized Keluang Pantai resettlement area in East Kalimantan's Pasir district did so not because they were irrationally rejecting progress or change but because they knew they could not obtain good harvests from fields in *imperata* grasslands. Similarly, in Dayak communities along the Telen River, the efforts of government extension workers to persuade the people to switch from shifting cultivation of dry rice to permanent wet-rice cultivation have consistently failed because the Dayak farmers know the lands proposed for such conversion are not fertile and well watered enough to sustain wet-rice cultivation without expensive additional effort. Their knowledge of the long fallows required for stable, shifting cultivation to maintain the

forests, has also made them resist official efforts to persuade them to confine their farming to smaller areas than previously used. Indeed, both here and in other areas of East Kalimantan, where soils, topography and water supply are appropriate (as, for example, in the Krayan area in the north-west of the province), the Dayak readily engage in wet-rice cultivation.

Adjustments and Variations

Thirdly, continuing capability for "situational adjustment."[20] By this we refer to people's modification of existing routines or habits and manipulation of existing norms so that the actions they take to gain their ends can be appropriate to their immediate situations. Thus a Bugis norm is that labour exchanges for important tasks should be restricted to kinsmen because non-kin, not being *sejiwa* (literally, "one spirit"), cannot be trusted. In frontier areas where kinsmen are few and labour is needed for such tasks as land clearance, Bugis migrants have been able to find help in accord with their norms by construing all people with a common village of origin in Sulawesi to be kin.

We may consider also the situations resulting from the granting of timber concessions on land used by shifting cultivators. Privation because of being denied access to land formerly used by people may be an expected result and has indeed been reported from another province of Indonesian Borneo.[21] It must be noted, however, that Indonesia's land laws include numerous conflicting stipulations (eg. that local people are entitled to use land in their customary manner, that people residing in timber concessions are restricted to certain areas; that all land within two kilometres of a river is available for use by local inhabitants). We are finding that some East Kalimantan shifting cultivators take advantage of the fuzziness of the laws by continuing to cut forest within the timber concessions. (We are also finding, incidentally, situational adjustment by timber-company personnel, some of whom have successfully argued that the activities of shifting cultivators have interfered with their production and that the government should therefore allow them to log more tracts in a given year than originally specified in their agreements.)

Fourthly, a great range of variation in the conditions under which the indicated capabilities and rationality are exercised.[22] If we look, for instance, at two Apo Kayan communities, Sungai Barang and Long Ampung, we can observe that the former is surrounded by a great deal of forest, whereas the latter is not. The people of Sungai Barang, then, have relatively easy access to the forest for hunting and for making their rice fields, and can readily obtain wood for building, firewood, and other uses. The differences between the two communities in forest accessibility are reflected in major differences in daily activities. Sungai Barang, unlike Long Ampung, is also near heath *(kerangas)* forest from which the best incense wood can be obtained. Such differences—and many more might be mentioned—are enough to make the exercise of rationality and decision-making capabilities in the two different communities produce very different results.

Fifthly, practical knowledge that people have gained, through experience, about the varying conditions under which they must make decisions and act.[23] A wide variety of information has already been brought to light in the course of this project, through the use of the people as consultants. In Long Segar, the people looked on with amusement as agricultural extension workers planted their experimental wet-rice fields in swampy, alluvial soil that the local inhabitants knew to be unsuitable. Similarly, the Sungai Barang people know about the unsuitability of heath-forest soils for their farms.[24]

Ecological and Socio-Economic Considerations

The policy implications of this view are considerably different from those of the other two views discussed. Combining recognition of the great diversity of existing ecological and socio-economic circumstances with the view that behaviour and beliefs are mutable (in response to changing external conditions) suggests that development-related human diversity is even greater than heretofore recognized. The development of effective strategies for change will require greater attention to this variability; different situations will require different approaches. Moreover, current land use strategies and the knowledge of people of their environment can be tapped in the effort to develop locally appropriate change. This view suggests also that diverse paths to improved living conditions exist, and that development efforts should focus on utilizing existing local-level knowledge, strategies, and creativity to solve particular development problems, rather than attempting to remake the people in a uniform and more advanced stage of development. As suggested in a recent article on upland "problem soils" in Indonesia, the local people might well be regarded as qualified consultants on how development in their areas can proceed.[25]

Besides having the policy implications noted above, this third model, with its focus on human adaptability, responsiveness, and initiative, has far-reaching implications for research in social science. The following five shifts or changes are particularly fundamental.

First, much research and analysis have been directed towards determining the goals of a society as a whole and ways in which it maintains itself. We are focusing instead on the ways particular individuals, acting together or separately and using whatever technological, organizational, and cultural means are available to them, respond to changing circumstances.

Secondly, a traditional concern in social science has been with the norms or rules people follow in their daily lives. In our research, we are investigating those areas of social life that are characterized by inconsistency, conflict, and ambiguity, we are interested in seeing how people utilize such indeterminacy to achieve certain immediate ends.

Thirdly, there has been a tendency to single out problems (e.g., over-population or protein deficiency) and ascribe them to people on a global scale or to broad categories of people, like "peasants" or "Amazon Indians."

Our research includes a recognition of the need to determine empirically which of many possible problems have urgency for particular people at particular times.

Fourthly, an orthodox disciplinary objective has been explaining culture or regularities of social process. We are replacing this with an attempt to understand, explain and predict specific human actions that have specific, practical significance.

Fifthly, the literature in social science is replete with statements which imply a basic dichotomy between rural and tribal peoples on the one hand, and modern urbanites on the other. But the third view, set forth in this section, implies no such dichotomy. Indeed, as we turn to the analysis of situations in the next section, the artificiality of such distinctions becomes clearer.

IV

Recognizing the responsiveness of people to changing circumstances, and wanting to provide useful information that is congruent with the policy implications outlined above, we have opted for a research strategy that focuses on situations rather than communities. We remain firmly within the anthropological tradition in our commitment to the holistic premise that problems can only be understood if they are considered part of a complex of interacting causes and effects. But we do not assume that the boundaries of that complex necessarily correspond to the boundaries of a community or its culture. The approach that we have developed includes identifying particular behaviours that affect or can affect the forest and then attempting to understand those behaviours by analyzing the situations in which they occur. Starting with a particular human behaviour, we trace the complex of relevant influences and impacts outward, obtaining, in the end, an understanding of the

important factors that must be attended to by the relevant actors. Such use of situational analysis to elucidate behaviour corresponds to the methods and goals of the situational analyses advocated by some philosophers.[26]

Consider, for example, certain activities observed by one of us among the Dayak of Telen River communities: cutting wood from the forest and making from it *balok* (beams, usually 10×10 cm) for sale. We discuss below some important factors that we have already discovered to be operating in the situations in which people decide to make *balok*. Selling *balok* represents a comparatively profitable utilization of time. In one day of hard work, using a chain-saw, two persons can expect to cut one cubic metre of *balok*, grossing approximately Rp. 20,000. This represents a much greater return than the available wage labour in the area which pays from Rp. 800 to 1,500 per day. Some of the people have established direct trading connections with Samarinda where they are paid Rp. 40,000 per cubic metre for *balok*, thereby increasing their profit.

The work setting is compatible with Dayak preferences. Specifically the cutter can work at his own rate, at times that are convenient to him (cf. the earlier discussion, page 108, of Dayak flexibility). Furthermore, the cutter can continue to live at home, in contrast to what is required by the other main sources of wage labour—the Georgia Pacific logging camp and the oil palm plantation— both of which are too far from the village for practical commuting and too close to fit into the traditional category of an income-seeking adventure.

Lastly, the legal status of these activities must be explained. Cutting and selling ironwood from within a concession is legal if a tax is paid to the government at the subdistrict, or *kecamatan*, level. Cutting other kinds of wood within a concession is legal only if a royalty (currently Rp. 5,500 per cubic metre) is also

---

* Compare, for example, the historical school of the *Annales*, currently led by Fernand Braudel, which takes an eclectic view embracing all elements of our environment that act holistically to affect human development.—Ed.

paid to the concession owner. These payments are rarely made because: (a) there are very few official personnel to enforce the regulations; (b) when *balok*-cutting comes to the attention of timber company personnel, the only actions taken by the latter are to confiscate the *balok* and to give some compensation to the cutters; and (c) there is informal agreement in the area that most *balok* cutting is done to feed or house one's family and is therefore an honest and proper activity, even if inconsistent with the rules mentioned.

Tracing the Threads of Influence

Decisions about what specific factors to investigate and how far to pursue them then are taken on the basis of empirically assessed impacts on the forests, the people, and important development questions in the region. Following this strategy we judge the ideas, goals and operating strategies of the personnel at Georgia Pacific, for instance, to represent more productive topics for investigation than do the details of the form of religion (Christianity) practiced within the confines of any particular community of shifting cultivators. We are not allowing the scope of inquiry to be limited by the geographical boundaries of conventional spatial units such as villages. Indeed, our research on the trade in incense wood is taking us from the Dayak collectors in the heath forests of Sungai Barang to Chinese traders in the river ports of East Kalimantan and ultimately to the buyers and warehouses of Hong Kong.[27]

The situational approach also provides a convenient framework for organizing our research in the Samarinda vicinity. Since the situation (rather than a "community"), defines the appropriate sphere of investigation, we are free—and indeed required—to pursue leads and trace threads of influence in many directions. The problem of defining the target population that has plagued researchers wanting to do holistic research in urban settings is obviated by this approach. One of our fundamental concerns is with human activities that change the forest. Therefore the

behaviour and beliefs of government officials and other professionals who clear logged-over forest near Samarinda with the intention of either having land for speculative purposes or establishing absentee-owned commercial plantations are as important to understand, from our perspective, as are the behaviour and beliefs of the poor Butonese who make farms on the hilltops near Samarinda and have migrated there because of poverty and land shortage in their home island.

Just as we are rejecting rigid spatial frameworks for inquiry, so too are we rejecting rigid temporal ones. Historical research is providing us with important insights regarding some of the actions and situations we are analyzing. An example are the movements of land-clearing Bugis pepper farmers in East Kalimantan. As a result of documentary research and the collection of case histories, we can see these movements not as discrete, individual migrations but rather as part of an ongoing and well-organized long-term colonization process with the potential for moving Bugis to almost all accessible areas of East Kalimantan where pepper can be profitably grown.[28]

Many developers have recognized the importance of understanding relevant human behaviour from a holistic perspective; but anthropological contributions have frequently been criticized as lacking in focus. Policymakers and planners do not want to read through pages of ethnographic description of cultural features that are only marginally relevant to development concerns. This situational approach provides a good framework for providing data that are germane, focused, and holistic.

V

In conclusion, we have planned a research project based on recognition of human flexibility, creativity, and responsiveness to changing conditions. We are documenting interactions of people in East Kalimantan with the tropical forest there and are making these interactions intelligible by showing the situations in which they occur. The research is resulting in information that will be useful to development planners and forest managers.

Our findings to date tend to indicate the heuristic value of this dynamic view of behaviour and suggest that this kind of situational analysis is an efficient and productive way to other policy-relevant information. Furthermore, this approach, in our view, represents a more realistic appraisal of human interaction with the biosphere than do the other views discussed. This human responsiveness to changing conditions is the characteristic that accounts for both creativity in problem-solving and the opportunism that is instrumental in creating problems.

The Inadequacy of Education

In our investigations we are finding that people typically act in what that consider to be their best interests; and, indeed, much of the people's forest-destroying or land-degrading action is profitable to them. An important, but often ignored, implication of this not too surprising finding is that education and propaganda will be insufficient to change what people do. Some concrete and profitable alternatives will have to be created if we want to protect the forests and other features of our biosphere.

To date, in development planning circles, the destructive aspect of human behaviour has been duly recognized. Yet the creativity that we are finding to be the other side of that coin has been vastly underestimated and correspondingly under-utilized. We are convinced that the decision-making capabilities, the capacity for situational adjustment and the rationality of people that we are finding in this project, combined with the knowledge these people have of their diverse environments, represent an important, neglected resource that, if used, could substantially improve the results obtained in development projects and resource management.

Notes

1. D. Poore, *Ecological Guidelines for Development in Tropical Forest Areas of South East Asia* (IUCN Occasional Paper No. 10, 1974).
2. *Laporan Universitas Mulawarman*, Pengaruh Ekspor Kayu dan Kesempatan Kerja, 1976.
3. C. Manning, "The Timber Boom, with Special Reference to East Kalimantan," *Bulletin of Indonesian Economic Studies*, Vol. 7, No. 3, 1971.
4. A. Sumitro, *Foreign Investment in the Forest-based Sector of Indonesia: Increasing Its Contribution to Indonesian Development*, Yogyakarta, Fakultas Kehutanan, Universitas Gadjah Mada, 1975.
5. K. Fischer; Y. Rasyid, *Population and Social Structure, TAD Report No. 8 (East Kalimantan Transmigration Development Project)*, Hamburg, Institute for International Economics, 1977.
6. K. Kartawinata; A. Vayda; R. Sambas Wirakusumah, "East Kalimantan and the Man and Biosphere Programme," *Berita Ilmu Pengetahuan dan Teknologi*, Vol. 21, No. 2, 1977 (reprinted in *Bornea Research Bulletin*, April 1978).
7. C. Hutton; R. Cohen, "African Peasants and Resistance to Change: A Reconsideration of Sociological Approaches," in I. Oxall, T. Barnett and D. Booth (eds.), *Beyond the Sociology of Development: Economy and Society in Latin America and Africa*, London, Routledge & Kegan Paul, 1975. See their discussion of "obstacle man."
8. G. Helleiner, "Smallholder Decision Making: Tropical African Evidence," in L. Reynolds (ed.)., *Agriculture in Development Theory*, New Haven, Conn., Yale University Press. See, for example, his review of the tropical African evidence.
9. R. Seavoy, "Social Restraints on Food Production in Indonesian Subsistence Culture," *Journal of Southeast Asian Studies*, Vol. 8, No. 1, 1977, pp. 15–30; and Indonesian Resettlement Team, Resettlement in Indonesia. ASEAN Workshop on Land Rehabilitation and Resettlement, Samarinda—Surakarta, 28 February–8 March 1979. See above for examples relating to Indonesia.
10. G. Foster, *Applied Anthropology*, p. 94, Boston, Little, Brown & Co., 1969.

11. See the references in T. Grandstaff, "The Development of Swidden Agriculture (Shifting Cultivation)," *Development and Change*, Vol. 9, 1978.

12. R. Stevens, *Tradition and Dynamics in Small-farm Agriculture: Economic Studies in Asia, Africa, and Latin America*, Ames, Iowa State University Press, 1977.

13. T. Schultz, *Transforming Traditional Agriculture*, New Haven, Conn., Yale University Press, 1964.

14. R. Watters, *Shifting Cultivation in Latin America*, Rome, FAO Forestry Development Paper No. 17, 1971.

15. M. Miracle, "The Smallholder in Agricultural Policy and Planning: Ghana and the Ivory Coast, 1960 to 1966," *Journal of Developing Areas*, Vol. 4, 1970.

16. A. Hoben, "Decision-making for Development: An Anthropological Perspective." Unpublished prospectus, 1979; M. Miracle, *Agriculture in the Congo Basin*, Madison, Wis., University of Wisconsin Press, 1967.

17. Cf. S. Ortiz, "Uncertainties in Peasant Farming: A Colombian Case," London, Athlone Press, 1973. (London School of Economics Monographs on Social Anthropology, No. 46.)

18. T. Jessup, Intra-project correspondence, 28 December 1979.

19. G. Castillo, "A Critical View of a Subculture of Peasantry," in C. Wharton (ed.), *Subsistence Agriculture and Economic Development*, Chicago, Ill., Aldine Publishing Company, 1969; see reference No. 7; and see Helleiner's (reference No. 8) concept of "the wise rejector."

20. Cf. S. Moore, "Epilogue: Uncertainties in Situations, Indeterminacies in Culture," in S. Moore and B. Myerhoff (eds.), *Symbol and Politics in Communal Ideology: Cases and Questions*, Ithaca, N.Y., Cornell University Press, 1975.

21. G. Adicondro, "The Jungles are Awakening," *Impact*, September 1979; J. Weinstock, *Land Tenure Practices of the Swidden Cultivators of Borneo*, thesis, Cornell University, Ithaca, N.Y., 1979.

22. R. Eckaus, *Appropriate Technologies for Developing Countries* (Chapter 6), Washington D.C., National Academy of Sciences; (see reference No. 16); P. Hill, *Studies in Rural Capitalism in West Africa*, Cambridge, Cambridge University Press, 1970.

23. D. Barker; J. Oguntoyinbo; P. Richards, *The Utility of the Nigerian Peasant Farmer's Knowledge in the Monitoring of Agricultural Resources. Report No. 4*, London, Monitoring and Assessment Research Centre (MARC), Chelsea College, University of London, 1977; R. Chambers, *Managing Rural Development: Ideas and Experience from East Africa;* Uppsala, Scandinavian Institute of African Studies (Africana Publishing Co.), 1974; A. Vayda, "Human Ecology and Economic Development in Kalimantan and Sumatra," *Borneo Research Bulletin*, Vol. II, No. I, 1979.

24. Cf. P. Richards, "Soil Conditions in Some Bornean Lowland Plant Communities," in *Symposium on Ecological Resources in Humid Tropics Vegetation*, Kuching, Sarawak, 1965.

25. P. Driessen; P. Buurman; Permadhy, "The Influence of Shifting Cultivation on a 'Podzolic' Soil from Central Kalimantan," in *Peat and Podzolic Soils and their Potential for Agriculture in Indonesia*, Bogor, Soil Research Institute. (Bulletin No. 3, 1976.)

26. K. Popper, *Objective Knowledge: An Evolutionary Approach*, Oxford, Clarendon Press, 1972; I. Jarvie, *The Revolution in Anthropology*, London, Routledge & Kegan Paul, 1964.

27. N. Peluso, Intra-project correspondence, 27 January 1980.

28. Cf. A. Vayda, "Buginese Colonization of Sumatra's Coastal Swamplands and its Significance for Development Planning," *Proceedings of the Programmatic Workshop on Coastal Resources Management, held in Jakarta, September 1979*, Tokyo, United Nations University (in press).

Section Two

19. *Countering a Major Blow to Garden State Economy* **Suzette Parmley** 113

20. *Food That Travels Well* **James E. McWilliams** 116

21. *Take a Short Route from Farm to Plate* **Froma Harrop** 118

22. *Can Sustainable Agriculture Be Profitable?* **Patrick Madden** 120

23. *Energy Conservation in Amish Agriculture* **Warren A. Johnson, et al** 131

24. *Catalog of Woes* **Richard N. Mack** 143

25. *Agricultural Change in Vietnam's Floating Rice Region* **R.C. Cummings** 147

26. *Food Revolution That Starts With Rice* **William J. Broad** 161

27. *The Great Sisal Scheme* **Daniel R. Gross** 164

28. *Plants, Genes and People: Improving the Relevance of Plant Breeding in Africa* **Angelique Haugerud and Michael P. Collinson** 170

29. *Three Ways Industrial Food Makes You Sick* **Turning Point Project** 188

30. *Opposition to Biotech Crops Is Groundless* **John K. Carlisle** 191

31. *Nutritional Ecology* **Bonnie McCay** 193

32. *Why People Go Hungry* **Kenneth J. Arrow** 202

33. *Facing Food Scarcity* **Lester R. Brown** 207

34. *What Are the Real Population and Resource Problems?* **Julian J. Simon** 219

35. *Growth in Population and Energy Consumption: More than a Matter of Interest* **Courtland L. Smith** 227

36. *Eating Fossil Fuels* **Dale Allen Pfeiffer** 233

37. *What's Your Consumption Factor?* **Jared Diamond** 241

Introduction to Section Two

The second section of the course touches on the constellation of issues revolving around agriculture, food, nutrition, and population. One way of envisioning their interconnections is as follows:

$$\text{Agriculture} \rightarrow \frac{\text{Food}}{\text{Population}} \rightarrow \text{Nutrition}$$

The ratio of food to population is a crude measure of nutrition, and the most important foods come to us via agriculture. In class, we'll see that this deceptively simple diagram has many more links within and without. For now, it is worth noting that as population grows, the food supply must grow at least as fast—at least barring redistribution of food—in order to simply maintain the existing level of nutrition. In turn, that means more pressure on agriculture.

We can, of course, attempt to reduce population growth. Population growth is derived from the "Population Component Equation," sometimes called the "Basic Demographic Equation." It looks like this:

$$\text{Population}_{\text{Time 2}} = \text{Population}_{\text{Time 1}} + \text{Births} - \text{Deaths} + \text{Inmigration} - \text{Outmigration}$$

We can rewrite this equation as:

$$\text{Population}_{\text{Time 2}} = \text{Population}_{\text{Time 1}} + (\text{Births} - \text{Deaths}) + (\text{Inmigration} - \text{Outmigration})$$

The difference between births and deaths is natural increase (or decrease, where deaths exceed births); the difference between inmigration and outmigration is net migration. At the *world* level, we only need to consider natural increase because there's no migration to or from the planet. That means that population growth is births—deaths. This, too, is misleadingly simple. In order to reduce population growth, we are left with three choices—decrease births, increase deaths, or both. For most us, increasing deaths is not an option—so all we are left with is to decrease births. Then the question is *how*?

Experts disagree about the role of population in such issues as food. At one extreme, Neo-malthusians believe that population is **the** in the world today—that it not only causes problems with food and nutrition, but also with economic development, resource consumption, pollution, political instability, and so on. Moderates believe that population is **a** problem—an important one, but one of many. At the other end of the spectrum, two groups come to similar conclusions, but for different reasons. Marxists see population as a **false** problem—a smokescreen for the real problem—as they see it—of inequitable economic and social relationships. High Techs view population as **no** problem—that population growth spurs us on to discover and invent bigger and better things and progress. You will these views represented in this part of the course and you may judge them for yourself.

To begin with agriculture, the Parmley piece gives the state of agriculture in New Jersey. Rutgers *is* the State University of New Jersey and the School of Environmental and Biological Sciences (nee "Cook College," the "Ag School" and the "College of Agriculture and Environmental Science") *is* the land grant division of Rutgers, so the article is an appropriate starting point. The op-ed pieces by Harrop and McWilliams discuss the ever-widening distances our food travels before it reaches us. On the one hand, improvements in such areas as transportation, storage, preservation, and so on have offered us as consumers ever-broader food choices and access to almost anything we want when we want it. On the other hand, we may pay a price for this as well—inferior quality, higher prices, more resource consumption and pollution, and the demise of local family farms, as has happened in New Jersey. Less land to feed a growing population then creates a whole new round of adaptive processes—as does our more global diet . . . the key is to make the best possible choices.

Madden asks a key question relevant to sustainable agriculture's viability—can it be profitable? Johnson, et al examine the Amish to see if we could increase or maintain our agricultural *productivity* (total output) by using their methods to increase agricultural *efficiency* (output per unit input). This piece of work came out of the energy crises in the 1970s—as did a couple of other articles in the reader, and may achieve heightened relevance again in the future. Mack illustrates one of my favorite—and to my thinking, underrated—social science concepts—unintended consequences. Cummings shows the other side of the "Green Revolution," the forerunner to today's work in biotechnology. Vietnam's conversion to HYVs (High Yield Varieties of rice) also illustrates one example of unintended consequences and perhaps shows similar potential pitfalls of the latest round of high tech agricultural developments. Broad describes how Uphoff provides a new, low-tech strategy for increasing yields that ultimately may prove more beneficial in terms of production, and with fewer side effects. Gross' article offers a different type of precautionary tale relating to international trade and growing for "the market." By contrast, Haugeraud and Collinson show one direction contemporary research might take.

The Turning Point Project advertisement and Carlisle's op-ed piece give opposing viewpoints on high tech food. McCay outlines nutritional basics, including some key terms, a causal scenario for why people may be malnourished, and some surprising observations about changes in nutrition when people's access to food increases. Arrow, in his review of Sen, offers an explanation of hunger. Lester Brown—a much-honored graduate of today's "SEBS" when it was still "The Ag School," has devoted his professional life to population-related issues, especially food. The picture he paints is not a particularly happy one.

Simon and Smith provide divergent views on other population-related issues, Smith on energy resources and Simon more generally. Pfeiffer ties this section together, integrating agricultural practices, food, population and sustainability. Diamond offers a new twist on Smith's argument. Food is often the first issue that comes to mind when speaking of population-related problems, but it is by no means the only one. Another course I teach, *"Population, Resources, and Environment,"* is devoted to a more in-depth examination of population dynamics and its role in the world today.

At the conclusion of this section, you should have some appreciation for the complexities involved in this set of topics and their interconnections and exposure to the spectrum of views concerning population's role in them. Since the experts—often looking at the same data—disagree, you are encouraged to think about them and to come to your own conclusion.

19

Countering a Major Blow to Garden State Economy

The outgoing agriculture secretary says state farmers are threatened by developers, competitors and costs.

Suzette Parmley

As Art Brown steps down today after 20 years as New Jersey's agriculture secretary, he worries about farming's future.

The more-than-$800-million-a-year state industry continues to be threatened by development, he said. And rising costs and increasing competition also are squeezing farmers.

"The major challenge is trying to keep young farmers on the farm," Brown said in a recent interview on his 40-acre farm in Egg Harbor, Atlantic County, leased to greenhouse operators. "We've got to have a profitable agriculture [industry]. I've already told the new agriculture secretary that that's his No. 1 challenge."

At his swearing-in ceremony this week, Charlie Kuperus, 43, a Sussex County farmer who succeeded Brown as agriculture secretary, was instructed by Gov. McGreevey "to keep the farms in New Jersey."

Farming remains one of the state's economic engines. In 2000, farming revenue in New Jersey totaled $812 million; farms employ about 25,000 people, not including about 7,000 farmers and their relatives who work full time at farming.

Brown's departure came as the state this week reported continued declines in some key crops while acreage devoted to farms and the total number of farms are stagnant. The state reported that:

❏ Acres harvested in tomatoes—a $30 million annual crop important to Gloucester, Cumberland and Salem Counties—hit a low of 3,400 last year, down nearly 6 percent from the year before and far from the record 13,000 in the late 1930s. Acreage for cabbage also hit a low last year, and acreage for bell peppers was at a low in 2000.
❏ Blueberries remain a big crop in Atlantic and Burlington Counties. The amount of acres in blueberries—about 7,500 over the last few years—produced a record $37 million crop last year.

---

* From *Philadelphia Inquirer,* 2/1/2002, by Suzette Parmley. Reprinted by permission of *Philadelphia Inquirer.*

❏ Soybean acreage was up slightly last year, producing a $40 million crop. Soybeans are key in Burlington, Salem, Cumberland and Gloucester Counties.

Farming in the Garden State has gone through tough times.

The rush to suburbia from the early 1950s through the 1960s produced deep farm losses in New Jersey. Each year, the state lost an average of 38,000 acres and more than 900 farms. In recent years, the decline has not been as sharp.

Today in New Jersey, there are 832,000 acres in farms. Burlington County—with 103,667 acres in farms—ranked a close second to Hunterdon County as the top farming county in the 1997 Agriculture Census.

And farming is not a full-time job for most.

Less than one-third of the state's 9,300 farms are full-time enterprises, and they account for 70 percent of production, according to the State Farm Bureau, a trade organization.

"For people making their living from full-time farming, it's a struggle staying in business due primarily to fluctuating commodity prices and also changing technology, and the whirlwind change of business in general," said Peter Furey, the bureau's executive director.

Furey said agriculture suffers from deflation when production outpaces demand, resulting in a glut and lower prices.

In a Farm Bureau survey last year, "farm viability" was listed as the top issue among farmers in the state.

"There's a squeeze play on, that's for sure," said Brown, 66, who first was named agriculture secretary when Tom Kean was governor. "When you look nationwide . . . they're all having a rough time."

Fred and Jean Wainwright are fourth-generation dairy farmers from Burlington County. The volatility of the dairy market has them on edge. Since last November, the price they get for milk has dropped from $16 per hundred pounds—about 12 gallons—to $13, due in part to a cheese glut in the Midwest.

Their 200-acre dairy farm straddles Florence and Mansfield, and it is hemmed in by highways and development.

"Nobody hardly ever gets started [farming] on their own unless it's in the family," said Fred Wainwright, 70, whose sons also are dairy farmers. "The economics are proving that we're in trouble. The industry has been depressed for the last three or four years."

Domestic competition also has caused a vegetable glut, as farmers in Southern states grow less tobacco and plant other crops instead.

"They are taking those [same] acres, and looking for an alternative crop, and so they put in some vegetables, and they compete with us," Brown said.

Another South Jersey farmer, Abe Bakker, who grows potatoes, soybeans and wheat on a 600-acre farm in Shiloh Borough, Cumberland County, said the industry had to do a better job of marketing itself and experimenting with new techniques.

"It's a new millennium, and we have to act differently about how we market our products, and how we farm within the most urban state in the United States," Bakker, a fourth-generation farmer, said.

That is what Adesoji Adelaja calls "New Age Agriculture."

"We need to explore new ways to market agriculture and give farmers potentially new markets," said Adelaja, the dean and research director at Rutgers University-Cook College and the New Jersey Agricultural Experiment Station. "New Jersey cannot grow the same thing as farmers in Iowa. Before we write off agriculture, we certainly have to step up the degree of innovation, and usher in a new age."

Brown, the outgoing secretary, said New Jersey's increasingly diverse population—the numbers of Latinos and Asians are growing—may provide new opportunities.

"We have to see what they want as far as food goes," he said. "They may like what came over from their home country, so we can grow a lot of that."

Former Gov. Christie Whitman's $1 billion initiative to preserve one million acres of open space and farmland was passed by the Legislature in 1999, and it provided a stable source of funding to save land from development over a decade.

But it also intensified the race among farmers and deep-pocketed developers for quality land.

Tom Polinski, 50, of Lumberton in Burlington County, said municipalities could do only so much against development. About 600 acres of farmland have been preserved in his township.

"The sentiment of the community is to save even more, but how many farms are left to save?" asked Polinski, who recently sold a landscape design business. "I knew every single farmer in Lumberton. We went from having five big farms down to two in the past 10 to 12 years."

20

Food That Travels Well

James E. McWilliams

THE term "food miles"—how far food has traveled before you buy it—has entered the enlightened lexicon. Environmental groups, especially in Europe, are pushing for labels that show how far food has traveled to get to the market, and books like Barbara Kingsolver's "Animal, Vegetable, Miracle: A Year of Food Life" contemplate the damage wrought by trucking, shipping and flying food from distant parts of the globe.

There are many good reasons for eating local—freshness, purity, taste, community cohesion and preserving open space—but none of these benefits compares to the much-touted claim that eating local reduces fossil fuel consumption. In this respect eating local joins recycling, biking to work and driving a hybrid as a realistic way that we can, as individuals, shrink our carbon footprint and be good stewards of the environment.

On its face, the connection between lowering food miles and decreasing greenhouse gas emissions is a no-brainer. In Iowa, the typical carrot has traveled 1,600 miles from California, a potato 1,200 miles from Idaho and a chuck roast 600 miles from Colorado. Seventy-five percent of the apples sold in New York City come from the West Coast or overseas, the writer Bill McKibben says, even though the state produces far more apples than city residents consume. These examples just scratch the surface of the problem. In light of this market redundancy, the only reasonable reaction, it seems, is to count food miles the way a dieter counts calories.

But is reducing food miles necessarily good for the environment? Researchers at Lincoln University in New Zealand, no doubt responding to Europe's push for "food miles labeling," recently published a study challenging the premise that more food miles automatically mean greater fossil fuel consumption. Other scientific studies have undertaken similar investigations. According to this peer-reviewed research, compelling evidence suggests that there is more—or less—to food miles than meets the eye.

It all depends on how you wield the carbon calculator. Instead of measuring a product's carbon footprint through food miles alone, the Lincoln University scientists expanded their equations to include other energy-consuming aspects of production—what economists call "factor inputs and externalities"—like water use, harvesting techniques, fertilizer outlays, renewable energy applications, means of transportation (and the kind of fuel used), the amount of carbon dioxide absorbed during photosynthesis, disposal of packaging, storage procedures and dozens of other cultivation inputs.

Incorporating these measurements into their assessments, scientists reached surprising conclusions. Most notably, they found that lamb raised on New Zealand's clover-choked pastures and shipped 11,000 miles by boat to Britain produced 1,520 pounds of carbon dioxide emissions per ton while British lamb produced 6,280 pounds of carbon dioxide per ton, in part because poorer British pastures force farmers to use feed. In other words, it is four times more energy-efficient for Londoners to buy lamb imported from the other side of the world than to buy it from a producer in their backyard. Similar figures were found for dairy products and fruit.

These life-cycle measurements are causing environmentalists worldwide to rethink the logic of food miles. New Zealand's most prominent environmental research organization, Landcare Research-Manaaki Whenua, explains that localism "is not always the most environmentally sound solution if more emissions are generated at other stages of the product life cycle than during transport." The British government's 2006 Food Industry Sustainability Strategy similarly seeks to consider the environmental costs "across the life cycle of the produce," not just in transportation.

"Eat local" advocates—a passionate cohort of which I am one—are bound to interpret these findings as a threat. We shouldn't. Not only do life cycle analyses offer genuine opportunities for environmentally efficient food production, but they also address several problems inherent in the eat-local philosophy.

Consider the most conspicuous ones: it is impossible for most of the world to feed itself a diverse and healthy diet through exclusively local food production—food will always have to travel; asking people to move to more fertile regions is sensible but alienating and unrealistic; consumers living in developed nations will, for better or worse, always demand choices beyond what the season has to offer.

Given these problems, wouldn't it make more sense to stop obsessing over food miles and work to strengthen comparative geographical advantages? And what if we did this while streamlining transportation services according to fuel-efficient standards? Shouldn't we create development incentives for regional nodes of food production that can provide sustainable produce for the less sustainable parts of the nation and the world as a whole? Might it be more logical to conceptualize a hub-and-spoke system of food production and distribution, with the hubs in a food system's naturally fertile hot spots and the spokes, which travel through the arid zones, connecting them while using hybrid engines and alternative sources of energy?

As concerned consumers and environmentalists, we must be prepared to seriously entertain these questions. We must also be prepared to accept that buying local is not necessarily beneficial for the environment. As much as this claim violates one of our most sacred assumptions, life cycle assessments offer far more valuable measurements to gauge the environmental impact of eating. While there will always be good reasons to encourage the growth of sustainable local food systems, we must also allow them to develop in tandem with what could be their equally sustainable global counterparts. We must accept the fact, in short, that distance is not the enemy of awareness.

21

Take a Short Route from Farm to Plate

Froma Harrop

An onion grown in Iowa travels an average 35 miles to the Iowa supermarket. An onion from the usual sources in other states treks an average 1,759 miles to the Iowa store.

We're talking "food miles," a growing concern of governments, environmentalists and gourmets. Food miles is the distance food travels from farm to plate.

It used to be that all food was local. New England has lousy soil and a cold climate. But the people there managed to feed themselves 300 years ago, even though there were no highways or California. They couldn't have asparagus in February or bananas ever, but they didn't starve.

Early in the 20th century, most food was still produced close to home. Even urban homemakers canned vegetables and fruits, buying bushels from nearby farms. Nowadays, food consumed in the developed world travels enormous distances.

Rising oil prices give the issue of food miles new importance. Transportation costs account for six to 10 percent of the retail cost of produce. A study at Iowa State University found that produce trucked to Des Moines from states outside Iowa used four to 17 times more fuel than that grown locally.

The farther produce is trucked, the more oil is burned. Fossil-fuel use contributes to global warming. Japan is studying how reducing food miles could help it comply with the Kyoto Protocol.

Researchers at Iowa State's Leopold Center for Sustainable Agriculture added up the distances that 16 types of locally grown fruit and vegetables traveled to markets in Iowa. Crops grown in the state traveled a total 716 miles, the distance between Des Moines and Denver. The produce coming to Iowa from the typical sources in other states journeyed 25,301 miles. That's the equivalent of circling the globe and going an extra 400 miles.

Even big farm states import soybeans for livestock feed," explains Rich Pirog, the Leopold Center's marketing and food systems program leader.

But agriculture in an urbanized state such as New Jersey centers on fruit, vegetables, seafood and some dairy. So in terms of feeding its people, Pirog says, New Jersey may be more self-sufficient than Iowa.

Measuring food miles is not easy when it comes to processed fare. Beef cows raised in Iowa may get sent to a feedlot in Colorado, then a packing plant in Nebraska, before the steaks get shipped.

Some foodstuffs are veritable jet-setters. British fish is sent to China for processing by low-wage workers, then returned to the United Kingdom for sale, according to a BBC report.

Locally grown food is usually fresher, but not always. Lettuce at a farmers' market may have been sitting in the back of a hot truck for six hours. It may be more tired than a head picked in California four days earlier but immediately refrigerated.

When food miles become a consideration, environmentally concerned shoppers face tough choices. Example: Organic broccoli is grown with fewer chemicals. That's good. But suppose the broccoli was shipped across the continent in a truck belching carbon dioxide. Bad.

States have become sensitive to the economic affect of food miles. Many now have food-policy councils that help farmers sell locally. For example, they may change laws requiring governments to accept only the lowest bids. Even if their own farms charge more, keeping them in business has its own economic benefits.

Finally, there's the emotional angle. We moderns often feel cut off from the natural world. Eating food grown on local soil restores some of that lost bond.

Harvest time reminds us that for almost all of human history, food came from a few surrounding square miles. More of what we eat today can again be local, if people start thinking seriously about food miles.

22

Can Sustainable Agriculture Be Profitable?

Patrick Madden

For a wide range of reasons—including low farm commodity prices, high debt loads, and declining land values—large numbers of U.S. farmers are in serious financial jeopardy. While about 40 percent of U.S. farms were found to be debt-free in January 1986, another 11 percent were deeply in debt and had a negative cash flow: their debts amounted to more than 40 percent of the current market value of their assets and they received too little income to meet family living expenses, farm operation expenses, and mortgage payments. Some 40,000 of these farms were technically insolvent—the farmers would be unable to repay their debts even through total liquidation of their assets.[1]

Another indicator of the seriousness of the situation is the plight of bankers and other farm lenders. One in every seven farmers in debt to a commercial bank or the Farmers Home Administration is insolvent. Neil Harl of Iowa State University has predicted that "unless something is done, or circumstances change, as many as one-third of the farmers nationally will move to insolvency, taking down their lenders, their suppliers and other

merchants, and inflicting incalculable damage upon the fabric of rural communities."[2]

Meanwhile, the public has grown increasingly concerned about the sustainability of agriculture. Several agricultural chemicals once thought to be benign actually pose serious health threats, and some of these chemicals are appearing in drinking water. In many locations soil is rapidly being eroded, and in addition, underground supplies of water and fossil deposits of energy and minerals are being depleted at rates that cannot be continued indefinitely.

The picture is not entirely grim, however. More-sustainable alternative technologies are being developed and adopted, featuring reduced dependence on chemical technologies[3] as well as soil-conserving methods of growing crops.[4] Farmers who consider their farming methods to represent organic, regenerative, or other alternative approaches are employing some of these increasingly popular farming technologies, in addition to a number of less-conventional methods. Thousands of these farmers have prospered, others have failed financially and have gone out of farming. Large

* *Environment, volume 29, no. 4*, pp. 19–20, 28–34, 1987. Reprinted with permission of the Helen Dwight Reid Educational Foundation. Published by Heldref Publications, 1319 Eighteenth St., NW, Washington, DC 20036–1802. Copyright © 1987.

numbers have reverted to use of chemical-intensive methods. Many are struggling valiantly and still hope to succeed while adhering to alternative methods. Others use a mixture of conventional and alternative farming technologies on various parts of the farm. Results of a recent farmer survey illustrate the connection between farm profit and sustainability and suggest directions that might enhance attainment of both.

Alternative Farming Concepts

The collage of alternative farming styles is called by many names, including organic, regenerative, biodynamic, natural, biological, and ecological farming. All these approaches and others are encompassed in the generic term "alternative agriculture" as used by Garth Youngberg at the Institute for Alternative Agriculture. These approaches also seem to be largely, if not entirely, compatible with "sustainable"[5] agriculture and "regenerative"[6] agriculture.

There are no hard-and-fast definitions or categories for such "soft" concepts as alternative, sustainable, organic, and regenerative agriculture. Technologies that are considered alternative today may become commonplace tomorrow. For example, a few years ago conservation tillage was considered an innovative alternative to the mold-board plow. Many farmers who replaced the traditional mold-board plow with the chisel plow were ridiculed as "trash farmers," because they left crop residues on the surface rather than turning them under.

In most communities that has now changed. Countless thousands of farmers have learned it is not necessary to turn the topsoil upside down every year. On many farms conservation tillage not only reduces soil erosion, it also increases profits, both immediate and long-term. And when farmers learned more profit could be made by using conservation tillage, many stopped laughing and bought chisel plows and heavy-duty planters and grain drills. Perhaps billions of tons of eroded soil are saved each year by farmers who use no-till farming or other forms of conservation tillage rather than the traditional plow. In many places conservation tillage has become so widespread that it is no longer considered an alternative technology,[7] although most people still consider it a sustainable technology.

Regenerative agriculture is characterized as a farming system in which an abundance of safe and nutritious food and fiber is produced using farming methods that are ecologically harmless, sustainable, and profitable. Following a transitional phase, chemical insecticides and other toxic compounds are replaced by reliance on natural biological controls to the maximum extent feasible. Renewable sources of soil nutrients are largely or totally substituted for chemical fertilizers. Methods of conservation tillage relying on routine applications of herbicides that find their way into water supplies or foodstuffs would not qualify as regenerative agriculture. Regenerative agriculture also incorporates profitability as part of the norm or goal: if farmers must commit financial suicide in quest of ecological harmlessness, their form of agriculture is neither sustainable nor regenerative. [8]

Although regenerative is conceptually a more-comprehensive term and a more-idealized goal than sustainable, sustainable and regenerative agriculture are here considered synonymous. They are defined as using on-farm, renewable resources instead of imported and nonrenewable resources to the fullest extent possible, while earning a return that is acceptable to the farmer. Specifically, the norm of regenerative agriculture implies use of a wide range of farming systems. These involve:

❏ emphasizing natural, on-farm, nonchemical approaches to pest control that do not destroy or decimate populations of earthworms and other beneficial life forms;
❏ maintaining and enhancing soil fertility by utilizing on-farm sources of nutrients such as manures and legumes to the fullest extent practical and profitable;

❏ using fertilizers only as necessary to supplement on-farm sources of soil nutrients and selecting those that are thought to be harmless to beneficial forms of life and to the soil structure and nutrient balances within plant tissues; and

❏ using on-farm sources of capital, both farm profits and off-farm earnings, to finance the ownership and operation of the farm, rather than depending heavily on borrowed capital.

Sustainablity may also be defined in a multidimensional, hierarchical fashion that includes agronomic, microeconomic, ecological, and macroeconomic aspects:

Agronomic sustainability refers to the ability of a tract of land to maintain productivity over a long period of time. Microeconomic sustainability is dependent on the ability of the farm, as the basic economic unit, to stay in business. Ecological sustainability depends on the maintenance of life-support systems provided by non-agricultural and non-industrial segments of a region. Macroeconomic sustainability is controlled by factors such as fiscal policies and interest rates which determine the viability of national agriculture systems. In our view, there are critical constraints to sustainability at different scales of the agricultural hierarchy.[9]

A farming practice or system may be beneficial to one dimension of sustainability and harmful toward another. For example, a certain kind of conservation tillage may effectively prevent soil erosion and help again crop production. But if it relies on regular use of pesticides that pollute water supplies or affect the health of farm workers and consumers, this method of crop production would be considered nonsustainable from a community and environmental standpoint. Another farming method might be considered salutary in terms of agronomic, ecological, and food safety considerations, but it might earn such low profits that it cannot be financially sustainable.

Profits and Sustainability

The norm of sustainable or regenerative agriculture bears some similarity to the definition of organic farming postulated in 1980 by the U.S. Department of Agriculture Study Team on Organic Farming,[10] namely, in approaches to pest control and soil fertility management. But regenerative agriculture has the additional feature of recognizing that the farm must be profitable enough to stay in operation more or less indefinitely. Specifically, to be truly sustainable and regenerative from generation to generation, the farm must earn a level of profit acceptable to the farmer as a return on his or her labor, management, risk bearing, and capital. Otherwise, when the farmer retires or ceases farming, the farm will be liquidated.

The profitability of regenerative farming methods is affected by all aspects of the hierarchy of sustainable agriculture.[11] At the macroeconomic level, national and state regulations banning the use of certain pesticides have the effect of making regenerative farming methods relatively more profitable. However, national policies allowing importation of foods produced with pesticides forbidden in the United States lead to reduced food prices and undermine the profitability of all U.S. farms. At the other end of the hierarchy, scientific advances at the molecular and cellular level as well as agronomic practices have a profound effect on the opportunities available and on the profitability of regenerative and conventional farming methods.[12]

The farm must ultimately be able to pay its own way through on-farm earnings rather than remain a bottomless sink for off-farm savings or borrowed capital. Consequently, the norm of sustainable or regenerative agriculture includes the ultimate goal of prosperous and debt-free farming, in contrast to the seemingly perpetual state of indebtedness many people consider "normal," "modern," and "smart" farm management strategy.[13]

Off-farm income is a major source of financial stability for U.S. farm families, providing an average of about 60 percent of total income in recent years.[14] The farmer who chooses to use regenerative farming methods may find it necessary at least temporarily to subsidize the farming operation with off-farm income while making a transition from chemical-intensive methods. But when the net return from regenerative farming is considered too low to justify continuation, the farmer may revert at least part of the farm to chemical-intensive methods or change occupation. To be truly sustainable, the farm must at least be capable of earning a sustained return large enough to make it worthwhile for the farmer to continue farming in an ecologically harmless, regenerative way.

Sustainability in Practice

The ideal way to assess the economic performance of any segment of agriculture is with a complete census, providing details on all income and expenses. Unfortunately, such a census has never been carried out for sustainable agriculture in the United States. The Census Bureau conducts a census of farms every five years, but that data base currently does not indicate the number or characteristics of farms using specific farming technologies that might be considered sustainable, alternative, organic, regenerative, or biodynamic.

However, surveys of regenerative farms have been conducted from time to time. These studies cover a limited geographic area, sometimes just one state or several states. Since there is currently no nationwide list that could provide a representative sample of organic or regenerative farms, the results of these surveys must be interpreted cautiously and their limitations recognized.

A recent survey of organic or regenerative farmers provides insight into the way these farmers have performed financially during the current depression in agriculture, and how their farm income affects their ability to use regenerative methods. The farmers surveyed were originally participants in two studies, one from Washington University in St. Louis, Missouri,[15] the other from The Pennsylvania State University in University

Park, in cooperation with the Rodale Research Center in Kutztown, Pennsylvania.[16]

The Washington University study of Midwest farmers who used organic methods between 1974 and 1979 has become a landmark in the literature. Sixteen of those farmers were contacted in 1986. Of those 16, the follow-up survey showed 3 had died. Another had continued to farm organically until he retired. Three had declared bankruptcy. In one case, the bankruptcy was precipitated by a fire that burned the dairy enterprise. Another farmer had gone through bankruptcy but was still operating the farm. His sons bought the farm at the foreclosure sale, and have hired him to continue operating it organically with some assistance from one son who lives nearby and has a full-time job in town. Two farmers could not be contacted. In total, 8 of the original 16 are still farming, and 7 of these 8 said they are still farming organically. One now uses a full spectrum of chemicals.

The much larger Penn State study was started in 1981. The subjects for this study were selected from lists of farmers who were likely to be using methods considered organic or regenerative.[17] Detailed questionnaires were obtained from 344 farmers from seven states. Of these, 142 respondents described their farms as organic, 188 as mixed organic and conventional, and 14 as conventional.

The 344 farmers were contacted again in August 1986; 250 responded to the follow-up survey.[18] Of the 142 farmers who in 1981 classified their farms as organic, 98 responded to the 1986 follow-up survey. A total of 76 (77.6 percent) said they are still farming, 60 of whom said their farms are still organic. One now categorized himself as a conventional farmer; 15 (20 percent) categorized themselves as mixed.

Of the 188 farmers who categorized their farms in 1981 as mixed organic and conventional, 139 responded in 1986. Of the 88.5 percent who are still farming, 79 (57 percent) said they still use mixed conventional and organic methods; 26 (19 percent) have switched to conventional, and 18 (13 percent) said they have become organic farmers.

Of 14 farmers who considered their farms conventional in the 1981 survey, 11 responded in 1986. However, no meaningful conclusions can be drawn from this small sample regarding the performance of conventional farms. Moreover, the results drawn from the survey should be interpreted as illustrative, providing suggestions for hypotheses for further research.

The Washington University Sample, 1974–1986

Seven of the 8 remaining farmers from the Washington University study in 1974 said they are still farming organically. Discussions with two of the principal investigators of that study revealed that the farmers who have prospered since 1974 were considered at the time of the original study to be the most capable managers.[19] One of the bankrupt farmers indicated he had speculated on rising land values and lost out when the land market fell in the early 1980s.

One of the success stories from the Washington University sample is of an organic grain and livestock farmer in Iowa, Clarence Van Sant. He reported that his income is over $50,000, of which about one-third comes from his farm and two-thirds from his two health food stores. His 175-acre farm includes 120 acres of cropland. He grows alfalfa for two years, followed by one year each of soybeans, corn, and oats nurse crop (planted to shade the alfalfa). In addition, Van Sant has a small beef enterprise of 13 Charlois cows, 2 bulls, and a dozen calves. He also raises about 300 chickens. He markets all his livestock and poultry products as organic food, part of it through his own stores.

Van Sant reported he has always had an aversion to debt. His farm and stores are virtually debt-free, with a total debt of only $14,000. He bought his farm for $125 an acre in 1948 and paid for it in ten years. In 1980 he could have sold the farm for $2,000 an acre. Now land prices are down to about half that price.

Illustrating the importance of good financial management, Van Sant told of an opportunity twelve years ago to buy another farm in need of a lot of capital improvements. The banker approved the loan, but Van Sant said no. "Why take on more debt?" he asked rhetorically. One of his neighbors bought the farm and invested in high-capacity equipment. Because he had such large equipment, five years later the farmer decided he should buy another farm. As a result, he had to drive 40 miles a day just to do the chores on both farms. Van Sant said the neighbor, with a debt of $369,000, is reported to be the county's largest borrower from the Farmers Home Administration and is unable to make mortgage payments.

Asked about the advantages of farming organically, Van Sant replied, "peace of mind. I get yields like my neighbors, but for a lot less cost." He said his fields have hardly any grass or broadleaf weeds. He plants as late as possible so weeds will sprout and can be tilled under before planting. He intends to continue farming organically.

The survey revealed another interesting example of a grain and livestock farmer in the sandhills of Nebraska. He reported that his yields of corn, soybeans, and hay are substantially higher than those of his conventional neighbors and higher than the county average, and that his production costs are a fraction of his neighbors' costs.

This farmer reported he has never irrigated, while his conventional neighbors must irrigate to prevent crop failure. Nor has he ever applied herbicides in more than forty years on his farm, again in contrast to his neighbors. According to this farmer, there is a synergistic relationship between his nonuse of herbicides and his ability to obtain above-average yields without irrigating. His analysis of the situation is as follows: The soil consists of a 1-foot layer of sandy loam above a shallow layer of clay. Underneath the clay is a water-bearing stratum of gravel. When herbicides are recurrently applied to control weeds, a residue of the herbicide collects in the clay layer. The farmer has observed that the roots of his neighbors' crops are chemically "pruned" as they attempt to penetrate the clay layer into the moist gravel. One result of this is a shallow root system, and the crops must consequently be irrigated when the sandy topsoil dries out in summer. In contrast, this farmer said his crops' roots reach through the clay into the moist gravel layer. Even though the topsoil becomes powder dry, his unirrigated crops do not show stress during dry months, while those of his neighbors would quickly wither without irrigation. His refusal to apply herbicides is apparently saving many times more money than simply the cost of the herbicide, since he does not have to buy center pivot irrigation systems or pay electricity bills for pumping the water.

The scientific validity of this alleged connection between herbicide use and the need for irrigation deserves more research. The Nebraska farmer said his only cost for producing a corn crop in 1986 was the seed, plus the cost of tillage, planting, and cultivation. (He did not apply the usual dose of liquid fish fertilizer, because the crops "simply grew too fast" and got ahead of him.) He reported a corn yield last year of 130 bushels per acre, compared with a county average of 100, and 55 bushels of soybeans, compared with an average of 47. His alfalfa hay yields were described simply as "very high"; he did not weigh the loads and fed most of the hay to his 100 head of sheep.

The Penn State Sample, 1981–1986

Although the Penn State sample is not adequate to provide statistical inferences about the total U.S. population of organic or regenerative farms, it does provide information from a large number of farmers over the crucial five-year period from 1981 to 1986, when the overall farm economy suffered a deep recession. Farmers were asked about acreage, gross sales, herd size, crops, pest control measures, fertility management, debt-to-asset ratio, cash flow, and other pertinent information regarding their current financial status and changes since 1981.

Of the 250 farmers who responded to the follow-up 1986 survey, 37 are in California. Of these farmers, 23 (62 percent) produce vegetables, fruits, or nuts. Twenty-one

(57 percent) of the California farmers said their farms are organic. The 20 Idaho farmers in the survey are predominately field crop producers or general crop farmers; half said they farm organically. Wheat is king in Kansas, and nearly half (16) of the 38 Kansas farmers classified themselves as grain farmers, another 16 percent said their major enterprise was beef. Fewer than 1 in 4 of the Kansas farmers in the study said their farms are organic. The 29 Maine farmers, 45 percent of whom said they farm organically, are more diversified in the type of enterprise farmed than are most of the farmers in other states. The most frequent crops encountered are vegetables and melons. Vegetables and melons are also the predominant crops grown by the 25 Oregon farmers, 80 percent of whom said they farm organically. In Pennsylvania about 40 percent of the 44 farmers said they are dairy producers. Only 5 percent (2 farmers) said they operate organic farms; 28 others said their farms are mixed organic and conventional. In Washington 6 of the 17 farmers reported they are grain (predominately wheat) farmers. Four of the Washington farmers said they farm organically.

One common measure of the financial stability of a business is its ratio of debts to assets. A ratio greater than 40 percent is considered highly leveraged and potentially vulnerable to failure. In this sample of 250 farmers, 32 percent reported they are highly leveraged, compared with the national average of 21 percent.[20]

When a farm is both highly leveraged and has a cash flow problem (lacking enough income to meet cash operating expenses, interest, and principal on outstanding debt as well as family living expenses), the farm is considered to be in financial trouble. Nationwide, 173,000 farms (11 percent) fell into this category in January 1986.[21] Among the 250 farms surveyed, 12 percent fell into the financially troubled category, with both negative cash flows and a debt-to-asset ratio greater than 40 percent.

During a telephone interview, one of these financially troubled farmers said she and her husband had not earned a positive income in any of the past five years. When asked if they planned to continue farming, she replied, "Well, what else can you do when you've been farming for fifty-five years?" Clearly, the level of profit from this farm is not adequate to meet the needs of the farm family, but for lack of a better alternative, they plan to continue farming. However, a farmer in Maine who had farmed organically for many years reported he had decided to stop farming and get another job, because "the farm was not supporting the family."

The operator of a 2-acre farm near Sebastopol, California, who has been farming organically for fifteen years, reported his sales increased 45 to 50 percent in the past five years because of "the growth in demand for restaurant specialty crops and crops not commonly found in markets" and because of access to effective distributors who handle 80 percent of his produce; the remaining 20 percent is sold through farmers' markets. The farm provides about 20 percent of the family income; off-farm work is the main income source.

In contrast, a vegetable producer near Sacramento, California, earns about 95 percent of his income from his 175-acre farm that has grown melons, cucumbers, and squash seed for twenty years. He has farmed organically for fifteen years except for application of anhydrous ammonia as fertilizer. Vegetable crops are rotated with wheat, barley, milo, sudan, and other gains. Weeds, vetch, and bell beans are used as cover, and the residues are turned under. This farmer reported his 1985 income was about $30,000, and his debt-to-asset ratio is less than 40 percent.

Farmers who produce fresh fruits and vegetables organically usually (but not universally) incur higher costs per unit of output and must charge higher prices to continue producing in this manner. One of the farmers in this sample had contracted with a crew to weed his 10-acre garlic field for $1,400 in 1982. He said he could have controlled the weeds much more effectively and at a fraction of the cost by using a herbicide. He hoped that he would be able to recover the higher cost by having an ample yield and securing a premium price in the organic market. The following year (1983) he had reverted to chemical methods of weed control because he could not support his family with the farm income when he used organic methods.

A few miles from this farm, a highly successful organic grower produces a large number of different varieties of tree fruits, vegetables, and walnuts. He has extensive facilities on the farm for sorting, packing, processing, and refrigerating his produce. In the past five years, the size of this operation has increased both in acreage (from 200 to 220 acres) and in the scope of value-added processing and marketing. Each week he loads his 28-foot refrigerated truck and hauls produce to farmers' markets and various restaurants in the San Francisco area, about an hour from the farm. The farm has a very low debt-to-asset ratio (less than 10 percent), and the income is adequate to support two families and to finance the cash purchase of capital items; the farmer avoids incurring debt.

This farmer relies on the premium prices he receives for produce that is either certified as organically grown or, in some instances is offered as grown using IPM (integrated pest management). In the farmers' markets and the restaurant trade, he has developed a loyal clientele over the years. Although he strongly favors the production of foods with as little use of toxic chemicals as possible, he recognizes the inherent fragility of the organic markets. He reported that competition is growing stronger. He prospers because of his effective marketing system and because of a very elaborate production plan that provides an even flow of fresh produce throughout the harvest season, with new varieties added each year in response to what he perceives as trends in market demand.

Not all farmers using methods characterized as organic or regenerative rely on premium prices. Examples include an 800-acre nonirrigated wheat farm in Washington, where yields are comparable to those of neighboring conventional farms, but costs are substantially lower. This farmer sells all his wheat and dry peas in conventional markets, for ordinary market prices.

Another example is a 32-cow dairy in Pennsylvania that earns a net farm income more than double the average of the Dairy Herd Improvement Association (DHIA) farms in the same herd size class, primarily because of reduced input costs. The farmer's veterinary expense per cow is 6 percent of the DHIA average; he attributes this to reduced stress on the cows from having no pesticide residues in the feed. He produces a higher percentage of his feed (68 versus 59 percent) because of higher crop yields, and his milk production per cow is 5 percent above the DHIA average. (He does not market his milk as organic or receive a premium price for it.)

Until 1986, this farmer relied entirely on crop rotations and cultivation to control weeds and reported that during dry summer months, his corn does not exhibit moisture stress the way his neighbor's fields do. But in 1986 he reported, "I used some herbicide due to time involved in cultivating. I hope to go back to all cultivation in the future." He distributes manure from his dairy barn lagoon each spring as a major source of fertilizer. This farmer's net farm income in 1982 was $33,000, compared with the DHIA average of $11,000 in the same herd size category.

One of the leading U.S. producers of fresh grapes, Stephen Pavich and Sons in Arizona, uses a number of sustainable farming methods. With 1,125 acres of vineyard in 1986, the Paviches produced about 1 percent of the nation's total crop. They reported that their pest control is based on innovative vineyard management practices including reliance on natural enemies to control mite and insect pests. A permanent ground cover used for weed control is flail-chopped periodically. Weeds close to the vines are controlled by hand weeding and hoeing. The Paviches reported that most years they have been able to produce all or nearly all their grapes without using chemical pesticides except for sulfur to control mildew. Spot spraying of pesticide is sometimes done. The Paviches consider plant nutrition, especially in avoiding an excessively high ratio of nitrogen to calcium in the plant tissue, an important element of pest

control. The principal source of nutrients is application of 2.5 to 3.0 tons of compost per acre. The Paviches sell 97 percent of their grapes on the conventional market, including supermarket chains serving all 50 states and a dozen foreign nations; only 3 percent of their grapes are sold to specialty organic markets, under the Pavich brand name. They charge a somewhat higher price for their certified organic grapes ($1 to $2 more per 23-pound box) to cover the cost of extra handling and certification.

These examples are not, of course, typical of all regenerative farms. There is no typical farm. However, three characteristics seem to be true of most successful regenerative farmers: they are superb managers; they have complete knowledge of their farms and the enterprises grown on them; and they have a reverence for life that motivates them to find safe and harmless ways to produce food.

When farmers in the Penn State sample in 1981 were asked for their perceptions of why farmers avoided adoption of "organic methods of farming," about 4 out of 5 reported that farmers hesitated because of concern that insects would reduce yields or that weed control could become a problem. About 60 percent considered the lack of reliable information on organic farming to be a major deterrent. On the other hand, they considered organic farming methods to have a number of advantages (see Table 21.1).

The Challenges

There is nothing magical about sustainable agriculture—whether it is organic, regenerative, or another variation—that guarantees its success, even in good times. And in bad times, many regenerative farms fail along with their conventional chemical-intensive cousins. It takes excellent management skills to succeed in any style of farming, but it seems that sustainable agriculture is more of a challenge.

In addition to providing superb management of the physical and biological aspects of the farm operation, the farmer must also be

Table 21.1 Advantages of Organic Farming Methods as Reported By Organic and Mixed Organic- Conventional Farmers, 1981

Perceived Advantage	Organic Farmers	Mixed Farmers
	(percent of respondents)[a]	
Improved soil tilth and fertility	95	85
Reduced health risk for farmer and family	91	79
Reduced pollution from farming	81	69
More satisfaction from farming as a living	75	54
Healthier livestock	71	55
Healthier yields several years after adopting organic practices	48	40
Reduced risk of crop failure from drought	46	32
Higher prices for organic farm products	42	22
Higher profits from organic farming	32	18

[a] A total of 344 farmers responded from seven states.

SOURCE: Partrick Madden, Stephan Dabbert, and Jean Domanico. *Regenerative Agriculture: Concepts and Selected Case Studies*. The Pennsylvania State University Department of Agricultural Economics and Rural Sociology. Staff Paper no. 111 (University Park, 30 April 1986).

adept at financial management. Recent history has shown that highly leveraged purchases of high-priced farmland is not financially sound. Those farmers who are debt-free or have very low debt-to-asset ratios along with a positive cash flow seem to be surviving.

Many farmers using regenerative methods report that their costs of production are lower than those of their conventional-method neighbors. Some farmers report somewhat lower yields than their neighbors, but the yield sacrifice is frequently more than offset by cost reductions. Other organic or regenerative farmers complain of yield-reducing weed problems, especially when rain comes at a critical time in cultivation. But in many circumstances, nonherbicide methods result in yields and incomes comparable to conventional methods. Farmers have also reported profitable production of many crops without use of insecticides for several years. But an extraordinary increase in an insect, mite, or other pest population can demolish a crop or require application of a pesticide to prevent major losses. In these instances, farmers report they usually apply the lowest possible dose of the least disruptive material and take measures to prevent a perpetual dependence on pesticides.

These claims have been documented in some instances. But further research is needed to more fully understand how larger numbers of commercial-scale farmers in various locations and types of farming can profitably make the transition from chemical-intensive to regenerative farming methods without incurring severe problems with weeds, insects, soil fertility, and other difficulties that could spell financial disaster.

One of the farmers surveyed, a walnut producer in California, summarized the philosophy of regenerative agriculture on the back of his questionnaire:

Instead of spraying to kill the weeds in the orchard, we encourage them to grow, then mow until the last of June or July, then till it under. The only herbicide we ever used was less than a half gallon of Roundup to kill a couple of small patches of Bermuda grass. The soil now holds moisture longer and is a lot easier to work, the clods are smaller and break apart, and the cultivator shovels last over twice as long. We heard one man say, "The commercial way will make father rich and son poor." "God put man in the garden of Eden to dress and keep it." (Gen. 2:15) Today man has undressed and not kept the ground he farms. Could this be the reason for the dilemma many farmers are in?

Notes

1. Tim Johnson, Richard Prescott, Dave Banker, and Mitch Morehart, "Financial Characteristics of U.S. Farms, January 1, 1986," National Economics Division, Economic Research Service, Agriculture Information Bulletin no. 500 (U.S. Department of Agriculture, Washington, D.C., August 1986), 11, 20.

2. Neil E. Harl, "The Two Crises in U.S. Agriculture: Causes and Possible Solutions" (Paper delivered at American Bar Association annual meeting, Chicago, April 1987), 21.

3. J. Lawrence Apple and Ray F. Smith, *Integrated Pest Management* (New York: Plenum Press, 1976); U.S. Congress, Office of Technology Assessment, *Pest Management Strategies* (Washington, D.C.: U.S. Government Printing Office, 1979); Kenneth F. Baker and R. James Cook, *Biological Control of Plant Pathogens* (San Francisco: W. H. Freeman and Company, 1974); R. L. Ridgeway and S. B. Vinson, *Biological Control by Augmentation of Natural Enemies* (New York: Plenum Press, 1977); Marjorie Hoy and Donald C. Herzog, eds., *Biological Control in Agricultural IPM Systems* (Orlando, Fla: Academic Press, 1985).

4. F. R. Troeh, J. A. Hobbs, and R. L. Donahue, *Soil and Water Conservation* (Englewood Cliffs, N.J: Prentice-Hall, 1980); M. R. Gebhardt, T. C. Daniel, E. E. Schweizter, and R. R. Allamaras, "Conservation Tillage," *Science* 230(1985):625–30.

5. As defined by Gordon K. Douglass, *Agricultural Sustainability in a Changing World Order* (Boulder, Colo.: Westview Press, 1984); Thomas C. Edens, Cynthia Fridgen, and Susan L. Battenfield, eds., *Sustainable Agriculture and Integrated Farming Systems* (East Lansing: Michigan State University Press, 1985); University of California, "Sustainability of California Agriculture," Symposium Proceedings (Davis, 1986).

6. As defined by Robert Rodale, "Breaking New Ground: The Search for a Sustainable Agriculture," *The Futurist* 1(1983):15–20; Patrick Madden, "Regenerative Agriculture: Beyond Organic and Sustainable Food Production." *The Farm and Food System in Transition*, no. FS 33 (East Lansing: Michigan State University Press, 1984).

7. Gebhardt et al., note 4 above.

8. Patrick Madden, Stephan Dabbert, and Jean Domanico, *Regenerative Agriculture: Concepts and Selected Case Studies*, The Pennsylvania State University Department of Agricultural Economics and Rural Sociology, Staff Paper no. 111 (University Park, 30 April 1986); see also U.S. National Research Council, *The Role of Alternative Farming Methods in Modern Agriculture* (Washington, D.C.: National Academy Press, forthcoming).

9. Richard Lowance, Paul F. Hendrix, and Eugene P. Odum, "A Hierarchical Approach to Sustainable Agriculture," *American Journal of Alternative Agriculture* 1, no. 4(1986):169–73.

10. U.S. Department of Agriculture Study Team on Organic Farming, *Report and Recommendations on Organic Farming* (Washington, D.C.: U.S. Government Printing Office, 1980).

11. Lowance, Hendrix, and Odum, note 9 above.

12. An elaborate classification scheme for categorizing publicly funded (U.S. Department of Agriculture and land-grant universities) research considered relevant to organic farming has been developed. A large number of research studies are listed on subjects such as crop rotations, green manure crops, composting, biological nitrogen fixation, and biological methods of pest control (see F. W. Schaller, H. E. Thompson, and C. M. Smith, "Conventional and Organic-Related Farming Systems Research: An Assessment of USDA and State Research Projects," Experiment Station Special Report 91 [Ames, Iowa, 1986]). Other relevant research is being done in the private

sector, most notably the Rodale Research Center conversion experiment, which compares the yields of plots farmed with organic versus conventional practices over a five-year period (M. N. Culik, J. McAlister, M. C. Palada, and S. Reiger, "The Kutztown Farm Report: A Study of Low-Input Crop/Livestock Farm" [Rodale Research Center, Kutztoon, Penn., 1983]). As well, economists have conducted research at the microeconomic level of the hierarchy of sustainability. For example, an eight-year experiment comparing the profits and net-return viability of various conventional and organic farming methods in Nebraska concluded that organic methods yielded higher profits and incurred less year-to-year variability in earnings than did the continuously cropped systems dependent on routine applications of chemical pesticides. Organic rotations compared favorably with rotation using conventional (chemical) methods of pest control and soil fertility management (Glenn A. Helmers, Michael R. Langemeier, and Joseph Atwood, "An Economic Analysis of Alternative Cropping Systems for East-Central Nebraska," *American Journal of Alternative Agriculture* 1, no 4 [1986] (:153–58).

13. Patrick Madden, "Debt-Free Farming is Possible," *Farm Economics*, March–April 1986.
14. Johnson et al., note 1 above, 2.
15. William Lockeretz, Georgia Shearer, Daniel H. Kohl, and Robert W. Klepper, "Comparison of Organic and Conventional Farming in the Corn Belt," in D. F. Bezdicek et al., eds., *Organic Farming: Current Technology and Its Role in a Sustainable Agriculture*, Proceedings of a Symposium, Atlanta, 29 November–3 December 1981 (Madison, Wis.,: American Society of Agronomy, Crop Science Society of America, Soil Science Society of America, 1984), 37–48.
16. Madden et al., note 8 above.
17. A combination of mail and telephone questionnaires was used. In 1981 names and addresses of 3,714 farmers thought to be practicing organic or regenerative farming were obtained primarily from *The New Farm* magazine, Maine Organic Farmers and Growers Association, Kansas Organic Producers, Tilth in the Pacific Northwest, and California Certified Organic Producers. A total of 905 responded to a screening questionnaire mailed in early 1981. Those who indicated they were farming and were interested in cooperating in the study (a total of 652 farmers) were sent a list of 112 questions. Completed questionnaires were received from 357 of these farmers; 344 were complete enough to use in further analysis.
18. The "Total Design Method" was used in this survey (see Don. A. Dilman, *Mail and Telephone Surveys: The Total Design Method* [New York: John Wiley & Sons, 1978]). The method includes sending follow-up questionnaires to those who did not respond promptly and contacting the reaming nonrespondents by telephone. The overall response rate in 1986 was 72.7 percent.
19. William Lockeretz and Roger Blobaum, telephone and personal interviews with author, 1986.
20. Johnson et al., note 1 above, 15.
21. Ibid., 11.

23

Energy Conservation in Amish Agriculture

Warren A. Johnson, Victor Stoltzfus, Peter Craumer

Amish farmers can cut energy use without reducing yields, but this cannot be achieved everywhere.

The increasing agricultural yields of the last half-century have been achieved largely through the utilization of steadily increasing amounts of energy. Until the mid-1950's, total agricultural yields increased more rapidly than energy usage, but since then, the rate of increase in energy use has been faster than the increase in yields.[1] Not only does a farm use energy directly to power machinery and in the form of fertilizers, for example, but energy has indirectly led to greater agricultural production by eliminating the necessity for woods formerly used for household fuel and for pastures required by draught animals. Transportation and the processing of foods have also reduced food imbalances over space and time, enabling the products of all agricultural land to be fully and efficiently used.

If the current concern about future scarcity of energy is justified, will there inevitably be a decline in food production? Certainly such a pessimistic hypothesis could be made on the basis of the historical record. On the other hand, an optimistic hypothesis could be based on the current profligate use of inexpensive energy and the potential for maintaining high production by increasing the efficiency of energy use. Which of these hypotheses is correct could make all the difference to the poorly fed people in the world today and to their children.

To decide between these hypotheses on other than a theoretical or conjectural basis is difficult. Of the many examples of energy-efficient forms of agriculture in less-developed countries, most have low yields.[2,3] The processes of population growth and economic development have been largely ones of increasing use of energy, first in terms of intensified human labor[4] and then in the use of fossil fuels.[5] In the developed countries, in which scientific knowledge and technology enable the development of productive and energy-efficient

* Reprinted with permission from *Science, vol. 198*, pp. 373–378 by W. A. Johnson, V. Stoltzfus, P. Craumer. Copyright © 1977 American Association for the Advancement of Science.

agriculture, economic factors have virtually forced the extensive use of energy to increase yields and reduce manpower in order for individual farmers to survive economically. Alternative forms of agriculture are still being developed.[6]

The Amish, however, are the exception because their religious beliefs have caused them to turn their backs on a number of energy-consuming techniques while still benefiting from modern scientific knowledge. Most Amish are not averse to having their soil and feed analyzed by specialists nor to purchasing scientifically bred stock, even though they plow with horses, ride in buggies, and live in homes without electricity. They provide an opportunity to shed some light on the question of whether high-yielding agriculture inevitably requires the heavy use of energy. This study was designed to determine (i) how much less energy the Amish use than their non-Amish neighbors and (ii) what penalty they pay in reduced yields because of their agricultural methods.

The Amish

The Amish in America and Canada now number 70,000, most of whom live in communities in Pennsylvania, Ohio, Indiana, and Illinois. They are becoming increasingly visible to the general public as a result of tourism, journalism, and television. Although the study of their agricultural methods was initiated in the early 1940's,[7] little has been done since, even though published materials on other aspects of Amish ways have increased rapidly.

The Amish have their roots in the upheavals of the Protestant Reformation.[8] The reaction against the authority of the Catholic church was carried over into resistance by nonconformists to the authority of the new Protestant hierarchy. The Amish were a part of this Anabaptist left wing of the Protestant Reformation, which believed in individual interpretation of the Bible and adult baptism. In the 16th and 17th centuries, they were forced from Switzerland and Germany to other coun-

tries, including Russia, where their skills as farmers were needed. But in each country their nonconformist ways led to persecutions until they reached North America in the 18th century. The Amish, who in religious and agricultural matters were progressive for centuries, are now felt to be one of the best available sources of information on the farming life of 16th-century Germany.[9]

The religious functions of Amish agriculture are complex. Farming is not one among many neutral occupations but is strongly preferred as the optimum setting for the good life. This orientation stems most directly from their interpretation of Genesis 1:28, which directs humanity to replenish the earth and have dominance over animals and the land. They have a strong affinity for nature as God's work, as beautiful and orderly. Secondary choices are trades related to farming, such as carpentry, blacksmithing, and harness-making. Hard work is a moral value, which provides a context for the generally disciplined life. A simple technology is constantly adjusted to the right mix of sufficient labor intensity to provide jobs for the family and sufficient profitability to buy land, pay taxes, and support the shared obligations of the Amish community to cope with such problems as fire losses and medical bills. Education through the 8th grade is provided in their own schools. No government assistance is accepted, including social security or agricultural support programs, although they will consult agricultural advisers. They speak a dialect of German, and they refer to their non-Amish neighbors as "English."

The Amish belief in the literal interpretation of the Bible provides the basis for community integration. The biblical mention of horses but not of motorized vehicles has kept the scale of Amish communities small, the size being based on the power of the horse-drawn plow and the range of the buggy. In II Corinthians 6:14 it says, "Be ye not unequally yoked together with unbelievers," which the Amish interpret as forbidding their being tied directly to secular society by electrical lines or natural-gas pipelines. But in the modern era, many interpretations must of necessity be arbitrary when biblical wording does not apply directly to current questions. This fact, when combined with the independence of each Amish community, has led to much differentiation among them. Some Amish drive cars and are almost indistinguishable from the Mennonites, from whom the Amish split in 1697. But even among the Old Order Amish, the most numerous group, there are the very conservative who permit only stationary engines to drive belts for power (most Old Order Amish pull motorized balers behind their horses and may have a number of engines to power milking machines, refrigeration units, feed grinders, washing machines, and so forth). A market town in central Pennsylvania may have buggies of four different colors—white, yellow, grey, and black—indicating these different groups of Old Order Amish.

The market system of the larger society sets important constraints that the Amish must adjust to.[10] The price of land, the market for agricultural commodities, interest rates, and national economic factors all influence Amish operations. Since the Amish draw an ethical line between owning a machine and hiring custom agricultural work, they are beginning to use their neighbors' machinery, especially for specialized operations such as soybean harvest and the production of silage. The constraints of an ethically determined intermediate technology produce spatial differences in Amish agriculture as well. The Amish are not likely to spread into the Great Plains because that region is not conducive to the labor-intensive, unirrigated agriculture at which the Amish are so skilled.[11] The Amish not only must find the right area, but they must be able to purchase enough small farms to support their community and institutions without driving land prices too high. It is also desirable that a local market be available where they can sell the products of their gardens, barnyards, and farmhouses.

The Amish must adjust to the economic conditions as they find them, but in one major way they create their own economic pressures. The Amish family includes an average of seven children,[12] and the greatest task facing an Amish farmer is to see his sons estab-

lished on farms. In their attitudes toward children, the Amish are like traditional agricultural societies worldwide.

Energy Analysis

With the increased realization that energy, which is essential to modern society, may become scarce, energy analysis has increasingly become a supplement to other methods of analyzing questions concerning resources and the environment. As with economic analysis, energy analysis permits different production processes to be compared, except that the costs are in terms of the energy degraded to obtain a desired product rather than of the dollars spent. Energy analysis is especially useful when imperfect markets or hidden subsidies distort prices and make economic analysis difficult, as is often the case with energy and agriculture. Energy analysis has provided a new understanding of policy questions as diverse as packaging,[13] housing,[14] and transportation.[15] One of its key advantages is that it is not culture bound, as economic analysis so often is. It has been used effectively, for instance, to show that the use of cows in India is a sensible practice in that cultural context. Cows provide milk (the major source of animal protein in the Indian diet), motive power for farm work and transport, and dung (which, in most cases, is the only fuel available). In addition, the cows are fed with materials that would otherwise be largely wasted.[16]

However, the process of carrying out an energy analysis is rarely as straight-forward or concise as the laws of thermodynamics would suggest. Many studies of the same processes have led to different findings,[17] and international efforts have been initiated to standardize approaches and terminology.[18] Although standardization will be a great help, it will not resolve all the difficulties because of the necessity for tailoring each analysis to the objectives of the study.

In this study, the energy uses of Amish and "English" farmers were compared by calculating their energy ratios (sometimes called

Table 23.1 Energy Values of Major Food Products[25]

Item	Energy Value (kcal)
Milk	650*
Eggs	972+
Hogs	3,040#
Cows	2,440#
Chickens	1,035#
Corn	3,480§
Wheat	3,300§
Soybeans	1,340§

* Per kilogram, with 3.5 percent butter fat. +Per dozen, large. #Per kilogram of live weight. §Per kilogram.

caloric gain), the amount of food energy produced per unit of energy spent to produce it.[2,19] An energy ratio greater than 1.0 indicates that the process is a net producer of energy, and an energy ratio of less than 1.0, that it is a net consumer. The energy inputs to the agricultural process are traced back to the point at which additional energy costs make an acceptably small difference in the total energy costs. Outputs are calculated at the farm gate, on the basis that they are subsequently dependent on the allocation decisions of society rather than on the decisions of the farm operator.

In order to determine the penalty paid in lost production for energy conservation, the yields per acre (1 acre = 0.405 hectare) of each farm were determined. The total farm output, expressed in terms of 1000 kilocalories (Mcal) is divided by a corrected figure for farm acreage. The corrected acreage is obtained by adding to the total tillable land an additional acreage that would have been necessary to produce the supplemental feed that many farmers purchase. Acreages of woods and waste were not included, and rough pasture was discounted according to its equivalence to tillable land: the farmer suggested the terms of the trade, such as 3 acres of hillside pasture for 1 acre of tillable land.

The energy values of the major farm products are given in Table 23.1. For some, such as milk, eggs, and grains, the energy values are obvious. These are homogeneous commodities of relatively little variation in quality or nutritive value. With animals, however, there are large variations based on size, age, and quality of the animal. The product itself is complex: how should the analysis distinguish between prime meat cuts of low caloric value with high caloric fat and animal byproducts? The approach used here is that of Cook,[20] which assumes a standard percentage of the carcass to be separable lean meat, with bone and excess fat removed. The energy output per animal is, of course, more a function of these assumptions than a straightforward energy accounting, and as a result, the matter of whether a process is a net energy producer or consumer becomes less meaningful. However, these necessary assumptions do not impair the *comparisons* of energy ratios and yields between Amish and English farmers; indeed, any assumption of caloric values that is based on the weight of a fairly standard animal product would lead to the same relative responses to the questions posed by this study.

Table 23.2 gives the energy values used to convert major inputs into caloric values. For the most part, they are averages of selected data available in the literature, weighted to account for completeness of analysis and appropriateness for this study. Most energy fig-

Table 23.2 Energy Costs of Major Inputs

Item	Energy Cost (Mcal)	Efficiency of Production (%)	References
Fuels			
Gasoline	9.30*	89.6	2,26
Diesel	10.40*	89.6	
Liquefied	6.45*	95.0	
Petroleum gas			
Kerosene	10.30*	84.6	
Naptha	7.70*	89.6	
Electricity	2.54+	34.0	
Fertilizer			
Nitrogen	15.9#		2,3,27,28
Phosphorus	3.5#		
Potassium	1.4#		
Pesticides			
Atrazine	45.2#		2,28–30
All others	33.0#		
Feed			
Corn	1,300§		28
Soybean meal	1,100§		2,3,30
Hay	400§		3,20,28,30
Transport	0.345¶		2,3,20
Farm equipment	160**		1–3

* Per liter. +Per kilowatt hour. #Per kilogram. §Per ton. ¶The total energy cost to produce a ton of soybeans, estimated to be 2200 Meal, is divided equally between the soybean oil and meal. Per ton per kilometer.

**Per horsepower per year. For Amish farms, the number of motors and their horsepower were recorded. For non-Amish, who power most of their farm implements from tractors, the horsepower of the tractors was doubled to account for their other equipment.

ures that are available for agricultural inputs vary considerably. Not only do major differences stem from the completeness of the analysis, but also, fertilizers are produced by different processes, feeds come from different regions (some with irrigation and others without), and the use of different forms of energy and transportation all contribute to the differences in conversion figures. Agricultural equipment is particularly difficult to handle since there are normally many pieces on a farm, each of which has different rates of use, which makes the calculation of energy depreciation rates awkward.

Solar and human energy are not included in the analysis. Solar energy is considered a free good; if it were not used by agriculture it would go essentially unused. Human energy, even on the Amish farms, is still a tiny fraction of the total energy used, even though the work begins early, often 5 a.m., and ends with the after-dinner chores. There is also the question of whether labor would be more correctly viewed from the Amish perspective, as a benefit rather than as a cost.

Research Procedure

Three groups of Amish were studied—in central Pennsylvania, eastern Illinois, and southwestern Wisconsin—in order to obtain results from different environments. A smaller number of English farmers in the same areas were also interviewed. In Wisconsin, several recently completed studies[21, 22] provided comparative data, which necessitated a somewhat modified analysis and different conversion figures. Each farmer interviewed was asked a series of questions about the quantities of materials brought onto the farm and of the products sent out. Data were confirmed where possible by checking with distributors of fuel, feed, and fertilizer.

The number of horses used on each Amish farm was quite consistent. There were usually eight work horses or mules, even though farm size varied considerably. The number of "driving" horses varied more, between one and two in Pennsylvania to between two and four in Illinois. The Amish contend that a work horse will eat as much as a cow, which is an indication of one energy cost the Amish must overcome if their yields are to equal the English.

An input-output analysis such as this has the advantage of simplicity, since it is essentially concerned with what comes onto each farm and what leaves it; however, it sheds little light on the internal operations of each farm. The farmer is assumed to be using his land reasonably, given the constraints he operates under. The analysis assumes that the results will reflect the different constraints of labor and energy operated under by both the Amish and the English. However, there are variations among the farms. The Amish produce much of their own food and sell surplus vegetables, fruits, eggs, and baked goods at local markets. Theoretically, the food purchased and sold by each farm family should be included in the energy analysis, but such data are hard to obtain and were not part of this study. Also, different farmers produce different crops and use different forms of crop rotation: the effects of these variables are unknown. It is not the highly controlled experiment that may be desired, but the results do reflect a substantial difference between Amish and English use of energy.

Results

Central Pennsylvania

The study area is one of ridges and valleys just east of the Allegheny Front. The Amish have moved here only within the last 10 to 15 years, as land prices, tourism, and industry in Lancaster County have made it difficult for them to find farms for their growing numbers in that traditional center of Amish life. The Amish are now found in 40 of Pennsylvania's 67 counties. The valleys of central Pennsylvania provide good limestone soils, a degree of isolation, wooded hills, and good supplies of water. The sample consisted of 12 farms belonging to the Old Order Amish, five to the most conservative group of Amish (locally known as Nebraska Amish), and six English farms. All are primarily milk producers.

The overall energy ratio of the Old Order Amish indicates that there is virtually no net gain in energy in their dairy operations (Table 23.3), but in its final form of milk, the energy is directly useful to man. The English farmers' energy ratio of 0.553 means that they use 83 percent more energy to produce a unit of milk than the Amish. The

Table 23.3 Energy Ratios and Yields per Farm (Central Pennsylvania). Summary data are shown in boldface type to facilitate comparison with data in Tables 23.4 and 23.5.

Group	Energy Ratio	Yield (Mcal/ha)	Output (Mcal)	Input (Mcal)	Size (ha)	Corrected Size (ha)	Cows (*N*)
Older Order Amish	**1.009**	**3,151**	134,527	113,367	32.6	42.7	31.0
English	**0.553**	**3,071**	245,715	444,453	73.4	80.0	47.3
Nebraska Amish	**1.508**	**1,710**	53,014	35,151	30.0	31.0	12.8

Table 23.4 Energy Ratios and Yields per Farm (Eastern Illinois). Summary data are shown in boldface type.

Group	Energy Ratio	Yield (Mcal/ha)	Output (Mcal)	Input (Mcal)	Size (ha)	Corrected Size (ha)
Data as Collected						
Amish	**0.974**	**3,165**	173,134	177,821	38.9	54.7
English	**2.003**	**11,444**	2,466,156	1,230,769	200.9	215.5
Assuming all grains fed to hogs						
Amish	**0.886**	**2,879**	157,494	177,821		
English	**0.707**	**4,644**	1,000,820	1,415,384		

Table 23.5 Energy Ratios and Yields per Farm (Southwestern Wisconsin). Summary data are shown in boldface type.

Group	Energy Ratio	Yield (Mcal/ha)	Output (Mcal)	Input (Mcal)	Size (ha)	Corrected Size (ha)	Cows (*N*)
Amish	**1.614**	**1,305**	50,631	31,379	60.8	38.8	14.5
English							
Small farms*	**0.274**	**1,668**	99,399	362,990	71.6	59.6	24.5
Large farms+	**0.395**	**2,079**	204,800	518,890	107.6	98.5	40.9

* Number of cows < 30. +Number of cows 30 to 49.

yields per hectare for the two forms of agriculture are much the same, with the Amish yields 4 percent higher. In this case, there is no penalty in reduced production stemming from the reduced energy use of the Amish, which supports the optimistic hypothesis that high production can be maintained with reduced use of energy.

For the Nebraska Amish, however, the historical relationship between energy use and yields appears. Their energy ratio is 49 percent higher than that of the Old Order Amish, but their yields are 47 percent lower. Since they use only one stationary engine, the Nebraska Amish must sell their milk as grade B milk, cooled only by spring water. In addition, they are less likely to take advantage of the services offered by agricultural extension agents and farm suppliers. Their farms are 27 percent smaller than those of the Old Order Amish, but they have many fewer cows, in part because they do not use milking machines. The Nebraska Amish generally reflect greater self-sufficiency. The farms appear noticeably poorer, and the farmers are more reluctant to be interviewed. The Nebraska Amish can perhaps best be thought of as failing to utilize the scientific developments as extensively as other Amish and are therefore similar to farms in less-developed countries.

Figure 23.1A provides a comparison of the major energy inputs per hectare for the three groups. The main energy savings of the Amish come in their use of fuel and equipment, as would be expected. The Old Order Amish use more purchased feed than the English: 100 acres (40.5 hectares) is about the limit of horse farming, and many farms have fewer tillable acres than that: if the Amish wish to have additional cows they must purchase additional feed.

An additional contrast between the Amish and the English is their household use of energy. The Amish use liquefied petroleum gas for cooking, refrigeration, and hot water; naptha for lighting (in Coleman lanterns); and wood for space heating. The English use energy in much the same way as most American families do. In our sample, the average Amish family used 15,330 Mcal per year, and the English families used 160,280 Mcal. The English, in fact, used 20 percent more energy in their homes than the Amish to produce 173,650 kilograms of milk, the average farm output. The conservation achievements of the Amish here are greater in their homes than in their farming.

Eastern Illinois

The Amish community in Douglas County, Illinois, was established in 1864 with the purchase of railroad land for $8.10 per acre. The land is excellent, with deep fertile soil, although its flatness creates some drainage difficulties. The uniformly good soil presents a problem to the Amish since it does not permit them to allocate any of it to woods and the 5 to 15 acres used as pasture on each farm are inefficiently used in comparison with the English farms. In the absence of woods, household heating is by fossil fuels, and in the absence of gravity-fed water systems, windmills are used to lift water to insulated water tanks.

As Amish farms dominate this part of Douglas County, it was not possible to pair Amish farms with adjacent English farms. The nearest English farms were substantially larger than the Amish farms: the five English farms surveyed averaged 495 acres (200 ha) compared with 96 acres (39 ha) for 11 Amish farms. The Amish use very little chemical pesticides and, because of the good soil in the area, they have traditionally not used chemical fertilizer, although some farmers are beginning to apply small amounts (some organic fertilizers are used). However, unlike another recent study of organic farming,[23] we found that the Amish yields of corn, 115 bushels per acre (7200 kg/ha), are less than the English figures of 165 bushels per acre (10,4000 kg/ha). The largest single energy input to an Amish farm is for supplementary feed (especially soybeans) which is grown in only limited quantities (Fig. 23.1B). Hogs are the major product in the area, although the English farmers export substantial amounts of grain as well.

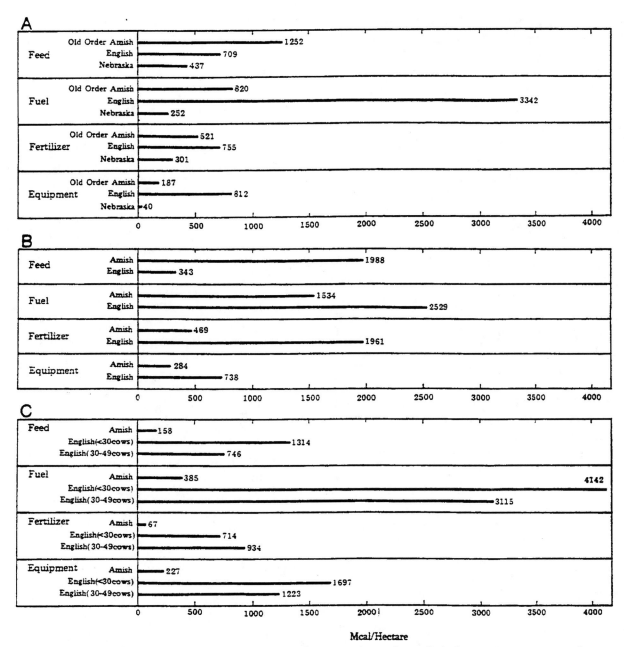

Figure 23.1 Major energy inputs per hectare for Amish and English farms in (A) central Pennsylvania, (B) eastern Illinois, and (C) southwestern Wisconsin.

The initial calculation of the energy ratios (Table 23.4) reflects the grains exported by English farmers, which pushes their energy ratios above 2.0. Since it would not be correct to compare outputs of animal products to grain, a calculation was made of the hogs that could be produced if the exported grain had been fed to hogs, using local feeding efficiencies of 4.25 kg of grain per kilogram of animal

weight gain. A 15 percent energy surcharge was added for the estimated energy cost of this hypothetical feeding operation. On this basis, the energy ratio of the Amish was 25.3 percent higher than that of the English, but their yields were 38.1 percent lower. These results support the pessimistic hypothesis, that a decline in energy available to agriculture would cause a decline in food production.

There are several possible explanations for the differences in the results from Illinois and Pennsylvania. The use of chemical fertilizers would increase Amish yields significantly, but it would also lower their energy ratios toward the English figures, thus generally reducing the differences between the two farming operations. It is also possible that hog farming, being less labor-intensive than dairy farming, is less amenable to energy conservation through Amish methods. However, since crop production is the major energy consumer, it seems unlikely that this factor would be important.

The differences between the two sets of results probably stem from the differences between the two environments. The diversity of central Pennsylvania, with its long narrow valleys, steep wooded hills, and marginal pasture, can be used efficiently by the Amish, while the uniformly good soil of Illinois is ideal for modern agricultural technology. Each environment presents certain obstacles and opportunities, and although it is easy to visualize the obstacles to using large machines on the irregular topography of Pennsylvania, it is not so easy to identify the obstacles to the Amish in Illinois. Household uses of energy are not included in these figures, In fact, since the energy ratios and yields of the Amish are similar in Illinois and Pennsylvania, it is probably more correct to say only that the Amish cannot utilize the Illinois site as effectively as the English.

The differences between the results for Illinois and Pennsylvania suggest that if energy were to become scarce in the future, the changes in agriculture would vary depending on the site. In diverse environments, agricultural practices may move away from energy-intensive methods more rapidly than in areas that are now treated most intensively by modern methods. If labor is substituted for increasingly expensive energy, idle small farms may be returned to production to the extent that they permit the utilization of local energy sources such as woods and pastures. Sites that enable farmers to avoid the high cost of equipment and fuel will increasingly be advantageous.

Fig. 23.1. Major energy inputs per hectare for Amish and English farms in (A) central Pennsylvania, (B) eastern Illinois, and (C) southwestern Wisconsin.

Southwestern Wisconsin

Vernon County and the adjacent part of Monroe County is the site of the Cashton-Westby Amish settlement. Consisting of approximately *55* farms, the community has been expanding as Amish have moved in from other areas where land pressure and prices are higher. The Amish here are conservative, in many ways similar to the Nebraska Amish in their use of stationary engines and belt power and the limited use they make of available scientific assistance. The region is characterized by a rolling upland topography cut by flat-bottomed valleys, with rocky, wooded slopes making up much of the landscape between. The soils are deep forest soils overlying dolomite and sandstone, but the farms are large because of the amount of unproductive land on the hillsides. Dairy farming predominates, and nearly all cropland is planted with corn, hay, and oats.

Data were collected from ten farms in this settlement and were compared with a statistical sample of 14 farms obtained from the 1975 Wisconsin Farm Business Summary[21] and with supplementary data from other sources.[22] While not providing a sample of farms in the same area, this sampling method did offer the opportunity to select English farms of the same approximate size and with the same number of cows, thus, differences in these variables should not affect the outcome. However, compared with English dairy farms in Pennsylvania, the small English farms (with an average of 24.5 cows) were relatively inefficient in their use of energy, and yields were less. Therefore, a sample of larger Wisconsin farms (30 to 49 cows) were also evaluated to see if the scale of operation affected the results.

The energy conservation of the Amish is striking (Table 23.5). The Amish yields are 22 percent less than those of the smaller English farms and 37 percent less than those of the larger ones, and yields on all types of farms are well below those in Pennsylvania. The Amish inputs for all major items—feed, fertilizer, fuel, and equipment—are low, whereas for the English farms they are high, especially for fuel (Fig. 23.1C). The data for English farms in all three study areas suggest that larger farms are more energy efficient than the smaller ones.

Conclusions

The data do not clearly support either the optimistic or the pessimistic hypothesis. The results from the more progressive Old Order Amish in Pennsylvania, who perhaps best approximate a traditional culture taking advantage of modern science and technology, do support the optimistic hypothesis, but the Amish in Illinois, who are progressive in most matters, do not. A number of other factors, such as the effects of different environments and the differences in farm size and operation, are also important. An input-output analysis such as this does not permit a detailed understanding of the specific reasons for the variations. To obtain the data necessary for such an analysis would require the collection of a vast amount of information from each farmer throughout the year and necessitate a degree of involvement in the farm operation that Amish farmers may not be willing to grant. Even with such data, the interrelationships might not become clear.

In one respect, however, the results are clear and do support the optimistic hypothesis, if slightly modified to pertain to energy conservation on farms in general rather than just in agricultural production. An Amish farmer told us that to buy a car he would have to milk five more cows. One may ask how many cows it would take to purchase a recreation vehicle or a color television or to pay an electric bill. If the Amish are conservationists, it is primarily in their consumption pattern. Their major contribution to energy conservation is in the limited demands they make on

available resources to support their way of life. Their major purchases are limited to clothing, bread flour, sugar and a few other food items, and household equipment and furnishings. The Amish buggies and harnesses, which are made by Amish craftsmen, will last 20 to 30 years, a horse may live that long as well, although the average life span is approximately 20 years. Probably more than any other group in this country, the Amish could survive without the support of industrial society.

Amish conservation and its economic consequences also account for the prosperity and expansion of Amish agriculture, a striking factor in itself in this era of poverty-stricken small farms and large commercial agriculture. The frugality of their consumption patterns and their willingness to use a labor-intensive intermediate technology has meant that the Amish could bank most of the proceeds of their farming operations and accumulate the funds to obtain land for their sons as the need arises. Their simple technology has enabled the Amish to avoid the major causes of small farm poverty and bankruptcy, the difficulty of obtaining the capital to purchase modern agricultural machinery or the heavy debt payments required if it is obtained.[24]

If energy becomes scarce in the future, the effects will not be felt uniformly. Agriculture would almost certainly be able to procure supplies needed for energy-efficient purposes such as fertilizing crops and preserving food. Even though the results we have described are mixed, they do suggest the potential for reintroducing human labor without major losses in production as long as key supplies such as fertilizers are available. The requirement of human labor could even be a benefit if energy shortages reduced the jobs available in other sectors of the economy.

The Amish experience should make us more confident about the future if energy should become progressively scarcer. It is often said that the Amish provide a vignette of early America: is it also possible that they may provide an image of the future?

Notes and References

1. J. S. Steinhart, and C. E. Steinhart, *Science* 184, 307 (1974).
2. G. Leach, *Energy and Food Production* (International Institute for Environment and Development, Washington, D.C., 1975).
3. M. Slesser, *J. Sci. Food Agric.* 24, 1193 (1973).
4. E. Boserup, *The Conditions of Agricultural Growth* (Aldine, Chicago, 1965).
5. R. G. Wilkinson, *Poverty and Progress: An Ecological Perspective on Economic Development* (Praeger, New York, 1973).
6. R. Merrill, Ed., *Radical Agriculture* (Harper & Row, New York, 1976).
7. W. M. Kollmorgen, *Rural Life Stud. No. 4* (U.S. Department of Agriculture, Washington, D.C., 1942): *Am. J. Sociol.* 49, 233 (1943).
8. J. A. Hostetler, *Amish Society* (Johns Hopkins Press, Baltimore, 1963).
9. W. I. Schreiber, *Our Amish Neighbors* (Univ. of Chicago Press, Chicago, 1962), pp. 88–98.
10. V. Stoltzfus, *Rural Sociol.* 38, (1973).
11. E. W. Schwieder and D. A. Schwieder, *A Peculiar People: Iowa's Old Order Amish* (Iowa State Univ. Press, Ames, 1975).
12. H. E. Cross, *Nature (London)* 262, 19 (1976).
13. B. M. Honnon. *Environment* 14, 11 (1972).
14. A. Mackillop, *Ecologist* 2 (No. 12), 4 (1972).
15. E. Hirst and J. C. Moyers, *Science* 179, 1299 (1973).
16. S. Odend'hal. *Hum. Ecol.* 1, 3 (1972).
17. B. F. Chapman, *Energy Policy* 2, 91 (1974).
18. International Federation of Institutes for Advanced Study, *Energy Analysis Methodology, Workshop Rep. No. 6* (Nobel House, Stockholm).
19. G. H. Heichel, *Am. Sci.* 64, 64 (1976).
20. C. W. Cook, *J. Range Manage.* 29, 268 (1976); A. H. Denham, E. T. Bartlett, R. D. Child, *ibid.,* p. 186.
21. *Wisconsin Farm Business Summary, 1975* (Univ. of Wisconsin Extension, Madison, 1976).
22. U.S. Department of Agriculture, *Agric. Inf. Bull. No. 230* (1968); *Selected U.S. Crop Budgets: Yields, Inputs and Variable Costs* (1971), vol. 2.
23. W. Lockeretz, R. Klepper, B. Commoner, M. Gertler, S. Fast, D. O'Leary, R. Blobaum, *Center for the Biology of Natural Systems Rep. No. CBNS-AE-4* (1975).
24. E. Higbee, *Farms and Farmers in an Urban Age* (Twentieth Century Fund, New York, 1963), p. 47.
25. A. L. Merrill and B. K. Watt, *Energy Value of Food, U.S. Department of Agriculture Handbook No. 74* (1963).
26. *Handbook of Tables for Applied Engineering Sciences* (Chemical Rubber Co., Cleveland, 1970), p. 304; V. Cervinka, W. J. Chancell, R. J. Coffelt, R. G. Curley, J. B. Dobie, B. D. Harrison, *Trans. Am. Soc. Agric. Eng.* 18, 246 (1975).
27. W. Lockeretz, R. Klepper, M. Gertler, S. Fast, D. O'Leary, *Center for the Biology of Natural Systems Rep. No. CBNS-AE-6* (1975).
28. D. Pimentel, L. E. Hurd, A. C. Bellotti, M. J. Forster, I. N. Oka, O. D. Sholes, R. J. Whitman, *Science* 182, 443 (1973).
29. M. B. Green and A. McCulloch, *J. Sci. Food Agric.* 27, (1976).
30. B. Commoner, *Center for the Biology of Natural Systems Rep. No. CNBS-AE-1* (1974).

24

Catalog of Woes

Richard N. Mack

Some of our most troublesome weeds were dispersed through the mail.

Like his modern-day counterpart, the winter-weary gardener of one hundred years ago could open his mailbox in late winter to find that long-awaited harbinger of spring—the wonderful new seed catalogue. While mail-order catalogs in general are a modern phenomenon, seed catalogs have been around for more than two hundred years, long enough to have influenced the vegetation of many parts of our country. The results have been both beautiful and disastrous.

Nineteenth-century nurseries introduced and helped spread many of the plants we now call weeds on our farms, waterways, lawns, and gardens. The word *weed* has several definitions. I will consider it to mean a plant that we think is out of place either in the wild or in the garden. In their native environments, the plants live alongside their predators, parasites, and plant competitors which limit their number and range. Removed from their natural enemies, they can run unchecked and become weeds.

For more than a century, botanists have been collecting information on the origins and life histories of the aggressive plants, and their data have been the basis for plant quarantine and state laws aimed at controlling the spread of weeds. Nevertheless, many weeds have marched across our continent, often showing up simultaneously in locations thousands of miles apart with no apparent explanation. Perhaps one reason for this mystery is that weed experts have held contaminated crop seeds, vehicles, and animals mainly responsible for the distribution of weeds, while underestimating another culprit: the nineteenth-century mail-order seed business.

In the first decades after the American Revolution, these catalogs were usually small circulars or handbills that advertised seeds, cuttings of fruit trees or a few ornamental plants sold locally. Some catalogues were undoubtedly mailed to potential customers, although the high cost of postage and the uncertainty of mail service in the new republic

---

probably limited the practice. It wasn't until the late 1840's that postal rates became affordable and opened the doors to a potentially lucrative mail-order market. The mail quickly became an efficient disperser of plants.

In the early 1800s, seed catalogs reflected the needs of their typical customers: self-reliant farmers who grew all the food they and their livestock ate, as well as the fiber they needed to make their clothes. Plants were also used to make home remedies. Catalogues of the time advertised horehound, an expectorant in cough syrups; catnip, which could be made into a tea to soothe the nerves; and absinthe, used as an antiseptic and a sedative (and also as an ingredient in a liqueur). Some medicinal plants, such as belladonna and digitalis, are still used by the pharmaceutical industry as sources of powerful drugs. Customers could also buy seeds of the opium poppy, which were sold for "medicinal purposes" as well as for their oil. As late as 1895, the catalog of the German Fruit Company of Los Angeles advertised the oil of the opium poppy as "an agreeable sweet oil, good for eating, painting and illuminating."

Another drug-producing plant that appeared regularly in seed catalogs more than a hundred years ago is marijuana. In those days, however the plant was planted for its physical, not its chemical, properties. Hemp, as the plant was commonly called, was sold mainly as a source of fiber. A local supply of fiber for rope production would have been essential to a largely rural population. Although cultivation was sporadic, hemp nevertheless was planted widely. Much of the so-called ditch weed growing in the Midwest today is probably the legacy of nineteenth-century local fiber production.

The seeds of the hemp plant, however, were most often used as bird seed. Other weedy plants were also introduced as bird seed, including canary grass, corn poppy, and rape. Although none of these species, including opium poppy and marijuana, are native to North America, today they are all naturalized and commonly found throughout the United States.

After the Civil War, Americans enjoyed an economic boom. Industries grew, and new railroads and highways crisscrossed the nation, connecting burgeoning cities and suburbs. Americans who now drew wages in factories and shops rather than on farms had more leisure time and discretionary income than ever before. Also, most people no longer had to grow their own food. All of this meant that, for the first time, many people could afford lawns and ornamental gardens. At the same time, the public's interest in natural history grew, particularly in plants and their scientific names. Collecting dried and pressed botanical specimens became a popular hobby. The seed catalogs in the United States (and in Europe, too) between 1870 and 1900 mirrored these great social and economic changes. Their pages were filled with hundreds of species of ornamental plants. Selections of medicinal and herbal plants shrank or disappeared altogether. Seed merchants discovered that there was a lot of money to be made in ornamentals, and they competeted to see who could offer the most diverse and exotic selection of plants. The catalogs of the late Victorian era were hundreds of pages thick and elaborately illustrated in a multitude of colors. Modern seed catalogs pale by comparison. Among the plants portrayed so enticingly are some of the most persistent weeds in many areas of the country today: baby's breath, Japanese honeysuckle, and bachelor's button.

Several introductions during this era proved particularly troublesome, most notably the water hyacinth. This plant first drew public attention in the United States at the 1884 International Cotton Exhibition in New Orleans. For unknown reasons, this native of the Amazon Basin was exhibited by the Japanese delegation, which probably handed out specimens to exhibition goers. The exhibition spurred interest in the water hyacinth, but it wasn't the first time this aquatic plant had been brought to our shores. At least one nursery owner in New Jersey was selling it at the time, and the plant had been available from European suppliers for at least twenty years.

By the early 1890's, the water hyacinth had attracted the attention of many other nursery owners who sold it by mail for as much as a dollar a plant, a large sum in those days, equivalent to about eleven dollars today. These nursery owners lavishly praised the beauty of this plant and described its easy care in the house or garden. Their catalogs included specific instructions on how to grow the plant and recommended that it be planted in ponds. At least one catalog illustrated its advertisement with an idyllic scene of water hyacinths floating down a stream. Little did these plant merchants know that they were contributing to what would become one of the worst weed disasters in the country.

Outside its home range in South America, where it is kept in check by its natural enemies, the water hyacinth runs wild. Its ability to float means that it can be carried miles downstream by the current. It can also be carried upstream, for instance, if it gets caught in the paddle wheels of a river steamer. Water-hyacinth grows at spectacular rates, each plant replicating itself hundreds of times each year. By the mid-1890s, many Florida rivers were clogged with dense mats that even steamers could not penetrate. Navigable rivers were quickly reduced to streams by impenetrable tangles of living and dead plants. Photographs of this period in Florida show long wooden boardwalks that had been constructed over the mats to allow passengers access to ships now confined to narrow channels far offshore. The water hyacinth is a particularly serious pest in regions where malaria and encephalitis are common, as the insect carriers of these diseases breed in the plant's extensive vegetative growth. By 1896 the water hyacinth had become such a problem that Congress appropriated funds for the study of the plant's control.

Today, water hyacinth remains a serious problem in much of the tropics and subtropics, as well as in parts of Florida and other states of the Gulf Coast. But it is not the only plant that was introduced with great enthusiasm, which later turned into regret. Hindsight tells us that bringing in Brazilian pepper, common ironwood, purple strawberry guava was also a mistake. Each of these attractive woody plants has escaped cultivation and become a threat to native plants in Florida and Hawaii.

Trouble lay hidden, too, in seeds that were never intended for planting. For example, dried flower arrangements and wreaths (often called immortelles in old catalogues) were popular among the late Victorians, as they are today. The wreaths were fashioned out of a wide variety of dried alien grasses, which today make up a virtual *Who's Who* of weedy grasses in the United States: soft chess, rattlesnake chess, compact brome, medusa head, and goose grass. Jointed goat grass is perhaps the most notorious of this group. A native of arid Eurasia, the grass is a close relative of wheat. It has a life history similar to that of wheat and occasionally even hybridizes with that grain in the field. By germinating and flowering at the same time as winter wheat, but with seeds that readily shatter before the wheat is harvested, jointed goat grass has become a stubborn pest in many wheat fields. When they were sold in dried flower bouquets, the grasses were ripe and ready to shed their seeds. There is no way of knowing for certain how many weeds were spread by the discarding of dried flower arrangements, but it is probably many.

Although few food crops have become serious weed problems (exceptions include weedy forms of some cereal grains), some forage plants have turned out to be bad choices. Johnson grass was introduced locally in the United States before the Civil War and was touted as a forage grass that regularly produced amazing amounts of hay. Its reputation grew, and by the end of the nineteenth century, it was being sold across the country, although mostly in the South. However, the high forage production of this grass came at a steep price for the farmer. In the course of its vigorous growth, Johnson grass forms tenacious tangles of rhizomes, among which few other plants can grow. Furthermore, the grass is practically impossible to eradicate in a field because it readily resprouts from these rhizomes, even if they remain only as small fragments in the soil. This ability to resprout was particularly troublesome before the advent of herbicides. Once a field was sown with Johnson grass, the farmer could not use it for any other purpose. The grass also can hybridize with cultivated sorghum, a close relative, and the result reduces a field of commercial sorghum to a worthless mixture of weedy sorghum offspring. The widespread popularity of Johnson grass in the late 1800's continues to cause problems for American agriculture today. Each year farmers from California to Georgia must cope with this aggressive plant.

Not all weeds are herbaceous plants. Woody ones, such as trees and shrubs, can also cause big problems. From the standpoint of its real and potential damage to American agriculture, the worst alien invader by far in the nineteenth century was common barberry. The shrub is not a particularly aggressive weed, but it is a terrible hazard nonetheless because it is the intermediate host for the devastating stem rust disease of wheat caused by the fungus *Puccinia graminis*. The earliest record of its sale in a catalog that I have seen is 1844, although other historical accounts place it in the United States before then. Certainly by the end of the century seeds and cuttings were widely available. Common barberry is an attractive, hardy shrub with bright scarlet berries that can be made into jelly. Perhaps for these reasons its popularity and range grew quickly. Common barberry was planted all over the country, including the wheat-growing states of the Midwest, and consequently threatened the wheat crop on a national level. During World War I, in an effort to save the crop for the war effort, a campaign was organized to eradicate every barberry shrub. Thousands of school children in the Midwest were enlisted to seek out common barberry while others specialized in destroying the plants once they were found. Schools held competitions and the child who found the most plants was awarded a medal. This quasi-military operation was an unparalleled success. Although the plant was not totally eradicated, it was controlled to the point where wheat crop losses due to stem rust dropped significantly.

Unfortunately, the commercial spread of undesirable alien plants did not end with the nineteenth century. A few of the weedy plants advertised in old catalogs are still sold today, along with some new potential disasters. Two examples are diffuse knapweed, which readily invades rangeland in the western United States, and Kahili ginger, which spreads quickly through mountain forests in Hawaii. The renewed interest in seed mixtures of "wildflowers" also has the potential for spreading alien species. Purveyors of these packets or cans of seeds often do not discriminate between native and alien species. How many more local naturalizations will occur as nature enthusiasts unwittingly sow these seeds?

I believe there are several lessons to be learned from the perusal of old seed catalogs, those dusty and now fragile remnants of a largely unrecognized nineteenth century industry. One has to do with the contribution these catalogues make to our understanding of how the alien weed flora grew and prospered in the United States and how good intentions can go amiss. Another concerns the wisdom of disseminating any wild plant before we have firm evidence that it is unlikely to become weedy. Introducing an aggressive weed is much like Pandora's box; once established, such a plant is virtually impossible to eradicate.

25

Agricultural Change in Vietnam's Floating Rice Region

R. C. Cummings

The problems of predicting the results of technological innovations are immense, and nearly all projects, in retrospect, seem vulnerable to criticism regarding unintended and unforeseen consequences. One particular source of perplexity is that the new advances in technology may result in environmental changes which themselves produce unexpected sociocultural consequences. This article examines one such case, the introduction of the green revolution, in the floating rice region of South Vietnam.[1]

In the Vietnamese case, the adoption of the new higher-yielding seed varieties (henceforth referred to as HYV) by a small number of farmers transformed the environment substantially; so much that the production of the region's traditional rice was adversely affected and all the remaining non-HYV farmers were eventually forced either to convert to HYV or abandon agriculture altogether. The social and economic consequences of these HYV-induced environmental changes, then, have been much more severe than would have been expected of the introduction of HYV in itself. The direct significance of the Vietnamese case is considerable in view of the fact that the environmental conditions discussed here are found not only in Vietnam, but in parts of Cambodia, Thailand, Burma, Bangladesh, India, Indonesia, and Africa.

The first section of this article briefly introduces the floating rice region of South Vietnam, providing the necessary geographic, demographic, and ethnographic background. Next, the traditional methods of rice cultivation and the new HYV methods are discussed and compared in term of their differential input and yields. The third section describes the environmental constraints operating in this part of Vietnam, how HYV changes this environment, and why the remaining traditional rice cultivators were forced to convert to HYV. The final section discusses the social and economic implications of this environmentally-forced conversion.

Background

The floating rice region of South Vietnam corresponds to that portion of the Mekong Delta in which the depth of the flood waters from the Mekong and Bassac Rivers during the monsoon season precludes the cultivation

---

* From *Human Organization, vol. 37, no. 3* by R.C. Cummings. Copyright © 1978 by Society for Applied Anthropology. Reprinted by permission.

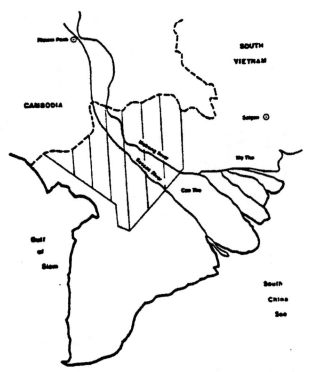

Figure 25.1 South Vietnam's floating rice region.

of all but "floating rice" varieties (discussed in the next section). It is a low alluvial plain lying between and extending roughly 60 kilometers on either side of these two rivers, beginning where these waters flow across the Cambodian-Vietnamese border and ending approximately 100 kilometers downstream (see map, Figure 25.1). The total land area is about 10,000 km².

The population of this region is about two and one-half million people, most of whom are ethnic Vietnamese. At least 70% of the population is engaged in agriculture, with most of the other 30% engaged in retail sales, transportation, services, and fishing. There is virtually no industry in the area.

Rural villages in this part of the Mekong Delta exhibit a lineal settlement pattern, the houses stretching almost endlessly along the major communication routes and the numerous streams and canals. Densities in some rural areas may reach as high as 650 people per km², though the density for the region as a whole averages less than half that figure. The individual household, which is generally a nuclear family or a bilateral stem family, is the most important social, economic, and religious unit in the village. Although there is a preponderance of kin as opposed to nonkin ties within small residential neighborhoods of the villages, there is only infrequent cooperation outside the individual household for any economic purpose; periods of peak labor demand, during which household labor is inadequate, require hiring additional laborers, who are usually nonkinsmen (cf. Hendry 1964:259–65).

During the mid-1970s, this area was characterized by numerous small-size holdings. For example, in Hoa Binh village,[2] a typical floating rice community, the total cultivable rice land was about 1,800 hectares, distributed among some 650 families (total population = 14,000 inhabitants, or about 2,200 families). The median holding was a little less than two hectares, with a range from 0.1 of a hectare to 14.9 hectares.

Rice Cultivation

In the western Mekong Delta the cultivation of rice has been strongly influenced by the high flood waters of the Mekong and Bassac Rivers. Beginning around April, these rivers begin to swell from the rains and melting snows to the north, and by October they have risen some three to five meters above their dry season level. This distension and overflow inundates the paddy fields with up to four meters of water, creating conditions which preclude growing any rice other than floating varieties. These rices are well-adapted to this deep water environment. By elongating their stems at a rate of up to 30 centimeters a day, they are able to keep their leaves above the surface of the rising flood waters and thus escape drowning. As the flood waters recede, the long-stemmed plants stretch out in all directions, ultimately lying in a tangled thicket as the fields begin to dry and harvesting begins. In extremely low-lying areas harvesting may be done from boats.

Floating rice requires relatively low labor and capital inputs. After plowing and harrow-

Table 25.1 Methods and Costs of Floating Rice Cultivation

Item	Rate	Cost per Hectare: In-kind	Cost per Hectare: Cash
Plowing[a]	6,000$VN[b]/hectare re		6,000$VN
Seeds	7 gia[c] of seed/hectare @ 2100$VN per gia		14,700$VN
Harvest	7 gia of paddy/hectare harvested	7 gia	
Labor for gathering cut paddy and assisting in threshing and winnowing	1 gia/worker/day	6 gia	
Threshing[d]	3 gia/100 gia threshed	3 gia	
Winnowing[e]	1 1/2 gia/100 gia winnowed	1 1/2 gia	
Transportation[f]	3 gia/100 gia hauled	3 gia	
TOTAL COSTS		20 1/2 gia	20,700$VN

a. Plowing includes one harrowing; additional harrowings, which are seldom needed, cost 3000$VN each. Most plowing and harrowing on floating rice paddy land is done by tractor.
b. The symbol $VN represents a Vietnamese piaster; in April of 1975, 750$VN = one U.S. dollar.
c. A gia is a dry volume measure equal to 22 kilograms of paddy.
d. Threshing is normally done by driving a tractor around and around on the dried paddy, the force of the tractor's tires twisting the paddy kernel from the stalks.
e. Winnowing is done either by pouring threshed paddy off a raised bamboo platform and allowing the wind to separate the chaff from the grain, or by using a winnowing machine, which is essentially a gasoline engine-driven fan in front of which the threshed paddy is poured. The labor cost for wind winnowing is roughly equivalent to the cost of renting the machine.

ing the fields in April, the farmer sows his seed, but then need not expend any more energy or cash until harvesting in December. At this time the farmer normally hires laborers to cut his rice, dry it, thresh it, and transport it back to his home. Plowing and harrowing of the fields is paid for in cash, but all other expenses are paid for in paddy. Table 25.1 summarizes the methods and costs involved in the cultivation of floating rice.

Yields from floating rice varieties average about 100 *gia* (2.2 metric tons; one gia = 22 kilograms) per hectare. Subtracting 22.5 gia for payments-in-kind plus 11.8 gia as the paddy equivalent of cash expenditures for plowing, seed, and interest for eight months,[3] the net yield from one hectare of floating rice is about 67 2/3 gia of paddy.[4]

The South Vietnamese National Institute of Statistics has estimated that the average rural family of seven requires about 77 gia of paddy per year.[5] My own data on household consumption indicates that this same family of seven will require in addition the equivalent of

100 gia of paddy to satisfy its nonrice food needs and its clothing, religious, educational, and miscellaneous expenses if it is to maintain a rural, "middle-class," standard of living. Since the median-size landholding in this region is a little less than two hectares, many families are unable to satisfy their total paddy requirement of 177 gia per year solely from floating rice cultivation. But because the labor requirements for floating rice are so minimal, there is sufficient time to seek supplemental income which can raise total family income above the subsistence level. Thus floating rice is not only well adapted to this deep-water environment but also to a situation characterized by numerous, small-scale, subsistence farms.

The methods and inputs involved in HYV cultivation, on the other hand, contrast sharply with the traditional ways. Most important, HYV production is highly capital and labor intensive. Moreover, it requires a new attitude toward agriculture, that is, one which is directed toward profit making and the market rather than subsistence and the household. In addition, because HYV is irrigated rice and is grown in the dry season, the farmer must work during a time traditionally devoted to the ritual rounds, merry-making, and leisure. HYV cultivation, in a sense, turns the social and agricultural calendars upside down.

New agriculture also requires that the farmer learn and master new skills and procedures, such as transplanting, irrigation, the application of fertilizer and insecticides, and weeding. It also requires that old tasks be performed in new ways. For example, due to the danger of crushing the bunds which retain the water in the irrigated fields, tractors can no longer be used for plowing or transporting paddy back to town. HYV cultivators must therefore use oxen or hand tillers to plow and must hire laborers to carry their paddy home. In addition, threshing must be performed by a threshing machine, which obviates winnowing. The methods and costs involved in HYV cultivation are summarized in Table 25.2.

The most striking difference between the floating rice and HYV types of cultivation[6] is the astronomically large capital input required for the latter,[7] more than ten times greater than for the floating varieties.[8] Plowing, seed, threshing, and transportation are more expensive, and fully half of the increase is due to the purchase of fertilizer and insecticide, which are not used in floating rice cultivation. Other costs include transplanting, weeding, the construction of bunds to retain the irrigation water, the leveling of the fields, and the digging of irrigation channels.

The high costs, however, are accompanied by high yields and high profits. HYV yields three to four times as much paddy as floating rice, depending upon the level of inputs applied to the production process. After paying cash and in-kind expenses, the HYV farmer can usually net more than 200 gia of paddy per hectare. In cash equivalences, net profits for HYV run about three times that obtained from the floating varieties.[9]

On the face of it, HYV cultivation appears to offer the small-scale subsistence farmer the opportunity to increase his profits and standard of living substantially. In fact, however, HYV cannot be cultivated profitably unless one can maintain the high level of capital and labor inputs. The farmer must have sufficient resources to purchase the necessary amounts of fertilizer and insecticide, to hire laborers to dig irrigation channels, to repair the bunds and level the fields, and to weed. If these minimal inputs are not applied, yields and profits fall geometrically and the farmer may ultimately be worse off than under his traditional methods of cultivation. In addition, there are extremely high risks involved in HYV production.[10]

Due to these high capital costs, high risks, loss of leisure, and the forced absence from the ritual rounds, many floating rice cultivators prefer to continue planting their traditional crop rather than adopt the new HYV rice. Given their values and the generally adequate yields from floating rice cultivation, their preference appears quite reasonable. I was thus quite surprised to find many poor, small-scale, peasant farmers foregoing their traditional seed and planting HYV, particularly when their profits from HYV were not much greater than profits from floating rice and in some cases were actually less. To understand

Table 25.2 Methods and Costs of Broadcasted and Transplanted HYV Cultivation

Item	Rate	Broadcasted In-kind	Broadcasted Cash	Transplanted In-kind	Transplanted Cash
Plowing[a]	24,500$VN/hectare		24,500$VN		24,500$VN
Seeds[b]	3,000$VN/gia		21,000$VN		10,500$VN
Bunds[c]	1,000$VN/man-day		15,000$VN		15,000$VN
Transplanting[d]	21,000$VN/hectare			21,000$VN	
Weeding[e]	450$VN/man-day		22,400$VN		2,700$VN
Irrigation	45 gia/hectare	45 gia		45 gia	
Fertilizer	350 kilo of Urea/hectare @ 9,000$VN/50 kilo bag		63,000$VN		63,000$VN
Insecticide[f]	42 kilo of dry DDT compound @ 900$VN/kilo		37,800$VN		37,800$VN
	6.7 liter of liquid DDT solution @ 2200$VN/liter		15,000$VN		15,000$VN
Harvest	7 gia/hectare	7gia		7 gia	
Miscellaneous					
Harvest labor	1 gia/man-day	6 gia*		7 gia**	
Threshing	4 gia/100 gia threshed	13 gia*		16 gia**	
Transportation[g]	By head pan, 10$VN/gia carried/100 meters		16,250$VN*		20,000$VN**
TOTAL COSTS		72 gia	214,950$VN	75 gia	209,000$VN

* based on average yield of 325 gia/hectare
** based on average yield of 400 gia/hectare

[a]Plowing includes two harrowings and a leveling; most plowing is done by oxen, which is much more expensive than tractor.

[b]Broadcasting HYV is at the same rate as floating rice—7 gia/hectare. Transplanted HYV, due to more careful and controlled spacing, requires only half that amount.

[c]Bunds and irrigation channel maintenance and repair expenses vary greatly depending upon the height of the land, the distance from the pump source, and the severity of silting from the previous year's flooding. No attempt is made to account for the cost of initially converting floating rice fields to HYV irrigation fields. This cost would vary with the level of the field, depth of the irrigation channels, distance from the main irrigation channel, etc.

[d]Seedbed preparation, seeding, and care are usually household tasks and no cash value is assigned here. Uprooting of seedlings and transportation of the latter to the fields is calculated in the total cost of transplanting.

[e]Weeding on broadcasted fields requires about 56 man-days because of the rampant growth of weeds and because of the caution required to avoid trampling the seedlings; weeding is almost negligible on transplanted fields, averaging only about 6 man-days/hectare.

[f]Insecticide usage varies greatly. Most farmers apply the basic dry mixture in three equal doses during the first three months of plant growth; they spray the liquid solution only if they observe the appearance of worms and insects. But due to the adulteration of insecticides by unscrupulous manufacturers and merchants, the dry insecticide may be ineffective and the farmer will need to spray almost daily. It is possible that the liquid solution may also be adulterated, in which case the spraying may occur on an even more feverish level. The maximum cost is estimated at 30,000$VN, with an average low among sprayers of 4,000$VN. The figure presented here represents a weighted average between these two extremes.

[g]Transportation costs are based upon an average distance of 500 meters from paddy field to the farmer's home.

why this change occurred, it is necessary to examine more closely the relationship between floating rice, HYV, and certain environmental conditions found in this part of the Mekong Delta.

Floating Rice, HYV, and Environmental Constraints

The major environmental constraints operating in the deep-water region of the Mekong Delta stem from the different levels of the paddy fields, the flood levels of the Mekong and Bassac Rivers, and the timing of the monsoon rains. These environmental forces are closely interrelated. The rains begin about the end of April, and flood waters from the rivers begin to enter the paddy fields sometime in May. Low-lying fields will experience the first flooding at this time; by June the middle-level field will be soaked from the floods; and by mid-July even the high fields will be inundated. The flood waters usually peak sometime in late October and begin to recede by November, by which time the monsoon rains have ended. The high fields of course begin to dry first; the middle-level fields will usually be above water by the first week of December or soon after; and the low-lying fields, with a few exceptions, should be free of surface water by the end of January. The relationship between these three environmental factors is sketched in Figure 25.2.

Floating rice fits nicely into this environmental pattern. The only constraint it faces is that there must be ample time for the seed to germinate, the root system to become firmly

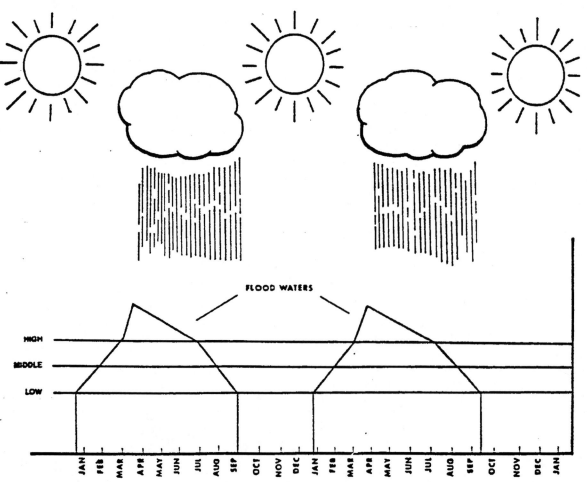

Figure 25.2 Field levels, flood depths, and the monsoon rains.

established, and the plant to attain a height of several centimeters before the field is inundated. The seed is sown dry (ungerminated) on relatively dry soil and is not covered. Because it depends on the spring rains for germination, the seed must be sown shortly after the first rains in April but sufficiently prior to the floods.[11] If one wishes to combine a dry season crop with floating rice, then the former must be planted early enough to permit its growth and harvest before the fields need to be prepared for the sowing of floating rice in the spring.

For the production of HYV, the major concern is how best to fit its 120-day growing season[12] into the period of year during which the fields are above the high flood waters; planning must be such that the crop is approaching maturity before the floods reach too high a level, otherwise the risk of loss from drowning or lodging is very high. This timing becomes critical if one wishes to double-crop, or plant two consecutive crops of HYV during one dry season. On a high-level field, for example, sowing broadcast, a crop could be planted in early December and harvested in March, with a second crop planted immediately afterwards and harvested just as the floods were rising in late June or early July. A middle-level field, on the other hand, has fewer months during which it is free from flood waters and it is not possible to broadcast two crops of HYV. The time during which the crop is actually in the field, however, can be reduced by sowing first in a seedbed and then three or four weeks later transplanting the seedlings to the fields. Owners of middle-level fields can thus still double-crop, but they must *transplant* both crops. Finally, on very low-lying fields, flood waters may recede so slowly that even with transplanting one can plant only one HYV crop per year.

Given the environmental conditions of the Mekong Delta's floating rice region, and the nature of the crops which can be grown there, a number of options are available to each farmer in term of what crops he will plant throughout the year. For example, a farmer owning a middle-level field would have at least four possible options: he could plant only floating rice, he could combine floating rice with a vegetable or other dry season crop; he could combine his floating rice with a single crop of broadcasted HYV; or he could transplant two consecutive crops of HYV and forego his crop of floating rice, since double-cropping would not allow sufficient time to prepare the fields and sow the floating rice before the floods come in June. Figure 25.3 shows the major options available for each paddy field level.

Figure 25.3 assumes that the only constraints on the farmer's choice are the differential levels of paddy fields, the depth of the floods, and the timing of the monsoons. Given these constraints, personal factors, such as preferences, availability of capital and credit, the willingness to take risks, and so forth, should be the determinants of just what option will actually be selected. In point of fact, however, this assumption holds only under the ideal condition that each farmer's choice of cultivation option is made independently of every other farmer, such that farmer X's decision to plant HYV has no effect whatsoever on farmer Y's decision regarding which crops he will plant. This condition of independence characterized agriculture in this deep-water region of Vietnam for only a few years after the introduction of HYV. After that time, the expansion of HYV began to affect adversely the cultivation of floating rice, eventually forcing the complete abandonment of the latter. To understand how this occurred, we must shift focus and trace the historical development of HYV in this floating rice region.

The Introduction of HYV

HYV was first introduced into the western Mekong Delta during the 1968–69 dry season.[13] The early pioneers were those who had sufficient capital or credit and had access to high, level land which could be easily converted for HYV production. A number of these early cultivators of HYV grew two crops of HYV and abandoned their traditional floating variety. Other farmers experimented, growing first one crop of HYV and then planting their traditional floating variety more or less as

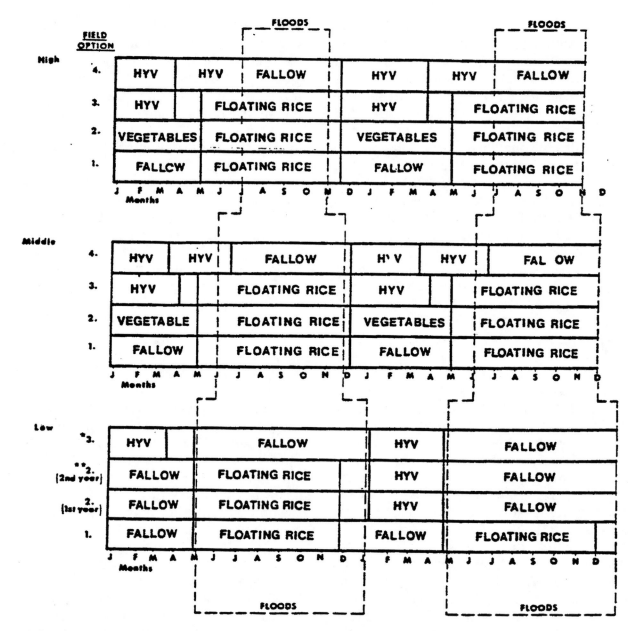

Figure 25.3 Cultivation options.

* In order to squeeze two HYV into the 6 months during which the mid-level fields are dry, both crops must be transplanted.

** On low-lying fields, the time during which the land is above floodwater is so short that it is impossible to plant three consecutive crops, either HYV-Floating Rice-HYV or Floating Rice-HYV-Floating Rice. Thus, in any given dry season during which HYV is planted, even if transplanted, floating rice cannot be grown; although in any year in which floating rice is planted, HYV can be grown immediately after its harvest.

subsistence insurance. Later, many of these farmers also began double-cropping HYV, and thus they too abandoned their floating rice varieties.

Most of the farmers on middle-level fields either continued planting floating rice or combined one crop of floating rice with one crop of HYV. Only a few of these farmers double-cropped HYV by transplanting. In fact, transplanting was rather rare throughout the region because it required an immediate cash outlay which not many farmers could afford and because sufficient numbers of experienced transplanters were not available. The great majority of HYV farmers thus broadcasted their seeds.

The early experimenters with HYV, due mainly to their wealth and thus their ability to maintain the required level of inputs, were generally quite successful and were quickly emulated. Within five years HYV occupied 15–20% of the paddy fields during the dry season.

When HYV was first introduced, there did not appear to be any problem in regard to its adaptability to this deep-water, environmental niche, nor to the accommodation between it and the traditional floating rice. After all, the one was grown in the dry season and the other during the floods; and except for the time limitation which necessitated abandoning floating rice if one wished to double-crop HYV, the two varieties did not appear to compete with each other or adversely affect one another. HYV, in general, only increased the farmer's cultivating options.

Later, however, as the number of individuals double-cropping HYV increased—and thus correspondingly the area of paddy fields under the cultivation of floating rice during the floods *decreased*—those, who continued to plant floating rice began to suffer crop losses due to drowning, lodging, and uprooting. These losses were the result of: (1) the strong flood currents that whipped and smashed the long-stemmed floating rice plants, uprooting them or lodging them beneath the water where they drowned; and (2) the large clumps of water hyacinth and other debris which enter the fields during the floods and can also uproot the floating rice plants by entangling their upper nodes, or, with their sheer mass, can force the plants under the surface where they drown. Current and debris are perennial problems for the traditional floating rice farmer, but when all farmers in a given area are cultivating floating rice these effects are dissipated and diminished; it is normally only on the perimeters of the great fields that the current can damage, and when everyone is cultivating floating rice those on the perimeter are instrumental in keeping floating debris out of the fields, either by periodically pushing the water hyacinth and debris out of the fields and back into the main current, or by building low bamboo fences which prevent the debris from entering the fields. When a good deal of the rice fields are abandoned during the flood season, as is true when a number of farmers doublecrop HYV and forego their floating rice crop, the effect of the current and debris are borne in greater proportion by each farmer. If the double-cropping becomes so extensive that numerous small paddy plots in the middle of the great field are completely isolated, then those farmers will experience the full force of the current and the debris on their field, and they will usually suffer severe losses.

This is what happened in Tan An District. Since most of the HYV cultivation began on the high, level land which could easily be converted into irrigated paddy fields and which was concentrated in four or five central villages of the district, it was on this land that farmers double-cropped in the greatest proportions, foregoing their floating rice during the flood season. When the number of double-croppers was such that about 20% of the floating rice fields were not cultivated, nearly half of the remaining floating rice farmers experienced some losses; when a third of the floating rice was abandoned, nearly all of the remaining floating rice farmers suffered some loss, and a number lost more than half of their crop: and, finally, when more than half of the floating rice fields were left uncultivated, it became no longer profitable for the remaining farmers to continue planting floating rice. Thus, within three years of the introduction of HYV, there were no longer any cultivators of floating rice in those central villages where HYV was so concentrated in its early development. This same transformation from floating rice to HYV is occurring in other villages as well but at a slower pace.

Thus this is not a situation where the peasants are led by profit-seeking motives to abandon their traditional rice and methods and undertake HYV cultivation, as one might be led to assume from a casual reading of agricultural statistics regarding the increased conversion of floating rice fields to HYV production. A more careful investigation of the process by which HYV has been introduced reveals that the abandonment of the traditional floating varieties has been forced by environmental factors, and that the shift toward HYV cultivation by a number of farmers is a reluctant one. Actually the floating rice farmer has little choice. He must either plant HYV or quit agriculture altogether, renting his land to others or selling it outright. While the HYV program might appear successful viewed from the capital down, closer inspection shows a number of problems. Some of the implications of this environmentally-forced transformation from floating rice to HYV production are discussed in the following section.

Implications

The most immediate effect of the forced adoption of HYV cultivation has been to increase the existing concentration of wealth and land, furthering the already great economic inequality of these rural arms. In the village surveyed for this study, for example, nearly half of the small-scale, relatively poor farmers who were forced to abandon floating rice cultivation are either renting to others or have sold their land. The poor smallholders who did shift to HYV generally lack the capital necessary to maintain the optimal level of production inputs. Their fields are yellow from insufficient fertilizer, and worms and insects seemingly feast there with impunity. Their yields are consequently low, 200–220 gia per hectare being common. Subtracting their payments-in-kind and a bare minimum for cash expenses, their net yield is not much greater than their floating rice yields. For these farmers, the green revolution has not signaled a new era of prosperity; they may actually be worse off now than they were previously. Rich farmers, on the other hand, with their large capital reserves and/or credit, are able to provide the necessary inputs, reap high yields and profits, and increase their already high standard of living.

There are a number of further specific social and economic consequences of this HYV-changed environment and subsequent forced shift to HYV. First, those forced out of farming usually become wage laborers, either remaining in the village and working for HYV cultivators, or, less frequently, moving to the urban areas and seeking what little work is available there. Conditions for those working as wage laborers on HYV farms is deteriorating. There are less payments-in-kind than under the traditional crops, and given the country's galloping inflation this represents a decrease in real per capita income. Furthermore, the actual demand for labor itself may be decreasing. There is a trend toward greater capital investment; hand tillers, threshers, reapers, and other labor-saving machinery are becoming more numerous. In addition, as the productivity of labor increases, fewer workers are needed to produce the same amount of grain. But this greater productivity is not being translated into higher wages. For example, the harvester receives the same wage in paddy for cutting one hectare of HYV as for one hectare of floating rice, although the amount of rice cut on the HYV field averages more than three times that of the floating rice field.

The opportunity for making high profits from HYV production naturally has an impact on land values. For example, rent on one hectare of floating rice land for one year was previously 25–35 gia, depending upon the level and quality of the land, the distance from the main road, etc. The same land developed for HYV cultivation goes for as much as 70 gia per season today. As more and more land comes under HYV production, existing tenancy rights become more tenuous: a tenant planting floating rice may be forced by a greedy landlord to convert to HYV or lose his tenancy.[14]

As the ranks of the smallholders are depleted, a new class of progressive, technology-minded, profit-seeking farmers emerges. These are primarily from nonagricultural sectors of the economy, such as the bureaucracy, the military, and the commercial sector. They usually rent three of four hectares of land, hire the necessary labor, provide the capital for the purchase of fertilizer, insecticides, and irrigation services, and receive huge profits from their investment.

The activities and behavior of these "gentlemen farmers" are having a profound effect upon the quality of village life. Most often they are outsiders and thus are able to avoid the obligations of traditional ties between landlord and tenant or landlord and laborer, contributing further to the deterioration of the tenants' and laborers' condition. In addition, the rich proprietors are often politically powerful and can pressure local legislative bodies into making decisions which serve their own interests. For example, I witnessed one case involving a small irrigation project (part of a large Delta-wide program for expanding HYV production) which was slated for one of Tan An District's villages in 1975. An existing canal was to be dredged to allow a number of smallholders to irrigate their HYV fields at lower cost. At the last minute, the village administration notified the higher authorities that cooperation for redigging the canal could not be obtained and that a new site was being designated for the project. Surprisingly, the number of beneficiaries at the new she was a fraction of those at the original site, or at any number of alternative sites. Later investigation showed that the police chief (a nonresident), two military personnel (also nonresidents), and a small number of local large landowners had conspired to persuade the village officials to change the site. The new canal will cut through the middle of a large tract of land recently converted to HYV production by this group.

There is, of course, no reason to expect these HYV-rich individuals to limit themselves to influencing local legislation. Their wealth, leisure, education, and experience make them prime candidates for direct participation in the political process at both the local and supra-local levels. Already in Hoa Binh Village, the number of village councilmen who are using HYV is in a majority, and two of the five hamlet chiefs are among the largest HYV cultivators in their respective hamlets. And although the 1974 provincial council elections did not produce more than a few HYV-cultivating candidates, the number of HYV farmers who were active in campaigning for other candidates appeared significant. It is safe to conclude that as these HYV cultivators gain greater control of both local and supra-local institutions and organi-

zations, the character of the latter will increasingly reflect the interests of these wealthy farmers. This, in turn, will have a direct effect on the quality of social life for the remaining villagers.

Another consequence of this forced transformation from floating rice to HYV is the adverse effect it has on land reform. The Land-to-the-Tiller Program, begun in 1969, was an admirable attempt to ameliorate the previous inequalities in land tenure. For the country as a whole, more than one million hectares of land were given to some 800,000 former tenants, with the government reimbursing the landlords for their loss. In Hoa Binh Village, for example, in which land tenure was characteristic of the Mekong Delta's floating rice region, 840 hectares of rice land were given to some 450 former tenants.[15] Nearly half of these tenants (45%) received less than two hectares, while a full one-fourth received less than one hectare. Many of these recipients of smallholdings were in the lower economic stratum of the village. But, as discussed previously, it is precisely this group which is being forced out of traditional rice farming, and thus much of the beneficial effect of land reform is being dissipated by the HYV program. If anything, tenancy is increasing (although many of today's tenants are "gentlemen farmers" using HYV) and the concentration of land among the few is accelerating.

The results of HYV cultivation vis-a-vis the smallholder have not all been so bleak, however. A number of the latter have been able to share in the new prosperity of the green revolution. Most of these were a little wealthier than their poorer counterparts, perhaps had access to credit or loans through kinship or other connection, were able to mobilize more household labor for working their fields, or maybe had enough land that they could rent out some and work some, using the return on the former to invest in the latter. For whatever reason, the green revolution affected this small minority exactly as its early advocates predicted: it raised incomes and standards of living and offered small-scale farmers a share of the good things in life. Unfortunately, the number of smallholders in the floating rice region of the Mekong Delta for whom the promises of the green revolution came true was small.

Conclusions

In light of the material presented in this paper, one must refrain from assuming that all cultivators of HYV are reaping a large profit and enjoying a new prosperity. Early criticism of the effects of the green revolution focused on the fact that the poor, small-scale farmer, due to his lack of capital inputs and limited access to credit, was unable to participate in the cultivation of HYV (cf. Wharton 1969:469–70; Falcon 1970:707–708; Ghosh 1969:87; Frankel 1971:204–08; Walters and Willett 1971:181–83; Blair 1971; Cohen 1974; Muthial 1971; Sen 1970; Schuh 1970:719; Mukherjee 1970:A.15; Shah 1970:44). The cast offered here demonstrates that inability to participate in the HYV program is not the only problem with the green revolution. The poor smallholder may indeed be cultivating HYV, but primarily because he has been forced to do so. Because these poor farmers are frequently marginal cultivators, their low capital inputs result in low yields, and their net profits are not much higher than they were under the traditional crop, but with a lot more headache, effort, and risk. Therefore, it must not be assumed by government planners and experts in economic development that solely because a farmer is cultivating HYV he is ipso facto on the road to prosperity.

Many writers have stated that in order for the poor smallholders to join the green revolution, there must be a "provision of joint services . . . both as regards the supply of inputs (capital, machinery, technical skills, etc.) and the sale of produce" (Ahmad 1972:16; cf. Wharton 1969:469–70; Falcon 1970:707–708; Ghosh 1969:87, Frankel 1971:204–208; Walters and Willett 1971:181–83). The emphasis on such statements has been on joining the HYV program, rather than on its continued success once the farmer has taken the initial step. Data presented here indicate that an effort should also be made to assist a number of marginal cultivators of HYV whose labors and results, despite a number of years at HYV production, still reflect subsistence farming. This latter group should not be neglected simply because they are already using HYV.

In general, the social and economic implications of the green revolution cited here do not differ greatly from those reported elsewhere. That is, there is an increased disparity of income distribution in the rural areas, the ranks of the rural wage laborer are increasing, unemployment due to mechanization and increased capital investment is rising, tenancy security for smallholders is becoming more tenuous, and concentration of landownership is increasing at the expense of small farming units. What is different in the floating rice region of Vietnam, however, is that these implications are likely to be more exaggerated and severe because they derive not just from HYV cultivation but also from an HYV-changed physical environment. These problems, in Vietnam and throughout the rest of the developing world where the green revolution has promised to eliminate rural misery and stagnation, must be tackled in terms of developing new institutions and formulating new policies which ensure that the technological development of HYV is coordinated with social justice and the raising of living standards for all sectors of the rural population. Unless such reform is undertaken, the problems of unequal income distribution and unemployment will worsen and will serve in the long run to offset all the potential benefits of the green revolution.

Notes

1. The green revolution has been defined as "the rapid spread in the use of highly productive new varieties of grain, together with increased supplies of cheaper fertilizer . . ." (Walters and Willett 1971:108); and as "the development of new improved varieties whose primary characteristic is that they have a greater response to the application of fertilizer" (Schuh 1970:719).
2. Hoa Binh Village, as all other place names used in this paper, is a pseudonym. It desig-

nates the village in which I lived during my fieldwork and from which the bulk of the data presented here was obtained.

3. A gia of paddy sells for 21000$VN (About U.S. $3.00) at harvest; interest costs average about 30% per annum.

4. This net yield figure could be increased considerably if there were greater utilization of household labor. The majority of households, however, rely upon internal labor to a very limited extent. First, it is prestigious not to use one's family members as farm laborers. Second, since most of the payments are in kind, the hiring of outside labor, particularly from among one's fellow villagers, represents a form of redistribution or a cultural leveling mechanism. Third, there is a great concern on the part of the farmers to harvest their paddy and get it out of the fields as rapidly as possible so as to prevent losses from theft and unlawful taxation or extortion. Reliance upon household labor would extend the time required to complete the harvest and would thus endanger the paddy crop.

5. Sansom (1970:37–38) cites the per capita paddy consumption as 240 kilograms. I have merely converted this figure into gia for a family of seven.

6. Caution must be exercised in comparing the HYV cost and yield figures with those for the traditional floating varieties. The figures for the later represent those obtained by the "average" floating rice cultivator—the majority of farmers interviewed reported figures which varied only slightly with those given here. The range of costs and yields reported by HYV cultivators, on the other hand, was quite large (yields, for example, varied from less than 200 gia to nearly 450 gia per hectare). The reason for this large variance is that there are a number of relatively poor farmers engaged in HYV production whose level of capital and labor inputs is significantly below the optimal level, resulting in rather low yields and net profits. The HYV figures presented here represent this optimal level. Although this optimum is attained only by a small majority of HYV farmers, *all* HYV cultivators recognize this optimal level and strive for it.

7. This large capital input could be reduced if the farmer utilized his household labor to a greater extent. The factors against this, discussed in note 4 in regard to floating rice, largely hold true for HYV, though for nonpeak

labor demands household labor is increasingly relied upon. As profit seeking and market orientation become more ingrained in the HYV farmers, a shift toward increased reliance upon household labor should manifest itself. Already there are isolated instances of individuals hoeing by hand instead of renting a plow, and irrigating fields by raising buckets of water by hand from a source and pouring them into irrigation channels.

8. Figures from India, in contrast, show an increase in investment "from around U.S. $9.00 at present to around U.S. $200.00 for rice production if the full-scale HYV program for rice production is to be adopted by a farmer" (*Economic Bulletin for Asia and the Far East* 1969:12, cited in Ahmad 1972:15). This figure, like those presented here for Vietnam, does not include a cost factor for the original construction of irrigation ditches, bundings, etc., which in the India case already exist since the traditional rice crop also is irrigated.

9. The net yield on flowing rice is 79.5 gia with a cash debt of 20,700$VN. The price of one gia of rice is 2100$VN, at 166,950$VN for the cash value of the net yield. Subtracting the cash debt plus 30% interest for eight months, the net profit is about 142,000$VN. For transplanted HYV, the net yield is 325 gia with a cash debt of 209,000$VN. The price of one gia of HYV paddy is 2,050$VN or 666,250$VN for the cash value of the net yield. Subtracting the cash debt plus 30% interest for four months, the net profit in cash is about 430,000$VN, which is about three times as great as that for floating rice.

10. For an example of just one of the risks HYV farmers face, see Note f to Table 2.

11. All the farmers I talked with insisted they could only sow dry seed on relatively dry soil, the seed was to be left uncovered, and if the soil was too wet and soggy they could not sow. Why this is so is not exactly clear. One critical problem facing these cultivators is the unreliability of the spring rains. If the farmers covered the ungerminated seed with earth, the flood waters might cover the fields before the rains had penetrated beneath the soil enough to germinate the seed, and the underdeveloped plant could not elongate its stem rapidly enough to escape drowning. On the other hand, the farmer cannot wait until the rains have soaked the land sufficiently and then sow pregerminated seed, because again

there would not be enough time for the plant to grow before the flood waters inundated the fields. But the timing of the rains and the inundation of the fields is not the only reason for sowing dry seed on dry soil. If the soil happens to be thoroughly soaked prior to or just at the beginning of the early rains, the farmers could conceivably sow pregerminated seed which would have sufficient time to grow before the flood waters entered the fields. But they don't and they will not plant at all if their fields are too wet and puddled. Some farmers mentioned that the plant could not develop a firm root system if the seed was sown pregerminated, and thus losses from uprooting due to high winds and rushing water would be high; others stated that pregerminated seed did not grow properly at

all and that the young plants become lodged in the mud. No conclusive answer to this problem could be found. See the discussion in Grist 1965:128–29.

12. The variety of HYV grown by 90% of the farmers in Tan An District was IR-8, with a growing season of 115–120 days. Other varieties, recently introduced and supposedly more resistant to insects, have a longer growing season but give slightly lower yields. These later varieties include IR-73/2, IR-26, and IR-20.

13. From April, 1969, until June, 1970, I served as a District Development Officer with the United States Agency for International Development in Tan An District and was able to witness first hand the early efforts at introducing HYV into the area.

26

Food Revolution That Starts with Rice

William J. Broad

Many a professor dreams of revolution. But Norman. T. Uphoff, working in a leafy corner of the Cornell University campus, is leading an inconspicuous one centered on solving the global food crisis. The secret, he says, is a new way of growing rice.

Rejecting old customs as well as the modern reliance on genetic engineering, Dr. Uphoff, 67, an emeritus professor of government and international agriculture with a trim white beard and a tidy office, advocates a management revolt.

Harvests typically double, he says, if farmers plant early, give seedlings more room to grow and stop flooding fields. That cuts water and seed costs while promoting root and leaf growth.

The method, called the System of Rice Intensification, or S.R.I., emphasizes the quality of individual plants over the quantity. It applies a less-is-more ethic to rice cultivation.

In a decade, it has gone from obscure theory to global trend—and encountered fierce resistance from established rice scientists. Yet a million rice farmers have adopted the system, Dr. Uphoff says. The rural army, he predicts, will swell to 10 million farmers in the next few years, increasing rice harvests, filling empty bellies and saving untold lives.

"The world has lots and lots of problems," Dr. Uphoff said recently while talking of rice intensification and his 38 years at Cornell. "But if we can't solve the problems of peoples' food needs, we can't do anything. This, at least, is within our reach."

That may sound audacious given the depths of the food crisis and the troubles facing rice. Roughly half the world eats the grain as a staple food even as yields have stagnated and prices have soared, nearly tripling in the past year. The price jolt has provoked riots, panicked hoarding and violent protests in poor countries.

But Dr. Uphoff has a striking record of accomplishment, as well as a gritty kind of farm-boy tenacity.

He and his method have flourished despite the skepticism of his Cornell peers and the global rice establishment—especially the International Rice Research Institute, which helped start the green revolution of rising grain production and specializes in improving rice genetics.

His telephone rings. It is the World Bank Institute, the educational and training arm of the development bank. The institute is making a DVD to spread the word.

"That's one of the irons in the fire," he tells a visitor, looking pleased before plunging back into his tale.

Dr. Uphoff's improbable journey involves a Wisconsin dairy farm, a billionaire philanthropist, the jungles of Madagascar, a Jesuit priest, ranks of eager volunteers and, increasingly, the developing world. He lists top S.R.I. users as India, China, Indonesia, Cambodia and Vietnam among 28 countries on three continents.

In Tamil Nadu, a state in southern India, Veerapandi S. Arumugam, the agriculture minister, recently hailed the system as "revolutionizing" paddy farming while spreading to "a staggering" million acres.

Chan Sarun, Cambodia's agriculture minister, told hundreds of farmers at an agriculture fair in April that S.R.I.'s speedy growth promises a harvest of "white gold."

On Cornell's agricultural campus, Dr. Uphoff runs a one-man show from an office rich in travel mementos. From Sri Lanka, woven rice stalks adorn a wall, the heads thick with rice grains.

His computers link him to a global network of S.R.I. activists and backers, like Oxfam, the British charity. Dr. Uphoff is S.R.I.'s global advocate, and his Web site (ciifad.cornell. edu/sri/) serves as the main showcase for its principles and successes.

"It couldn't have happened without the Internet," he says. Outside his door is a sign, "Alfalfa Room," with a large arrow pointing down the hall, seemingly to a pre-electronic age.

Critics dismiss S.R.I. as an illusion.

"The claims are grossly exaggerated," said Achim Dobermann, the head of research at the international rice institute, which is based in the Philippines. Dr. Dobermann said fewer farmers use S.R.I. than advertised because old practices often are counted as part of the trend and the method itself is often watered down.

"We don't doubt that good yields can be achieved," he said, but he called the methods too onerous for the real world.

By contrast, a former skeptic sees great potential. Vernon W. Ruttan, an agricultural economist at the University of Minnesota and a longtime member of the National Academy of Sciences, once worked for the rice institute and doubted the system's prospects.

Dr. Ruttan now calls himself an enthusiastic fan, saying the method is already reshaping the world of rice cultivation. "I doubt it will be as great as the green revolution," he said. "But in some areas it's already having a substantial impact."

Robert Chambers, a leading analyst on rural development, who works at the University of Sussex, England, called it a breakthrough.

"The extraordinary thing," he said, "is that both farmers and scientists have missed this—farmers for thousands of years, and scientists until very recently and then some of them in a state of denial."

The method, he added, "has a big contribution to make to world food supplies. Its time has come."

Dr. Uphoff grew up on a Wisconsin farm milking cows and doing chores. In 1966, he graduated from Princeton with a master's degree in public affairs and in 1970 from the University of California, Berkeley, with a doctorate in political science.

At Cornell, he threw himself into rural development, irrigation management and credit programs for small farmers in the developing world.

In 1990, a secret philanthropist (eventually revealed to be Charles F. Feeney, a Cornell alumnus who made billions in duty-free shops) gave the university $15 million to start a program on world hunger. Dr. Uphoff was the institute's director for 15 years.

The directorship took him in late 1993 to Madagascar. Slash-and-burn rice farming was destroying the rain forest, and Dr. Uphoff sought alternatives.

He heard that a French Jesuit priest, Father Henri de Laulanié had developed a high-yield rice cultivation method on Madagascar that he called the System of Rice Intensification.

Dr. Uphoff was skeptical. Rice farmers there typically harvested two tons per hectare (an area 100 by 100 meters, or 2.47 acres). The group claimed 5 to 15 tons.

"I remember thinking, 'Do they think they can scam me?'" Dr. Uphoff recalled. "I told them, 'Don't talk 10 or 15 tons. No one at Cornell will believe it. Let's shoot for three or four.'"

Dr. Uphoff oversaw field trials for three years, and the farmers averaged eight tons per hectare. Impressed, he featured S.R.I. on the cover of his institute's annual reports for 1996 and 1997.

Dr. Uphoff never met the priest, who died in 1995. But the success prompted him to scrutinize the method and its origins.

One clear advantage was root vigor. The priest, during a drought, had noticed that rice plants and especially roots seemed much stronger. That led to the goal of keeping fields damp but not flooded, which improved soil aeration and root growth.

Moreover, wide spacing let individual plants soak up more sunlight and send out more tillers—the shoots that branch to the side. Plants would send out upwards of 100 tillers. And each tiller, instead of bearing the usual 100 or so grains, would puff up with 200 to 500 grains.

One drawback was weeds. The halt to flooding let invaders take root, and that called for more weeding. A simple solution was a rotating, hand-pushed hoe, which also aided soil aeration and crop production.

But that meant more labor, at least at first. It seemed that as farmers gained skill, and yields rose, the overall system became labor saving compared with usual methods.

Dr. Uphoff knew the no-frills approach went against the culture of modern agribusiness but decided it was too good to ignore. In 1998, he began promoting it beyond Madagascar, traveling the world, "sticking my neck out," as he put it.

Slowly, it caught on, but visibility brought critics. They dismissed the claims as based on wishful thinking and poor record keeping, and did field trials that showed results similar to conventional methods.

In 2006, three of Dr. Uphoff's colleagues at Cornell wrote a scathing analysis based on global data. "We find no evidence," they wrote, "that S.R.I. fundamentally changes the physiological yield potential of rice."

While less categorical, Dr. Dobermann of the rice research institute called the methods a step backward socially because they increased drudgery in rice farming, especially among poor women.

In his Cornell office, Dr. Uphoff said his critics were biased and knew little of S.R.I.'s actual workings. The method saves labor for most farmers, including women, he said. As for the skeptics' field trials, he said, they were marred by problems like using soils dead from decades of harsh chemicals and monocropping, which is the growing of the same crop on the same land year after year.

"The critics have tried to say it's all zealotry and religious belief," Dr. Uphoff sighed. "But it's science. I find myself becoming more and more empirical, judging things by what works."

His computer seems to hum with proof. A recent report from the Timbuktu region of Mali, on the edge of the Sahara Desert, said farmers had raised rice yields 34 percent, despite initial problems with S.R.I. guideline observance.

In Laos, an agriculture official recently said S.R.I. had doubled the size of rice crops in three provinces and would spread to the whole country because it provided greater yields with fewer resources.

"Once we get over the mental barriers," Dr. Uphoff said, "it can go very, very quickly because there's nothing to buy."

The opponents have agreed to conduct a global field trial that may end the dispute, he said. The participants include the rice institute, Cornell and Wageningen University, a Dutch institution with a stellar reputation in agriculture.

The field trials may start in 2009 and run through 2011, Dr. Uphoff said. "This should satisfy any scientific questions," he added. "But my sense is that S.R.I. is moving so well and so fast that this will be irrelevant."

Practically, he said, the method is destined to grow.

"It raises the productivity of land, labor, water and capital," he said. "It's like playing with a stacked deck. So I know we're going to win."

27

The Great Sisal Scheme

Daniel R. Gross

With dreams of riches, the peasants of northeastern Brazil planted crops of "green gold." They harvested instead malnutrition and misery.

In northeastern Brazil, the lush green coastal vegetation almost hides the endemic human misery of the region. Unless you look closely, the busy streets of Salvador and Recife and the waving of palm trees mask the desperation of city slums, the poverty of plantation workers. When you leave the well-travelled coastal highways and go—usually on a dusty, rutted road—toward the interior, the signs of suffering become more and more apparent.

The transition is quick and brutal. Within 50 miles the vegetation changes from palm, tropical fruit, and dark-green broad-leafed trees to scrawny brush only slightly greener than the dusty earth. Nearly every plant is armed with spines or thorns. The hills are jagged, with hard faces of rock exposed. This is the *sertão,* the interior of northeastern Brazil.

If the *sertão* were honest desert, it would probably contain only a few inhabitants and a fair share of human misery. But the *sertão* is deceitful and fickle. It will smile for several years in a row, with sufficient rains arriving for the growing seasons. Gardens and crops will flourish. Cattle fatten. Then, without warning, another growing season comes, but the rains don't. The drought may go on, year after dusty year. Crops fail. Cattle grow thin and die. Humans begin to do the same. In bad droughts, the people of the *sertão* migrate to other regions by the thousands.

The bandits, the mystics, the droughts and migrants, the dreams and schemes of the *sertão* hold a special place in Brazilian, folklore, literature, and song. Even at its worst, the *sertão* has been a fertile ground for the human imagination.

For two years, I studied the impact of sisal crops—a recent dream and scheme—on the people of the *sertão.* Taking an ecological approach, I found that sisal, which some poetic dreamers call "green gold," has greatly changed northeastern Brazil. But the changes have not been what the economic planners anticipated. And misery has not left the *sertão.*

I lived in Vila Nova, a small village with a population of less than 500 about an hour's drive from the town of Victoria in Bahia State. Vila Nova is striking only for its drabness. Weeds grow in the middle of unpaved streets. Facing the plaza is an incomplete series of nondescript row homes. Some have faded pastel façades, others are mud brown because their owners never managed to plaster over the rough adobe walls. The village looks decadent, yet the oldest building is less than 20 years old and most were built after 1963.

Cattle raisers settled the *sertáo* 400 years ago when the expanding sugar plantations of the coast demanded large supplies of beef and traction animals. A "civilization of leather" developed, with generations of colorful and intrepid cowboys *(vaqueiros)* clad entirely in rawhide to protect themselves against the thorny scrub vegetation. As the population of the *sertáo* grew, many *sertanejos* settled down to subsistence farming. Gradually the entire region became a cul-de-sac, with many small and medium-sized estates occupied by descendants of the *vaqueiros* and others who had drifted into the region.

Life was never easy in this thorny land, for the work was hard and the environment cruel. Yet cooperation and mutual assistance provided assurance of survival even to the poorest. The chief crops were manioc, beans, and corn, and most of what was grown was consumed by the cultivator's family. Most families received some share of meat and milk and consumed highly nutritious foods like beans and squash, in addition to starchy foods like manioc flour.

When droughts menaced the region all but the wealthiest ranchers migrated temporarily to the coast to work on the sugar plantations. When the rains came again to the *sertáo,* they nearly always returned, for the work in the cane fields was brutal and labor relations had not changed greatly from the time when slaves worked the plantations.

Originally from Mexico, sisal was introduced to Brazil early in this century and reached the *sertáo* in the 1930's. Farmers found sisal useful for hedgerows because its tough, pointed leaves effectively kept out cattle. The cellulose core of the long sisal leaf contains hard fiber which can be twisted together into twine and rope. When World War II cut off the supply of Manila hemp to the United States, buyers turned to Brazil for fiber. At first only hedgerow sisal was exploited, but the state of Bahia offered incentives for planting sisal as a cash crop. Since sisal plants require about four years to mature, Brazil did not begin to export the fiber in significant quantities until 1945. The demand persisted, and by 1951, Brazil was selling actively in the world market as prices rose.

In Vila Nova, a young entrepreneur who owned a mule team, David Castro, heard about the prices being paid for sisal fiber and planted the first acres of sisal in 1951. By 1968, in the county of Victoria where Vila Nova is located, so many people had caught "sisal fever" that half of the total land area was planted in the crop. Sisal is easily transplanted and cultivated, requires little care, and is highly resistant to drought. It has some drawbacks as a cultivated plant, however. At least one annual weeding is necessary or else the field may become choked with thorn bushes, weeds, and suckers (unwanted small sisal plants growing from the base of parent plants). A field abandoned for two years becomes unusable, practically unreclaimable. Despite these difficulties, many landowners planted sisal, especially in 1951 and 1962, years of high prices on the world market.

From the outset, sisal produced differential rewards for those who planted it. Owners of small plots (ten acres or less) planted proportionately more of their land in sisal than did large landowners. Many who owned just a few acres simply planted all their land in sisal in expectation of large profits. This deprived them of whatever subsistence they had managed to scratch out of the ground in the past. But work was easy to find because the need for labor in the sisal fields grew rapidly. When, after four years, the crops were ready to harvest, many small landholders discovered to their dismay that prices had dropped sharply, and that harvest teams did not want to work small crops. They had planted sisal with dreams of new clothes, new homes, even motor vehicles purchased with sisal profits, but found their fields choked with unusable sisal and became permanent field laborers harvesting sisal on large landholdings. In this way, sisal created its own labor force.

The separation of sisal fiber from the leaf is known as decortication. In Brazil, this process requires enormous amounts of manual labor. The decorticating machine is basically a spinning rasp powered by a gasoline or diesel motor. Sisal leaves are fed into it by hand, and the spinning rasp beats out the pulp or residue leaving only the fibers, which the worker pulls out of the whirling blades. Mounted on a trailer, the machine is well adapted to the scattered small-scale plantations of northeastern Brazil.

The decortication process requires constant labor for harvesting the year round. Sisal leaves, once cut, must be defibered quickly before the hot sun renders them useless. Each decorticating machine requires a crew of about seven working in close coordination. The first step is harvesting. Two cutters move from plant to plant, first lopping off the needle-sharp thorns from the leaves, then stooping to sever each leaf at the base. A transporter, working with each cutter, gathers the leaves and loads them on a burro. The leaves are taken to the machine and placed on a low stage for the defiberer to strip, one by one. A residue man removes the pulpy mass stripped from the leaves from under the motor, supplies the defiberer with leaves, and bundles and ties the freshly stripped fiber. Each bundle is weighed and counted in the day's production. Finally, the dryer spreads the wet, greenish fiber in the sun, where it dries and acquires its characteristic blond color.

For the planters and sisal buyers, this method of decortication operates profitably, but for the workers it exacts a terrible cost. The decorticating machine requires a man to stand in front of the whirling rasp for four or five hours at a shift, introducing first the foot and then the point of each leaf. The worker pulls against the powerful motor, which draws the leaf into the mouth of the machine. After half of each leaf is defibered, the defiberer grasps the raw fiber to insert the re-

maining half of the leaf. There is a constant danger that the fiber will entangle his hand and pull it into the machine. Several defiberers have lost arms this way. The strain and danger would seem to encourage slow and deliberate work: but in fact, defiberers decorticate about 25 leaves per minute. This is because the crew is paid according to the day's production of fiber. Although the defiberer is the highest-paid crew member, many of them must work both morning and afternoon shifts to make ends meet.

A residue man's work is also strenuous. According to measurements I made, this job requires that a man lift and carry about 2,700 pounds of material per hour. The residue man, moreover, does not work in shifts. He works as long as the machinery is running. The remaining jobs on the crew are less demanding and may be held by women or adolescents, but even these jobs are hard, requiring frequent lifting and stooping in the broiling semidesert sun.

With their own fields in sisal, to earn money the villagers had to work at harvesting

sisal for large landowners. And because wages were low, more and more people had to work for families to survive. In 1968 two-thirds of all men and women employed in Vila Nova worked full time in the sisal decorticating process. Many of these were youths. Of 33 village boys between the ages of 10 and 14, 24 worked on sisal crews. Most people had completely abandoned subsistence agriculture.

Sisal brought other significant changes in the life of Vila Nova. Because most villagers no longer grew their food, it now had to be imported. Numerous shops, stocking beans, salt pork, and manioc flour, grew up in the village. A few villagers with capital or good contacts among wholesalers in the town of Victoria built small businesses based on this need. Other villagers secured credit from sisal buyers in Victoria to purchase sisal decorticating machinery.

The shopkeepers and sisal machine owners in the village formed a new economic class on whom the other villagers were economically dependent. The wealthier group enjoyed many advantages. Rather than going to work on the sisal machines, most of the children of these entrepreneurs went to school. All of the upper group married in a socially prescribed way: usually a church wedding with civil ceremonies as well. But among the workers, common-law marriages were frequent, reflecting their lack of resources for celebrating this important event.

The only villagers who became truly affluent were David Castro and his cousin. These men each owned extensive sisal plantations and several decorticating units. Most importantly, each became middlemen, collecting sisal in warehouses in the village and trucking the fiber into Victoria. David, moreover, owned the largest store in the village. Since the village was located on David's land, he sold house plots along the streets. He also acted as the representative of the dominant political party in Victoria, serving as a ward boss during elections and an unofficial but effective police power. There was a difference between David and the large ranch owners of the past. While wealthy men were formerly on close terms with their dependents, helping them out during tough times, David's relations with the villagers were cold, business-like, and exploitative. Most of the villagers disliked him, both for his alleged stinginess and because be never had time to talk to anyone.

During my stay in Vila Nova I gradually became aware of these changes in the social and economic structure. But I hoped to establish that the introduction of sisal had also resulted in a quantitative, ecological change in the village. At the suggestion of Dr. Barbara A. Underwood of the Institute of Human Nutrition at

Calorie Budget of a Sisal Worker's Household

	Average Daily Calorie Intake	Minimum Daily Calorie Requirements	Percent of Need Met	Percent of Standard Weight of Children
Household	9,392	12,592	75%	
Worker	3,642	3,642	100	
Wife	2,150	2,150	100	
Son (age 8)	1,112	2,100	53	62%
Daughter (6)	900	1,700	53	70
Son (5)	900	1,700	53	85
Son (3)	688	1,300	53	90

Columbia University, I undertook an intensive study to determine what influence sisal had on diet and other factors of a few representative households. When I looked at household budgets, I quickly discovered that those households that depended entirely on wages from sisal work spent nearly all their money on food. Families with few or no children or with several able-bodied workers seemed to be holding their own. But families with few workers or several dependents were less fortunate. To understand the condition of these families, I collected information not only on cash budgets but also on household *energy budgets.* Each household expends not only money, but also energy in the form of calories in performing work. "Income" in the latter case is the caloric value of the foods consumed by these households. By carefully measuring the amount and kind of food consumed, I was able to determine the total inflow and outflow of energy in individual households.

For example, Miguel Costa is a residue man who works steadily on a sisal unit belonging to a nearby planter. He lives in Vila Nova in a two-room adobe hut with his wife and four small children, ranging in age from three to eight. During the seven-day test period, Miguel worked at the sisal motor four and a half days, while his wife stayed home with the children. I was able to estimate Miguel's calorie expenditures during the test period. During the same period, I visited his home after every meal where his wife graciously permitted me to weigh the family's meager food supplies to determine food consumption. Each day the supply of beans diminished by less than one-half pound and the weight of the coarse manioc flour eaten with beans dropped by two or three pounds. Manioc flour is almost pure starch, high in calories but low in essential nutrients. At the beginning of the week about half a pound of fatty beef and pork were consumed each day, but this was exhausted by midweek. The remainder of the family's calories were consumed in the form of sugar, bread, and boiled sweet manioc, all high in calories but low in other nutrients.

Estimating the caloric requirements of the two adults from their activities and the children's by Food and Agriculture Organization minimum requirements, the household had a minimum need of 88,142 calories for the week. The household received only 65,744 calories, or 75 percent of need. Since the two adults did not lose weight while maintaining their regular levels of activity, they were apparently meeting their total calorie requirements. Miguel, for example, had been working steadily at his job for weeks before the test and continued to do so for weeks afterward. Had he not been maintaining himself calorically, he could not have sustained his performance at his demanding job. Despite his small stature (5 feet, 4 inches) Miguel required some 3,642 calories per day to keep going at the job. And Miguel's wife evidently also maintained herself calorically—pregnant at the time of my visit, she later gave birth to a normal child.

The caloric deficit in Miguel's household, then, was almost certainly being made up by systematically depriving the dependent children of sufficient calories. This was not intentional, nor were the parents aware of it. Nor could Miguel have done anything about it even if he had understood this process. If he were to work harder or longer to earn more money, he would incur greater caloric costs and would have to consume more. If he were to reduce his food intake to leave more food for his children, he would be obliged by his own physiology to work less, thereby earnings less. If he were to provide his household with foods higher in caloric content (for example, more manioc), he would almost certainly push his children over the brink into a severe nutritional crisis that they might not survive for lack of protein and essential vitamins. Thus, Miguel, a victim of ecological circumstances, is maintaining his family against terrible odds.

Miguel's children respond to this deprivation in a predictable manner. Nature has provided a mechanism to compensate for caloric deficiencies during critical growth periods: the rate of growth simply slows down. As a result, Miguel's children, and many other children of sisal workers, are much smaller than properly nourished children of the same age. The longer the deprivation goes on the more pronounced the tendency; thus Miguel's youngest boy, who is three, is 90 percent of standard weight for his age. The five-year-old boy is 85 percent; the six-year-old girl, 70 percent; and the oldest boy, at eight, is only 62 percent of standard weight. Caloric deprivation takes its toll in other ways than stunting. Caloric and other nutritional deficiencies are prime causes of such problems as reduced mental capacity and lower resistance to infection. In Vila Nova one-third of all children die by the age of 10.

When I surveyed the nutritional status of the people of Vila Nova, I found a distinct difference between the average body weights of the two economic groups formed since the introduction of sisal (shopkeepers and motor-owners on the one hand and workers on the other). Since the introduction of sisal the upper economic group exhibited a marked improvement in nutritional status (as measured by body weight) while the lower group showed a decline in nutritional status. The statistics showed that while one group was better off than before, a majority of the population was actually worse off nutritionally.

This conclusion was unexpected in view of the widespread claim that sisal had brought widespread benefits to the people of the *sertão,* that sisal had narrowed the gap between the rich and the poor. Clearly, changes had come about. Towns like Victoria had grown far beyond their presisal size.

But outside the towns, in the villages and rural farmsteads, the picture is different. Having abandoned subsistence agriculture, many workers moved to villages to find work on sisal units. In settlements such as Vila Nova wages and profits depend on the world price for sisal. When I arrived in 1967, the price was at the bottom of a trough that had paralyzed all growth and construction. Wages were so low that outmigration was showing signs of resuming as in the drought years. In spite of local symbols of wealth and "development," my observations revealed a continuation of endemic poverty throughout most of the countryside and even an intensification of the social and economic divisions that have always characterized the *sertão.*

Sisal is not the only example of an economic change that has brought unforeseen, deleterious consequences. The underdeveloped world is replete with examples of development schemes that brought progress only to a privileged few. The example of sisal in northeast Brazil shows that an ecological approach is needed in all economic planning. Even more important, we must recognize that not all economic growth brings social and economic development in its true sense. As the sisal example shows, a system may be formed (often as part of a worldwide system) that only increases the store of human misery.

28

Plants, Genes and People: Improving the Relevance of Plant Breeding in Africa

Angelique Haugerud and Michael P. Collinson

Plant breeders cannot respond to every quirk of farmers' circumstances but the relevance of breeding research in poor nations can be improved. Recent innovations in germplasm screening programmes for developing nations highlight important differences in selection criteria between farmers and scientists, and among farmers themselves. Drawing on the authors' African experience with International Agricultural Research Centres working on maize and potatoes, the paper explores how breeding programmes benefit from an understanding of farmers' own detailed knowledge about the crop varieties they already cultivate. Issues considered include farmers' use of cultivar diversity, the trade-off between yield and maturity class as selection criteria, defining appropriate experimental conditions, and innovative techniques to increase farmer participation in germplasm screening.

Introduction

Plant breeding dominates international agricultural research, accounting for about 50% of the budgets of the International Agricultural Research Centres (IARCs) (Simmonds, 1984). Recent innovations in breeding programmes for developing nations highlight differences in selection criteria between farmers and scientists, and among farmers themselves. Scientists' and farmers' assessments of new crop varieties diverge, not because farmers lack formal scientific knowledge, but because scientists often fail to use farmers' knowledge and to accommodate their constraints. Farmers' own cultivar preferences vary according to characteristics such as farm size, family structure, gender, wealth, and market opportunities. Overlooking both types of divergence in breeding criteria carries the twin risks of releasing new crop varieties farmers do not adopt, and rejecting germplasm farmers find

---

valuable. Ignoring the differences can also mean a breeding programme's new cultivars reach only a narrow range of farmers. This paper addresses ways to reduce such risks.

Plant Breeding and the IARCs in Africa

In Africa, the International Agricultural Research Centres have spent more per head, hectare and tonne of food, with less to show (as yet) for the effort than elsewhere (de Janvry and Dethier, 1985). Africa's position in the world economy, its diverse environments, economies and sociopolitical systems all contrast sharply with the conditions of the Asian "Green Revolution." Communications, food transport costs, the means to distribute agricultural inputs on time, water availability, soils and climatic conditions are all less favourable in Africa than in Asia. Foreign exchange to import chemicals and fertilizers is scarce, and both foreign and domestic terms of trade often work against agriculture. African farmers diversify their economic pursuits and limit their dependence on uncertain markets and government services.

Wheat and rice, Asia's food staples, are luxuries in Africa. African staples such as sorghum, millet, cassava, chickpeas and cowpeas have only recently received research attention from both national programmes and IARCs, as have regions with poor soils and low and unreliable rainfall.

Africa's national research institutions often retain the orientations of western agricultural education (Collinson, 1988). University agricultural curricula are still centred on large fields, machines, straight lines and intensive management. These biases threaten the long-term sustainability of African agricultural systems, and limit the relevance of national and international research. Relevance is also jeopardized by a single-discipline focus, narrow peer group evaluation, unquestioning adherence to inherited breeding strategies, and inadequate exposure of plant breeders to small farmers' circumstances.

Traditional western agricultural curricula, for example, discount intercropping, though many plant scientists today recognize that insufficient research has been done on possible positive interactions of species and cultivars planted in mixtures (Altieri, 1985; Thresh, 1982; Willey 1979). Complementary effects involving the uptake of soil nutrients or water, for example, are poorly understood (Willey, 1979), as is the degree to which crop and cultivar mixtures may slow the spread of pathogens and pests. Yet intercropping research in Africa is often considered a retrograde step.

Attempts in the last decade to institutionalize processes for agricultural researchers (both national and international) to learn directly from farmers, and for farmers themselves to do more than react to scientists' proposals have been dominated by various types of farming systems research (FSR) (Byerlee *et al.*, 1982; Collinson, 1982, 1985, 1988; DeWalt, 1985; Eicher and Baker, 1982; Gilbert *et al.*, 1980; Hildebrand, 1981; Horton, 1986; Merrill-Sands, 1986; Moock, 1986; Norman, 1980; Norman *et al.*, 1982; Rhoades, 1985b; Shaner *et al.*, 1982). Though the term FSR itself has become controversial, its basic principles are of lasting importance. These include the need for close collaboration among technical scientists (both physical and biological) and social scientists; the usefulness of multi- rather than single-commodity approaches (since farmers themselves pursue multiple enterprises and evaluate technical innovations in any one crop in the context of the systems they operate); and explicit recognition that the farmer and other agents in the food system are the primary clients of agricultural research, and that farmers' current production systems must be understood in order to design and assess on-farm and on-station experimental programmes intended to improve production (see IARCs, 1987).

The less effective alternative has been for researchers to seek the optimal way to grow crops and to expect farmers to adjust to these requirements. When scientists' selections of new crop varieties are based solely on features of the natural environment (such as rainfall, soils and temperatures), farmers may reject the high-yielding varieties scientists most admire. More than maximum yield, African cultivators often favour yield stability, short maturation periods, suitability for intercropping, storability and particular taste or cooking characteristics.

This paper focuses on two important modern African food staples—maize and potatoes—and draws on the authors' east African experience with the two IARCs concerned with these crops. Collinson, an economist, was with the International Maize and Wheat Improvement Centre (CIMMYT) regional office in Nairobi from 1976 to 1987. Haugerud, an anthropologist, was a postdoctoral research fellow (funded in part by the Rockefeller Foundation) with the International Potato Centre (CIP) in eastern Africa from 1984 to 1986.

An essential starting point when defining breeding criteria is farmers' own detailed knowledge about cultivars. Plant selection can be oriented, at least in part, to replacing specific cultivars important to farmers.

How African Farmers Use Cultivar Diversity

Breeding programmes have rarely exploited small farmers' sophisticated knowledge of differences among cultivars, and their use of these differences in cropping strategies. (One recent exception is a participatory rice breeding programme in India described by Maurya *et al.*, 1988). Cultivators classify varieties, and value particular characteristics, for different purposes. They often manage a combination of cultivars in the production process, and multiply or eliminate varieties as they evaluate their performance over time (see Brush *et al.*, 1980; Conklin, 1980, 1988; Rhoades, 1985a; Richards, 1985).

Farmers themselves are expert experimenters with new plant materials (see Johnson, 1971; Ninez, 1984; Rhoades, 1987; Richards,

1985). When testing promising new plant genotypes, scientists can improve the relevance of their research by drawing upon farmers' own informal methods of experimenting with unfamiliar cultivars and practices. Farm innovators over thousands of years have enabled the human population to double ten times since agriculture began, including eight doublings *before* industrialization and the use of fossil fuels:

The human population expanded as traditional agricultural societies learned to domesticate animals, select crop varieties, manage weeds and insects, and enhance nutrient recycling. Both ecosystems and social systems were modified to sustain improved agricultural technologies. The transformations occurred through experimentation, fortuitous mistakes, and natural selection. (Norgaard, 1985)

African farmers are less likely than scientific breeders to seek a single best cultivar for any given crop. Instead, an accepted new cultivar usually joins other valued genotypes of the same crop in a farmer's fields. Mixed stands (of cultivars as well as species) are conventional. Plant breeders can ease their own task by combining groups of relatively compatible traits into different cultivars in the knowledge that farmers will readily manage more than one.

Yield stability in Africa, unlike that in industrial economies, depends on a patchwork of many different varieties planted on the same farm, rather than on a continuous supply of new cultivars (Plucknett and Smith, 1986). In the West, rapid evolution of new races of pathogens prompts a frequent turnover of cultivars of such crops as wheat, for which the average lifespan of a new variety in northwestern U.S. is only five years (Plucknett and Smith, 1986). Wheat mixtures have recently been rediscovered as a means of managing pathogens. The biological hazards of genetic homogeneity in the U.S. are demonstrated by the speed with which Florida's citrus crop succumbed to citrus canker bacterial infection in the mid-1980s, and by the devastating southern corn leaf blight in 1970. In

1983, for example, 86% of Florida's commercial orange harvest consisted of just three varieties, while two-thirds of its grapefruit crop was made up of a single strain (MacFadyen, 1985).

In developing countries, cultivar specialization may increase short-term profits for a few large farmers, but threaten the long-term environmental and economic sustainability of production. The IARCs can help national programmes to reduce the likelihood of epidemics caused by breakdown of monogenic resistance in popular cultivars.

In addition to epidemiological reasons for monitoring cultivar specialization in Africa, the local relevance of breeding agendas depends upon understanding farmers' everyday strategies of cultivar diversification. Some maize and potato examples illustrate this point.

How Rwandan Farmers Use Potato Cultivar Diversity

In Rwanda, the surprising popularity of one degenerated potato cultivar (degeneration refers to accumulation of viruses), together with other aspects of existing diversification strategies, contributed to a shift in emphasis in the national germplasm screening programme.

Farmers in Rwanda recognize several dozen different potato varieties, which they distinguish according to plant and tuber traits, as well as agronomic and culinary characteristics. In Haugerud's field research, over 65 different names of potato varieties were elicited from farmers across several agroecological zones of Rwanda. Cultivar names are not necessarily consistent across localities or regions, and electrophoretic protein band analysis suggested that possibly 20% of the names are synonyms.

Most Rwandan potato farmers grow three to eight different cultivars at once. They mix cultivars within fields, and use variability in traits such as the length of the growth cycle, dormancy (time elapsed between physiological maturity and sprouting), disease resistance (particularly late blight), tolerance of rainfall

excesses and deficits, and dry matter content (which affects taste and storability) to manage the vagaries of both nature and the market (see Durr, 1980; Poats, 1981; Scott, 1988).

Since most potato varieties introduced into Rwanda before the late 1970s were from a relatively narrow genetic base (European-adapted *Solanum tuberosum*), cultivar diversity provides less protection against environmental hazards than in the crop's Andean homeland. Nonetheless, Rwandan farmers do use the available diversity to help reduce their production, consumption and marketing risks, and to spread labour requirements and food supplies more evenly across the annual cycle. Cultivar mixtures allow the use of staggered harvests and varied growth cycles, which permit farmers to extend the period of fresh food and cash availability.

Distinctions between "traditional" and "modern" varieties, always problematic, are quickly blurred in Rwanda, where potatoes have only been grown for about a century, and where in recent decades dozens of cultivars have been introduced, from Europe and South America in particular. The four most frequently grown potato cultivars in Rwanda (Montsama, Sangema, Gashara, and Muhabura) have diverse origins. Agricultural research institutions introduced Montsama and Sangema into Rwanda from Mexico in the 1970s, and Gashara from Europe a number of decades ago. Farmers and traders probably brought Muhabura into Rwanda from Uganda. Montsama, Muhabura and Sangema were multiplied and distributed by the Rwandan national potato research programme (PNAP) in the late 1970s and early 1980s.

Farmers rate these four popular cultivars as having distinctly different maturity and dormancy periods, water content, cooking time, storability, late blight resistance, market acceptability, response to moisture stress, and suitability for intercropping (see Table 28.1 and Haugerud, 1988). The variety Muhabura, for example, though disliked for its taste and poor storability, is appreciated for its short dormancy. Farmers appreciate Sangema for its taste, market acceptability, yields under good

Table 28.1 Farmers' Assessments of the Four Most Frequently Grown Potato Cultivars in Rwanda (Percentage of 186 farmers interviewed from four cultivation zones citing each characteristic)

	Cultivar			
	Montsama	Sangema	Gashara	Muhabura
Growth cycle				
Long	1	59	0	55
Medium	22	25	0	28
Short	77	16	100	17
Dormancy				
Long	8	86	13	14
Medium	23	7	4	42
Short	69	7	83	44
Taste				
Good	93	84	100	14
Medium	6	15	0	39
Poor	1	1	0	46
Starch content				
High	88	60	97	4
Medium	12	28	3	25
Low	0	12	0	71
Cooking time				
Long	0	9	0	48
Medium	18	18	2	26
Short	82	73	98	26
Storability				
Good	38	58	67	22
Medium	22	23	17	36
Poor	40	19	15	42
Yield under good rainfall				
Good	57	84	41	63
Medium	34	12	43	12
Poor	9	4	16	25
Yield under poor rainfall				
Good	44	49	35	30
Medium	31	34	33	42
Poor	25	17	32	28
Late blight resistance				
Good	38	50	14	27
Medium	26	32	26	22
Poor	36	18	60	51
Bacterial wilt tolerance				
Good	47	56	53	40
Medium	19	20	26	30
Poor	34	24	21	30
Market acceptability				
Good	89	88	33	9
Medium	11	11	14	30
Poor	0	1	52	61
Suitability for intercropping				
Good	64	33	55	12
Medium	32	32	28	45
Poor	4	35	17	43

rainfall, and late blight resistance (which Rwandan farmers equate with good yield under heavy rain), though they appreciate less its long dormancy and long growth cycle.

The degenerated cultivar Gashara would have been abandoned long ago if disease resistance and yield were farmers' sole decision criteria. Many farmers continue to cultivate Gashara, however, because of its short growth cycle, short cooking time, short dormancy, and good taste (low water content). The continued popularity of this cultivar suggests one neglected strategy for current breeding and germplasm screening. We return later to this and other implications of the farm survey work for germplasm screening in Rwanda.

East African Farmers' Use of Maize Cultivar Diversity

Farmers recognize in maize, as in potato cultivars, important differences in taste, texture, storability, marketability, disease and pest resistance, and response to moisture stress. At least nine possible end uses, many of them simultaneously relevant on a single farm, help to determine the maize genotypes eastern African farmers prefer. The crop may, for example, be consumed at home green or dry, brewed for beer, or sold green or dry. In addition, the plant and grain may be used green at various stages of maturity, or dry as food for livestock. Cultivar mixtures in maize, a sexually-reproduced, allogamous species, behave differently from those in an inbred, vegetatively-propagated crop such as potatoes. The "purity" of individual cultivars planted in field mixtures is less in an outbreeder such as maize, while the possibilities for farmers themselves to improve the crop through rustic forms of recurrent selection are greater.

As in the case of potatoes, many farmers plant both early and late maturing maize cultivars in order to manage seasonal food gaps, to meet varied end uses of the crop, and to manage environmental hazards (uncertain rainfall, diseases, pests). Maize farmers in parts of Zambia, for example, plant traditional short-term cultivars (100–120 days) early in the season to obtain food and because they taste better as green maize than do the later-maturing hybrids SR52 and ZH1 (170 days), which are produced mainly for sale. Some farmers respond to poor maize harvests and impending food scarcity by planting local early-maturing maize varieties before the start of the new season in low-lying areas with a high water table (CIMMYT, 1978). Zambian farmers give priority to the planting of traditional varieties, which delays planting of the hybrids that require a 170-day season; 25% of the hybrids are planted with only 125 remaining days of rain. When asked whether an improved 120-day cultivar would be useful to them, 96% of the farmers thought it would, and 63% mentioned the advantage of early food (CIMMYT, 1978).

In Zimbabwe, farmers in Mangwende use maize varieties with differing times to maturity (such as SR52, R201 and R200) to manage the variable timing of the rains. An October start to the rainy season results in first plantings of SR52, a 170-day variety with high yield potential. If farmers have to replant because of early drought, or delay planting because of late onset of the rains, they switch to shorter-cycle cultivars such as R201 or R200 (both 135–140 days). Multiple plantings are common, and late plantings of R201 or R200 extend into January. Late plantings help to insure against losses in the crop planted earlier and allow a spread of oxen use over a longer period (Shumba, 1985).

The relative economic value of maize stover and grain also affects farmers' choice of cultivar. Breeders need to determine the appropriate harvest index (ratio of stover to grain) in the context of local production priorities. Where pressures on dry season feed are increasing, the market for fodder expands and maize stover quality and quantity become increasingly important criteria in farmers' cultivar choice. Maize stover markets are emerging in Zimbabwe, where cattle owners collect their stalks for dry-season feed, and where noncattle owners traditionally exchange access to stover in their fields for access to hired draught power from cattle owners (CIMMYT, 1982). In Somalia, there is a market for maize stalks that have been cut

Table 28.2 Sources of Feed for Dairy Animals in Western Kenya

	Farmers (%)	Relative Importance of Source (% farmers)				
		1	2	3	4	Less Important
Grazing						
own farm	100	100	—	—	—	—
commons	79	—	25	4	4	46
neighbouring farms	67	—	—	—	—	67
Maize						
green stalks	96	—	42	42	8	4
dry stalks	83	—	4	29	17	33
leaves	25	—	—	—	—	25
Banana leaves/stems	42	—	—	—	—	42
Sugar cane tops	50	—	—	—	—	50

and dried. In land-scarce central Kenya, some farmers prefer to plant a proportion of their land to the 600-series maize hybrids, rather than the 500-series recommended for the zone, because its larger plant structure provides more biomass for stall feeding of dairy cattle, a major source of cash for many households.

Farmers in the densely-settled parts of western Kenya show the same interest in maize stover. Both green plant material and dry maize stover are important sources of cattle feed. Identification of this interest by farm surveys (Table 28.2) led to proposals for two adaptive experimental programmes (Wangia, 1980). One was to examine the increase in maize plant density needed to increase fodder production without sacrificing grain yields in both the long and short rains. The second was to examine the effects on grain and fodder yields of alternative times of picking the leaves and tops of maize when green.

Breeding Implications of Farmers' Cultivar Diversification

In industrialized economies, field mechanization and consumer markets favour genotypic and phenotypic uniformity. Standardized plants and products are less relevant to Africa's resource-poor farmers. Crop breeding in Africa can benefit from the comparative advantage of the skilled labour of small farmers in handling cultivar diversity, and in giving detailed attention to individual plant types. Understanding decisions about the adoption of new cultivars requires knowledge of farmers' present diversification strategies. This is not to suggest that scientists cannot stimulate changes in existing cropping patterns or husbandry practices, or that farmers will adopt only those new cultivars that are higher-yielding replicates of currently popular varieties. Rather, researchers must consider carefully the costs and risks farmers face, before investing time and money in developing particular types of new cultivars.

Balancing Yield and Maturity Period as Selection Criteria

Conventional varietal selection based on yield favours later-maturing cultivars (given the correlation of yield and period of photosynthetic intake). Farmers, however, may adopt shorter-term varieties in agroclimatic zones where long-duration cultivars offer higher biomass and yields. The rationale for such a choice becomes apparent once the scientist's analytical framework shifts from the individual cultivar to a multi-crop and multiple season perspective. Rather than assume farmers will accommodate any maturity period in a high-yielding cultivar, breeders must first assess local constraints on maturity periods and then select for high yields within locally appropriate maturity classes.

Although farmers are skilled at managing cultivar diversity (including multiple maturity periods), even minor departures from current types can have wide ramifications for cash flow and food security. If land is scarce, for example, adoption of a longer-maturing cultivar may mean an unaffordable delay in the planting of another essential food staple on the same plot. A new variety may require earlier planting or harvesting of a previous season's crop on the same land. It may compete for scarce labour at critical points in the production cycles of other crops. A later-maturing cultivar may introduce a constraint in the family consumption calendar if its longer period in the field coincides with a period when food substitutes are unavailable. It may introduce a family cash constraint if delayed harvest prolongs a period of cash shortage. In short, single-crop or commodity research programmes cannot ignore other crops and enterprises that compete for farmers' land, labour and cash resources, and that help farmers meet their food and cash needs.

In addition, under conditions of bimodal rainfall and land scarcity, single season yields may be less important to small farmers than annual productivity. In this situation farmers may choose to plant the combination of cultivars that gives the best yields in two growing seasons, rather than a single cultivar that gives the best yield in one season but precludes a second crop the same year and therefore forces the farmer to purchase food on an expensive preharvest market. Some examples from areas where land is scarce and rainfall bimodal illustrate these points.

Maize Maturity Classes in Western Kenya

Farming systems research has highlighted the disadvantage of the highest-yielding hybrids in western Kenya's densely settled, high rainfall zone. Here rainfall averages 1500+

mm (bimodally distributed), and with up to 600 persons km^{-2} a high proportion of holdings are little more than one-half hectare per family. The long maturation period of the high-yielding 600-series Kitale hybrids makes it difficult to plant a second maize crop. The hybrids are planted in March and not harvested until mid-September. Because rainfall is unreliable from December to February, the late-standing 600-series crop leaves only 100 days for replanting with a second maize crop in the last months of the year. The second maize crop is essential to poorer families who have little land because maize prices in July and August (before the new long rains harvest) often reach three or four times the post-harvest prices. Unless they plant a second crop, small farmers are forced to buy maize for food at high prices and then, for lack of cash, or because they have mortgaged the crop to buy food earlier, they are forced to sell their crop at low post-harvest prices. Such food purchases take precedence over input purchases from their limited cash resources.

In recognition of farmers' need to secure a second crop, new on-farm experimental research began to reconsider cultivar recommendations. Trials were designed to compare the performance of maize varieties in the 130- to 180-day range in the long (March to August) and short (August to December) rainfall periods and to identify the varietal combination that gives the best production over the two seasons (Collinson, 1985).

Experiments were also designed to evaluate the profitability of earlier maturing maize cultivars. An early-planted, early-maturing cultivar can command three to four times the price of the normal post-harvest maize. A short-duration cultivar could be grown either for food security, to avoid the need to buy maize on the expensive pre-harvest market, or for profit to exploit this market. Such a cultivar, even with only half the yield potential, will still be twice as profitable as a full-season cultivar if its earliness allows it to catch the high prices (until wide adoption of short-duration cultivars reduces seasonal price fluctuations).

Short-duration cultivars are also advantageous in managing climatic as well as market hazards. Research in southern Zimbabwe, for example, showed that a shorter-duration maize cultivar (shorter than the 135–140 day R201 variety currently in use) would improve farmers' flexibility to manage mid-season droughts (CIMMYT, 1982).

Maize Maturity Classes in Burundi

Farmers in Burundi rejected a new late-maturing (220-day), high-yielding maize variety although it yielded 20 to 40% more than cultivars released previously (Zeigler, 1986) because they had to wait six weeks longer to harvest it, so that the new variety did not permit a good second pea crop. Field trials based on farmers' traditional practices showed that the higher yields of the late-maturing maize cultivar occurred at the expense of family food security and nutritional balance, since it did not fit into the complex local system of intercropping maize and beans and relay cropping maize with peas. The late maize also had less stable yields.

In such a situation, selecting a new cultivar on the basis of single crop yield trials (rather than the mixed cropping and relay cropping actually practised by local farmers) may result in the release of a cultivar that is incompatible with farmers' needs and limitations, and that actually decreases their nutritional and economic well-being.

Potato Maturity Classes in Rwanda

In Rwanda (the most densely populated country in sub-Saharan Africa) extreme land scarcity (see UNICEF, 1985), bimodal rainfall, and late blight all affect farmers' potato maturity class preferences. Rainfall distribution permits double, and in some zones multiple, cropping of potatoes. Late blight increases with the spread of fungal spores in heavy rain, and farmers' traditional means of coping with the disease is to plant late in the rainy season. Although higher-yielding, later-maturing (120+ days) potato cultivars resistant to late blight became locally available in the late 1970s, by the mid-1980s few farmers chose to rely on

them. Short-duration cultivars allowed them greater flexibility in managing very scarce land resources, in dealing with uncertain rainfall distribution, and in managing food and cash needs.

For example, some farmers in the northern volcanic soils zone (e.g., at 2300 m altitude) intercrop potatoes (planted in April/May and harvested in August/September) with maize (planted in May and harvested in January). After the potato harvest, they plant beans in the same maize field in September and harvest them in December and January. The longer the cycle of the potato crop, the more difficult it becomes to get the bean relay crop planted in time to catch the short rains.

In zones where peas are grown, potatoes enter the type of intercrop and relay crop system Zeigler (1986) describes for maize in Burundi. Potatoes and beans are intercropped with maize, then peas are added to the maize field once the potatoes and beans have been harvested. Here again, shorter-cycle potato cultivars are an advantage.

Nearly all of 186 Rwandan farmers interviewed in four production zones stated a preference for either short-duration cultivars alone (70–90 days), or for a mixture of early, medium and late cultivars (see Haugerud, 1988). Almost none (2%) preferred to rely on long-cycle cultivars alone. One rationale for the mixed strategy is that short-cycle cultivars, by filling food and cash gaps, enable some farmers to grow longer-cycle varieties as well. Wealthier farmers with large land holdings can devote more land to late cultivars. Given the nearly universal demand for some early cultivars, the Rwandan germplasm screening and seed production programme, which had previously emphasized late cultivars, recently increased the emphasis on short-duration cultivars. Previously, the programme had taken insufficient account of the multi-crop and multiple-season framework in which farmers decide what cultivars to adopt.

Most Rwandan farmers also prefer either to maintain diversity in length of dormancy by planting some cultivars with short and some with longer dormancy (54% of the farmers surveyed), or to plant only short-dormancy cultivars (43%). Nearly all farmers reject exclusive reliance on cultivars with longer dormancies (over three months), since the trait is a disadvantage under the highland cropping calendar and rainfall pattern. To avoid long seed storage, some farmers use treatments such as pit storage to break dormancy earlier.

Defining Appropriate Maturity Classes

Land and labour availability, rainfall distribution and reliability, and farmers' wealth are all crucial determinants of appropriate maturity classes. Farmers' flexibility in managing environmental hazards and domestic food and cash needs is greater if they cultivate either short-duration cultivars or a mixture of long and short, than if they rely only on long-duration cultivars, in spite of the latter's yield advantage. Short-duration cultivars in some environments have more stable yields, and are a particular advantage for resource-poor farmers who face volatile food markets, extreme land scarcity, and rainfall regimes that permit double cropping of the same land (see also Voss, 1989, on beans). Early cultivars are also an advantage in some unimodal rainfall systems where a draught power constraint prevents farmers from planting on time, or where unreliable rainfall means longer-duration cultivars have much less stable yields.

Once breeders determine appropriate maturity classes they must define experimental conditions for varietal selection. Like the trade-off between yield and maturity class, the definition of appropriate experimental conditions also challenges traditional research assumptions.

Defining Appropriate Experimental Conditions

Efforts to match the conditions of resource-poor farmers in experimental fields are controversial (Ter Horst and Watts, 1983). Should varietal selection on the research station be conducted under husbandry conditions beyond the reach of most African farmers? Identification of superior genotypes is more difficult under low input conditions, where heterogeneity makes it difficult to apply equal selection pressure over an entire plant population. More experimental replications are required, since differences in productivity may be small and statistical error large. Adjusting on-station research to farmers' practices and priorities can complicate experimental design and analysis. Moreover, it is impossible for scientists to evaluate breeding material over the full range of field conditions and cropping systems to which it will be exposed (Arnold and Innes, 1984).

Classic experimental methodology, however, has its own shortcomings. Both conscious and unconscious decisions by crop scientists produce more favourable crop environments on research stations than in farmers' fields, and lead breeders to select genotypes that respond well to favourable environments (see Maurya *et al.*, 1988; Simmonds, 1981, 1984). Non-experimental variables "may often represent future technical recommendations to farmers rather than farmers' current practices" (Ashby, 1986). Researchers disagree, however, about the implications of the well-known yield gap that results from differences between conditions on the research station and in the farmers' fields (see IRRI, 1979; Matlon and Spencer, 1984).

One problem is to identify the changes to farmers' practices and priorities which it is reasonable to expect them to adopt. The yield is in part due to circumstances beyond farmers' control (e.g., whether fertilizer or irrigation water arrives on time), as well as to farming practices that make good biological, economic or nutritional sense. Small farmers may use low inputs for a number of reasons: the mix of production, consumption, and marketing priorities within the farming system; limited cash resources; inadequate personal influence to obtain inputs; and limited capacity to risk high losses. Small cultivators operate multiple enterprises as an integrated system, which requires compromises in management, and therefore productivity, of any one constituent enterprise. Traditional mixed cropping is a further dimension of this systems context with its own implications for germplasm selection.

Dual selection strategies—with high input levels for wealthier farmers and low levels for resource-poor farmers—may be justified if, for the crop in question, there is significant intra-species variability under the selection pressures in the local environment (*i.e.*, important local differences in yield stability and average yields among cultivars of one species), and where a substantial proportion of farmers use low inputs in managing the species and are unlikely to change this practice because of their priorities and resource limitations.

Another way in which germplasm screening can take greater account of the diversity of actual farm conditions is to decentralize screening by the earlier release of promising material to farmers for testing in on-farm trials, as in a successful rainfed rice breeding programme in India (Maurya *et al.*, 1988).

When scientists define treatment and non-experimental variables for cultivar selection, they manipulate management practices such as time of planting, soil fertility, water availability, chemical protection against diseases and pests, intercropping, relay cropping, cultivar mixtures, crop rotation and plant spacing. The more explicitly they take such decisions from a knowledge of farmers' practices, and the less tied they are to traditional textbook experimental design, the more useful research results are likely to be. Some illustrations follow.

Time of Planting and Maize Performance

Maize yields are substantially reduced each day that planting is delayed after the onset of the rains (see Cooper and Law, 1977). Acland (1971) reported reductions of 55–110 kg ha^{-1} for each day planting was delayed in Kenya's Rift Valley Province, and as much as 170 kg ha^{-1} d^{-1} in the Eastern and Central Provinces, where the season is shorter. Labour and draught power constraints, however, lead many small farmers to continue to plant maize for two or even three months after the start of the rains. Seedbed preparation with a hand hoe, when the soil is inverted, requires up to 50 labour days per hectare.

In Zimbabwe, as population densities rise, the cultivated areas increase, grazing areas shrink, available draught power declines and the period required for cultivation lengthens. In addition to experimentation on reduced tillage to counter this trend, research has begun to focus on short-duration maize cultivars that can be planted late and still avoid the cut-off of the rains. Agronomic research must also address the significant interactions between time of planting, plant density and fertilizer level.

Contrary to conventional wisdom that late planting demonstrates small farmers' irrationality, scientists now recognize that labour and power constraints limit farmers' ability to plant at the "optimal" time. Indeed, the appropriate variety for small farmers will often be 20–30 days quicker maturing than the breeders' preferred full-season cultivar. In addition, some cultivators intentionally avoid planting early in order to reduce the risks from hazards such as uncertain rainfall or diseases and pests associated with rainfall. Interest has therefore grown in the effects of late planting on varietal choice, and in the selection of cultivars adapted to small farmers' power constraints.

Fertilizers and Maize

Agronomic recommendations aimed solely at yield maximization underestimate the importance of yield stability and hazard management to resource-poor farmers. Improved maize cultivars tested without fertilizers in on-farm trials in Malawi, for example, were more than twice as unstable as local maize. With fertilizer, yield stability improved for both local and improved maize, though the latter remained significantly less stable than the local maize (Hildebrand and Poey, 1985).

Farmers limit their use of purchased inputs such as fertilizers when they fear damaging losses from environmental hazards. Producers in southern Zimbabwe, for example, apply a basal dressing of compound fertilizer after rather than before the maize crop emerges, in order to reduce their losses from poor germination (Shumba, 1985). Such strategies will sometimes be sufficiently widespread to be included as non-experimental variables in varietal selection. The improved yield stability associated with such strategies can itself provide the foundation for a shift to higher inputs and more intensive husbandry.

Experimental Conditions and Potato Varietal Selection in Rwanda

One potato research programme in Rwanda owes its success in part to the screening of germplasm without fertilizers or fungicides. The programme recognized early that most farmers' only commercial inputs would be occasional seed purchases; since degeneration rates (accumulation of viruses) are low in the highlands, farmers can multiply their own seed for five to ten years. In order to benefit the minority of farmers who can afford other inputs, scientists in the Rwanda programme also carry out separate fungicide trials and train extension officers in their use. In its first five years Rwanda's low-input screening programme introduced six improved cultivars whose yields without chemical inputs were two to five times the previous national average (Bicamumpaka and Haverkort, 1983; Nganga, 1983; PNAP, 1984, 1985). Germplasm sources for the improved cultivars included South America, Mexico and Europe. Two previously introduced cultivars which the programme re-released in 1980 (Sangema and Montsama) were found in all the country's major potato producing regions in 1985. In nearly two-thirds of 360 potato fields observed in 1985, either Montsama or Sangema occupied the largest area (Haugerud, 1988).

Farmer surveys demonstrated the prevalence of intercropping in Rwandan potato fields. Recorded observations of 360 potato fields in all of the country's major production zones showed nearly half (47%) to be intercropped (Haugerud, 1988). The crops most often associated with potatoes were maize, beans, sorghum, colocasia and sweet potatoes. Government survey data showed that over half of Rwanda's total cultivated area was intercropped and that 48% of the area under potatoes was planted with crop mixtures (Government of Rwanda, 1985).

On-station trials then began to consider the comparative performance of the potato programme's improved cultivars in various crop associations. Trials of potatoes intercropped with maize in 1987 showed that land equivalent ratios increased with increasing plant densities, even when plant densities of associated crops were those normally used in pure stands (7.2 potato plants and 8.0 maize plants m^{-2}; preliminary results are reported by Jeroen Kloos in the 1987 CIP regional progress reports). Other trials are evaluating the performance (at varying plant densities) of early, medium and late potato cultivars planted in association with an early maize cultivar. Trials to test the performance of field mixtures of improved potato cultivars were also recommended, after farm surveys showed that most farmers grow three to five different potato cultivars at once, most of their fields being planted with cultivar mixtures.

Participatory Breeding Research

It is easy to assert that defining appropriate varietal screening priorities and experimental conditions requires frequent and direct communication both between farmers and researchers and between researchers of different disciplines (economists, anthropologists, breeders, agronomists, phytopathologists, soil specialists). Few biological scientists, however, are trained in techniques to elicit and to apply knowledge from farmers (see Richards, 1985; Brokensha *et al.*, 1980):

Although it sounds straightforward for scientists to learn from farmers, and to convene groups or panels or innovator workshops, how to do this is rarely part of scientists' training, and good methods are anyway not well known. Nor has discussion of such methods penetrated the harder professional literature. (Chambers and Jiggins, 1985)

After a decade of rhetoric about "feedback" of farmers' problems to extension workers and scientists, a large gap remains between the ideal and the reality.

Innovations in both training and methods are required to bridge this gap. To the usual on-station and on-farm trials, and formal and informal surveys, must be added less familiar approaches such as panels of farmers who regularly meet with and advise scientists, one-shot group interviews, the training of scientists in role reversal, workshops with innovative farmers, and village meetings in which farmers decide on the design of on-farm trials (see Ashby, 1986; Chambers and Jiggins, 1985; Biggs, 1988).

Farmers included in the design of on-farm trials can "contribute to defining evaluation criteria, before researchers screened out most of the options by fixing the experimental design" (Ashby, 1986). When setting up on-farm variety trials, scientists can begin by asking farmers how they themselves would test a new cultivar on their own land (Biggs, 1988). In addition, researchers can track farmers' own innovations, which take them beyond the limitations of reductionist methods of on-station trials, as they adapt new cultivars to complex intercropping, rotation and agroforestry practices, and as they exploit diverse microenvironments (Chambers and Jiggins, 1985).

The late 1970s saw a shift in emphasis in agricultural research from large, formal farm surveys to reconnaissance and exploratory surveys (see Chambers and Jiggins, 1985; Collinson, 1981; Hildebrand, 1981; Horton, 1986; Rhoades, 1985b). Collinson (1981) and Crawford and Franzel (1987) found that no major results from rigorous informal exploratory surveys contradicted those of later formal surveys. Formal surveys and systematic sampling by agroecological zone, farm size, or other criteria are sometimes useful at a later stage to refine or confirm findings from field observations and interviews in exploratory surveys, particularly if the latter suggest the need for programme changes.

Large-scale formal surveys, with their well-known problems of data reliability, sampling biases, logistical costliness, and lengthy processing requirements, are increasingly replaced by less formal and more innovative techniques. In such attempts, team work, rather than "lone ranger" research (Robert Rhoades' term) increases the credibility of results.

Farmer Participation in On-Station Germplasm Screening

In experimenting with methods in Rwanda's national potato research programme, some small farmers were invited to join scientists on the research station in the seasonal selection of advanced clones in the germplasm screening programme. Each year the Rwandan national potato research programme (PNAP) screens thousands of potato genotypes (a few of which are local crosses and most of which are imported from CIP's international and regional breeding programmes). PNAP selects and multiplies seed of improved cultivars after a number of seasons of testing on the experiment station, in multilocal trials, and finally in farmers' fields (see Bicamumpaka and Haverkort, 1983; Nganga, 1983; PNAP, 1984, 1985). Normally when on-station germplasm plots were harvested, the entire research team (breeder, agronomist, pathologist, anthropologist) were present to select by consensus genotypes to keep for further stages of testing and multiplication. In a novel initiative, farmers were invited to make their own selections from the station fields, and to explain their reasoning to scientists. Researchers found that they had previously assumed too narrow a range of local acceptability in traits such as tuber colour, size, shape and uniformity. Whereas some researchers, for example, had for years favoured red-skinned clones, farmers found red, white and purple skins all to be acceptable. The only skin types farmers strongly rejected were russets, which they believed to be diseased.

In other words, the scientists were more conservative than the farmers, and their misconceptions led to unnecessary rejection of some potentially useful potato germplasm.

Formal farm surveys of existing varieties and preferences confirmed these findings. Incorporating farmers into on-station germplasm screening can produce useful information at little cost.

Participatory research, then, can become a two-way flow that both takes scientists to farmers' fields and brings farmers to the scientists' fields. CIAT's bean research programme in Rwanda subsequently adopted this approach. Female bean seed experts now participate in on-station bean varietal assessment (Sperling, 1988). Women farmers (since they rather than men tend the crop) visit on-station germplasm trials at two or three critical points in bean growth (at flowering and formation of pods, at maturation, and at harvest). Also valuable to both the scientists and visiting farmers are the observations of station field labourers (themselves usually small farmers) who see the scientists' trials through the entire crop cycle. In the Rwandan potato research programme, local scientists knew that some station labourers were both very keen observers of experimental germplasm, and experimenters with promising plant material on their own farms. These labourer-farmers were among those who assessed potato germplasm in the exercise mentioned. This technique is a useful complement to farmer-managed trials in farmers' fields.

Conclusions

Plant breeders cannot respond to every quirk of farmers' circumstances. Their task becomes more complicated, costs increase, and progress slows as the number of selection criteria increases. Breeders require general guidelines based on accurate prior identification and ranking of cultivar traits that particular categories of producers and users find important, discarding less relevant screening criteria, and assessing farmers' capacities to change existing practices. Crop breeding is a long-term investment; decisions taken at the outset have implications for many years to come (see Lipton, 1989).

If farmers in Africa, Asia and Latin America are to influence agricultural research more directly, researchers and extensionists need better incentives and improved ability to address farmers' needs. Skills to bridge the social distance between "authoritarian" scientists and "deferential" farmers are essential, so that "when farmers experiment with low fertilizer applications to find out what works and pays best for their conditions," researchers will see them as experimenters rather than as "deviants who do not adopt recommended practices" (Chambers and Jiggins, 1985; Ashby, 1986).

Ashby (1986), Biggs (1988), Martin and Farrington (1987), Merrill-Sands et al. (1989), Rhoades (1987) and Richards (1985), among others, have discussed useful innovations in training, methods and approach. The procedures involved are not complicated, but do require a willingness to spend time in the field and to learn directly from farmers. Farmers' participation in on-station activities such as germplasm screening, as in Rwanda's potato and bean research programmes, can yield useful information at little cost.

Social science skills are often underutilized in the design and analysis of on-station and on-farm experiments. In on-farm trials, for example, anthropologists' field skills and knowledge of rural social organization are helpful in selecting collaborators, judging their representativeness, monitoring experiments and farmers' opinions of them, exploring the implications of innovations in particular crops, and reformulating hypotheses for further testing (Tripp, 1985). Although increasing the participation of both farmers and social scientists in agricultural research has been one aim of farming systems research, progress has been slow. Fundamental changes in the organization of agricultural research, and in the attitudes of agricultural scientists, remain necessary.

The gap between what is technically or biologically possible, and what is practicable for small farmers sometimes translates into conflict between excessively optimistic biological scientists and excessively pessimistic social scientists. In defining relevant breeding priorities, however, the essential starting point is for anthropologists, economists and breeders alike to give close attention to farmers' own detailed knowledge of existing crop varieties and to how they select, manage and use them. On-station trials to test improved cultivars should take farmers' cropping systems and husbandry practices explicitly into account (as in the Burundi maize and Rwanda potato programmes). Monocrop and intercrop/relay crop systems, for example, are likely to produce contradictory experimental results when new cultivars are tested. The selection of new cultivars solely on the basis of single crop yield trials can lead to the introduction of locally unsuitable cultivars, with detrimental nutritional and economic consequences for farmers (as in the Burundi maize trials). On-farm trials should incorporate farmers' own methods of informal experimentation, their standards of judgement, and their suggestions concerning experimental design. As scientists adjust their research priorities and experimental techniques to solve clients' problems, they will require the courage to depart from textbook experimental design and disciplinary paradigms.

Although appropriate plant breeding priorities vary across Africa's diverse microenvironments and cropping systems, a few guidelines have broad application. One concerns cultivar maturity classes. Scientists' failure to identify locally appropriate maturity classes before attempting to maximize yield and biomass can increase the gap between on-station and off-station yields. This occurs, for example, if breeders have not recognized the advantages of short-duration cultivars in the context of resource limitations (e.g., in mechanized power, labour, cash or land) that prevent farmers from planting on time or from specializing in long-duration varieties. Short-duration cultivars or a mixture of early and late cultivars often increase small farmers' flexibility in managing environmental hazards, family labour supply, and domestic food and cash needs. Africa's farmers are skillful managers of cultivar sets with diverse agro-nomic and culinary traits, including multiple maturity periods.

Bimodal rainfall and scarcity of land and cash in eastern Africa are associated with complex systems of double cropping, intercropping and relay cropping. Under these conditions farmers are likely to prefer a rapid turnover of crops and the combination of cultivars that gives the best annual rather than single-season yield. Within such production zones (e.g., in the highlands of Kenya, Uganda, Rwanda and Burundi), cultivars of different maturity class sometimes have socioeconomically distinct clienteles. Late-maturing varieties, for example, sometimes suit the wealthier farmers better than the poorer farmers with less land and cash. Scientists must then consider the possibly conflicting interests of wealthy and poor farmers, and may vary experimental design (both on and off the research station) by category of farmer.

Finally, researchers should keep in mind that farmers' powers of observation and skills in innovation contributed to eight doublings of the human population before industrialization and the discovery of fossil fuels (Norgaard, 1985). Sustainable agriculture in all nations will require greater scientific respect for, and more effective collaboration with, those who possess the wisdom of generations of "nonscientific" farming.

Acknowledgements

The authors gratefully acknowledge helpful comments on an earlier draft of this paper from many colleagues. A. H. thanks the Rockefeller Foundation, the Rwandan Institute of Agronomic Sciences (ISAR), the Burundi Institute of Agronomic Sciences (ISABU), and the International Potato Centre (CIP) for generous support of post-doctoral research in Rwanda, Burundi and Kenya between 1984 and 1986.

The views expressed in this paper are those of the authors alone and do not necessarily reflect the official positions of the institutions with which they have been affiliated.

References

Acland, J. D. (1971). *East African Crops.* London: Longman.

Altieri, M. A. (1985). Developing pest management strategies for small farmers based on traditional knowledge. *Development Anthropology Network* 3(l):13–18.

Arnold, M. H. & Innes, N. L. (1984). Plant breeding for crop improvement with special reference to Africa. In *Advancing Agricultural Production in Africa* (ed. by D. L. Hawksworth). Wallingford, Oxford: CAB.

Ashby, J. A. (1986). Methodology for the participation of small farmers in the design of on-farm trials. *Agricultural Administration* 22:1–19.

Bicamumpaka, M. & Haverkort, A. (1983). The PNAP approach to potato development in Rwanda. In *Agricultural Research in Rwanda: Assessment and Perspectives.* The Hague: ISNAR.

Biggs, S. (1988). Resource-Poor Farmer Participation in Research: Political, Administrative and Methodological Considerations. Working Paper Draft. The Hague: ISNAR.

Brokensha, D., Warren, D. M. & Werner, O. (1980). *Indigenous Knowledge Systems.* Lanham, Maryland: University Press of America.

Brush, S., Carney, J. J. & Huaman, Z. (1980). The Dynamics of Andean Potato Agriculture. Social Science Department Working Paper Series 1980–85. Lima: CIP.

Byerlee, D., Harrington, L. & Winkelmann, D. (1982). Farming systems research: issues in research strategy and technology design. *American Journal of Agricultural Economics* 64:897–904.

Chambers, R. & Jiggins, J. (1985). Agricultural Research for Resource-Poor Farmers: A Parsimonious Paradigm. Manuscript for discussion. Sussex: Institute for Development Studies.

CIMMYT (1978). Demonstrations of Adaptive On-Farm Research, No. 3. Part of Serenje District, Central Province, Zambia. Nairobi: CIMMYT East and Southern African Office (with Research Branch, Ministry of Agriculture, Lusaka).

CIMMYT (1982). Demonstrations of Adaptive On-Farm Research No. 5. Part of Chibi District, Zimbabwe. Nairobi: CIMMYT East and Southern African Office (with Department of Research and Specialist Services and University of Zimbabwe, Harare, Zimbabwe).

Collinson, M. P. (1981). A low cost approach to understanding small farmers. *Agricultural Administration* 8:433–450.

Collinson, M. P. (1982). Farming Systems Research in Eastern Africa: The Experience of CIMMYT and some National Agricultural Research Services, 1976–1981. International Development Paper, No. 3. East Lansing Michigan: Michigan State University.

Collinson, M. P. (1985). On-farm research with a systems perspective: its role in servicing technical component research in maize and some examples from eastern and southern Africa. In *To Feed Ourselves: Proceedings of the First Eastern, Central and Southern Africa Regional Maize Workshop, Lusaka, Zambia.* Mexico: CIMMYT.

Collinson, M. P. (1988). The development of African farming systems: some personal views. *Agricultural Administration and Extension* 29:7–22.

Conklin, H. C. (1980). Folk Classification: A Topically Arranged Bibliography of Contemporary and Background References Through 1971. New Haven: Yale University, Department of Anthropology.

Conklin, H. C. (1988). Des orientements, des vents, des riz ... pour une étude lexicologique des savoirs traditionnels. *Journal d'Agriculture Traditionnelle et de Botanique Appliquée* 33:3–10.

Cooper, P. J. M. & Law, R. (1977). Soil temperature and its association with maize yield variations in the highlands of Kenya. *Journal of Agricultural Science,* Cambridge 89:355–363.

Crawford, E. & Franzel, S. (1987). Comparing formal and informal survey techniques for farming systems research. *Agricultural Administration and Extension* 27:13–33.

De Janvry, A. & Dethier, J. (1985). Technological Innovation in Agriculture: The Political Effects of Its Rate and Bias. CGIAR Study Paper No. 1. Washington, DC: World Bank.

DeWalt, B. R. (1985). Farming systems research. *Human Organization* 44:106–114.

Durr, G. (1980). *Potato Production and Utilization in Rwanda.* CIP: Lima.

Eicher, C. & Baker, D. (1982). Research on Agricultural Development in Sub-Saharan Africa. International Development Paper No. 1. East Lansing, Michigan: Michigan State University.

Gilbert, E. H., Norman, D. & Winch, F. (1980). Farming Systems Research: A Critical Appraisal. Rural Development Paper, No. 6. East Lansing, Michigan: Michigan State University.

Haugerud, A. (1988). Anthropology and interdisciplinary agricultural research in Rwanda. In *Anthropology of Development and Change in East Africa* (Eds. David Brokensha and Peter D. Little). Boulder, Colorado: Westview Press.

Hildebrand, P. (1981). Combining disciplines in rapid appraisal: The Sondeo approach. *Agricultural Administration* 8:423–432.

Hildebrand, P. & Poey, F. (1985). *On-Farm Agronomic Trials in FSR/E.* Boulder, Colorado: Lynne Rienner Press.

Horton, D. (1986). Farming systems research: twelve lessons from the Mantaro Valley project. *Agricultural Administration* 23:1–15.

IARCs (1987). Statement of the Representatives of the IARCs Workshop on Farming Systems Research. Proceedings of a Workshop on FSR. Hyderabad, India: ICRISAT.

IRRI (International Rice Research Institute) (1979). *Farm Level Constraints to High Rice Yields in Asia: 1974–77.* Los Banos, Philippines: IRRI.

Johnson, A. (1971). Individuality and experimentation in traditional agriculture. *Human Ecology* 1:149–159.

Kahn Jr, E. J. (1984). Profiles: the staffs of life. *New Yorker,* November 11.

Lipton, M. (1989). *New Seeds and Poor People.* Baltimore: Johns Hopkins University Press.

MacFadyen, J. T. (1985). United Nations: a battle over seeds. *The Atlantic Monthly* (November), 36–39.

Martin, A. & Farrington, J. (1987). Abstracts of Recent Field Experience with Farmer-Participatory Research. Agricultural Administration Network Paper No. 22. London: Overseas Development Institute.

Matlon, P. J. & Spencer, D. S. (1984). Increasing food production in subSaharan Africa: environmental problems and inadequate technical solutions. *American Journal of Agricultural Economics* 671–676.

Maurya, D. M., A. Bottrall & Farrington, J. (1988). Improved livelihoods, genetic diversity and farmer participation: a strategy for rice breeding in rainfed areas of India. *Experimental Agriculture* 24:311–320.

Merrill-Sands, D. (1986). Farming systems research: clarification of terms and concepts. *Experimental Agriculture* 22:87–104.

Merrill-Sands, D., Ewell, P., Biggs, S. & McAllister, J. (1989). Issues in Institutionalizing On-Farm Client-Oriented Research in National Agricultural Research Systems. Paper presented at International Workshop on Development in Procedures for Farming Systems Research, 13–17 March, 1989, Bogor, Indonesia.

Moock, J. L. (1986). *Understanding Africa's Rural Households and Farming Systems.* Boulder, Colorado: Westview Press.

Nganga, S. (1983). The PNAP (Programme Nationale d'Amélioration de la Pomme de Terre) in Rwanda: institutional development, organization and achievements. In *Agricultural Research in Rwanda: Assessment and Perspectives.* The Hague: ISNAR.

Ninez, V. K. (1984). *Household Gardens: Theoretical Consideration on an Old Survival Strategy.* Lima: CIP.

Norgaard, R. B. (1985). Traditional agricultural knowledge: past performance, future prospects, and institutional implications. *American Journal of Agricultural Economics* 66:874–878.

Norman, D. W. (1980). The Farming Systems Approach: Relevancy for the Small Farmer. Rural Development Paper, No. 5. East Lansing, Michigan: Michigan State University.

Norman, D. W., Simmons, E. B. & Hays, H. M. (1982). *Farming Systems Research in the Nigerian Savannah.* Boulder, Colorado: Westview Press.

Plucknett, D. L. & Smith, N. J. H. (1986). Sustaining agricultural yields, Part II. *Biological Science* 36: 40–45.

PNAP (Programme National d'Amélioration de la Pomme de Terre) (1984). Rapport Annuel. Ruhengeri, Rwanda: PNAP/ISAR.

PNAP (1985). *Rapport Annuel.* Ruhengeri, Rwanda: PNAP/ISAR.

Poats, S. (1981). La pomme de terre au Rwanda: résultats preliminaires d'une enquête de consommation. *Bulletin Agricole du Rwanda* ND 14:82–91.

Rhoades, R. (1985a). Traditional Potato Production and Farmers' Selection of Varieties in Eastern Nepal. Potatoes in Food Systems Research Series, Report No. 2. Lima: CIP.

Rhoades, R. (1985b). Informal survey methods for farming systems research. *Human Organization* 44:215–218.

Rhoades, R. (1987). Farmers and Experimentation. Discussion Paper No. 21. London: Overseas Development Institute.

Richards, P. (1985). *Indigenous Agricultural Revolution.* Boulder, Colorado: Westview Press and London: Hutchinson.

Rwanda, Government of (1985). Résultats de l'Enquête Nationale Agricole 1984, Vol. I. Kigali, Rwanda: Ministry of Agriculture.

Scott, G. (1988). *Potatoes in Central Africa: A Study of Burundi, Rwanda and Zaire.* Lima: CIP.

Shaner, W. W., Philipp, P. F. & Schmehl, W. R. (1982). *Farming Systems Research and Development: Guidelines for Developing Countries.* Boulder, Colorado: Westview Press.

Shumba, E. M. (1985). On-Farm Research Priorities Resulting from a Diagnosis of the Farming Systems in Mangwende, a High Potential Area in Zimbabwe. Research Report No. 5. FSRU, DR and SS, Ministry of Agriculture, Zimbabwe.

Simmonds, N. W. (1979). *Principles of Crop Improvement.* London: Longman.

Simmonds, N. W. (1981). Genotype (G), environment (E) and GE components of crop yields. *Experimental Agriculture* 17:355–362.

Simmonds, N. W. (1984). The State of the Art of Farming Systems Research. Washington, DC: World Bank.

Sperling, L. (1988). Farmer Participation and the Development of Bean Varieties in Rwanda. Paper prepared for joint Rockefeller Foundation/International Potato Center Workshop on Farmers and Food Systems held in Lima, Peru, September 26–30, 1988.

Ter Horst K. & Watts, E. R. (1983). *Plant Breeding for Low Input Conditions.* Lusaka, Zambia: Ministry of Agriculture and Water Development.

Thresh, J. M. (1982). Cropping practices and virus spread. *Annual Review of Phytopathology* 20:193–218.

Tripp, R. (1985). Anthropology and on-farm research. *Human Organization* 44:114–124.

UNICEF (1985). Inventaire O.N.G. Kigali, Rwanda.

Voss, J. (1989). Integrating social science research into the development and testing of new agricultural technology: The case of CIAT's Great Lakes Bean Project. In *Social Science Perspectives on Managing Agricultural Technology,* (Eds. David Groenfeldt and Joyce L. Moock). Sri Lanka: International Irrigation Management Institute.

Wangia, S. M. M. (1980). Dairy Farmer Survey Report, Parts of Kakamega District. Nairobi: Scientific Research Division, Ministry of Agriculture.

Willey, R. W. (1979). Intercropping: its importance and research needs. *Field Crop Abstracts* 31(1).

Zeigler, R. S. (1986). Application of a systems approach in a commodity research programme: evaluating Burundi highland maize. *Experimental Agriculture* 22:319–328.

29

Three Ways Industrial Food Makes You Sick

Industrialized agriculture puts animals in concentration camps where they become crazy and diseased. It puts chemicals on our vegetables and fruit. It slips bacteria genes into our lettuce and biotech growth hormones into our milk without telling us. Then we serve it all to our kids for "dinner."

1. Increased Cancer Risk

It is not possible to say with certainty that any particular cancer in your family or community has been directly caused by the massive use of chemicals in industrial food production. But many studies implicate pesticides in incidences of leukemia and lymphoma, as well as cancers of the brain, breast, testes and ovaries.

According to the U.S. Food and Drug Administration (FDA), over 35% of the food that they tested in 1998 contained pesticide residues. 53 pesticides classified as "carcinogenic" are presently registered for use on major crops, including apples, tomatoes, and potatoes. 71 different ingredients in pesticides have been found to cause cancer in animals and humans. Consumers Union reported that tests of apples, grapes, green beans, peaches, pears, spinach and winter squash have shown toxicity at hundreds of times the levels of other foods. And many U.S. products have tested as being more toxic than those from other countries.

A National Cancer Institute study found that farmers who used industrial herbicides had six times greater risk than non-farmers of contracting non-Hodgkin's lymphoma, a type of cancer. (American farms use nearly a billion pounds of pesticides each year.) The Environmental Protection Agency (EPA) says it has identified 165 pesticides as potentially carcinogenic.

The EPA also reports that more than 1,000,000 Americans drink water laced with pesticides that have run-off from industrial farms. Agricultural chemicals have also leeched into hundreds of rivers, making fish unsafe to eat, water unsafe to drink or to swim in. Toxic sludge is another worry: heavy metals, chemicals and low-level radioactive wastes are now used as fertilizers in industrial farming. Eventually these find their way into groundwater.

Industrial agriculture advocates argue that the link between pesticides and cancer is not proven; but corporations have said things like that about everything from cigarette safety to asbestos to global warming. We are dealing with the health of families here; *shouldn't the precautionary principle be the standard to apply?*

2. Increase in Food-borne Diseases

Every week the media carry stories about people becoming sick from bacteria in food. Researchers at the Centers for Disease Control (CDC) estimate that food-borne pathogens infect up to 80 million people a year, and cause over 9,000 deaths in the U.S. alone. The bugs are passed to humans through beef, chicken, or pork, but sometimes from cheese, fruit and vegetables that are carelessly processed.

Food-borne diseases have increased in recent years largely because of the industrialization of animal-raising. Most animal products now come from animals raised in *concentration camp* conditions: thousands are jammed together in tiny cages or on the floors of poorly ventilated stadium-sized buildings; covered with each other's excrement; gone crazy from the crowding; injected with growth-inducing hormones and antibiotics. The CDC says that reported cases of diseases from *Salmonella* and *E. coli* pathogens are ten times what they were two decades ago, and cases of *Campylobacter* are more than double. The CDC saw none of these bugs in meat until the late 1970s when factory farming became popular.

The use of antibiotics in animal-feed may also be accelerating the alarming growth of antibiotic resistance. *Infections resistant to antibiotics have now become the 11th leading cause of death in the U.S.* Most reports blame doctors for over-prescribing antibiotics for people. But nearly 50% of U.S. antibiotics are given to animals, not people.

Antibiotics fed to animals eventually cause disease organisms to mutate stronger. *Salmonella, E. coli, Campylobacter* now have antibiotic resistant strains. If you eat a chicken with antibiotic resistant *E. coli,* you might become very sick, and antibiotics may not be able to help. If we don't immediately stop using antibiotics on factory farm animals, we could eventually produce an uncontrollable "supergerm," even a global pandemic.

Scarier still is "Mad Cow Disease." In England, more than 4 million cattle were destroyed, because of fear of infection. No such outbreak is yet admitted in this country, but what of the 100,000 "downed cows" that die each year for unexplained reasons? Since "downed cows" have previously been ground-up and fed to other cows, serious concern is appropriate. The CDC is studying them.

The response from the industrial food industry is to build hundreds of nuclear irradiation stations to kill the bugs. The average pound of hamburger may receive the equivalent of millions of chest x-rays. But is the proliferation of nuclear power stations the right answer to a problem that could be solved by raising animals in a healthy environment? We don't think so.

3. Biotechnology Is Not the Answer

An alarming percentage of our food has been genetically engineered (GE): nearly 50% of U.S. soybeans (and soybean products) and cotton; 35% of corn and canola. Some estimates are that 50% of packaged foods contain at least one GE ingredient, *but none are labeled for consumers.* Certain tomatoes have virus genes; certain lettuce has bacteria genes; among hundreds of other examples.

Why are no genetically engineered products labeled? The companies refuse to do it, asserting the foods are safe. (None have had independent long-term testing.) And the FDA, intimidated by industry, does not require testing or labels. But wouldn't you like to be informed?

The FDA *has* warned that some genes contain toxins whose effects can be amplified by gene splicing; and that certain GE foods can produce serious allergic reactions. There is also the possibility of "horizontal gene transfer," where viruses spliced into one gene sequence "infect" other species, bringing grave risks. Why doesn't the FDA warn us of these?

Finally, the point is this: The massive changeover from farming to *corporate* farming—with its corresponding change in values—has produced a level of health risk that never existed before.

But you can protect yourself: (1) Buy "certified organic" foods. (2) *Call us* at the number at the bottom of the page. We will send you lists of genetically engineered products. (3) *Call the FDA.* (1-888-463-6332). Tell them you want mandatory testing and labeling on all genetically engineered foods, and an end to factory farming of animals.

Center for Food Safety
The Humane Society of the United States
Organic Consumers Association
Mothers & Others for a Livable Planet
Food & Water
EarthSave International
Sustainable Cotton Project
Food First/Institute for Food and Development Policy
Humane Farming Association
David Suzuki Foundation
Earth Island Institute
Institute for Agriculture and Trade Policy
International Forum on Food and Agriculture
The Land Institute
Organic Farming Research Foundation
GRACE Factory Farming Project
Corporate Agribusiness Research Project
Grassroots International
International Society for Ecology and Culture
International Forum on Globalization

Signers are all part of a coalition of more than 60 non-profit organizations that favor democratic, localized, ecologically sound alternatives to current practices and policies. This advertisement is #3 in the Industrial Agriculture series. Other ad series discuss the extinction crisis, genetic engineering, economic globalization and megatechnology. For more information, please contact:

Turning Point Project, 310 D St. NE, Washington, DC 20002 1-800-249-8712 • www.turnpoint.org • email:info@turnpoint.org

30

Opposition to Biotech Crops Is Groundless

John K. Carlisle* *

WASHINGTON—Environmentalists frequently urge industry to adopt "clean technologies" that reduce pollution and promote conservation. Why is it, then, that those same environmentalists advocate a ban on agricultural biotechnology that significantly reduces the use of potentially harmful pesticides, decreases soil erosion by up to 98 percent and helps prevent the destruction of ecologically important rainforests?

Their opposition makes no sense. Indeed, environmentalists should be stumbling over themselves advocating the rapid development of this amazing new technology.

Under traditional crossbreeding methods, which farmers have been doing for thousands of years, it would take 10 to 12 years to develop hybrid plants and animals. Agricultural biotechnology enables scientists to transfer the desired gene traits much more efficiently and quickly.

Environmental activists claim genetically enhanced crops are poorly regulated and pose a public threat. These arguments are without merit.

The U.S. Food and Drug Administration, the U.S. Department of Agriculture and the Environmental Protection Agency require all genetically enhanced products to go through a rigorous regulatory review. It takes a company about eight to 10 years to bring a genetically enhanced product from the laboratory to the marketplace.

In addition to U.S. regulatory agencies, leading national and international organizations have endorsed the safety of genetically enhanced food, including the American Medical Association and the World Health Organization.

Already, biotechnology has yielded many benefits. Strains of cotton, corn, potatoes, rice, squash and papaya have been "vaccinated" with genes that make them resistant to a variety of crop-destroying viruses.

That means that farmers can significantly increase yields, so much so that it is estimated that food biotechnology could meet up to 25 percent of the world's food needs in the next 50 years. The higher yield also means farmers won't have to clear as much land, including tropical rainforests.

Another environmental benefit is that farmers have dramatically reduced their reliance on pesticides and herbicides. In 1996 corn farmers used 1.5 million fewer pounds of insecticides to fight the European corn borer thanks to "genetically vaccinated" corn plants.

One final environmental plus: Farmers can preserve valuable topsoil because they would no longer have to plow under harmful weeds before and after harvesting and planting. Estimates of the topsoil that can be saved by no-till farming range from 70 percent to 98 percent.

Still, environmentalists insist that agricultural biotechnology is a genetic apocalypse waiting to happen. They derisively call disease-resistant corn and vitamin enhanced tomatoes "Frankenfoods" that could unleash some sort of nightmarish genetic domino effect with ramifications for human health and the ecosystem.

However, they never offer credible scientific evidence for their claims. Dr. Norman Borlaug, the Nobel Prize-winning scientist who is considered the father of the Green Revolution, accuses the environmental movement of playing upon peoples' fears for short-term political gain.

"You get a few extremists into the movement and they stir up controversy and confuse people for their own interests," he says.

Former President Jimmy Carter defines biotechnology, saying: "Responsible biotechnology is not the enemy; starvation is."

One gets the impression that it is not really science that motivates many environmentalists but a bizarre brand of New Age-like religion.

Dr. Mae Wan-Ho, one of the most vocal of the few scientists who oppose biotechnology, condemned agricultural biotechnology as a morally bankrupt product of a "reductionist-mechanistic science" that has "taken the poetry out of farming" by turning the farmer into a tractor driver.

While Dr. Wan-Ho may find poetry in a farmer breaking his back using discarded techniques, it is doubtful many farmers share her opinions.

Sadly, there is just no pleasing the environmental movement when it comes to technological progress—even if it means a world with fewer hungry people and a better environment.

31

Nutritional Ecology

Bonnie McCay

Key definitions in nutritional ecology include:

"Malnutrition": dietary causes of lowered "health" in the sense of ability to rally from insults. It may also be caused by "health" lowered because of infectious and other diseases.

Under- and Over-Nutrition: both lead to reduced life expectancy, increased susceptibility to disease, reduced quality of life (and "productivity")

Prevention: the only effective means of control.

Undernutrition: old and new "world food problems"

Malnutrition is most noticeable when a famine occurs and/or when food prices escalate. These are interconnected: when food reserves (especially grain) run low and prices escalate, famine becomes more likely—as does less dramatic undernutrition. For example, in Ethiopia civil war and revolutions have played a role as well. This illustrates the politics of hunger and starvation.

Per capita consumption in the world has actually increased in recent years at rate of .8% a year as world grain production – the major source of calories (energy) has out paced world population growth. Why, then, is there a "world food problem?"

Poverty, Distribution, and Differential Access to Strategic Resources

Developed, industrialized countries, per capita food consumption increased at ca. 1.5% a year; in the underindustrialized, "developing," Third World countries, the average is less than .4% a year, and for some a net decline.

The magnitude of the problem: 86% of the world's population growth is in very poor areas, where up to 1/3rd of the population are on the borders of bare subsistence.

The basic, less noticed problem: chronic malnutrition, especially among the poor. What does being poor have to do with it?

❑ more of income is spent on food (60–80%); thus less flexibility when times are rough in terms of reallocating money from other things to food; "belt-tightening" with consequences for nutritional status one of the few recourses.

- poverty assoc. with lower education; "ignorance and superstition" contribute to failure to take full advantage of available foods.
- poverty sometimes associated with striving for upward mobility, being like the rich and the famous, having aspirations that you cannot easily fulfil. Among health results: inappropriate infant feeding practices: bottle feeding of babies despite inability to buy adequate amounts of formula or to have clean and reliable water supplies. (we will address this later)
- nutritional stresses often go together with other stresses: poor housing, often very constricted resource base (few opportunities in urban, industrial jobs; poor, marginal farmlands in rural areas), inadequate medical care, higher incidence of infectious and other disease.

These associations are not just correlational: "synergism" of nutrition and infection (via effects on immune system, etc.); of bottle-feeding, nutrition, and infection; perhaps (the evidence is a little shakier on this) of nutrition and "education" (ability to learn, ability to adapt to new jobs, etc.) through effects of undernutrition when young on mental development, learning capabilities, as well as physical growth and development rates (slower).

Distribution Problem Is Not New

With the rise of agriculture ca. 10,000 yrs. B.C. began also the rise of complex societies with structured inequality in access to food and other basic resources – MALNUTRITION STRATIFICATION.

In a study of European diet, from 1400–1800 Braudel found that Genoa Italy the rich had diets in which cereals accounted for 52% of total calorie intake, while for the poor, 81% of their diets consisted of "bread, more bread, and still more bread and gruel." The poor: in towns, rural peasants, lowest working-class. In 1782, the French peasant or laborer ate 2–3# of bread per day. This was the cheapest food (elsewhere, by this time, maize in the

Mediterranean [polenta], potatoes in Scandinavia, Scotland, Ireland), and not the fragrant, light, freshly baked loaf, but often hard, moldy; some places cut with an axe. Bread baked every month or so. In times of famine, even bread was often not available, especially to the rural poor, forced to "famine diets," e.g., "cabbage runts" with bran soaked in cold water; wild plants, dogs, human flesh.

- associations between poverty and disease in history (Braudel 1973:38):

Between the 15th and 18th centuries European populations were hit over and over by great epidemics of plague (bubonic) and other infectious diseases (smallpox, diphtheria, etc.). Braudel called these "social massacres" (p. 38) because the poor were always the first to suffer the effects of the epidemic and seemed to have suffered the most—partly because of low nutritional health, partly because of "fewer options":

Plague: the rich fled to country houses, while the poor remained penned up in contaminated towns, isolated in the name of quarantine and "observation" by local governments. As their death rates declined the rich were then told it was safe to return!

Geography of Poverty and Malnutrition Changed with Industrialization: in Europe, shifted more to urban poor, workers; with growth of colonial empire, shifted across the seas, intensifying problems of poverty and malnutrition in already stratified, heavily-populated societies like India (where today the poorest 1/3rd of the population receives 20–30% less food than the national average) and transforming other societies into ones full of poverty and malnutrition.

IN THE HISTORICAL, EVOLUTIONARY, PERSPECTIVE, A REDUCED RANGE OF FOOD CHOICE AND INCREASED RELIANCE ON DIETARY "STAPLES" HAS ALSO PLAYED A ROLE IN MALNUTRITION. The rise of agriculture was not only accompanied by the rise of social stratification. It was a mixed blessing in another way. The prehistory and history of human agricultural and economic development is one of progressive limitation of choice in food (Doughty 1979).

There is safety in numbers (of food eater). A rule of nutritional health is that dietary diversity is the best bet. Even Popeye can eat too much spinach and have it be dangerous to his health (oxalic acids, tying up calcium, etc.).

We do not need tables of food composition, computers, and nutritionists if we have varied and ample diets. This rule is a good one to follow also because nutrition science does not know enough to offer you many better ones, past research has concentrated on isolated nutrients and foods, and recommended that a "good" diet is one in which the intake of nutrients is adjusted to meet the needs of the individual. But: what nutrients are actually in particular foods? This is hard to answer. For example, the potato, lowly as it is, has over 250 different compounds (Doughty 1979). Foods are eaten in combinations, not alone, making it more complicated. And "need" is not easy to determine: requirements and nutrient absorption vary by individuals, even by situations, and are not known for some nutrients, especially some vitamins and trace elements (Doughty 1979).

The Problem: With Rise of Agriculture, Dietary Diversity Declined; in Addition, Poverty Is Often Associated with a Decline in Dietary Diversity

The estimated population of humans before rise of agriculture was about 5 million hunter-gatherers, 1 person per 25 sq. km; about 5000 edible plants in their environment. Studies of contemporary hunter-gatherers have shown a tendency to utilize a large sample of these: e.g., the Kung San of NW Botswana, southern Africa, use 150 species of wild plants and animals. They and others studied show few if any signs of malnutrition

("over" or "under"), and after the first few years of life, when infectious disease takes a heavy toll, they tend to be strong and active.

Today there are billions of people; more or less involved in a modern market economy. 25 persons per sq. km; less than 150 food plants entering the world market, and only 15 of them account for most of the energy (calories) consumed by the human population (Doughty 1979: 279)

What happened? About 10,000 years ago people began gathering seeds and sowing plants in plots, propagating plants with cuttings, etc. and intensifying tendency to rely on starchy roots, tubers, and seeds to provide the main bulk of their energy needs in their diets.

These dietary patterns consisted of starchy staple plus tasty tidbits or sauces:

> cereal seed: millet, rice, barley, maize, wheat
> root or tuber: potato, cassava, yams, taro
> starchy fruit: breadfruit, plantain.

These tend to have monotonous taste or texture, so made more appetizing by dipping them in or serving with sauce, stew, relish made from a great variety of foods cultivated or collected from the wild, including fish and game too. Dietary diversity provided this way (Doughty 1979). In addition, in many areas and some until recently, several different "staples" were used: ex.: Zanda of the southwestern Sudan, in 1950: 8 cereals, 11 starchy-roots and fruits; 7 legumes; 16 oilseeds; 31 leafy vegetables; 11 other vegetables; 47 fruits; 11 plant foods used for flavoring only; 27 plants burnt, ashes added to stews; 52 plants used for medicines (Doughty 1979: 279?)

In setting like this, the nutritional problems are associated with the seasonality of harvests, infectious diseases, and the weaning period, when child is being weaned onto low-protein starchy staples and has little variety in the diet ("kwashiorkor," PCM). Long-term, widespread drought, too.

What is happening and has happened is the loss of diversity in the rural diet, reducing the options and making people more dependent on the starchy staples, together with the nutritional risks they carry.

Protein Quantity

One concern is the *quantity* of protein available from a food in the diet:

Grams of protein per 100 kcal (from McElroy and Townsend 1979: 188):

Cassava	<1
Plantain	1
Sweet potato	1
Yam	2
Taro	2
Potato	3
Rice, highly milled	2
Maize	3
Wheat	
Lentils (legumes)	7
Soybeans	9
Milk, cow whole	5
Milk, cow skim	10
Eggs	8
Beef, lean	9
Poultry	14
Fish (freshwater)	19

Quality and Amino Acids

Another concern is the *quality* of the protein available: foods differ in the composition of the proteins they have: the amounts and relationships among the amino acids present. Amino acids that are critical ("essential") to the human diet include lysine, leucine and isoleucine, methionine, cystine, tryptophan. A diet that has high quantity protein (e.g., lots and lots of maize or rice) but low quality may produce some nutritional deficiency syndromes. "Protein complementarity" refers to the ability of different foods, when eaten in combination, to provide an adequate balance of the essential amino acids.

Calories, Proteins, Vitamins, and Minerals

Two key definitioner are in order:

Calories: the energy available in foods, from carbohydrates, lipids, proteins.

Proteins: etymology: *proteno* (Greek): original, first; used in 1840 for food component: "without it no life is possible"

Proteins are the structural part of animal cells, complex molecules polymers of amino acids with peptide linkages, with an average of 20 amino acids per protein about half the dry weight

Amino acids essential in adult human diet (i.e. not synthesized or not synthesized enough by the body):

valine	leucine, isoleucine
threonine	methionine
phenylalanine	tryptophan
lysine	

Protein quality varies with its amino acid composition (examples: gelatin and zein, a protein in corn, have very low quality; animals fed exclusively these proteins will die; if fed glycinin [soybean] or glutenin [from wheat] they will be fine in terms of maintenance, growth, health; if fed gliadin [also from wheat] young animals will not grow, but adults will be maintained adequately)

Vitamins are chemically unrelated to each other and are a functional category of elements essential in the diet in small amounts, each involved in specific metabolic reactions within the cell. They have "Water-soluble" and "fat-soluble," properties which determine patterns of transport, storage, and secretion within the body. They were first discovered not by presence but by absence through clinical "deficiency" diseases, e.g., beriberi (thiamin deficiency).

Minerals are calcium, phosphorus, magnesium, sodium, chloride, potassium, sulphur, iron. Trace elements include copper, iodine, manganese, molybdenum, fluoride, selenium, zinc, chromium. Trace elements are the "ash" of oxidized biological materials. Some implicated in specific deficiency diseases, e.g., iodine and thyroid problems, including goiter and cretinism; perhaps Ca combined with vitamin D in nervous system disorders, like Arctic hysteria (and Victorian hysteria?).

Protein-Calorie Malnutrition

It is a mistake to focus solely on protein: associated with these low or unbalanced protein foods are called PCM or "protein-calorie malnutrition," reflecting the difficulty of separating protein and calorie deficiencies and the importance of both in the diet: without adequate calories, a seemingly adequate amount of protein can result in one of the classic "protein deficiency" diseases: *marasmus* or *kwashiorkor*.

Marasmus is usually found among very young children and infants; it involves gross weight loss, the wasting away of subcutaneous fat and muscles (the extremely thin children shown in news photos of Ethiopia now); once diagnosed and treated, the case fatality rate is ca. 15–40%.

Kwashiorkor (in the Ga language of Ghana: "the disease the first child gets when the next one is on the way") looks quite different: think of the famine children with large bellies, puffy faces: enlarged fatty liver, edema; also flaky skin, thin, often discolored hair; "petulant apathy"; it is a disorder of amino acid metabolism and is more difficult to cure (with food, electrolyte solutions) than marasmus since more of the body's system is involved.

Gerlach (1961): childrearing practices among the Digo of Tanzania: adult diet is adequate: porridge of maize, plantains, or cassava served with side dishes of green leaves, dried fish, beef, or milk. Children 8 years and up: adult diet. Children 6–7: less so, but eat meat and fish at weekly feasts. Children under 5: breast milk and a watery gruel. The mother is expected to breastfeed her child of or 3 or 4 years. Taboo on sexual relationships until the child has reached the ideal weaning age. Child thus has minimally adequate diet from mother's milk and gruel—unless mother has another child. In that case, the child is at risk of protein malnutrition, here called "chirwa," meaning the taboo was broken. This cultural belief and practice is meaningful and perhaps adaptive in a setting of low protein diets—helping to ensure that mother's milk is available longer (Whiting on postpartum sex taboo in the tropics); however, it can be mal-adaptive too: for example, because of shame from diagnosis of child's problem as "chirwa"—the taboo is broken—the mother may hide her sick child and prevent it from getting medical care (Gerlach 1961).

Both: prevent proper growth and development, since the child with marasmus does not have enough energy to grow, and the child with kwashiorkor does not have enough interest in food (anorexia) to grow.

These are extreme types of PCM. Much more common is "nutritional dwarfism" in its many levels: the body adapts to under and unbalanced nutrition by slowing down growth and development. The rate of growth is slowed; in some cases the person eventually reaches "normal" height and weight, but much later (e.g., 25 instead of 15 or 16); in others, the adult is small, too. "Sub-clinical malnutrition," ranging from people with just enough dietary intake to be slightly underweight and underheight to those who show stunted growth and are prone to many illnesses. Malnutrition in a population is usually detected by measuring children for height and weight/age and comparing the results with a "standard" population. Marasmus and kwashiorkor and other "deficiency" syndromes are much rarer than "nutritional dwarfism" but they are all part of the same problem.

Here is a list of some of the most important starchy staples, nutritional risks—and adaptive behaviors found in populations long accustomed to a limited dietary variety. These are sometimes called SUPERFOODS when a population is culturally and economically focused on one of them.

The emphasis is on protein, because this tends to be limiting in a starchy staple-based diet:

1. Rice (South Asia, SE Asia, E Asia): *quantity* of protein is limiting as are thiamine and other water-soluble vitamins, which tend to get lost when rice is milled, washed, and boiled. The classic "malnutrition" syndrome found is endemic BERIBERI and PCM. The adaptive behaviors, widespread, including adding dried or fresh fish, fish sauces, soy products, fresh vegetables, even in small amounts, to a rice meal (Chinese restaurants). For vegetarians, the presence of legumes in the meals adds protein and complements amino acids of rice. In addition, in India there is less adult beriberi because in some areas the practice is to parboil unhusked rice, dry it before milling, thus diffusing the water-soluble vitamins throughout the grain.

2. Corn [Maize] (South and North America originally; diffused to Africa and much of the rest of the world after Columbus): amino acids (components of protein) are unbalanced in relation to human needs: the critical amino acids lysine, leucine, and tryptophan in particular are proportionally low. The B vitamin niacin is also limited (in utilizable form). A *low quality* protein source, but excellent source of carbohydrates (energy). The classic malnutrition syndrome is PELLAGRA and PCM. The adaptive behaviors include (1) eating corn with beans, at the same time (the beans provide complementary amino acids) [THE BURRITO]; (2) treating corn with alkali (lye, lime, wood ashes) before grinding (this adjusts the ratio of leucine to isoleucine to reduce its antagonistic effect on the conversion of tryptophan to niacin) (Katz et al).

3. Wheat, barley and rye (Middle East, Europe . . .): fairly good quantity and quality of protein, especially when the diet includes dairy products, as it usually does where wheat is the staple (people who grow wheat also have tended to be "mixed farmers" who keep cattle, etc. Isoleucine and lysine are the limiting amino acids in wheat, complemented by their sources from dairy products). Malnutrition syndromes: PCM [wheat alone, "bread, bread, and more bread"; the "sugar babies" of the late 19th century probably had kwashiorkor—and if moldy, risks of ergotism, etc.-rye]; ZINC DEFICIENCY, CALCIUM DEFICIENCY, IRON DEFICIENCY. These deficiency syndromes are most likely where the diet is not diversified and where the wheat is unrefined and the bread is unleavened—i.e., parts of the Middle East. Results: hypogonadal dwarfism (Zinc); rickets, osteomalacia (CA); anemia (FE, complicated by parasitic infestation—schistosomiasis, hookworm, whipworm). Why? unrefined wheat, unleavened, is very high in fiber and "phytates," which combine with Ca, Fe, Zn and reduce the body's ability to absorb these critical trace elements. Dietary fiber [good for you in other ways] may also interfere with mineral absorption.

4. Tropical "high bulk, low-protein" starchy staples, e.g., cassava, sago, plantain, sweet potato, taro? See chart above: you must eat an awfully large amount to get enough protein out of them; complementary sources, esp. fish, chickens, pigs, are critical here. PCM is a real problem, particularly for children being weaned (kwashiorkor). Some trade-offs involved: these are very productive, easy to grow, excellent sources of calories, and perhaps some other dividends. Cassava, for example, may be therapeutic for people who have

"Mild" or "benign" sickle-cell anemia: cyanate is used in treating crises; inhibits sickling; cyanate's precursor, thiocyanate, is found in cassava in impressive amounts (also, to lesser degree, in yams, sorghum, millet).

"The World Food Problem" stems from increased reliance on starchy staples with the hazards they represent; rapid social and environmental change reducing the effectiveness of human "adaptations" to hazards; overpopulation; and pauperization with associated problems, including fewer dietary options.

1. Internal causes of loss of dietary diversity (Doughty 1979):
   examples: (typically related to population increase and/or increased involvement in market economy): having to clear land farther from home because of loss of soil fertility nearby: increased traveling time, less time for and interest in gathering wild foods, greater reliance on smaller variety available from fields and gardens or markets [plus loss of inherited knowledge about wild foods]
   intensification of agriculture, from forest swidden to plow and other farming on cleared, permanently farmed land; this often means reduction in the kinds of food grown as well; rice became the "superfood" of Japan through this process.
   loss of "common property" natural resources—forests, wildlife, fish, etc. through population pressure (converting to farmlands, housing, etc.) and through takeover by competitors or outsiders (see below): deforestation, for example, with consequent loss of firewood and wild plants and animals (and loss of soil fertility).
2. External causes:
   examples: loss of land because of political takeover by others, i.e. North American Indians forced to small reservations, compounded by population increase: Hopi of Arizona and New Mexico: 1900 A.D. used more than 25 different wild leafy plants;

1937 only 5; today: none, only occasionally in seasonal special foods. Zulus of South Africa, who lost land to Boers and British conquerors: 1900: 14 types of maize, 20 diff. ways of cooking and serving with sauces, 10 types of sorghum with 10 methods of preparation. Many kinds of yams, other tubers, pumpkins, gourds, beans. 27 wild herbs. Today: pellagra: monotonous diet, no use of green leaves, etc.

Situations like this have led to outright starvation of hundreds of thousands, millions of people, as well as to chronic undernutrition. A famous instance: the Irish potato famine of the mid 19th century: ca. 1.5 million Irish people died between 1845 and 1851 from starvation or related diseases. Why? All they had was the potato, and not much of that. The potato had become a "superfood" because it would grow well in the climate and, in particular, would grow fairly abundantly on tiny plots of otherwise marginal land. The question is, why tiny plots of marginal land? The answer is twofold: (1) system of inheritance allowing fragmentation among male heirs, combined with population growth; and (2) takeover of the better lands in Ireland by the English, in the south, and by the Scots—forced out of Scotland by conversion of farm land to sheep ranches—in the north. Why the famine? Add to the above a fungal disease of potatoes and a weather system conducive to it: the "potato blight." Population growth and political/economic factors made the Irish vulnerable to this, and gave them few options: starve or leave. They did both, and also changed their mode of inheritance and marriage system.

The Landlord System (Doughty 1979)

With social stratification, large numbers of people lose direct control over their land and what they do with it. Chiefs, kings, emperors, presidents maintain power by giving land (or people) to nobles, warlords, priests, political favorites. Colonial powers do the same.

Under these systems of social stratification came the creation of slaves, serfs, and landless labourers and/or share croppers and tenant farmers.

People lose choice about food, payment for work typically in the cheapest and simplest foods available. Tenants and sharecroppers are often forced by indebtedness and terms of contracts to deliver more food to the landlord, less for own consumption. They are also forced to farm what the landlord or the market wants: chiefly staples that can be marketed.

Accompanying this is the reservation of "common lands" for landlords, nobles, kings: e.g., "parks" of England, King's forests: taking firewood, trees, deer, rabbits, even birds became illegal, poaching, at times a capital offense (Thompson 1975).

Agricultural Development and the "Green Revolution"

Back in the countryside the transformation of farming, is occurring via agricultural development and the "green revolution." The goal is to increase world food production, but the effects for millions of people are not improved diets. (1) again, loss of land to the more enterprising growers; (2) focus on "high yielding crops with good storage properties"—selection for fewer varieties, with less regard for nutritional values than total productivity, harvesting ease, and adaptability to drought, frost, floods, insect plagues. The emphasis is on uniformity and limited variety for efficiency of international trade, large-scale processing by corporations. The "Green Revolution" (wheat, especially in India and Pakistan; rice, esp. in Southeast Asia) includes breeding new cereal seeds for high yielding qualities, resulting in abandonment and genetic loss of diverse native varieties (including some more resistant to insects, drought, etc.); increased cereal production at the expense of other plants; high risks and losses; tendency to benefit wealthier farmers, increasing gap between rich and poor (Punjab; Sikhs), increased price of land, sharecroppers

and tenant farmers become landless; mechanization resulting in unemployment, loss of intercropping source of diversity, etc.

Industrialization, Migration, Urbanization

The above processes result in an increase in "landless," drift to urban areas or to work in distant mines, plantations, factories.

These have subtle effects on diets, e.g., seasonal labor migration of male household head or sons: mother and children left to grow food, etc., with little time for growing extras or gathering wild foods, lowered incentive to prepare appetizing dishes; increased reliance on cash remittances from the migrant laborers and what is available in markets and stores.

They also have blatant effects on diets; e.g., the urbanization and the creation of "company towns," virtually total reliance on market economy and the wages of labor; on the food available in the "company store" or urban stores. For the majority this means low wages, hard working conditions, no or little place for own food production, reliance on limited range of affordable foods in markets, limits on food storage, hygiene, food preparation (e.g., cost of fuel and time required)

Example (Jelliffe and Jelliffe): general decline in the use of animal protein in Western European diet since the Middle Ages (Wallerstein); rise in consumption of carbohydrates, especially refined ones—sugars—with development of colonial empires of trade. In the U.K. in 1903 infant mortality was 132/1,000 live births (compare U.S., late 1970s, 23.2 [lower now]; 40+ in poverty areas); 1903 deaths mostly due to "nutrition-related" diseases, including diarrhea, marasmus, etc. Urban/rural differences in the rates, and problems observed in the U.K. and Scotland then mirror those of slum areas and shanty towns in tropical countries and here today: i.e. working mothers leaving their babies at home with inadequate care; weaned early, "handfed" rather than breast fed; rickets (even in sunny tropics, where in cities children spend more time indoors or, in some areas, are kept indoors or overclothed because of "evil eye" beliefs; vitamin D deficiency).

Example: 19th century Scotland (Frisch): when women began working in factories, they had less time to make oat and barley porridge, and increased their use of unfortified white-bread and sugar syrup or "treacle" for their families, with probable effects in the creation of PCM in children, as well as delayed sexual maturity and fertility in women.

Example: studies of PCM in South Africa among urbanized black Africans: working mothers, difficulties in taking adequate care of their children.

The general pattern with urbanization and industrialization is that PCM problems tend to be those like "marasmus" and "weanling diarrhea" rather than "kwashiorkor"; but in general, diets become limited and amounts and quality controlled by wages. "Poverty" = "Malnutrition" (this is not necessarily so for rural areas, where the lack of money and material goods need not mean the lack of adequate food). The nutritional stresses accompanying urbanization are now being experienced most seriously in the less developed, largely tropical countries of the world.

These are several causes in the relationship between urbanization and infant/child health. (Jelliffe and Jelliffe): 1. decline in breast-feeding; 2. rise in attempted bottle feeding with formula or cow's milk; 3. tendency to buy expensive, processed infant foods; 4. less effective child care (in cities, often fewer relatives to help out); 5. earlier weaning; 6. less sunlight; 7. less variety and quality of foods available; AND 8. a new kind of poverty.

Synergism of Nutrition and Infection

Infection may result in reduced food intake (anorexia), increased metabolic losses, if gastrointestinal tract is involved, decreased absorption of available nutrients; increased needs for nutrients, especially during recovery phase, or depletion of body reserves of protein, calories, fat. In this way, bouts of infectious disease can "cause" nutritional diseases—i.e. kwashiorkor and marasmus.

Gambian village study: generally adequate food, but frequent infections (measles, whooping cough, malaria, etc.) result in disease and death "due to malnutrition" but infectious disease the underlying cause.

Inadequate and imbalanced diets can result in an intensification of infectious disease, as is common in Central America (Guatemala INCAP studies): otherwise common, transient, even mild infections of infants and young children become killing diseases, in the context of poor diets of mothers and children: "weanling diarrhea," for example, the major cause of infant mortality in many poor countries: disease and death "due to infectious disease" with malnutrition the underlying cause. In general, being poor means having fewer dietary resources and fewer options.

32

Why People Go Hungry

Kenneth J. Arrow

Poverty and famines: an essay on entitlement and deprivation. Amartya Sen.
Oxford University Press. 257 p.

A localized famine is commonly thought of as resulting from a local failure of crops that is not mitigated by importing food, as happened in the Sahel region of Africa in the late 1960s. Countries where hunger is widespread are frequently blamed, moreover, for allowing excessive population growth. The simple Malthusian ratio of food supply to population is further simplified so that the cause of misery is often seen as a matter of overpopulation alone; we even hear advocates of "lifeboat ethics," whereby countries should be abandoned to their fates.

Mr. Sen makes a strong case against such views and is highly qualified to do so. He is a scholar of unusually wide interests in an era in which most economists have become highly specialized. As Drummond professor of political economy at Oxford, he holds the oldest chair in the United Kingdom. He has been a student of economic development since his first work that became widely known, his monograph *Choice of techniques,* where his cool insistence on proper economic principles argued against simplistic planning and political doctrines in India. He is known for highly technical studies, particularly on the meaning and measurement of social welfare; indeed, he has been elected to be president of the Econometric Society, a worldwide association of the mandarins of mathematical and statistical methods in economics. He is also known among philosophers for his ideas on ethics and the basis of good social action.

In brief, he argues that famine results from the working of the economic system in allocating the ability of people to acquire goods. Famine cannot be explained by a simple relation between food supply and population. Sen illustrates this argument by detailed studies of four famines: the great Bengal famine of 1943–1944, in which perhaps three million people died (mostly by lowered resistance to disease); the famine in several provinces of Ethiopia between 1972 and 1974; the highly publicized drought and famine in the Sahel between 1968 and 1973; and the famine in Bangladesh in 1974 (the same region as the 1943–1944 famine, but under a different political regime).

Most striking are the statistics on the two Bengal famines, the first of which Sen analyzes in the greatest detail. The 1943 crop of rice and other foods was somewhat low, especially in relation to the extraordinarily large harvest of 1942, but it was distinctly higher than the crop of 1941, which was not a famine year. Sen finds that the per capita availability of food supply was 9 percent higher in 1943 than in 1941 and only about 10 percent less than the average of the five preceding years.

Therefore, he concludes, famine cannot be accounted for simply by lack of available food. Relatively small changes in the food supply can be accompanied by dramatic increases in the number of deaths from famine. Why should this occur? Sen points to the simple fact that goods reach people through their ability to "command" that they have goods, as provided by the workings of the socioeconomic system. At any given moment, each economic agent has an "entitlement," a range of different goods that he or she can acquire. This concept can most easily be understood in a private-enterprise economy with little government intervention, though, as Sen emphasizes, the concept is much broader than that.

In a free-enterprise economy every good or service has a price, and each economic agent starts out by owning some goods or services. The rice farmer owns some land, used for producing rice, which can then be sold on the market at the going price or reserved for use by the farmer and his family. The receipts from sales can be spent on other goods—different foods, spices, clothing, and so forth. The agricultural laborer has only his or her labor to sell; the proceeds can be spent on rice or other goods. Similarly the cities contain workers who sell labor for money to buy food, shelter, and clothing; and entrepreneurs who buy goods and labor, produce other goods, sell them, and have the proceeds for personal consumption and investment in business expansion.

People will starve, then, when their entitlement is not sufficient to buy the food necessary to keep them alive. The food available to them, in short, is a question of income

distribution and, more fundamentally, of their ability to provide services that others in the economy are willing to pay for.

This, of course, does not mean that the supply of food is irrelevant. A decrease in the supply of food will usually increase its price, as people compete for the scarcer quantity. This will in turn decrease their ability to buy food by using their entitlement and, if they start close enough to the margin of hunger, may drive them to the point of starvation. Further, the entitlement approach, simple as it is, enables the analyst to say something about the distribution of the burden of starvation. Farm owners and, to a lesser extent, sharecroppers, should be less affected than others because the reduction in the amount they sell is at least partly offset by the higher prices. If the reduction in supply is caused by some factor, like flood, that reduces the amount to be harvested, farm laborers are thereby more likely to be seriously affected.

Thus, studies of different entitlements and how they are affected by variations in food supply, alone or in conjunction with other shifts in the economy, are capable of giving a much greater insight into the causes of famine than a simple measure of the amount of food available. But the real point of Sen's analysis is to show that relatively small changes in food supply may nevertheless be accompanied by famine. Indeed the economic theory he presents would allow for the possibility that, with no changes in the food supply at all, famine could be caused by other economic factors.

In his analysis of the Bengal famine of 1943 and 1944, Sen points to just such factors. Predominant among them, in his view, is the effect of the war against the Japanese in increasing demand. (He is careful to add that the evidence is not strong enough to establish one sequence of causes as against another.) Government expenditures, especially on construction, rose sharply. This clearly increased the entitlements of the newly employed urban workers; and since the total supplies were unchanged, the entitlements of the rural groups had to fall. Indeed, rice prices rose sharply even before any evidence that crops had failed.

In Bengal, when conditions are sufficiently desperate, a person will, if necessary, spend the whole of his or her income on food. Even many of those who do not live in fear of starvation will be hungry enough so that a large fraction of any increase in income will be spent on food.* Indeed, in the poorer, less-developed countries, roughly two-thirds of total income goes for expenditures on food. Hence, as groups like urban workers newly employed in war work gain increased entitlements, their willingness to buy additional food is high. Prices rise, and the entitlements of other groups will necessarily fall unless there is a corresponding rise in food supply. If these other groups are already on the margin of sustainable life, then indeed a famine may be created without any decline in food supply.

Sen offers additional explanations. Perhaps the most controversial is that of hoarding, either for oneself or for speculation. When situations of scarcity arise, hoarding is always blamed. The evidence for the degree and the effects of hoarding is usually difficult to come by, but, apart from this empirical question, there is a significant theoretical problem concerning its implications. If the famine is prolonged, then hoarding at the beginning means greater stores will be available later on. In fact, if the hoarder was correct in his expectations, that is, if the farmer does need to consume his own grain at a later date or if the speculator makes money by selling at a higher price, then hoarding will have improved the availability of food later on, at, to be sure, the cost of making things worse initially.

A still better result might be achieved if the government took over some part of the hoarded stores and distributed them to the needy; but it should also withhold some from immediate use. Such a policy would amount to changing the entitlements. Indeed, when a famine occurs it would certainly require an inhuman preference for established property rights over human needs not to redistribute

purchasing power and other forms of entitlements. But that does not alter the basic point about hoarding: if we consider the entire period of famine, hoarding will only worsen the famine if it turns out to be excessive, that is, if some of the hoards are retained beyond the end of the famine.

In view of the absence of detailed data on famines, it is not surprising that Sen's analysis does not explain everything. His point of view would suggest that if the total food supply changed only mildly the terrible losses of some people should be reflected in greater food consumption by others. Yet in Table 6.7 (p. 71), concerning the Bengal famine of 1943–1944, the proportionate increase in destitution is much the same for noncultivating landowners (admittedly a poor group in the best of times) as for peasant cultivators or for those who worked partly for themselves and partly for others. If the rice crop failure is treated as minor, the landowners should have gained; any reduction in quantity would have been more than offset by the rise in the price of rice compared with other prices. However, the table covers only some rural regions; it may well be that greater supplies of grains were to be found in the urban regions. In Calcutta itself, only migrants from the rural areas seem to have suffered from famine.

Many other insights are to be gained from Sen's emphasis on entitlement, especially concerning the subtlety of the interaction between pastoralists and farmers, a subject he discusses in his chapters on the famines in the Sahel and in Ethiopia.

What policies does an entitlement approach suggest? Sen is surprisingly chary of answers to this question. A brief chapter mostly tends to emphasize the complexity of the analysis introduced by the entitlement approach. He correctly points out that the market mechanism cannot be relied upon, for it is precisely the failure of market power that chooses the victims of famine. He does speak of insurance arrangements, that is, ways by

---

*   T. T. Poleman, *Qunatifying the nutrition situation in developing countries*. Food Research Institute Studies, XVIII (1981), p. 25.

which entitlement of a particular group, for instance rural laborers, could be automatically increased under famine conditions. However, he seems to emphasize the difficulties rather than the advantages of such a device.

For example, he points out that general famine conditions affect only selected persons, and an insurance program based on aggregate food supply, for example, would therefore miss its intended beneficiaries. If, on the other hand, insurances were highly individualized, this would, in my view, affect the incentives people have to work and to plan for the future. Still, it does not seem to me so difficult to propose that, at certain levels, a program for insurance (or, what is equivalent, relief) should go into effect, based on the ability of some designated fraction of the population to buy food; not does it seem excessively difficult to direct aid to the groups most likely to be affected. This will not feed every starving person, since some will receive help who do not need it and some who need help will not receive it; but no system will avoid problems of this sort.

Although famine is a fairly unusual event, and improvements in transportation and communication have made it less and less likely, the need to respond to specific famines is no less urgent. The three famines of the mid-1970s discussed by Sen, though apparently much less severe than the 1943–1944 famine in Bengal, are horrifying enough. Indeed, the fact that famine is becoming less frequent and intense should make it all the easier to provide prompt aid. On a world scale, hunger and malnutrition are far greater problems. Of course, they are intimately related. As is obvious from Sen's analyses, famine is the result of pushing already hungry populations over the relatively low threshold that separates them from genuine starvation.

The extent of world hunger as expressed in protein-calorie malnutrition has been much disputed. Estimates range from 100 million to 2.5 billion people affected. In any case, it is certainly very large. Since the various aid programs that nations and international organizations are now willing to support are sure to be inadequate to deal with even the lowest estimates, the exact figure is really of little practical consequence.

Among experts there is an increasing tendency to regard hunger as primarily a problem of income distribution, of purchasing power. In this sense, Sen's book can be seen as part of a larger effort to make a fresh analysis of hunger. His entitlement approach adds to the emphasis on income distribution by stressing its causes, rather than merely taking the distribution as a given. But since the analysis of causation is necessarily complex and uncertain, the two approaches are similar. The pioneering work in connecting income distribution with hunger is that of Shlomo Reutlinger and Marcelo Selowsky for the International Bank for Reconstruction and Development (the World Bank).[*] They estimated (very imperfectly) a relation between calorie consumption and income; then, with the aid of the fragmentary income distribution data available, they estimated the calorie consumption for different income classes. On this basis, they could estimate the number of people whose supply of calories fell below some critical level. Because there is little data available, the possibilities for error are enormous; but this approach gets at the underlying determinants of hunger.

What has become clear is that hunger and ultimately famine are basically questions of the distribution of income and the entitlements to food. That does not of course mean that food supply is irrelevant, but that it is far from determining who will go hungry. At higher levels of consumption, hunger fades away as a basic problem but is replaced by other needs, including medicine, shelter, and the like. In short, averages are insufficient guides to economic performance, though they cannot be ignored.

The appropriate measures to change income and food distribution, especially those

---

[*] *Malnutrition and poverty: magnitude and policy options,* World Bank Staff Occasional Paper No. 23 (1976).

that relieve famine, hunger, and poverty, partly depend on the information available; but they also require conceptual definitions, and these are intimately tied to value judgments and measures of welfare. As a counterpoint to his analysis of famines, Sen discusses some of the problems of measuring poverty. He shows the inadequacy of the usual United States measure, the number of people whose incomes are below the so-called "poverty line." He would equally reject a measure of hunger based on the number of people whose food consumption falls below a fixed level defined as "adequate." The distribution of income below the poverty line or of calorie consumption below the critical level may still allow for sharp differences among poor people. In the case of calorie consumption, the difference may be between widespread hunger and appalling famine.

Sen's book, together with other recent work on the world problem of hunger, should alert us even more strongly to the need for studying the distribution of income and of improving the relative situation of the very poor in order to curb the worst consequences of the economic system. The political implications of this shift in emphasis may be serious indeed, pointing up the responsibilities of the governments of the less developed countries. Poor as they may be, these countries generally have more control over their domestic income distribution than the advanced nations they deal with.

33

Facing Food Scarcity

Lester R. Brown

At 1:30 a.m. on Tuesday, September 12, a small group of high-ranking agricultural economists, meteorologists, and remote-sensing satellite experts entered a corridor on the fifth floor of the U.S. Department of Agriculture's massive "South Building" in Washington, D.C. Behind them, an armed guard closed a heavy steel door, which was then locked. Inside, the blinds were drawn down on all windows, the stairwells and elevators were locked, and the telephones switched off.

Through the night, the group pored over the data they had brought—information on grain crop supply and demand that had been compiled from more than 100 agricultural countries and confirmed by a sophisticated array of satellite observations and weather analysis. At 5 a.m., the group—known as the World Agricultural Outlook Board—assembled around a table in a conference room inside the locked area, and began a final review of their findings.

Around dawn, a score of international wire service reporters—all with security clearances—began converging on the building, and at 7 o'clock they were admitted to a guarded room inside the locked area. Under heavy surveillance, they were given computer discs and secured phone lines, and permitted to begin looking at what the Board had found. At exactly 8:30, the "lockup" ended: the reporters' phone lines were switched on, the blinds were raised to the morning sun, and the steel door was opened. Simultaneously, the Board's report went out over the Internet.

At first glance, what the various tables that had been compiled through the night revealed was that the world's stocks of rice, wheat, corn, and other grains had fallen to their lowest level in two decades. But a mile away at the Worldwatch Institute, we aggregated the crop totals and linked them to global population data, with an even more disturbing result. Measured in days of global consumption, the world's estimated carryover stocks of grain for 1996 had fallen to 49 days—the lowest level ever.

The Outlook Board's report, which is released each month, is little known to the public but of incalculable value to commodities traders and agribusinesses—some of whom stand to gain or lose fortunes on the information it contains. But on this occasion the data had even more meaning: in a world of rapidly expanding human population, carryover grain stocks are the key indicator of the world's capacity to meet that population's growing demand for food. Grain is the planet's largest source not only of food for direct consumption, but of feed for livestock and poultry products, and farm-raised fish—of the major protein sources on which humans depend.

The Outlook Board reported that crop-withering heat waves had lowered grain harvests in the northern tier of industrial countries, including the United States, Canada, parts of Europe, and Russia. In many farming regions, the summer of 1995 was the hottest ever recorded. Thus, many of the world's farmers found themselves contending not only with the usual vagaries of weather but with temperatures higher than they have ever known—much as global climate models had projected would result from the planet's rising levels of atmospheric carbon dioxide. As that trend continues, shrunken harvests could become the price of our addiction to fossil fuels.

The scarcity implicit in the reported trends and the higher food prices that would result was bad news for the world's low-income consumers. Already spending nearly all their meager incomes on food just to survive, many will not make it to the next harvest. In the global race between food and people, they would be among the early losers.

For decades, grain stocks remained more or less adequate; as population has surged, so has food production. Boosted by new crop varieties, fertilizers, and irrigation, yields improved dramatically. But in recent years, farmers have faltered, and much of the optimism engendered by those ever-rising yields is evaporating. Since the bumper crop of 1990, there has been no growth in global grain production at all—while population has grown by some 440 million people, or the equivalent of 40 New York Cities.

In 1995, a small amount of cropland was held out of production under commodity set-aside programs, including some 7.5 percent of U.S. cornland and 12 percent of the grain-land in Europe. But even if all this land *had* been in production, the additional 34 million tons or so of grain that it would have produced would not be enough to offset the year's 49-million-ton drop in global stocks. In fact, world stocks have now been drawn down for three consecutive years, helping to cushion the lack of growth in world production. But now that they are down to 49 days (little more than pipline supplies), the cushion is nearly gone.

In effect, the world's food economy may be shifting from a long-accustomed period of overall abundance to one of scarcity. Of course, the abundance of the past half-century hasn't eliminated hunger, as the episodes of starvation in Ethiopia and Somalia arrest—not to mention the less publicized deprivation of many of the world's billion "absolute poor." But that deprivation has been largely a result of poverty, not of overall supply. In the coming era, the supply itself will be limited, and the effects of shortages will be felt everywhere. Already, the 90 million being added to the global population each year are being fed only by reducing the consumption of those already here.

If the September World Outlook report came as coveted business intelligence for shrewd commodities traders, it did not come as any great surprise to those who have been studying the earth's carrying capacity. Environmentalists and scientists have long argued that the environmental needs of the past few decades could not continue. We could be heading for unimaginable trouble, they said, if we continue to strip the planet of its forest cover, to erode its cropland, overgraze its rangelands, overpump its aquifers, deplete its oceans, pollute its air, pump excessive amounts of carbon dioxide into the atmosphere, and destroy the habitats of our fellow creatures.

Some thought the crisis might come in the form of an epidemic of pollution-induced illnesses and rising death rates. Others thought the effects might first show up in the collapse of local ecosystems. Indeed, such perturbations have become increasingly visible at the regional level—in the surging death rates of Russians, or the desertification of once productive land in Africa. But globally, it is food scarcity that may soon become the principal manifestation of continuing population growth and environmental mismanagement. If so, the first economic indicator of environmental stress will be rising food prices.

The Shrinking Land

One reason the world's opinion-makers find it hard to believe there will be any problem with food is that they have lived in a period of unbroken abundance, with much of that abundance concentrated in the same regions where the most influential news media are concentrated. Tragedies like the starvations in Ethiopia and Somalia are thus seen as isolated aberrations. But perhaps the most compelling reason for thinking there's no problem is the assumption that if it really comes to the crunch, farmers can always bring more land into cultivation. After all, on every continent there are vast areas of unpopulated, uncultivated territory.

That assumption is unwarranted. Food cannot be grown just anywhere; it can't be grown in places where the land is too cold, too dry, too steep, or too barren. It also can't be grown where there is no water or where the soil has been degraded by erosion. Of the land that is still free of all these constraints, nearly all is already in cultivation. Moreover, some of the most erodible land is slowly *losing* its productivity.

All over the world, farmers have begun pulling back, abandoning much of the marginal land they first plowed in the mid-1970s. That land had been pressed into service after the Soviet Union's surprise decision, in 1972, to import massive quantities of wheat after a poor harvest. The decision had caused world grain prices to double, and gave farmers a strong incentive to raise output. But today, with much of that land being depleted still further by erosion, it is no longer worth tilling. In the former Soviet Union, the harvested grain area has shrunk from its peak of 123 million hectares in 1977 to 94 million in 1994. In the United States, the Conservation Reserve Program established in 1985 retired much of the highly erodible land that was plowed in the late 1970s, paying farmers to return it to grass before it became wasteland.

While the United States, Russia, and Ukraine are abandoning or retiring marginal grainland, some of the more densely populated countries are losing prime cropland to nonfarm uses. As Asia industrializes, the construction of thousands of factories, roads, parking lots, and new cities is wiping once-productive crop land off the map. Japan, South Korea, and Taiwan, the Asian countries that industrialized first and can serve as models of what may happen elsewhere, have collectively lost about 40 percent of the grain harvested area they had in 1960. Each year, Indonesia is losing an estimated 20,000 hectares of cropland on Java alone, which is enough to supply rice for 360,000 people, even as it adds 3 million people per year.

Even so, the losses in those countries may be dwarfed by what now appears likely—and perhaps inevitable—in China and India. The two population giants rank first and third as food producers (the U.S. is second), and both are gearing up for automobile-centered transportation systems. As recently as three years ago, China had only one car for every 200 people—a mere 1 percent of the U.S. ownership rate. But an increase to 22 million cars on the road by 2010, as now projected, would cause heavy cropland losses.

Yet, shortsighted as that may seem, it is a global trend with enormous momentum. It is epitomized, perhaps, by how quickly Vietnam, now a rice exporter, managed to break its own vow not to let industrialization undermine essential food production. Last spring, Vietnamese Prime Minister Vo Van Kiet established a ban on building factories in rice paddies. Just four months later, he changed his mind—in order to allow Ford Motor Company and other firms to build on 6,310 hectares of farmland near Hanoi.

While development encroaches on farmland, most farmers have nowhere else that they can retreat to in turn—and in fact, many are giving up farming and moving to the cities. In most countries, the agricultural frontiers have disappeared and nowhere is there any large areas of highly productive cropland waiting to be plowed. In a few places, such as the cerrado (a dry plain) in Eastern Brazil, there is marginally productive land that can be used if grain prices rise high enough. But that will do little more than help to satisfy local demand. Brazil, now the largest grain importer in the western hemisphere, is facing a population increase of more than 100 million people over the next half-century. If it can feed its own people, it will be doing well, it is unlikely to do much for China or Bangladesh.

The Dehydration of the Land

The human body consists largely of water, as does the food that sustains it. But the water in an ear of corn or a quarter-pound of beef is a mere drop in the bucket compared to the water needed to produce it. A pound of wheat takes about 1,000 pounds of water to grow. A pound of beef takes much more. A large part of the world's food production therefore depends on supplementing rainfall with irrigation—either from underground aquifers or from rivers. Yet, both groundwater and surface water are becoming scarce. While the quantity of water on the planet remains unchanged, the proportion of it diverted to uses other than agriculture—to residential and industrial needs—is climbing hand-in-hand with population and industrialization. At the same time, pressures are growing in many watersheds to limit both agricultural *and* other human uses of water in order to protect threatened ecosystem.

Water tables are now falling in major flood-producing regions. In the U.S. Great Plains, farmers from South Dakota through Nebraska, Kansas, eastern Colorado, parts of Oklahoma, and the Texas panhandle were able to greatly expand their irrigation from mid century through 1980, by pumping from the great Ogallala Aquifer. But the Ogallala is mostly a fossil aquifer—meaning that most of it is not recharged by rainfall. Reliance on it, therefore, is ultimately unsustainable. And, in its more shallow southern reaches, it is already largely depleted. As a result, since 1982 irrigated area in Texas has shrunk 11 percent, forcing farmers to return to traditional—and less productive—dryland farming. Irrigated area is also shrinking in Oklahoma, Kansas, and Colorado. An estimated 21 percent of U.S. irrigated cropland is watered by the unsustainable practice of drawing down underground aquifers.

In India, water tables are falling in several states including the Punjab—the country's breadbasket. In the Punjab, the double cropping of winter wheat and rice has dramatically boosted the overall grain harvest in recent years, but it has also pushed water use beyond the sustainable yield of the underlying aquifers. In such areas, the rate of pumping for irrigation will eventually be reduced to the rate of recharge. If water is being pumped out twice as fast as rainfall is recharging it, for example, the supply of irrigation water will one day have to be cut by half. In an area like the Punjab, this may mean that the double-cropping of wheat and rice will have to be modified by substituting a lower yielding dryland crop, such as sorghum or millet, for the rice. For India, which is adding 18 million people each year, that is not a pleasant prospect.

In China, which is trying to feed 1.2 billion increasingly affluent consumers, much of the northern part of the country is a water-deficient region. Around Beijing, for example, the water table has dropped from 15 feet below ground level in 1950 to more than 150 feet below today. In the northern provinces of Shanxi, Hebei, Henan, and Shandong, the amount of water available for irrigation has fallen to a fraction of that needed to maximize yields. And Vaclav Smil, a China scholar at the University of Vancouver in Canada, observes that the growing water needs of China's cities and industrial areas "will tend to lower even those modest irrigation rates."

If that is the case—if groundwater is falling not just in China, but all over the world—it becomes a question of some urgency whether the difference can then be made up from surface water. The planets great rivers, after all, are perpetually renewing. Yet here, too, there are signs of trouble. In more populated regions, rivers have been tapped, diverted and dammed until often there is little water left to continue on its way. In fact, many rivers now run dry before they reach the ocean.

Several months before the World Agricultural Outlook Board issued its September report, for example, China's great Yellow River completely disappeared some 620 kilometers from its mouth on the Yellow Sea. At the same time, on the opposite side of the globe, the Colorado River was disappearing into the Arizona desert; since 1993, it has rarely reached the Gulf of California. In central Asia, the Amu Darya is drained dry by Turkmen and Uzbek cotton farmers well before it reaches the Aral Sea, thus contributing not only to the sea's gradual disappearance but also to that of the huge fishery it once supported.

Draining rivers dry may be rationalized as essential to human food production, but the benefits that draining confers on one front have to be weighed against the heavy toll it takes on another. Dried-up or diminished outflows threaten the survival of those fish that spawn in them. Estuaries that have served as breeding grounds for oceanic species are destroyed.

Accordingly, some governments are moving to restore river flow to protect these fisheries—even though it means reducing irrigated area. In California, for example, officials have decided to restore nearly a million acre-feet of water to the annual flow of the Sacramento River in an effort to maintain the health of the San Francisco Bay estuary. Thus the irrigated area in California is declining even as the demand for food is climbing. Worldwide, with some two-thirds of all the water that is diverted from rivers or pumped from underground now used for irrigation, any cutbacks in water supply affect the food prospect. In regions where all available water is now being used, the competition between farmers and cities is intensifying.

The dilemma is that as population grows, the resulting increases in urban and industrial demand can be satisfied only by diverting water from the very irrigation needed to supply that population's food. In Colorado, the small town of Thornton, which lies northwest of Denver, has purchased water rights from farmers and ranchers in Weld County on Colorado's northern border. It plans to build a 100-kilometer pipeline to transport the water as its needs begin to exceed local supplies in the years ahead.

Similarly, in 1995, the city of Fukuoka in southern Japan bought irrigation water from some 700 rice growers to avoid a water shortage. In China, officials decided in early 1994 to ban farmers from the reservoirs around Beijing, so the water could be used to meet the city's soaring residential and industrial demands. Those demands are further heightened by the population's growing affluence, which increases per-capita water use as more people get indoor plumbing, replete with flush toilets. These diversions of irrigation water to nonfarm uses are but three isolated examples of a practice that is fast becoming commonplace.

Could More Fertilizer Help?

If the cropland area is no longer expanding, then the prospects for producing food from land come down to raising the output from the existing cropland. That was the global strategy for four decades, and it worked. . . . As long as farmers kept increasing the amount of fertilizer they used, the amount of cropland per person could continue to shrink, as it did, without noticeably disrupting the food supply. In effect, more fertilizer made up for having less land. But of course, adding more and more fertilizer to the land can't go on forever. It's like a baker adding more and more yeast to the dough.

Historically, of course, abundant increases in output have been achieved by this strategy. Between 1950 and 1989, fertilizer use expanded ten-fold—from 14 million tons to 146 million tons, helping to nearly triple the world's grain harvest. But now it appears that the limits have been reached, and in some regions exceeded. In country after country, farmers have discovered that they are already using the maximum amount of fertilizer that existing crop varieties can effectively use. Over the past six years, global fertilizer use has actually fallen, to 122 million tons.

The principal reason for the drop can be traced to an excessive use of fertilizer in the former Soviet Union before the agricultural economic reforms that were launched in 1988. During the preceding decades, Moscow had hoped that heavy fertilizer use would eliminate dependence on imported grain. When the farmers were faced with real-world prices for both grain and fertilizer, however, their use of fertilizer became far less profligate—falling some 60 percent between 1988 and 1995.

Other countries have also retrenched on this front. In the United States, fertilizer use peaked around 1980 and has dropped some 10 percent since then as new soil fertility tests have enabled farmers to more precisely determine fertilizer needs and avoid overuse. In both western Europe and Japan, fertilizer use has been refined to the point where adding more would have little effect on production.

The substitution of fertilizer for land, the formula that worked so well for farmers for nearly half a century, is now failing them. Unless plant breeders can develop new varieties that can effectively use still larger quantities of fertilizer, the world's farmers will have trouble reestablishing steady growth in food output. The challenge to agricultural scientists, to find a new formula to expand world food output as needed, has thus far gone unanswered.

The Limits of Fisheries

Jules Verne long ago suggested that when we reached the limits of food production on the land, we could turn to the oceans. Unfortunately many countries have been doing just that over the past several decades. Between 1950 and 1989, the fish catch expanded more than four fold, climbing from 22 million tons to 100 million tons. During the six years since then, the catch has leveled off. United Nations marine biologists count 17 major oceanic fisheries, and report that all are now being fished at or beyond capacity; thirteen are in a state of decline. Contrary to the prognosis of Jules Verne, we reached the limits of the oceans first.

Between 1950 and 1989, the seafood catch per person went from 9 kilograms to 19 kilograms. Since 1989, it has declined 8 percent. Predictably, seafood prices are rising. As a result of our failure to stabilize population before reaching the limits of oceanic fisheries,

we now face a declining seafood catch per person—and rising seafood prices for as far as we can see into the future.

Cessation of growth in the world fish catch is putting additional pressure on land-based food sources. If the annual growth in the world's animal protein supply—the 2 million more tons we were once able to haul from the sea—is now replaced with fish reared in ponds by fish farmers, it will require roughly 4 million tons of grain, approximately the amount of grain consumed each year in Belgium.

The Demand Side

While there has been no growth in the last five years in either ocean- or land-based food production, the demand for food has continued to expand, driven by population growth and rising affluence. Although the rate of world population growth has declined from the historical high of 2 percent in 1970 to 1.6 percent in 1995, the annual addition of some 90 million is now greater than at any time in history. Feeding that many more people each year requires that the world's farmers annually expand their production capacity by 28 million tons of grain per year, or 78,000 tons per day.

Even as population grows at a record pace, those with low incomes, who account for most of humanity and who typically depend on a starchy staple, such as rice, for 70 percent or more of their calories, want to diversify their diets by consuming more livestock products. This desire to move up the food chain appears to be universal. In every society where incomes have risen, so has consumption of livestock products. Our long existence over evolutionary time as hunter-gatherers may have created an innate taste for meat and eggs, while the taste for milk and milk-products, such as butter, cheese and yogurt, followed the development of agriculture.

As incomes have risen since 1950, world meat consumption has leaped four-fold, from 44 million tons to 184 million tons. Consumption per person has nearly doubled—from 17 kilograms in 1950 to 33 kilograms in 1994.

Within the last two years, rising meat consumption has transformed China from a net grain *exporter* of 8 million tons to a net *importer* of 16 million tons. Its overnight emergence as a leading importer of grain, second only to Japan, is helping drive up world grain prices. Over the next few decades, as China's population continues to balloon by another half-billion people, and as rapid industrialization continues to drive up incomes and the demand for grain even as it paves over cropland, the country's import deficit will continue its dramatic expansion.

It is only a matter of time until China's grain import needs overwhelm the export capacity of the United States and other exporting countries. But before that happens, the shortage will spread, because even as China is bidding for a growing share of the wood's exportable supplies, so are scores of other countries. The grain import needs of countries such as Indonesia, Iran, Pakistan, Egypt, Ethiopia, Nigeria, Mexico, Bangladesh, and India could easily triple by 2030. In the competition for high-priced exportable supplies, the weaker economies will lose out. In more human terms, so will many of the world's poor.

Even among the affluent, however, spending money on food is not unaffected by the growing shadow of global limits. As people shift toward more meat-based diets, the pattern of meat consumption itself is changing. The production of beef and mutton has leveled off in recent years, largely because the number of cattle, sheep, and goats being raised has pushed the limits of rangeland carrying capacity much as the quantity of fish being taken has reached the sustainable yield limits of the ocean. Most future gains in beef production will have to come from the feedlot, which puts beef in competition with pork and poultry for available grain supplies.

Carrying Capacity

As both fishermen and farmers fall behind the growth in world population, that growth raises a fundamental question about how many people the earth can support. The answer depends on a second question: At what level of consumption?

Grain use per person measures both the amount of grain consumed directly, which accounts for half of human caloric intake, and the amount consumed indirectly in the form of livestock products, which accounts for a large share of the remainder. Grain use varies from a high of roughly 800 kilograms per person in the more affluent societies, such as the United States, to a low of 200 kilograms per person in low-income societies, such as India. If the current world grain harvest, averaging 1.75 billion tons thus far during the 1990s, were boosted by roughly 15 percent to 2 billion tons, that harvest—if equitably distributed—could support 2.5 billion people at the American level of consumption, 5 billion at the Italian level, or 10 billion at the Indian level.

These numbers point to a looming gap between the projected growth of world population to 10 to 14 billion, and the strains on both oceanic- and land-based food production imposed by the current population of 5.7 billion—most of whom would like to move up the food chain. This gap underscores the need for governments to assess their *national* carrying capacities so that they and the people they serve can understand the difficult choices that lie ahead.

Now that the global fish catch has leveled off, we have a good sense of just how much food the oceans can sustainably provide. We are also beginning to develop a clearer sense of what can reasonably be expected from the land. Barring any new technologies that could lead to quantum jumps in food production, the way the discovery of fertilizer did, there is no possibility that the entire world can adopt the American diet. Indeed, for the first time in history, humanity is facing the prospect of a steady decline in both seafood and grain consumption per person for as far as we can see into the future.

The Politics of Scarcity

The fall in world grain carryover stocks in each of the last three years may mark the early stage of a transition from a buyer's market to a seller's market, one in which long-term grain prices are more likely to be rising than falling, and in which the politics of surplus, which have dominated the period since World War II, will be replaced by a politics of scarcity. Instead of a few exporting countries competing for markets that were never quite large enough, more than a hundred importing countries will compete for supplies that never seem adequate. Already, 1995 has witnessed the steepest rise in prices of wheat, rice, and corn seen in many years.

Experience with world food scarcity in the last half century has been limited to a few years in the mid-1970s, after the Soviet Union secretly cornered the wheat market in 1972 and drove gain prices abruptly upward. The U.S. government, in an effort to keep domestic food prices from rising in response to the scarcity, imposed an export embargo on soybeans, a crop that supplies much of the world's cooking oil and a large share of the protein meal fed to livestock. Since the United States was supplying over half the world's soybean exports, the economic shock waves from this decision reverberated throughout the world.

It was during this time of relative grain scarcity that the use of food for political purposes became an international issue. The U.S. State Department was accused of maintaining a blacklist of countries that voted against U.S. interests in the United Nations, and of putting blacklisted countries at the end of the line awaiting scarce food aid.

In the integrated economy of the 1990s, the effects of food scarcity sweep even more quickly across international borders than they did two decades ago; as USDA statistician Fred Vogel observed on the morning of the Outlook Board report, once the news was released at 8:30, it was "around the world in seconds."

Governments of exporting countries, sensitive to the speed with which the vagaries of a global market can generate food scarcities and inflation at home, are often tempted to impose export embargoes. Last May, Vietnam imposed a partial embargo on rice. Because grain prices in neighboring China had risen well above the world market level, large amounts of rice from Vietnam were crossing into China. But with rice prices climbing by up to 70 percent in northern Vietnam, making it difficult to control inflation, the government restricted exports while waiting for the new harvest to come in. Since Vietnam is the third largest rice exporter, after Thailand and the United States, this raised the world rice price. Meanwhile, in China, some provinces have even banned grain shipments to other provinces *within* the country in an effort to stop price rises.

The prospect of chronic world food scarcity raises new questions about the morality, of restricting or banning food exports. One question is whether a grain-exporting country can be justified in restricting exports in order to quell domestic food price rises, even though it will lead to even more rapid price rises—with potentially tragic effects—in the rest of the world. Another question concerns the role of the international community in protecting national versus international interests. The General Agreement on Tariffs and Trade, or GATT, is not well equipped for this task; it has been designed mainly to ensure access to markets. The challenge now is to

---

In a Nutshell

Why even with advances of modern agricultural technology, we are falling behind Years needed for the human population to reach . . .

Its 1st billion 2,000,000

2nd billion	105
3rd billion	.30
4th billion	15
5th billion	12
6th billion	11

One billion people is equal to 100 cities the size of Cairo or Los Angeles.

devise a set of trade institutions and rules that will assure access to *supplies*.

In the world of the late 1990s, many more countries will be seeking food supplies—some of them desperately—than will be in the market to sell. Even now, only a handful of countries consistently export grain on a meaningful scale: Argentina, Australia, Canada, France, Thailand, and the United States. Current world grain exports add up to roughly 200 million tons per year, of which the United States accounts for close to one-half. That puts great power in the hands of one government; and the possibility that food could be used for political purposes may be of growing concern to a majority of countries.

The politics of commodity control gained world-wide notoriety in 1973, when the Organization of Petroleum Exporting Countries successfully engineered a tripling in the world price of oil. Of course, there are differences between grain and oil. First, people can survive without oil, but not without food. Oil can be replaced with other energy sources, but there's no replacement for grain. And second, the United States controls a larger share of grain exports than Saudi Arabia does of oil.

With seafood, the politics of scarcity is raising its head in the increasingly frequent clashes among countries over access to fisheries. Although only a few of these disputes actually make international news, they are now an almost daily occurrence. Their pervasiveness is evident in a Greenpeace statement released at the U.N.-sponsored conference on regulating fishing on the high seas in July 1995: "Tuna wars in the northeast Atlantic, crab wars in the North Pacific, squid wars in the southern Atlantic, salmon wars in the North Pacific, and pollock wars in the Sea of Okhotsk are all warning signs that fish stocks are in serious trouble."

No other economic indicator is more politically sensitive than rising food prices. If the grain scarcity that will now continue at least until the 1996 harvest should continue indefinitely, millions of low income breadwinners could find that soaring food prices threaten the survival of their families. Food scarcity could bring into question the legitimacy of numerous national governments that have failed to address the growing imbalance between human reproduction and food production. Food prices rising out of control could trigger not only economic instability, but widespread political upheaval.

As of 1995, many aid donor countries, including the United States, are cutting food assistance budgets. These cuts, combined with higher procurement prices for grain, have reduced food aid from the historical high in fiscal 1993 of 15.2 million tons to an estimated 7.6 million tons in 1996.

The world is moving into a new era, one in which the problems we face will be vastly different from those with which most governments and news organizations are now preoccupied. With the world fish catch no longer expanding, if some people raise their consumption of seafood (as seems virtually certain), it will now be at the expense of others. Given the reality of rising prices, and of the wide disparities in income worldwide, the same may soon be said of food in general. In the past, as long as the pie was expanding, political leaders could always urge patience, arguing that everyone's lot would soon improve. But when the pie stops expanding, not because of a temporary lag of technology or planning, but because our collective consumption has finally overtaken some of the planet's productive limits, the political dynamic changes. The question of how the pie is sliced takes on a new prominence.

Our Greatest Change

For the first time during the half century since population growth accelerated after World War II, the world's farmers do not have the technologies needed to match the growth in population. If farmers cannot rely on the steadily expanding use of fertilizer to boost their grain harvests, and if agricultural scientists cannot quickly come up with a new technology that will lead to a quantum jump in world food output, then the world will need a new strategy for balancing human numbers and food supplies. With neither fishermen nor farmers able to keep up with population growth, most of the responsibility for achieving a humane balance between food and people rests with family planners. Beyond that, every effort will be needed to exploit each technological potential, however small its contribution, to expand food output.

As the difficulty in feeding 90 million more people each year becomes apparent, food security may replace military security as the principal preoccupation of governments. For many countries, security now depends more on protecting their territory from soil erosion than it does on protecting it from military invasion. As the food balance becomes more fragile, national security may depend more on stabilizing population than on developing new weapon systems.

In scores of developing countries, the population-driven growth in demand for food is now overrunning the capacity of local agricultural support systems, generating potentially huge import deficits. Given the over-population of so much of the world today, it may now be time to ask whether couples anywhere can morally justify having more than two children, the number needed to replace themselves.

The challenge is to quickly make the transition to smaller families everywhere. Historically, two countries have managed to reduce their population growth rates by half in a matter of years, and what was learned from those experiences is both painful and instructive. Japan did this during the seven years from 1949 to 1956, after it had to adjust to surviving without the overseas territories lost as a result of its defeat in World War II. China did the same thing between 1970 and 1976, when it first introduced family planning and adopted the two-child family as a goal.

The urgency of implementing the U.N. World Plan of Action adopted in Cairo in September, 1994, which calls for linking a global population strategy to more equitable development for poor nations and for women, increases as food scarcity spreads. One of the key components of the Plan is to fill the family planning gap as soon as possible. There are an estimated 120 million women in the world,

mostly in developing countries, who want to limit the size of their families but lack access to the family planning services needed to do so.

The Plan also emphasizes the importance of educating females. There is no social indicator that correlates more closely with the shift to smaller families than the level of female education, and this is a correlation that holds across all cultures. Few investments by the international development community can yield a higher return—in economic productivity, human well-being, and ultimately in political stability—than these.

If national governments undertake carrying capacity assessments, some may find that they cannot provide even for the projected growth in their populations, much less the aspirations of these populations for more varied diets. Under these circumstances, any hope the world's poor have of improving their diets depends on stabilizing world population long before it reaches the 10 to 14 billion now projected. Those countries that wait too long to address the population threat, as China did, may find themselves choosing between the reproductive rights of the current generation and the survival rights of the next.

There are a number of steps that can be taken to expand food production and buy additional time to stabilize population. These include:

❑ Returning to production the cropland in the United States and Europe that has been idled under supply management programs. This could boost grain production by an estimated 34 million tons, enough to cover world population growth for nearly 15 months.

❑ Discontinuing the use of grain to produce ethanol in the United States. Releasing the 10 million tons of corn now used for this purpose would support world population growth for an additional four months.

❑ Converting the land to produce tobacco into the production of food. If the 5 million hectares of cropland now used to grow tobacco were turned over to growing grain, it would not only provide enough grain to support world population for six months, but it would also reduce mortality rates and sharply lower health care costs.

❏ Investing more in agricultural research, specifically in developing more fertilizer responsive varieties *or* an alternative formula that will replace the use of fertilizer in expanding world food production. This effort demands an all-out effort using both conventional plant breeding techniques and those of biotechnology.

❏ Raising the efficiency of water use by shifting from free distribution of water to water marketing, a step that would permit more land to be irrigated.

❏ Designing a world action plan to stabilize soils, recognizing that every ton of topsoil lost to erosion today diminishes the food supply for the next generation.

❏ Devising national programs to protect cropland, particularly the most productive land, from being converted to nonfarm uses. This could be done either through zoning or through the adoption of a cropland conversion tax, one that would be large enough to reflect the land's long-term contribution to food security.

❏ Encouraging home gardening, particularly in affluent societies where land is available, much like the U.S. "victory gardens" of World War II.

There are also opportunities for reducing per-capita consumption, which in some societies is conspicuously excessive. In affluent societies, overeating today is regarded as unattractive; in the future it may be unconscionable. There are several ways of lowering per capita grain consumption to alleviate the effects of scarcity.

❏ One is to let the market do it. When grain prices doubled in the 1970s, Americans lowered their consumption of meat, milk and eggs enough to reduce grain feeding by 46 million tons, which would cover 20 months of world population growth. The disadvantage of this approach is that prices that are high enough to move the affluent down the food chain can inflict severe suffering on the poor.

❏ A second way is to educate people about the health risks associated with excessive consumption of fat-rich livestock products. The healthiest people in the world are not those living at the top of the food chain or those at the bottom, but those in the middle. Italians who use abut 400 kilograms of grain per year, for example, live longer than Americans who consume twice that, even though the Italians spend much less on health care. The growing popularity of semi-vegetarian diets in the United States in the early 1990s, when grain and meat prices were relatively low, demonstrates the possibility.

❏ A third technique, one widely used by industrial countries during World War II, is the rationing of the consumption of livestock products. The disadvantage of this approach is that it requires a nation-wide bureaucracy to administer the program and to enforce compliance.

❏ Fourth, and perhaps the most effective and efficient technique, is a tax on livestock products, one not unlike that applied by most governments to alcoholic beverages, another grain-based product. Although a tax on livestock products might not be politically popular among the affluent, it does moderate grain price rises, and in a time of acute scarcity it could be the price of political stability.

❏ Reducing the consumption of fat-rich livestock products, through whatever means, could help buy some additional time to stabilize population size. If the world's affluent could reduce their consumption of grain fed livestock products by 10 percent, they could free up 64 million tons of grain for direct human consumption. This would cover world population growth for another 26 months. A 20 percent reduction would buy more than four years.

One of the sustaining forces of modern civilization has been the expectation of a better life in the future. If the food situation continues to deteriorate, with no prospect of reversal, people in those societies least able to compete for these supplies will begin to lose hope. With the loss of hope comes the risk of social disintegration.

The economically integrated world of the late nineties is moving into uncharted territory, facing a set of problems on a scale and of a nature quite different from those faced in the past. If we are unable to reverse the trends of recent years, food scarcity may well become the defining issue as we exit this century and enter the next. History judges political leaders by whether or not they respond to the great issues of their time. For today's leaders, the challenge is to achieve a humane balance between food and people on a crowded planet.

34

What Are the *Real* Population and Resource Problems?

Julian J. Simon

Is there a natural-resource problem now? Certainly there is—just as there has always been. The problem is that natural resources are scarce, in the sense that it costs us labor and capital to get them, though we would prefer to get them for free.

Are we now "entering an age of scarcity"? You can see anything you like in a crystal ball. But almost without exception, the best data—the long-run economic indicators—suggest precisely the opposite. The relevant measures of scarcity—the costs of natural resources in human labor, and their prices relative to wages and to other goods—all suggest that natural resources have been becoming *less* scarce over the long run, right up to the present.

How about pollution? Is this not a problem? Of course pollution is a problem—people have always had to dispose of their waste products so as to enjoy a pleasant and healthy living space. But on the average we now live in a less dirty and more healthy environment than in earlier centuries.

About population now: Is there a population "problem"? Again, of course there is a population problem, just as there has always been. When a couple is about to have a baby,

they must prepare a place for the child to sleep safely. Then, after the birth of the child, the parents must feed, clothe, guard, and teach it. All of this requires effort and resources, and not from the parents alone. When a baby is born or a migrant arrives, a community must increase its municipal services—schooling, fire and police protection, and garbage collection. None of these are free.

Beyond any doubt, an additional child is a burden on people other than its parents—and in some ways even on them—for the first fifteen or twenty-five years of its life. Brothers and sisters must do with less of everything except companionship. Taxpayers must cough up additional funds for schooling and other public services. Neighbors have more noise. During these early years the child produces nothing, and the income of the family and the community is spread around more thinly than if the baby were not born. And when the child grows up and first goes to work, jobs are squeezed a bit, and the output and pay per working person go down. All this clearly is an economic loss for other people.

Almost equally beyond any doubt, however, an additional person is also a boon. The child or immigrant will pay taxes later on, contribute

---

energy and resources to the community, produce goods and services for the consumption of others, and make efforts to beautify and purify the environment. Perhaps most significant of all for the more-developed countries is the contribution that the average person makes to increasing the efficiency of production through new ideas and improved methods.

The real population problem, then, is *not* that there are too many people or that too many babies are being born. It is that others must support each additional person before that person contributes in turn to the well-being of others.

Which is more weighty, the burden or the boon? That depends on the economic conditions, about which we shall speak at some length. But also, to a startling degree, the decision about whether the overall effect of a child or migrant is positive or negative depends on the values of whoever is making the judgment—your preference to spend a dollar now rather than to wait for a dollar-plus-something in twenty or thirty years, your preferences for having more or fewer wild animals alive as opposed to more or fewer human beings alive, and so on. Population growth is a problem, but not *just* a problem; it is a boon, but not just a boon. So your values are all-important in judging the net effect of population growth, and whether there is "overpopulation" or "underpopulation."

An additional child is, from the economic point of view, like a laying chicken, a cacao tree, a new factory, or a new house. A baby is a durable good in which someone must invest heavily long before the grown adult begins to provide returns on the investment. But whereas "Travel now, pay later" is inherently attractive because the pleasure is immediate and the piper will wait, "Pay now, benefit from the child later" is inherently problematic because the sacrifice comes first.

You might respond that additional children will *never* yield net benefits, because they will use up irreplaceable resources. Much of this book is devoted to showing that additional persons do, in fact, produce more than they consume, and that natural resources are not an exception. But let us agree that there is

still a population problem, just as there is a problem with all good investments. Long before there are benefits, we must tie up capital that could otherwise be used for immediate consumption.

Please notice that I have restricted the discussion to the *economic* aspect of investing in children—that is, to a child's effect on the material standard of living. If we also consider the non-economic aspects of children—what they mean to parents and to others who enjoy a flourishing of humanity—then the case for adding children to our world becomes even stronger. And if we also keep in mind that most of the costs of children are borne by their parents rather than by the community, whereas the community gets the lion's share of the benefits later on, especially in developed countries, the essential differences between children and other investments tend to strengthen rather than weaken the case for having more children.

Food

Contrary to popular impression, the per capita food situation has been improving for the three decades since World War II, the only decades for which we have acceptable data. We also know that famine has progressively diminished for at least the past century. And there is strong reason to believe that human nutrition will continue to improve into the indefinite future, even with continued population growth.

Land

Agricultural land is not a fixed resource, as Malthus and many since Malthus have thought. Rather, the amount of agricultural land has been, and still is, increasing substantially, and it is likely to continue to increase where needed. Paradoxically, in the countries that are best supplied with food, such as the U.S., the quantity of land under cultivation has been decreasing because it is more economical to raise larger yields on less land than to increase the total amount of farmland. For this reason, among others, land for recreation and for wildlife has been increasing rapidly in the U.S. All this may be hard to believe, but solid data substantiate these statements beyond a doubt.

Natural Resources

Hold your hat—our supplies of natural resources are not finite in any economic sense. Nor does past experience give reason to expect natural resources to become more scarce. Rather, if the past is any guide, natural resources will progressively become less scarce, and less costly, and will constitute a smaller proportion of our expenses in future years. And population growth is likely to have a long-run *beneficial* impact on the natural-resource situation.

Energy

Grab your hat again—the long-run future of our energy supply is at least as bright as that of other natural resources, though political maneuvering can temporarily boost prices from time to time. Finiteness is no problem here either. And the long-run impact of additional people is likely to speed the development of a cheap energy supply that is almost inexhaustible.

Pollution

This set of issues is as complicated as you wish to make it. But even many ecologists, as well as the bulk of economists, agree that population growth is not the villain in the creation and reduction of pollution. And the key trend is that life expectancy, which is the best overall index of the pollution level, has improved markedly as the world's population has grown.

Pathological Effects of Population Density

This putative drawback of population growth is sheer myth. Its apparent source is faulty biological and psychological analogies with animal populations.

The Standard of Living

In the short run, additional children imply additional costs, though the costs to persons other than the children's parents are relatively small. In the longer run, however, per capita income is likely to be higher with a growing population than with a stationary one, both in more-developed and less-developed countries. Whether you wish to pay the present costs for the future benefits depends on how you weigh the future relative to the present; this is a value judgment.

Immigration

Immigration usually has a positive effect on most citizens. The few persons whom the immigrants might displace from their jobs may be hurt, of course, but many of them only temporarily. On balance, immigrants contribute more to the economy than they take, in the U.S. and most other places.

Human Fertility

The contention that poor and uneducated people breed like animals is demonstrably wrong, even for the poorest and most "primitive" societies. Well-off people who believe that the poor do not weigh the consequences of having more children are simply arrogant or ignorant, or both.

Future Population Growth

Population forecasts are publicized with confidence and fanfare, but the record of even the official forecasts made by U.S. government agencies and by the UN is little (if any) better than that of the most naive predictions. For example, experts in the 1930s foresaw the U.S. population as declining, perhaps to as little as 100 million people, long before the turn of the century. And official UN forecasts made in 1970 for the year 2000, a mere thirty years in advance, were five years later revised downward by almost 2 billion people, from 7.5 billion to 5.6 billion. Nor is the record better with more modern statistical methods. Perhaps most astonishing is a forecast made by the recent President's Commission on Population Growth and the American Future. In 1972 the commission published its prediction that "there will be no year in the next two decades in which the absolute number of births will be less than in 1970." But in the year *before* this prediction was made—1971—the number of births had *already* fallen lower than in 1970. The science of demographic forecasting clearly has not yet reached perfection.

World Population Policy

Tens of millions of U.S. taxpayers' money is being used to tell the governments and people of other countries that they ought to take strong measures to control their fertility. The head of the Population Branch of the U.S. State Department Agency for International Development (AID)—the single most important U.S. population official for many years—has publicly said that the U.S. should act to reduce fertility worldwide for its own economic self-interest. But no solid economic data or analyses underlie this assertion. Furthermore, might not such acts be an unwarranted interference in the internal affairs of other countries?

Domestic Population Activities

Other millions of U.S. taxpayers' funds go to private organizations making up the population lobby, whose directors believe that, for environmental and related reasons, fewer Americans should be born. These funds are used to propagandize the rest of us that we should believe—and act—in ways consistent with the views of such organizations as the Population Crisis Committee, the Population Reference Bureau, the Worldwatch Institute, the Environmental Fund, and the Association for Voluntary Sterilization.

Still more tens of millions of U.S. taxpayers' funds are being spent to reduce the fertility of the poor in the U.S. The explicit justification for this policy (given by the head of Planned Parenthood's Alan Guttmacher Institute) is that it will keep additional poor people off the welfare rolls. Even were this to be proven—and as far as I know it has not been proven—is this in the spirit or tradition of America? Furthermore, there is statistical proof that the public birth-control clinics, which were first opened in large numbers in

the southern states, were positioned to reduce fertility among blacks.

Involuntary Sterilization

Tax moneys are being used to involuntarily sterilize poor people (often black) without medical justification. As a result of the eugenics movement, which has been intertwined with the population-control movement for decades, there are now laws in thirty states providing for the involuntary sterilization of the mentally defective, and many thousands have been so sterilized. And these laws have led to perfectly normal women being sterilized, without their knowledge, after being told that their operations were other sorts of minor surgery . . .

About This Author and His Values

This book originated in my interest in the economics of population. In order to show that population growth is not a straightforward evil, I had to show that more people need not cause scarcities or environmental decay in the long run. That's how this book came to be written.

Ironically, when I began to work on population studies, I assumed that the accepted view was sound. I aimed to help the world contain its "exploding" population, which I believed to be one of the two main threats to mankind (war being the other). But my reading and research led me into confusion. Though the standard economic theory of population (which has hardly changed since Malthus) asserts that a higher population growth implies a lower standard of living, the available empirical data do not support that theory. My technical book, which is the predecessor of this volume, is an attempt to reconcile that contradiction. It leads to a theory that suggests population growth has positive economic effects in the long run, though there are costs in the short run.

When I began my population studies, I was in the midst of a depression of unusual duration (whose origins had nothing to do with population growth or the world's predicament). As I studied the economics of population and worked my way to the views I now hold—that population growth, along with the lengthening of human life, is a moral and material triumph—my outlook for myself, for my family, and for the future of humanity became increasingly more optimistic. Eventually I was able to pull myself out of my depression. This is only part of the story, but there is at least some connection between the two sets of mental events—my population studies and my increasing optimism.

One spring day about 1969 I visited the AID office in Washington to discuss a project intended to lower fertility in less-developed countries. I arrived early for my appointment, so I strolled outside in the warm sunshine. Below the building's plaza I noticed a sign that said "Iwo Jima Highway." I remembered reading about a eulogy delivered by a Jewish chaplain over the dead on the battlefield at Iwo Jima, saying something like, "How many who would have been a Mozart or a Michelangelo or an Einstein have we buried here?" And then I thought, Have I gone crazy? What business do I have trying to help arrange it that fewer human beings will be born, each one of whom might be a Mozart or a Michelangelo or an Einstein—or simply a joy to his or her family and community, and a person who will enjoy life?

I still believe that helping people fulfill their desires for the number of children they want is a wonderful service. But to persuade them or coerce them to have fewer children than they would individually like to have—that is something entirely different.

The longer I read the literature about population, the more baffled and distressed I become that one idea is omitted: Enabling a potential human being to come into life and to enjoy life is a good thing, just as enabling a living person's life not to be ended is a good thing. Of course a death is not the same as an averted life, in part because others feel differently about the two. Yet I find no logic implicit in the thinking of those who are horrified at the starvation of a comparatively few people in a faraway country (and apparently more horrified than at the deaths by political murder in that same faraway country, or at the deaths by accidents in their own country) but who are positively gleeful with the thought that 1 million or 10 million times that many lives will never be lived that might be lived.

Economics alone cannot explain this attitude, for though the economic consequences of death differ from those of non-life, they are not so different as to explain this difference in attitude. So what is it? Why does Kingsley Davis (one of the world's great demographers) respond to the U.S. population growth during the 1960s with, "I have never been able to get anyone to tell me why we needed those 23 million." And Paul Ehrlich: "I can't think of any reason for having more than one hundred fifty million people [in the U.S.], and no one has ever raised one to me."

I can suggest to Davis and Ehrlich more than one reason for having more children and taking in more immigrants. Least interesting is that the larger population will probably mean a higher standard of living for our grandchildren and great-grandchildren. A more interesting reason is that we need another person for exactly the same reason we need Davis and Ehrlich. That is, just as the Davises and Ehrlichs of this world are of value to the rest of us, so will the average additional person be of value.

The most interesting reason for having additional people, however, is this: If the Davises and Ehrlichs say that their lives are of value to themselves, and if the rest of us honor that claim and say that our lives are of value to us, then in the same manner the lives of additional people are of value to those people themselves. Why should we not honor their claims, too?

If Davis or Ehrlich were to ask those 23 million additional Americans born between 1960 and 1970 whether it was a good thing that they were born, many of them would be able to think of a good reason or two. Some of them might also be so unkind as to add, "Yes, it's true that you gentlemen do not *personally* need any of us for your own welfare. But then, do you think that we have greater need of *you*?"

What is most astonishing is that these simple ideas, which would immediately spring to the minds of many who cannot read or write, have never even come into the heads of famous scientists such as Davis and Ehrlich—by their own admission.

The same absence of this basic respect for human life is at the bottom of Ehrlich's well-known restatement of Pascal's wager. "If I'm right, we will save the world [by curbing population growth]. If I'm wrong, people will still be better fed, better housed, and happier, thanks to our efforts. [He probably *is* wrong.] Will anything be lost if it turns out later that we can support a much larger population than seems possible today?"

Please note how different is Pascal's wager: Live as if there is God, because even if there is no God you have lost nothing. Pascal's wager applies entirely to one person. No one else loses if he is wrong. But Ehrlich bets what he thinks will be the economic gains that we and our descendants might enjoy against the unborn's very lives. Would he make the same sort of wager if his *own* life rather than others' lives were the stake?

A last, very personal word: I may come through the print to you as feisty or even tough, and able to take care of myself in this argument. But I am not very feisty in person. I have been trying—mostly unsuccessfully—to get a hearing for these ideas since 1969, and though times have changed somewhat, the difficulties of espousing this unpopular point of view do get to me; until recently they were near the point of shutting me up and shutting me down. If there weren't a handful of editors like Sandy Thatcher of Princeton University Press, you wouldn't hear from me at all. Some others hold a point of view similar to mine. But there are far too few of us to provide mutual support and comfort. So this is a plea for love, printer's ink, and research grants for our side. All contributions gratefully accepted.

Now let's see if my facts and arguments persuade you of the claims I have made. . . .

Conclusion

In the short run, all resources are limited—natural resources such as the pulpwood that went into making this book, created resources such as the number of pages Princeton University Press can allow me, and human resources such as the attention you will devote to what I say. In the short run, a greater use of any resource means pressure on supplies and a higher price in the market, or even rationing. Also in the short run there will always be shortage crises because of weather, war, politics, and population movements. The results that an individual notices are sudden jumps in taxes, inconveniences and disruption, and increases in pollution.

The longer run, however, is a different story. The standard of living has risen along with the size of the world's population since the beginning of recorded time. And with increases in income and population have come less severe shortages, lower costs, and an increased availability of resources, including a cleaner environment and greater access to natural recreation areas. And there is no convincing economic reason why these trends toward a better life, and toward lower prices for raw materials (including food and energy), should not continue indefinitely.

Contrary to common rhetoric, there are no meaningful limits to the continuation of this process. There is no physical or economic reason why human resourcefulness and enterprise cannot forever continue to respond to impending shortages and existing problems with new expedients that, after an adjustment period, leave us better off than before the problem arose. Adding more people will cause us more such problems, but at the same time there will be more people to solve these problems and leave us with the bonus of lower costs and less scarcity in the long run. The bonus applies to such desirable resources as better health, more wilderness, cheaper energy, and a cleaner environment.

This process runs directly against Malthusian reasoning and against the apparent common sense of the matter, which can be summed up as follows: The supply of any resource is fixed, and greater use means less to go around. The resolution of this paradox is not simple. Fuller understanding begins with the idea that the relevant measure of scarcity is the cost or price of a resource, not any physical measure of its calculated reserves. And the appropriate way for us to think about extracting resources is not in physical units, pounds of copper or acres of farmland, but rather in the services we get from these resources—the electrical transmission capacity of copper, or the food values and gastronomic enjoyment the farmland provides. Following on this is the fact that economic history has not gone as Nalthusian reasoning suggests. The prices of all goods, and of the services they provide, have fallen in the long run, by all reasonable measures. And this irrefutable fact must be taken into account as a fundamental datum that can reasonably be projected into the future, rather than as a fortuitous chain of circumstances that cannot continue.

Resources in their raw form are useful and valuable only when found, understood, gathered together, and harnessed for human needs. The basic ingredient in the process, along with the raw elements, is human knowledge. And we develop knowledge about how to use raw elements for our benefit only in response to our needs. This includes knowledge for finding new sources of raw materials such as copper, for growing new resources such as timber, for creating new quantities of capital such as farmland, and for finding new and better ways to satisfy old needs, such as successively using iron or aluminum or plastic in place of clay or copper. Such knowledge has a special property: It yields benefits to people other than the ones who develop it, apply it, and try to capture its benefits for themselves. Taken in the large, an increased need for resources usually leaves us with a permanently greater capacity to get them because we gain knowledge in the process. And there is no meaningful physical limit—even the commonly mentioned weight of the earth—to our capacity to keep growing forever.

Perhaps the most general matter at issue here is what Gerald Holton calls a "thema." The thema underlying the thinking of most writers who have a point of view different from mine is the concept of fixity or finiteness of resources in the relevant system of discourse. This is found in Malthus, of course. But the idea probably has always been a staple of human thinking because so much of our situation must sensibly be regarded as fixed in the short run—the bottles of beer in the refrigerator, our paycheck, the amount of energy parents have to play basketball with their kids. But the thema underlying my thinking about resources (and the thinking of a minority of others) is that the relevant system of discourse has a long enough horizon that it makes sense to treat the system as not fixed, rather than finite in any operational sense. We see the resource system as being as unlimited as the number of thoughts a person might have, or the number of variations that might ultimately be produced by biological evolution. That is, a key difference between the thinking of those who worry about impending doom, and those who see the prospects of a better life for more people in the future, apparently is whether one thinks in closed-system or open-system terms. For example, those who worry that the second law of thermodynamics dooms us to eventual decline necessarily see our world as a closed system with respect to energy and entropy; those who view the relevant universe as unbounded view the second law of thermodynamics as irrelevant to this discussion. I am among those who view the relevant part of the physical and social universe as open for most purposes. Which thema is better for thinking about resources and population is not subject to scientific test. Yet it profoundly affects our thinking. I believe that here lies the root of the key difference in thinking about population and resources.

Why do so many people think in closed-system terms? There are a variety of reasons. (1) Malthusian fixed-resources reasoning is simple and fits the isolated facts of our everyday lives, whereas the expansion of resources is complex and indirect and includes all creative human activity—it cannot be likened to our own larders or wallets. (2) There are always immediate negative effects from an increased pressure on resources, whereas the benefits only come later. It is natural to pay more attention to the present and the near future compared with the more distant future. (3) There are often special-interest groups that alert us to impending shortages of particular resources such as timber or clean air. But no one has the same stake in trying to convince us that the long-run prospects for a resource are better than we think. (4) It is easier to get people's attention (and television time and printer's ink) with frightening forecasts than with soothing forecasts. (5) Organizations that form in response to temporary or non-existent dangers, and develop the capacity to raise funds from public-spirited citizens and governments that are aroused to fight the danger, do not always disband when the danger evaporates or the problem is solved. (6) Ambition and the urge for profit are powerful elements in our successful struggle to satisfy our needs. These motives, and the markets in which they work, often are not pretty, and many people would prefer not to depend on a social system that employs these forces to make us better off. (7) Associating oneself with environmental causes is one of the quickest and easiest ways to get a wide reputation for high-minded concern; it requires no deep thinking and steps on almost no one's toes.

The apparently obvious way to deal with resource problems—have the government control the amounts and prices of what consumers consume and suppliers supply—is inevitably counter-productive in the long run because the controls and the price fixing prevent us from making the cost-efficient adjustments that we would make in response to the increased short-run costs, adjustments that eventually would more than alleviate the problem. Sometimes governments must play a crucial role to avoid short-run disruptions and disaster, and to ensure that no group consumes public goods without paying the real social cost. But the appropriate times for governments to play such roles are far fewer than the times they are called upon to do so by those inclined to turn to authority to tell others what to do, rather than allow each of us to respond with self-interest and imagination.

I do not say that all is well. Children are hungry and sick; people live out lives of physical and intellectual poverty, and lack of opportunity; war or some new pollution may do us all in. What I *am* saying is that for most of the relevant economic matters I have checked the *trends* are positive rather than negative. And I doubt that it does the troubled people of the world any good to say that things are getting worse though they are really getting better. And false prophecies of doom can damage us in many ways.

Is a rosy future guaranteed? Of course not. There always will be temporary shortages and resource problems where there are strife, political blundering, and natural calamities—that is, where there are people. But the natural world allows, and the developed world promotes through the marketplace, responses to human needs and shortages in such manner that one backward step leads to 1,000 steps forward, or thereabouts. That's enough to keep us headed in a life-sustaining direction. The main fuel to speed our progress is our stock of knowledge, and the brake is our lack of imagination. The ultimate resource is people—skilled, spirited and hopeful people who will exert their wills and imaginations for their own benefit, and so, inevitably, for the benefit of us all.

35

Growth in Population and Energy Consumption: More Than a Matter of Interest

Courtland L. Smith

Fifteen years after Paul Ehrlich drew attention to *The Population Bomb*, The United Nations midrange projection is that world population growth will peak in 2100 at 10.5 billion.[1] The Department of Commerce estimates the United States population will reach a maximum of 309 million about 2050.[2] While these projections foresee limits to growth, increased energy consumption and goals for economic growth will further multiply population impacts. A perspective from human history shows the relative magnitude of population and energy consumption changes and suggests concepts for coping with them.

Population Growth Rates

In the last 10,000 years human population has increased from an estimated 5 million to 4.4 billion.[3] Fig. 35.1 plots this increase and the constant growth rate, i, required to achieve it. The growth rate is equivalent to an annual interest rate of less than 7/100 of a percent (0.00068).

population in n years
= initial population $x\ (1 + i)^n$

Since the actual curve is below the constant growth rate, this indicates the rate of population growth progressively increased. From 8,000 B.C. to A.D. 1, the population growth rate was less than 5/100 of a percent (0.00046). From 1850 to 1945, it increased to almost 9/10 of a percent (0.0088). From 1945 to 1990, population growth occurred at a rate of 1.45 percent.

What is the fastest rate at which human populations can grow? Physical anthropologists estimate that assuming the average woman has a 20-year reproductive period, "The total fertility should be about 8."[4] This is one child every 2 1/2 years "and allows for some miscarriages and some temporary sterility." If medical practices are such that all these children live to be adults, the growth rate could be as high as 7 percent, i.e., almost quadrupling in 20 years.

Kenyan women currently average 8.0 births per lifetime. This results in a 4 percent growth rate—the highest in the world

---

for the period 1975 to 1980.[5] The preference for Kenyan women is for even larger families.[6]

Population and Energy Equivalents

Does the Earth have sufficient resources and how should they be distributed to feed 10.5 billion people? Questions about the distribution of resources imply the problem is more than just numbers of people. High energy utilization places greater pressure on natural resources and creates more pollution. People of high energy cultures are not equal to those from low energy cultures in the share of the world's life support system they take.

Both the United States and China have approximately the same amount of arable land. How carefully must the Chinese use land to feed an estimated one billion people? The Chinese, however, do not use large portions of their land to grow feed for livestock, nor are they contemplating schemes to grow oil producing plants. In terms of energy consumption, one Chinese citizen does not equal one from the United States.

A measure comparing the proportional share by nation or region is the population and energy equivalent ratio (PEER). It is calculated by multiplying the population of each nation by its per capita energy consumption, and this value is divided by the world average. The PEER shows, according to population and energy consumption, the relative population of each nation.

Data from the United Nations *Statistical Yearbook* report the 1979 average annual world energy consumption at 2002 kilograms of coal equivalent per capita.[7] This is an average per capita energy consumption of 38,400 calories per day. In 1979 the United States population was 221 million. This times the daily average per capita energy use of 215,300 calories divided by the world average yields

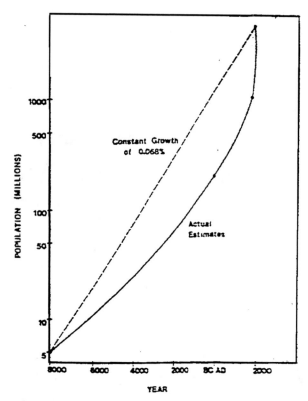

Figure 35.1 World population growth plotted on a logarithmic scale from 8000 B.C. to present. The straight line indicates the simple interest rate that would achieve this increase over 10,000 years.

$$\text{U.S. PEER} = 221 \times (215{,}300/38{,}400) = 1{,}239 \text{ million}$$

For China, the population estimate of 945 million times their average daily energy consumption of 12,000 calories per capita divided by the world average gives PEER of 295 million.

From the population and energy consumption perspective, the United States population in 1979 was over 1.2 billion and China's was less than 300 million. According to population and energy, the United States is the one with the more serious population problem. One birth in the United States has nearly 20 times the energy consumption effect it would in China, and over 60 times the effect in India. Table 35.1 ranks the world's largest population and PEER nations and regions.

Table 35.1 Population and PEERS for Nations and Regions, 1979

Population Million	Nation or Region	PEER Million
945	China	295
699	Mid & South Asia (less India)	89
651	India	60
482	East and West Europe (less USSR)	1,188
456	Africa	81
265	USSR	730
239	South America	137
221	USA	1,239
120	Mid-America	69
116	Japan	204
95	West Asia	52
24	Canda	127
18	Australia	54
5	Oceania	11
4,336	Totals	4,336

Source. United Nations, note [7] above.

Figs. 35.2–35.4 show relative areas, populations, and PEERS for these major geographic areas. The land area dominance (Fig. 35.2) of South America, Africa, and Asia contrasts with the population dominance of South and East Asia (Fig. 35.3). On the basis of population and energy equivalent ratio, the dominance of the United States and Europe, including the USSR, becomes evident (Fig. 35.4).

Economic Growth

While population growth may be waning, economic planners talk of stimulating 3–5 percent growth rates. Nations with growth rates of more than 10 percent are held out as special successes. From a population and energy perspective this raises new questions about the ability of the world's environment to support future generations.

The energy required to support an individual 10,000 years ago is estimated at 5,000 calories per day.[8] For societies with simple agriculture which predominated during the next 8,000 years, daily energy consumption more than doubles to 12,000. Irrigated agricultural activities before the industrial revolution increase the average daily use to 26,000 calories. The 1979 world average was 38,400, and the average U.S. citizen used 215,300.[9]

The per capita energy consumption estimates in Table 35.2 are based on assumptions about the mix of societies using technologies described above. The population and energy equivalent ratio grew at an average rate of 9/100 of a percent (0.00088) over the last 10,000 years. From 1850 to the present, the PEER growth rate was 1.7 percent. Figuring

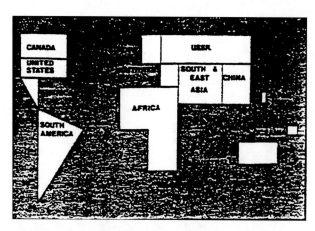

Figure 35.2 World map with continental polygons representative of land area, 1979

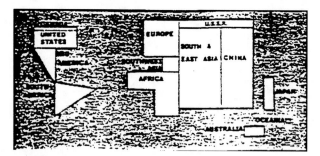

Figure 35.3 World map adjusted along vertical axis so that polygons are proportional to population, 1979 (from United Nations, Ref. [7]).

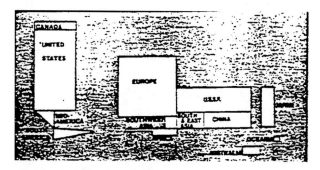

Figure 35.4 World map adjusted along vertical axis so that polygons are proportional to population and energy equivalent ratios (PEERS), 1979 (From United Nations, Ref. [7]).

population and PEER growth using calculations of simple interest suggests that long term average annual growth rates have been very low, less than 1/10 of a percent. This also shows that low growth rates over long periods produce very large increases.

Table 35.2 projects world population and energy equivalent ratios backward and forward in time using 1979 as the base year. Relative to 1979 average per capita world energy consumption, the energy equivalent population 10,000 years ago equalled 650,000. In equivalent U.S. citizens this would have been only 116,000 people. If the 10.5 billion people in 2110 achieve an energy standard of living equal to that of the United States, world population would be equivalent to 50 billion people in terms of 1979 energy consumption. This is an average annual population and energy growth rate of 2 percent over the next 130 years. This is only slightly greater than the growth rate for the 130 years from 1850 through 1979.

Economist, Julian Simon, suggests that population increase spurs economic growth.[10] This appears to be the association with human history since the dawn of the agricultural revolution. During the exponential phase of growth, more population does seem valuable. The question for humanity is, when does exponential growth become logistic? That is, rather than continuing to increase, when does it approach a limit that cannot be exceeded?

Associated with new technologies, increase in energy consumption, and economic growth has been greater economic inequality.[11] Growth is justified on the assumption that even if there is greater inequality, the average person is better off than before. Data from development projects do not support this assumption. In many cases, people were actually worse off after economic development. A World Bank economist summarizes the results of development, "It is now clear that more than a decade of rapid growth in underdeveloped countries has been of little or no benefit to perhaps a third of their population."[12]

Growth and the associated inequality raise new questions. To assume technology will lift humanity to new levels of productivity is to project the pattern of the last 10,000 years into the future. Is it in humanity's best interest to continually convert new technological breakthrough into more people? But the notion of well-being is so tied to the concept

Table 35.2 Population and PEER Projections Standardized to 1979 Energy Consumption Rates

Population Millions	Time	Per Capita Energy	PEER Millions
5	8000 BC	5,000	0.65
200	AD 1	10,000	52
1,000	1850	20,000	520
4,336	1979	38,400	4,336
10,500	2110	215,300	59,000

of growth, it seems impossible to break the shackles. Further, the assumption that higher levels of productivity will improve the human condition is not borne out by recent development experience. The transition from exponential to logistic growth requires new planning horizons and concepts.

Implications of Logistic Growth

With logistic growth, limits are known. Concern, then, has to be with how to use and allocate what is available. To cope with this, more careful planning over longer time periods is necessary. Questions need to be asked regarding the life span of an activity. The demands of the activity need to be projected as carefully as possible through the expected lifetime. This could be a person's life; the expected life of a satellite or technological system; or the lifetime of a community which comes into being to extract a nonrenewable resource.

Over what time span should the minimum economic plan for the future extend? When a child is born, its parents need a concept and plan for what kind of world that child will experience. For preagricultural societies the lifetime plan would have been about 35 years. For mechanized societies the plan is more like 75 years and needs to project energy consumption, employment opportunities, agricultural productivity, resource availability,

and the overall ability of the world ecosystem to support the child over its expected lifetime.

A society with a 2 percent population growth rate will more than quadruple in size over 75 years. If the resource base of the society is fixed, then this means there will be one fourth as much to go around. If, in addition, the desired energy consumption growth rate is 5 percent, then this means close to 40 times as much in the way of new energy productivity. On a simple interest basis, the population and energy equivalent to sustain 2 percent population growth along with 5 percent annual energy growth for 75 years is 200 fold.

Logistic growth demands planning that encompasses a lifetime, plus greater interest in quality and equality. Concern with quality and equality rather than production and quantity is a key indicator in the transition from exponential to logistic growth. With exponential growth, society is preoccupied with increases in raw quantity, for numbers and increments of growth are most important There is little consideration of how to distribute what is produced.

With logistic growth, there is an absolute quantity that cannot be exceeded. Concern, therefore, is with quality of life and how it is distributed. When more is not better, necessity dictates focusing on the quality of what exists. The decade of the 1970's was a period where interest in quality of life, environment, and workspace expanded. Nowhere was the ideal reached, but the very fact that more and more people are making decisions regarding quality is a reflection of the philosophic shift that accompanies logistic growth.

Polio vaccine inventor Jonas Salk and his son Jonathan note the epochal nature of the population growth changes taking place. These changes are comparable with those of the agricultural revolution, which ignited exponential growth some 10,000 years ago.[13] The Salks conclude that we can "emerge from the present period not merely as survivors, but as human beings in a new reality." To do this, population and energy cannot continue to be compounded at interest. Planning must be based on lifetimes and focus on questions of quality, equality, and distribution.

References

1. U.N. Population Division, Department of International Economic and Social Affairs, *Long-Range Global Population Projections*, (New York: United Nations, 1981, pp. 16–17.
2. U.S. Bureau of the Census, "Population Estimates and Projections," *Current Population Reports, Series P-25*, 922, p. 1, Oct. 1982.
3. Arthur H. Westing, "A Note on How Many Humans That Have Ever Lived," *BioScience*, vol. 31, pp. 523–524, July/Aug. 1981.
4. G. A. Harrison, J. S. Weiner, J. M. Taner, and N. A. Barnicot, *Human Biology*, New York: Oxford University Press 1964, p. 498.
5. U. N. Department of International Economic and Social Affairs, *World Population Prospects as Assessed in 1980*, New York: United Nations, Population Studies, No. 78, 1981, pp. 70–74; and Robert Lightbourne Jr. and Susheeia Singh, "The World Fertility Survey: Charting Global Childbearing, *Population Bulletin*, pp. 1–55, March 1982.
6. "Fastest Growing," *Parade Magazine*, p. 11, Dec. 5, 1982.
7. United Nations, Department of International Economic and Social Affairs, *Statistical Yearbook, 1979/80. Thirty-first Issue*, New York: United Nations, 1981, Tables 11, 18, and 189.
8. Earl Cook, "The Flow of Energy in an Industrial Society," *Scientific American*, vol. 224, pp. 134–147, Sept. 1971
9. United Nations, note 7 above, Tables 11 and 18.
10. Julian Simon, *The Ultimate Resource*, Princeton, NJ: Princeton University Press, 1981.
11. Irma Adleman and Cynthia Taft Morris, *Economic Growth and Social Equity in Developing Countries*, Stanford, CA: Stanford University Press, 1973; Hollis Chenery, Montek S. Ahluwailia, C. L. G. Bell, John H. Duloy, and Richard Jolly, *Redistribution with Growth*, London: Oxford University Press, 1974; T. Scarlett Epstein, *South India: Yesterday, Today and Tomorrow: Mysore Villages Revisited*, New York: Macmillan Co., 1973; and Gunnar Myrdal, *Asian Drama: An Inquiry into the Poverty of Nations*, New York: Twentieth Century Fund, 1978.
12. Chenery et al., [11] above, p. xiii.
13. Jonas and Jonathan Salk, *World Population and Human Values*, New York, Harper & Row, 1981, p. 164.

36

Eating Fossil Fuels

Dale Allen Pfeiffer

Expanded to become *Eating Fossil Fuels: Oil, Food and the Coming Crisis in Agriculture,* 2006, New Society Publishers.

Human beings (like all other animals) draw their energy from the food they eat. Until the last century, all of the food energy available on this planet was derived from the sun through photosynthesis. Either you ate plants or you ate animals that fed on plants, but the energy in your food was ultimately derived from the sun.

It would have been absurd to think that we would one day run out of sunshine. No, sunshine was an abundant, renewable resource, and the process of photosynthesis fed all life on this planet. It also set a limit on the amount of food that could be generated at any one time, and therefore placed a limit upon population growth. Solar energy has a limited rate of flow into this planet. To increase your food production, you had to increase the acreage under cultivation, and displace your competitors. There was no other way to increase the amount of energy available for food production. Human population grew by displacing everything else and appropriating more and more of the available solar energy.

The need to expand agricultural production was one of the motive causes behind most of the wars in recorded history, along with expansion of the energy base (and agricultural production is truly an essential portion of the energy base). And when Europeans could no longer expand cultivation, they began the task of conquering the world. Explorers were followed by conquistadors and traders and settlers. The declared reasons for expansion may have been trade, avarice, empire or simply curiosity, but at its base, it was all about the expansion of agricultural productivity. Wherever explorers and conquistadors traveled, they may have carried off loot, but they left plantations. And settlers toiled to clear land and establish their own homestead. This conquest and expansion went on until there was no place left for further expansion. Certainly, to this day, landowners and farmers fight to claim still more land for agricultural productivity, but they are fighting over crumbs. Today, virtually all of the productive land on this planet is being exploited by agriculture. What remains unused is too steep, too wet, too dry or lacking in soil nutrients.[1]

Just when agricultural output could expand no more by increasing acreage, new innovations made possible a more thorough exploitation of the acreage already available. The process of "pest" displacement and appropriation for agriculture accelerated with the industrial revolution as the mechanization of agriculture hastened the clearing and tilling of land and augmented the amount of farmland which could be tended by one

---

person. With every increase in food production, the human population grew apace.

At present, nearly 40% of all land-based photosynthetic capability has been appropriated by human beings.[2] In the United States we divert more than half of the energy captured by photosynthesis.[3] We have taken over all the prime real estate on this planet. The rest of nature is forced to make due with what is left. Plainly, this is one of the major factors in species extinctions and in ecosystem stress.

The Green Revolution

In the 1950s and 1960s, agriculture underwent a drastic transformation commonly referred to as the Green Revolution. The Green Revolution resulted in the industrialization of agriculture. Part of the advance resulted from new hybrid food plants, leading to more productive food crops. Between 1950 and 1984, as the Green Revolution transformed agriculture around the globe, world grain production increased by 250%.[4] That is a tremendous increase in the amount of food energy available for human consumption. This additional energy did not come from an increase in incipient sunlight, nor did it result from introducing agriculture to new vistas of land. The energy for the Green Revolution was provided by fossil fuels in the form of fertilizers (natural gas), pesticides (oil), and hydrocarbon fueled irrigation.

The Green Revolution increased the energy flow to agriculture by an average of 50 times the energy input of traditional agriculture.[5] In the most extreme cases, energy consumption by agriculture has increased 100 fold or more.[6]

In the United States, 400 gallons of oil equivalents are expended annually to feed each American (as of data provided in 1994).[7] Agricultural energy consumption is broken down as follows:

❑ 31% for the manufacture of inorganic fertilizer
❑ 19% for the operation of field machinery
❑ 16% for transportation
❑ 13% for irrigation
❑ 08% for raising livestock (not including livestock feed)
❑ 05% for crop drying
❑ 05% for pesticide production
❑ 08% miscellaneous[8]

Energy costs for packaging, refrigeration, transportation to retail outlets, and household cooking are not considered in these figures.

To give the reader an idea of the energy intensiveness of modern agriculture, production of one kilogram of nitrogen for fertilizer requires the energy equivalent of from 1.4 to 1.8 liters of diesel fuel. This is not considering the natural gas feedstock.[9] According to The Fertilizer Institute (http://www.tfi.org), in the year from June 30 2001 until June 30 2002 the United States used 12,009,300 short tons of nitrogen fertilizer.[10] Using the low figure of 1.4 liters diesel equivalent per kilogram of nitrogen, this equates to the energy content of 15.3 billion liters of diesel fuel, or 96.2 million barrels.

Of course, this is only a rough comparison to aid comprehension of the energy requirements for modern agriculture.

In a very real sense, we are literally eating fossil fuels. However, due to the laws of thermodynamics, there is not a direct correspondence between energy inflow and outflow in agriculture. Along the way, there is a marked energy loss. Between 1945 and 1994, energy input to agriculture increased 4-fold while crop yields only increased 3-fold.[11] Since then, energy input has continued to increase without a corresponding increase in crop yield. We have reached the point of marginal returns. Yet, due to soil degradation, increased demands of pest management and increasing energy costs for irrigation (all of which is examined below), modern agriculture must continue increasing its energy expenditures simply to maintain current crop yields. The Green Revolution is becoming bankrupt.

Fossil Fuel Costs

Solar energy is a renewable resource limited only by the inflow rate from the sun to the earth. Fossil fuels, on the other hand, are a stock-type resource that can be exploited at a nearly limitless rate. However, on a human timescale, fossil fuels are nonrenewable. They represent a planetary energy deposit which we can draw from at any rate we wish, but which will eventually be exhausted without renewal. The Green Revolution tapped into this energy deposit and used it to increase agricultural production.

Total fossil fuel use in the United States has increased 20-fold in the last 4 decades. In the US, we consume 20 to 30 times more fossil fuel energy per capita than people in developing nations. Agriculture directly accounts for 17% of all the energy used in this country.[12] As of 1990, we were using approximately 1,000 liters (6.41 barrels) of oil to produce food of one hectare of land.[13]

In 1994, David Pimentel and Mario Giampietro estimated the output/input ratio of agriculture to be around 1.4.[14] For 0.7 Kilogram-Calories (kcal) of fossil energy consumed, U.S. agriculture produced 1 kcal of food. The input figure for this ratio was based on FAO (Food and Agriculture Organization of the UN) statistics, which consider only fertilizers (without including fertilizer feedstock), irrigation, pesticides (without including pesticide feedstock), and machinery and fuel for field operations. Other agricultural energy inputs not considered were energy and machinery for drying crops, transportation for inputs and outputs to and from the farm, electricity, and construction and maintenance of farm buildings and infrastructures. Adding in estimates for these energy costs brought the input/output energy ratio down to 1.[15] Yet this does not include the energy expense of packaging, delivery to retail outlets, refrigeration or household cooking.

In a subsequent study completed later that same year (1994), Giampietro and Pimentel managed to derive a more accurate ratio of the net fossil fuel energy ratio of agriculture.[16] In this study, the authors defined two separate forms of energy input: Endosomatic energy and Exosomatic energy. Endosomatic energy is generated through the metabolic transformation of food energy into muscle energy in the human body. Exosomatic energy is generated by transforming energy outside of the human body, such as burning gasoline in a tractor. This assessment allowed the authors to look at fossil fuel input alone and in ratio to other inputs.

Prior to the industrial revolution, virtually 100% of both endosomatic and exosomatic energy was solar driven. Fossil fuels now represent 90% of the exosomatic energy used in the United States and other developed countries.[17] The typical exo/endo ratio of pre-industrial, solar powered societies is about 4 to 1. The ratio has changed tenfold in developed countries, climbing to 40 to 1. And in the United States it is more than 90 to 1.[18] The nature of the way we use endosomatic energy has changed as well.

The vast majority of endosomatic energy is no longer expended to deliver power for direct economic processes. Now the majority of endosomatic energy is utilized to generate the flow of information directing the flow of exosomatic energy driving machines. Considering the 90/1 exo/endo ratio in the United States, each endosomatic kcal of energy expended in the US induces the circulation of 90 kcal of exosomatic energy. As an example, a small gasoline engine can convert the 38,000 kcal in one gallon of gasoline into 8.8 KWh (Kilowatt hours), which equates to about 3 weeks of work for one human being.[19]

In their refined study, Giampietro and Pimentel found that 10 kcal of exosomatic energy are required to produce 1 kcal of food delivered to the consumer in the U.S. food system. This includes packaging and all delivery expenses, but excludes household cooking).[20] *The U.S. food system consumes ten times more energy than it produces in food energy.* This disparity is made possible by nonrenewable fossil fuel stocks.

Assuming a figure of 2,500 kcal per capita for the daily diet in the United States, the 10/1 ratio translates into a cost of 35,000 kcal of exosomatic energy per capita each day. However, considering that the average return on one hour of endosomatic labor in the U.S.

is about 100,000 kcal of exosomatic energy, the flow of exosomatic energy required to supply the daily diet is achieved in only 20 minutes of labor in our current system. Unfortunately, if you remove fossil fuels from the equation, the daily diet will require 111 hours of endosomatic labor per capita; that is, *the current U.S. daily diet would require nearly three weeks of labor per capita to produce.*

Quite plainly, as fossil fuel production begins to decline within the next decade, there will be less energy available for the production of food.

Soil, Cropland and Water

Modern intensive agriculture is unsustainable. Technologically-enhanced agriculture has augmented soil erosion, polluted and overdrawn groundwater and surface water, and even (largely due to increased pesticide use) caused serious public health and environmental problems. Soil erosion, overtaxed cropland and water resource overdraft in turn lead to even greater use of fossil fuels and hydrocarbon products. More hydrocarbon-based fertilizers must be applied, along with more pesticides; irrigation water requires more energy to pump; and fossil fuels are used to process polluted water.

It takes 500 years to replace 1 inch of topsoil.[21] In a natural environment, topsoil is built up by decaying plant matter and weathering rock, and it is protected from erosion by growing plants. In soil made susceptible by agriculture, erosion is reducing productivity up to 65% each year.[22] Former prairie lands, which constitute the bread basket of the United States, have lost one half of their topsoil after farming for about 100 years. This soil is eroding 30 times faster than the natural formation rate.[23] Food crops are much hungrier than the natural grasses that once covered the Great Plains. As a result, the remaining topsoil is increasingly depleted of nutrients. Soil erosion and mineral depletion removes about $20 billion worth of plant nutrients from U.S. agricultural soils every

year.[24] Much of the soil in the Great Plains is little more than a sponge into which we must pour hydrocarbon-based fertilizers in order to produce crops.

Every year in the U.S., more than 2 million acres of cropland are lost to erosion, salinization and water logging. On top of this, urbanization, road building, and industry claim another 1 million acres annually from farmland.24 Approximately three-quarters of the land area in the United States is devoted to agriculture and commercial forestry.[25] The expanding human population is putting increasing pressure on land availability. Incidentally, only a small portion of U.S. land area remains available for the solar energy technologies necessary to support a solar energy-based economy. The land area for harvesting biomass is likewise limited. For this reason, the development of solar energy or biomass must be at the expense of agriculture.

Modern agriculture also places a strain on our water resources. Agriculture consumes fully 85% of all U.S. freshwater resources.[26] Overdraft is occurring from many surface water resources, especially in the west and south. The typical example is the Colorado River, which is diverted to a trickle by the time it reaches the Pacific. Yet surface water only supplies 60% of the water used in irrigation. The remainder, and in some places the majority of water for irrigation, comes from ground water aquifers. Ground water is recharged slowly by the percolation of rainwater through the earth's crust. Less than 0.1% of the stored ground water mined annually is replaced by rainfall.[27] The great Ogallala aquifer that supplies agriculture, industry and home use in much of the southern and central plains states has an annual overdraft up to 160% above its recharge rate. The Ogallala aquifer will become unproductive in a matter of decades.[28]

We can illustrate the demand that modern agriculture places on water resources by looking at a farmland producing corn. A corn crop that produces 118 bushels/acre/year requires more than 500,000 gallons/acre of water during the growing season. The production of 1 pound of maize requires 1,400 pounds (or

175 gallons) of water.[29] Unless something is done to lower these consumption rates, modern agriculture will help to propel the United States into a water crisis.

In the last two decades, the use of hydrocarbon-based pesticides in the U.S. has increased 33-fold, yet each year we lose more crops to pests.[30] This is the result of the abandonment of traditional crop rotation practices. Nearly 50% of U.S. corn land is grown continuously as a monoculture.[31] This results in an increase in corn pests, which in turn requires the use of more pesticides. Pesticide use on corn crops had increased 1,000-fold even before the introduction of genetically engineered, pesticide resistant corn. However, corn losses have still risen 4-fold.[32]

Modern intensive agriculture is unsustainable. It is damaging the land, draining water supplies and polluting the environment. And all of this requires more and more fossil fuel input to pump irrigation water, to replace nutrients, to provide pest protection, to remediate the environment and simply to hold crop production at a constant. Yet this necessary fossil fuel input is going to crash headlong into declining fossil fuel production.

U.S. Consumption

In the United States, each person consumes an average of 2,175 pounds of food per person per year. This provides the U.S. consumer with an average daily energy intake of 3,600 Calories. The world average is 2,700 Calories per day.[33] Fully 19% of the U.S. caloric intake comes from fast food. Fast food accounts for 34% of the total food consumption for the average U.S. citizen. The average citizen dines out for one meal out of four.[34]

One third of the caloric intake of the average American comes from animal sources (including dairy products), totaling 800 pounds per person per year. This diet means that U.S. citizens derive 40% of their calories from fat-nearly half of their diet.[35]

Americans are also grand consumers of water. As of one decade ago, Americans were consuming 1,450 gallons/day/capita (g/d/c),

with the largest amount expended on agriculture. Allowing for projected population increase, consumption by 2050 is projected at 700 g/d/c, which hydrologists consider to be minimal for human needs.[36] This is without taking into consideration declining fossil fuel production.

To provide all of this food requires the application of 0.6 million metric tons of pesticides in North America per year. This is over one fifth of the total annual world pesticide use, estimated at 2.5 million tons.[37] Worldwide, more nitrogen fertilizer is used per year than can be supplied through natural sources. Likewise, water is pumped out of underground aquifers at a much higher rate than it is recharged. And stocks of important minerals, such as phosphorus and potassium, are quickly approaching exhaustion.[38]

Total U.S. energy consumption is more than three times the amount of solar energy harvested as crop and forest products. The United States consumes 40% more energy annually than the total amount of solar energy captured yearly by all U.S. plant biomass. Per capita use of fossil energy in North America is five times the world average.[39]

Our prosperity is built on the principal of exhausting the world's resources as quickly as possible, without any thought to our neighbors, all the other life on this planet, or our children.

Population and Sustainability

Considering a growth rate of 1.1% per year, the U.S. population is projected to double by 2050. As the population expands, an estimated one acre of land will be lost for every person added to the U.S. population. Currently, there are 1.8 acres of farmland available to grow food for each U.S. citizen. By 2050, this will decrease to 0.6 acres. 1.2 acres per person is required in order to maintain current dietary standards.[40]

Presently, only two nations on the planet are major exporters of grain: the United States and Canada.[41] By 2025, it is expected that the U.S. will cease to be a food exporter due to domestic demand. The impact on the U.S. economy could be devastating, as food exports earn $40 billion for the U.S. annually. More importantly, millions of people around the world could starve to death without U.S. food exports.[42]

Domestically, 34.6 million people are living in poverty as of 2002 census data.[43] And this number is continuing to grow at an alarming rate. Too many of these people do not have a sufficient diet. As the situation worsens, this number will increase and the United States will witness growing numbers of starvation fatalities.

There are some things that we can do to at least alleviate this tragedy. It is suggested that streamlining agriculture to get rid of losses, waste and mismanagement might cut the energy inputs for food production by up to one-half.[35] In place of fossil fuel-based fertilizers, we could utilize livestock manures that are now wasted. It is estimated that livestock manures contain 5 times the amount of fertilizer currently used each year.[36] Perhaps most effective would be to eliminate meat from our diet altogether.[37]

Mario Giampietro and David Pimentel postulate that a sustainable food system is possible only if four conditions are met:

1. Environmentally sound agricultural technologies must be implemented.
2. Renewable energy technologies must be put into place.
3. Major increases in energy efficiency must reduce exosomatic energy consumption per capita.
4. Population size and consumption must be compatible with maintaining the stability of environmental processes.[38]

Providing that the first three conditions are met, with a reduction to less than half of the exosomatic energy consumption per capita, the authors place the maximum population for a sustainable economy at 200 million.[39] Several other studies have produced figures within this ballpark (Energy and Population, Werbos, Paul J. http://www.dieoff.com/page63.htm; Impact of Population Growth on Food Supplies and Environment, Pimentel, David, et al. http://www.dieoff.com/page57.htm).

Given that the current U.S. population is in excess of 292 million,[40] that would mean a reduction of 92 million. *To achieve a sustainable economy and avert disaster, the United States must reduce its population by at least one-third.* The black plague during the 14th Century claimed approximately one-third of the European population (and more than half of the Asian and Indian populations), plunging the continent into a darkness from which it took them nearly two centuries to emerge.[41]

None of this research considers the impact of declining fossil fuel production. The authors of all of these studies believe that the mentioned agricultural crisis will only begin to impact us after 2020, and will not become critical until 2050. The current peaking of global oil production (and subsequent decline of production), along with the peak of North American natural gas production will very likely precipitate this agricultural crisis much sooner than expected. Quite possibly, a U.S. population reduction of one-third will not be effective for sustainability; the necessary reduction might be in excess of one-half. And, for sustainability, global population will have to be reduced from the current 6.32 billion people[42] to 2 billion-a reduction of 68% or over two-thirds. The end of this decade could see spiraling food prices without relief. And the coming decade could see massive starvation on a global level such as never experienced before by the human race.

Three Choices

Considering the utter necessity of population reduction, there are three obvious choices awaiting us.

We can-as a society-become aware of our dilemma and consciously make the choice not to add more people to our population. This would be the most welcome of our three options, to choose consciously and with free will to responsibly lower our population. However, this flies in the face of our biological imperative to procreate. It is further complicated by the ability of modern medicine to extend our longevity, and by the refusal of the Religious Right to consider issues of population management. And then, there is a strong business lobby to maintain a high immigration rate in order to hold down the cost of labor. Though this is probably our best choice, it is the option least likely to be chosen.

Failing to responsibly lower our population, we can force population cuts through government regulations. Is there any need to mention how distasteful this option would be? How many of us would choose to live in a world of forced sterilization and population quotas enforced under penalty of law? How easily might this lead to a culling of the population utilizing principles of eugenics?

This leaves the third choice, which itself presents an unspeakable picture of suffering and death. Should we fail to acknowledge this coming crisis and determine to deal with it, we will be faced with a die-off from which civilization may very possibly never revive. We will very likely lose more than the numbers necessary for sustainability. Under a die-off scenario, conditions will deteriorate so badly that the surviving human population would be a negligible fraction of the present population. And those survivors would suffer from the trauma of living through the death of their civilization, their neighbors, their friends and their families. Those survivors will have seen their world crushed into nothing.

The questions we must ask ourselves now are, how can we allow this to happen, and what can we do to prevent it? Does our present lifestyle mean so much to us that we would subject ourselves and our children to this fast approaching tragedy simply for a few more years of conspicuous consumption?

Author's Note

This is possibly the most important article I have written to date. It is certainly the most frightening, and the conclusion is the bleakest I have ever penned. This article is likely to greatly disturb the reader; it has certainly disturbed me. However, it is important for our future that this paper should be read, acknowledged and discussed.

I am by nature positive and optimistic. In spite of this article, I continue to believe that we can find a positive solution to the multiple crises bearing down upon us. Though this article may provoke a flood of hate mail, it is simply a factual report of data and the obvious conclusions that follow from it.

Notes

1. Availability of agricultural land for crop and livestock production, Buringh, P. Food and Natural Resources, Pimentel. D. and Hall. C.W. (eds), Academic Press, 1989.
2. Human appropriation of the products of photosynthesis, Vitousek, P.M. et al. Bioscience 36, 1986. http://www.science.duq.edu/esm/unit2-3
3. Land, Energy and Water: the constraints governing Ideal US Population Size, Pimental, David and Pimentel, Marcia. Focus, Spring 1991. NPG Forum, 1990. http://www.dieoff.com/page136.htm
4. Constraints on the Expansion of Global Food Supply, Kindell, Henry H. and Pimentel, David. Ambio Vol. 23 No. 3, May 1994. The Royal Swedish Academy of Sciences. http://www.dieoff.com/page36htm
5. The Tightening Conflict: Population, Energy Use, and the Ecology of Agriculture, Giampietro, Mario and Pimentel, David, 1994. http:// www.dieoff.com/page69.htm
6. Op. Cit. See note 4.
7. Food, Land, Population and the U.S. Economy, Pimentel, David and Giampietro, Mario. Carrying Capacity Network, 11/21/1994. http://www.dieoff.com/page55.htm
8. Comparison of energy inputs for inorganic fertilizer and manure based corn production, McLaughlin, N.B., et al. Canadian Agricultural Engineering, Vol. 42, No. 1, 2000.
9. Ibid.
10. US Fertilizer Use Statistics. http://www.tfi.org/Statistics/USfertuse2.asp
11. Food, Land, Population and the U.S. Economy, Executive Summary, Pimentel, David and Giampietro, Mario. Carrying Capacity Network, 11/21/1994. http://www.dieoff.com/page40.htm

12. Ibid.
13. Op. Cit. See note 3.
14. Op. Cit. See note 7.
15. Ibid.
16. Op. Cit. See note 5.
17. Ibid.
18. Ibid.
19. Ibid.
20. Ibid.
21. Op. Cit. See note 11.
22. Ibid.
23. Ibid.
24. Ibid.
25. Op Cit. See note 3.
26. Op Cit. See note 11.
27. Ibid.
28. Ibid.
29. Ibid.
30. Op. Cit. See note 3.
31. Op. Cit. See note 5.
32. Op. Cit. See note 3.
33. Op. Cit. See note 11.
34. Food Consumption and Access, Lynn Brantley, et al. Capital Area Food Bank, 6/1/2001. http://www.clagettfarm.org/purchasing.html

35. Op. Cit. See note 11.
36. Ibid.
37. Op. Cit. See note 5.
38. Ibid.
39. Ibid.
40. Op. Cit. See note 11.
41. Op. Cit. See note 4.
42. Op. Cit. See note 11.
35. Op. Cit. See note 3.
36. Ibid.
37. Diet for a Small Planet, Lappé, Frances Moore. Ballantine Books, 1971-revised 1991. http://www.dietforasmallplanet.com/
38. Op. Cit. See note 5.
39. Ibid.
40. U.S. and World Population Clocks. U.S. Census Bureau. http://www.census.gov/main/www/popclock.html
41. A Distant Mirror, Tuckman Barbara. Ballantine Books, 1978.
42. Op. Cit. See note 40.
43. Poverty 2002. The U.S. Census Bureau. http://www.census.gov/hhes/poverty/poverty02/pov02hi.html

37

What's Your Consumption Factor?

Jared Diamond

To mathematicians, 32 is an interesting number: it's 2 raised to the fifth power, 2 times 2 times 2 times 2 times 2. To economists, 32 is even more special, because it measures the difference in lifestyles between the first world and the developing world. The average rates at which people consume resources like oil and metals, and produce wastes like plastics and greenhouse gases, are about 32 times higher in North America, Western Europe, Japan and Australia than they are in the developing world. That factor of 32 has big consequences.

To understand them, consider our concern with world population. Today, there are more that 6.5 billion people, and that number may grow to around 9 billion within this half-century. Several decades ago, many people considered rising population to be the main challenge facing humanity. Now we realize that it matters only insofar as people consume and produce.

If most of the world's 6.5 billion people were in cold storage and not metabolizing or consuming, they would create no resource problem. What really matters is total world consumptions, the sum of all local consumptions, which is the product of local population times the local per capita consumption rate.

The estimated one billion people who live in developed countries have a relative per capita consumption rate of 32. Most of the world's other 5.5 billion people constitute the developing world, with relative per capita consumption rates below 32, mostly down toward 1.

The population especially of the developing world is growing, and some people remain fixated on this. They note that populations of countries like Kenya are growing rapidly, and they say that's a big problem. Yes, it is a problem for Kenya's more than 30 million people, but it's not a burden on the whole world, because Kenyans consume so little. (Their relative per capita rate is 1.) A real problem for the world is that each of us 300 million Americans consumes as much as 32 Kenyans. With 10 times the population, the United States consumes 320 times more resources than Kenya does.

People in the third world are aware of this difference in per capita consumption,

---

although most of them couldn't specify that it's by a factor of 32. When they believe their chances of catching up to be hopeless, they sometimes get frustrated and angry, and some become terrorists, or tolerate or support terrorists. Since Sept. 11, 2001, it has become clear that the oceans that once protected the United States no longer do so. There will be more terrorist attacks against us and Europe, and perhaps against Japan and Australia, as long as that factorial difference of 32 in consumption rates persists.

People who consume little want to enjoy the high-consumption lifestyle. Governments of developing countries make an increase in living standards a primary goal of national policy. And tens of millions of people in the developing world seek the first-world lifestyle on their own, by emigrating, especially to the United States and Western Europe, Japan and Australia. Each such transfer of a person to a high-consumption country raises world consumption rates, even though most immigrants don't succeed immediately in multiplying their consumption by 32.

Among the developing countries that are seeking to increase per capita consumption rates at home, China stands out. It has the world's fastest growing economy, and there are 1.3 billion Chinese, four times the United States population. The world is already running out of resources, and it will do so even sooner if China achieves American-level consumption rates. Already, China is competing with us for oil and metals on world markets.

Per capita consumption rates in China are still about 11 times below ours, but let's suppose they rise to our level. Let's also make things easy by imagining that nothing else happens to increase world consumption—that is, no other country increases its consumption, all national populations (including China's) remain unchanged and immigration ceases. China's catching up alone would roughly double world consumption rates. Oil consumption would increase by 106 percent, for instance, and world metal consumption by 94 percent.

If India as well as China were to catch up, world consumption rates would triple. If the whole developing world were suddenly to catch up, world rates would increase elevenfold. If would be as if the world population ballooned to 72 billion people (retaining present consumption rates).

Some optimists claim that we could support a world with nine billion people. But I haven't met anyone crazy enough to claim that we could support 72 billion. Yet we often promise developing countries that if they will only adopt good policies—for example, institute honest government and a free-market economy—they, too, will be able to enjoy a first-world lifestyle. This promise is impossible, a cruel hoax: we are having difficulty supporting a first-world lifestyle even now for only one billion people.

We Americans may think of China's growing consumption as a problem. But the Chinese are only reaching for the consumption rate we already have. To tell them not to try would be futile.

The only approach that China and other developing countries will accept is to aim to make consumption rates and living standards more equal around the world. But the world doesn't have enough resources to allow for raising China's consumption rates, let alone those of the rest of the world, to our levels. Does this mean we're headed for disaster?

No, we could have a stable outcome in which all countries converge on consumption rates considerably below the current highest levels. Americans might object: there is no way we would sacrifice our living standards for the benefit of people in the rest of the world. Nevertheless, whether we get there willingly or not, we shall soon have lower consumption rates, because our present rates are unsustainable.

Real sacrifice wouldn't be required, however, because living standards are not tightly coupled to consumption rates. Much American consumption is wasteful and contributes little or nothing to quality of life. For example, per capita oil consumption in Western Europe is about half of ours, yet Western Europe's standard of living is higher by any reasonable criterion, including life expectancy, health, infant mortality, access to medical care, financial security after retirement, vacation time, quality of public schools and support for the arts. Ask yourself whether Americans' wasteful use of gasoline contributes positively to any of those measures.

Other aspects of our consumption are wasteful, too. Most of the world's fisheries are still operated non-sustainably, and many have already collapsed or fallen to low yields —even though we know how to manage them in such a way as to preserve the environment and the fish supply. If we were to operate all fisheries sustainably, we could extract fish from the oceans at maximum historical rates and carry on indefinitely.

The same is true of forests: we already know how to log them sustainably, and if we did so worldwide, we could extract enough timber to meet the world's wood and paper needs. Yet most forests are managed non-sustainably, with decreasing yields.

Just as it is certain that within most of our lifetimes we'll be consuming less than we do now, it is also certain that per capita consumption rates in many developing countries will one day be more nearly equal to ours. These are desirable trends, not horrible prospects. In fact, we already know how to encourage the trends; the main thing lacking has been political will.

Fortunately, in the last year there have been encouraging signs. Australia held a recent election in which a large majority of voters reversed the head-in-the-sand political course their government had followed for a decade; the new government immediately supported the Kyoto Protocol on cutting greenhouse gas emissions.

Also in the last year, concern about climate change has increased greatly in the United States. Even in China, vigorous arguments about environmental policy are taking place, and public protests recently halted construction of a huge chemical plant near the center of Xiamen. Hence I am cautiously optimistic. The world has serious consumption problems, but we can solve them if we choose to do so.

Section Three

38. *Deal Is Reached to Save California Redwood Forest* **Frank Clifford** 249

39. *A Revisionist View of Tropical Deforestation and Development* **Michael R. Dove** 251

40. *Social Forestry for Whom?* **Vandana Shiva, et al** 265

41. *Organizing for Sustainable Development: Conservation Organizations and the Struggle to Protect Tropical Rain Forests in Esmeraldas, Ecuador* **Thomas K. Rudel** 271

42. *The Price of Everything* **Thomas Michael Power and Paul Rauber** 281

43. *Putting a Value on Environmental Quality* **John A. Dixon** 289

44. *Solution or Mess? A Milk Jug for a Green Earth* **Stephanie Rosenbloom** 296

45. *Are People Acting Irrationally?* **Abraham H. Wandersman and William K. Hallman** 298

46. *Black Lung: The Social Production of Disease* **Barbara Ellen Smith** 308

47. *Multi-Party Responses to Environmental Problems: A Case of Contaminated Dairy Cattle* **George E. B. Morren, Jr.** 323

48. *National Priority List Sites in New Jersey* **Environmental Protection Agency** 336

49. *Social Responses to Commodity Shortages: The 1973-1974 Gasoline Crisis* **Thomas K. Rudel** 337

50. *Fueling National Insecurity (Advertisement)* **Washington Legal Foundation** 352

51. *America's Green Recession* **Washington Legal Foundation** 353

52. *America's Apathy on the Environment* **Geneva Overholser** 354

53. *Green Fatigue* **Susan Nielsen** 356

54. *The Age of Eco-Angst* **Goleman** 358

55. *The Elusive Process of Citizen Activism* **Celene Krauss** 360

Introduction to Section Three

This section of the course touches on resource issues, environmental impact, policy, and strategies for change. Students often finish the course wanting to know what they should or could do. I would not pretend to tell you what you *should* do, but there are plenty of examples in the last section pertaining to what you *could* do. Each of us has to make the decision of what we can and want to do for ourselves.

The Clifford article outlines the settlement of one of our longer and more hotly contested environmental resource issues—the fate of virgin redwoods (Headwaters Canyon) in California. The film *"The Last Stand"* was made about the controversy, which made an environmental celebrity of Julia "Butterfly" Hill for her two year "tree-sit" in Luna. In my early years of doing this course, I showed the film *"Mad River"* (made in the late 1970s) and then *"Forest through the Trees"* (made in the early 1990s) until recently about the redwoods issue. These three are not the only films about the battle over redwoods and the time span they encompass indicate (again) how long a controversy can endure. The Dove and Rudel articles look at forest preservation approaches used in attempting to maintain the Amazon rainforest—somewhat similar situations in many respects, but in different locations. Shiva, et al look at an innovative yet failed attempt to re-forest an area in India. Again, human ecology looks at human-environment interactions across time and space to see what we can learn and improve.

The articles by Power and Rauber and by Dixon discuss two economics-based strategies for improving our relationship with the environment—"free market environmentalism" and "benefit-cost analysis". The latter has been around for some time and is familiar to most of us; the former is newer and represents a different method of pollution reduction apart from command and control regulation. See what you think of them as applied to environmental controversies. The Rosenbloom article offers an example of a technological advancement for your consideration and analysis.

Wandersman and Hallman examine the perception of risk and its relation to how we make choices about what we see as being "risky" and what we don't, and how we act on those perceptions. Another of my favorite social science concepts is Thomas's "definition of the situation"—if a situation is perceived as real, it is real in its consequences. The best-known example is the distinction between riding in a car and in an airplane. Statistically, the car is the real risk, but for many of us, the airplane is perceived as riskier—to the point where many of us refuse to fly or get nervous about it, but few of us refuse to ride in a car or get anxious about it.

Smith adds to this in different ways. Smith's piece on black lung shows how diseases are at least in part socially defined. The common sense view is that through science, technology, and medicine, disease is an "objective fact"; Smith demonstrates that this is most definitely not the case—that we often negotiate what a "disease" is and is not.

Morren's article provides an interesting case study of contaminated cattle in Michigan and how it happened, how it came to be exposed, and the major players involved. It also provides a framework of typical responses (or, non-responses) used by officials and other parties to keep a problem from being uncovered and addressed. In our last film, In *Our Water,* you'll see many of these tactics at work—employed by a variety of local, state, and national bureaucrats and political figures. The map of New Jersey Superfund sites is offered for your consideration.

Rudel's article is another that came out of the energy crises of the seventies. Although you are obviously too young to have experienced it, the potential for another is with us and it would behoove you to imagine what another gas crisis would be like today. As you read this, you might also think about how much—or how little—we learned. Further, this question could be asked about any resource or commodity—witness the mad rush to supermarkets and convenience stores in New Jersey whenever there's a hint of snow in a winter weather forecast. Given that we never have blizzards that isolate us in our homes for very long, why *do* we seem compelled to denude the stores of bread, milk, and snacks? The relatively high gas prices of recent years and the unsettled situation in the Middle East at least temporarily focused public and political attention on the energy issue. The advertisements by the Washington Legal Foundation express one viewpoint on how we might meet our energy needs while protecting the environment—and the prices we have paid (according to them) for the environmental measures we have taken. Solomon presents a native's view of what it would mean to drill in ANWAR (the Alaskan National Wildlife Refuge). See what you think.

We end with Overholser's op ed piece on what she sees as our apathy about the environment. Our school's existence might be seen as evidence to the contrary; on the other hand, Earth Day barely rates a mention these days by contrast to its import in 1970, when the first one was observed. Nielsen describes environmental "fatigue"—something you may be feeling at the end of the semester, while Goleman offers a different take on "eco-angst". Krauss discusses "the click"—the connection between the personal and the political. For her, that is a prerequisite to citizen activism and a difficult one to make—unless and until, perhaps, we are directly affected ourselves by a construction project or a toxic waste site.

By the end of this section, you will have seen a smattering of resource and environmental impact issues from a variety of perspectives. You'll see some policies that have worked and others that have not. You will have been exposed to many different ways of trying to effect environmental change. Whatever you make of these, there is no "magic bullet" or "one size fits all" strategy—if it were that simple and easy, if we did have all of the answers (and, for that matter, all of the right questions), perhaps there would be little need for this course, this department, or this school. I hope by the end of the course you'll understand and appreciate why that's not the case. Again, "now that you know, you can't not know".

38

Deal Is Reached to Save California Redwood Forest

Frank Clifford

About 10,000 acres go into public hands. Estimates of the allowable timber harvest were raised.

In a dramatic reversal, the Pacific Lumber Co. agreed to $480 million deal to save California's Headwaters Forest after government officials substantially raised their estimates of the amount of timber the company would be allowed to cut.

The agreement was reached last week, just before the federal share of the purchase price would have been withdrawn, and the 12-year-old campaign to save the last large stands of privately owned ancient redwoods would have been lost.

"This agreement accomplishes what many people worked toward for so many years," said John Campbell, president of Pacific Lumber. "We were able to preserve Headwaters and at the same time give the company the stability it needs to remain a vital part of the north coast economy."

The agreement transfers roughly 10,000 acres of the forest, about 250 miles north of San Francisco, into public ownership and sets strict new guidelines for protecting water quality and wildlife habitat on over 200,000 acres of surrounding forest that will remain in Pacific Lumber's hands.

The majestic trees are a remnant of the redwood empire that once extended from the Oregon border to Big Sur. Today, only about 5 percent of the original forest is still intact, almost all of it in publicly owned parks and preserves.

The trees and streams of the Headwaters Forest are home to several dwindling species of wildlife, including the northern spotted owl; the marbled murrelet, a small sea bird that nests in large trees; and the coho salmon, whose numbers have plummeted in recent years.

The strategy for protecting wildlife was at the heart of the agreement because it determined how much of Pacific Lumber's land would remain off-limits to logging.

State officials had estimated that Pacific Lumber would be able to cut 138 million board-feet of timber annually. But by last

---

week, officials said that the initial estimate had been in error and that the proper figure was closer to 180 million.

Campbell said he expected his firm to be able to cut close to 200 million board feet under the terms of the agreement.

State and federal officials insisted the conditions had not been altered and they said that the resulting pact would prove historic.

"This will go down in history as one of the great achievements of our time along with [the creation of] Yosemite, Sequoia and Kings Canyon National Parks," said Interior Secretary Bruce Babbitt at a news conference in Washington.

The agreement could also bring an end to one of the longest-running environmental battles in the nation. The siege of Headwaters has been marked by massive civil disobedience, thousands of arrests of people protesting the logging of 1,000-year-old trees and the death of a protester killed by a tree that was being cut down by a logger last fall.

The conflict dates back to the takeover of Pacific Lumber in 1986 by Houston-based Maxxam Inc. and that company's decision to triple the rate of logging, a course of action that eventually would have liquidated all of the big trees.

Many environmental groups hailed the agreement, although some feared that it was accomplished at the expense of weakened environmental protections.

"It is a terrific accomplishment to bring the largest groves into public ownership, plus it breaks new ground on the protection of timber on private land," said Jay Watson of the Wilderness Society. "The prohibitions on logging near streams far exceed state standards."

Besides prohibiting logging near streams, terms of the deal bar cutting trees for 50 years in roughly a dozen old-growth groves that remain in private ownership.

Moreover, the agreement establishes penalties "that are higher than any ever imposed" on timber companies in the past, according to Mary Nichols, California's secretary of resources.

If Pacific Lumber takes down a tree in a no-cutting zone, the company would be fined $1,000 to $3,000, plus up to 250 percent of the tree's pre-milled value, state officials said.

Some environmentalists were not happy with the agreement.

"We have some very serious concerns about the loopholes that have been created in the plan and we are prepared to use legal means at our disposal to address them," said Kevin Bundy of the Environmental Protection Information Center, a Northern California group that has been at the forefront of Headwaters protests for years.

39

A Revisionist View of Tropical Deforestation and Development

Michael R. Dove, MA, PhD

Introduction

The "Rain-forest Crunch" Thesis

A widely-accepted explanation of tropical deforestation attributes it to the poverty of its native human inhabitants. However, a number of scholars have criticized this theory, maintaining that deforestation is better explained by other factors, such as financial greed or political-economic dynamics. The purpose of the present study also is to criticize the "poverty" theory of deforestation, but from a rather different approach from the usual one. This critique will accordingly be based not on alternative explanations of deforestation, but on "deconstruction" of the poverty theory itself, focusing on its proposed solution to the problem: exploitation of the forest for marketable non-timber products as opposed to subsistence agriculture. The implication is that, if the return to the former use is raised sufficiently high, the latter use will cease. The underlying thesis, therefore, is that the problem of tropical deforestation is a product of economic miscalculation: the forest is being cleared because its riches have been overlooked.

This thesis is represented on U.S. grocers' shelves in the form of "Rain-forest Crunch" and "Rain-forest Crisp." The boxes of these products state that this marketing venture helps to raise the income of forest residents by anywhere from 500 to 2,000%, which "makes the trees too valuable to cut down." The implication, therefore, is that when the incomes of local forest dwellers are too low, the forest is *not* too valuable to cut down. Deforestation thus is linked to local poverty, which in turn is linked to exploitation of the wrong products of the tropical forest in the wrong way. The key is presumed to be finding the right products and the right way. Considerable resources are being devoted to this search, in the form of studies of non-timber forest products.

These efforts are salutary not only in their attempts to improve the economic position of tropical forest communities, but also in their attempts—through retail marketing—to educate the citizens of the U.S. and other industrialized

---

countries about the issue of tropical deforestation. It is with some hesitation, therefore, that I suggest that the premises of this approach are problematic and possibly inimical to the very cause which they espouse. The key to my critique is the fact that the poverty thesis and the "rain-forest crunch" *(see* preceding paragraph) solution is based on "helping."

The Implications of "Helping"

In an insightful study of the political consequences of linguistic forms, Edelman (1974, p. 295) wrote:

"Each linguistic form marshals public support for professional and governmental practices that have profound political consequences..."

I suggest that the linguistic form of "helping" tropical forest-dwellers to avoid deforestation marshals support for a highly problematical government stance towards these populations and this problem. Edelman (1974 p. 296) further writes:

"The most fundamental and long-lasting influences upon political beliefs flow . . . from language that is not perceived as political at all, but nonetheless structure perceptions of status, authority, merit, deviance, and the causes of social problems."

I suggest that the "rain-forest crunch" dialogue, while appearing to be apolitical, helps to structure perceptions of tropical deforestation as a problem of the poor forest-dwellers. As Edelman (1974 p. 305) puts it:

"The professional interpretation . . . also serves . . . the more far-reaching political function of shaping public perceptions so as to mask the appropriateness of change in economic and social institutions."

This is the real "nut" of the issue. I suggest that the "rain-forest crunch" approach, by focusing attention on the micro-economics of forest-dwellers, diverts attention from the broader political-economic bases of deforestation and thereby masks the need for fundamental change in political-economic institutions—a need which outweighs any potential economic benefits that the approach offers to forest dwellers.

I propose to examine in some detail the theoretical basis of the "rain-forest crunch" approach: the idea that deforestation can be combated by the development of non-timber forest products for the benefit of forest dwellers. I will suggest—drawing mostly on Southeast Asian data, in particular from Indonesia—that this idea is completely at odds with the historical development of such products, which has typically been carried out not for the benefit, but rather at the expense, of indigenous forest peoples. I will begin with an illuminating parable, which I recorded in the Meratus Mountains of Southeastern Kalimantan (comprising the major portion of the great island of Borneo, and now part of Indonesia).

The Little Man and the Big Stone

The Parable

Among the forest dwellers who search for diamonds in the hills above Martapura, there is a saying: "Whoever finds a big stone, he will eventually suffer [as a result]." Tales are told in the area of the woe that befell men who found truly large, valuable stones. The problem with such stones is that they cannot be sold: their value is out of proportion to the marketing channels that are normally used by these part-time miners (who gather diamonds in the same way that forest dwellers else-

---

*   These benefits may, in any case, be illusory. Saw *et al.* (1991, pp. 127, 129), in their study of Malaysian fruit-trees, write:

"It has become commonplace to suggest that the sale of wild fruit-crops and other non-timber products could offer a nondestructive means of exploiting forest resources to the benefit of a local community and in contrast to conventional logging practice . . . We can contribute no evidence to support that notion."

where in Kalimantan gather rattan or birds' nests). Big gemstones become sources of "dissonance" within the local and regional political-economic structure: they represent great wealth held by *orang kecil*—"little men"—but never for long. News of such finds quickly comes to the attention of *orang besar* ("big men") in Martapura, Banjarmasin, and even Jakarta (Indonesia's capital, on the island of Java).

A problem is then posed: how can the finder of the stone be relieved of it without giving him more wealth than is deemed appropriate for a poor tribesman in a remote corner of the country? To put the question in more structural terms, how can the "centre" extract such wealth from the "periphery" while still maintaining the appearance of a just society, which is demanded by the national ideology of *Pancasila?* The answer typically is to carry out this extraction in the name of the nation, with, for example, the announced intention of depositing the stone in a "national museum" and paying the finder a nominal "honorarium."

In some cases the stone actually may go to a museum, while in other cases it goes to state elites. In either instance the essential injustice of the extraction is perceived by most of the parties involved. This is reflected in the fact that it typically estranges the finder from the political-economic power-structure. He is estranged, he suffers (he is *susah),* because of the ill-luck which brought him fortune that would never have come to him by virtue of his place in society and that thereby revealed the political-economic inequity of this society.

The lesson of the parable of the big stone and the little man applies to much of the resource development in the tropical forests. The more successful the development is, the more likely is it that external political and economic forces will become involved, and the less likely is it that local inhabitants will be able to retain control (given a non-democratic political tradition such as exists in Indonesia). The reverse is also true: resource development by local peoples that is encouraged by the outside world, and that is left in the hands of the local people, is almost by definition likely to be development that is of less interest to the outside world and less successful for the local people themselves.

Accordingly I suggest that today's search for "new" sources of income for "poor forest-dwellers" is often, in reality, a search for opportunities that have no other claimants—a search for unsuccessful development alternatives. This raises the question: do tropical forest-dwellers need to be *helped* to develop by the broader political-economic systems in which they are enmeshed, or do they need to be *allowed* to develop? Am tropical forest peoples poor because they are not allowed to be rich?

Other Examples

This question is raised not just in folk parables but also in contemporary government policies regarding tropical forest-products development. An illustrative case is currently taking place in the goldfields of Southeastern Kalimantan (and elsewhere in Indonesia's outer islands). These goldfields were initially developed by local smallholders. Their modest successes drew the attention of the National Government several years ago, which responded by licensing the mining rights out to corporate concessionaires and declaring the smallholders who originally developed the goldfields to be "illegal" (Jhamtani, 1989, p. 11). The Government claimed that the attraction of increasing numbers of miners to these goldfields necessitated some form of regulation, but this does not, by itself, justify a shift in beneficiary from local (or even immigrant) smallholder to corporate outsider.

Another illustrative case involves rattan (stripped stems of climbing palms, commonly species of *Calamus*). This forest product, which has been gathered and traded by the

---

*   *Pancasila* literally translates as "five principles," including *Ketuhanan* "belief in God," *Kebangsaan* "nationalism," *Perikemanusiaan* "humanitarianism," *Keadilan Sosial* "social justice," and *Demokrasi* "democracy."

forest dwellers of Kalimantan for centuries, and has been cultivated for almost a century and a half (I. H. Burkill cited in Tsing, 1984 p. 247), began to enjoy a boom in the mid-1980s, providing Indonesia with export revenue of $80 millions annually (Jhamtani, 1989 p. 17). In 1989, after long ignoring the smallholder rattan industry (*cf.* Tsing, 1984 p. 255), the Government banned the export of either raw or half-finished rattan and placed all export of finished rattan under the control of the Indonesian Association of Furniture Producers (Jhamtani, 1989 p. 17: *Environesia,* 1990 p. 13). The political-economic tone of this move is reflected in the fact that this producers' association is headed by Bob Hasan, the self-proclaimed "king" of Indonesia's timber industry. Such favouring of an already-privileged elite is not justified by the Government's desire (in itself laudable) to increase the nation's benefit from rattan by adding-on value before exporting it. The domination of this association by a member of the political-economic elite is no accident: it is predictable from this study's thesis regarding the development of tropical forest products. It would only be surprising (because of not being predicted) if this association was headed by someone from outside the elite!

A third case involves exploitation of the forest biomass itself, one of the most important resources of tropical forests. This biomass (in addition to being heavily exploited for lumber and pulp by commercial interests) is exploited for crop-sustaining ash—obtained through swidden, i.e., shifting or slash-and-burn agriculture—by the local forest peoples, and also by non-local, market-oriented "truck farmers." These are lowlanders who have been outfitted (in many cases with chain-saws and trucks) by urban entrepreneurs, or transmigrants who turned to slash-and-burn agriculture when their World Bank-devised farming systems failed.

The truck farmers follow the logging roads into the hills and, as soon as logging operations have been completed, burn the remaining timber and plant cash-crops. After 2–3 years of cropping, the land succeeds to *Imperata cylindrica* (the ubiquitous pioneer-

ing Saw-grass of Southeast Asia), and they move up the logging road and begin again. The first reports of this type of shifting cultivator began to appear about ten years ago (Vayda, 1981), but their existence is now generally recognized. A recent report calls them "urban-based entrepreneurial shifting cultivators" or "transitional or opportunistic shifting cultivators," in contrast to the *"bona fide* or traditional shifting cultivator" (Ohlsson, 1990 pp. 29–31).

The Government stance towards these various types of shifting cultivation reveals, again, a political-economic bias in the management of tropical forest resources. Most government officials continue to blame practically all forest clearance on forest-dwelling tribesmen practising traditional, sustainable swidden agriculture. Although the shifting cultivation of truck farmers and transmigrants is far more destructive than the traditional swidden agriculture, the political power of the urban business class and the transmigration programme make it virtually impossible for officials to even acknowledge, much less curtail, their involvement in shifting cultivation. As Hurst (1990 p. 24) says, "The government . . . consistently blames the tribal groups for the environmental havoc caused by wandering transmigrants." While it is non-local "shifted cultivators" who do most of the damage, therefore, it is local "shifting cultivators" who take the blame (Westoby, 1983 pp. 243–4). Nor is switching the blame to the "shifted cultivators" (e.g., Indonesian transmigrants) strictly correct: it is the political-economic factors behind this displacement of rural populations, which are typically external to them, that are in fact blameworthy (*cf.* Thiesenhausen, 1991 p. 7).

Also blameworthy are the concessionaires who build the logging roads and then shirk their legal responsibility for controlling their use. But, again for political reasons, it is usually impossible for government officials to acknowledge this dimension of the problem (*cf.* Brown, 1991 pp. 79–80). In short, what is, in reality, as Ohlsson (1990 p. 31) writes, a straightforward "law-and-order problem" involving exploitation of the forest by out-

Figure 39.1 Pattern of tropical forest development.

siders, instead is officially construed as a "cultural" problem involving the forest dwellers—most unfairly to them and unfortunately for the world.

There is some evidence to suggest that this pattern is beginning to change, however: in the past 2–3 years, high Indonesian officials, such as the Governor of South Kalimantan (Ir. H.M. Said), have publicly acknowledged the existence of a traditional *non*-destructive variant of shifting cultivation. This can be attributed to the addition of human ecology and ecological anthropology to the curricula of many of the nation's universities, the gradual development of a tradition of empirical study of shifting cultivation, and the growing political voice of the *bona fide* shifting cultivators themselves.

Para Rubber

One of the most revealing examples of the contested development of a forest product is Para rubber.*

Para Rubber *(Hevaa brasiliensis)*

The bulk of Indonesia's rubber (75% at the most recent count [GOI, 1991 pp. 215–6]) is produced in small gardens of a hectare or so, by "smallholders" (defined as people with less than 25 hectares [Barlow & Muharminto, 1982 p. 86]), who are ordinary farmers who produce rubber with household labour to meet part of their household's income requirements. Most smallholders also cultivate food-crops, which helps them to cope with market risk in the rubber system—much as rubber cultivation helps them to cope with environmental risk in the food-crop system.

Such a combination of market- and subsistence-oriented agricultural activities is common among the forest-dwelling peoples of Indonesia (and also Malaysia, *cf.* Cramb, 1988). Other examples are swidden agriculture and rattan production in East Kalimantan (Peluso, 1983a, 1983b; Weinstock, 1983; Lindblad, 1988 pp. 59–60), swidden agriculture and coffee in Sulawesi (Burch, 1986), swidden agriculture, coffee, and damar, in Sumatra (Mary & Michon, 1987), and sago (obtained from various palms and cycads) extraction and spice cultivation in the Moluccas (Ellen, 1979).

The combination of the two systems is extremely flexible and resilient, and it has conferred unusual autonomy on smallholders with respect to both the external market and government forces. This is reflected in the fact that the smallholders' share of Indonesia's rubber production has grown in every decade since smallholders first started planting rubber early in the present century, while the share held by government and private estates (which pioneered rubber cultivation) has shrunk just as steadily.

Cultivation of Para Rubber has many of the characteristics that are purportedly sought in current schemes to develop tropical forest peoples and conserve their environment. It

---

* While Para rubber is a forest product in South America, and while it fitted into the economic niche of forest products in Southeast Asia, it is technically not a forest product in Southeast Asia because the tree producing it, *Hevea brasiliensis,* is a native of the New World.

involves local peoples in production for national and international markets, moderates their dependence upon forest-based food-cropping, and is adopted with alacrity. But while smallholder rubber development suits these manifest goals, it does not suit certain latent goals that are better fulfilled by estate development. Estate development suits the general, over-arching governmental imperative of centralized control and extraction of resources (*cf.* Booth, 1988 p. 237), while smallholder development frustrates it.

Smallholders, as a result, have received little official support and considerable official opposition. Until relatively recently, the Government directed virtually all of its technical, material, and regulatory, support to the estate sector (*cf.* Booth, 1988 pp. 206, 225). In the mid-1970s, the Government began to direct some resources towards the smallholder sector, but the number of smallholders who benefited was limited (in the 1980s, only 8% of rubber smallholders had been included in governmental extension programmes [Booth, 1988 p. 217]), and the predominant pattern of development—consisting of satellite smallholder estates surrounding a "nuclear" Government estate (called *Perkebunan Inti Rakyat* or *PIR*)—was less an attempt to improve traditional smallholdings than an attempt to remake them in the image, and under the control, of the Government estates (*cf.* Barlow & Tomich, 1991 p. 44). As a result, these schemes were highly problematical, and this approach has now been largely abandoned (*ibid*, p. 48).

There was a colonial precedent for this official lack of support for native rubber cultivation in the form of the international rubber regulation agreements of the 1920s and 1930s. These agreements were ostensibly designed to stabilize world rubber prices by limiting production through taxation, imposition of sales quotas, and prohibition of planting (Bauer, 1948). In practice, however, the agreements were employed to preserve the *status quo*—particularly to protect the early domination of the industry by European estates from an increasingly competitive smallholder sector.

The smallholders' competitive edge was based on the fact that they could establish rubber at less than 10% of the cost of the estates and they were willing to tap it for prices which were as little as one-fifth of those that the estates demanded to give a reasonable return (Bauer, 1948 pp. 68, 206). The earlier-referred-to resiliency of smallholder cultivation enabled them to survive these punitive schemes. Despite the fact that export taxes on smallholder production were increased to the point where they equalled from 2,000 to 6,500% of net profit (Bauer, 1948 p. 142), smallholders continued to increase both the quantity and quality of their production. Then, and today, smallholders flourished less because of government policy, than in spite of it.

Natural Forest Rubber

The unwelcome entry of the native population into rubber cultivation was stimulated. ironically, by colonial intervention in Para Rubber's historical antecedent in Southeast Asia—namely, the gathering of natural forest rubber. Forest rubbers, resins, and gums played a prominent role in the long history of Southeast Asian trade in forest products. Large-scale trade with Europe in natural rubbers dates from the 1840s and the discovery that "gutta-percha"—a generic name for latex from a number of different plants, but especially from *Palaquium* spp. (Burkill, 1962 II p. 1651)—could be used for insulating marine telegraph cables, among other purposes (Lindblad, 1988 p. 14). A second boom in the European trade occurred during the first decade of this century, following the discovery that fire-resistant plates and tiles could be made from "jelutong"—again a generic term for latex from a number of different plants, but especially from *Dyera* spp. (Burkill, 1962 I p. 889; Lindblad, 1988 p. 18).

As this commercial boom developed, the Colonial Government progressively restricted exploitation by local smallholders. By 1908 the Colonial Government in parts of Kalimantan was requiring a license to tap the trees; in 1910 the Government awarded all tapping rights to foreign concessionaires; and in 1913 the Government imposed export levies on the native tappers (Potter, 1988 pp. 131–3). The Government justified these measures either in terms of the need to avoid overexploitation of the latex-yielding trees (Potter, 1988 p. 131), or of the need to protect the smallholders against middlemen (Lindblad, 1988 p. 19). But the attendant abuse of native rights in pursuit of European profit was so glaring that the Dutch legal scholar, J. van Vollenhoven, called it a textbook case of the Colonial Government's abuse of its right to "wastelands" (Potter, 1988 p. 134).

These examples all suggest the existence of a common pattern of resource development in the tropical forest (again, assuming a nondemocratic political-economic tradition): forest people develop a resource for the market, and if and when this market attains sufficient importance, central economic and political interests assume control of it, based on self-interest rhetorically disguised as the common good (Figure 39.1).

This generalization is based on Southeast Asian data, and while there are important differences in the historical development of forest resources in South America and Africa, there are important similarities as well. For example, the control of forest rubbers (and attempted control of Para Rubber) by the State in Indonesia has a close parallel in the Amazon region, where absolute rule over native rubber tappers (the *serenguieros)* by political-economic elites has persisted almost up to the present day.

Non-Timber Forest Products

This historical pattern throws into question the premises of contemporary efforts to develop non-timber forest products.

UNESCO/FAO Study

The premises of these efforts are stated explicitly by one contributor to the field (Keff,

1991 p. 33): "Recent studies on indigenous peoples and the impact of their traditional life-styles on tropical forests appear to indicate that crafts development represents a constructive alternative to destructive land-use practices." The problems with this approach are illustrated by a recent United Nations (UNESCO/FAO) study of the prospects for contributing to forestry development and protection in Kalimantan through development of forest-based handicrafts and other sources of income (Ohlsson, 1990). The Authors of the study conclude that, in addition to handicrafts, the income of rural and isolated people can be supplemented by "agriculture or other activities, such as butterfly farms, crocodile farms, fish farms, and medicinal plant collection" (Ohlsson, 1990 p. 69). Yet notably absent from this list are the tropical forest products which are of the greatest interest to external society: trees for timber or pulp, valuable hardwoods, gems and other minerals, what may well be the world's greatest botanical gene-pool, and rubber and other smallholder export crops such as Coffee (*Coffea arabica*), Tobacco (*Nicotiana tabacum*), and Coconuts (*Cocos nucifera*).

This study's list of potential sources of income is a list not of what the broader society values *most,* but of what it values *least*. It is a list of what the broader society is likely to allow the forest peoples to keep—so long, as the story of the "big stone" suggests, some twist of fate does not suddenly render one of these products more valuable than is deemed appropriate for a poor forest dweller. For an environment as rich in resources as Southeast Asia's tropical forests, a list of potential income sources that cannot transcend butterfly and crocodile farms is a recommendation, however unintentional, not for the *empowerment* of the forest peoples but for their *impoverishment.* In the context of heightened competition for access to tropical forest resources, this "sin of

---

*   As Blaikie (1985 p. 84) writes: ". . . Conservation practices left undone, legislation remaining unheeded, projects that only serve to keep research officers in salary and which never leave the experimental station (those things *not* done) are, also, political acts and not just omissions, or non-events which do not need explanation."

omission"—which strengthens the position of outside interests and weakens the position of the forest dwellers—is no accident: it is a product of the ideology and rhetoric of the dominant political-economic interests.

IUCN Study

Another revealing study on non-timber forest products in Southeast Asia was carried out recently for the World Conservation Union (IUCN). Its Authors call these products a "neglected resource," whose role in the national and local economies of Southeast Asian countries has been "overlooked" (Beer & McDermott, 1989 pp. 13, 125). They blame this on a lack of study, writing "That policymakers tend to forget the role of non-timber forest products is not surprising, given the lack of readily available information on the subject" (*ibid.* p. 13).

I suggest that the recent absence of attention to this topic is not simply a scholarly lacuna, but is a function of the political-economic context. When these products are important to governments, they are studied; and the reverse also is true. For example, the colonial Dutch Government's economic interest in *gutta percha* and *jelutong*—products that are today of minimal economic importance—is clearly reflected in the Netherlands East Indies' colonial forestry literature, a recent compendium of which lists 64 and 32 references, respectively, to these two products alone (CAPD, 1982). The association between state interest and research attention is reflected in the observation by the Authors of the IUCN study that research interest in rattan canes has increased significantly in the past few years (Beer & McDermott, 1989 p. 17), a development that nicely matches the recent increase in the value (and state involvement in the production) of Indonesian rattan.

The Authors of the IUCN study call the scholarly inattention to these resources, which continued even into the 1980s, an "imbalance" (Beer & McDermott, 1989 p. 17). I suggest that this imbalance is one not of scholarship but of state interest (and I suggest that the research priority, when faced with such an anomaly, is not simply to redress it—as implied in Beer & McDemott's work—but first to ask why it exists, following Thompson *et al.* [1986].) Non-timber forest products have been ignored during much of this century; they acquired the label "minor," because central governments were focusing their extractive interest on timber. It is precisely this preoccupation with timber that made possible the current "discovery" (or, more properly, "rediscovery") of some formerly prominent non-timber forest products.

Discussion

This pattern of resource exploitation is at variance with the "rain-forest crunch" premise, that forest reserves are being overexploited by forest dwellers; that this is due to the absence of non-timber sources of income, and the solution is to help forest dwellers to find and develop such sources. My study suggests that there has been no lack of such sources in the past, and that the problem has been in maintaining the forest peoples' control of them. The nature of the relationship between forest degradation and underdevelopment of forest peoples is the reverse of that which is commonly claimed: forests are not degraded because forest peoples are impoverished; rather, *forest peoples are impoverished by the degradation of their forests and other resources by external forces.* In a perverse irony, the instrument of the forest peoples' impoverishment, deforestation, is blamed on them! Their proximity to the forest makes

---

*   The forest peoples of Indonesia physically and culturally distant from the seats of power. Residence in the forest is associated, for related reasons (*see* Dove, 1985), with anti-establishment political views, which has been one of the principal justifications for ongoing government programmes to resettle people out of the forests.

them an easy target for blame, and their lack of political capital makes it difficult for them to refute this charge.

The problem is not that the forest peoples are poor, therefore, but that they are politically weak (and the problem is not that the forest is environmentally fragile, but that it is politically marginal). The problem for the forest peoples is that they inhabit a resource which is coveted by groups that are more powerful than they are (while the problem for the forest is that it is inhabited by peoples who are too weak to insist on its sustainable use). These problems therefore stem not from imbalances in attention by scholars, development officials, or markets; they stem from a more fundamental imbalance in political economy. This imbalance (as in the parable of the big diamond found by the little man) stems from an association of rich resources and weak peoples. The imbalance operates on several different levels. At the level of the individual, it makes it difficult for a poor man to hang on to resources that are incommensurate with his social and political status. At the level of the community, the imbalance makes it difficult for marginal forest dwellers to contest appropriation of their resources by the political and economic institutions of the Central Government. At the level of the nation, it makes it difficult for countries with poorly-developed political and economic institutions to contest the undervalued purchase of their resources by powerful industrialized nations.

The exploitation of Malaysia's timber by Japan is a good example of the latter situation. Japan can import valuable hardwoods from Malaysia, for use as throw-away chopsticks and concrete shuttering, at less than the cost of using local plantation trees (Goodland *et al.,* 1990 p. 314; *cf.* Myers, 1986 pp. 297–8), because Malaysia's political and economic institutions permit its timber to be sold at far below its true value. The political-economic

institutions of Malaysia are, in the context of this exchange, found wanting. A political-economic imbalance between Malaysia and Japan makes this inequitable extraction of hardwoods possible at the international level (with Japan taking from Malaysia), practically as a political-economic imbalance within Malaysia makes it possible at the national level (with national elites taking from local communities). They are two sides of the same coin. In both cases, the nation and the local people are "smallmen," too weak to hang on to their "big wealth."

Conclusions and Recommendations

Conclusions

The lesson of this analysis is not to ignore minor forest products, but to place them clearly—and their potential development value for indigenous forest peoples—within their proper political-economic context, with all of its associated constraints.* One of these constraints is discursive: this analysis suggests that state elites do not just control valuable forest resources: they also control discourse regarding these resources. Demystification of the debate over tropical deforestation and development is needed, therefore, and this depends on untying what we may call "discursive knots" (from Rabinow, 1986 p. 253). These knots are tied by asking, for example. "How can we help?" instead of "How are we hurting?", and "What do we need to give *to* tropical forest peoples?", instead of "What have we taken away *from* tropical forest peoples?"

Any resolution of the problems of tropical forest development and conservation must begin, not by searching for resources that forest dwellers do not already have, but by first

---

* This contextualization may help to explain both over- and underemphases of minor forest product—the latter occurring when local exploitation of a product competes with external exploitation of other products. Thus, Caldecott (1988 p. 55) claims that the Sarawak government underestimates by over 99% the importance of feral pigs in the diet of forest dwellers, apparently as part of an effort to downplay the value of the forests for other purposes than commercial logging.

searching for the institutional forces that restrict their ownership and use of existing resources. The first approach has obvious attractions, because it is less problematical to assume that rural peoples have no resources than to explain why the resources that they had have been taken away (*cf.* Jhamtani, 1989 pp. 24–5). It is no coincidence (to return to Edelman's [1974] analysis of the language of "helping") that the emphasis on what society needs to do *for* rural peoples effectively precludes attention to what society has already done *to* them. It is no accident that the emphasis on rural peoples' poverty tends to preclude attention to their actual resource-wealth. Identification of "the problem" as a lack of resources rhetorically—and ironically—supports the resource *disenfranchisement* of rural communities. We may also note the comment of Shiva (1989 p. 86), writing on the privatization of the commons in South Asia: "As usual, in every scheme that worsens the position of the poor, it is the poor who are invoked as beneficiaries."

The problem involves not just an economic calculus but also a political-economic one. The tropical forest is being cut, not because its products are improperly valued, but because the beneficiaries and victims are improperly identified. There is less need to find "nuts" that will counterbalance the local peasants' or tribesmen's purported interest in clearing the forest, than to find institutional mechanisms that will counterbalance the political-economic forces favouring self-interested resource-use by national and international elites. With such mechanisms in place, the study and development of non-timber forest products would take on new meaning; in the absence of such mechanisms, these efforts are premature at best and chimerical at worst.

Recommendations

Many things are possible if the political-economic will to develop rather than under-develop tropical forest peoples is ever attained. Consider, for example, the possibilities for developing smallholder Para Rubber

cultivation. Among the major rubber producers, Indonesia's smallholders have the most primitive technology (Barlow & Muharminto, 1982 pp. 92–3). Almost all smallholders employ genetic material and techniques of cultivation and production that have remained unchanged since the initial decades of rubber's introduction to Southeast Asia (*cf.* Barlow & Tomich, 1991 pp. 31, 35), so that it is not surprising that the rubber which they produce has the lowest quality and fetches the lowest price (Barlow, 1978 p. 411; Ching, 1985 p. 81). Malaysia, whose smallholders were in a similar position a generation ago, shows what can be accomplished (*cf.* Barlow & Tomich, 1991 p. 50): between 1965 and 1980, government efforts to assist Malaysian smallholders (stimulated by some degree of democratization of the political process) raised average yields by 126%. By comparison, yields in Indonesia rose just 17% during the same time-period (Booth, 1988 pp. 211–2).

The productivity of Indonesia's smallholdings could be greatly improved by the introduction of such elementary inputs as high-quality planting material and extension advice (*cf.* Barlow & Tomich, 1991 p. 51). This offers one of the best avenues for development of Indonesia's tribal, swidden-cultivating minorities (as Geddes [1954 p. 98] concluded for the Dayaks of Sarawak) and, in general, it offers one of the few ecologically sound avenues for development in the tropical forest (*cf.* Goodland's [1990 p. 191]) recommendation to "reactivate Asian sleeping [namely, under-exploited] rubber").

One of the most important principles to follow in planning development interventions, whether with Para Rubber or some other resource, is to avoid centralization. All available evidence suggests that centralized control leads too easily (at least in Indonesia) to local economic hardship and resource degradation instead of the reverse. In the case of smallholder rubber, therefore, instead of developing problematic (and expensive) nucleus estate projects under the wing of state plantations, the Government should assist traditional smallholders *in situ* (and at far less cost). In the case of rattan, if some type of export organization is deemed necessary, a nongovernmental organization (NGO) would be preferable to an elite-dominated trade association such as the Indonesian Furniture Producer's Association. In many cases it may be preferable to let the smallholder interact with the market either on his/her own, or through the medium of local NGOs. While the logic of the market is not infallible, it often does better by the smallholder than the formal organizations that central governments create on his/her purported behalf.

Afterword

The belief that tropical forest peoples will better conserve their environment if permitted rights to "minor" forest products is doubly flawed. Not only do such people not represent the primary threat to the tropical forest (which comes instead from logging, ranching, plantations, government resettlement schemes, and political-economic refugees), but their interest in conservation is not likely to be heightened by this strategy—quite the reverse! The parable of the little man and the big stone is illuminating in this regard.

That story of the little man and the great treasure occurs (in varying forms) in many different societies. The most famous exposition in English literature may be Steinbeck's "The Pearl" (1945), set in Latin America. Steinbeck tells of a great pearl—the "Pearl of the world"—found by a poor pearl diver, Kino, and of the conspiracy by society to defraud him of it. Instead of bringing him wealth and happiness, the pearl brings Kino and his family only violence and tragedy, so that at the end of the story he hurls it back into the ocean from which it came. Robbed of his proper right to benefit from the pearl, Kino (in effect) destroys it.

There is an analogy here to conservation of tropical forests. If indigenous people are deprived of rights to all but the least and meanest of forest resources, they may well follow the example of Kino and destroy that which was theirs by right but the enjoyment of which was denied to them.* If left with access only to the most truly "minor" forest products, forest dwellers are unlikely to feel any "major" commitment to forest conservation. National elites and international agencies may delude themselves by continued mystification on this point, but they are not likely to delude the forest peoples.

Acknowledgements

The data presented in this study were gathered during a total of eight years of residence and research in Indonesia, between the years 1974 and 1985. Two of these years were spent conducting research in a longhouse in West Kalimantan, and six years were spent as a visiting professor and research adviser at a government university in Java, during which time research was continued in Kalimantan and several of Indonesia's other outer islands, in addition to Java itself.

This research was successively supported by the U.S. National Science Foundation (Grant Nr GS-42605), the Rockefeller Foundation, the Ford Foundation, and the East-West Center's Environment & Policy Institute. The current analysis was partially supported by a fellowship in Yale University's Program in Agrarian Studies. Earlier versions of this paper were presented at The New York Botanical Garden and Yale University's School of Forestry and Environmental Science. The Author is grateful to two anonymous referees for constructive comments, to Terese Leber for assistance with literature searches, and to Helen Takeuchi for assistance with graphics. The Author alone is responsible for the final analysis presented here.

---

* An historical example of this is Indonesia's Sandalwood Tree (*Santalum album* L.). Because of the interest of native Rajahs, and subsequently of the Dutch colonists, in controlling and profiling from this trade, it "caused the common Timorese more pain than pleasure" (Ormeling, 1957 p. 177). The commoners' response was predictable: "Wherever possible the population tried to get rid of the troublesome sandalwood tree by clandestine felling, or by other means" (*ibid.* pp. 177–8).

Summary

This study critiques one of the prevailing theories of tropical deforestation, namely that the forest is being cleared because its riches have been overlooked (the purported solution to which is the marketing of "rain-forest crunch"). Edelman's work on the language of "helping" is drawn on to suggest that a focus on the micro-economics of forest dwellers diverts attention from macro-economic and political issues whose impact on the forest is far more serious.

The study begins with a parable from Kalimantan, relating how the discovery of a big diamond can bring misfortune to a poor miner. It is suggested that this parable applies more generally to resource development in tropical forests, and that the major challenge is not to give more development opportunities to forest peoples but to take fewer away.

This principal is illustrated with respect to gold mining, rattan gathering, and truck-farming, in Indonesia. In each case, when a forest resource acquires greater value in the broader society, it is appropriated by external entrepreneurs at the expense of local communities. A detailed case-study is presented of the development of Para Rubber cultivation. Smallholders currently dominate this cultivation, despite steadfast opposition by both contemporary and colonial governments, whose self-interests are better served by the cultivation of the Rubber on large estates.

Each of these cases illustrates the predisposition of political and economic forces in the broader society to take over successful resource development in the tropical forest. Contemporary efforts to develop "non-timber forest products" are reinterpreted, in this light, as attempts to allocate to the forest dwellers the resources of least interest to the broader society. The absence of research in this area is attributed not to academic oversight but to conflicting political-economic interests.

This thesis of resource exploitation is at variance with the "rain-forest crunch" premise: namely that forest reserves are being overexploited by forest dwellers, that this is due to the absence of other sources of income, and that the solution is to help forest dwellers to find such sources. It is suggested that there has been no lack of such sources in the past, and that the problem has been in maintaining the forest peoples' control of them. The lesson of this analysis is not to ignore minor forest products, but to place them—and their potential development value for indigenous forest peoples clearly within their proper political-economic context.

Any resolution of the problems of tropical forest development and conservation must begin, not by searching for resources that forest dwellers do not already have, but by *first* searching for the institutional forces which restrict the forest dwellers' ownership and productive use of *existing* resources. One of these institutional forces is discourse. It is widely understood that state elites seek to control valuable forest resources; it is less widely understood that an important means to this end is the control of resource-related discourse. De-mystification of the current debate over tropical deforestation and development is thus sorely needed.

References

Australian Centre for International Agricultural Research (ACIAR) (1985). *Smallholder Rubber Production and Policies: Proceedings of an International Workshop held at the University of Adelaide.* ACIAR. Canberra. Australia: 151 pp., illustr.

Barlow, Colin (1978). *The Natural Rubber Industry: Its Development, Technology, and Economy in Malaysia.* Oxford University Press, Kuala Lumpur, Malaysia: xxiv + 500 pp., illustr.

Barlow, Colin and Muharminto (1982). The rubber smallholder economy. *Bulletin of Indonesian Economic Studies.* XVIII(2), pp. 86–119.

Barlow, Colin and Tomich, Thomas (1991). Indonesian agricultural development: the awkward case of smallholder tree crops. *Bulletin of Indonesian Economic Studies.* XXVII(3). pp. 29–54.

Bauer, P. T. (1948). *The Rubber Industry: A Study in Monopoly and Competition.* Longmans, Green, London, England, UK: xiii + 404 pp.

Beer, Jenne H. de and McDermott, Melanie J. (1989). *The Economic Value of Non-timber*

Forest Products in Southeast Asia: With Emphasis on Indonesia, Malaysia, and Thailand. Netherlands Committee for IUCN, Amsterdam, The Netherlands: 175 pp., illustr.

Blaike, Piers (1985). *The Political Economy of Soil Erosion in Developing Countries.* Longman Inc., New York, NY, U.S.A.: 188 pp., illustr.

Booth, Anne (1988). *Agricultural Development in Indonesia.* Asian Studies Association of Australia. Southeast Asia Publications Series No. 16. Allen & Unwin, Sydney, Australia: vii + 295 pp., illustr.

Brown, Lester R. (1991). *State of the World 1991: A Worldwatch Institute Report on Progress Toward a Sustainable Society.* W.W. Norton, New York, NY, U.S.A.: xvii + 254 pp., illustr.

Burch, Carol-Carmen (1986). *Coffee as Cash in Highland Indonesia: Evidence on a Debate.* Paper read at the Annual Meeting of American Anthropological Association. Philadelphia, Pennsylvania, U.S.A.: [not available for checking].

Burkill, I. H. (1962). *A Dictionary of the Economic Products of the Malay Peninsula.* Ministry of Agriculture and Cooperation, Kuala Lumpur, Malaysia: xiv + 2444 pp. (in 2 vols).

Caldecott, Julian (1988). *Hunting and Wildlife Management in Sarawak.* International Union for Conservation of Nature and Natural Resources. Gland/Cambridge: xx + 150 pp., illustr.

Centre for Agricultural Publishing and Documentation (CAPD) (1982). *Indonesian Forestry Abstracts: Dutch Literature until about 1960.* CAPD, Wageningen. The Netherlands: xvii + 658 pp., illustr.

Ching, Lim Sow (1985). Malaysian smallholders: issues and approaches in further processing and manufacturing. Pp. 73–85 *in* ACIAR (*q.v.*).

Cramb, R. A. (1988). The commercialization of Iban Agriculture. Pp. 105–34 *in* Cramb & Reece (*q.v.*).

Cramb, R. A. and Reece, R. H. W. (Eds) (1988). *Development in Sarawak: Historical and Contemporary Perspectives.* Monash Paper on Southeast Asia Nr 17, Center of Southeast Asian Studies, Monash University, Clayton, Victoria, Australia: 191 pp., illustr.

Dove, Michael R. (1985). The agroecological mythology of the Javanese, and the political economy of Indonesia. *Indonesia.* XXXVI, pp. 1–36.

Edelman, Murray (1974). The political language of the helping professions. *Politics and Society,* IV(3), pp. 295–310.

Ellen, Roy F. (1979). Sago subsistence and the trade in spices: a provisional model of ecological succession and imbalance in Moluccan history. Pp. 43–74 in *Social and Ecological Systems* (Eds P.C Burnham & R. F. Ellen). Academic Press, London, England, UK: viii + 314 pp., illustr.

Environesia (1990). ITTO meeting promotes unsustainable logging. Vol. IV(2). pp. 12–5. illustr.

Geddes, W. R. (1954). *The Land Dayaks of Sarawak.* Colonial Research Study Nr 14, HMSO, London, England, UK: 113 pp., illustr.

Goodland, Robert (1990). How to save tropical forests—a conspectus. Appendix A in *Race to Save the Tropics: Ecology and Economics for a Sustainable Future* (Ed. Robert Goodland). Island Press, Washington, DC, U.S.A.: xvi + 219 pp.

Goodland, Robert J. A., Asibey, Emmanuel O. A. and Post, Jan C. (1990). Tropical moist forest management: the urgency of transition to sustainability. *Environmental Conservation,* 17(4). pp. 303–18 (5 tables).

Government of Indonesia (GOI) (1991). *Statistik Indonesia: Statistical Yearbook of Indonesia.* Biro Pusat Statistik (Central Bureau of Statistics), Jakarta, Indonesia: xlix + 597 pp., illustr.

Hurst, Philip (1990). *Rainforest Politics: Ecological Destruction in Southeast Asia.* Zed Books, London, England, UK: xiv + 303 pp.

Jhamtani, Hira (1989). *An Overview of Forestry Policies and Commercialization in Indonesia.* Paper presented in the Workshop on the U.S. Tropical Timber Trade: Conservation Options and Impacts: 28 pp., illustr.

Kerr, K. (1991). The economic potential of handicraft enterprises in rural development: focus on Indonesia. *Unasylva,* CLXV(42), pp. 31–6. illustr.

Lindblad, J. Thomas (1988). *Between Dayak and Dutch: The Economic History of Southeast Kalimantan. 1880–1942.* Verhandelingen Nr 134. Foris Publications, Dordrecht, The Netherlands: x + 282 pp., illustr.

Mary, F. and Michon, G. (1987). When agroforests drive back natural forests: a socio-economic analysis of a rice-agroforest system in Sumatra. *Agroforesty Systems,* V, pp. 27–55.

Myers, Norman (1986). Economics and ecology in the international arena: the phenomenon of "linked linkages." *Ambio,* XV(5), pp. 296–300, illustr.

Ohlsson, Bo (1990). *Socio-economic Aspects of Forestry Development. (Indonesia Forestry Studies VIII-3.)* Ministry of Forestry/Food and Agriculture Organization, Jakarta, Indonesia: ix + 77 pp.

Ormeling, F. J. (1957). *The Timor Problem: A Geographical Interpretation of an Underdeveloped Island.* (Groningen/Djakarta: J.B. Wolters.) Martinus Nijhoff, 's-Gravenhage, The Netherlands: viii + 284, illustr.

Peluso, Nancy P. (1983a). Networking in the Commons: a tragedy for rattan? *Indonesia.* XXXV, pp. 95–108.

Peluso, Nancy P. (1983b). *Markets and Merchants: The Forest Product Trade of East Kalimantan in Historical Perspective.* MSc thesis. Cornell University, Ithaca, NY, U.S.A.: ix + 246 pp., illustr.

Potter, Lesley (1988). Indigenes and colonisers: Dutch forest policy in South and East Borneo (Kalimantan), [ad] 1900 to 1950. Pp. 127–49 in *Changing Tropical Forests: Historical Perspectives on Today's Challenges in Asia, Australasia and Oceania* (Eds John Dargavel, Kay Dixon & Noel Semple). Centre for Resource and Environmental Studies, Canberra, ACT, Australia: ix + 446 pp., illustr.

Rabinow, Paul (1986). Representations are social facts: modernity and post-modernity in anthropology. Pp. 234–61 in *Writing Culture: The Poetics and Politics of Ethnography* (Eds J. Clifford & G.E. Marcus). University of California Press, Berkley, California, U.S.A.: ix + 305 pp.

Saw, L. G., Frankie, J. V., Kochummen, K. M. and Yap, S. K. (1991). Fruit trees in a Malasian rain forest. *Economic Botany,* XLV(1), pp. 120–36.

Shiva, Vandana (1989). *Staying Alive: Women, Ecology and Development.* Zed Books, London, England, UK: xx + 224 pp., illustr.

Steinbeck, John (1945/1974). *The Pearl.* Bantam Books, New York, NY, U.S.A.: 118 pp.

Thiesenhausen, William C. (1991). Implications of the rural land tenure system for the environmental debate: three scenarios. *The Journal of Developing Areas,* XXVI(1), pp. 1–24.

Thompson, M., Warburton, M. & Hatley, T. (1986). *Uncertainty on a Himalayan Scale: An Institutional Theory of Environmental Perception and a Strategic Framework for the Sustainable Development of the Himalaya.* Ethnographica, London, England, UK: ix + 162 pp.

Tsing, Anna Lowenhaupt (1984). *Politics and Culture in the Meratus Mountains.* (PhD dissertation, Stanford University.) Ann Arbor, Michigan, U.S.A.: University Microfilms, 2 vols, xi + 635 pp., illustr.

Vayda, Andrew P. (1981). Research in East Kalimantan on interactions between people and forests: a preliminary report. *Borneo Research Bulletin,* XIII(1), pp. 3–15.

Weinstock, J. A. (1983). Rattan: ecological balance in a Borneo rainforest swidden. *Economic Botany,* XXXVII(1), pp. 58–68.

Westoby, Jack (1983). Who's deforesting whom? *Australian Forestry,* LXIV(4), pp. 244–50.

40

Social Forestry for Whom?[1]

Vandana Shiva, H. C. Sharatchandra and J. Bandyopadhyay

Throughout Asia declining forest reserves and related environmental deterioration have brought a substantial interest in the concept of social forestry, which looks to the community to assume a major role in forest management. The Indian government has been at the forefront of this interest, adopting an ambitious social forestry program based on broad participation in forest management to rebuild the country's forest wealth while directly meeting the needs of rural populations for the forest products. While the program has contributed to an expansion of forest cover through the stimulation of private forestry, the primary beneficiaries have been landowners and industry and, contrary to its stated objectives, it has in fact contributed to a decrease in the availability of both forest and food products to the rural poor. This study documents the nature and causes of the gap between an enlightened policy based on the concept of community management and the results of the program through which that policy has been implemented.

The Setting

Between 1947 and 1977, India's forest cover decreased from 40 to 20 percent, with only about 11 percent of the total land area actually under adequate tree cover.[2] Besides having a deleterious effect on agriculture, deforestation has caused severe ecological damage in many areas of rural India and hardship for the 90 percent of the Indian population that continues to depend on forests for its domestic needs, fodder for animals, poles and posts for housing, and for organic fertilizer for agriculture.

For centuries prior to British rule, the rural people of India had made use of forestry products according to locally agreed upon practices that ensured their continued supply and distribution to those who needed them. The roots of the current problem trace back to British rule and the policy of reserving large forest areas for the monopolistic use of the British government. This resulted in a sudden and drastic reduction both of the public forest lands open to public use, and the forests belonging to the local *panchayats* (village councils). An irreversible trend in forest management and land-use was thus initiated involving the alienation of the whole rural population from the forest, which in its eyes, now came under the exclusive control of such "external" authorities as forest officers and contractors. The sudden restriction of the population's access to large parts of the reserved forest led, in the absence of any alternatives, to the remaining panchayati forests being rapidly stripped of their trees to meet the needs of the local people. The reserve forests, in the meantime, dwindled through inefficient management oriented to commercial exploitation.[3]

The structure and orientation of forestry management which had led to this sorry state was adopted from the British by the Indian government after the close of British rule. The problem was subsequently exacerbated by the food production priorities of the Indian government during the 1960's, which brought thousands of hectares of forest land under the plough.

Social Forestry: The Concept

Under the joint crisis of unsatisfied basic needs and ecological instability, the rebuilding of India's forest wealth has, in recent years, become one of the major issues in land-use policy, and social forestry has been proclaimed as the leading instrument for forest regeneration. The announced aim of the government's social forestry program is primarily the development of firewood resources, since the shortage of domestic energy, predominantly firewood for food preparation, is expected to be more critical in future years than shortages of food itself. Furthermore, the fuel crisis diverts agricultural waste and dung from its use as organic manure to fuel for cooking, thus sabotaging sustainable agricultural activity. It also undermines agricultural activity by diverting some 20 percent of available farm labor and 18 percent of domestic household labor to firewood gathering.

Of course, forests also provide a wide variety of other products essential to rural life, including fodder for draught animals and timber for housing. This is in addition to the role of forests in stabilizing both hydrological and soil systems. By planting trees in areas now devoid of tree cover, social forestry aims to prevent soil erosion and the silting up of tanks and reservoirs; to arrest the surface run-off of rain water from hillsides; to recharge springs, streams, and underground water aquifers; and finally, in areas which have been severely deforested, to halt the process of desertification.

The basic concept of social forestry is quite simple. Young saplings planted on common lands are likely to be quickly ruined by uncontrolled grazing if the local community is not committed to their protection. They must feel they have a stake in insuring the productive development of the forest resource to meet their own needs for forest products, both for consumption and for income generation, and they must be organized to enforce the rules upon which they agree regarding the management of that resource.

Social Forestry: The Karnataka Program

In 1980 the government of Karnataka submitted a proposal to the World Bank requesting Rs. 600 million for a five-year social forestry program. The stated aim was to combat ecological degradation and meet the basic firewood, fodder, and timber needs of the rural population. The scheme called for development of 110,000 hectares of private land as forests—some 60 percent of the total area of the scheme. A significant feature of the proposal was that the main species to be encouraged was eucalyptus. No mention was made of such traditional farm trees as *honge, neem* and mango.

A quotation from the proposal expresses the lofty expectations of its drafters regarding expected benefits for the rural population.

> *[The purpose of social forestry] is the creation of forests for the benefit of the community through active involvement and the participation of the community. In the process, the rural environment will improve, rural migration will reduce, rural unemployment substantially cease. . . . The overall concept of social forestry aims at making the villages self-sufficient and self-reliant in regard to their forest material needs.*[4]

The present study examines the early results of the on-going social forestry scheme in the Kolar district of Karnataka, in which essentially the same program model proposed to the World Bank has been in operation for a number of years. The evidence from this experience suggests that this particular approach to social forestry, far from achieving its goals, has in many ways exacerbated the problems it sought to solve.

In part this is because the emphasis has in fact been on private farm forestry to the neglect of communally owned forests from which the entire community *may* benefit. It also relates to the choice of species, since eucalyptus, which the program emphasizes, fulfills fewer ecological functions than traditional tree species. It cannot be browsed by animals and provides no fodder, it produces no fruit or nuts, and it is not favored as a fuel.[5] There is also evidence that the development of eucalyptus plantations results in the displacement of labor.

To understand the actual and prospective impact of the program currently being implemented, it is necessary to put it in the context of the traditional agricultural pattern in the area.

Traditional Agriculture in Kolar: Private versus Communal Ownership

Traditionally agriculture in Kolar featured a rich variety of predominantly rain-fed food and cash crops, though a few areas are sustained by well and tank-fed irrigation systems. These crops have been supplemented by a mixture of carefully chosen, multipurpose farm trees like honge (Pongamia sp.), *ala (Ficus* sp.), tamarind (Tamarindus sp.), pale *(Acacia sp.),* and neem *(Melia Azadimenta)*. These preferred tree species provided a broad range of benefits to the local population. For example, the most popular among them in the Kolar region was the honge. Its leaves provide fodder and green manure. Its oil is used for lighting. And its wood makes an extremely good fuel. Neem is used as a pesticide, and as medicine, food, oil and firewood. Tamarind, mango, and jackfruit provide fruits that are an essential part of the diet. This mix of species made the local population self-sufficient with respect to a number of needs without making conflicting demands on the land for food, fodder, fuel, and manure.

Some were planted on privately owned land, either along field bunds or in the fields themselves. In addition to these privately owned trees, there were community owned trees on the village commons and along roadsides. Other communal lands, designated as *gomal* lands, were used predominantly for grazing, but also produced communally available tree products.

All of the traditional species played a significant role in maintaining soil fertility, preventing soil erosion and conserving underground and surface water resources. Using its traditional store of knowledge of silviculture, the species chosen by the community and the lands on which they were planted were carefully chosen to maximize their ecological, as well as their economic, value. Thus, trees were planted along the tank bunds, field boundaries, and on common land to hold the soil and conserve moisture. Hence, the distribution of trees, together with the choice of species, lent itself to maximizing material benefits for the community as a whole.

Erik Eckholm has argued that the cooperation required for communal forestry is largely ruled out in settings of significant social inequality such as exist in Kolar.[6] This goes against the evidence of India's historical reality. Relics of village woodlots or roadside plantations can still be easily found. In the traditional village, private and unequal landholdings existed side-by-side with common and equally shared resources.

The Breakdown of Community Norms

While self-interest might guide a landlord's use of his own land, the use of common resources such as village woodlots was guided by shared community norms, even for the private landlord. The efficacy of these norms was sustained until the simultaneous operation of individual and community obligations was made impossible through the opening up of the village economy to large urban and industrial markets. By and large, access to the larger markets was, and still is, possible only for the most privileged members of the community who had easy access to educational, bureaucratic, and financial institutions. That started a process that gradually broke down the traditional social bonds between the rich and the less fortunate members of the village—leading gradually to a breakdown of the community. Furthermore, the introduction of new agricultural techniques that were adopted only by the rich farmers made them less dependent on local resources, as for example, the substitution of chemical fertilizer for green manure. Under such circumstances, the participation of rich villagers in community efforts to maintain local resources was reduced, leading ultimately to the slow decay of those community norms that had previously governed the use of local resources. Where social organization is based on cooperation amongst members and production based on need, the logic of gain is entirely different from that of societies based on competition and profits through exchange.

The survival of such community property as pastures and village woodlots, or "common goods" like a stable ecosystem, is only possible under a social organization where checks and controls on the use of resources are built into the organizing principles of the community. On the other hand, the breakdown of a community, with the associated collapse in concepts of joint ownership and responsibility, can trigger the degradation of common resources. This is what has happened in forest ownership and land use in India.

Eucalyptus: The Great Encroacher

In the second half of the 1970's, significant changes in land use in Kolar emerged as a result of the Karnataka social forestry program. Through the distribution of free seedlings, farmers have put a large amount of land under farm forests. Although the social forestry scheme was supposed to make a variety of species available for farm forestry, in fact very few species other than *Eucalyptus tereticornis* (also called Mysore hybrid) have been planted. According to our observations in Kolar district, about 55,000 acres had been committed to eucalyptus by 1980-81. The government estimated that 14,000 acres had been planted to eucalyptus in that year alone, and that 93.1 percent of the extension had taken place on agricultural and cultivatable waste lands.[7]

As was noted earlier, the primary objective of the social forestry program is to meet the basic needs of the rural population for forest products, in particular for firewood and fodder. Yet, while for cooking purposes the need is for a slow, controlled heat, eucalyptus—the primary product of the social forestry project—burns too fast to be a preferred cooking fuel among residents of the area. Furthermore, because it is so fast burning, the quantities of eucalyptus wood required to sustain a fire for the length of time required to cook a meal can be prohibitively expensive at its current market price, which is set by the demand for it as a pulp source for the manufacture of paper and rayon. (More than 80 percent of the eucalyptus from Kolar is earmarked for the polyfibre industry in Harihar.) The small number of families using eucalyptus for cooking are usually poor families who collect it from reserved forests in the absence of any other species.

Because of the decline in traditional tree species like honge, tamarind, etc., the supplies of traditional cooking woods that were once available are becoming increasingly restricted. If that trend continues, the firewood crisis will worsen during the years to come, despite the impressive growth of eucalyptus plantations in the villages. Furthermore, eucalyptus tereticornis provides no fodder and in arid regions where it drives out herbaceous annuals, which cannot compete with it for the limited available water, thus allowing no undergrowth which might be used for grazing. Consequently the widespread planting of this species on farmland and communal lands has succeeded in further depleting the already scant fodder resources of the area.

By increasing fodder shortages, the planting of eucalyptus has also indirectly affected the viability of two alternative, renewable energy resources: animal energy and biogas energy. Less fodder reduces the inputs to biogas plants, thus accentuating the already acute problem of firewood shortages.

Simplistic Assumptions

Why has the social forestry program failed so conspicuously to achieve its primary objective of satisfaction of the basic biomass needs of the rural population? The answer, in our view, lies in the simplistic assumptions that have been made about the production and distribution of primary forest products. It has been assumed implicitly that just growing more trees will satisfy basic needs. No distinction has been made between what trees are grown or who grows them, even though the evidence suggests that the tree species that get planted determine to a large extent which groups will benefit. It has also been assumed erroneously that if more of a particular commodity is produced in a particular area, that commodity will automatically become more available to the local people. That assumption takes little account of the nature of the market economy. In a market economy, it is those with the highest purchasing power who have command over resources. And in this case, those with the highest purchasing power are not the local people but distant urban based industries.

Also neglected is the relationship between wood fibre production and food production. There has been a tendency for the government to be concerned with food productivity, food shortages, and food surpluses only in relation to urban consumption needs. Thus, we have instances of importing wheat to check inflation in response to a rising price of wheat, but wheat is not the staple food of most of the rural poor in India. In Karnataka the basic staple is *ragi*, a millet. Price increases of 200 percent in two years have made ragi nearly as expensive as wheat and rice, with little reaction from the government. Among the consequences is a decline in physical health and nutritional status as a result of shifting from the traditional staple diet of millets and pulses to diets (made possible through debt or food for work programs) of wheat or rice.[8]

Significantly the area under ragi has been systematically shrinking in Kolar (from 141,772 acres in 1977-78 to 48,406 in 1980-81) as it has throughout Karnataka, primarily through the conversion of these lands to eucalyptus plantations. It may be anticipated that this conversion will continue in response to further expansion of the social forestry program.

A related consequence is a decline in the demand for labor. By growing eucalyptus, a farmer becomes relatively independent of labor for his farm operations while simultaneously retaining the returns from his land. The cost of mixed and rotational cropping of traditional food crops in rain-fed areas requires an annual expense of at least Rs. 1,500 per hectare, with a labor requirement on the order of 250 man-days. By contrast, eucalyptus plantations require only an initial expenditure of Rs. 1,500 per hectare plus harvesting costs, with a guaranteed high return. Labor costs during the growth period are negligible. Farmers currently sell eucalyptus at around Rs. 300 per ton to the pulp based industries, easily Providing an annual return of Rs. 2,500 per hectare.

Despite its proclaimed objectives, the present social forestry program thus appears to be little more than yet another policy for supplying industrial raw materials. Unlike conventional forestry, which simply supplied industry its raw material from land specially earmarked for reserved forests, social forestry is ultimately performing the same function by putting new demands on lands that have been used for production of the basic food requirements of the rural population. At worst, such calculated displacement of basic food production must lead to slow emaciation and death through starvation of a significant number of the rural poor.

Perversely this in turn may in fact have a detrimental impact on noneucalyptus forest production, since the survival of the displaced labor is dependent on searching out alternative means of livelihood. One such option is the collection of firewood in the reserve forests, not for their own consumption, but for sale in urban and semi-urban centers. In one of the villages in our survey, fifteen out of sixty households were found to be fully dependent on the firewood trade. Villagers spend nearly eight hours a day walking six to eight kilometers to the local market where a headload of firewood sells for some Rs. 4.00. Further deforestation is one of the consequences of this firewood trade, and the theft of firewood through stripping forest reserves of their remaining trees is the only option left to more and more villagers.

Earlier afforestation programs of the forest department, which raised eucalyptus on forest land, presented the argument that eucalyptus was often the only species that could survive on degraded soils. But now, through social forestry, eucalyptus is being introduced for the first time on fertile land in arid and semi-arid regions where crops could grow. Since eucalyptus leaves do not contribute to the building up of humus, and the tree does not allow undergrowth, the long-term impact of eucalyptus on the fertility of agricultural lands in these regions is quite deleterious.[9]

The Challenge

Our study has demonstrated a substantial gap between the high-sounding objectives of social forestry and the realities of its implementation in the Indian district studied. Unfortunately the evidence suggests that the negative consequences described are not limited to this district. The task of developing social forestry programs that can in fact meet their intended objectives becomes a major challenge for those who believe in people's participation in development. The organized will of the people, instead of the availability of foreign funds, should be the starting point for social forestry. In various parts of the country, nongovernmental organizations have done excellent afforestation without foreign aid. Perhaps ultimately the answer can be found in some form of collaboration between the government foresters, nongovernmental organizations, and the village people.[10] Only if the people and the government learn to work together in a new relationship is it likely that the laudable objectives of social forestry will be realized.

Notes

1. Revised and abstracted version of "The Challenge of Social Forestry" by the same authors published in W. Fernandez and S. Kulkarni, *Towards a New Forest Policy*, Indian Social Institute, New Delhi 110003 (1983). Reprinted by permission.
2. B. B. Vohra, "The Greening of India" in J. Bandyopdahyay, N. D. Jayal, U. Schoettli, and Chhatrapati Singh (eds.), *India's Environment: Crises and Responses*, (Dehradun: Natraj Publishers, 1985), p. 27.
3. C. T. S. Nair, "Crisis In Forest Resource Management" in Bandyopadhyay, *loc. cit.*, pp. 10–3.
4. Government of Karnataka. *Social Forestry Programme with World Bank Aid* (Bangalore), 1980, p. 9.
5. Vandana Shiva and J. Bandyopadhyay, *Ecological Audit of Eucalyptus Cultivation*, (Dhradun: The English Book Depot, 1985), pp. 31–46.
6. Erik Eckholm, *Planting for the Future: Forestry for Human Needs*, World Watch Paper No. 26. World Watch Institute, Washington, D. C. 1979, p. 36.
7. See Bureau of Economics and Statistics, Government of Karnataka, *Report on the Impact of Social Forestry Programme on Land Use in Kolar and Bangalore Districts*, Bangalore, 1984, p. 6.
8. Vandana Shiva, et al., unpublished, 1979.
9. Shiva and Bandyopadhyay, *Ecological Audit*, op. cit.
10. Vandana Shiva, J. Bandyopadhyay and N. D. Jayal, "Afforestation in India: Problems and Strategy," *AMBIO* (forthcoming).

41

Organizing for Sustainable Development: Conservation Organizations and the Struggle to Protect Tropical Rain Forests in Esmeraldas, Ecuador

Thomas K. Rudel

Specialists in tropical rain forest conservation have recently begun to suggest that forests facing imminent destruction in deforestation "hot spots" can not be saved, and that conservation organizations would use their resources more effectively if they focused on preserving "cold spots," remote places with intact rain forests. The advocates of the cold spot strategy contend that sustainable development efforts in deforestation "hot spots" are ineffective. A case study of sustainable development in a rapidly deforesting region of coastal Ecuador questions this contention. Sustainable development in this region takes two organizational forms, one focused on the adoption of sustainable forestry techniques in a small set of villages and the other centered around the creation of a civic arena for discussing and resolving regional sustainable development issues. This two-pronged effort has achieved some success and may provide a model for sustainable development in places experiencing rapid tropical deforestation.

Introduction

At a recent meeting about global processes of tropical deforestation convened by the TREES (Tropical Ecosystem Environment Observation by Satellite) project of the European Commission's Joint Research Centre, tropical rain-forest ecologists argued that, because environmentalists can not stop deforestation in the "hot spots" where forests disappear rapidly, they would be more effective if they focused their efforts on preserving "cold spots," intact rain forests in remote locations (1). In effect the ecologists argued for a type of "biological triage" in which conservationists abandon some rain forests because the social and economic forces which encourage their destruction are so overwhelming that the probabilities of implementing conservation plans in these regions are virtually nil. The draconian effects of this proposal underscore the need to evaluate sustainable development efforts in

* From *Ambio: A Journal of the Human Environment,* vol. 29, no. 2, 2000. Published by the Royal Swedish Academy of Sciences. Reprinted by permission of the Royal Swedish Academy of Sciences.

places experiencing rapid deforestation. In addition to assessing effectiveness, the evaluations should identify those organizational factors which have influenced program effectiveness. This paper addresses both of these issues through an assessment of recent sustainable development efforts in the rain forests of Esmeraldas, Ecuador, a region experiencing one of the highest rates of deforestation in South America (2). The paper begins with a discussion of the optimal organizational form for sustainable development projects. The focus then shifts to Esmeraldas. The paper describes the region, outlines the process of deforestation, and presents a narrative history of recent efforts to slow deforestation in the region. It concludes with an assessment of the two pronged Esmeraldas approach as a model for sustainable development efforts in other deforestation "hot spots."

Organizing for Sustainable Development

The most widely used operational definition of sustainable development comes from a 1987 article by Barbier in which he outlines three overlapping sets of considerations, the biological, the economic, and the social, that people should use in formulating programs of sustainable development (3). To qualify as sustainable development, a program must conserve biological riches at the same time that it increases incomes and promotes social equity in the communities who use these resources. This definition suggests two paths to sustainable development, one involving new technologies and the other involving new institutions for arriving at compromises among resource users.

Because some technological innovations promise to achieve the goals of conservation, equity, and economic growth simultaneously, one path to sustainable development has a narrow, technological focus. Like earlier development projects, these projects promote the creation, adoption, and diffusion of technologies among small sets of users. The success of these demonstration projects should

in turn encourage the spread of the new, ecologically benign technologies to other users. The projects represent the focal point of sustainable development efforts in a place. A second path to sustainable development acknowledges that the three goals are frequently incompatible; economic growth usually exploits natural resources and increases economic inequalities. Under these circumstances people usually achieve sustainable development through a series of "trade offs"; for example, people moderate their expectations of economic gain in order to conserve natural resources in a region (4) For them sustainable development means "bringing together economy, ecology, and society . . ."(5). Operationalizing this concept requires the creation of encompassing organizations whose members include all of the stakeholder groups in the region of interest (6). These organizations play an important procedural role because they create "civic arenas" for crafting plans for sustainable development (7). By bringing together groups of people with different interests in a natural resource, civic arenas provide occasions for negotiating the trade offs that permit sustainable development in a region.

Watershed associations exemplify encompassing organizations. Formed in the aftermath of a severe drought, a watershed association in the western United States brings together ranchers, farmers, federal land managers, and the owners of ecotourist enterprises to manage the use of water. The ties and commitments created through encompassing organizations engender the trust that makes it possible for the participants to agree on the tradeoffs that move them towards sustainability. Initiatives may come up from the bottom, from stakeholder groups, but power differentials between these groups shape the substance of the compromises that emerge from negotiations within the organization.

In impoverished regions both demonstration projects and encompassing organizations often begin as initiatives sponsored by outsiders. Because poor, rural regions of developing countries have fewer local organizations than more affluent regions (8), a higher pro-

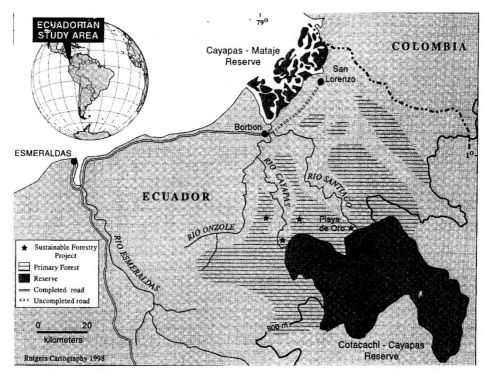

Figure 41.1 The forests of Esmeraldas, mid-1990s.

portion of the programmatic initiatives for these places come from outsiders who work in agencies and NGOs. The interventions proposed for rain-forest regions usually promote recently created global norms about sustainable development. The recent history of sustainable development in the rain-forest region of the province of Esmeraldas, Ecuador fits this pattern. It illustrates how externally sponsored demonstration projects and encompassing organizations can advance sustainable development in a rapidly deforesting region (9).

Esmeraldas: A Case Study of Sustainable Development

The Regional Context

The forests of Esmeraldas, Ecuador, represent the southernmost extension of tropical rain forests on the Pacific Coast of South America. Myers refers to them as a "deforestation hot spot," one of 10 places in the world with particularly large numbers of endemic species at risk of extinction and particularly high rates

of deforestation (2). Only the northern portions of the province, close to the border with Colombia, remain forested. While other parts of coastal Ecuador contain small, remnant patches of rain forest, only this region, outlined in Figure 41.1, contains a large area of intact rain forest. Its unique status has attracted timber companies who want to exploit the forest and conservationists who want to conserve it.

High rates of tropical deforestation provided the impetus behind recent efforts at sustainable development in the forest zones of Esmeraldas. The estimates of the rate of deforestation vary with the time period and measurement techniques, but all of the estimates are high, ranging from 2.0% to 4.0% per annum (10, 11). This is the highest rate for any province in Ecuador and one of the highest rates for any region in South America (2). A variety of forces explain the high rates of deforestation. First, Esmeraldas' forests are more accessible to the major urban markets for wood in Ecuador than the other forested regions in the country, and its forests contain commercially valuable hardwood species like chanul (*Humiriastrum procerum*) and laurel (*Cordia alliodora*), so the demand for logs is unrelenting. Second, the government has committed itself to building a road north along the coast to the Colombian border (Fig. 1). Expecting windfall profits from the rising value of land in the corridor along the road, an estimated 25,000 colonists have settled in the corridor, logged the nearby forests, and cleared land for agricultural uses. Third, shrimp farmers have moved into the area and begun cutting down mangrove trees to create shrimp ponds. Fourth, the populations of Chachis and Afro-Ecuadorians, the long resident peoples of the region, began to increase after 1970 when the infant mortality rate in the region began to decline. In 1990 the region contained approximately 90,000 people. Their incomes are low. While per capita incomes in Ecuador average around USD 1200 yr^{-1}, incomes in forest zone of Esmeraldas average around USD 400 (12). The region is not a particularly hospitable place for humans. Onchocerciasis (river blindness) has afflicted large numbers of Chachi (13). Chloroquine resistant strains of malaria occur in the region, and cholera is common. The weather is hot and humid; temperatures average 25°C. Annual rainfall in the region ranges from 2500 to 4500 mm, with a marked rainy season each year between December and June (14).

The settlement pattern is riverine, and most transport is by river. On the southern and western fringes of the forested regions companies have built logging roads, and farmers have settled along them; elsewhere the deforestation follows the rivers. All of the forests abutting rivers have been cleared (Fig. 1) (15). To reach primary forest, you have walk at least 2–3 km inland from the river. The lands closer to the river are dedicated to a variety of food crops, cassava, bananas, sugar cane, almost all of which are consumed at home. People in the Afro-Ecuadorian communities are poor, and over the years they have acquired what some might call some expensive tastes—in particular outboard motors.

The story about how people came to acquire outboard motors illustrates the persistent economic dilemmas of the region's residents to which any program of sustainable development must respond. Up until the early 1970s, people paddled up and down the river in dugout canoes. At that point Yamaha tried to create a market for themselves by "giving" away outboard motors. At least that is how people say it happened. Yamaha did not really give the motors away; they sold them through a variety of "no money down" deals.

The convenience of the outboard motors is undeniable. People can get to the regional center of Borbon in 45 minutes in an outboard powered water taxi, covering a distance that once took an entire day of paddling. The difficulties have to do with the cost of the outboards. At current prices they go for about USD 3000. Few people have that kind of money, so communities buy them, and they go into debt in order to purchase the motors. One of the few ways to raise the money to pay off the debt is by selling the commercially valuable wood on the village's lands (Anonymous interviews, Esmeraldas, April 1996). Working with contracts from the timber companies, comuna (village) members have cleared land at rapid rates since the early 1980s (14).

Processes of Deforestation

Afro-Ecuadorian comunas claim most of the land in the most intensely logged zone, but they do not have secure title to land, so comuna leaders worry about land invasions by colonists. These concerns about continued possession of the forests create incentives to exploit them for their present day value. Four timber companies work in the region, and they are eager to draw up contracts to log village lands. The margin between the prices the companies pay for wood and the prices they obtain for lumber have been very large. In 1996, the companies paid the people selling the wood USD 3–5 ft^{-3} for the right to take out commercially valuable species of trees. When that wood arrived at the factory door in one of Ecuador's large cities, it was worth about USD 65 ft^{-3} (16). The wood would be worth more if the companies could export it, which under Ecuadorian law they can not. After agreeing on a price for the timber, the companies' workers, some of them hired locally, fell the trees with chain saws. Then they drag the logs to the river with vehicles. In less highly capitalized operations, workers drag the logs to the nearest creek, and wait for the next heavy rain to float the logs out to the river. Because many logs get stuck in the shallow creeks and never make it to the river, there is a great deal of waste. At the river's edge the workers construct rafts of the newly cut logs and float them downstream to a landing where workers with cranes load the logs onto trucks for the trip to the sawmill. The processed lumber is then sold on the Ecuadorian market.

The timber companies that do the work are not impersonal, multinational enterprises. Rather they are family run firms, based in the provincial capital, which serve as intermediaries between village organizations and the outside world. The companies currently process and merchandize wood, but they have a long history of working with villagers to market other commodities from the region. Some of the same families that operate timber companies purchased gold, rubber, and bananas from villagers during earlier commodity booms (Anonymous interview, Mexican community organizer, Esmeraldas, Ecuador, April 1996). The ties between villagers and the companies resemble patron-client relationships. Loggers on the southern fringes of the forest, who use roads rather than rivers to extract logs, promised to build a road into a previously isolated village in return for an agreement to allow the logging of the forests around the village (Anonymous interview, President, Private Esmeraldas Forest Reserve, Quito, July 1998). In another instance, a company received permission to log the forests of a Chachi community after agreeing to build a medical dispensary for the village and staff it with a nurse for a limited period of time (13). In general, the companies give the villagers something that they want, and in return several villagers sign a contract giving the companies access to tropical wood at a low price. The companies are not completely happy with this arrangement; they would like to buy village lands outright and exploit them without having to go through third parties, but Ecuadorian law does not permit indigenous peoples to sell their land to non-natives.

Conservation Organizations

Instituto Ecuatoriano Forestal y de Areas Naturales (INEFAN), the forest and parks agency for Ecuador, has the responsibility of protecting two biological reserves in the zone: the Cayapas-Mataje Reserve which protects mangrove forests along the coast and the Cotacachi-Cayapas Reserve which extends from the tropical forests or the coastal plain to the alpine environments of the high Andes (Fig. 1). Given the domain that it controls, INEFAN has very few employees. In 1996, it had 150 employees in its field offices. Of these people 60 worked in the Galapagos Islands, which left 90 persons to manage the timber trade and guard the 17 parks in the rest of Ecuador. In 1998, INEFAN had only eight park guards for the 200,000 ha Cotocachi-Cayapas reserve (17). These employees are also charged with collecting royalties on logs for the central government. INEFAN employees in the Esmeraldas region concentrate on collecting taxes rather than managing forests. They maintain an office and boats with outboard motors in Borbon at the confluence of the two major rivers, the Cayapas and the Santiago, that drain the interior where most of the logging is done. When rafts of freshly cut logs float by the INEFAN office on their way to the landing downstream, INEFAN employees go out to collect the royalties from people on the rafts or the truckers. The employees do not get to keep the revenue that they collect. It goes to the treasury department which returns a small portion to INEFAN in the form of salaries. The incentives behind the royalties are exploitative. The more exploitation that occurs in a given time period, the higher the government's receipts, so from a revenue point of view the government would want to encourage deforestation.

To promote biodiversity conservation, INEFAN concludes numerous agreements with foreign aid missions. In the spring of 1996, the agency had 32 cooperative agreements with foreign aid missions like USAID (United States Agency for International Development) and the GTZ (Deutsche Gesellschaft für Technische Zusammenarbeit), the German overseas technical assistance mission. Each agreement requires the participation of INEFAN personnel who, given their small numbers, find it difficult to honor their commitments to their foreign counterparts. In this sense, INEFAN represents an administrative bottleneck. There would be more technical assistance projects if INEFAN could administer them.

The SUBIR Project: Demonstrating Sustainable Forestry

Several of INEFAN's foreign assistance agreements concern sustainable forestry in the Esmeraldas region. The agreements have a tripartite structure. The funding comes from a foreign aid mission; Ecuadorian environmental NGOs provide field personnel, and INEFAN legitimates the activity. In the SUBIR (Sustainable Use of Biological Reserves) project USAID has financed work by Ecuadorian ecologists who have designed a plan for the sustainable harvesting of wood from primary forests in the comuna of Playa de Oro in the buffer zone of the Cotacachi-Cayapas Ecological Reserve (Fig. 1). Village leaders in Playa de Oro have also started an ecotourist enterprise which makes use of the surrounding forests. So far these enterprises look like a modest success. With assistance from USAID the village obtained legal title to their lands and began the sustainable harvest of wood. Since 1996, sustainable forestry has continued without subsidies from USAID, and the ecotourist enterprise has begun to attract a small stream of visitors (12, 18).

People in the surrounding communities have noticed the Playa de Oro demonstration project. By late 1998, 20 villages had contacted the SUBIR promoters, decided to manage their lands communally, and appointed forestry committees (12). The committee members have begun to draw up plans for land use, designating some lands for forest reserves and other lands for agriculture. The governing bodies in nine villages have decided to adopt simplified versions of the Playa de Oro program. With the help of SUBIR officials these communities are in the process of securing titles to their lands. All nine of the villages are located in the buffer zone of the Cotacachi-Cayapas Reserve. The concentration of sustainable forestry efforts in the buffer zone around the reserve reflects a judgement by SUBIR's planners, bitterly disputed by some environmentalists, that it is impossible to save all of the remaining forests in Esmeraldas. A more achievable conservation goal would focus on conserving forests in those communities that border on and serve as an ecological buffer for the Cotacachi—Cayapas Reserve. This debate repeats at a more localized scale the global controversy about the efficacy of cold vs. hot spot strategies of forest conservation.

There has been some progress on equity issues. When representatives of the comunas gather for coordinating unit meetings, they compare notes about their contracts with the timber companies, and this comparative perspective makes it difficult for the companies to negotiate particularly abusive agreements with individual comunas. For example, comuna leaders have agreed not to sell standing wood to the timber companies because under these contracts comuna residents never get any of the value added to the wood. A limited version of a "united front" of comunas emerged during 1997 and 1998 when a group of the SUBIR comunas negotiated in common with the timber companies and secured prices for their wood that were more than twice the prices obtained during the same period by individuals who contracted with the companies in the traditional manner. The comunas even withheld wood from the market for a short period during the 1998 El Niño rainy season when damaged logging roads made it difficult for companies to get their product to market (19). The market share of the SUBIR comunas is small, but their success in negotiating higher prices is well known. In several recent instances communities have also marketed their wood without middlemen.

The Coordinating Unit: An Encompassing Organization for Esmeraldas

The idea of creating an encompassing organization emerged in 1995 when GTZ foresters got the foreign forestry assistance missions in Ecuador to endorse the idea of creating an organization of villages that would bargain collectively with the timber companies in an attempt to raise the price that the villages receive for a cubic meter of wood. This idea originated in Mexico where German forestry technicians helped a group of ejidos in the province of Quintana Roo organize a similar united front in the 1990s. To drum up support for the project in Ecuador, the Germans enlisted the support of the governor of Esmeraldas and flew him up to Quintana Roo to see how an association of community forestry enterprises worked. GTZ also brought community organizers from Mexico to Ecuador to help comuna leaders create an association of villages. In effect the Germans were trying to implant a foreign model in Ecuador (20).

To implement the Mexican plan in Ecuador, GTZ officials, the director of INEFAN, and the governor of Esmeraldas province agreed to establish a coordinating unit to discuss the management of the region's rain forests. As of July, 1997, this organization had had six meetings. The coordinating unit includes members from fifty Afro-Ecuadorian comunas, the lumber companies, INEFAN, the provincial government, environmental NGOs, and international aid missions with interests in the region. The coordinating unit differs in its composition from most other politically active organizations. Unlike special interest organizations which represent selected interests in the society, the coordinating unit's membership includes most of the groups active in the forests of northwestern Ecuador. It has created a civic arena for the discussion of sustainable forestry issues in Esmeraldas. The members of the coordinating unit meet regularly, and this practice represents progress for environmentalists because it insures that sustainable development issues will get some attention on a regular basis. Previously, interest and activity on environmental issues would decline as soon as environmentally concerned politicians left office.

Environmentalists do not always set the agenda for coordinating unit meetings. For example, the coordinating unit has served as a forum for a discussion initiated by the timber companies over whether they should be permitted to buy timber land. After much dis-

cussion the members agreed that, while the companies could not buy land from indigenous peoples, they could buy land from colonists. The companies want to purchase land because, with the logging of primary forests likely to end soon, they would like to start forest plantations on their own land.

In the coordinating unit's first year, comuna leaders found the meetings rewarding because they provided an occasion for creating social networks across villages and between villagers and NGO personnel. The meetings also provided a forum for discussing the success and failure of the SUBIR experiments in harvesting and marketing wood. They also get discussed at workshops that the coordinating unit has held for comuna leaders on the marketing and sale of roundwood (21). In its second year, with personal networks established, participants in the meetings began to consider ways in which the organization could provide new services to its members. One proposal involved creating the organizational infrastructure to export green certified tropical wood from Ecuador (Anonymous interview, GTZ consultant, Quito, July 1998). To receive green certification, wood would have to come from sustainably managed forests. Selling these woods in the international markets would raise their price. Both the timber companies and the environmentalists support the proposal. If the coordinating unit decides to support this idea, it would lobby for a repeat of the ban on exporting certified logs, identify an organization to certify logging operations, set the standards for certification, and oversee the process. Launching a project of this type requires a great deal of communication between interested members of the organization. In other words, the "cross-cutting," "inclusive" nature of sustainable development projects implies a need for many consultations in the formulation of the projects and unusually high transaction costs. An encompassing organization can reduce these costs by making them part of the internal workings of the organization (22).

Who provides the funds and the initiative to create encompassing organizations? Ostrom calls this problem "a second order collective dilemma" (23). In Esmeraldas the dilemma has been resolved for the moment by the German forestry assistance program. The GTZ has paid the expenses associated with the meetings of the coordinating council, and it pays the salaries of the coordinating unit's professional staff who convene the meetings and lobby on behalf of the organization. Clearly, this "external" solution to the problem of creating and maintaining the encompassing organization can not endure for long. The national government, the provincial government, or local stakeholders must "take ownership" of the coordinating unit if it is to endure. Finding the right time and way to disengage represents a major challenge for the German foresters.

Conclusion

Demonstration Projects, Encompassing Organizations, and Outside Intervention

As the focal point of sustainable development efforts in the Esmeraldas forest zone, the SUBIR demonstration project initiates social change, but, because it co-evolves with the local social order, it also comes to resemble the existing institutional order in the province. The comuna leaders see the promoters of sustainable forestry efforts as potential sources of funds for a wide variety of projects, and the officials of the aid organizations do not want their projects to fail for lack of local support. Out of this interpersonal dynamic a new set of patron-client ties can emerge with the aid officials as patrons and villagers from community forestry projects as clients. This dynamic contributes to the creation of "islands of sustainability" like the Playa de Oro forestry project. This pattern of environmental clientilism has contradictory effects. The project itself has a valuable demonstration effect, but the impetus behind the projects, the patron-client pattern of support, may convince observers in other communities that sustainable forestry can only be done with extensive outside support. The adoption of the Playa de Oro model in other communities in the Cotacachi-Cayapas buffer zone suggests that, when the meetings of an

encompassing organization provide occasions for examining experiments like Playa de Oro, concerns about environmental clientilism and change confined to islands of sustainability may be exaggerated. The SUBIR project has initiated a set of important institutional changes in the management of Esmeraldas' forests, and, while the eventual magnitude of these changes remains unclear, the initial pattern indicates that conservation gains are possible in areas experiencing rapid deforestation.

The history of the coordinating unit indicates the value of encompassing organizations in promoting sustainable development. The coordinating unit created a civic arena in which the competing parties negotiated directly with one another, and in several instances the direct negotiations facilitated the creation of workable plans of sustainable development. In a peripheral place like Esmeraldas where few formal organizations exist and informal patron-client ties play a large role in the operation of the economy, a formal encompassing organization, usually supported with resources from outside sources, may represent the only way to create a civic arena to address and resolve issues of sustainable development. Only a regional organization can address issues like the certification of wood for export or legislation to permit the purchase of lands by timber companies.

The demonstration projects promoting new technologies and the encompassing organizations providing arenas for compromise, interact in ways that strengthen both efforts. By adopting new forestry techniques and creating a coalition of comunas to market wood products, the SUBIR village leaders gave the much more numerous comuna leaders in the coordinating unit examples of how they might change the timber industry if they acted collectively. By providing a forum for assessing the SUBIR initiative, the coordinating unit probably accelerated the diffusion of sustainable forestry in the province, and, in so doing, demonstrated its own value to participating comuna leaders.

Events in the forest zone of Esmeraldas reinforce Tendler's conclusions about the conditions for effective governance in the tropics (24). Tendler has argued on the basis of a case study in Ceara in Brazil's northeast that the absence of a vigorous civil society does not condemn people to a pattern of ineffective governance because effective governance does not always begin with initiatives from local communities. Rather effective governance emerges from a creative tension between different levels of government. Initiatives at the state level can invigorate local governance just as initiatives from local groups can invigorate provincial government. The history of SUBIR and the coordinating unit in Esmeraldas supports this contention. Outside intervention did provide the impetus for some sustainable forestry in local communities and a more persistent engagement with issues of sustainable development in provincial government. For this reason the Esmeraldas experience argues for continued attempts to foster sustainable development in the deforestation hot spots of the world.

References and Notes

1. Pearce, F. *Beyond Hope: Poverty and Politics are Putting end to Rainforest Conservation. New Scientist. October 31.* 1998. For information on the TREES project, see their website, http://wwwjrc.it/gvm/trees.

2. Myers, N. 1993. Tropical forests: the main deforestation fronts. *Environ. Cons. 20,* 9–16.

3. Barbier, E. 1987. The concept of sustainable economic development. *Environ. Cons. 14,* 101–110.

4. Pearce, D. 1988. The economics of natural resource degradation in developing countries. In W. Turner (ed.), *Sustainable Environmental Management: Principles and Practices.* Westview, Boulder, pp. 15–31.

5. Trzyna, T. 1995. *A Sustainable World: Defining and Measuring Sustainable Development.* California Institute of Public Affairs, Claremont, pp. 17, 20.

6. Olsen, M. 1982. *The Rise and Decline of Nations: Economic Growth, Stagflation, and Social Rigidities.* Yale University Press, New Haven, pp. 47–53.

7. A civic arena is "a cluster of public settings in which sectorally diversified actors provisionally suppress their particularistic projects in order to formulate and pursue an emerging common purpose." Mische, A. 1998. *Civic Arenas and Political Process in Brazlian Society.* Unpubl. manuscript, Sociology Department, Rutgers University.

8. Esman, M. and Uphoff, N. 1984. *Local Organizations: Intermediaries in Rural Development.* Cornell University Press, Ithaca.

9. The following account of sustainable development efforts in Esmeraldas is based on a visit to the villages carrying out sustainable forestry projects in 1996. Key informant interviewing and archival research in Ecuador in 1996, 1997, and 1998 supplemented the site visit.

10. Sierra-Maldonado, R. 1996. *La Deforestacion en el Noroccidente del Ecuador, 1983–93.* Ecociencia, Quito. (In Spanish).

11. Van der Hammen, C. and Rodriguez, C. 1997. *Excursion a Esmeraldas en Derecho y el Manejo del Basque Amazonico.* Tropenbos Foundation, Wageningen. Pp. 135–37. (In Spanish).

12. Stallings, J. 1998. An Overview of the SUBIR project. *III International Symposium on Sustainable Mountain Development,* Quito, Ecuador.

13. Medina, V.H. 1992. *Los Chachi: Supervivencia y Ley Tradicional.* Ediciones Abya-Yala, Quito, 49 p. (In Spanish).

14. Sierra-Maldonado, R. 1994. *Land Use Strategies of Household Based Enterprises, the Timber Industry, and Deforestation in Northwest Ecuador.* Ph.D. Dissertation, Ohio State University, U.S.A. pp. 29–30.

15. The geographic extent of the primary forest in Figure 38.1 is based on a 1993 remote sensing image of the region in Sierra-Maldonado (10), p. 137.

16. Gesellschaft für Technische Zusammenarbeit (GTZ). 1996. *El Reto de la Deforestacion en Esmeraldas.* Quito, Ecuador. (In Spanish).

17. Morales, M. 1998. Legal aspects of the SUBIR community based conservation projects. *III International Symposium, Sustainable Mountain Development.* Quito, Ecuador.

18. Care-Ecuador. 1998. Subir-Fase II. Quito, Ecuador. (In Spanish).

19. Guevero, M. 1998. The SUBIR Community Forest Network. *III International Symposium on Sustainable Mountain Development.* Quito, Ecuador.

20. For a description of the Mexican sustainable forestry project, see Prell, D. 1992. *Mexican and Mayan Environmentalism: Physical, Economic, and Cultural Factors that Influence*

the *Environmental Movement in Quintana, Roo, Mexico.* Ph.D. Dissertation, University of Wisconsin-Milwaukee, U.S.A.

21. Unidad Coordinadora. 1997. *Proceso hacia el Desarrollo Forestal Sustentable en Esmeraldas, Informe de Actividades.* 1996. Esmeraldas, Ecuador. (In Spanish).

22. Williamson, O. 1986. *Economic Organization: Firms, Markets, and Policy Control.* New York University Press, New York.

23. Ostrom, E. 1990. *Governing the Commons: The Evolution of Institutions for Collective Action.* Cambridge University Press, Cambridge.

24. Tendler, J. 1997. *Good Government in the Tropics.* Johns Hopkins University Press, Baltimore.

25. Funds from the Tropenbos Foundation, The Netherlands, and the National Science Foundation, United States (SBR-96-18371) facilitated this research.

26. First submitted 24 August 1998. Accepted for publication after revision 24 August 1999.

42

The Price of Everything

Thomas Michael Power and Paul Rauber

Maybe it has something to do with the approaching millennium: the lion will lie down with the lamb, and toxic polluters will drink herbal tea with environmental activists. The wonderful new development is lauded in the press and preached from scores of think tanks. No longer, we are told, do we have to rely on threats of fines or jail time in order to get industry to do the right thing. The business leaders of today, working together with enlightened environmentalists, have discovered in the magic of the marketplace a cheaper, more effective, and less contenious remedy to just about any environmental ailment.

The debate over environmental protection in the 1990s fills the ideological vacuum left by the end of the Cold War. It is now fashionable, for instance, to compare government regulation to the "command-and-control" economic arrangements of the former Soviet Union. As the Soviet system failed, the analogy suggests, so too will a regulatory system based on the *diktat* of federal bureaucrats telling industry how much pollution to reduce and how to reduce it. "Command and control" is said to cost U.S. businesses $140 billion a year, handicapping the economy, hobbling the recovery, and unfairly vilifying many environmentally concerned Americans who just happen to own polluting industries.

The alternative to this clumsy, old-fashioned, and vaguely unpatriotic-sounding system is "free-market environmentalism" (a.k.a. "new resource economics"), which promises to harness the vigor and inventiveness of capitalism to heal the earth. To do so, it proposes to vastly expand our present notion of private property, to sell that property to the highest bidder, and then to let the logic of the market sort things out.

Already a new property right has been created: the right to pollute. One section of the 1990 Clean Air Act allows plants that pollute below certain levels to sell pollution "credits" to dirtier concerns; innovative, clean industries profit from their cleanliness, while the dirty industries pay for their sins until they can get around to cleaning up their acts. A market in these "pollution credits" has been established at the Chicago Board of Trade, where rights to emit tons of sulfur dioxide are bought and sold like pork bellies or soybean futures.

Having set prices on pollution, free marketers are also trying to figure out what those who enjoy environmental quality should be made to pay for it. What will the market bear for the use of a regional park? Hopefully the public will pay more for Sunday hikes than the local developer will for condos, because if not, farewell forest. And if people want

---

* Reprinted by permission from the November/December issue of *Sierra*.

wolves in Yellowstone National Park, free marketeers argue, they should be willing to pay for them, cash on the barrelhead. It's just a question of settling on the price.

Not all proponents of free-market environmentalism subscribe to all of its logical but occasionally wacky conclusions. Every ideology has its ideologues; in this case, they are the libertarian-minded think tanks and academics who have provided the theoretical spadework for the new discipline. More common, however, are those who seek to pick and choose at the free-market table, ignoring dishes that don't coincide with their interests. Many businesses, for example, are enthusiastic about market solutions, but only when they result in a further giveaway of public resources. Contrarily, some environmentalists advocate market mechanisms in the name of efficiency, reasoning that making environmental responsibility cheaper will result in a corollary reduction of political opposition, the end result being the possibility of greater protection.

This, crudely put, is the position of the Environmental Defense Fund, the most market-oriented of the major environmental groups, as well as of some individuals within the Sierra Club. "We're finally getting past the debate about whose position is morally superior and moving on to a point where we will accomplish real reductions in pollution and resource use," says Dan Dudek, a senior economist at the EDF. His organization, which helped write the pollution-credit section in the Clean Air Act, looks forward to the establishment of national markets for nitrogen oxides, and perhaps even global markets for CFCs and carbon dioxide.

A big plus for free-market environmentalism has been its bipartisan support; neo-liberal Clintonian Democrats and anti-regulatory Bob Dole Republicans embrace it with equal enthusiasm. *Mandate for Change*, candidate Clinton's policy blueprint, contained a chapter ("The Greening of the Market") calling for a harnessing of the "daily self-interest" of firms and individuals to replace "command-and-control" regulations. During the campaign, Clinton himself said that we must "recognize that Adam Smith's invisible hand can have a green thumb," and called for a "market-based environmental-protection strategy."

This is a bitter draught for many environmental activists, weaned on regulatory triumphs like the National Environmental Policy Act and practiced in lobbying the government to toughen environmental laws, not abandon them. Most environmentalists are innately suspicions of economists anyway. They are the ones, after all, who tend to portray environmental quality as an expensive frivolity; who tell us that pollution controls hamper productivity and threaten private property; that zero levels of toxic releases are a naively impossible goal, and that protecting endangered species without regard for the economic consequences is irrational—as, perhaps, are many environmentalists.

(This suspicion of the dismal science is well warranted historically. From its beginning, the intellectual mission of Anglo-American economics has been to demonstrate the secret logic of allowing businesses to maximize profits, unfettered by social controls. That was, after all, Adam Smith's goal—to depict the selfish, even antisocial actions of private commerce as ultimately benefiting the public. No wonder the business community enthusiastically supported the intellectual venture that came to be known as economics.)

Yet these same wary environmentalists frequently endorse the use of economic instruments—perhaps without quite realizing it, and often to the profound distress of the affected industry. They insist, for example, that a price be put on empty beverage containers to create an economic incentive for recycling. (The deposit idea is now being considered for other, more dangerous solid wastes, such as automobile batteries, or refrigerators containing CFCs.) They argue that water "shortages" in arid regions result from the absence of incentives to conserve when the low price of government-subsidized irrigation reflects neither what the water costs to provide nor its value in alternate uses. They attack government subsidies for destructive programs such as the U.S. Forest Service's below-cost timber sales. Yet they remain queasy about extending this approach to all other environmental problems—with good reason, as it turns out.

This ambivalence reflects a healthy respect for the limitations of market "solutions." Economic instruments are tools, but using them does not require us to embrace a new ideology or to jettison all government regulation. It *does* require environmentalists to determine when such tools can be used productively, and which specific sort of tool is appropriate to a given situation or industry. It requires the adoption of an explicitly pragmatic approach to solving environmental problems. Most importantly, it requires that political problems be faced first.

Whenever environmental policy is made, three crucial issues must be resolved:

❏ What level of environmental protection is desired in each particular location?
❏ Who is going to pay the direct costs of achieving the targeted level of protection?
❏ What policy tools will be used to achieve these levels and to impose the costs?

Since economic instruments are merely policy tools, it's no use talking about them until the first two far more contentious questions have been settled. Otherwise, market mechanisms will end up doing what they have always done, i.e., maximizing profits by ignoring pollution or shifting environmental costs elsewhere. Market measures, then, are appropriate in situations with firmly established pollution-control objectives, where conventional environmental regulation would result in pure economic waste. Say, for example, that we have decided to reduce the amount of solid waste going into a city's landfill. Instead of issuing a decree ordering such a reduction by every citizen and business, we change the way garbage fees are paid; instead of extracting them from property taxes, as is usually the case, we start charging by weight or volume, and institute curbside recycling at the same time. Recyclers get a break, and others pay in relation to the amount of garbage they produce. Here economic instruments have something to offer, but only after the basic political questions have been settled.

This was not entirely the case in the pollution-permit market created by the 1990 Clean Air Act and implemented earlier this year. This pet program of the free-market environmentalists was designed to ease the pain for industries required to halve their 1980 level of SO_2 emissions by 2000. While promising in theory, however, its actual implementation revealed a number of hidden problems.

Unaddressed, for instance, was the question of who had to live with continued high levels of pollution. When the geographic area over which pollution credits can be traded is very large—nationwide in the case of SO_2—the effect of the market can be to stick some people in dirty areas with the bill. In some parts of the country air quality dramatically improves; in others, serious pollution problems persist with the full blessings of the market and the law. (The geographic question is what got World Bank Chief Economist Lawrence Summers in such hot water last year when his memo about the "impeccable" logic of dumping toxic waste in the "underpolluted" Third World was leaked to the press.) At its worst, trading pollution rights can legitimize continuing pollution. In one of the very first acid-rain trades under the new program, the Wisconsin Electric Power Company sold a Pennsylvania utility 20,000 tons of pollution credits. Under Wisconsin law, however, the company would not have been entitled to emit the pollution in the first place—yet federal law still allowed it to be peddled to Pennsylvania.

Meanwhile, East Coast utilities have been selling their SO_2 credits to midwestern power plants, allowing them to continue burning high-sulfur midwestern coal. But what goes around comes around: the midwestern emissions ultimately drift back through the Atlantic and New England states, where they fall as acid rain.

Since it was concern over acid rain in the Northeast that led to the Clean Air Act's SO_2 caps in the first place, New York is now trying to prevent its utilities from selling SO_2 permits to upwind states. In the Midwest, on the other hand, ratepayers pay higher bills in order to finance their utilities' SO_2 purchases, but don't see any reduction in local SO_2. Had their utilities been forced by regulation to reduce emissions, at least the higher bills would have been offset by cleaner air; now the public pays for "pollution control," but gets none.

Supporters of emission trading argue that New York's fears are overstated, and that the benefits of local utilities cleaning up enough to sell credits far exceed the relatively small excess SO_2 blown in from upwind. Indeed, the Sierra Club itself has intervened with Ohio's public utilities commission in support of an acid-rain-reduction plan consisting of emission trading, energy efficiency, and use of low-sulphur eastern coal. "By forcing the marketplace to the lowest-cost solution that really works," says Sierra Club Ohio Chapter Energy Chair Ned Ford, "environmentalists gain credibility and enhance the opportunity for further reduction."

Of course, a simpler market mechanism could have been employed by taxing emissions above a certain level. While this would have had the same effect of rewarding the clean and punishing the dirty, it is anathema to free-market ideologues, whose interest is the creation of new private-property rights—in this case, a right to pollute.

Ironically, some of the businesses pollution-trading systems are supposed to assist don't want to play ball. The Ohio Power Company would prefer simply installing a scrubber. In Southern California, two dozen major businesses are opposing an emission-trading scheme proposed by the South Coast Air Quality Management District, claiming that it would "substantially raise the costs" of pollution control, and pleading to be allowed to continue with "command and control."

Many environmentalists also attack pollution-credit trading as fundamentally flawed. That is not necessarily true. The real problem is that the program was established before all the basic questions were answered—in this case, what level of environmental quality should be assured for *all* areas covered by the trade. Those answers can only be reached through a political process, not bought at the market.

There is a fundamental conflict here that goes far beyond the use of economic instruments. Environmental protection necessarily involves the transfer of control over very valuable resources from one group of people to another. These resources are the wealth of the natural world, extractable and otherwise, and the limited capacity of the air, water, and land to assimilate the wastes associated with economic activity. Historically (and to a considerable extent today), this natural wealth has been the province of industry. The Forest Service sells the national forests for a song to giant timber companies; the Bureau of Land Management allows gentlemen ranchers to denude the public range for a pittance; the 1872 Mining Law gives away the public's mineral wealth to multinational corporations. Until very recently, the cost of waste disposal was however much it took to build a smokestack, or a drainpipe to the nearest river.

Taken for granted, these hidden subsidies—economists call them "externalities"—are not reflected in the price of commodities. Timber is cheap because the Forest Service gives it away; driving is cheap because drivers don't pay for air pollution. The real cost, of course, is paid in sick children, eroded farmlands, vanished fisheries, and extinction of species, and is shunted to the public, preferably the public of future generations.

Over the past several decades, the environmental movement has attempted to transfer control of these natural resources—worth, literally, trillions of dollars—from the commercial sector to the public. A transfer of wealth of this magnitude cannot take place without considerable conflict. In the past, such power shifts have required revolutions.

The continuing struggle over environmental policy, therefore, is hardly surprising. Economic instruments can make a modest contribution toward resolving it, to the extent that they can reduce the cost of environmental protection. But the fundamental conflict over who controls the use of our air, water, and landscapes cannot be decided merely through a change in the instrument of enforcement.

Business sometimes argues that it doesn't really matter *who* pays the direct costs of pollution control, since the costs will ultimately be borne by the general citizenry in the form of higher prices anyway. But in this case environmentalists have Econ 1-A on their side: it is elementary economic theory that markets can change behavior only if the full costs of an activity—the externalities—are incorporated into the immediate prices paid. If the price of gasoline included the direct costs of maintaining a permanent fleet (let alone fighting a war) in the Persian Gulf, our transportation system would reform itself in a hurry.

If the free marketeers based their program on charging the true environmental costs for all resources used, the environmental movement would sign up *en masse*. But ideological freemarket environmentalists often seem more concerned with the market than with the environment; they tend to feel that equity—the distribution of access to scarce resources, or the right to a clean and healthful environment—is less important than economic efficiency and property rights.

This is exactly what is being demanded in the current attempt to expand the legal concept of "takings" to include environmental regulations. By this theory, any environmental regulation that results in lost profits requires government compensation. This assumes, of course, that people have a "property right" to pollute or damage the environment in any way they wish, and that the public has to pay them if that right to damage the environment is changed or revoked. Oddly, free marketeers somehow always assign property rights to those doing the polluting rather than to those being damaged by the pollution.

This is one example of the huge ideological gulf that separates the vision of a good society shared by most environmentalists from that of the free-market enthusiasts. Environmentalists act collectively to preserve certain qualities associated with the natural and, often, social environments. In this sense, they are fundamentally conservative: they wish things to remain the same, or even to return to a previous preferred condition. It is ironic, then, that their suspicion of market instruments is sometimes taken as proof of their "watermelon" character: green on the outside but red on the inside.

Free marketeers, on the other hand, are enthusiastic about the constant change that a market economy encourages, and are suspicious of any efforts to guide the direction of the economy or society collectively. They see such attempts as authoritarian, economically destructive, and tantamount to socialism. The economy for them is an adventure of unknown destination. Columnist George Will, for instance, writes fondly of the "billions of daily decisions that propel a free society into an exhilaratingly unknown future." We should learn to enjoy the excitement and change, and trust that the overall result, whatever it may be, will be much better than anything we could collectively arrange.

Ideological free marketeers insist that we should not use individual market tools without buying the whole package. Advocates such as John Baden of the Foundation for Research on Economics and the Environment (FREE) object strenuously to the use of market instruments "simply as tools for the Efficient delivery of environmental goals . . . [while] the goals themselves remain collectively determined." Again, environmentalists are plainly the conservatives to the radical free marketeers, who are willing to trust everything to their faith in the inevitably positive outcome of market forces.

It is not necessary for the environmental movement to respond to one type of extremism and ideological wishful thinking by adopting another. Incentives *do* matter, and market instruments can help us, collectively, to protect the environment. Consider, for example, the following possibilities:

❑ In western rural areas, streams often run dry during peak summer irrigation periods. Because irrigation water is usually provided at very low cost to farmers, it is often used inefficiently (growing rice in California's Central Valley, for example). One solution is to allow government fish-and-wildlife agencies, water-quality agencies, or private-sector environmental groups to purchase water rights from farmers and use them to protect streams and their associated fisheries. These rights could be purchased on the basis of a willing buyer and a willing seller, a straightforward market transaction. Another approach is simply to raise the price of the water to the farmers to more closely approximate its real cost, thus discouraging ecologically foolish uses.

❏ Many of the most serious urban environmental problems—congestion, air pollution, noise—are associated with the automobile. Driving is rewarded in many ways, such as when businesses provide free parking for employees. But what if employers paid employees the cash value of parking privileges in higher wages, and then charged full cost for the parking? Those who choose to use mass transit or car pools would have higher net incomes, but no one would be worse off. Resources might well be saved and environmental costs reduced. Similarly, public agencies could charge commuters the full costs—including environmental costs—of using private automobiles. Increasing rush-hour tolls for lone drivers while forgiving them to carpoolers are steps in this direction.

❏ In the same vein, dramatically raising the price of gasoline to reflect its real costs—a ready military, poisoned ecosystems in Alaska, polluted low-income neighborhoods next to refineries—would shortly result in increased fuel efficiency and reduced automobile usage. Other auto-related costs, like collision insurance, could also be included in the gas price.

These examples are purposely speculative to give a feeling for the range of environmentally productive uses for economic instruments. Once environmentalists begin to think in this direction, they are likely to generate many more ideas. Call it "the magic of the marketplace."

Some free-market ideas, while undeniably creative, need careful scrutiny. A good example is the proposal to charge increased fees to recreational users of public lands. The idea is to provide a positive incentive for bureaucrats whose revenues are closely tied to the amount of econonmic activity they generate. The more timber they harvest, the more mines they permit, the more land they lease for grazing, the larger are their budgets. (Since the government does not factor externalities into the equation, these activities show up as pluses on bureaucratic balance sheets, even when the activity results in a net loss to the public.)

Because recreationists pay few if any fees, the argument goes, no revenue is associated with their interests and the land managers ignore them. Hence the notion to charge hikers, campers, and skiers whatever the market will bear, thus producing a cash flow that will impress the bureaucrats enough to preserve and enhance recreational values. This, we are told, will automatically provide protection for public lands, because recreational fees would bring in far more than the timber, forage, and mineral charges that now largely finance these agencies.

Recreation-fee advocate Randal O'Toole explicitly suggests that if public lands were in private hands, the widespread environmental damage we observe in the West would be much reduced. This is hard to believe for anyone who has ever flown over the Pacific Northwest and seen the checkerboard of clearcut private lands next to still-intact bits of public forests, or peered beyond the beauty strips in Maine. There is no doubt that when an agency develops a financial stake in serving a particular clientele, it becomes a strong advocate for that clientele's interests. Consider the many state fish-and-game agencies. Funded primarily by the sale of fishing and hunting licenses, they are single-minded defenders of fishing and hunting interests. In Montana and Wyoming, fish-and-game agencies have resisted wolf reintroduction because they fear that wolves will reduce the number of ungulates available to hunters. The Montana agency has opposed listing of the grizzly bear as an endangered species because it would ban grizzly hunting, and has also refused to support the reintroduction of bighorn sheep in any area where they could not be hunted. The moral is that when cash flow alone guides government agencies, some perversity almost always follows. In order to imagine how a recreational-fee system might work, one need look no further than those national-forest areas that have been surrendered to intensive downhill-ski development. Nor does giving recreationists more influence in the management of wild areas necessarily guarantee a haven for backpackers and birdwatchers. The Bureau of Land Management could well find that more money could be made sponsoring off-road-vehicle rallies than from either backpackers or cattle. Perhaps currently roadless wildlands would produce a larger cash flow were they open to motorized tours: snowmobile trails, helicopter lifts into campsites, Going-to-the-Sun-type roads through all of the spectacular mountain country. Already the solitude of the Grand Canyon is marred by the noise of sightseeing aircraft; in the Wasatch Mountains of Utah, backcountry skiing has been almost completely displaced by heli-skiing. There is an important distinction to be made here. When we are talking about relatively common commodities such as timber or forage or minerals, it is perfectly reasonable to expect market approaches to work. After all, we already trust the production and use of those commodities to commercial markets. But to most of us, the management of our public lands is not (or should not be) primarily about adjusting slightly upward or downward the quantity of 2x4s or sheep pasture or phosphate rock that make it onto the market. The issues at stake in the management of public lands—biodiversity, wilderness, sustainability—go far beyond the world of commodities and the language of economics. The problem with this method of influencing public-land management is that many of the things we want public lands managed for do not and cannot have dollar values attached to them. There is no way for cash-flow analysis to put an accurate price tag on a spotted owl or a grizzly bear, nor to indicate what wilderness is worth. Rather, we seek to protect wilderness and grizzlies not as playgrounds and playthings for tourists and fee-payers, but because we wish at least some small part of our natural heritage to continue to exist apart from us and our cash registers. Wilderness is "valuable" to us precisely to the extent that it is not used by humans; consequently, "use" is meaningless as a measure for accurately valuing it. MARKETS ARE NOT NEUTRAL, technological devices. They are social institutions whose use has profound consequences. All societies purposely limit the extent of the market in order to protect their basic values. We, for instance, do not allow the buying and selling of votes and judicial decisions; we do not allow the selling of the sexual services of children; we do not allow human beings to be sold into slavery. Free-market enthusiasts assume that market-oriented, calculating, self-regarding (i.e., "greedy") behavior is all that is needed for a good, responsible society. Such behavior, they assert, should be encouraged, not constrained. But what kind of decent society can depend upon this type of motivation alone? Selling certain things, in fact, degrades them: selling praise, spiritual favors, intimacy, the privileges of citizenship, or the outcomes of athletic events does not enhance their value, but reduces or destroys it. Even the commercial market is built on a basic morality that takes the larger society and its values into account. Well-functioning markets do not simply spring into being spontaneously. Rather, they are regulated by elaborate public and private social institutions like courts, contract law, industrial associations, and our stock, bond, and commodity exchanges. When the regulatory apparatus breaks down, so do the markets, as can be seen in the recent history of the savings-and-loan industry. Without social structures the pursuit of commercial gain degenerates into banditry, as is evident in the drug trade, in frontier societies (such as our own in the last century), or in countries like Somalia where those social institutions have collapsed. Unadorned market-oriented behavior leads to "gangster capitalism," not to the good society. This raises a disturbing aspect of the use of economic instruments to solve environmental problems. A basic assumption of the free-market approach is that motives don't matter, only results. If bribing polluters out of polluting works, fine. If giving civil servants bonuses for obeying the law is effective, pay them. Assume the worst of all human beings and arrange incentives to harness the basest of human motives. This is the social logic of freemarket environmentalism. But to most of us, motives do matter. A lie is not the same as a mistake; murder is not the same as self-defense or manslaughter; prostitution is not the same as love. Oliver Wendell Holmes once said that even a dog distinguishes between being stumbled over and being kicked. Most of us have at least the sensibilities of that dog. We do care about the motives of our fellow citizens; it matters if someone seeks to protect the community and its land base because they actually care, as opposed to doing it only to protect their pocketbooks (or pick ours). Ethics and conscience matter, and markets can undermine both.

The basic operating principle behind a "free market society" is an anti-democratic one: that peoples' preferences, whatever they may be, should be accepted and given an importance in proportion to the dollars that back them up. But most of us—including those without a great deal of money—have moral and social values that lead us to be very critical of some preferences, the expression of which we seek to block regardless of their financial backing. Even when we do not support the use of legal restrictions to constrain their expression, most of us would be uncomfortable passively accepting all market outcomes as legitimate. Instead, we seek social and cultural means to discourage some and encourage others. That is what "manners" and "public opinion" and "community standards" are all about. One of the worrisome things about allowing the use of public lands to be determined entirely by the highest bidder is the implicit legitimization of those outcomes. Destructive behavior should not automatically become legitimate and acceptable simply because it is backed by the largest wad of cash.

Environmentalists should be concerned with the waste of *all* resources: natural, social, and political. Policies that are unnecessarily costly and that do not accomplish their objectives involve pure waste, and should be reexamined. Economic instruments for controlling pollution and managing public lands can offer more efficient ways to reach our objectives; at the very least, by reducing the cost of environmental control, they open up the possibility of attaining higher standards of quality. Many market plans begin by setting a goal, and then proceed to attain it in the least costly way. That is a positive approach. Finally, economic instruments can solve certain types of environmental conflicts to the mutual satisfaction of all involved—a rare and attractive option in an otherwise contentious struggle.

But this mutual satisfaction can never be achieved by the commercial-market mentality alone. On the contrary, that mentality tends to gnaw away at the ethical underpinning of society, and can even undermine the foundations of markets themselves: witness the insider trading, market manipulation, and regulatory corruption scandals of the 1980s. The social and community values that environmentalists hold should not be abandoned to an ideological fad. They are crucial to building a healthy society, and should form the basis for the pragmatic decisions that will get us there.

43

Putting a Value on Environmental Quality

John A. Dixon

A tested evaluation technique of economists is cursed by environmentalists in America but welcomed by their counterparts in developing countries.

Asoybean field in Korea is eroding. Hot geothermal waste water from an electricity generating plant in the Philippines needs to be disposed of. A middle class Thai government official goes to Lumpinee Park in Bangkok for an early morning walk.

What could these events possibly have in common? All are examples of the myriad problems or activities that can be addressed by economic analysis—and are daily.

In these examples, something called benefit-cost analysis (BCA) has been used to, respectively, 1) place a value on the benefits gained from preventing soil erosion, 2) help select from among various alternatives an appropriate wastewater disposal method, and 3) estimate the social value of a free public park in a crowded Asian capital.

The use of benefit-cost analysis, a common evaluation technique, is not new. It has been around almost 50 years. What is new—and controversial, in both developing and highly industrial countries—is its application in putting a dollar value on environmental consequences of development projects.

"The benefit-cost analysis controversy," according to Maynard Hufschmidt of the East-West Center's Environment and Policy Institute, "comes down to the question: what weight, if any, should be placed on the results of benefit-cost analysis in making public decisions on environmental quality?"

It is, Hufschmidt explains, a systematic method of identifying the "goods" and the "bads"—the economic benefits and costs—of any project, program, or policy. "It is a tool to aid decision-making in the public sector," Hufschmidt says. "Not a complete decision rule in the sense that any project or program would be accepted or rejected solely on the basis of a given benefit-cost analysis. But it can be a very useful aid in making decisions."

East-West Center researchers have just finished a two-and-a-half year study aimed

* From *East-West Perspective, vol. 3, no. 1*, Summer 1982. "Putting a Value on Environmental Quality" by John A. Dixon. Reprinted with kind permission of Kluwer Academic Publishers.

at helping those concerned with promoting environmental quality goals in Asia and the Pacific. The study sought to show how environmental concerns can be incorporated into traditional project analysis. In the process, the study hoped also to contribute to the credibility of environmentalists in developing countries, where development decisions by governments, multinational corporations, and financial aid institutions are usually made primarily on economic grounds with little regard for the deterioration of ecosystems or landscapes.

Many environmental agencies in those countries now view benefit-cost analysis as a positive tool rather than as an impediment, as it is still viewed by environmentalits in the United States.

Benefit-cost analysis is "about as neutral as asking a fox into a henhouse to observe the color of the eggs," according to Ida Hoos, a research sociologist at the University of California at Berkeley. "There is nothing magic or scientific about it. It is almost always an ex post facto justification of a position already taken." she said. (*New York Times,* Feb. 14, 1982.)

A more moderate, though still critical view was expressed by Norman Cousins in a *Saturday Review* editorial (April 14, 1979): "One of the least attractive terms in the American language is 'cost benefit ratio.' In the refrigerated patois of the budgeteers it means that any proposed action must produce tangible returns equal to or greater than its expense. The term descends like a death sentence on any proposal that would apply creative imagination to socially essential programs or long-range goals. If ideas are offered that seek to upgrade the quality of education, or that would improve the nutrition of the nation's children, or that would make life a little less squalid or agonizing for millions of Americans . . . someone is certain to say the idea cannot be justified because of CBR (cost-benefit ratio)."

Economic analysis, for better or worse, is a fact of life. Whether it is done implicitly, as is usually the case for personal decisions, or explicitly, as required increasingly by the federal government or by banks and various international aid agencies, most decisions that involve spending money and time (or, as, economists say, allocating resources), are based to some extent on economic analysis.

In personal decision making, we routinely evaluate the costs and potential benefits from an action, consider the alternatives or trade-offs, and reach a decision. The process is carried out daily: Should I bring my lunch to work or eat out? Do I prefer to watch TV or go to a movie? Both questions involve potential benefits and measurable costs.

In such a case, you are carrying out an implicit benefit-cost analysis of various options. This example is self-contained, as an individual you both receive the benefits and pay the costs. When broader institutional or public projects are considered, some of the benefits or costs may be incurred by others and some of the effects may result in environmental benefits and costs, outcomes that are hard to measure and to price.

Here's how it works. Any project or activity, whether it is cooking a dinner, building a freeway, constructing a factory, or reforesting an entire watershed, combines a set of resources to produce a variety of goods and services. Most projects also generate by-products or residuals, that is, products other than those for which the project was undertaken.

Cooking a dinner, for example, requires a combination of items (food, heat, water, cook's time) to produce the main product— the meal. Byproducts are also generated and may be either good (tempting aromas of cooked food, heat from the stove when it's cold in the kitchen) or bad (pots to wash, scraps, the odor of burnt food, heat from the stove when it is hot in the kitchen). Benefit-cost analysis (BCA) is one of many techniques that provide formal economic evaluations of resources, results, and byproducts alike.

Benefit-cost analysis includes three steps for any given project or activity: 1) It lists and quantifies all of the resources that go in and the products and byproducts that result: 2) it places values on, or monetizes, these items; and 3) it uses various mathematical techniques to summarize the total benefits and costs of the project.

The process of evaluation is important because, given limited money or time, we cannot usually do everything we would like to and therefore have to make decisions about both what we do and in what order.

The environment, as well as the goods and services provided by our natural or manufactured surroundings, is also a scarce resource, just as money or time are. Clean air, uncrowded beaches, mountain views, and pleasant urban areas are not unlimited in supply. However, since many such considerations are not easily priced or measured, they are frequently ignored in conventional benefit-cost analyses of development projects. This wouldn't be important if the projects did not have a measurable effect on the environment. Most large projects, however, do have environmental consequences:

❏ A large dam project both opens up to human settlement a previously inaccessible watershed and disrupts fish movements and the livelihood of downstream fishermen.

❏ An agricultural land settlement project removes primary forest cover which in turn affects soil erosion and the waterflow characteristics of the watershed.

❏ A coastal industrial development project produces air and water pollution that adversely affects bordering mangrove areas and a coastal fishery.

Recent work has focused on how environmental effects can be included in traditional economic analysis by quantifying, valuing, and then presenting the environmental dimensions as part of a complete economic analysis.

In principle, there is no difference between carrying out an economic evaluation of a project that includes environmental dimeneions and an analysis that does not include these dimensions. In practice, however, this is frequently not the case because of the greater difficulty in defining and quantifying environmental aspects of a project. Certain common factors apply to any analysis and must be recognized and taken into consideration.

These include: the *boundaries* of the project considered, the *time horizon,* and *discount rates.* Once these factors have been considered and the various resources used and products and byproducts measured, the actual process of economic evaluation is quite straightforward. The way a project is defined, therefore, becomes very important in determining how useful and sensitive the ultimate analysis is, especially if concern for the environment is given high priority.

Project boundaries are the limits placed on the analysis—that is, where the line is drawn between what is included as part of the activity and what is excluded. If a benefit is received or a cost incurred by someone outside of the project area, these amounts are not included in the analysis.

For example, farmers in an upland area in Korea are growing crops on moderately steep hillsides. Heavy summer rains lead to soil erosion which goes into streams and ends up deposited in fields in the lowlands or in reservoirs behind dams (thereby decreasing their useful life). A project is proposed to stabilize upland soils by use of appropriate mulching techniques. What is the proper project boundary? If the farmer's own field is used as the unit of analysis, only those resources used on the field and the products from the field will be included. These include the costs involved in the new soil stabilizing techniques (mulch, labor, tools) and the projected benefits (less soil lost, a possible increase in crop yields). The benefits are measured only to the extent that they benefit the farmer, not the wider community. If a wider area is included in the analysis (perhaps a whole watershed), the costs and benefits measured would be those of many individual farmers as well as other public concerns. In the wider analysis, the benefits from decreased soil erosion and sedimentation could include the increased economic life of dams and reservoirs and the prevention of soil deposition on lowland fields.

Defining the limits of the analysis is in part dependent on the type of project being considered. A project affecting a major river, such as a large dam for irrigation, would appropriately require consideration of the area above the dam, the watershed, and the area below the dam, the command area served by the dam's water and power. Projects relating to individual decision makers, such as small farmers, however, may need to be evaluated at a level that ensures that the benefits and costs as seen by the individual farmers are such that they will adopt the recommended change or support the project.

Here is a common problem: A project such as the soil stabilization program in Korea may be beneficial when viewed by the government at a broad level and yet not worth doing when viewed by each individual farmer. That's because most of the costs are borne by the individual farmers but most of the benefits, such as the increased economic life of dams and reservoirs, are received by other people or society at large. Such a divergence of views frequently occurs between the private perspectives (the level of the individual farmer) and that of society (a broader level).

When environmental dimensions are included in project analysis, the problem becomes more acute. Frequently the actions of many individuals, while desirable by themselves, jointly lead to undesirable environmental effects. For example, when a narrow individual focus is taken, a person may choose to own a car to drive to work. When a million people do this in a large city like Los Angeles, smog, traffic congestion, and other undesirable effects result. An economic analysis done on a city-wide basis may well suggest that the costs of private car ownership outweigh the benefits, while each individual has reached the opposite conclusion. Appropriate taxes and subsidies can sometimes be used to ensure that the private and social analyses yield the same conclusion.

Singapore was faced with a worsening traffic congestion problem in its central business district. A major cause was single occupant commuter cars. A system was devised whereby during the morning and afternoon rush hours, admission to the central business district was restricted to buses and to cars with prepaid passes. All others had to pay a substantial fee to enter the zone. While not solving the problem, congestion has decreased.

The appropriate *time horizon* is the second major concern in an analysis. After the project boundaries have been selected it is necessary to decide how long to continue the analysis. In general, a proper time horizon will be long enough to include most of the anticipated effects from a project. It can vary greatly, from one day to several decades. Cooking a meal at home will involve only a few hours from beginning to end while a major construction project could take years to finish, and its benefits are reaped for many more years. When a project involves a natural system, the effects may last for years or take years to be felt. Reforestation and consequent timber production from a newly forested area may require 20, 30, or more years of analysis to properly assess benefits and costs.

When environmental concerns are explicitly considered, the time horizon is often longer than otherwise. Frequently, periods of 10, 15, or 20 years are included in project evaluations. Such periods are long enough to include the usually significant start-up costs in the early years as well as the benefits from later periods. If capital investment is an important component of the project, the proper time horizon should usually be long enough to include its expected useful life.

Time horizons used in project evaluation need not be 30, 50, or 100 years. Because economists use *discounting rates* to place future benefits and costs into present-day dollars, the value of a benefit or cost occurring many years in the future is very small today. The practice is based on the principle of known behavior that the value of a dollar of benefits, or costs, today is greater than the same amount of benefits, or costs, next year or any time in the future.

There is nothing magical, mysterious, or tricky about discounting. It merely is an orderly way to compare a series of costs and benefits that occur at various times and to calculate present values.

Many conservationists carry their distrust of economic analysis generally over to discounting specifically because it frequently produces results unfavorable to their positions. They argue that because of increasing population and decreasing availability of natural settings or open spaces, the value of these natural resources will increase in the future. This view may well be correct but should not be confused with discounting.

The fact that discounting and rigorous economic analysis may produce results that certain groups do not like should not be used to dismiss such analysis. Rather, it points out that not all decisions can or should be made based solely on economic criteria.

The question of which discount rate to use is more controversial. A low discount rate weighs future costs and benefits much more hevily than a high discount rate.

As seen in the Table 43.1, $100 received 20 years from now is worth $67.30 today at a 2 percent discount rate, $21.45 at an 8 percent rate, and only $6.11 at a 15 percent rate. Because benefits and costs in any project occur at various times, and the time when they occur can vary greatly from one project to another, the discount rate used can have very important effects on how profitable any given project is seen to be by an individual. For example, a project such as reforestation that may have large initial costs in the first few years and sizable benefits 10 to 15 years later may be viewed as very profitable by someone with a low discount rate (the present value of future benefits is still substantial) and very unattractive by someone with a very high discount rate (the present value of future benefits is very low).

Poor people frequently need money, food, and other products and services today and cannot afford to wait for future benefits. Implicit discount rates of 20, 30, or even 50 percent have been measured in some countries. Governments currently use discount rates of 10 to 15 percent that are thought to reflect the scarcity value of money. Some environmentalists use very small or zero discount rates for environmental goods and services in the belief that their scarcity, and hence value, will increase in the future.

The divergence in the discount rates used by various people (a farmer, a government planner, a forester) viewing the same planned reforestation project can, and often does, lead to very different views on the profitability, and hence adoption, of the proposed project. If this divergence is not acknowledged, a project can be designed, funded, and implemented only to meet with complete rejection or non-participation on the part of those individuals who are supposed to carry it out. Therefore, the question of what is the "correct" discount rate is not really answerable.

Several analyses of the same project may need to be made using different discount rates. Each analysis would then illustrate how a proposed project was viewed from various perspectives. If all of these analyses produced similar results, so much the better. If the use of different discount rates produced very different results with regard to net benefits, this

Table 43.1 The Present Value of $100 Received at Different Times in the Future with Various Discount Rates

Time (Years)	Discount Rate %				
	2	5	8	10	15
0 (present)	$100.00	$100.00	$100.00	$100.00	$100.00
10	82.03	61.39	46.32	38.50	24.72
20	67.30	37.68	21.45	14.92	6.11
30	55.21	23.14	9.94	5.73	1.51
50	37.15	8.72	2.13	0.85	0.09

would indicate potential problems that would need to be carefully considered.

In the example cited earlier—the problem of erosion from an upland soybean field in Korea—erosion led to soil loss and the depositing of soil and sediment downstream, both on other fields and in streams. Mulching techniques were introduced to prevent most of the erosion, but these also imposed costs—financial costs. The benefits from mulching, however, were two-fold: the upland farmer's own fields were stabilized and hence yields increased, and downstream losses were reduced.

In an analysis carried out by Sung-Hoon Yim, an economist from Chung-Ang University, Seoul, the farmer's field was selected as the unit of analysis but the project boundary was extended to include the directly traceable costs of erosion from that field. Each year soybeans and barley were grown in rotation and, under the existing system, soil loss was measured at 40 metric tons per hectare. In addition, the excessive water runoff carried away nutrients in the soil and these lost nutrients were measured. Because of the rapid runoff of rainwater, little water soaked into the soil and its moisture content was low. Consequently, during certain dry months, irrigation was required.

The existing system, therefore, produced soybeans and barley at a certain level but had yearly losses of soil, soil nutrients, and water that had to be replaced to maintain productivity. The proposed new system involved the use of straw mulch and vertical drilling in the soil to encourage deep percolation of rainwater and reduce soil erosion. It involved considerable initial expense but provided a number of benefits. Was the new system profitable from the farmer's point of view? Was it profitable from the government's perspective?

The project boundaries had been defined and a time horizon of 10 years selected. It was felt that 10 years was long enough to include the various costs and benefits involved in the proposed change. Two discount rates were used: 10 percent as the government's estimate of the social cost of capital and 20 percent as an estimate of the farmer's own private discount rate. The farmer, therefore,

would value immediate rewards more highly than the government since future benefits are worth less to the farmer (with a 20 percent discount rate) than would the same benefits to the government (with a 10 percent rate).

The analysis compared the two alternatives: the existing cropping system (with substantial erosion) and the proposed system (the project) using mulching with greatly reduced erosion. For each option, the resources used and the products and byproducts for each of the 10 years were listed and then valued. Costs had negative values and benefits, positive values. For some items—mulching or irrigation or fertilizer—the costs were readily calculated. But how to value soil lost each year under the existing system? In this case the cost of physically removing the soil deposited on lowland fields each year was counted as the "cost" of the erosion. In addition, soil nutrients lost from the upland field were replaced by chemical fertilizer and this was an additional "cost" of the existing system.

A table was created that listed the value of all benefits and all costs for each year for the ten-year period under study. For each year the total costs were subtracted from total benefits. This net benefit figure was usually positive (greater than zero) but in some years, when costs were very high, it was negative, indicating a cash loss for that year. The two options were then compared by discounting the net benefit figures by 10 percent and then by 20 percent, and adding up the total values for each option for the ten years. This yielded the present value of net benefits for each option (the Net Present Value, NPV), and showed the current worth of each option today at two discount rates—10 percent and 20 percent.

In this case, the present value of net benefits of the proposed new system (mulching) was larger than for the existing system. Hence, the new system was more "profitable."

Economics generally, and benefit-cost analysis specifically, can create a logical and rigorous framework that can be used to examine various policies. The techniques used should not be seen as providing final answers or the only basis for decisions. Most decisions are made in a complicated institutional setting that combines political, cultural, economic, and other considerations. The goal of economic analysis is to provide the policymaker with more complete information and to help determine what are the real options, what are the tradeoffs, what are the benefits and the costs.

Granted, consideration of environmental aspects of a project makes the task of the economic analyst more difficult. Problems arise with both quantifying the environmental goods and services and then valuing them. It may be that the final answer reached is not one that a conservationist or an environmentalist hoped for. For example, the value of a downtown park may be much greater when used for real estate development than as a green open space. In cases such as this the political and social aspects of decision making may take precedence and the park may be preserved as a green space regardless of its value when developed for office buildings.

Obviously, the use of benefit-cost analysis for some sensitive or controversial decisions can lead to reactions such as those of Cousins and Hoos. There will always be cases when decision makers use a straight economic analysis to justify an unpopular decision. But if benefit-cost analysis is used carefully and the assumptions embodied in it are made explicit, it can be a very useful tool to value environmental aspects of projects and present the options available to decision makers. In those cases where society has not already decided in favor of preservation or some other course of action as a matter of principle, benefit-cost analysis, properly applied, need not be an "after-the-fact justification of a position already taken" but rather, can be an aid to society in the rational allocation of scarce resources.

44

Solution, or Mess? A Milk Jug for a Green Earth

Stephanie Rosenbloom

A simple change to the design of the gallon milk jug, adopted by Wal-Mart and Costco, seems made for the times. The jugs are cheaper to ship and better for the environment, the milk is fresher when it arrives in stores, and it costs less.

What's not to like? Plenty, as it turns out.

The jugs have no real spout, and their unorthodox shape makes consumers feel like novices at the simple task of pouring a glass of milk.

"I hate it," said Lisa DeHoff, a cafe owner shopping in a Sam's Club here.

"It spills everywhere," said Amy Wise, a homemaker.

"It's very hard for kids to pour," said Lee Morris, who was shopping for her grandchildren.

But retailers are undeterred by the prospect of upended bowls of Cheerios. The new jugs have many advantages from their point of view, and Sam's Club intends to roll them out broadly, making them more prevalent.

The redesign of the gallon milk jug, experts say, is an example of the changes likely to play out in the American economy over the next two decades. In an era of soaring global demand and higher costs for energy and materials, virtually every aspect of the economy needs to be re-examined, they say, and many products must be redesigned for greater efficiency.

"This is a key strategy as a path forward," said Anne Johnson, the director of the Sustainable Packaging Coalition, a project of the nonprofit group Green Blue. "Re-examining, 'What are the materials we are using? How are we using them? And where do they go ultimately?'"

Wal-Mart Stores is already moving down this path. But if the milk jug is any indication, some of the changes will take getting used to on the part of consumers. Many spill milk when first using the new jugs.

"When we brought in the new milk, we were asking for feedback," said Heather Mayo, vice president for merchandising at Sam's Club, a division of Wal-Mart. "And they're saying, 'Why's it in a square jug? Why's it different? I want the same milk. What happened to my old milk?'"

Mary Tilton tried to educate the public a few days ago as she stood at a Sam's Club in North Canton, about 50 miles south of Cleveland, luring shoppers with chocolate chip cookies and milk as she showed them how to pour from the new jugs.

"Just tilt it slowly and pour slowly," Ms. Tilton said to passing customers as she talked about the jugs' environmental benefits and cost savings. Instead of picking up the jug, as most people tend to do, she kept it on a table and gently tipped it toward a cup.

Mike Compston, who owns a dairy in Yerington, Nev., described the pouring technique in a telephone interview as a "rock-and-pour instead of a lift-and-tip."

Demonstrations are but one of several ways Sam's Club is advocating the containers. Signs in the aisle laud their cost savings and "better fridge fit."

And some customers have become converts.

"With the new refrigerators with the shelf in the door, these fit nice," said April Buchanan, who was shopping at the Sam's Club here. Others, even those who rue the day their tried-and-true jugs were replaced, praised the lower cost, from $2.18 to $2.58 a gallon. Sam's Club said that was a savings of 10 to 20 cents a gallon compared with old jugs.

The new jug marks a sharp break with the way dairies and grocers have traditionally produced and stocked milk.

Early one recent morning, the creators and producers of the new tall rectangular jugs donned goggles and white coats to walk the noisy, chilly production lines at Superior Dairy in Canton, Ohio. It was founded in 1922 by a man who was forced to abandon the brandy business during Prohibition. Five generations of the founder's family, the Soehnlens, have worked there.

Today, they bottle and ship two different ways. The old way is inefficient and labor-intensive, according to members of the family. The other day, a worker named Dennis Sickafoose was using a long hook to drag plastic crates loaded with jugs of milk onto a conveyor belt.

The crates are necessary because the shape of old-fashioned milk jugs prohibits stacking them atop one another. The crates take up a lot of room, they are unwieldy to move, and extra space must be left in delivery trucks to take empty ones back from stores to the dairy.

They also can be filthy. "Birds roost on them," said Dan Soehnlen, president of Superior Dairy, which spun off a unit called Creative Edge to design and license new packaging of many kinds. He spoke while standing in pools of the soapy run-off from milk crates that had just been washed. About 100,000 gallons of water a day are used at his dairy clean the crates, Mr. Soehnlen said.

But with the new jugs, the milk crates are gone. Instead, a machine stacks the jugs, with cardboard sheets between layers. Then the entire pallet, four layers high, is shrink-wrapped and moved with a forklift.

The company estimates this kind of shipping has cut labor by half and water use by 60 to 70 percent. More gallons fit on a truck and in Sam's Club coolers, and no empty crates need to be picked up, reducing trips to each Sam's Club store to two a week, from five—a big fuel savings. Also, Sam's Club can now store 224 gallons of milk in its coolers, in the same space that used to hold 80.

The whole operation is so much more efficient that milk coming out of a cow in the morning winds up at a Sam's Club store by that afternoon, compared with several hours later or the next morning by the old method. "That's our idea of fresh milk," Greg Soehnlen, a vice president at Creative Edge, said.

Sam's Club started using the boxy jugs in November, and they are now in 189 stores scattered around the country. They will appear soon in more Sam's Club stores and perhaps in Wal-Marts.

The question now is whether customers will go along.

As Ms. Tilton gave her in-store demonstration the other day at the Sam's Club here, customers stood around her, munching cookies and sipping milk. "Would you like to take some home today?" she asked.

A shopper named Jodi Kauffman gave the alien jugs a sidelong glance.

"Maybe," she said.

45

Are People Acting Irrationally?

Understanding Public Concerns About Environmental Threats

Abraham H. Wandersman and William K. Hallman

News stories about environmental events illustrate public concerns about environmental policy and regulations. Increasingly, public perceptions of risk and fear of cancer are influencing the development of public policy regarding the environment. Policymakers have often regarded these public concerns as irrational. The purpose of this article is to describe how psychological research can be used to understand the public's concerns about environmental threats and to discuss the "irrationality" of these concerns. Examples are drawn from research on perceived risk and fear of cancer, and roles are suggested for psychology and psychologists in informing environmental policymaking.

We recently received the following telephone call from a reporter for the *Los Angeles Times:*

I'm doing an article on towns that have been hit by cancer clusters that have killed a number of children. The scientists have come in and done their research and have found no explanation for what caused the cancers. I'm trying to look at how this leaves these communities adrift and confused and scared. Are people acting irrationally? Can you help my readers understand this situation?

Because of our studies on hazardous waste, we are often contacted by citizens, mental health professionals, government agencies, and reporters about how communities respond when residents believe they have been harmed by toxic chemicals, radiation, or other environmental threats. The scenario has become familiar, particularly because these dramas are often played out in the morning newspaper or evening news.

Often in these communities there is an apparent high rate of cancer, birth defects, mysterious rashes, or other unexplained illnesses. Community members may believe that there are possible links between these illnesses and toxic substances such as pesticides or materials escaping from a landfill or industrial site. Some residents may also feel unfairly stigmatized as news accounts seem to suggest that their community is unhealthy

---

or unsafe. There are sometimes disagreements among scientists about whether the risk is real or not. Frequently, there are controversies about who is responsible for the problem and who is responsible for the solution. Often there is a heated conflict between government and citizens over what should be done. Throughout, there is uncertainly, ambiguity, and apprehension.

Public officials often have difficulty understanding public reactions to perceived environmental threats. "Public fear of risk has been frequently dismissed as 'technophobia,' and the American public has been criticized as 'risk aversive,' as 'healthy hypochondriacs,' as 'misguided or uninformed'" (Nelkin, 1989, p. 99). Officials ask, Why should the public be concerned with the seemingly minute risks posed by some environmental problem when they assume greater risks by smoking, drinking and driving, or not wearing seatbelts?

As community psychologists, we have attended public meetings in towns facing environmental threats. Often a local official will rise to the podium and explain, "Look, if you people would just listen to the facts, you would understand that there is nothing to worry about." Not surprisingly, this incantation holds little magic. Yet, some public officials continue to be astonished by the "irrationality" of their constituencies. They do not seem to understand that resolving questions about environmental threats goes beyond simply trying to convince the public of the validity of numbers derived through quantitative methods. Many also fail to appreciate public skepticism and do not understand how little these numbers seem to help people.

Groups of experts from the National Research Council, the General Accounting Office, the Science Advisory Board of the U.S. Environmental Protection Agency, and others have called for a better understanding of how people respond to environmental threats. We agree that to respond effectively to environmental problems, policymakers must know as much about the social, emotional, and behavioral impacts of environmental threats as they do about the biological effects of such hazards.

Psychologists can play a key role in helping others to understand these impacts and in interpreting the "irrationality" that often accompanies them. Over the past two decades, psychologists and other social scientists have studied the impacts of technological catastrophes on communities. Although no comprehensive model of individual and community dynamics in coping with toxic hazards currently exists, several middle-range models incorporate coping style, social support, uncertainty, attribution of responsibility, culture, and context (economic, social, physical, environmental, and political factors; see Baum, Fleming, & Singer, 1983; Cvetkovich & Earle, 1992; Hallman & Wandersman, 1992). Each of these models suggests that responses to environmental threats follow patterns, are largely predictable, and are not as irrational as they appear.

To provide examples of how psychological theory and empirical research can shed light on controversies over environmental threats, we focus on risk perception and, specifically, fear of cancer. We chose these because they appear to be major influences on the degree to which the public responds to environmental threats. Although much of what we discuss relates specifically to hazardous chemicals, many ideas also apply to environmental risks posed by ionizing radiation and other hazards such as electric and magnetic fields emitted by power lines, appliances, and cellular telephones.

We will discuss why quantitative risk assessment does not provide all the information needed to make policy decisions, and we will examine empirical evidence on the components of risk perception and on the "rationality" of public risk perception. The difference between risk *assessment* (made by health and environmental agencies) and risk *perception* (made by the public) is at the heart of much of the misunderstanding and outrage over environmental threats (Hance, Chess, & Sandman, 1988). Cancer and fear of cancer are often at the center of attention in risk assessment and in environmental controversies over hazardous chemicals. Yet, fear of cancer is often difficult to quantify. As such, we will discuss a research effort to define and measure fear of cancer and outline its connections with hazardous chemical situations.

Risk Assessment and Risk Perception

"Sure, it's going to kill a lot of people, but they may be dying of something else anyway." Othal Brand, recently appointed to the Texas pesticide regulatory board on the termite killer Chlordane. ("Perspectives," 1990, p. 17)

Hazardous chemicals and their disposal present a major environmental challenge to society. According to Sandra Lee of the Environmental Protection Agency (cited in Upton, Kneip, & Toniolo, 1989), there are approximately 30,000 toxic chemical waste disposal sites that may pose a threat to public health in the United States, and the number is still growing. In their review on the public health aspects of toxic chemical disposal sites, Upton et al. concluded that the sites are a source of potential risk to the health of a large segment of the population. The public *is* concerned about these risks. A June 1989 Gallup poll (Kohut & Shriver, 1989) found that 69% of the public personally worried a great deal about contamination of soil and water by toxic waste, and a 1986 Roper poll found that chemical waste disposal was the highest ranked environmental problem (Allen, 1987). A June 1992 *USA Today* (Tyson, 1992) poll showed that the environment was the number one concern in the United States.

Quantitative Risk Assessment

In an effort to understand and respond to the risks posed by environmental hazards, scientists and engineers have tried to quantify them. By quantifying risks, assessors hope to rationalize the debate about what to do about risks. Furthermore, formal quantitative risk assessments are often required by government agencies as a prerequisite to remediation. For example, the Environmental Protection Agency requires a quantitative risk

analysis to estimate the potential risks posed by hazardous waste sites before cleanups can begin. Such assessments use what is known about the toxicity of the chemicals involved, combined with estimates of the quantity of chemicals involved, and the number of people exposed. It is important to point out that quantitative estimates of risk are based on only two dimensions, the probability of a negative outcome and the severity of that outcome.

Why Quantitative Risk Assessments Are Not Enough

Although the idea of using science to quantify risks is appealing, risk assessments can be complex. It is often difficult to identify the chemicals that are present at a contaminated site. It may be difficult or impossible to determine how many people have been exposed and to what extent. In addition, even when the chemicals involved are known and the extent of exposure of the population is known, complete toxicological data exists for only a small subset of the chemicals used in the United States (Shodell, 1985). As a result, Sjoberg (1980) warned that even the best quantitative risk analysis is enveloped in uncertainty. Quantitative risk assessments must make some assumptions given the frequent absence of reliable empirical data. For example, the need to use mathematical models to extrapolate scientific data to real-world exposure situations creates uncertainty because different models can result in vastly different estimates of risk.

Quantitative risk assessments depend on the assumptions of the model used, and the results of the assessment depend a great deal on the integrity of the assessors. Often these assessments are conducted without citizen participation, and the results are poorly communicated to the public. As such, community members sometimes fear that money or politics can influence the results of such assessments.

Both because of the lack of certainty, particularly in the context of conflicting expert opinions, and because of the possibility of potential bias, quantitative risk assessments often do little to calm the fears of potentially affected residents. Nor do they necessarily address many of the questions important to community members. Typically, quantitative risk assessments focus only on the possible risks to human health. Also, the aggregate nature of a risk assessment (e.g., number of deaths per million) does not make prediction possible for a specific individual (E. Vaughan, personal communication, August 8, 1990).

In addition, health risks are not the only issues people face when confronted with environmental threats. Our research on communities located near a hazardous waste landfill found that besides health concerns, residents were also concerned about their property values, crop damage, harm to pets and farm animals, increased truck traffic from the landfill, and the public image of their community (Hallman, 1989).

Perceptions of the acceptability of a risk implicitly involve personal and societal value judgments. To measure quantitatively how risky something is, it is necessary to identify its adverse effects on those things that individuals consider to be valuable. But science provides no special insights into what society should value (Fischhoff, Watson, & Hope, 1984).

W. R. Freudenburg (1988) argued that there are at least three ways social science can improve quantitative risk assessment. He suggested that social science can help clarify the differences between scientists and the public when it comes to the assessment of technological risks. In addition, he maintained that social scientists should have input into the actual calculations of the probabilities of undesired consequences. He also suggested that social science can offer insights into the processes by which risk assessments are carried out.

Perceptions of Risk

Finding benzene, a carcinogen, in Perrier bottled water led to an expensive effort to regain the confidence of the public and restore Perrier's image of credibility: "At stake was the pristine reputation of the bubbly mineral water 'It's perfect. It's Perrier,' . . . Perrier astutely realized that these days the *perception* of risk is as important to the

health-conscious American public as the reality of risk" (Russell, 1990, p. 45).

If the data from quantitative risk assessments is not particularly helpful, how do people decide whether a risk is acceptable or not? Several researchers suggest that people's perceptions of risks are influenced by the characteristics of the perceivers and the contexts of their perceptions (Vaughan, 1993, this issue). Douglas and Wildavsky (1982) suggested that perceptions of risk should be thought of in a cultural context and that such perceptions may be biased by political, economic, and cultural propensities. Similarly, the theory of social amplification of risk (Kasperson et al., 1988; Renn, Burns, Kasperson, Kasperson, & Slovic, 1992) suggested that psychological, social, institutional, and cultural processes can interact in ways that may amplify or attenuate responses to perceived risks.

A large body of research has also found that people's perceptions of the acceptability of risks are largely influenced by the characteristics of the hazards they face (see Fischhoff, Slovic, Lichtenstein, Read, & Combs, 1978; Hallman & Wandersman, 1989; Johnson & Tversky, 1984; Slovic, Fischhoff, & Lichtenstein, 1980; Slovic, Fischhoff, & Lichtenstein, 1986; Starr, 1969). Drawing on this research, Hance et al. (1988) suggested that people do not simply disregard scientific information about risks. Rather, people use this information in combination with information about the social, political, and ethical characteristics of the risk to make decisions about its acceptability. Hance et al. called these characteristics of the risk *outrage* factors, to differentiate them from *hazard* dimensions, which are typically measured quantitatively, often through risk assessments. The more outrage factors that surround a risk, the more likely people will be concerned (or outraged) about it, despite scientific data indicating that a risk is low.

According to this model, given two risks of equal magnitude, a risk that is voluntary is more acceptable than an involuntary risk. Similarly, risks under individual control are seen as more acceptable than those under government control. Risks that seem fairly distributed are more acceptable than those that seem unfairly distributed. Natural risks are more acceptable than artificial risks. Familiar risks are more acceptable than exotic risks. Risks that are detectable are more acceptable than risks that are undetectable. Risks that are well understood by science are more acceptable than those that are not. Risks that are associated with other memorable events (like Love Canal or Chernobyl) are seen as more risky. Risks that seem ethically wrong are less acceptable.

Vlek and Stallen (1980) took a comprehensive approach to risk that includes many of the ideas mentioned above. They proposed 32 specific aspects of risk that determine the nature and context of a risky decision problem, grouped under 11 categories. They suggested that the acceptability of risky activity varies with voluntariness of exposure, controllability of the consequences, distribution of consequences in time, distribution of consequences in space, context of probability assessment, context of accident evaluation, combination of accident probability and seriousness, knowledge about the risky activity, condition of the subject, social considerations, and confidence in experts/regulators. They proposed that perceptions of risk are predictable to a large extent.

Some of our research used variables suggested by Vlek and Stallen (1980) to predict residents' perceptions of health risks associated with a nearby hazardous waste landfill (Hallman, 1989). We obtained R^2 values as high as .53 in the prediction of perceptions of health risk. The fact that risk perceptions can be predicted is important. The pattern of correlations between these variables and perceived risks has face validity. That is, the beliefs people hold are logically consistent with their overall perceptions of risk. In our study, perceptions of health risks are positively correlated with such beliefs as these: There are not enough written regulations that govern the landfill; the experts who are supposed to ensure the safety of the landfill are not well trained; the operators of the landfill are not using proper equipment or techniques; an accident could easily be caused by human error; a leak at the landfill would be

extremely difficult to remediate; and so forth. Risk perceptions, then, are supported by a set of beliefs that are sensible and not simply composed of senseless or irrational fears and unbridled emotions.

Fear of Cancer and Environmental Threats

There are two things that motivate Americans: Money and fear of cancer. (Annas, 1989)

One force that has enlarged the debate about environmental health issues is a preoccupation by Americans with the risks of developing cancer. The Office of Technology Assessment (U.S. Congress, 1981) issued a report that described the importance of cancer in shaping public health actions, public perceptions, and legislative response. The report also described laws that attempt to reduce exposure to carcinogens and concluded that the "existence of the laws clearly states that Congress has seen cancer risks as deserving government attention" (p. 176). Moreover, cancer risks are often the focus of lawsuits, particularly because the courts are becoming more willing to treat cancerphobia as a compensable injury (Willmore, 1989).

The risks of cancer often spark grassroots efforts to resolve environmental problems. In a survey of 110 community organizations involved in environmental health issues, N. Freudenberg (1984) found that nearly half these groups were formed because concerned citizens were afraid or angry about a suspected health hazard. Although exposure to toxins can cause a variety of physical effects, the most common concern cited in Freudenberg's survey was fear of cancer resulting from an environmental hazard.

Other research has suggested that fear of cancer may exist among residents in communities near hazardous sites. Long-term chronic fears have been documented among some of the residents of Legler, New Jersey (Edelstein, 1982, 1988), who feared that the consumption of the contaminated water in their town could cause cancer up to 20 years later, and among residents of Love Canal, who feared that children in the community might contract cancer sometime in the future (Stone & Levine, 1985).

Definition of Fear of Cancer

Berman and Wandersman (1990) reviewed the literature on fear of cancer. They defined *fear* as a rational response to an imagined or actual threat and contrasted it with *phobia*, a special form of fear that is out of proportion to the demands of the situation and cannot be explained or reasoned away by the afflicted. Phobias are beyond voluntary control and lead to avoidance of the feared situation.

Cancerphobia has been defined as the fear or belief that one is afflicted with cancer despite a lack of medical evidence or medical evidence to the contrary (Sanborn & Seibert, 1976). Berman and Wandersman (1990) proposed that if a person is in a situation where there is reason to fear contamination from toxic chemicals, such as living near a hazardous waste landfill or working in or residing near a factory that manufactures toxic chemicals, fear of cancer can be a rational response and should not necessarily be considered phobic.

Relationship Between Fear of Cancer and Outrage Characteristics of Hazardous Chemicals

Berman and Wandersman (1990) proposed that there are at least three reasons why the fear of contracting cancer is expected to be a major source of psychological disruption in the lives of individuals facing a perceived toxic hazard. First, synthetic chemicals are highly feared in our society because of much publicized carcinogenic properties of a few of these substances and because in extreme cases exposure may prove fatal to humans (Tschirley, 1983).

Second, it is difficult to detect many chemical toxins without sophisticated soil, groundwater, and organic tissue analysis, particularly if the chemicals are present in small quantities. As a result they represent unknown hidden dangers. As such, they are much more feared. Although there is only a small body of knowledge about the effects of toxic chemicals at low levels in the environment and although these effects are difficult to discern and measure, low-level exposures are the foci of most public concerns (Higginson, 1984).

Third, most people fear cancer as a loathsome fatal disease that can cause prolonged suffering, pain, disability, disfigurement, dependence, social stigma, isolation, and disruption of life-style (Brooks, 1979; Linn, Linn, & Stein, 1982). Media reports and public discussion addressing the potential physical dangers created by toxic exposure may lead people to interpret and label physical and behavioral symptoms of distress as ominous warning signs of cancer.

Combining Berman and Wandersman's (1990) analysis of fear of cancer with the outrage model of perceived risks (Hance et al., 1988) makes it clear that people's fears of getting cancer should heavily influence the acceptability of the risks of hazardous chemicals because fear of cancer should increase the level of outrage. For example, in most contamination situations, the chemicals are synthetic (not natural), difficult to detect, unfamiliar, and not well understood by science, and the risks are inescapable, are under the control of the government or industry, and may be seen as unfairly and unethically imposed. Moreover, cancer is among the most dreaded of diseases. As such, the number and seriousness of these outrage factors may overshadow quantitative estimates of cancer risks, prompting public rejection of even the smallest of risks.

Measuring Fear of Cancer

Environmental policy and litigation have been hampered by a lack of established measures of concepts important to the public, such as fear of cancer. Psychologists can develop measures for relevant constructs. In our study of residents living near a hazardous waste landfill (Wandersman, Berman, & Hallman, 1989), we investigated fear of cancer in the community. Because there were few measures of fear of cancer (Berman & Wandersman, 1990), Berman and Wandersman (1992) developed a survey (The Knowledge of Cancer Warning Signs Inventory) in which respondents rate the extent to which they believe each of 25 symptoms is a warning sign of cancer. Respondents are then asked to rate the extent to which they have been distressed by each symptom in the past week. The two scores for each item are multiplied and summed for The Fear of Cancer Index (FCI) score. Using the FCI, we compared samples located near the landfill with two samples located further away (Wandersman et al., 1989) and found that fear of cancer was significantly higher ($p < .05$, one-tailed) in the near landfill sample.

Conclusion

Throughout this article we have tried to make two basic points. First, risk perceptions that do not match scientific estimates of risk are not necessarily irrational. For example, if one believes that regulators cannot be trusted, experts are not well trained, and accidents can easily be caused by human error, then it is rational to view that risk as unacceptable. Moreover, this rationality should be understood by experts and factored into the policy process. This does not mean that quantitative risk assessments should be abandoned or ignored but that they should not be the only basis for decision making.

Second, we have suggested ways in which psychologists can play a role in informing environmental policymakers. We believe that psychologists can play many other important roles in making environmental policy as researchers, practitioners, and citizens. Many areas of psychology contain relevant theories for environmental problems, and psychologists should be encouraged to become participants in environmental research by using clinical psychology (e.g., psychological distress and coping styles), cognitive psychology (e.g., cognitive biases and decision making), community psychology (e.g., community dynamics and citizen participa-

tion in toxic hazards), environmental psychology (e.g., environmental stress), law and psychology (e.g., validity of expert testimony), and social psychology (e.g., attribution of blame and responsibility for the problem and for solutions).

There are also professional roles for psychologists to play in mediating conflict resolution, providing expert testimony, treating environmentally distressed populations, and working effectively in the fields of organizational behavior and industrial workplace safety.

As industry and government officials discover that the public can thwart potentially hazardous projects and products, they appear more willing to negotiate with the public. Psychologists can play a useful role by identifying the focus of perceptions and the way conflict resolution can proceed. Psychologists can develop reliable measures of key constructs, such as fear of cancer, that can help describe and quantify important public concerns other than mortality and morbidity.

Gathering information about these constructs and understanding their bases can be helpful in risk communication. For example, our research suggested that higher perceptions of health risk near a hazardous waste site were associated with a lack of trust of environmental regulators and workers. Attempts to communicate with the public about risks that are based only on established cancer rates or other measures of morbidity or mortality fail to address other important public concerns. More responsive risk communication efforts are necessary, such as those advocated in *Improving Risk Communication* (National Research Council, 1989).

Although policymakers seem more willing to turn to social science to help them understand public sentiment, psychologists must be careful. As Fischhoff (1990) warned, "Psychologists often *seem* needed by policymakers primarily when some of the public's behavior threatens their policies" (p. 647). In such cases, policymakers may seek the expertise of psychologists to gain public acceptance of the policymakers' views. In other cases, policymakers may use the expertise of psychologists as a substitute for public involvement. In both cases, Fischhoff warns that there is a danger that the expertise of psychologists may shift the political balance against the public's best interest, contributing to a kind of disenfranchisement.

We have argued that psychologists can help policymakers understand people's perceptions of risk and have discussed how to communicate better with the public about risks. We do not believe that consultation with psychologists should supplant citizen participation efforts, nor should insights into risk perception, fear of cancer, or risk communication be used as a tool to simply assuage public fears. Rather, consultation with psychologists should facilitate participation in policymaking by all the major stakeholders, including citizens.

There is an extensive literature on citizen participation (e.g., Heller, Price, Riger, Reinharz, & Wandersman, 1984; Wandersman & Florin, in press) that can be used to help policymakers understand participation and when and why it does and does not work. This literature can also help inform citizens in their efforts to make citizen participation effective and efficient.

Every state and locality has cause to be concerned about environmental safety. Therefore, psychologists also have roles and responsibilities *as citizens* to understand environmental issues. There are no easy answers to environmental policy issues. But putting unquestioning trust in scientists, government regulators, or politicians is clearly not the solution. All citizens need to take responsibility for becoming knowledgeable about environmental threats and the trade-offs that are necessary to counter them. By demonstrating such understanding, they can participate more effectively in developing environmental policy without having to defend themselves against charges of irrationality.

Psychologists have had a long history of involvement in helping policymaking at many levels of government. We have come a long way in understanding peoples' concerns about environmental problems and how to help citizens and policymakers talk to one another. Psychologists have the tools to contribute to the development of environmental policy that is responsive to the needs of all of the stakeholders involved. It is time for psychologists, citizens, and the government to make better use of those tools.

References

Allen, F. W. (1987). Towards a holistic appreciation of risk: The challenges for communicators and policymakers. *Science, Technology, and Human Values, 12*, 138–143.

Annas, G. (1989, October). *Ethics in modern waste management.* Paper presented at the meeting of the American Public Health Association, Chicago.

Baum, A., Fleming, R., & Singer, J. E. (1983). Coping with victimization by technological disaster. *Journal of Social Issues, 39*, 117–138.

Berman, S., & Wandersman, A. (1990). Fear of cancer and knowledge of cancer: A review and proposed relevance to hazardous waste sites. *Social Science and Medicine, 31*(1), 81–90.

Berman, S., & Wandersman, A. (1992). Measuring fear of cancer. The fear of cancer index. *Psychology and Health, 7*, 187–200.

Brooks, A. (1979). Public and professional attitudes toward cancer: A view from Great Britain. *Cancer Nursing, 2*, 453–460.

Cvetkovich, G., & Earle, T. C. (Eds.) (1992). Public responses to environmental hazards. *Journal of Social Issues, 48*(4), 1–187.

Douglas, M., & Wildavsky, A. (1982). *Risk and culture.* Los Angeles: University of California Press.

Edelstein, M. R. (1982). *The social and psychological impacts of groundwater contamination in the Legler section of Jackson, New Jersey.* Report to the law firm of Kreindler & Kreindler, New York.

Edelstein, M. R. (1988). *Contaminated communities: The social and psychological impacts of residential toxic exposure.* Boulder, CO: Westview Press.

Fischhoff, B. (1990). Psychology and public policy: Tool or toolmaker? *American Psychologist, 45*, 647–653.

Fischhoff, B., Slovic, P., Lichtenstein, S., Read, S., & Combs, B. (1978). How safe is safe enough? A psychometric study of attitudes towards technological risks and benefits. *Policy Sciences, 9*, 127–152.

Fischhoff, B., Watson, S. R., & Hope, C. (1984). Defining risk. *Policy Sciences, 17*, 123–139.

Freudenberg, N. (1984). Action for environmental health: Report of a survey of community organizations. *American Journal of Public Health, 74*, 444–448.

Freudenburg, W. R. (1988). Perceived risk: Social science and the art of probabilistic risk assessment. *Science, 242*, 44–49.

Hallman, W. K. (1989). Coping with an environmental stressor: Perception of risk, attribution of responsibility, and psychological distress in a community living near a hazardous waste facility (Doctoral dissertation. University of South Carolina). *Dissertation Abstracts International, 51/01B*, 474.

Hallman, W. K., & Wandersman, A. H. (1989). Perception of risk and toxic hazards. In D. Peck (Ed.), *Psychosocial effects of hazardous waste disposal on communities*. Springfield, IL: Charles C Thomas.

Hallman, W.K., & Wandersman, A. H. (1992). Attribution of responsibility and individual and collective coping with environmental threats. *Journal of Social Issues, 48*, 4. 101–118.

Hance, B. J., Chess, C., & Sandman, P. M. (1988). *Improving dialogue with communities: A risk communication manual for government*. Trenton, NJ: Department of Environmental Protection.

Heller, K., Price, R., Riger, S., Reinharz, S., & Wandersman, A. (1984). *Psychology and community change: Challenges for the future*. Homewood, IL: Dorsey Press.

Higginson, J. (1984). Existing risks for cancer. In P. F. Deisler (Ed.), *Occupational health and safety: 9. Reducing the carcinogenic risks in industry* (pp. 1–19). New York: Marcel Dekker.

Johnson, E. J., & Tversky, A. (1984). Representations of perceptions of risks. *Journal of Experimental Psychology: General, 113*, 55–70.

Kasperson, R. E., Renn, O., Slovic, P., Brown, H. S., Emel, J., Gobel. R., Kasperson, J. X., & Ratick, S. (1988). The social amplification of risk: A conceptual framework. *Risk Analysis, 8*, 177–187.

Kohut, A., & Shriver, J. (1989, June). *The environment* (Report No. 285). Princeton, NJ: The Gallup Report.

Linn, M., Linn, B., & Stein, S. (1982). Beliefs about causes of cancer in cancer patients. *Social Science and Medicine, 16*, 835–839.

National Research Council. (1989). *Improving risk communication*. Washington, DC: National Academy Press.

Nelkin, D. (1989). Communicating technological risk: The social construction of risk perception. *Annual Review of Public Health, 10*, 95–113.

Perspectives. (1990, April 23). *Newsweek*, p. 17.

Renn, O., Burns, W. J., Kasperson, J. X., Kasperson, R. E., & Slovic, P. (1992). The social amplification of risk: Theoretical foundations and empirical applications. *Journal of Social Issues, 48*(4), 137–160.

Russell, C. (1990, June). What, me worry? *American Health*, pp. 45–51.

Sanborn, D., & Seibert, D. (1976). Cancerphobic suicides and history of cancer. *Psychological Reports, 238*, 603.

Shodell, M. (1985). Risky business. *Science 85, 6*, 43–47.

Sjoberg, L. (1980). The risks of risk analysis. *Acta Psychologica, 45*, 301–321.

Slovic, P., Fischhoff, B., & Lichtenstein, S. (1980). Facts and fears; Understanding perceived risk. In R. C. Schwing & W. A. Albers (Eds.), *Societal risk assessment: How safe is safe enough*? (pp. 181–216). New York: Plenum Press.

Slovic, P., Fischhoff, B., & Lichtenstein, S. (1986). The psychometric study of risk perception. In V. T. Covello, J. Menkes, & J. Mumpower (Eds.), *Risk evaluation and management* (pp. 3–24). New York: Plenum Press.

Starr, C. (1969). Social benefit versus technological risk. *Science, 165*, 1232–1238.

Stone, R. A., & Levine, A. G. (1985). Reactions to collective stress: Correlates of active citizen participation at Love Canal. In A. Wandersman & R. Hess (Eds.), *Beyond the individual: Environmental approaches and prevention* (pp. 153–177). New York: Haworth Press.

Tschirley, F. (1983, November–December), Covering toxics: Put dioxin in perspective. *Scope, Scientists Institute for Public Information*, pp. 3–5.

Tyson, R. (1992, June 1). Poll: Environment tops agenda. *USA Today*, p. 1.

Upton, A., Kneip, T., & Toniolo, P. (1989). Public health: Aspects of toxic chemical disposal sites. *Annual Review of Public Health*, pp. 1–25.

U.S. Congress, Office of Technology Assessment. (1981). *The assessment of technologies for determining cancer risks from the environment.* Washington, DC: U.S. Government Printing Office.

Vaughan, E. (1993). Individual and cultural differences in adaptation to environmental risks. *American Psychologist, 48,* 673–680.

Vlek, C., & Stallen, P. (1980). Rational and personal aspects of risk. *Acta Psychologica, 45,* 273–300.

Wandersman, A., Berman, S., & Hallman, W. (1989). *Hazardous wastes, perceived risk, fears about cancer, psychological distress and health.* Paper presented at the 97th Annual Convention of the American Psychological Association, New Orleans.

Wandersman, A., & Florin, P. (in press). Citizen participation in community organizations. In J. Rappaport & E. Seidman (Eds.), *Handbook of community psychology.* New York: Plenum Press.

Willmore, R. L. (1989). Cancerphobia liability: Will this be "Tort of the decade" in the '90s? *Occupational Health & Safety, 58*(1), 18.

Note

Abraham H. Wandersman, Department of Psychology, University of South Carolina; William K. Hallman, Department of Human Ecology, Cook College, Rutgers—The State University of New Jersey.

This research was supported by an institutional grant from the American Cancer Society (ACS-IN-107). We would like to thank the following for their helpful comments on one or more of the 12 previous drafts of this article: Irwin Altman, Andrew Baum, Barbara Brown, Boyd Keenan, Lester Lefton, Elaine Vaughan, Lois Pall Wandersman, Neil Weinstein, and Brian Wilcox.

We are grateful to Steven Berman for his significant role in the research on a community located near a hazardous waste landfill reported in this article, especially the work on fear of cancer.

Correspondence concerning this article should be addressed to Abraham H. Wandersman, Department of Psychology, University of South Carolina, Columbia, SC 29208.

grassroots movements = focussed on treatment

Coal companies went from being w/o machines. mechanized. Loss of jobs, only some companies could afford to do this. Tried to blame disease on other things (silica)

46

Black Lung: The Social Production of Disease

Barbara Ellen Smith

The black lung movement that erupted in West Virginia in 1965 was not simply a struggle for recognition of an occupational disease; it grew into a bitter controversy over who would control the definition of that disease. This article examines the historical background and medical politics of that controversy, arguing that black lung was socially produced and defined on several different levels. As a medical construct, the changing definitions of this disease can be traced to major shifts in the political economy of the coal industry. As an occupational disease, the history of black lung is internally related to the history of the workplace in which it is produced. As the object of a mass movement, black lung acquired a political definition that grew out of the collective experience of miners and their families. The definition of disease with which black lung activists challenged the medical establishment has historical roots and justification; their experience suggests that other health advocates may need to redefine the diseases they hope to eradicate.

The recognition that certain forms of ill health are socially produced and therefore possibly preventable is one of the most important sources of progressive political vitality in the United Stats today. During the past decade, sporadic protest has erupted over hazardous situations in isolated workplaces and communities, from the controversy over toxic waste disposal in the Love Canal area to the protest against use of dioxin-contaminated herbicides in the Pacific Northwest. In some instances, more prolonged and widespread struggles have developed, such as the movement for black lung compensation and the current mobilization against nuclear power. These phenomena are admittedly quite diverse in their social bases, ideologies, and political goals. However, to varying degrees, all have involved the politicization of health hazards and illness, and thereby have drawn into the arena of political controversy one of the most elite professional domains in the United States-scientific medicine.

These controversies characteristically have originated in the bitter suspicions of lay people who fear that certain of their health problems are caused by industrial practices and products, but who have no scientifically credible proof to substantiate their concern. In some cases, scientists have scornfully dismissed as "housewife data" lay efforts to document these health problems.[1] Indeed, health advocates' demands for compensatory or preventive action have often encountered their most formidable ideological opposition from the ranks of the medical establishment, who come armed with the seemingly unassailable authority of "science" and characteristically argue that no action is justified until further evidence is collected. Especially in contexts like that of the petrochemical industry, where workers and sometimes residential communities are exposed to manifold hazards about which little is known and whose effects may not be manifested for decades, health advocates can be forced into a no-win situation: they must prove their case with data that do not exist, using a model of disease causation that is ill suited to multiple and/or synergistic hazards, and which a growing chorus of critics argue is structurally incapable of explaining the major health problems of our place and time, such as heart disease and stress.[2]

This article examines one health struggle, the black lung movement, during which the scientific authority of the medical establishment was itself questioned in the course of an intense political controversy over the definition of disease. The movement arose in southern West Virginia in 1968 and had as its initial goal the extension of workers' compensation coverage to victims of "black lung," a generic term for the ensemble of respiratory diseases that miners contract in the workplace. To elucidate the medical politics of this struggle, this article looks at three aspects of the history of black lung. The first section explores the major changes in medical perception of black lung and presents evidence suggesting that these shifting perceptions have been occasioned by social and economic factors ordinarily considered extrinsic to science. This section also points out the ideological and political functions of the medical definitions of this disease. The second part focuses on the history of black lung itself and argues that the respiratory disease burden is intimately related to the political economy of the workplace, the site of disease production. The final section describes the recent battle over black lung compensation, focusing on the strikingly different definitions of disease that miners and the medical establishment elaborated.

Medical Constructions of Black Lung

The history of science is popularly conceived as a continuum of concepts and paradigms evolving through time toward an ever more comprehensive and accurate understanding of a "given" external reality. However, there is a growing tradition of literature that challenges this positivist approach by classifying the scientific knowledge of any society as part of its historically specific belief systems, and viewing scientific concepts as both a consequence of and an influence upon the overall structure of social relations. Efforts to pursue this approach with regard to medical science have been especially fruitful and abundant. Scholarship has focused primarily on the ways in which medical practice has tended to reflect and uphold socially structured inequality (especially that based on class, sex and race). Some analysts have also begun to investigate the exceedingly complex correspondence between the structures, forces, and dynamics of social relations in the "body politic."[3]

The case of black lung provides an exceptionally clear example of the ways in which factors external to science have shaped and changed medical knowledge. In the United States, medical perceptions of black lung fall into three periods, bounded by major shifts in the political economy of the coal industry. Observations of miners' unusual respiratory disease burden and speculation as to its workplace origins characterized the first medical construction of black lung. This viewpoint originated in the anthracite coalfields of Pennsylvania during a period when medical knowledge and practice, health care delivery arrangements, and industrial relations between miners and operators were all in a state of flux. A completely different concept of black lung emerged in a later period from the expanding bituminous coalfields, where tight corporate control over the health care system, a stark class structure, and other factors were relevant to the medical outlook. A third concept of black lung developed gradually after World War II in the context of a highly unionized, increasingly capital-intensive industry with a union-controlled health plan for miners and their families.

The first written documents concerning miners' unusual respiratory trouble originated from the anthracite region of eastern Pennsylvania; here were located the first large-scale coal mining operations in the United States, dominated by the affiliates of nine railroads. During the 1860s and 1870s, a few physicians acquainted with this region began to publish articles remarking on miners' respiratory difficulties and speculating that they were related to the inhalation of dusts and gases in the workplace. These articles are remarkable for their detailed accounts of unhealthy working conditions and their inclusion of statements by miners themselves on their workplace health.[4]

This period prior to the hegemony of scientific medicine was characterized by a relative eclecticism and fluidity in medical knowledge, practice, and health care delivery arrangements. Some medical historians argue that the uncertain financial, professional, and social status of physicians lent more equality and negotiability to the doctor-patient relationship than is customary today.[5] In the anthracite coalfields, miners were beginning to finance their health and welfare needs through mutual benefit associations that gave financial assistance in cases of sickness, disability and death.[6] This brief period of relative fluidity in the health care system was soon eclipsed, however, by the simultaneous eradication of the benefit associations and the growth of the company doctor system. The most significant episode in this process was the strike of 1874–1875, which led to the famous Molly Maguire murder trials and resulted in the disintegration of the major anthracite trade union, the Miners' and Laborers' Benevolent Association. The powerful Philadelphia and Reading Railroad, whose affiliate Coal and Iron Company was the largest anthracite coal producer, subsequently attempted to replace the union's health and welfare functions with a Beneficial Fund financed by miners and controlled by the company. During the last two decades of the nineteenth century, as mining corporations gradually extended their control over health care delivery through the company doctor system, physicians in the anthracite fields grew silent on the subject of miner' occupational lung disease. The anthracite industry subsequently entered a period of decline from which it never recovered; the center of U.S. coal production shifted to the bituminous fields, where physicians elaborated a completely different concept of black lung.

The bituminous industry of southern Appalachia achieved national economic importance around the turn of the century and by the end of World War I was rapidly becoming the heart of U.S. coal production. In the coal camps of this rural and mountainous region, physicians did not simply ignore the existence of black lung, as many have suggested, rather, they viewed miners' diseased state as normal and nondisabling, and therefore unworthy of scientific investigation. The sources of this perception may he found partly in the political economy of the coal industry, which left a peculiarly impressive stamp on the structure of health care delivery in Appalachia.[7]

In the southern bituminous industry, coal operators initially assumed a direct role in establishing, maintaining, and controlling many social and political institutions, such as the public schools, churches, and the police. Their activities derived in part from practical necessity: companies often had to import much of their labor force into this sparsely populated area, and in order to keep these workers had to provide housing, food, and a minimum of public services. However, the operators' role was neither benign nor merely practical. The profits to be made from housing, food, and to a lesser extent medical care were often quite significant to companies attempting to survive in the highly competitive, unstable business environment of bituminous coal. Moreover, totalitarian control of coal communities, including issuance of a separate currency (scrip), domination of the police, and even control of the physical access to the towns, enabled these companies to forestall what they perceived as one of the most pernicious threats to their economic status—unionization.

Health care did not escape the logic of this competitive environment and direct domination of the work force. The company doctor was the only source of medical care in almost all rural Appalachian coal camps. Under this system, the coal company controlled the employment of a doctor, but mines were required as a condition of employment to pay for his services. The company doctors' accountability to the coal operators is one of the most obvious and fundamental reasons for the medical concepts of miners' occupational health developed during this period. Work-related accidents and later diseases spelled economic liability for the coal operators under the workers' compensation system. Any agitation for preventive action would have represented an even greater nuisance. There was instead a uniform tendency to ascribe accidents and diseases to the fault of the miner—his carelessness and personal habits, such as alcoholism. Thus, one physician in 1919, after reciting a litany of occupational safety and health hazards, including dust, gob piles, electricity, poisonous gases, and contaminated water supplies, managed to conclude: "Housing conditions, and hurtful forms of recreation, especially alcoholism, undoubtedly cause the major amount of sickness. The mine itself is not an unhealthful place to work."[8]

The medical ideology surrounding black lung was more complex than this outright denial of occupational causation. Physicians dubbed the widespread breathlessness, expectoration of sputum, and prolonged coughing fits "miners' asthma." These symptoms of lung disease were *constituted as a norm;* as such, they were to be expected and by definition were nondisabling. For example, in 1935, one physician in Pennsylvania wrote:[9]

As for as most of the men in this region are concerned, so called "miners' asthma" is considered an ordinary *condition that needs cause no worry and therefore the profession has not troubled itself about its finer pathological and associated clinical manifestations (emphasis added).*

A miner who complained of disability due to respiratory trouble was diagnosed as a case of "malingering," "compensationitis," or "fear of the mines." The social control aspects of this ideology are obvious: if disease was natural, inevitable, and nondisabling, then prevention was unnecessary. Moreover, exhibiting disability from a respiratory disease was a medically stigmatized sign of psychological weakness or simplicity.[10]

Although the company doctor system provides one explanation for this medical concept, it may also be related to class interactions in the coalfields and to some of the basic precepts of scientific medicine. It may be speculated that the company doctor's social as well as medical perspective on the coal miner and his family was influenced by the relative status of each within the coal camp environment.[11] The monoeconomy of the Appalachian coalfields produced a rather simple and vivid class structure, in which physicians, lawyers, and a few other professionals formed an island in a working-class sea. On the one hand, the superiority of the doctors' status relative to the working class was everywhere apparent—in their standard of living, language, etc. On the other hand, these physicians were in a distinctly inferior position by the standards of the medical profession as a whole, and moreover were denied numerous amenities available in more cosmopolitan surroundings. Their degraded social and physical environment was embodied in and no doubt in many cases attributed to coal miners themselves—their ramshackle houses, coarse language, "lack of culture," and so on. What was "normal" for miners, including even a chronic respiratory condition, was by no means normal for the company doctor.[12]

The outlook of scientific medicine, which around the turn of the century was gaining hegemony over other forms of medical theory and practice, is also relevant to the company doctors' conceptualization of black lung. With the rise of scientific medicine, production of medical knowledge gradually became the province of research scientists, divorced from the human patient by their location in the laboratory. Building on the precepts of cell theory and the discovery of bacteria, their efforts focused on the isolation of specific aberrations in cell function, and their correlation with discrete disease agents. The "germ theory" of disease causation, which essentially holds that each disease is caused by a specific bacterium or agent, became the basis of scientific medicine. This theory confounded the microscopic *agent* of disease with the *cause* of disease; it thus implicitly denied a role to social and economic factors in disease causation and displaced the social medicine of an earlier period.

At the level of medical practice, diagnosis became a process of identifying separate disease entities, with confirmation of the diagnosis sought in the laboratory; the patient's own testimony as to his/her condition was relegated to a decidedly secondary status. Indeed, scientific medicine involved what Jewson[5] termed the "disappearance of the sick-man" from the medical world view. The patient increasingly appeared almost incidentally as the medium for disease, eclipsed by the focus on identifying discrete pathologies. In the absence of a verifiable clinical entity, the patient was by definition (health is the absence of disease) pronounced healthy. His/her protestations of feeling ill became a matter for the psychiatrist.[13]

These features of the scientific medical outlook dovetailed with previously mentioned factors to produce the company doctors' conceptualization of black lung. To the extent that any company doctor seriously attempted to diagnose a miner's respiratory condition, the effort was informed by the search for previously established clinical entities, especially silicosis and tuberculosis. Up until very recently, silica was considered the only dust seriously harmful to the respiratory system. Moreover, silicosis possesses characteristics that scientific medicine is most conducive to recognizing as a legitimate clinical entity: it is associated with one specific agent; it produces gross pathological change in lung tissue, apparent upon autopsy; and it reveals itself relatively clearly in a characteristic pattern on an X-ray. Most coal miners were not exposed to silica in significant quantity, and their X-rays did not exhibit the classic silicotic pattern. To the extent that their X-rays revealed the pathological changes now associated with coal workers' pneumoconiosis, these too were considered normal—for coal miners.[14] Moreover, as a group, miners seemed to experience a low mortality rate from tuberculosis, considered the prime public health problem of this period. Hence developed the perversely ironic "coal dust is good for you" theory: "It is in the highest degree possible that coal-dust possesses the property of hindering the development of tuberculosis, and of arresting its progress."[15]

The company doctor system did not go unchallenged by coal miners; unrest over its compulsory character occasionally led to strikes and generated the demand for a health care plan organized on the opposite basis— union control and industry financing. Following a protracted strike and federalization of the mines in 1946, miners finally won a contract establishing such a system, the Welfare and Retirement Fund. Financed by a royalty assessed on each ton of mined coal, the Fund provided pensions, hospitalization, and medical cafe for miners and their families. Although officially directed by a tripartite board composed of representatives from industry, the union, and the public, in reality the Fund was controlled by the United Mine Workers. At the time of its creation, progressives in the health care field almost unanimously viewed the Fund as an innovative leap forward in health care delivery. Contradictions embedded in coal's postwar industrial relations subsequently compromised this vision and constricted the Fund's activities. Nevertheless, in its first decade and heyday, the Fund transformed the structure and quality of health care in the Appalachian coalfields.[16]

The establishment of the Fund made possible the beginning of a third period in the medical conceptualization of miners' respiratory disease. Progressive physicians, many organized in prepaid group practice financed through the Fund, undertook clinical research on the respiratory problems of their coal miner patients. The Fund also employed in its central office a physician whose primary responsibility was to educate the medical profession about coal miners' dust disease. These physicians were largely responsible for the trickle of literature on coal workers' pneumoconiosis that began to appear in U.S. medical journals during the early 1950s; of the articles they did not write, most depended on data from Fund-officiated hospitals and clinics. All argued essentially that "authoritative opinion to the contrary notwithstanding," coal miners suffer from a "disabling, progressive, killing disease which is related to exposure to coal dust."[17]

Despite these efforts, medical recognition of coal workers' pneumoconiosis did not evolve in an orderly, linear fashion, advanced by the inquiring gaze of these scientists. They remained a minority within the medical establishment, and coal miners in most states continued to be denied workers' compensation for occupational lung disease. The recognition that black lung was rampant among U.S. coal miners did not evolve of its own accord within the boundaries of medical science. It was forced on the medical community by the decidedly political intervention of miners themselves.

Black Lung and the Transformation of the Workplace

Since the changing medical concepts of black lung reveal more about the development of the coal industry and health care systems than the nature and extent of respiratory disease among coal miners, observers may well wonder what the history of black lung actually entails. It is extremely difficult to reconstruct satisfactorily.

Epidemiological data on miners' lung disease are simply nonexistent, except for the very recent period. The early commentaries cited previously suggest that pervasive respiratory problems accompanied the growth of the anthracite and bituminous coal industries, a conclusion corroborated by nonmedical sources;[18] however, acceptance of "miners' asthma" and a dearth of medical literature swiftly followed. Between 1918 and 1940, a few scattered studies, primarily by the U.S. Public Health Service, uncovered "extraordinary" excess mortality from influenza and pneumonia among anthracite and bituminous coal miners; their susceptibility was likely due to the work-related destruction of their respiratory systems. However, all U.S. Public Health Service research on miners' occupational respiratory disease focused on silicosis; the resulting data were mixed, but the invariable conclusion was that bituminous miners were not exposed to silica in significant quantity and were not seriously disabled by work-related lung disease.[19]

Although the lack of statistics precludes documentation of the extent of black lung, it is possible to trace the changing causes of disease by analyzing the site of disease production—the workplace. By "workplace" is meant not only the physical characteristics of the site of coal production but also the social relations that shape and are part of the workplace. The interaction between miners and operators under historically given circumstance has shaped the timing and character of technological innovation, the nature of the work process, the pace of work, and other factors relevant to the production of occupational disease. The history of black lung is thus internally related to the history of the workplace, as a physical site and a social relationship.

This history may be divided into two major periods, distinguished by their different technologies, work organizations, industrial relations, and sources of respiratory disease: handloading and mechanized mining. During the initial handloading era, which persisted until the 1930s, of utmost importance to the production of coal and disease was the highly competitive and labor-intensive character of the industry. Fragmented into thousands of competing companies, bituminous coal suffered from chronic bouts of overproduction, excess capacity, low profit margins, and fluctuating prices. Because labor represented approximately 70 percent of the cost of production, a prime tactic in the competitive struggle was to cut the cost of labor, principally by lowering the piece rate. In addition, the craft nature of the labor process rendered companies relatively powerless to control productivity and output, except by manipulating the miners' wages.[20]

These economic dynamics had important implications for the workplace as a site of disease production. The instability of the industry frequently resulted in irregular work and a lowering of the piece rate, both of which forced miners to work faster and/or longer hours in an attempt to maintain their standard of living. The impact on health and safety conditions was almost invariably negative, as miners necessarily reduced nonproductive, safety-oriented tasks, such as roof timbering, to a minimum.[21] Working longer hours in mines where "towards quitting time [the air] becomes so foul that the miners' lamps will no longer burn"[22] no doubt increased the respiratory disease risk. Moreover, a financially mandated speedup encouraged miners to re-enter their work areas as soon as possible after blasting the coal loose from the face, an operation that generated clouds of dust and powder smoke.[23]

Respiratory hazards often were especially grave in non-gassy mines, where ventilation tended to be poorest. The prospect of losing their entire capital investment in one explosion encouraged mine owners to install better ventilation systems in mines where methane gas was liberated; the non-gassy mines, however, tended to "kill the men by inches."[4, p. 244] Writing around the turn of the century, one mine inspector described in detail the ventilation problem and its implications for miners' health:[22, pp. 449–450]

> ... adequate ventilation is not applied in such [non-gassy] mines, because they can be wrought without going to the expense of providing costly and elaborate furnaces or fans, air-courses, stoppings, and brattice. From four to six cents a ton are thus saved in mining the coal that should be applied in ventilating, but saved at the expense of the workmen's health. ... Constant labor in a badly-aired mine breaks down the constitution and clouds the intellect. The lungs become clogged up from inhaling coal dust, and from breathing noxious air; the body and limbs become stiff and sore, the mind loses the power of vigorous thought. After six years' labor in a badly vented mine—that is, a mine where a man with a good constitution may from habit be able to work every day for several years—the lungs begin to change to a bluish color. After twelve years they are black, and after twenty years they are densely black, not a vestige of natural color remaining, and are little better than carbon itself. The miner dies at thirty-five, of coal-miners' consumption.

During the 1930s, the introduction of mechanical loading equipment dramatically altered the workplace, while the organizing successes of the United Mine Workers transformed relations between miners and operators. Although mechanical cutting devices were introduced into underground coal mines as early as 1876, their adoption was gradual and associated with only a partial reorganization of the craft work process. The classic changes produced by mechanization and Taylorization, such as elevated productivity, loss of job control, de-skilling, and an increased division of labor, appeared slowly in bituminous coal during the first three decades of the twentieth century. However, the widespread introduction of loading machines in the 1930s broke the craft organization of work once and for all. More technological innovation swiftly followed, with the introduction of continuous mining technology after World War II. This technology did not increase the already specialized division of labor as much as it replaced several tasks (and miners) with one central production worker—the continuous miner operator.

Virtually all sources agree that the mechanization of underground mining greatly increased dust levels and magnified the existing problems with respiratory disease.[24] Miners were quick to rename the Joy loaders "man killers" and to protest the unemployment, physical hardships placed on older miners, and health and safety problems that attended their introduction. For example, at the 1934

UMWA convention, miners debated at length a resolution demanding the removal of these machines from the mines; the few delegates who spoke against it were nearly shouted down by the tumultuous convention. One miner argued:[25, p. 192]

I heard one of the brothers say that they don't hire miners over forty years of age in their locality. I want to tell you brothers that there is no miner that can work in the mines under those conveyors [loading machines] and reach the age of forty. Those conveyors are man killers and I believe this convention should do its utmost to find some way whereby those conveyors will be abolished. . . . The young men after they work in the mine six or eight hours daily become sick, either getting asthma or some other sickness due to the dust of the conveyors and they can no longer perform their duty.

Another miner, during debate over continuous mining machinery at a UMWA Convention 22 years later, echoed those comments:[26]

. . . [T]hey are putting cost moles [continuous miners] in our mines, and I hope they don' put them in anybody else's mines. We had one man die from the effects of that procedure. We had to give them a 15-minute shift. We have had any number who have had to get off because of health. It seems that someone forgot the miners who have [to operate] the moles. . . . He stands up there and inhales the fumes and the oil and the steam that is created by the heat from the mole. He doesn't get sufficient oxygen. . . .

It would be mistaken to conclude that because mechanization was associated with increased dust levels, machines themselves were the cause of this problem. Here again the economic and political circumstances of technological innovation were critical in determining its impact on the workplace. The large coal operators introduced continuous mining technology in the midst of a desperate competitive struggle with oil and natural gas, which by the 1950s had usurped coal's traditional markets in home heating and the railroads. By making coal a capital-intensive industry and vastly increasing labor produc-

tivity, the large operators hoped to force the small, labor-intensive producers into bankruptcy and win a respectable share of the growing utility market. Of crucial importance to pace, nature, and success of this mechanization strategy was the role of the union. Headed by the authoritarian but charismatic John L. Lewis, the United Mine Workers not only accepted but aggressively promoted mechanization, believing that it would lead to institutional security, high wages, and economic prosperity.[27] Although there was widespread rank-and-file discontent with mechanization, the very process replaced labor with machinery, rendering miners redundant and their protest ineffective. Despite scattered strikes and other expressions of unrest, miners were unable to modify the policy of their union or exert significant control over the impacts of mechanization on their workplace and communities.

The result was not simply increased respirable dust in the workplace, but social and economic disaster in the coalfields. In the space of 20 years, between 1950 and 1969, the work force shrank by 70 percent. For the unemployed, the monoeconomy of the Appalachian coalfields left no alternative but migration. Coal-dependent communities became ghost towns, as some counties lost half their population in the space of 10 years. Those who managed to keep their jobs in large mines confronted increased dust, noise, high-voltage electricity, and other hazards. Supervision intensified, as the operators attempted to recoup their investments in machinery by pushing productivity higher and higher.[28]

The black lung controversy that erupted in 1968 was very much a product of and a challenge to this history. The movement represented an effort by miners and their families to reclaim the political and economic potency denied them for almost 20 years. Black lung disease in a sense became a metaphor for the exploitative social relations that had always characterized the coalfields, but worsened during two decades of high unemployment, social dislocation, and rank-and-file weakness vis-a-vis the coal industry. The goal of black lung compensation represented, in part, a demand for retribution from the industry for the devastating human effects of its economic transformation.

The Battle Is Joined

By 1968, when the black lung movement arose, the union's overt cooperation with the large operators had outworn its usefulness to the industry and outlived it tolerability for the rank and file. The major producers had thoroughly mechanized their mines, reduced intraindustry competition from small companies, and held their own against external competition from alternative fuels. Capital was flowing into the industry not only through the enormously increased productivity of its workers, which tripled between 1950 and 1969, but also in the form of investment by the oil industry. Electric utilities seemed to offer unlimited market potential. Threatening the rosy forecasts, however, were an increasingly rambunctious work force and a projected manpower shortage. An enormous turnover was beginning in the work force, as the miners who managed to keep their jobs during postwar mechanization were now retiring en masse, replaced by young workers with no necessary allegiance to the UMWA leadership. The economic prosperity rankled workers already beginning to question the sluggish collective bargaining advances of their union leaders and made strikes a more potent weapon.[29]

The first unmistakable evidence that rank-and-file rebellion was afoot erupted in the winter of 1968–1969 with the birth of the black lung movement. Originating in southern West Virginia, the movement was based in the older generation of workers who were leaving the mines. They faced retirement with a sparse pension of $100 per month (if they could meet the Fund's increasingly arbitrary and strict eligibility requirements), without the traditional cushion of the extended family and without compensation for the respiratory disease from which so many suffered.[30] Discontent focused on the demand that the West Virginia legislature pass a bill recognizing black lung as a compensable disease under the state's workers' compensation statutes.

Opposing the movement were the combined forces of the coal industry and the medical establishment. A member of the latter insisted, "There is no epidemic of devastating, killing and disabling man-made plague among coal workers."[31] Another argued, "The control of coal dust is not the answer to the disabling respiratory diseases of our coal miners."[32]

Exasperated by strident opposition and legislative inaction, miners began to quit work in February 1969 in a strike that eventually brought out 40,000 workers and shut off coal production throughout the state. Their solidarity and economic muscle forced a black lung compensation bill through the legislature; although less liberal than what miners had hoped for, they declared a victory and returned to work after the governor signed the bill into law.

This was the most dramatic and widely reported phase of the black lung movement, but it marked only the beginning. Coupled with the death of 78 miners in the violent Farmington mine explosion in November 1968, the black lung movement generated a national political debate over health and safety conditions in U.S. coal mines. In December 1969, the Congress passed a Coal Mine Health and Safety Act, which detailed to an unprecedented degree mandatory work practices throughout the industry and offered compensation to miners disabled by black lung and the widows of miners who died from the disease. Large coal companies vigorously opposed certain, but not all of the act's provisions. Most notably, they fought the extremely strict respirable dust standard of 3.0 mg/m^3, scheduled to drop to 2.0 mg/m^3 after three years; this was designed to prevent black lung. The compensation program, by contrast, was to their liking; not only did it seem to promise that the turmoil over black lung would dissolve, the program also relieved them of liability for compensation by financing benefits with general tax revenues from the U.S. Treasury.

Ironically, passage of the act ensured that the issue of black lung compensation would not die but remain the focus of a continuing movement. In 1970, the Social Security Administration began administering the claims process for compensation benefits; within the program's first week of operation, 18,000 claims poured into agency offices.[33] By the fall of the same year, letters of denial began to flow back into the coalfields. The bitterness and confusion that ensued derived partly from a pattern that repeated itself throughout thousands of these rural communities: several disabled miners and widows received black lung benefits, but their brothers or uncles or neighbors down the road were denied, even though by all appearances they were equally or even more disabled by lung disease. In other words, the criteria by which the Social Security Administration judged claimants' eligibility appeared completely arbitrary and violated local perceptions of who was disabled by black lung. Thus miners and their families pitted themselves against Social Security and the medical establishment in a bitter struggle over who would control the definition of disease and disability.

The Social Security Administration initially based its eligibility criteria on the orthodox medical conception of black lung, a view that reflects the rigidity and narrowness of the germ theory. According to this perspective, black lung is limited exclusively to one clinical entity—coal workers' pneumoconiosis (CWP); this is the only lung disease considered occupational in origin and therefore compensable. The agent (and cause) of CWP is, by definition (pneumoconiosis means "dust-containing lung"), the inhalation of respirable coal mine dust, which produces certain pathological changes in one organ (the lungs) and which are revealed in a characteristic pattern on an X-ray. The disease process is linear and quantitative; the stage of CWP is determined by the number and size of opacities on the lung field, as revealed through an X-ray. The first stages of disease, categorized as "simple" pneumoconiosis, are considered compatible with health, whereas advanced or "complicated" pneumoconiosis is severely disabling and sometimes fatal.[34]

This conception of black lung has highly significant political and ideological functions. Most important, it minimizes and depoliticizes the problem. If the *cause* of CWP is respirable dust, then prevention is a technical matter of controlling this inanimate object, rather than a political question involving the relations of power in the workplace. Moreover, most surveys find a 3 percent prevalence of complicated CWP; if this is the only stage of disease considered disabling, then a relatively small number of coal miners are functionally impaired by occupational lung disease and deserve compensation. Respiratory disability in miners with simple CWP is attributed to nonoccupational factors, above all the victims themselves and their cigarette smoking. Obviously, this entire train of thought functions to shift medical and political emphasis away from the workplace as a source of disease and onto the worker.[35]

The entire diagnostic and claims procedure also functioned to individualize what miners and other activists considered a collective problem. On a practical level, the dominant medical concept of black lung meant that claimants with evidence of complicated CWP, even if they experienced little disability, automatically received compensation; some with lesser stages who met a complex combination of other criteria also received benefits. But thousands of miners and the widows of miners, who by all appearances were equally or more disabled by respiratory disease, were denied compensation.

In the course of their movement to achieve more liberal eligibility criteria, miners and other activists implicitly elaborated a completely different understanding of black lung and its causes. Their view was not articulated by a single spokesperson or written down in a single position paper; it was woven into the culture and ideology of the movement, and in almost all respects ran counter to the dominant medical view of black lung. Indeed, the very act of insisting collectively on the reality of their own disease experience was in itself a challenge to scientific medicine, insofar as the latter tends to individualize health problems and denigrate the patients' perceptions of their own condition.

It should be stressed that the movement's ideology did not involve a wholesale rejection of science and was not based on fundamentalist religion or other antiscientific sensibilities. Indeed, some activists made skillful use of the scientific arguments of a few physicians who, because of their research findings, lent support to the black lung cause.[36] Overall, the movement's ideology was based in the collective experience of its participants. Their skepticism toward the medical establishment had historical roots in the company doctor system, which for many activists was a bitter and living memory. Their view of black lung itself was based in their own holistic experience of disease—its physical as well as psychological, social, and economic aspects. And their understanding of the causes of black lung derived from their experiences with the coal industry, as workers, as widows of men killed by the mines, and as residents of coal towns where "there are no neutrals"[37]—even scientists.

For movement participants, the medical definition of black lung as a single clinical entity principally affecting one organ of the body had little meaning, because black lung meant a transformation in their whole way of life. As one 56-year-old miner, disabled by black lung since the age of 48, described:[38]

Black lung is a cruel disease, a humiliating disease. It's when you can't do what you like to do; that's humiliating. I had to lay down my hammer and saw, and those were the things I got the most pleasure out of. The next thing I liked to do was work in my garden; now my garden's the biggest weed patch in Logan County. There were times in 1971 when I was still working that it was difficult for me to get to the bedroom when I was feeling bad. Now, of course, that's humiliating.

Many miners' analysis of the agents and causes of black lung also contrasted with the orthodox medical view. They argued that many features of the workplace had damaged their lungs, such as working in water over their ankles or breathing the fumes from cable fires. Moreover, they asserted that although respirable dust was the agent of CWP, the cause of the whole disease experience ultimately was economic:

Where do we get the black lung from? The coal companies! They've had plenty of time to lessen the dust so nobody would get it. It's not an elaborate thing to keep it down: spray water. They just don't put enough of it on there. They don't want to maintain enough in materials and water to do that. . . .[39]

Should we all die a terrible death to keep those companies going?[40]

Thus, miners developed a belief that they were *collectively entitled* to compensation, not at all because of individualized medical diagnoses of CWP but because of the common health-destroying experience that defined them as a group: work in the mine. Implicit in this view was the idea that black lung is a destructive process that begins when a miner starts work, not something that acquires legitimacy only when a radiologist can find it on an X-ray.

A disabled coal miner reported:[41]

I worked in the cleaning plant, an outside job. I had four conveyors to bring to the storage bin. I had, I'd say, 16 holes in this galvanized pipe, two rows, that's 32 holes in all, little tiny holes, to keep down the dust. I stood many a time across from that conveyor and somebody'd be on the other side, and all you could see was their cap lamp. And that's in the cleaning plant: that's outside! That's not even at the face.

In the Black Lung Association, we're asking due compensation for a man who had to work in the environment he worked in. Not that a man can't choose where he works. But he's due more than just a day's wages. He and his family ought to be compensated for the environment he worked in.

These beliefs found expression in a multitude of political demands concerning the black lung compensation program, eventually and most clearly in the demand for automatic compensation after a specified number of years' work in the mines. Federal legislation to effect this change went down to defeat in 1976. However, medical and legal eligibility requirements for compensation were so liberalized by amendments passed in 1972 and 1978 that most miners and the widows of miners who worked a substantial period of time in the mines are now receiving black lung benefits.[42]

The black lung movement has been rightly criticized for its lack of a preventive focus. Despite the clear and widely held perception that the coal companies were to blame for black lung, activists never directed their struggle at the heart of the problem, prevention in the workplace. This was partly due to the initial, erroneous view that the cost of state compensation (financed by industry) would force the companies to improve health conditions in the mines. A lasting and effective prevention campaign would have required a tighter alliance between working miners, disabled miners, and widows; a much firmer conviction that black lung is not inevitable; and, at least eventually, a political vision of how miners might improve their occupational health by asserting greater control over the workplace.

However, the black lung movement suggests that even within the confines of an after-the-fact struggle for compensation, important and intensely political issues may be at stake. This article has explored the history of black lung on many levels—as a medical construct, a product of the workplace, a disease experience, and a political battle. The evidence presented suggests that miners' experientially based view of black lung and challenge to the medical establishment have historical justification. Medical science's understanding of black lung has not derived from observation unencumbered by a social and economic context, but has been profoundly shaped by that context; as a result, it has performed crucial political and ideological functions. In one era, it served to "normalize" and thereby mask the existence of disease altogether; in the more recent period, it has tended to minimize and individualize the problem.

By contrast, black lung activists succeeded in challenging the scientific medical establishment by insisting on the validity of their own definition of disease. They viewed black lung as an experience affecting the whole person in all aspects of life. Rather than

focusing on a causal relationship between one discrete agent and one disease, they looked at the workplace as a total environment where the miner confronts an array of respiratory hazards. Finally, activists defined black lung as a collective problem whose ultimate cause was economic. In its entirety, the history of black lung suggests that a similar task of redefinition awaits other health advocates if they wish to challenge effectively the social production of disease.

Acknowledgments—This article was written under a research fellowship at the International Institute for Comparative Social Research in Berlin, West Germany. I wish to thank the Institute and its staff for their financial support, friendship, and intellectual stimulation. Conversations and correspondence with Norm Diamond, Gerd Göckenjan, and Meredeth Turshen were also an invaluable part of the process that led to this article.

References

1. NOVA. A plague on our children. WGBH Educational Foundation, Boston, 1979, film transcript, p. 35.

2. For a clear presentation of the overall argument, see Doyal, L. (with Pennell. I.). *The Political Economy of Health*. Pluto Press, London, 1979. See also Turshen, M. The political ecology of disease. *Review of Radical Political Economics* 9(1): 45–60, 1977. See also Eyer, J. Hypertension as a disease of modern Society, *Int. J. Health Serv.* 5(4): 539–558, 1975.

3. Many analysis have pointed out this relationship on a theoretical level, but only a few have attempted to apply it in concrete investigation. See the discussion concerning the relationship between capitalist work relations and technology and the scientific model of brain function (as factory manager, telephone exchange, and, today, computer) in Rose, A. *The Conscious Brain*. Alfred A. Knopf, New York, 1974. For a more general discussion, see Figlio, K. The historiography of scientific medicine: An invitation to the human sciences. *Comparative Studies in Society and History* 19: 262–286, 1977. See also Foucault, M. *The Birth of the Clinic*. Vintage Books, New York, 1973.

4. The most comprehensive discussion I found was Sheafer, H. C. Hygiene of coal-mines. In *A Treatise on Hygiene and Public Health,* edited by A. H. Buck. vol. 2. pp. 229–250. William Wood and Company, New York, 1879. Shearer wrote: "Any one who has seen a load of coal shot from a cart, or has watched the thick clouds of dust which sometimes envelop the huge coal-baskets of the anthracite region so completely as almost to hide them from sight, can form an idea of the injurious effect upon the health of constant working in such an atmosphere. The wonder is not that men die of clogged-up lungs, but that they manage to exist so long in an atmosphere which seems to contain at least fifty per cent of solid matter" (p. 245). See also Carpenter, J. T. Report of the Schuylkill County Medical Society. *Transactions of the Medical Society of Pennsylvania,* fifth series, part 2, pp. 488–491, 1869.

5. Figlio (3). Jewson, H. D. The disappearance of the sick-man from medical cosmology, 1770–1870. *Sociology* 10(2): 225–244, 1976.

6. On early financing of medical care in the coalfields, see Ginger, R. Company-sponsored welfare plans in the anthracite industry before 1900. *Bulletin of the Business Historical Society* 27(2): 112–120, 1953. See also Falk, L. A. Coal miners' prepaid medical care in the United States—and some British relationships. 1792–1964. *Med. Care* 4(1): 37–42, 1966.

7. A comprehensive survey of health care under the company doctor system was extracted from the U.S. government by the United Mine Workers of America during temporary federation of the mines in 1946. The result was the so-called Boone report. U.S. Department of the Interior. Coal Mines Administration. *A Medical Survey of the Bituminous-Coal Industry.* Government Printing Office, Washington, D.C., 1947.

8. Hayhurst, E. R. The health hazards and mortality statistics of soft coal mining in Illinois and Ohio. *J. Ind. Hygiene* 1(7): 360, 1919.

9. Rebhorn, E. H. Anthraco silicosis. *Med. Soc. Reporter* 29(5): 15, Scranton, Pennsylvania, 1935.

10. Those who persisted in their complaints of breathlessness were eventually referred to psychiatrists, according to the testimony of miners and their families during interviews with the author. The argument that miners' symptoms of lung disease were psychological

in origin may be found in Ross, W. D., et al. Emotional aspects of respiratory disorders among coal miners. *J.A.M.A.* 484–487, 1954.

11. My thought on this relationship were stimulated and clarified by Biglio, K. Chlorosis and chronic disease in 19th century Britain: The social constitution of somatic illness in a capitalist society. *Int. J. Health Serv.* 8(4): 589–617, 1978.

12. This view persists today. Abundant examples may be found, especially in journalistic and sociological literature on Appalachia. Miners are alternately romanticized and reviled, in either case, they are "a breed apart."

13. See Brown, E. R. *Rockefeller Medicine Men.* University of California Press, Berkeley, 1979. On the germ theory and its implications for the doctor-patient relationship, see Jewson (5), Figlio (3), and Berliner, H. S., and Solmon, J. W. The holistic health movement and scientific medicine: The naked and the dead. *Socialist Review* 9(1): 31–52, 1979.

14. "One radiologist in southern West Virginia says until five years ago he regularly encountered chest X-rays from physicians that showed massive lung lesions labeled 'normal miner's chest.'" Aronson, B. Black lung: Tragedy of Appalachia, *New South* 26(4): 54, 1971.

15. Meiklejohn, A. History of lung disease of coal miners in Great Britain: Part II, 1875–1920. *Br. J. Ind. Med.* 9(2): 94, 1952. This view apparently originated in Britain and was picked up by physicians in the United States.

16. See Seltzer, C. Health care by the ton, *Health PAC Bulletic* 79: 1–8, 25–33, 1977.

17. Martin, J. E., Jr. Coal miners' pneumoconiosis, *Am. J. Public Health* 44(5): 581, 1954. See also Hunter, M. B., and Levine, M. D. Clinical study of pneumoconiosis of coal workers in Ohio river valley. *J.A.M.A.* 163(1): 1–4, 1957. See also the numerous articles by Lorin Kerr in this period, especially Coal workers' pneumoconiosis, *Ind. Med. Surg.* 25(8): 355–362, 1956.

18. Nonmedical literature from all over the world suggests that coal miners have long experienced black lung. Friedrich Engels discusses miners' "black spittle" disease in *The Condition of the Working Class in England,* Alden Press, Oxford, 1971. Emile Zola's character Bonnemort in the novel *Germinal* is clearly a victim of black lung. And John Spargo, a progressive era reformer intent on the

prohibition of child labor, discusses the respiratory problems of the anthracite breaker boys in *The Bitter Cry of the Children*, Macmillan Company, New York, 1906, p. 164.

19. U.S. Public Health Service. The health of workers in dusty trades, Part III. Public Health Bulletin Number 208, Government Printing Office, Washington, D.C., 1933: U.S. Public Health Service. Anthraco-silicosis among hard coal miners. Public Health Bulletin Number 221, Government Printing Office, Washington, D.C., 1936: U.S. Public Health Service and Utah State Board of Health. The working environment and the health of workers in bituminous coal mines, non-ferrous metal mines, and non-ferrous metal smelters in Utah, 1940.

20. A lucid discussion of the labor process in this period may be found in Dix, K. *Work Relations in the Coal Industry: The Hand-Loading Era, 1880–1930*. Institute for Labor Studies, West Virginia University, Morgantown, West Virginia, 1977. On the economics of the industry, see Suffern, A. E. *The Coal Miners' Struggle for Industrial Status*. Macmillan Company, New York, 1926. See also Hamilton, W. H., and Wright, H. R. *The Case of Bituminous Coal*. Macmillan Company, New York, 1925.

21. One study actually found an inverse statistical relationship between employment levels and the rate of fatal accidents. See the discussion in Dix (20), pp. 101–104.

22. Roy, A. *History of Coal Miners of the U.S.* J. L. Prauger Printing Company, Columbus, Ohio, 1907, p. 119.

23. In some cases, state law or local practice dictated that coal be shot down at the end of the day, allowing the atmosphere to clear overnight. However, this was not uniform practice throughout the industry.

24. Physician, miners, and government officials seem to agree on this point: representatives from industry in some cases demur. There is also disagreement about the magnitude of any increase in respiratory disease. See *Papers and Proceedings of the National Conference on Medicine and the Federal Coal Mine Health and Safety Act of 1969, Washington, D.C.*, 1970. Debate on these questions also runs through the many volumes of testimony on the 1969 act. See U.S. Senate, Committee on Labor and Public Welfare, Subcommittee on Labor, *Coal Mine Health and Safety.* Hearings, 91st Congress, 1st session, Government Printing Office, Washington, D.C., 1969.

25. United Mine Workers of America, *Proceedings of the 33rd Consecutive Constitutional Convention*. United Mine Workers of America, Indianapolis, Indiana, 1934, vol. 1.

26. United Mine Workers of America, *Proceedings of the 42nd Consecutive Constitutional Convention*. United Mine Workers of America, Washington, D.C., 1956, see pp. 306–331.

27. Lewis clearly articulated this position in his book, *The Miners' Fight for American Standards,* Bell Publishing Company, Indianapolis, Indiana, 1925.

28. This paragraph compresses an enormous social and economic transformation into a few sentences. For a detailed description of the changed industrial relations in this period, see Seltzer, C. The United Mine Workers of America and the coal operators: The political economy of coal in Appalachia, 1950–1973. Ph.D. dissertation, Columbia University, 1977.

29. See David, J. P. Earnings, health, safety, and welfare of bituminous coal miners since the encouragement of mechanization by the United Mine Workers of America, Ph.D. dissertation, West Virginia University, 1972. David demonstrates how miners fell behind workers in certain other unionized industries during this period.

30. In 1969, the U.S. Surgeon General estimated that 100,000 coal miners were afflicted with CWP. A study of 9,076 miners, conducted between 1969 and 1972, found a 31.4 percent prevalence of the disease among bituminous miners; among those who had worked 30 to 39 years in the mines, prevalence rose to over 50 percent. See Morgan, W. K. C., et al. The prevalence of coal workers' pneumoconiosis in U.S. coal miners. *Arch. Environ. Health* 27: 222, 1973. Current prevalence in the work force runs around 15 percent. These data are all on CWP. Black lung, i.e., the whole disease experience that miners consider occupational in origin, is not considered a legitimate concept by scientific medicine, and its prevalence is unknown. In scientific medical terms, black lung includes CWP, bronchitis, emphysema, and possible other unrecognized disease processes. The prevalence of this ensemble of diseases is of course higher than that of CWP alone.

31. Dr. Rowland Burns, as quoted in the Charleston (West Virginia) *Daily Mail*, January 15, 1969.

32. Dr. William Anderson, as quoted in the Charleston (West Virginia) *Gazette*, April 16, 1969.

33. U.S. House, Committee on Education and Labor, *Black Lung Benefits Program.* First Annual report. Government Printing Office, Washington, D.C., 1971.

34. The views of W. K. C. Morgan and his associates represent the dominant position of the medical establishment on CWP. See Morgan, W. K. C. Respiratory disease in coal miners. *Am. Rev. Resp. Dis.* 113: 531–559, 1976.

35. For example: "The presence of severe shortness of breath in a coal miner with simple CWP is virtually always related to a nonoccupationally related disease, such as chronic bronchitis or emphysema, rather than to coal mining. . . . Smoking is by far the most important factor in producing respiratory symptoms and a decrease in ventilatory function." Morgan (34), pp. 540–541.

36. Several physicians took the side of miners in the black lung controversy, arguing that the degree of respiratory disability does not correlate with X-ray stages of CWP and that disability of miners with simple CWP is often occupationally related. Some explained this phenomenon by hypothesizing that the disease process is pulmonary vascular in nature, i.e., it affects the vessels of the lungs, impairing their ability to exchange gases with the bloodstream. Hyatt, R. E., Kistin, A. D., and Mahan, T. K. Respiratory disease in southern West Virginia coal miners. *Am. Rev. Resp. Dis.* 89(3): 387–401, 1964. See also Rasmussen, D. L., et al. Respiratory impairment in southern West Virginia coal miners. *Am. Rev. Resp Dis.* (10): 658–667, 1968.

37. As in a line from a famous song by Florence Reese, "Which Side Are You On?", inspired the mine wars in Harlan County, Kentucky, during the 1930s.

38. Author's interview with disabled coal miner, Logan Country, West Virginia, September 6, 1978.

39. Author's interview with disabled coal miner, Raleigh County, West Virginia, September 19, 1978.

40. Author's interview with disabled coal miner, Raleigh County, West Virginia, August 24, 1978.

41. Author's interview with disabled coal miner, Raleigh County, West Virginia, September 19, 1978.

42. By 1978, approved claims exceeded 420,000 and amendments enacted in that year are pushing the total even higher. This does not mean, however, that eligibility requirements will not be tightened in the future. Indeed, the current trend is to do so. See General Accounting Office, *Legislation Allows Black Lung Benefits To Be Awarded without Adequate Evidence of Disability*. Report to the Congress, Government Printing Office, Washington, D.C., 1980.

47

Multi-Party Responses to Environmental Problems: A Case of Contaminated Dairy Cattle

George E. B. Morren, Jr.

ABSTRACT: This paper presents a framework for exploring the temporal and behavioral aspects of the responses of various involved parties that may lead to governmental intervention in situations involving exposure of the public to hazardous substances. The activities of key individuals are closely scrutinized. Relevance of the framework to agricultural and food concerns is also indicated. The exemplary case is the contamination of livestock in Michigan that began in 1973, but other cases are discussed that conform closely to the pattern described by the framework.

Introduction

This paper presents a framework for exploring the courses of action taken by the various parties involved in incidents in which large numbers of people have been exposed to hazardous substances. Debates about the nature of the problems and the appropriateness of remedial responses that precede governmental interventions are of particular concern. I focus specifically on the characteristic responses of victims, officials, and responsible parties (such as industrial firms) and link them to changing awareness and political activity. I am also concerned to explain the actions of key individuals who seem to rise from obscurity in crises and extend their capabilities to influence overall results.

To accomplish these objectives, I closely examine a specific case, the contamination of Michigan's milk supply by polybrominated biphenyl and related isomers that began in 1973. This was an early incident of a *type* involving large scale chemical tainting of livestock and poultry that was to occur with some frequency in the U.S. over the next 15 years. For example, in addition to Michigan, serious incidents involving contaminated milk have been reported in the states of Arkansas, Texas, Indiana, Mississippi, Louisiana, and Hawaii.

* From *Agriculture and Human Values, vol. 6, no. 4,* Fall 1989. "Multi-Party Responses to Environment Problems" by George E. B. Morren, Jr. Reprinted with kind permission of Kluwer Academic Publishers.

Since 1981 alone, Arkansas has had at least four serious incidents affecting its livestock, dairy, and poultry industries. These cases seem to be of a piece, not only with the Michigan case, but also with other local problems involving chemical and radiological hazards, such as Three Mile Island (Ford, 1982), Love Canal (Brown, 1981; Gibbs, 1982; Levine, 1982), and Woburn, Massachusetts (DiPerna, 1985).

As the public generalizes its concerns about environmental risk and its distrust of industry and government becomes more volatile, the food and agriculture industry and related government agencies will be increasingly caught up in the kinds of contentious situations that formerly were the domain of the manufacturing and service sectors. National debates on food and agriculture-related issues are already firmly established and have been assimilated by federal agencies.

In some cases, local controversies have been sufficiently intense as to put some growers and firms out of business, to induce others to change basic features of their operations, and to generate high levels of uncertainty for the industry as a whole. Food-related industries are increasingly (even particularly) vulnerable to this kind of scenario, even as the performance of responsible governmental agencies remains spotty and their vulnerability to external (and even internal) criticism increases. Here my focus is primarily on the local and state arenas where controversies currently surround such issues as aerial pesticide applications, contaminated packaging (including dioxin in milk cartons), agricultural nuisances, pure food, the manufacture of agricultural chemicals, non-point source impacts on local water quality, biotechnology, food irradiation, antibiotics in feed and in food, and agricultural applications of sewage sludge.

A Processual Outline of Responses

In the best of all possible worlds, government intervention occurs only[1] when responses at lower levels prove inadequate to the task due to the magnitude and scope of the problematical situation and[2] if the people experiencing a problem request it. Of course, we do not live in an ideal or even a parsimonious world; some governments and processes are more democratic than others, politicians and bureaucrats in all systems seem to have totalitarian impulses, some parties to a situation have more influence or power than others, some policies were designed to deal with problems that no longer exist (Gardner, 1963), and so on. Experience also suggests a third condition for governmental action, the existence of appropriate policy and the machinery to implement it. For issues below the policy threshold—often involving novel problems treated as familiar ones—actions appear not to be purposeful. Thus, Lindblom (1959) has described public planning as involving, not systematic problem solving and rational weighing of fundamental issues, but a process of "muddling through."

There are always people somewhere who are experiencing difficulties that *might* be addressed by their governments, but are not. Some students of public policy have asserted that it is just as interesting and productive to study "unpolitics"—inaction, the absence of debate, or non-decision-making on issues that objectively exist—as to study action in the public-policy arena (Crenson, 1971). Indeed, inaction is as characteristic a pose of government as action. This is because officials have a vested interest in keeping their own bureaucratic situations on an even keel, of changing how they do business as little as possible (Reich, 1970). Another source of inaction is that people have an interest in husbanding their autonomy by keeping government at arms length *most of the time.* This is because government sponsored interventions are frequently felt as uninvited, authoritative, inappropriate, costly and hard to reverse. Hence, too, they are often seen as a last resort.

Nevertheless, situations arise in which people not only need to mobilize resources beyond their own but, having recognized the need, demand intervention by government. What often ensues, however, is not mutual learning and constructive debate among concerned citizens, officials, and industry representatives, but rather a pattern of non-debate, denial, inaction, and efforts to convince people that their concerns are imaginary or that the state has a monopoly on concern and expertise. This seems generic to novel problems and situations (or those perceived to be novel) for which there is no explicit policy or official pattern of response.

Thus with issues that are still "below the surface," in what is sometimes described as a "policy-vacuum," a complex and interactive process unfolds. This is presented in outline form in Figure 47.1. This outline should not be interpreted as a hard and fast *thing* or system, but rather as a heuristic device for examining and comparing cases. Thus, in the account which follows, I distinguished between *victims* who are initially the first people to feel the lash of a problem but are subsequently joined by a larger concerned public, *officials* who are the bureaucratic decision-makers and scientists, and *industry representatives* who are business executives or their spokespeople who may present themselves as victims too.

For convenience of presentation, I group responses and related processes into four sectors, each describing an escalatory process; official responses, victims' responses, *awareness* of victims and the larger public, and *political activity*. The four sectors involve acts, events, and consequences that are broadly interactive. *Awareness* is viewed as setting the bias of the three other sectors, affecting the level at which a particular situation enters the trajectory and promoting or resisting escalation. Clearly, officials do not always ignore problems. More importantly, by responding to a problem in one locality they foster awareness and a heightened sense of risk in others (see below). In addition, the activities listed under the rubric of political activity in particular serve to articulate the other three by establishing the mix of participants, interests, and value-laden worldviews *(weltanschauungen)* represented in public

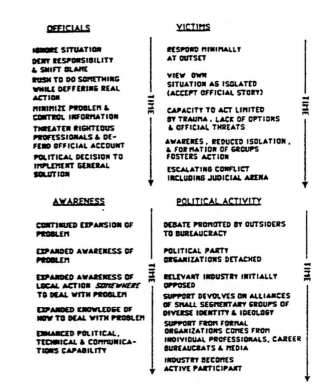

Figure 47.1 Outline model of multi-party responses to a hazard.

and private debates that may lead to policy making and regulatory action. Politics also brings yet other kinds of actors into play; e.g., journalists. I begin by discussing the responses of stereotypical "officials."

Officials

Government officials, and sometimes executives of large businesses accused of responsibility for a situation, adhere to a scenario that repeats itself over and over again:

1. Authorities ignore the situation as long as possible.
2. If passed, they deny responsibility and attempt to shift blame to others, possibly including the victims.
3. In response to mounting pressure they may rush to be seen doing something (anything) on the basis of preliminary information on the situation.

4. Their preferred style, however, is to defer action based on the need to do more studies according to their own priorities (and to ignore the priorities of the people concerned).

5. They then minimize the extent of the problem, while also controlling all information about it including the existence of other victims, a reflexive coverup that slows the spread of awareness and political activity.

6. Outside interveners, such as experts employed by concerned citizens or righteous professionals, who attempt to falsify the emerging official description of the situation, do so at the risk of physical threats or of being called dissidents or professional incompetents when, in fact, they are "whistle blowers." Although not inevitable, at this point in the process, the action can cross a threshold and shift from the bureaucratic arena to a more broad based political debate on the way to new policies.

7. As a result of actions taken by victims and advocates to force an issue into the political arena, new policies may emerge. These are often in the form of legislation, providing officials with a general solution that assimilates problems previously viewed as novel to established models and routines.

Victims

The behavior of victims of a serious spreading problematic situation also seems to follow a typical scenario that interacts with industrial and official behavior in unfortunate ways:

1. Victims also respond minimally at the outset and try to deal with novel and unprecedented problems as if they were familiar ones.

2. They may view their situations as isolated and accept official accounts (if any), even guilt and blame.

3. Resisting escalation to higher levels, the capacity of victims to act effectively may be inhibited by physical and emotional trauma as well as limited resources and conflicting objectives.

4. In any event, action usually depends on awareness that they, as victims, are not alone. In other words, awareness falsifies the perception of novelty or restricted scope and promotes escalation.

5. With regard to the foregoing, expertise is no guarantee against victimization, although sophisticated victims may have an enhanced ability to "learn their way" through a situation and the confidence to resist official or industry denigration, obfuscation, and coercion.

6. Victims achieve their greatest success when they band together with other concerned people to form an advocacy group or make use of existing local institutions to take action. Such actions typically force escalation and reduce the options of other parties to the situation while possibly increasing their own.

Advocacy groups have a mixed character (see Gerlach & Hine, 1973; Zald & McCarthy, 1987). Important features may include, (1) how long they have persisted after a catalyzing situation or the emergence of the problems that form their reason for being, (2) their evolving organizational structures, and (3) whether or not they have looked beyond local issues and advocacy to take on other problems and roles. Advocacy groups have important roles to play in forcing debates about change, broadening the participatory base of debates, and mobilizing people and resources. New, highly local groups form around specific situations such as a hazardous waste dump, a nuclear power plant, a resource development proposal or some other source of perceived risk. They raise funds, organize demonstrations, lobby local political leaders, hire "experts" such as lawyers, and engage in litigation. Beginning as totally independent cells, they may also form alliances with similar groups for specific actions and join together in regional or even national "clearinghouse" organizations that serve as information exchanges. By the same token, they may also fade away once closure has been achieved regarding the situation that led to their original formation. Emergent leaders are unlikely to enter and rise in formal institutions, but rather make a career of being outsiders.

Established organizations such as the Sierra Club and other national environmental groups and the National Farm Bureau Federation have the characteristics of formal organizations (although local chapters may have some autonomy). Unlike grass roots advocacy groups, they have a formal hierarchical structure, permanent salaried staff for managerial and even operational functions and to provide expertise in science and technology, lobbying, law, public relations and so on. They are able to sustain efforts across a broad front on issues affecting their constituencies rather than being single-issue "adhocracies." They also tend to establish close working relationships with legislative and executive agencies, relevant science organizations, and industrial groups in order to operate backstage as well as in public. It is not unusual for ranking members of established movement groups to make careers of moving among these institutions; e.g., from "club" to industry or agency to university, and so on, as social movement organization professionals or even entrepreneurs (McCarthy & Zald, 1987:380ff).

Awareness

In a study of the circumstances surrounding the passage of air pollution control legislation, Crenson claims that, "the only way to prevent air pollution legislation from being enacted is to prevent *the issue* from coming up in the first place (1971:87; emphasis mine)." A technique commonly employed to keep "the cat in the bag" for as long as possible (in hopes that the issue will go away by itself) is to avoid sharing knowledge, especially knowledge of the existence of other concerned people or victims, to maintain that the victims' situations are unique, and that somehow they brought them on themselves. The "cat can be let out of the bag," the novelty challenged, and the action or policy vacuum broken regarding such an issue by:

1. Continued expansion of the problem;
2. Increased and widening awareness of the expansion of the problem;
3. Increased and widening awareness of a localized event involving a comparable problem and/or action *somewhere* to deal with it;
4. Increased knowledge of how to deal with the particular kind of problem based on experience and models developed in pioneering localities;
5. The decision by policy-makers to implement a general solution affecting all localities where local solutions have not been implemented or have not been effective, as well as localities that haven't even experienced or discovered the problem in the first place;
6. The ability of victims of new incidents to place credible claims is now greatly enhanced due to official redefinitions of problems and the scope of agency responsibility. Thus, after the Love Canal episode, environmental and health agencies around the country behaved differently than they had before when confronted by the public with a case involving hazardous waste.

The reference in number 3, above, to "a localized event . . . 'somewhere'" is not an appeal to chance, but a statement of the contingent nature of the process. Arguably, situations involving actual or potential hazards of many kinds occur everywhere and remedial actions may even be advancing for some. People in many places that are subject to a hazard may be totally or marginally ignorant of it and its potential implications. That changes when a "major" event occurs as signalled by broad media coverage. I refer to such situations as "catalyzing" events because, until they occur, all the other necessary ingredients of a situation may be present in many localities or agencies, but lacking awareness, nothing happens. Possible examples of catalyzing events include the Denora, Pa. air pollution disaster, Love Canal, N. Y., Times Beach, Mo., and Bhopal, India. With respect to the framework, this means that escalation is not linked inevitably to the objective magnitude of the problem, but rather depends on the growth of awareness and the strength of forces resisting escalation.

Political Activity

The political activity surrounding this emergence also follows a pattern with these features:

1. The people who first promote the debate are outsiders to the relevant bureaucracies or political bodies, for example, leaders of local *ad-hoc* advocacy groups.
2. Conventional political party organizations are detached from the issue.
3. Relevant business and industry, after *initial* and even prolonged opposition, sooner or later become active participants in policy-making to shape it to their interests.
4. Support for action on the issue does not become consolidated in formal organizations, but rather is carried forward by individuals and a myriad of small groups and grass roots organizations of diverse identity and orientation that form alliances and coalitions.
5. Support from formal organizations is by *individual* professionals and career bureaucrats in relevant agencies and from the news media.

Print and electronic journalists play a crucial role because, by disseminating information about common problems and improvements, they promote debate. Their "nose for news" can be sharpened through understanding of the local situation and the performance of government agencies. Employees of government agencies can themselves benefit from exposure to the "big picture" if it makes them more critical of their own and colleagues' biases. Such insiders do, however, run the risk of being seen as disloyal and insubordinate.

The following case, involving widespread contamination of the human food chain with an exotic chemical, illustrates many of the points raised in the foregoing discussion. It shows the very rapid divergence between victims and officials regarding the identification of the problem and possible remedies due, at least in part, to the inability of official scientists to explore novelty with an open mind and to listen to citizen concerns. It describes an advocacy organization unable to fulfill its perceived mission and role by conflicts of interest and structural constraints. The fact that a key victim possessing excellent scientific credentials was only marginally better off than less sophisticated victims tends to give the lie to the claim frequently made by government and industry scientists that people are to blame for their own ignorance. It is a revealing and ironic situation that highlights the frequent dominance of worldview over science.

The Contamination of Michigan's Food Chain[3]

In the spring of 1973, a truck belonging to St. Louis Freight Lines, a common carrier, loaded a ton of polybrominated biphenyl (PBB) from the Michigan Chemical Corporation (MCC) and delivered it to a feed mill of Farm Bureau Services (FBS), a subsidiary of Michigan Farm Bureau (MFB), ostensibly the farmers' own advocacy and support organization.[4] FBS, with 87 mills and more than 200 dealers, was the largest agricultural feed supplier in the state.

MCC is a subsidiary of Northwest Industries, itself a subsidiary of Velsicol Chemical Corporation, one of the most heavily penalized firms in the chemical industry (Epstein, et al., 1982:49). This kind of corporate structure has functioned in the past to compartmentalize legal responsibility and buffer "parent" companies from potentially serious damage claims and other risks.[5]

The delivery was a catastrophic mistake. The feed plant had ordered a ton of magnesium oxide (also known as "Milk of Magnesia"), an innocuous substance used to enhance the digestion of livestock and marketed by MCC under the trade name Nutrimaster. MCC was also a supplier of PBB, a fire retardant used in industry, under the trade name Firemaster. Due to a paper strike at this time, many of its chemical products were packed in plain 50 pound brown sacks distinguished only by crudely stenciled labels.

Workers at the mill routinely mixed the bags' contents into succeeding batches of feed, which were then sold all over the state. Other feed mixtures prepared in the same machines were also tainted. FBS shipped bags of supposed magnesium oxide to other mills and dealers as well. Soon entire farm herds and flocks were dead or dying. Dairy animals, the usual consumers of the augmented feed, were especially hard hit, but sheep, beef cattle, and poultry also were affected. Ultimately, as many as 100,000 cattle died or were destroyed, as well as millions of chickens and thousands of swine and sheep. While animals were dying, livestock continued to be slaughtered and contaminated animal products, including milk, meat and eggs, marketed throughout the region to be eaten by urban dwellers as well as farm families who consumed their own produce. In the end, medical authorities estimated that 9 million people, the entire population of the State of Michigan, had measurable levels of PBB in their tissue. The worst symptoms occurred in farm families.

PBB belongs to a novel family of chemical called *halogenated hydrocarbons.* They are made from "basic hydrocarbon" or petroleum fraction molecules by adding atoms of elements known as halogens; chlorine, bromine or iodine. Bromine is the element that contains the desired fire-retardant character, which is added to the hydrocarbon benzene to produce PBB. In order to reduce the fire death rate in the U.S., use of fire retardants is mandatory in certain consumer goods. Unfortunately, many of the substances used for this purpose are suspected carcinogens and mutagens as well as being extremely toxic.

Measuring toxicity is hardly straightforward. One of many complicating factors is that there is no such thing as a "pure" chemical. Manufacturing gives rise to chemical variations known as *isomers,* small differences in molecules, so that there are more than 100 different PBBs. These are thought to have varying toxicities and their presence complicates the task of identification. Moreover, products include accidental contaminants as well as intentional additives that may increase their toxicity while also making medical and veterinarial diagnosis more difficult. When authorities finally got around to testing for PBB, they only looked for one isomer and contaminents were overlooked entirely.

In the Michigan case, the health of hundreds of thousands of people who consumed large quantities of PBB-contaminated animal food products was seriously affected. PBB and other halogenated hydrocarbons are novel toxicological agents because they do not act in organisms the way familiar poisons do. PBB accumulates in the tissues of exposed people and animals alike and it is thought that repeated small doses are potentially more injurious than a few massive exposures. Symptoms included extreme fatigue, dizziness, headache, neurological deterioration, skin problems including chloracne, stomach ailments, unusual nail growth, hair loss and increased susceptibility to disease (Epstein et al., 1982:49n). Most scientists and technical people, including veterinarians, physicians, and university and government experts, confronted these problems with fatal ignorance compounded by arrogance. Farm families, the early victims, initially faced the situation with bewilderment, fear and guilt and later with hurt, anger and a sense of betrayal. Their physical ailments were difficult to separate from the emotional effects of the economic impacts.

The mysterious symptoms did not begin to appear in the herds of FBS customers until the summer of 1973 as farmers exhausted their supplies of farm-grown silage and substituted purchased feed. An early victim with a singular role to play was Rick Halbert, a third generation Michigan dairy farmer, who held an

M.S. in chemical engineering from Michigan State. Between August and October, 1973, he and his father, who operated a neighboring dairy farm, bought 65 tons of magnesium oxide enriched feed from FBS. Ironically, the feed mixture itself had been produced to Mr. Halbert's specifications. For some time after problems emerged, he was convinced that it was custom blended for him alone and that therefore his problem was unique. In fact, FBS had appropriated the idea and distributed the mixture widely in the state.

For the Halberts, "the story . . . began to unfold with a vague uneasiness about dropping milk production" (Halbert & Halbert 1978:7). The first sick cows were observed on 20 September, with the first death in October. Symptoms included loss of appetite, sudden drop in milk production, grotesquely curling hoofgrowth, dull, matted coat, thick, wrinkled skin, loss of balance, still born and grossly deformed calves, reduced disease resistance, mastitis and metritis, uterine problems, and teeth grinding due to abdominal pain.

Rick Halbert suspected feed problems right away. He even focused on the additive and *queried FBS directly about it* to seek assurance that magnesium oxide had been used. FBS was explicitly reassuring. He noted the resemblance of the symptoms to those reported in incidents involving other chemical contaminants including pesticides and also one involving chlorinated napthalenes (in the end, brominated napthalenes were found as a contaminant of the PBB!). At the request of Halbert's vet, two diagnostic veterinarians from the Michigan Department of Agriculture (MDA) visited the Halbert farm and gathered samples to test for routine bacterial, viral, and fungal problems. A dairy scientist from MSU who also visited the farm concurred that it seemed to be a non-specific feed problem, and recommended that they change every item in the cows' diet. The general health of the herd improved somewhat after that although milk production continued to plummet, from 33,000 to 8000 pounds and later a general deterioration of the herd set in.

The Halberts lost $80,000 in the remaining four months of 1973. Most important, due

to sharply reduced milk production, they lost their "milk base," the annual quota assigned by the Federal Milk Market Administration. This meant that even if the family's herd returned to former levels of production, the difference between the old and the new quotas would have to be sold at a punishingly low price (Halbert & Halbert 1978:54–59).

At this point everyone, except possibly Rick Halbert himself, treated the situation as a routinely familiar and isolated problem. Apparently, none of the Halberts neighbors used the same feed and when, as late as February, 1974, he queried FBS directly about other complaints, they claimed he was the only one. This was a falsehood that was to be maintained in various guises throughout the crisis as FBS and government agencies consistently minimized the magnitude and scope of the problem as a rationale for inaction. Later it was revealed that *all* the hundreds of farmer victims had been told that their problems were unique and that *their own* poor husbandry practices were to blame.

"They thought it was like Watergate and they called it Cattlegate. But there was no big coverup. It was not what was done that was wrong, but what was not done by a number of people in authority who did not realize the magnitude of the problem." Harry Iwasko, state official cited in Egginton (1980:84).

Halbert quickly learned that "little but frustration was to be gained in making a formal approach to a government institution, even though this was usually the place with the expertise (Egginton 1980:59)." The Michigan Department of Agriculture and Michigan State University were unresponsive as were the federal Department of Agriculture and the Detroit office of the Food and Drug Administration. He had contacted all directly and was brushed off on the basis that this was one farmer's problem and thus highly localized. Some private labs out of state could do some of the work, but at a price (FBS commissioned such work but held the results privately). Under these circumstances, Halbert developed his own technique for penetrating state and federal agencies, taking circuitous routes around them until he found an *individual* who was interested in the case and willing to do some research. In this way he reached USDA research scientists at Ames (reproduction specialist), Baton Rouge (mycologist), and Beltsville (toxicologist) to pick up pieces of the problem. It was at Ames where samples were subjected to gas chromatography because of Rick's suspicions about pesticides. *By accident,* the lab left the machine turned on over lunch time and the peaks that were later found to represent the heavy PBB molecules were first discovered.[6]

Finally a Beltsville livestock toxicologist, to whom Rick Halbert had speculatively sent a sample of feed, identified PBB. This was in April 1974, 8 months after the sickness had first appeared in the Halbert cattle. By this time, more than 90 percent of the PBB was already in the environment, in livestock, in food products on grocery shelves, in refrigerators and freezers, and in human tissue. This was the cost of bureaucratic delay.

Although Rick Halbert thought that now his and other farmers' problems were over, they were really only beginning. The Food and Drug Administration responded to the Beltsville report by ordering a check of feed stocks in the state. MDA introduced a quarantine program barring shipment of milk from herds in which contamination levels exceeded 1 part per million (ppm) of PBB. In the years to come, however, no ban was ever placed on marketing meat from quarantined or otherwise contaminated herds, not even after a program to dispose of contaminated cattle by burial was introduced. Little was done to prevent contamination or even "re-recontamination" of feed plants, farm and barns. Indeed, a "Silent Spring" situation developed on many farms, with a wide range of fauna disappearing, even earthworms.

Undoubtedly, part of the problem was the absence of press notice and coverage. Studies of news reporting on a wide range of environmental disasters show that reporters depend on government spokespeople disproportionately as news sources (Media Institute, 1985). Since the government was denying the existence of a problem, there was *no news.* It is also the case that the big aggressive newspapers are typically located in cities and, hence, reporters are removed from rural issues.

The first news story on the disaster appeared on an inside page of the *Wall Street Journal* on 8 May 1974; Michigan papers were largely silent until as late as 1977. The story of what actually occurred inside the feed plant back in 1973 was "broken" by a trade paper, the *Michigan Farmer*, in November, 1975. The Michigan Farm Bureau immediately cancelled its $45,000 per year advertising account. It was not until early 1977 that the two biggest papers in the state, the *Detroit Free Press* and the *Detroit News* produced any indepth reporting at all. This was probably because the authorities' success in preventing the consuming public from making the connection between farmer's difficulties and their food supply was finally unravelling due to the actions of a health advocacy group and a small number of state legislative aides.

State health authorities were virtually inactive. The State Department of Public Health carried out one poorly conceived study comparing families living on officially quarantined farms with other farm families but, since the criteria for quarantine were so arbitrary, it is likely that many unquarantined farms were highly contaminated too. Nevertheless, for several years this study was used as a rationale for not carrying out more thorough work.

The first disturbing health information came from a survey conducted by a citizens group. It was not until 1977 that the state Health Department carried out a serious study, this time of maternal milk. They were shocked to find PBB in 96 percent of the women sampled and levels up to 4 times that allowed in cows milk sent to market, 1.22 ppm, in certain rural areas. In the summer of 1976, a state legislative aide contacted Dr. Irving Selikoff, head of the Environmental Sciences Laboratory of New York's Mount Sinai Hospital. Almost two years *earlier* Selikoff had informally agreed to send a team to Michigan, but state authorities never issued an invitation. Now such authority was forthcoming from the legislative leadership and Selikoff's large team of specialists arrived to begin their work in an unused wing of a Grand Rapids hospital in 1976. Preliminary results announced in January, 1977 found a variety of PBB isomers in subjects, that 40 percent had some neurological disorders with memory lapse the most dramatic symptom, and also that many had skin, breathing, and joint problems. Later analysis also confirmed that many suffered from damage to their immuno-suppressive system. Selikoff urged that the so-called tolerance level established by state authorities be reduced to as close to zero as possible. Later, with state support, the study was extended to include urban residents and Selikoff's team was the source of the finding that all 9 million Michigan residents carried PBB in their systems.

An exchange between Selikoff and a Michigan State University scientist at a conference in October, 1977 summarizes the four-year stance and worldview of official science during the catastrophe. The M.S.U. scientist, "I've got to stick up for the Department of Agriculture. . . ." Replied Selikoff, "You have to stick up for the truth. You have no other options."

Conclusions

This case should be compared with other incidents involving chemical contamination to see if all follow similar patterns along the lines described earlier in this paper. In my view, a critical element in this unfolding situation was the absence of awareness, common expressions of concern, and the development of public discussion and debate. Hence, in this seemingly novel situation, timely and effective action by agencies with appropriate capacities was also lacking. Without intending to blame them directly, the silence of the press was critical. This was fostered by the success of Michigan Farm Bureau and Farm Bureau Services in controlling both the flow of information and state governmental processes including regulatory performance.

The farmers certainly had strong grievances against all of the institutions they thought had originally been set up to serve them; their advocacy organization, their college of agriculture, and the various state and federal agencies that existed to deal with this kind of issue (Coyer & Schwerin, 1981).

From time to time, national organizations or their local cells became "derailed" when they take on ancillary functions for their constituents that develop into serious structural constraints on their advocacy roles. Even quotidian activities such as selling advertising space in an organization's publications or taking ads in trade media can compromise a group's proclaimed mission. This is one interpretation of what happened to the Michigan Farm Bureau. From being the (at least large) farmer's advocate it branched out into farm supplies. When those operations went bad it dealt with its constituency/clientele like many other companies have in the past, attempting to contain the problem and to minimize liability. This left Michigan farmers with *no effective advocate.*

It is also important to note that the *novelty* issue affected how the various parties performed. Notwithstanding his technical credentials and real expertise, Rick Halbert's claim lacked credibility precisely because it appeared to the authorities he contacted to be unprecedented. For their part, the authorities responded to what we now understand to be a novel problem as if it were a familiar one— "a farmer with some sick cows."

Halbert's key role and the Michigan PBB situation resembles in some respects the role of Lois Gibbs in the notorious Love Canal toxic waste dump case in Lewiston, New York (Brown, 1981; Gibbs, 1982; Levine, 1982), but there are also some important differences. Halbert pursued a technological fix; due to a combination of his own worldview and a lack of information on the scope of the problem, he was unable to see it "whole." Somewhat later, a public advocacy group in Michigan seems to have looked more broadly at the situation, organizing, engaging the media and launching its own health survey (with the results described above).

Seen in isolation, the official response in Michigan appears to have been painfully slow and inadequate. Yet general and official awareness developed in the span of a year and most of the other events described above occurred within three years after the problem's onset. In Love Canal, residents first noticed seepage of suspicious materials into their homes and other frightening occurrences in the late 1950s and waited almost 20 years for an official response. On that scale, Gibbs took the stage late in the game to play the key role of forming a community group that designed strategies, initially aimed to press authorities for more effective action, but finally at initiating an increasingly public debate. Once engaged, the media played a critical role, particularly in expanding the arena in which debate was occurring, until it was a truly national debate, engaging the Congress, most state legislatures, and myriad localities.

In Michigan, the PBB contamination and the state's handling of it became little more than an issue in a gubernatorial election. Yet, the Michigan incident exposed some 9 million people to a toxic chemical, while Love Canal directly exposed a few hundred residents near the site and as many as 100 thousand people dependent on local ground water supplies. The Halberts' book was made into a Hollywood film, *Bitter Harvest*, but the incident as well as the film seem largely forgotten. Love Canal has come to symbolize the threat posed by chemicals in the environment. Ultimately the activities of Gibbs and her neighbors made it possible for anyone in the United States to press a credible claim regarding toxic waste. Gibbs went on to found the Citizens Clearinghouse for Hazardous Wastes, a national networking organization devoted to facilitating citizen action and a persistent thorn in the sides of authorities and "mainline" environmental groups alike. It produces two newsletters and publishes an extensive list of informational, technical, and "how-to" materials.

Contrastingly, incidents involving milk contamination continue to occur around the country, tend to be treated as novel events and, in many cases, relevant agencies are slow to respond. Incidents in Hawaii from 1982 to 1985 and in Arkansas between 1985 and 1989 (McCartney, 1986; Schneider, 1989a & b), pursued familiar courses: in each, the contaminant was the pesticide heptachlor and it was disseminated to dairy cattle in feed by suppliers who initially denied responsibility. There were accusations of inordinate delay on the part of the federal (the FDA) and state authorities who also rushed to reassure the public. During the period of seeming delay, contamination spread to other livestock and ultimately significant concentrations were detected in maternal milk and consumer food stuffs. Widespread economic and emotional distress ensued among farmers and other individual victims were largely ignored by officials, who became preoccupied with the impacts on "corporate victims," processors and retailers. The press reports of these incidents also have much in common, the tendency to treat them in isolation, as state or regional problems, restricted to a specific contaminant or class of contaminants. In other words, like their largely official sources, journalists have difficulty seeing these situations "whole." Even as I write, the news media seem to be gearing up for another onslaught on regulatory agencies, this time for failing to monitor adequately the presence of antibiotics in milk. These reports ignore previous media campaigns on similar topics[7] and, more significantly, take no notice at all of other kinds of contaminants. This illustrates a key feature of the framework presented in this paper, the role of expanding awareness. Even as public awareness grows, a catalyzing event has not yet occurred in the dairy industry, and perhaps in the food industry at large, that would produce the kind of large scale regulatory changes that have transformed the environmental field.

Acknowledgements

The research and writing upon which this paper is based has been partially supported by the National Agricultural and Natural Resources Curriculum Project and the New Jersey Agricultural Experiment Station (Publication J-26104-1-89). I am grateful to Kathleen Wilson, Tom Ruehr, Ernest Schusky, Michael Schulman, Bonnie McCay, and anonymous reviewers for comments on earlier versions.

Notes

1. For purposes of describing the process, which is outlined in Figure 43.1, I have taken certain liberties with the real variability that exists among cases (as among individual people).
2. The empirical literature on whistle-blowing is sparse. It consists mostly of news stories and journalistic exposes, first person accounts by ex-employees (e.g., Agee, 1976), and works of advocacy (Nader *et al.,* 1972). There are several analyses and reviews that might be useful to readers. Near and Micelli (1985) present a model that focus on the process of decision making by the whistleblower and the reactions of authorities within the organization. Jensen (1987) depicts the procedural and substantive "tension points" faced by the prospective whistleblower. Greenberger and associates (1987) examine the interactions among whistleblowers and their co-workers. Loeb and Cory (1989) illuminate the ethical plight of a key professional in organizations, namely the management accountant, when wrongdoing is uncovered. These along with Westin (1981), also give access to other analyses and cases.
3. This brief narrative of the course of the disaster is principally based on *Bitter Harvest* by Frederick and Sandra Halbert (1978), themselves victims, and *The Poisoning of Michigan* by Joyce Egginton (1980), a journalist. Other books and articles have also been consulted (Chen, 1979; Coyer & Schwerin, 1981; Peterson, 1978).
4. Since its battle with the Farmers Union in the 1930s, the Farm Bureau has been criticized for its advocacy of agribusiness, its denigration (even exclusion) of the small and part-time farmer, who are viewed as "non-commercial", and its cosiness to politically conservative economic interests (Durrenberger, 1985/86). Of course, the same criticisms are leveled at cooperative extension and the Land Grant colleges. Nevertheless, many farmers view Farm Bureau as their own

organization and in many states it has effectively, even innovatively, represented the interests of a significant segment of the industry. Here the concern is with the perceptions of the farmer-victims.
5. A notorious example emerged in the Hopewell Va. vs. Kepone contamination case in which it was shown that the responsible party, Life Sciences, Inc., was a *de facto* subsidiary of Allied Chemical Corporation.
6. Under the protocol for the lighter pesticide molecules, the scan should have been terminated earlier.
7. For example, see Orville Schell's (1984) roundup of the parties to an earlier conflict over antibiotics in livestock feed.

References

Agee, Philip. *Inside the Company*. New York, Bantam, 1976.

Brown, Michael. *Laying Waste: The Poisoning of America by Toxic Chemicals*. New York: Pocket Books, 1981.

Chen, Edwin,. *PBB: An American Tragedy*. Englewood-Cliffs, NJ: Prentice Hall, 1979.

Coyer, Brian and Don S. Schwerin, "Bureaucratic Regulation and Farmer Protest in the Michigan PBB Contamination Case," *Rural Sociology.* 46(4,1981): 703–723.

Crenson, Mathew A. *The Un-Politics of Air Pollution: A Study of Non-Decisionmaking in the Cities*. Baltimore: The Johns Hopkins University Press, 1971.

Diperna, Paula. *Cluster Mystery: Epidemic and the Children of Woburn, Mass.* St. Louis; C.V. Mosby, 1985.

Durrenberger, E. P., "Notes on the Cultural-Historical Background to the Middlewestern Farm Crisis," *Culture and Agriculture.* 28 (Winter): 15–17, 1985/86.

Egginton, Joyce. *The Poisoning of Michigan.* New York: Norton, 1980.

Epstein, Samuel, Lester O. Brown and Carl Pope. *Hazardous Waste in America.* San Francisco: Sierra Club Books, 1982.

Ford, Daniel. *Three Mile Island: Thirty Minutes to Meltdown.* New York, Viking, 1982.

Gardner, John. *Self-Renewal.* Evanston: Harper & Row, 1963.

Gerlach, Luther P. and Virginia Hine. *Lifeway Leap.* Minneapolis: University of Minnesota Press, 1973.

Gibbs, Lois. *Love Canal: My Story*. Albany: State University of New York Press, 1982.

Greenberger, D. B., M. P. Micelli, and D. J. Cohen, "Oppositionists and Group Norms: The Reciprocal Influence of Whistle-blowers and Co-workers," *Journal of Business Ethics*. 6(7): 527–542, 1987.

Halbert, Frederick and Sharon. *Bitter Harvest*. Grand Rapids, William B. Erdman, 1978.

Jensen, J. Vernon, "Ethical Tension Points in Whistleblowing," *Journal of Business Ethics*. 6(4): 321–28, 1987.

Levine, Adeline G. *Love Canal: Science; Politics and People*. Lexington, MA: Lexington Books, 1982.

Lindbloom, Charles E., "The Science of Muddling Through," *Public Administration Review*. (Spring, 1959): 79–88.

Loeb, S. E. and S. N. Cory, "Whistleblowing and Management Accounting: An Approach," *Journal of Business Ethics*. 8(12):903–916, 1989.

McCarthy, John D. and Mayer N. Zald, "The Trend of Social Movements in America: Professionalization and Resource Mobilization." In: *Social Movements in an Organizational Society*, M. N. Zald and J. D. McCarthy, eds., New Brunswick, N.J., Transaction Books, pp. 337–391. 1987.

McCartney, Scott. "Dairymen Say Pesticide in Cattlefeed Brought a Nightmare that Won't End," Associated Press *Philadelphia Inquirer* March 30, 1986.

Media Institute. *Chemical Risks: Fears, Facts and the Media*. Media Research Series, Washington DC: Media Institute, 1985.

Nader, R., P. J. Petkas and K. Blackwell. *Whistleblowing: The Report of the Conference on Professional Responsibility*. New York, Grossman, 1972.

Near, J. P. and M. P. Micelli, "Organizational Dissidence: the Case of Whistle-Blowing," *Journal of Business Ethics*. 4(1): 1–16, 1985.

Peterson, Iver, "Michigan PBB: Not a Comedy but Plenty of Errors," *New York Times,* (September 2): E16, 1978.

Reich, Charles. *The Greening of America*. New York: Bantam, 1970.

Schell, Orville, "A Reporter at Large (Antibiotic Feed Additives–Parts I & II), *The New Yorker*. April 23 & April 30, 1984.

Schneider, Keith, "Pesticide Barred in 70s is Found to Taint Poultry," *New York Times*, March 16, 1989 (a).

Schneider, Keith, "Tainted Milk and Meats Raise Vigilance," *New York Times*, May 11, 1989 (b).

Westin, A., ed. *Whistle Blowing: Loyalty and Dissent in the Corporation*. New York, McGraw Hill, 1981.

Zald, Mayer N. and John D. McCarthy, eds. *Social Movements in an Organizational Society*. New Brunswick, N.J., Transaction Books, 1987.

48

National Priorities List Sites in New Jersey

United States Environmental Protection Agency

S ite-specific resources available from this page include Site Progress Profiles, site narratives, and Federal Register notices.

Access these resources ...

❑ by map, click on the site of interest.
❑ by list, of all NPL sites in New Jersey by county.

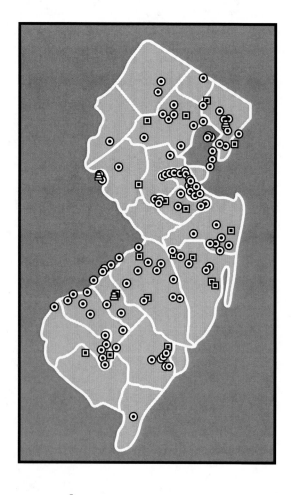

Map Key :   ⚠ Proposed : 2   ⊙ Final : 114   ▣ Deleted : 25

49

Social Responses to Commodity Shortages: The 1973-1974 Gasoline Crisis

Thomas K. Rudel[1]

This paper examines social responses to the 1973–1974 gasoline crisis in the United States, using newspaper reports of automobile driver behavior in two metropolitan areas and American Automobile Association data on the adoption of rationing plans and the availability of gasoline in 48 states. From these data it is possible to identify two types of responses: individual responses by automobile drivers, which occurred in every region affected by the shortages, and collective responses in the form of rationing plans adopted by governments and gas station operators in the regions with the most severe shortages. In the latter regions the responses occurred in sequence, with individual responses emerging first and collective responses developing later.

Introduction

In the past 10 years periodic interruptions in the supply of food and fuel flowing to consumers in advanced industrial societies have raised questions about the ways in which individuals and societies cope with sudden declines in the availability of basic commodities. Because these questions concern the ways in which societies provision themselves with basic resources, they address issues of long-standing importance to social scientists, but they raise these issues in

a new context. Rather than focusing on conditions of prolonged scarcity which affect economies in the less developed countries or on conditions of temporary scarcity which affect economics in the more developed countries during recessions, these questions focus on the temporary scarcity of one resource in an otherwise affluent economy.

Under these conditions consumers alter their purchasing patterns and government officials search for policies to ease the shortage or moderate its effects. The search for policies would be greatly facilitated if policy-makers had some knowledge about (1) the ways in which consumers and governments usually respond to shortages and (2) the effects which the responses and the interaction of the responses have on the society's capacity to cope with shortage.[2] To begin this inquiry, it would be valuable to know whether or not there are general patterns of response to commodity shortages. The answer to this question can only come from close scrutiny of responses to particular shortages, a task which I undertake here with an analysis of the 1973–1974 gasoline crisis.

The 1973–1974 Gasoline Crisis

The 1973–1974 gasoline crisis is probably the best-known commodity shortage to have occurred in the United States in recent years. Several special circumstances shaped consumer responses to the shortage. First, it involved an item which could not be conserved in significant amounts without drastic changes in daily routines. In this circumstance short-term conservation efforts yielded only limited reductions in demand for gasoline. Second, the suddenness with which the shortages developed made it difficult for the society to take actions which would bring the supply of gasoline into line with the demand for gasoline. Technological innovations, such as mixing alcohol with gasoline or constructing cars which consume less fuel, required long periods of implementation and had no effect on the supply of gasoline during the shortage. Unable (or unwilling) to decrease their demand for gasoline and unable to influence its supply, individual consumers responded by investing more time and energy in the purchase of gasoline, a change which affected transactions at gas stations.

To identify the changes in gasoline transactions, I collected two types of data: to investigate the types of changes, I studied newspaper reports of automobile driver behavior in two metropolitan areas, Atlanta and New York; to identify regional and temporal patterns in the changes, I collected data on the availability of gasoline and the regulation of its sale in 48 states during the shortage.

Trends in Two Metropolitan Areas

Several considerations governed the choice of New York and Atlanta as sites for studying driver behavior during the shortage. First, the shortage developed to a greater extent in metropolitan than in nonmetropolitan areas (American Automobile Association, 1974). The decision on which metropolitan areas to study rested in part on theoretical considerations. To capture the full range of variation in responses I wanted to study one metropolitan area where the shortage was mild and short in duration and another where it was severe and long. Using newspaper reports and American Automobile Association (AAA) data to gauge the extent of the shortage in each major metropolitan area, I eliminated from consideration such cities as Chicago and Los Angeles because they experienced moderate shortages and chose Atlanta and New York because they experienced typically mild (Atlanta) and severe (New York) shortages.[3]

Atlanta

Intimations of a local gasoline shortage first appeared in early December 1973, when President Nixon introduced his gasless Sundays program. The day before the first of these, on December 2, the *Atlanta Constitution* headlined "Fill 'Er Up with Anything, Stampeding Motorists Cry." The next day, however, gasoline supplies seemed plentiful. As one reporter wrote, "While authorities in many states reported thousands of stranded, out of gas motorists caught on the roads on gasless Sunday," Georgia officials had no such reports.[4]

Adequate gasoline supplies persisted throughout the month of December in Georgia; motorists and transportation officials complained not about the availability of gasoline but about the prices which they had to pay for it.[5] Over the holiday weekend stories concerning automobile travel in Georgia focused on the number of traffic accidents rather than the gasoline shortage.[6] Enough stations continued to pump gasoline throughout January to enable drivers to "shop around" for inexpensive fuel. Stories on the gasoline shortage emphasized rises in price and variations in price from station to station. One story began with the headline "38.6 Cent Gallon Draws a Crowd," cars were backed up a quarter mile in either direction to buy the cheap gasoline on a Saturday during the middle of the month.[7] Evidently drivers reacted to the rapidly rising gasoline prices at some stations by patronizing other stations with lower prices. Weekly surveys by the Georgia chapter of the AAA on the availability of gasoline across the state confirmed the impression of adequate gasoline supplies in January: the number of stations out of fuel never rose above 7% of Georgia's gas stations. From the end of January to the end of February gasoline supplies declined steadily until almost 30% of Georgia's stations had run out of fuel) American Automobile Association, February 26, 1974). Under these conditions drivers adopted such elaborate search strategies that gas station operators began to take note. The *Atlanta Constitution* reported: "Shell dealer in Woobury complains . . . of motorists from Greenville, about 10 miles away, who rush down to soak up his small supply. 'They call down here wantin' to know if I've got any gas.'" Another gas station operator observed, "It's like Grand Central Station when we open up in the morning. People are already waiting at the pumps when we get to the station at seven in the morning."[8]

Gasoline never became so scarce that motorists would purchase it at any price. As one Atlanta gas station reported, "I've got plenty of fuel for two reasons. First is that my company allocated it to me, and second is that at these prices nobody will buy it from me."[9]

Throughout the remaining weeks of the shortage Atlanta drivers continued to mix their strategies, shopping around for inexpensive gasoline on the few occasions when it was available, traveling considerable distances to find gasoline on other occasions, and scrambling for a place at the head of a line of waiting cars on still other occasions. In early March state officials prepared a rationing plan but because gasoline supplies in the state began to increase in early April 1974, the plan was never implemented.[10]

Compared with other metropolitan areas, Atlanta experienced a mild gasoline shortage, and responses to the shortage by consumers never went beyond changes in individual practices in purchasing gasoline. The companies raised the price of gasoline; a few gas stations ran out of fuel, and drivers responded by altering their individual search strategies.

New York

Although accurate information on the availability of gasoline in the New York metropolitan area did not become available until AAA began doing weekly surveys of gasoline supplies in mid-January 1974, it is apparent from newspaper accounts that New York drivers began to experience severe gasoline shortages toward the end of December 1973 when monthly supplies of gasoline gave out at numerous gas stations. Drivers responded to the scarcity by "topping off" their tanks at frequent intervals so as to insure that they would not run out of gasoline. The topping-off process doubled the number of customers which a station had to service in order to sell 1000 gallons of fuel and increased by a slightly smaller percentage the total number of stops which drivers made at gas stations.[11] The larger number of stops translated into long lines at the service stations by the end of December. A 20% increase in the price of gasoline accompanied its decline in availability during the month of December.[12] As gasoline became scarcer, transactions involving the resource became more complicated. Some stations imposed service charges of $1.00 to $2.00 above the cost of the gasoline, while other stations created tie-in arrangements in which drivers who wanted to buy gasoline had to purchase a car wash or cigarettes in addition. If customers did not participate in these arrangements, they could not buy gasoline.[13]

Not only the customers faced increased complications in gasoline transactions; so did the gas station managers. In order to conserve supplies and insure that most drivers received at least some gasoline, operators began limiting gasoline purchases to so many gallons or so much money per car. As soon as the station managers set down rules, they had to listen to drivers pleading for relaxation of the rules in special cases. The comments of a gas station owner in northern New Jersey are apt:

People are trying all kinds of tricks to get front of the line and get more gasoline. Most of them have to go to the hospital; their wives are sick; they're about to have a baby. I've never heard of so many babies being born, and the husbands don't have the gasoline.[14]

By early January the growing shortage of gasoline in the New York area had induced price rises in gasoline, complicated transactions involving gasoline, and caused friction between people buying and selling gasoline. This last problem become so acute in the first days of 1974 that the City of New York began stationing police around the most congested stations. As one of them explained, keeping the peace around gas stations was no easy task.

Near the station . . . drivers don't do much beyond just getting out of their cars and yelling at one another. What happens three blocks back is another story. They come up one way streets the wrong way, trying to sneak into line by jumping ahead of the car that's waiting at the intersection. That starts the yelling and the horn blowing, and only the bravest man will insist on staying in line. Or, if there is the least space beyond the intersection, you'll got some clown trying to sneak in there. If somebody pulls in front of a big husky truck driver, he had better be as big as the truck driver.[15]

What would cause a reasonable person to cut in line at a gas station? Another reporter had the answer.

People are spending up to six hours a week in line waiting for gas. Because they equate time with money, they are willing to cut in line. As one line cutter explained,

"Well, in my case it is either gas or welfare; I need the gas and I need the time. I don't use this thing (the van) for pleasure anymore . . .

I use it only for deliveries, but if I spend forever waiting for gas, I can't get to fill my orders."[16]

The long lines and frequently chaotic conditions at area gas stations increased popular discontent with the "business as usual, except on Sundays" policies pursued by local governments and increased popular support for rationing schemes which would give priority at the pumps to select groups of drivers. These sentiments ran so strongly among New York taxicab drivers that they organized several protests in which they blockaded filling stations with their cabs.[17] By the second week in January at least 20% of the station operators in the New York metropolitan area had established their own system of priorities in which they gave preferential treatment to their regular customers. Some stations in New York City supplemented their regular customer plan with preferential treatment for "important" people, such as diplomats, doctors, and law enforcement officials.[18] In effect gas station managers established their own rationing plans which created privileged and underprivileged groups of users. In mid-January the federal government outlawed "regular customer" arrangements, but a survey conducted in the New York metropolitan area in late January reported widespread violation of the new federal law.[19]

By the middle of January most gas stations had received their January allotments from suppliers, and the gasoline shortage eased somewhat. Toward the end of the month the shortages grew more severe again as numerous stations exhausted their monthly supplies, and by the last week in January over 25% of the stations in New York State reported that they had no fuel (American Automobile Association, 1974). Truckers prolonged the end of the month gasoline drought with a protest against the 55 m.p.h. speed limit in which they prevented fuel trucks from leaving northern New Jersey oil refineries by blocking the refinery exits with their trucks. At the same time, governments serving large populations in the New York metropolitan area began rationing gasoline.[20]

On February 4th the mayor of Elizabeth, New Jersey instituted the first mandatory gasoline rationing plan in the region. He linked the adoption of the plan to the problem of maintaining order around gas stations. "Mayor Thomas G. Dunn of Elizabeth said he head moved after '200 serious incidents' in a month had taken his police force from other duties."[21] Several days later the mayor of Bridgeport cited difficulties in maintaining public order around gas stations as an important reason for instituting the second gasoline rationing plan in the metropolitan area.[22] On February 12th New Jersey instituted the first statewide odd-even rationing plan in the New York metropolitan area, and on February 26th New York adopted a similar plan. Perhaps because rationing represented a new political issue, the lines of the political cleavage were not clearly drawn, and partisan political activity did not mark the passage of the laws. As one observer of the New York State legislature commented:

There is surprisingly little conflict between the two parties on the issue. There is some carping, but until most politicians can determine which way the wind blows and how freely gasoline flows . . . they would rather steer clear of this issue and suffer silently like motorists.[23]

Clamorous demands for government intervention after the severe shortages of early February dispelled the legislators' reluctance to act on the issue. In both New Jersey and New York the state legislatures voted overwhelmingly to empower the governors to establish rationing plans by decree. The only votes against the New York state plan came from legislators representing upstate regions where the shortages did not exist.

The odd-even rationing plans gave preference at the pumps to commercial vehicles on all days, to cars with license plates ending in an even number on even-numbered days, and to cars with license plates ending in an odd number on odd-numbered days. The plans had an immediate impact on the business of buying and selling gasoline. One seemingly representative New Jersey dealer summed up his experience on the first day of his state's odd-even rationing plan.

I haven't had a bit of trouble. Everyone, and I mean everyone, has been cooperating. In fact, this morning the lines were much shorter, and I was able to sell gas for one extra hour.[24]

Generally, lines shortened, stations returned to unlimited purchases, and relations between customers and gas station operators improved.[25]

The order introduced by the mandatory odd-even plans proved short-lived, however, and February's end of the month gasoline drought created chaotic scenes at area gas stations. In the words of one reporter,

Panic buying compounded the problem as motorists hunted from station to station in search of an open pump . . . At open stations lines of cars were commonly six blocks long in the city and a mile or more in the suburbs, and after waiting several hours, a buyer was likely to find a limit on his purchases.

In these circumstances local public officials became

almost competitive in their claims of hardship. "Rockland County (N.Y.) is being cheated more than any other area in its gas supply," said District Attorney Robert Meehan, who announced plans to summon a grand jury to investigate the situation. Ocean County (N.J.) officials consider their area to be the hardest hit with 90% of their service stations closed and others open for only limited periods, . . . Fist fights broke out at several stations in Ocean County, where the lines of cars were up to four miles long.[26]

The end of the month allocation processes clarified the relationship between individual and collective responses to the gasoline shortage. First, the collective responses constrained but did not eliminate individual responses to the problem. At the end of February, with the odd-even rationing plans in effect, individual drivers continued to search for gasoline, but they confined their searches to alternate days of the week. Second, because the rationing plans stipulated only who should be patronizing gas stations on a particular day, they restored order only in situations marked by disputes over who could buy gasoline. As several residents of Ocean County presumably found out, there were numerous other issues about which one could fight. To restore order in this situation would have required more detailed rationing plans than the ones in operation.

Metropolitan area governments never enacted more comprehensive rationing plans because in the first few weeks of March gasoline supplies in the New York metropolitan area returned to near normal levels. With the return of adequate gasoline supplies, consumers resumed the pre-crisis patterns of purchasing gasoline. By the middle of March numerous drivers had abandoned their regular gas stations for other stations offering less expensive gasoline, and by early May the legislatures in both New Jersey and New York had repealed their gas rationing laws.[27]

The history of consumer responses to the scarcity in Atlanta and New York suggests two types of responses to the gasoline shortage. First, drivers begin searching for gasoline in new places at unusual times almost as soon as the shortages become apparent. Drivers continued these sometimes frenzied, sometimes devious search strategies throughout the shortage. Second, in New York, the metropolitan area with the worst shortages, first gas station operators and then governments developed collective responses to the shortage in the form of gas rationing plans. The events leading up to the adoption of the rationing plans suggest a sequence of social responses to the gasoline shortage. Individual responses came first, but the aggregate effect of the individuals searching for gasoline proved so chaotic in regions characterized by the worst shortages that it generated a collective response in the form of rationing plans designed to restore order around gas stations. If this line of argument, developed for two metropolitan areas, proves correct for the entire nation, the adoption of rationing plans by state governments should be positively associated with the severity of statewide shortages in gasoline. Data collected

by the American Automobile Association and the Federal Energy Office during the winter of 1973–1974 for each state makes it possible to test this hypothesis.

Trends Across the Nation

In mid-January 1974 the American Automobile Association began conducting weekly state surveys of gasoline availability at 5000 gas stations throughout the country in an attempt to keep the driving public informed of local variations in availability which might affect their travel plans.[28] So that the data would be useful to interstate as well as intrastate travelers, the national AAA office issued common guidelines to each state office to insure the comparability of data across state lines. The guidelines stipulated that the state office gather data through telephone interviews with gas station operators located on heavily traveled routes throughout the state. They also required that the state offices ask each operator if he or she (1) was out of gasoline, (2) was limiting purchases to a certain quantity of gasoline per car, and (3) was staying open on weekends and during the evenings on weekdays. The national office of AAA compiled and published this data in weekly Fuel Gauge Reports beginning on January 15, 1974.

With this data we can develop indirect measures of the availability of gasoline from week to week for each state. The percentage of surveyed stations which had no fuel is the most direct indicator of the gasoline shortage. Data on the percentage of stations limiting the amount of gasoline purchased by a car and the percentage of gas stations operating for limited hours provide additional measures which suggest but do not directly indicate a shortage.

The states fall into one of three categories depending on the type of rationing plan which they adopted.[29] The first consists of those states which adopted no rationing plan whatsoever; the second consists of those which adopted partial rationing plans but adopted no statewide plan and those which adopted voluntary odd-even rationing plans; and the

Table 49.1 Rationing Policies and the Gasoline Shortage: Group Means, January to March 1974[a]

Policy	Number of States	Percentage of Stations Out of Fuel	Percentage of Stations Limiting Hours	Percentage of Stations Limiting Sales
No rationing	25	4.8	53.1	15.3
Partial rationing	17	11.2	77.0	34.2
Complete rationing	6	13.0	82.5	32.5

[a]SOURCE: American Automobile Association (1974).

third consists of those which adopted mandatory odd-even rationing plans. The three categories form an ordinal scale of rationing with category 1 equivalent to no rationing and category 3 equivalent to complete rationing.

The cross-tabulations in Table 49.1 of state rationing policies with measures of the gasoline shortage indicate association between the policy adopted and the extent of the shortage but leave unclear the sequence of events surrounding the adoption of the policies.

Scattered evidence indicates that gasoline shortages first appeared in different parts of the country in the early weeks of December 1973. From early December to early January the percentage of respondents in the Continuous National Survey who reported experiencing difficulty in obtaining gasoline increased from 17% to 37%.[30] In mid-January Oregon adopted the first rationing plan when Governor Tom McCall established a voluntary odd-even rationing plan. On January 28th Hawaii instituted the first mandatory odd-even plan. Between February 8th and 26th 18 more states adopted various types of rationing plans. In March three more states enacted laws which rationed gasoline. Newspaper accounts of the circumstances surrounding the adoption of the first statewide mandatory rationing plan underscore the association observed in the New York metropolitan area between frantic individual searches for gasoline and the appearance of collective responses to the shortage. One reporter described the adoption of gas rationing in Hawaii in the following terms.

Growing traffic congestion and clashes around filling stations as panic buying mounted persuaded acting Governor George Arlyoshi to invoke emergency power Thursday and order gasoline controls.[31]

In other words, the conditions which precipitated collective responses to the shortage required a population which was already responding individually to the problem. The frantic individual searches for gasoline generated an increasing number of violent incidents around gas stations which led to the imposition of rationing plans by government officials attempting to restore order.

The map in Fig. 49.1, indicating the location of the states which adopted rationing, offers a different perspective on the spread of gas rationing plans. The clustering of states with plans on the east and west coasts suggests an explanation which emphasizes the diffusion of a policy innovation. Officials in one state adopt the plan, and officials in the neighboring states, heartened by the plan's success in the first state, adopt it in their state as well. In this interpretation the extent of the gasoline shortage does not predict the adoption of gas rationing; rather, proximity to a state which already has a rationing plan predicts the adoption of a plan.

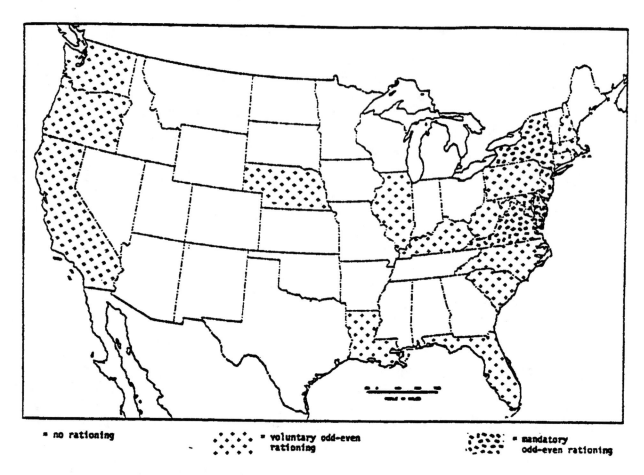

no rationing

= voluntary odd-even
rationing

= mandatory
odd-even rationing

Figure 49.1 Gas rationing plans in the continental United States, March 1974.

Weekly data on the percentage of gas stations out of fuel, grouped by the three categories of gas rationing policies in Fig. 49.2, casts doubt on the diffusion explanation by suggesting a connection between the extent of the gasoline shortage in a state at the end of January and the rationing policy adopted, usually in February, by the state. A discriminant analysis of the rationing policies permits a more detailed assessment of the shortage and diffusion explanations. The number of stations out of fuel, limiting hours, and limiting purchases provide measures of the shortage. A dummy variable which indicates whether or not a neighboring state had already adopted a rationing plan when a state adopted its own plan measures the diffusion of the policy innovation.

The results of the discriminant analysis in Table 49.2 indicate that the combination of gasoline scarcity and diffusion of innovation variables discriminates efficiency between the states on the basis of the rationing policies adopted. The relative size of the standardized discriminant coefficients indicates that, while geographical proximity to states with rationing plans did have some effect on the adoption of gas rationing plans, the primary determinant of gas rationing policies in a particular state was the number of gas stations out of fuel in the state.

This evidence, along with the evidence from the Atlanta and New York metropolitan areas, permits us to draw the following conclusions about social responses to the 1973–1974 gasoline crisis: (1) the residents of regions with mild shortages developed individual responses to the problem, while the residents of regions with severe shortages developed both individual and collective responses to the problem; (2) in the latter regions the responses occurred in a sequence,

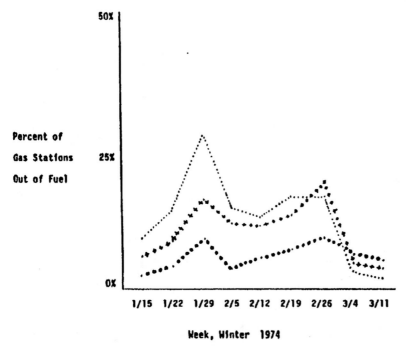

Percent of
Gas Stations
Out of Fuel

Week, Winter 1974

Figure 49.2 Percentage of stations out of fuel by rationing policy and week for 48 states, (00000) states with no gas rationing: (+ + + + +) states with voluntary rationing; (. . . . .) states with mandatory rationing. Source: American Automobile Association (1974).

with individual responses developing first and collective responses emerging later.

The Pattern of Response: An Explanation

Explanations for variations in the incidence of gas rationing plans and the timing of their adoption must begin with variations in the extent of the gasoline shortage, but this relationship is mediated by variations in the social organization of competition between motorists for gasoline. According to this line of argument, the increased scarcity of gasoline causes changes in the competition between motorists for gasoline, which in turn causes local authorities to institute gas rationing plans.

The 1973–1974 gasoline shortage created a dilemma for automobile drivers, and this dilemma affected both the setting and the ways in which motorists competed for gasoline. On the one hand, the evening, weekend, and end of the month closings of gas stations increased the probability that drivers would not find any stations open on a trip, so if they wanted to minimize the risk of running out of gasoline on the road, they had to top off their gasoline tanks at frequent intervals. On the other hand, if numerous drivers began topping off their tanks, the number trying to purchase gasoline in any given time period would increase dramatically, and each one would face a long wait each time. A willingness by some drivers to let their tanks run down to near empty levels before refueling would ease the dilemma faced by other drivers; they could continue to top off their tanks without encountering particularly long waits. Because few drivers proved willing to risk running out of fuel, the shortage generated long lines of waiting cars at gas stations. In other words the similar behavior of drivers during the shortage produced long waits and frayed nerves among the people buying and selling gasoline. In game theory terminology, drivers generated a "commons dilemma" at gas stations by becoming participants in an "N-person, mixed motive game with a dominating strategy for defection" (Dawes, 1973, cited in Edney and Harper, 1978; Edney and Cass, 1978: 372).

As the shortages grew more acute and more gas stations closed, the calculations of individual drivers began to change; fewer and fewer of them allowed their gas tanks to become nearly empty before stopping to fill up. This change in individual calculations combined with the additional gas station closings caused a change in the pattern of competition

Table 49.2 The Discriminant Function

Canonical Correlation	Wilk's Lambda	Chi-Square	Degrees of Freedom	Significance
.758	.397	40.156	8	.000

Standardized discriminant function coefficients	Percent of grouped cases correctly classified: 75.0
Out of fuel = -0.643	Percent of grouped cases that would have been correctly classified in a random assignment: 39.3
Diffusion = -0.454	
Hour limits = 0.233	
Purchase limits = 0.031	

for gasoline which worsened the situation at gas stations.

Work by population ecologists illuminates the changed nature of competition between motorists. According to MacArthur,

Two species that compete by depleting the resource supply (resource competition) are having a "scramble" while two who compete by combat or interspecific territoriality (behavior competition) are having a "contest." (1972: 25)

Scrambles ensue when individuals push and shove each other momentarily while pursuing a scarce resource. The conflicts between individuals over a particular resource are fleeting: one gets the resource, and the others turn away in search of another resource. Because competitors pay relatively little attention to each other and devote themselves to searching for the resource, scrambling is referred to as resource competition. Throughout the gasoline crisis drivers competing for places in the shorter lines at filling stations engaged in behaviors which approximated scrambles. Motorists looking for gasoline along major thoroughfares would gauge the length of the lines at gas stations and pull over quickly when they spotted a gas station with short lines. Although drivers competed with one another for places at the head of

lines, they rarely took any note of the personal characteristics of their competitors. They got whatever gasoline they could and went their way as quickly as possible.

Contests develop when two individuals or two groups of individuals compete with each other for a prolonged period of time over a particular resource. Because individuals pay a relatively large amount of attention to the behavior of their competitors when they contest, it is often referred to as behavior competition. The New York City police officer's comment about the size of the driver who cuts in front of a truck driver waiting in line illustrates the kind of situation in which contesting is likely to arise. Someone cutting in line had better be larger than the waiting driver in front of whom he cuts because the waiting driver may become so incensed that he may try to do physical harm to the driver cutting in line. In this kind of situation drivers pay particular attention to the personal characteristics of their competitors.

The two modes of competition are interrelated:

We note that there is a natural priority: competition for resources can exist by itself, with no aggressive overtones, while aggressive (behavior) competition would be pointless unless, in its absence, there would be resource competition; there would be no reward for fighting if some new resource were not gained. Hence we conclude that behavior competition is a modification of an underlying resource competition. (MacArthur, 1972: 27)

In other words, competition by contesting does not develop until the population has also engaged in competition by scrambling. A closer look at the particular forms of competition reveals the reason for the natural priority. The widespread presence of scrambling in a population suggests that the desired resource is still relatively abundant. After a cursory glance at the lines at one gas station, drivers turn their attention to another gas station farther down the road which may have shorter lines. This pattern of behavior suggests that enough gasoline is available that the driver will eventually find a gas station with short lines.

Individual behavior in contesting situations suggests that the desirable resource exists in smaller quantities. In this form of competition, rather than turning away to search for other gas stations with shorter lines, drivers either take up and begin holding a place at the end of the line or they begin thinking of a devious maneuver which will, almost magically, deposit them at the head of the line. Presumably neither the driver who goes to the end of the line nor the driver who thinks of cutting in line would place himself in a situation in which he might have to contest with other drivers if shorter lines existed nearby. In other words, arguing with other drivers or at least fixing your attention on other drivers so as to exploit or resist exploitation becomes sensible only when all gas stations have such long lines that further searching for stations with short lines yields no dividends.[32]

In regions characterized by acute gasoline shortages drivers probably scrambled less and contested more as the shortages became more severe. To prevent violence from breaking out between individuals contesting for favored positions in the gas lines, gas station operators and state governments established regulations which stipulated who had priority at the pumps.[33] The priorities established by the plans discriminated between some drivers in arbitrary ways, giving preference to drivers with one type of license plate on one day and preference to drivers with another type of license plate on another day. Under these provisions one group of drivers had preferential access on any given day, but over the course of several days all drivers received equal access to the pumps. Other provisions in these plans established preferential groups of drivers on a more permanent basis. Economic considerations usually underlay the selection of some groups of drivers for preferential treatment. For instance, when the regular Customers at particular gas stations began purchasing gasoline at whichever stations had the shortest lines, gas station operators began to think that they would lose their regular customers. The loss of customers who only bought gasoline did not perturb gas station operators, but the loss of customers who, in addition to buying gasoline at frequent intervals, had repair work done at the station, made station operators apprehensive because the lost repair work could amount to a significant portion of a gas station's revenues. This prospect forced political considerations on gas station operators who wanted to weather the crisis with a minimum amount of disruption to their business. To avoid the economically damaging loss of their regular customers, gas station operators began giving priority at the pumps to their regular customers. Faced with a similar threat of damage to the local economy, governments in many states exempted commercial vehicles from the odd-even rationing plans. The conditions which compelled the creation of these preferential groups of consumers suggest that, as the shortage of a given commodity grows more acute, the number of preferred groups of consumers and the degree of preference given to these groups will increase.

By establishing preferential groups of consumers, the rationing plans reduced the size of the pool of drivers eligible to buy gasoline and forced the remaining drivers to either conserve fuel or at least allow their tanks to run down to near empty levels before refueling. By limiting access to the pumps in this way, the rationing plans promised to ease the common dilemma around gas stations in the states with the worst shortages.[34]

Summary and Conclusion

Responses to commodity shortages occur in a two-stage sequence. When the resource is still relatively abundant, individuals respond primarily by searching for it in other places or by searching for substitutes. The sudden disappearance of a resource or the sudden appearance of a substitute resource provokes scrambles for the available resource. As the shortage grows progressively worse, the social organization of competition for the resource changes. The search becomes more chaotic, opportunistic behavior proliferates as the rules governing the allocation of the resource through the market disintegrate, and scrambles, a momentary pushing and shoving for possession, evolve into contests, protracted struggles between two contestants who often suffer injury during the contest and privation after the contest. In this circumstance societies organize to restore order to the competitive process. Authorities establish privileged and underprivileged groups of resource users, and articulate rules for the allocation of the resource between the groups. In these arrangements the privileged resource users are usually specialists who claim to make the most indispensable use of the resource.

Until data on consumer behavior in 20 to 30 commodity shortages become available, the generality of the response process described above will remain subject to question. In considering different commodity shortages, the limited set of shortages which conform to the conditions prevalent during the 1973–1974 gasoline shortage becomes more obvious. First, the gasoline shortage involved a resource with low elasticities of demand and supply. During the period of the shortage consumers could neither decrease their demand for the resource, nor could they increase the supply of the resource in significant ways.

Second, this shortage involved a resource which had not been in short supply in recent years and for which governments did not have rationing plans already prepared. Finally, the shortage occurred in the political economic context of a mixed economy in which both market processes and government authorities allocate resources. When the shortage occurs in a markedly different political-economic context, the process of response may take a different form. For instance, in Poland, where the government rations basic commodities such as meat even during periods of relative abundance, shortages in 1978 convinced the government to undertake a partial deregulation of meat marketing. This action caused an immediate fourfold increase in the price of meat in some shops and made differences in ability to pay more important in determining who purchased meat and who did not. Consumers accepted these changes without protest.[35] This example suggests that in countries where governments intervene more decisively in markets, shortages often become evident to consumers in different ways, and consumer responses often take a different form. Despite these limits on the generality of the process described above, there still seem to be numerous commodity shortages which have generated patterns of social response similar to the one which developed during the 1973–1974 gasoline crisis. Obvious examples include salmon fisheries in the North Atlantic (McCoy, 1978) and water in the western United States.

Acknowledgments

This research was supported by Grant No. HD05876 from the National Institute for Child Health and Human Development to the Center for Demography and Ecology, University of Wisconsin-Madison. I want to thank Jon Light, Steve Messner, Stephanie Morgan, Christine Padoch, and David Rosen for critical readings of an earlier draft of this paper.

Notes

1. Department of Human Ecology and Social Sciences, Cook College, Rutgers University, New Brunswick, New Jersey 08903.

2. Ecological interpretations of war (Vayda, 1976) and sociological work on natural disaster (Erikson, 1976; Quarentelli and Dynes, 1977) also focus on response processes.

3. It would be stretching a point to call two cases of anything a sample. Had a larger number of metropolitan areas been selected, the criteria used to select New York and Atlanta would have resulted in a stratified, random sample of metropolitan areas.

4. David Morrison, "Sunday Was Quite Gasless," the *Atlanta Constitution,* December 3, 1973.

5. Beau Cutts and David Morrison, "Many Gas Stations Overcharge," the *Atlanta Constitution,* December 11, 1973; Beau Cutts, "IRS to Fine Price Gougers," the *Atlanta Constitution,* December 12, 1973.

6. Beau Cutts, "State Holiday Toll Reaches 9," the *Atlanta Constitution,* December 27, 1973; Jim Merrimer, "19 Die in Georgia in Holiday Traffic," the *Atlanta Constitution,* January 2, 1974.

7. "Gas Here—Some Cheap," the *Atlanta Constitution,* January 17, 1974; Gary Hendricks, "38.6 Cents Draws a Crowd," *the Atlantic Constitution,* January 17, 1974.

8. Mike Christensen and Chet Fuller, "Gas Outside of Atlanta near Bottom of Barrel," the *Atlanta Constitution,* Match 3, 1974.

9. "See March Pinch: State Oil Official to Appeal Supply," the *Atlanta Constitution,* March 5, 1974.

10. Jeff Nesmith, "Simon Scoffs at Gas Shortage Forecasts while Georgia Readies Even-Odd Rationing Plan," the *Atlanta Constitution,* March 6, 1974.

11. Although the average amount of gasoline purchased in each transaction dropped by approximately 50% in a matter or weeks, the number of stops made at the gas stations did not double largely because conservation efforts during the crisis reduced the amount of driving done by the residents of the New York metropolitan area by 10–15%. See "Dealers Attribute Long Lines at Gas Stations to Panic Buying," The *New York Times,* January 3, 1974.

12. Paul Montgomery, "Drivers Face Another Weekend of Lines and Rising Prices," *The New York Times,* January 5, 1974.

13. P. L. Montgomery, "Fuel Supply and Tempers Grow Short in City Area," *The New York Times,* January 1, 1974.

14. P. L. Montgomery, "Fuel Supply and Tempers Grow Short in City Area," *The New York Times,* January 1, 1974.

15. Laurie Johnston, "Policeman Faces Own Crisis Keeping Pace at Pumps," *The New York Times,* January 3, 1974.

16. Michael T. Kaufman, "Drivers Waiting to Fill Empty Tanks Pour Out Their Many Tales of Woe," *The New York Times,* January 3, 1974.

17. Edward C. Burks, "Cabbies Stage Brooklyn Blockade over Fuel Crisis," *The New York Times,* January 5, 1974.

18. David Bird, "Filling Stations Play Favorites," *The New York Times,* January 8, 1974.

19. Gerald Gold, "Fuel Crisis Stirs and Stymies Consumerists," *The New York Times,* January 27, 1974.

20. Several small town governments engineered rationing plans in early January. One New Jersey community required that local gas station operators limit their sales to local residents. In another New Jersey community the town government passed an ordinance establishing special hours at local gas stations during which only local residents could purchase gasoline. See Frank J. Prial, "Massachusetts to Start Rationing Plan, Monday," *The New York Times,* February 9, 1974.

21. Peter Kihss, "Elizabeth Adopts Gas Rationing," *The New York Times,* February 4, 1974.

22. "Area Pumps Go Dry as the End of January Nears," *The New York Times,* January 27, 1974.

23. Frank Lynn, "Politics and Gasoline," *The New York Times,* February 12, 1974.

24. P. L. Montgomery, "Jersey Gasoline Plan Cuts Tension and Long Lines," *The New York Times,* February 12, 1974.

25. J. F. Sullivan, "Jersey's Start Successful," *The New York Times,* February 12, 1974; L. Von Gelder, "Controls Reduce Gasoline Tie-Ups on First Day Here," *The New York Times,* February 27, 1974.

26. Robert D. McFadden, "Lack of Gasoline Worst Ever Here." *The New York Times,* March 1, 1974.

27. Michael C. Jensen, "Drivers Begin to Shop for Best Gasoline Prices," *The New York Times,* March 15, 1974.
28. The analysis does not include Alabama or Nevada because the AAA chapters in those states failed to file reports for several weeks during the period under analysis.
29. The Federal Energy Office compiled the data on rationing plans in March 1974. It was published in an American Automobile Association news release on March 19, 1974. The total number of stations surveyed rose from 4200 in mid-January to 6200 in mid-March. The increase in the number of stations sampled does not seem to reflect any change in the sampling strategies used by AAA state offices.
30. The Continuous National Survey (CNS) was a "small, weekly nationwide probability sample designed to provide multiple federal agencies with data relevant to programs and policy issues" (Murray *et al.*, 1974: 258). The Department of Transportation and the Federal Energy Office commissioned the survey in 1973 in order to gain information on the impact of the energy crisis on the American consumer.
31. Tillman Durden "Hawaii First State to Set Gasoline Sales Controls," *The New York Times,* January 28, 1974.
32. The work of Albert O. Hirschman on consumer responses to declines in the quality of goods throws new light on the shift in the social organization of gasoline purchasers which occurred during the crisis. Hirschman sees two general set of responses to declines in the quality of goods and services: (1) the "exit" option, in which people stop buying one good and purchase another, or quit one job and begin another (1970: 4); and (2) the "voice" option, in which "the firm's customers or the organization's members express their dissatisfaction directly to management or to some other authority" (1970: 4). In the initial stages of the gasoline shortage drivers responded by exiting; later, as the shortages worsened, customers began to complain more frequently about prices, services, and the availability of gasoline—in Hirschman's terms they began to exercise voice. In this circumstance market processes (exit) are of little use to seller because they provide no information about prospective

purchasers other then the price which they are willing to pay. Because political processes (voice) rely on discussions, reports, and briefs in deciding how to allocate a resource, they are information-rich compared to market processes (Hirschman, 1976: 386) and are more likely to yield information which will enable sellers to choose between two economically acceptable purchasers.

33. After the institution of a rationing system, gasoline resembled a public good more than a private good. A private good is a resource which if X_1 in a group $X_1 X_n$ consume it, then no one else in the group can consume it. In contrast, a public good is a resource which if X_1, consumes it, cannot be withheld from the other members of the group $X_1 \ldots X_n$ (Olson, 1971: 14). Oakland (1972: 356–357) makes the point that public and private goods are polar cases; he maintains that there is a continuum between purely private goods, such as food, and purely public goods, such as air, along which different resources can be ranked. Resources in intermediate positions on the continuum usually share with private goods the attribute that they can be rationed and share with public goods the attribute that numerous individuals can use the good simultaneously. When gas rationing was instituted, individuals in the privileged group of users could not be denied the resource if they could pay. In this respect gasoline resembled a public good. On the other hand individuals in the disadvantaged group often could not gain access to the resource when individuals from the advantaged group had access. In this respect gasoline resembled a private good. In effect, when governments instituted rationing plans, gasoline assumed the characteristics of an impure public good.
34. This progression of events lies behind Brian Berry's suggestion that, in the face of declines in the quality of a good, the chief alternative to individual exit is group voice (reported in Rokkan, 1974: 132). One would expect that shifts in consumer attitudes would accompany the shifts in consumer social organization. Specifically, the shift from the individual to the collective response should be paralleled by a shift in consumer motivation. In the initial stages of the shortage, changes in the price of the resource should motivate lower rates of consumption; in the later, more

severe stage of the shortage, altruism, in the form of responses to appeals to limit consumption so as to minimize the social disruption caused by the shortage, should assume a more important role in motivating lower rates of consumption. Honnold and Nelson's (1978) findings in a study of the evolution of consumer attitudes during the 1977 natural gas shortage in Virginia suggest empirical support for this argument.

35. Paul Hofmann, "Poland Combats Meat Shortage By Opening Commercial Shops," *The New York Times,* November 27, 1980. This policy change should not be confused with the dramatic government-ordered increases in food prices which touched off a wave of riots and strikes by Polish workers in June 1976.

References

American Automobile Association (1974). Fuel Gauge Reports, January-March.

Dawes. R. M. (1973). The commons dilemma: An N-person mixed motive game with a dominating strategy for defection. *Oregon Research Institute Bulletin* 13: 1–12.

Edney, J. J., and Harper. C. S. (1978). The effects of information in a resource management problem: A social trap analog. *Human Ecology* 6(4): 387–395.

Edney, J. J., and Cass, R. C. (1978). The commons dilemma: A simulation testing the effects of resource visibility and territorial division. *Human Ecology* 6(4): 371–386.

Erikson. K. T. (1976). *Everything in It's Path: Destruction of Community in the Buffalo Creek Flood.* Simon and Schuster, New York.

Hirschman, A. O. (1970). *Exit, Voice, and Loyalty: Responses to Declines in Organizations, Firms, and States.* Harvard University Press, Cambridge, Mass.

Hirschman, A. O. (1976). Comment. *American Economic Review* 66(May): 386–389.

Honnold, J. A., and Nelson, L. D. (1978). Structural and situational determinants of conservation: An analysis of consumer response to the 1977 fuel crisis. Paper presented at the annual meeting of the American Sociological Association, San Francisco.

MacArthur, R. H. (1972). *Geographical Ecology: Patterns in the Distribution of Species.* Harper and Row, New York.

McCay, B. J. (1978). Systems ecology, people ecology, and the anthropology of fishing communities. *Human Ecology* 6(4): 397–422.

Murray, J. L., Minor. M. J., Bradburn, N. M., Cotterman, R. F., Frankel, M., and Pisarski, A. E. (1964). Evolution of public response to the energy crisis. *Science* 184 (April 19): 257–263.

Oakland, W. H. (1972). Congestion, public goods and welfare. *Journal of Public Economics* 1: 339–357.

Olson, M., Jr. (1971). The *Logic of Collective Action: Public Goods and Public Policy,* 2nd Ed., Schocken, New York.

Quatentelli, E. L., and Dynes, R. R. (1977). Response to social crisis and disaster, in Inkeles, A. (ed.), *Annual Review of Sociology.* Annual Reviews, Palo Alto, pp. 23–50.

Rokkan, S. (1974). Entries, voices, exits: Towards a possible generalization of the Hirschman model. *Social Science Information* 13(l): 39–53.

Vayda, A. P. (1976). *War in Ecological Perspective,* Plenum, New York.

Fueling National Insecurity

While most of us suffer from the escalating cost of filling our gas tanks, some "public interest" activists likely don't share our concern. After all, increasing the price of natural resources, mostly by curtailing domestic energy production, has been a longstanding goal of environmental elitists. They think this is the best way to reduce supposedly rampant automobile pollution and force development of "alternative" fuels. Less reliance on oil should be a laudable goal, but professional environmentalists' misguided approach carries with it serious consequences for the public — more economic and national insecurity.

These activists should call themselves "Environmentalists for Foreign Energy Dependence" — as we have them to thank for the decades of regulations and lawsuits that make it nearly impossible to discover and refine oil here. And then, when we must rely on oil from unstable regions of the world, like the Middle East, these very same activists hypocritically scream "no blood for oil." Such dependence empowers erratic foreign regimes and power-hungry terrorists to hold our economy and national security, hostage. American energy consumers shouldn't be funding Saddam Hussein wannabes who would turn the Middle East into one huge arsenal of terror.

Daniel J. Popeo
Chairman
Washington
Legal Foundation

Paying at the pump for activism

Nor do we have to. America has abundant, untapped energy resources. But a maze of regulations makes exploring for energy on public lands prohibitively expensive, and extracting gas or oil essentially impossible. Significant improvements in technology have made resource extraction more environmentally friendly than ever. Yet, activists and politicians continue to stall offshore exploration and drilling in a barren patch of Alaskan wasteland. And on the rare occasion that approval to explore public lands is granted, extremists and their lawyers bombard energy companies with lawsuits. All this adds up to flat domestic energy production and higher prices.

Once oil is drilled, even more government mandates make it costly to turn crude into gasoline. Demand for gas in the U.S. is simply outstripping the capacity of domestic refineries, adding to what we pay at the pump and furthering our reliance on overseas production. Thanks to activist-driven federal rules, a new refinery hasn't been built here for almost thirty years, while other regulations make it almost prohibitively expensive even to upgrade existing plants. Also, federal regulations require that refiners create over twenty different kinds of fuel that can only be sold in specified regions of America.

Protecting the environment and pursuing new domestic energy development aren't conflicting goals. Responsible, authentic environmentalism, in fact, contemplates the balanced use *and* enjoyment of our resources. But today's no-growth activists must sell gloom and doom to stay in business, so it is fair to wonder whose interest they have in mind when they oppose practical solutions to our foreign energy dependence.

Washington Legal Foundation
Advocate for freedom and justice®

WASHINGTON LEGAL FOUNDATION • 2009 MASSACHUSETTS AVE., NW • WASHINGTON, DC 20036 • http://www.wlf.org

In All Fairness is produced through WLF's Civic Communications Program.

IN ALL FAIRNESS

America's *Green* Recession

America is in the midst of its first green recession, an economic downturn caused in no small part by irrational ideological activism. Thirty years of punitive laws, restrictive environmental regulations, and special interests' obstructionist lawsuits have come home to roost in our dangerous dependence on foreign oil, escalating fuel prices, and the collateral consequences of those costs.

OPEC is a "Made in the USA" monopoly. Environmental extremism has long dominated American energy policy-making, and as a result, we are the **Activism has consequences** only oil-producing nation in the world that limits access to its own abundant energy resources like oil, coal, and natural gas. Significant improvements in technology have made resource extraction more environmentally friendly than ever. However, on the rare occasion that the federal government grants approval for oil exploration on public lands, activists and their lawyers bombard energy companies with lawsuits. Finally, even if we were able to tap into new domestic crude oil sources, a thicket of federal rules ensnares the expansion of existing U.S. oil refineries; a new refinery hasn't been built here since Gerald Ford was President.

Activism has consequences. All Americans are suffering from this self-inflicted energy paralysis. We feel the pain every time we go to the grocery store, commute to work, or shuttle our kids around to after-school activities. No sector of the economy is immune, and unfortunately those who can least afford price increases of basic staples like gas and food are suffering the most.

Federal and state policy makers are failing to confront our stagnant domestic energy production. For instance, instead of making energy cheaper in California, that state's unelected Public Utility Commission (PUC) is tacking on an audacious fee to customers' electric bills to fund a $600 million climate change "think tank." Environmental activists, perhaps angling for a piece of the research pie, wholeheartedly supported the concept. One Californian, who objected to ratepayers being

Daniel J. Popeo
Chairman
Washington
Legal Foundation

singled out for such funding, asked of the PUC commissioners, "Are they consumer advocates? I just wonder." So should every-one.

Politicians are eager to tout "alternative" sources of electricity, but they follow in lock-step with their environmental elitist allies when it comes to dismissing nuclear power. Activists' and politicians' hypocritical stance on such energy has deprived the U.S. of new nuclear power plants for twenty years. Europe has long embraced this safe and reliable energy source. If it's good enough for the highly risk-averse French, why not us?

If special interests want to further their Luddite agenda, the rest of us shouldn't have to pay for it. It's time to put Americans to work tapping into the abundant energy supply we have right here at home. Until our leaders make this commitment, Americans' paychecks will continue to be on direct deposit to foreign energy producers.

Washington Legal Foundation
Advocate for freedom and justice®

WASHINGTON LEGAL FOUNDATION • 2009 MASSACHUSETTS AVE., NW • WASHINGTON, DC 20036 • http://www.wlf.org

In All Fairness is produced through WLF's Civic Communications Program.

---

* From *The New York Times Op-Ed* (May 19, 2008) by Daniel J. Popeo for The Washington Legal Foundation. Copyright © 2008 by Washington Legal Foundation. Reprinted by permission.

52 *lack do interest*

America's Apathy on the Environment

Geneva Overholser

There are a lot of reasons not to get too worked up over the impact we're having on our planet. Environmental changes seem so nebulous (would global warming be so bad?) and so distant in time and place. Politicians don't appear very concerned. Business people say calls to action are alarmist. And—the ultimate justification for complacency—even science seems divided.

No wonder most Americans, while professing environmentalism, remain unmoved by the looming but shadowy questions. It's enough to make active environmentalists want to grab us by the lapels—as a group assembled by the nonprofit Environmental Media Services attempted to do in Washington recently.

"The story of the last decade," said Bill McKibben, an environmental writer, is that "human beings crossed a certain threshold: We became big enough as a species to affect everything around us. The story of the next decade is increasingly going to be the story of the effects of crossing that threshold."

It's true that we don't know precisely what these effects will be, said Jane Lubchenco, a professor at Oregon State University and past president of the American Association for the Advancement of Science. "Scientists are only beginning to understand how . . . the massive changes are playing out." But scientists agree—overwhelmingly—that "we are disrupting the function of the systems on which we depend."

It's no accident that Americans are confused about what science thinks. People heavily invested in our patterns of behavior put a lot of money into assuring us that we shouldn't be worried enough to change those patterns. Lubchenco says that, thanks to groups like the Global Climate Coalition—which calls itself "a voice for business in the global warming debate"—"We've seen junk science, ignorance and misinformation drown out good, credible scientific information and public understanding."

The evidence that we're dramatically changing the world around us is unmistakable. Take an international study combining 46 years of data on the shrinking of sea ice in Arctic waters. Results indicated a less than 2 percent probability that the melting of the past 20 years was caused by normal climate variation, the Washington Post reported.

The business world is increasingly parting ranks with the do-nothings, as executives see the weight of science and public

---

opinion shifting. European companies have led the way. But American firms are following. Ford Motor Co. announced that it is resigning from the Global Climate Coalition because it believes there is enough evidence of global warming that companies must begin working together more effectively to reduce carbon emissions. Dow Chemical Co. had resigned previously.

Our current method, Lubchenco says, is simply "full steam ahead: It's better to ignore the possibility of a problem until it hits us in the face." Instead, she said, we should see that "uncertainty warrants precaution."

Also at the gathering was Denis Hayes, coordinator of the first Earth Day, 30 years ago. His current project is Earth Day 2000, whose aim is "to forge a global majority around environmental values." Americans should be leading the way toward engagement with the environment, he said. "But our credibility elsewhere depends on our succeeding at home."

While Americans brought about huge environmental improvements after the first Earth Day, we have been backsliding lately. Over the last 10 years, said Hayes, we've had a 12 percent growth in the harmful emissions—mostly from automobiles—that contribute to global warming.

The challenge for Americans is to move out of the complacency we're lulled into by the seeming distance and uncertainty of environmental challenges and to act on the values we profess.

53

Green Fatigue

We need a break from the Daily Doom Report
Susan Nielsen

Now that every day is Earth Day, we need a new kind of holiday. We need an annual break from bad environmental news.

The year-round glumfest about drowning polar bears, dying honeybees and the general futility of it all is raising consciousness but crushing spirits (or at least mine). We need a day of rest—a time to pretend, as we did in the 1990s, that the party could last forever.

—The other 364 days we can stick to the new normal, flogging ourselves about carbon and fretting about an uncertain future.

Lately, each week brings a fresh variation on the theme of "we're doomed." The stories come in three varieties. First, we're destroying the environment with our old bad habits, like building golf courses in the desert.

Second, we're making things worse with our new good habits, like embracing corn-based ethanol, which is contributing to a global food crisis and (wait, there's more!) deforestation.

Third, we're too late. We can sell our cars and walk on our knees to work, but the oceans will continue to rise. People in China and India, seeking a higher standard of living, will cancel out any of our feeble attempts to consume less. The furry little cubs will sink beneath the surface of the sea, unable to overcome forces set in motion a century ago.

It's a miracle we're able to function at all, weighed down by the Daily Doom Report.

"Dude, where's my iceberg?" the news headline blares, prompting a familiar mix of irritation and despair.

"Do you have time to save a polar bear today?" the Green-peace solicitors ask, so chipper that you want to punch them.

I think you see what I'm getting at here.

We need a break.

The new holiday could be a special national reprieve. Everyone would agree to give it a rest for 24 hours. No pestering from environmental groups. No grim stories about five-legged frogs or collapsing salmon runs. No one would be allowed to bring up peak oil, water shortages, dead zones or the chemicals in your favorite shampoo.

Best of all, everyone would be pardoned from feeling anxious about their big clomping carbon footprints. Just for a day, we could all drive our cars for as many miles as we can afford, and no one would open their piehole about taking the bus.

The idea of an environmental holiday may not be popular with some readers. They will write and say it's PEOPLE LIKE YOU who ruin the environment by being FLIPPANT and THOUGHTLESS. To them I apologize in advance, as part of a personal initiative to conserve energy by avoiding conflict.

But I'd also add this. Look, you won. The world now realizes that you are right. You were right back in the 1970s, when environmentalism was a lifestyle choice rather than a global necessity. You are right that it will take a worldwide, nonstop effort to limit the damage.

This is precisely why we now need an annual day of rest. Just one day. We'd go to the history museum and gaze fondly at the model Ford F-150, next to the dinosaurs. We'd reminisce about old road trips to Vegas, fast food in Styrofoam containers and Costco multipacks of batteries.

Then we'd turn on all the lights and crank the A/C and heat simultaneously. And just for a while it would be morning in America, when green was just a color and everything was free.

54

The Age of Eco-Angst

Daniel Goleman

My grandson's third birthday is at hand, and I'm looking at a toy racing car I won't be giving him. Painted a bright yellow, this nifty little toy seemed just right for him when I paid a buck for it at a big box store. But before I could give it to him, I learned that cheap toys made in China, like this one, can have lead in their paint—particularly reds and yellows—to make them more shiny.

My pleasure at picturing his delight at the toy car melted into something between disgust and outrage. That nifty toy sits on my desk months after I bought it.

Call it eco-angst, the moment a new bit of unpleasant ecological information about some product or other plunges us into a moment (or more) of despair at the planet's condition and the fragility of our place on it.

Eco-angst, it turns out, is but one version of a widely studied psychological phenomenon, one well-known in the world of retailing. Take a bargain bin cabernet, tell people it's an expensive, estate-bottled varietal, and they'll tell you they like it. They'll even linger longer over their dinner, enjoying not just the wine but the rest of their food more. Now describe the same wine as a low-end variety from North Dakota, and they'll tell you it's not so good—and finish their meal faster, enjoying it less.

We will no longer be impressed by an organic T-shirt if its cotton was grown by hogging water in an arid and impoverished land, or if its dye puts workers at heightened risk for leukemia.

The difference lies, of course, in the perception, not the reality. The emotional power of this perceptual skew has been documented in experiments not just with wines, but even pain relievers—the more expensive ones always seem better. Mindset drives our experience of a product, a fact known intuitively by advertisers long before the era of "Mad Men." Back in the 1920s, Edward Bernays, a nephew of Sigmund Freud, became an influential pioneer of public relations by capitalizing on the power of psychological manipulation of the public to sell products. Advertising and psychology have been intertwined ever since.

What's more, brain imaging now reveals that tasting what we think is a high-end wine produces heightened activity in a key strip of neurons in the orbitofrontal cortex, which lights up during moments of keen interest—a pattern some neuroeconomists see as the brain signature for brand preference. The "low-end" wine, on the other hand elicits not a budge in orbitofrontal chatter, a pattern indicating disinterest or disgust. (Study data can be found here.)

The neural signature for disgust may soon become more prevalent in the aisles of stores with the advent of heightened transparency about the ecological impacts of retail products like deodorants, foods and toys. A new generation of information systems has begun to offer detailed evaluations of once-hidden ecological impacts for tens of thousands of items, and the picture is not always pretty.

Eco-angst dawns with the discovery that some children's sunblock contains a chemical that becomes a carcinogen when exposed to the sun, or that the company that makes a popular organic yogurt operates in ways that result in significantly more greenhouse gases than their competitors. The moral here, or course, is not to stop using sunblock nor to give up yogurt, but to choose the brands without these downsides.

Such distasteful information has predictable consequences for marketing, particularly if the eye-opening data comes at the moment we're comparing two brands. Psychologists call it the "contrast effect": as Item A suddenly looks bad, we get an even stronger preference for Item B. It is also a marketing boon for products that do no harm.

Eco-angst among consumers may soon spread as information about products is increasing easy to get. GoodGuide.com, is a Web site (with its own iPhone application) that instantly compares any of 75,000 consumer products on their environmental, health, and social impacts. Another Web site, SkinDeep.com, analyzes every ingredient in personal care products to match them with findings from medical databases; it ranks, for example, more than a thousand shampoos on their likely levels of toxicity.

The blockbuster for ecological transparency was the announcement in July by Wal-Mart that they are developing a similar sustainability index with the help of an academic consortium. One day shoppers, it seems, will get ecological ratings of products along with price in Wal-Mart (and likely other major retailers as well) as they stroll the aisles.

These rating systems herald the death of "greenwashing," the advertising sleight-of-hand that plucks a single virtue from a multitude of a product's ecological impacts and touts its environmental goodness. We will no longer be impressed by an organic T-shirt if its cotton was grown by hogging water in an arid and impoverished land, or if its dye puts workers at heightened risk for leukemia, or if it was stitched together in a sweatshop where young women suffer from needless injuries.

Industrial ecology, the fledgling discipline that renders precise analyzes of the multitude of ecological impacts any man-made item has over its life cycle, tells us that there is little or nothing manufactured today that nature loves. Ours is an age of eco-angst because virtually all our industrial platforms, processes and chemicals were developed in a day when people were oblivious to their ecological impacts.

It's not that no one cared—no one really knew. Industrial ecology has only come of age in the last decade or two, and has yet to make its findings widely known. But as ecological transparency comes to the aisles of stores near you and me, it opens an opportunity for us to vote with our dollars with unprecedented precision for better ecological impacts.

Rather than taking the ascetic route of "No Impact Man," we can together become high impact shoppers, tipping market share to products with gentler ecological imprints. But to do so we need to face the often unattractive truths behind the making of our favorite stuff, and so risk a stiff dose of disgust.

55

The Elusive Process of Citizen Activism

Celene Krauss

Summary:
More people were fighting for rights / used citizen activism to fight for things which pertained to them (dangers to health).
small protests are not by tough gov't, have to be confident + able to fight. Small resistance = ability to challenge political authority. public excluded from decisions of gov't

Contrary to popul... protest did not die i... commentators such as Ch... Tom Wolfe present an ima... the "Me Decade," charac... sism, passivity, and a retre... tivity. Yet, in the hidden, le... daily life, something more...

Citizen activism expl... roots level in the 1970s ar... the 1980s. During those y... ple awakened to defend th... from corporate and governmental bulldozers. Ecologists fought against the destruction of the natural environment and human life. Workers exposed the problems of health and safety on the job. Consumer groups investigated carcinogens in our food and water. During this time women also fought for their rights in various arenas, and older people, veterans, and the handicapped formed coalitions to gain political power and recognition.

The protests of the '60s did not die completely; if anything, they became more and more rooted in the lives of ordinary men and women. People who had never regarded themselves as political activists became

...onse to concrete dangers to ...s, their health, and even ...tinue to see the 1970s as a ...decade? Why do we con... the citizen protests that ...d continue to grow even ...If citizen activism is poorly ...y be because we have no ...ich to think about these ...-lived protests of daily life. ...art, the deeper meanings and importance of these protests have been either ignored or trivialized. However, in a decade dismissed for its quiescence, the existence of citizen activism suggests an opposite view. In these struggles, ordinary people bring to bear unsuspected energy, intelligence, impact. These protests are not highly visible. There are few mass movements and even fewer celebrated leaders. These citizen struggles suggest that we need to treat as important the ways in which people experience and wrestle with crisis in bits and pieces, in the moments of daily life.[1]

Another view of citizen protest reveals the more elusive process of resistance, the activity

---

below the surface. The analysis of these protests brings out the ways in which people develop a critical world view as they penetrate the obfuscating analysis advanced by the powerful. These are the moments when, as C. Wright Mills once wrote, people see the link between their "personal troubles and public issues . . . the intricate connections between patterns of their own lives and the course of history."[2]

These protests, which appear sporadic, may have far-reaching implications. George RudÈ, a French social historian, made this point about food riots during the seventeenth and eighteenth centuries. These protests were sporadic outbreaks that occurred at different times for nearly two centuries before they became connected with a more far-reaching analysis and helped spur the French Revolution. Under certain conditions, Rudé implies, everyday protests create new, unanticipated possibilities for social change.[3]

Love Canal

Examining some examples of citizen protests allows as to clarify how this process of resistance develops. Consider the fight against toxic wastes at Love Canal.[4] Love Canal was a heterogeneous working- and middle-class community built in the 1950s adjacent to a landfill that contained carcinogenic chemicals. For two decades, residents unwittingly lived with the effects of inhaling carcinogenic compounds such as tetradioxine and benzene. These chemicals penetrated their homes and contaminated the waters where children swam. Residents lived with and accepted as personal tragedies high rates of miscarriage, birth defects, cancer, and various other illnesses. Michael Brown captured this insidious process when he wrote, "While people watched television, gardened, slept, and ate, they were inhaling a mixture of damaging chemicals."[5] Residents complained to the Niagra County Health Department about problems associated with toxic wastes such as black sludge seeping into their basements and pesticide smells permeating their

homes. This local agency characterized these problems as "nuisance conditions" and assured people that there was no real danger. Hooker Chemical, the company involved, knew that the situation was dangerous. Yet until the 1970s, residents of the area were kept in the dark. Their own health problems were perceived as "acts of capricious genes, a vicious quirk of nature."[6]

In the 1970s, a decade during which people became aware of the dangers of environmental pollutants, the residents of Love Canal pieced together the terrible story. Lois Gibbs describes that moment of truth, that shock of recognition that politicized her thinking. "All around me I saw things happening to my neighbors—multiple miscarriages, birth defects, cancer deaths, epilepsy, central nervous disorders, and more. . . . We were never warned. We had no idea we were living on top of a chemical graveyard. I never thought of myself as an activist or an organizer—I was a housewife, a mother—but all of a sudden it was my family, my children, and my neighbors."[7] This is an example of how it is sometimes possible for ordinary citizens to break through the obfuscating analysis of the powerful and make the connections between events in their own lives and larger public and political issues. Feminists call moments such as these "the click."[8]

As residents uncovered the dangers of toxic wastes, they once again approached their local government for help. They believed, as Gibbs wrote, that "If you had a complaint, you went to the right person in government. If there was a way to solve the problem, they would be glad to do it."[9] But they faced a government that, when confronted by residents with hard data on the effects of chemical wastes, dismissed them as overemotional "hypochondriacs." "The most difficult part of the struggle," notes Gibbs, "is that no one would take us seriously . . . It took Love Canal to open my eyes. I bought the American Dream when I moved to Love Canal only to learn it wasn't there because government and industry abused my rights."[10]

In the end, their response to the government's indifference led these residents to become more autonomous and militant. They became activists who justified civil disobedience on the grounds that they were making the system "do what it's supposed to do." They vandalized a construction site, burned effigies of the governor, and were arrested during a baby-carriage blockade. Confronted with continuing official indifference, residents of Love Canal finally took drastic action. They captured and held hostage two officials of the Environmental Protection Agency and offered President Carter an ultimatum. The next day the President bowed to the public outcry. Love Canal was declared a national disaster and $15 million was allocated for relocating its residents. In this case, the initial shock came from the existence of the dangerous toxic-wastes situation and the chemical company's cover-up of the danger, but people became even more disillusioned when they realized that "their" government would take no steps to remedy the situation. A more political position was a response to government indifference.

In the end, Love Canal had consequences that went beyond this grass-roots struggle. It sensitized the nation to the dangers of toxic wastes, influencing the creation of a federal superfund to clean up similar unsafe dump sites across the country. Lois Gibbs, who once described herself as a shy, apolitical housewife, became a national figure helping to organize grass-roots struggles to fight toxic wastes across the country. A new interracial coalition is now being formed around-this issue. Spearheaded by a Black community in North Carolina. Thus, we see how a small grass-roots protest was able to make its point clearly and forcefully and helped to stimulate the development of a larger movement.

Westway

We see this same deepening critique of power in anti-highway protest campaigns such as the one over Westway in New York City. When we look at the Westway issue, a struggle that seems to be about building a highway, there doesn't appear to be much

relationship to the kind of issue which people struggled about at Love Canal. We might even find the highway issue less controversial, viewing it as a situation in which, at least on the surface, there are plausible arguments to be made on both sides. Love Canal was a dramatic and moving struggle that had clear heroes and villains. The community residents who fought the insidious poisons of toxic wastes are clearly the good guys; and the government and industry officials who colluded to cover up this tragedy are clearly the bad guys. We are less likely to be moved, or take seriously, fights to stop highways. Citizen struggles, such as these, seem less urgent than such issues as toxic wastes or nuclear power. But when we look at the ways in which so-called single-issue struggles uncover a world of power and special interests, then the history of Westway issues reveals a more dramatic story.

In the early 1970s, the West Side Highway Project, a New York State agency, developed a plan for an immense eight-lane highway on Manhattan's waterfront. This development project would include a massive landfill to be used for industrial and residential development and parkland. The proposed highway project, costing over $1 billion, would be a financial boon to such business interests as banks, construction companies, and real-estate developers who stood to make millions. The project's proponents justified the construction of Westway by claiming it met the needs of city automobile drivers and that it would create much needed jobs for city workers. Further, it was claimed that the project would neither increase air pollution nor damage the marine life of the Hudson River. The project's opponents, who wanted to stop construction of Westway, argued that a trade-in of highway funds would benefit most New Yorkers by improving a dangerously deteriorated system of mass transit.

In this case, the public good was by no means clear or self-evident in the early stages of the struggle. It was necessary for activists to make a careful analysis of official projections used to justify the project in order to demonstrate the potential harm and injustice that would result from construction of the highway. Over a ten-year period, a growing coalition of ecologists, community activists, transit workers, and members of minority groups developed a complex analysis that raised fundamental questions about who would benefit and who would pay the costs of the highway. This "single-issue" protest ultimately connected seemingly disparate issues such as ecology, neighborhood integrity, race, and class.

One group of activists researched the inequities of highway use and were able to show that most residents of New York City would not benefit from the construction of the highway because more than half of all the city's households and three-fourths of Black and Hispanic families do not own a car.[11] Other activists showed how the attempt to separate the job and ecology issues was a red herring. A governmental trade-in of Westway funds would aid a deteriorating system of mass transit and thereby create more permanent jobs for transit workers as opposed to temporary jobs for construction workers. The trade-in not only would create one-third more jobs but most of those jobs would go to New Yorkers, whereas the Westway jobs would also go to workers in manufacturing plants outside the region.[12]

Finally, ecologists challenged claims that the construction of the highway would not increase air pollution. They produced data that showed that the construction of new highways always leads to increased highway use. Ecologists also exposed a massive governmental cover-up that hid data indicating that the highway would endanger marine life in the Hudson.[13] Over the years, citizen groups coalesced and brought repeated court actions on issues such as air quality permits, state water quality standards, and the consequences of dredging the Hudson. Marcy Benstock, one of the important leaders of this struggle, believed that "the thing to do is to get people to enforce these existing laws through citizen pressure."[14] This form of protest prolonged the highway fight for years and prevented construction from the beginning.

This year, almost a decade after Westway was first proposed, it may be the "Striped Bass Scandal" that stops the highway. It was held by the U.S. Court of Appeals for the Second Circuit that the government both ignored and withheld from the public evidence that the project's landfill would endanger the many species of fish that inhabit the Hudson River.[15] By forcing the government to make good on its own laws, struggles such as this one utilize contradictions inherent in the system.

For those who read about Westway in the popular press, it may have seemed a protest about highways and fish. Highways and fish do not appear to be urgent political issues. Yet this protest, no less than the one at Love Canal, raises deeper issues about the connection of state and private power. In the course of protest, anti-highway activists challenge far more than highway construction. They strike at a powerful historical relationship between the state and the private economy. Since 1945, the federal government has spent most of its transportation budget on roads and highways, and thereby stimulated capital accumulation. This has proven highly profitable for such industries as contracting, trucking, oil, steel, automotive, and real estate. When anti-highway activists slow down or stop the construction of a highway, they hurt this system of power and profit. In the course of struggle, activists learn about far more than the problems caused by a highway; they learn that the government values the wishes of powerful business interests above the needs of ordinary citizens.

Redlining

In grass-roots struggles throughout the decade, people broke through the cover-ups of government and business officials. We see this important work of discovery illustrated in struggles around neighborhood deterioration. Countless working-class neighborhoods were saved as working people refused to accept the inevitability of their neighborhood's decline or destruction. Many social analysts blamed inner-city neighborhood deterioration on racism and "white flight." By inquiring below the surface, working people uncovered other reasons such as blockbusting, gentrification, and redlining.

Redlining, for example, was discovered by working-class homeowners in a Chicago neighborhood who were trying to stem their community's decline. This is a process in which savings banks and other lending institutions arbitrarily refuse to grant mortgages or home loans to residents of a particular neighborhood that they define as "risky." Incredibly, these banks were investing the money of urban working depositors in developing the more profitable suburbs and sunbelt areas.

Gail Cincotta led the fight to stop redlining and organized National People's Action, a nationwide coalition of grass-roots organizations. The problem with redlining, notes Cincotta, is that the bank's projection of a "risky" neighborhood becomes a self-fulfilling prophecy. Banks disinvest in areas where housing is often structurally sound but old and in need of upgrading. When banks withdraw money in "anticipation" of neighborhood deterioration, these neighborhoods do deteriorate. Homeowners who wish to improve their building often feel that they have to sell when they are denied loans for this purpose. As more and more homeowners and businesses leave the neighborhood, real-estate speculators begin to buy neighborhood property, housing code violations increase, and absentee landlords become the rule.[16]

The inequities of this policy are well illustrated by data on redlining in New York City. Here only 13 cents out of every dollar that New Yorkers put into savings banks is reinvested in home mortgage loans. The remaining 87 cents of each dollar is invested in suburban and out-of-state mortgages and stocks and bonds. While only 13 percent of all of New York City's deposits are reinvested in mortgage loans locally, 62 percent of savings banks in Nassau and Suffolk counties invest locally. In other words, the suburbs not only get investments from local banks, but from

the city's as well. Clearly, city residents are discriminated against, and not surprisingly city neighborhoods decline.[17]

Throughout the '70s, citizen groups attempted to pressure local banks into disclosing redlining patterns and reinvesting in their communities. They found, however, that it was impossible to get banks to admit that the policy of redlining even existed. In response to citizen pressure, banks developed a counteroffensive. In New York City, for example, they took out full-page ads in city newspapers disclaiming the existence of redlining. The influential bank lobby in New York State granted special favors to state legislators in return for their opposition to anti-redlining legislation. When banks were asked to account for the granting of so few mortgages locally, they justified their actions by saying, as one bank president in Brooklyn put it, "very few applications came in."[18]

In the early 1970s, National People's Action tried to pressure the federal government into passing legislation that would require financial institutions to disclose where they grant loans. At the very least, this law would help residents substantiate the extent of redlining. But citizen groups were met with official indifference for years. Finally, in the mid-1970s, they won the passage of the disclosure bill and antiredliners now had the ammunition with which to begin to document their claim.

The campaign to stop redlining resembles the one at Love Canal. In both protests we see how difficult it is to get anyone in power to admit that a problem even exists. The burden of proof rests with ordinary citizens who have to break through the cover-up and develop their own analysis. Beginning with a simple desire to stem neighborhood decline, one grass-roots struggle in Chicago mushroomed into a powerful nationwide campaign to stop redlining. In the end, this struggle continued for many years as organizations not only made redlining patterns visible but also fought for neighborhood reinvestment.

In the process of protest, working people developed a complex analysis showing how neighborhood deterioration was not their fault: rather it resulted from the inequities of bank policy and real-estate speculation. It is not that banks set out to destroy neighborhoods and the lives of its people in some predetermined fashion, but that these are the incidental "costs" in a larger process of economic growth and profit making. By asserting the right of working-class neighborhoods to survive, working people stopped business as usual. They stemmed the flow of capital out of their communities and slowed down a system of growth and profit.

Redlining is one important issue that threatens working-class neighborhoods, but there are others as well. Working-class neighborhoods had always seemed like easy marks for city administrations and local industries. As Herbert Gans noted in his study of the redevelopment of Boston's West End, residents tended to be fatalistic about their capacity to influence the outside world and generally remained politically apathetic. These neighborhoods were seen as "placid villages" whose way of life guaranteed passive reactions to disruptive policies.[19] But in the 1970s, the concept of "neighborhood" took on new political meanings for community residents who fought against neighborhood destruction. Because these activists believed in the justice of American society, they became even more indignant when they realized that it did not work.

Consider the fight at Poletown in 1980, which was the latest in a series of working-class struggles across the country. The city of Detroit used its power of eminent domain to condemn this tightly knit Polish American neighborhood so that General Motors could build a Cadillac plant. The people of Poletown reacted strongly to this proposal. Many fought back, occupying a local church. They were religious and patriotic people. It was difficult for them to believe that their church could be condemned in the name of progress or justice.

We saw similar fights to preserve various neighborhoods in New York City. One example is the protest of the "fighting 69" of Corona, Queens, in the early 1970s. The city government promised a Queens developer,

Sam Lefrak, that they would build a public school adjacent to a Lefrak housing development. In Corona, a cohesive Italian-American neighborhood, 69 homes were slated for demolition so that the city could build an athletic field for the school. The residents of Corona saw themselves as good citizens and law-abiding people. They could not believe that this tragedy was happening to them. Like the people of Poletown, they fought back and refused to pay the price of loss of their homes and community so that Sam Lefrak could benefit.[20]

Social commentators are quick to compare the 1970s to the seemingly passive '50s. Once we look at citizen protests, however, our view of the '70s changes. From neighborhood to ecology, from consumer issues to technology, ordinary citizens called into question prevailing ideologies. On a day-to-day level, they ended a romance with the symbols of progress of the '50s. They asked important questions such as who benefits from economic growth and, similarly, from dangerous technology and political bureaucracy. This was a time of lost innocence for people who once believed in the system. As one resident at Three Mile Island sums it up, "In the Fifties, I was afraid we'd be invaded by a foreign country. It never occurred to me we would be invaded by America."[21]

Elusive Gains

The elusive process of citizen protest that is stressed here reveals the activity below the surface. Frank Riessman illuminates this hidden dimension of protest when he says, "People gain skills, some success, and knowledge about the enemy. They also build contacts and coalitions. In these ways, small politics may become the basis for big politics."[22]

These protests may go in different directions. Sometimes people win their protest, and sometimes they lose. Sometimes protests are co-opted and destroyed, and sometimes they mushroom into larger social movements. But the more elusive gains are the changes in people who take an active stance. These everyday struggles show the ways in which these people are neither narcissistic nor passive victims. People do indeed fight back. In the course of their struggles, they develop a critical world view, and they come to believe in their own ability to act. They are transformed by their experience. These personal chances allow people to pull aside the veil and glimpse the machinations of the powerful.

The actions described here show the small and hidden gains that emerge from this more elusive type of protest. As a first step in the process of resistance, we noted how people were provoked to make sense of troubles that seemed difficult to understand. In these moments they were able to link the personal and political in their own lives and act on this understanding. Ordinary citizens uncovered the dangers of toxic wastes, redlining, and highways.

Consider how difficult it is for citizens to initiate protests such as these. In each case those in power attempt systematically to distort the links between personal troubles and political issues. For the most part people are excluded from making those decisions that have far-reaching social and political consequences. Consequently, they are faced with a number of problems of seemingly indeterminate origin. People's neighborhoods deteriorate and they aren't sure why. Miscarriages get chalked up to unfortunate tragedies, as do serious illnesses.

Discovering the political nature of personal troubles is a difficult step in a society that covers up these connections. Consider how both Hooker Chemical and the local government continued to deny the dangers of toxic wastes when confronted with hard data. Similarly, banks refused to admit that they engaged in any discriminatory lending practices such as redlining. At Westway, activists had to penetrate the obfuscation of government and industry officials who justified the highway by claiming it would serve "the public interest." In each case, we see how the burden of proof falls on residents of the local community.

Discovering the causal link between the personal and political seems like a small act. But when viewed in the context of both gov-ernmental and corporate cover-ups, it is a major breakthrough. It implies a critique of the dominant ideology, and an unmasking of the connections that those in power disguise. This small change in consciousness, as we saw, empowered people to fight back. Whatever else may happen in these struggles, the awareness is won. This is a small act of resistance that may not seem to measure up to grand expectations for social change. Yet linking the personal and political is a critical gain: no click, no resistance.

As a second step in the process of resistance, we note how people become increasingly critical and militant. Engaging in struggles around "single issues" led ordinary citizens to learn about far more than their initial problem, as "one little click turns on a thousand others."[23] People became more and more disillusioned as they turned to government for help and attempted to participate in the system in even a minimal way. In each case they found that their expectations were violated when government failed to protect them from the abuses of the private economy.

Thus, we see that those in power not only obscure the links between the personal and political but obfuscate their own power as well. Terms like "objectivity," "efficiency," and "in the public interest" are used to mask the highly political connection between the private economy and the state. But this chicanery cannot hold up in the face of people's confrontation with the hidden exercise of power. In struggle after struggle, people learn the lesson that they are systematically excluded from decisions that affect and often harm their lives. This was no less true for the life-and-death fight against toxic wastes at Love Canal than for the fight to stop the construction of the Westway highway. The far-reaching gain of such citizen protests is this: ordinary people break through the obfuscating language of the powerful and develop an oppositional analysis.

The current emphasis on the positive aspects of these struggles does not mean that we should ignore their constraints. These protests are often short-lived and may make only ambiguous material gains or none at all.

For example, working-class people fight hard to stop redlining. They may win their objective and improve their neighborhood by pressuring lending institutions to reinvest in their community. Yet their very success makes them vulnerable to gentrification and therefore ripe for a new group of real-estate speculators. Every gain that people win, they win against great obstacles. People are held back by a system that constrains, represses, and co-opts resistance.

On their own, these everyday protests do not transform the whole of society. These struggles are, in truth, modest. They are small, fragmented, and sometimes contradictory efforts by people to change their lives. But, in some measure, they are anything but modest. They make possible important changes in people's lives in the here and now. They also change the ways people see themselves and their world. Change becomes possible as people overcome their fear and passivity and become critical, self-confident, and ready to fight back. The people of Love Canal and Westway and Poletown create change as they challenge our top-down view of politics and shape a politics from below, a "modest" politics that not only begins with everyday life but stays close to it.

Notes

1. For an excellent analysis of citizen activism see Harry C. Boyle, *The Backyard Revolution Understanding the New Citizen Movement* (Philadelphia: Temple University Press, 1980).
2. C. Wright Mills, *The Sociological Imagination* (New York: Oxford University Press, 1959), p. 4.
3. George Rudé, *Ideology and Popular Protest* (New York: Pantheon Books, 1980).
4. Information to illustrate Love Canal is drawn primarily from Michael Brown, *Laying Waste: The Poisoning of America by Toxic Wastes* (New York: Pantheon, 1980); and Lois Mane Gibbs, *Love Canal: My Story* (Albany: State University of New York Press, 1982)
5. Brown, *Laying Waste*, p. 21.
6. Ibid. p. 7.
7. Lois Gibbs, president, Love Canal Homeowners Association, letter on behalf of Stop Environmental Cancer Project. Santa Monica, Calif. (February, 1982).
8. Jane O'Reilly, "The Housewife's Moment of Truth." *Ms. Magazine* (Spring, 1972).
9. Gibbs, *Love Canal*, p. 12.
10. Lois Gibbs, lecture at Cooper Union, New York, N.Y., rebroadcast on WBAI, May, 1982.
11. For an excellent overview and analysis of issues involved in Westway see Joe Conason, "New York to Goldschmidt: Drop Westway," *The Village Voice* (Aug. 20, 1979).
12. Study by the Open Space Institute and the Sierra Club, cited in *The New York Post*, (Dec. 29, 1977).
13. Conason, *The Village Voice*.
14. Jack Newfield. "The Woman Who Blocked Westway," *The Village Voice* (Aug. 3, 1982).
15. Joe Conason, "Striped Bass Scale Down Westway," *The Village Voice* (Mar. 8, 1983).
16. Gail Cincotta, "Redlining: Problems and Tactics: The Chicago Experience," *STREET* (Summer, 1975); also see Ann Meyerson, "Redlining: How Banks and Other Financial Institutions Determine the Decline of Neighborhoods," paper written for Homefront Action Groups, 1976.
17. New York State Banking Study cited in Peter Freiberg, "Banks Draining Local Savings Banks," *The New York Post* (May 10, 1977).
18. Jack Newfield, "Redline Fever," *The Village Voice* (Mar. 13, 1978); bank president cited in *The New York Times* (Dec. 6, 1976).
19. Herbert Gans, *The Urban Villages* (New York: The Free Press, 1962).
20. On Poletown see Jeanie Wylie, "A Neighborhood Dies So General Motors Can Live," *The Village Voice* (July 8, 1981); Jay Shapiro, "Corona: Destruction of a Community," *The Township* (Nov. 30, 1970).
21. Cited in Paul Cowan, "Harrisburg: The Aftermath," *The Village Voice* (June 11, 1979), p. 27.
22. Interview with Frank Riessman, editor of *Social Policy*, New York, N.Y., April 22, 1983.
23. O'Reily, *Ms. Magazine,* p. 54.

End Note

I sincerely hope that you enjoyed and got something of value both from this reader and from the course as a whole. In the comic strip *"Peanuts,"* Charles Schulz once likened teaching to bowling—to the effect that you throw the ball and hope that you knock down all of the pins. We who teach never know how or in what way we influence our students or how successful our efforts have been. We don't and can't know, really, what our students take away from their time with us. Here's (some of) what I hope you leave us with.

On the tangible side, I hope you have some feel for what human ecology is about, its key attributes, some concepts, and the perspectives it includes. I hope you have some appreciation for the variety of human-environment interaction across time and space. I hope you realize that we don't have all of the answers, that we can learn from our own past—even if it's what not to do in a given situation—and that we can learn from other cultures—even traditional ones. I hope you can see the value of human ecology and the social sciences in general. I would submit that we cannot meaningfully address environmental issues purely from the natural science side and that our prospects for success are diminished unless we take humans as individuals and as societies and their cultures into account. "Technological fixes" are frequently not "fixes" at all, and often come with unintended consequences and a prohibitive price. Great policies on paper and advanced technologies can be subverted by the human element. Will we take any more solace from a nuclear accident if the cause is "human error" rather than a flaw in design or construction? I don't think so.

Less tangibly, perhaps, I hope what we've done has caused you to *think*—that is, after all, what you're supposed to be doing here (above and beyond obtaining a degree and a passport to greater material success). I hope you think about not only the issues and problems we've covered, but also (maybe especially) about *your* role in the environment and in the world generally. I hope your brush with human ecology and social science has been enlightening and liberating for you as an individual. As we have seen, the world is a complicated, confusing place . . . it is sometimes difficult to find our way in it. For me and, I hope, for you—the social sciences give us more options than we might otherwise be aware we have. Perhaps one of those less obvious options is a better way—for us as a society and for each of us as a person. I hope you see the world around you—your environment—in a new and different way.

If we have accomplished these things this semester, then we have been successful and done a great deal. As you leave us, I hope you will take away something of value to you and continue to learn throughout your lifetime. Take care.